EARLY BIOGRAPHICAL WRITINGS OF DR JOHNSON

Early Biographical Writings

of

Dr Johnson

With an introduction

by

J. D. FLEEMAN

1973

GREGG INTERNATIONAL PUBLISHERS LIMITED

CT
102
J63

ISBN   0 576 02301 9

Published in 1973 by Gregg International Publishers Limited
Westmead, Farnborough, Hants, England

Reprinted in Great Britain by Kingprint Limited
Richmond, Surrey.

CONTENTS

INTRODUCTION

As a biographer Johnson is best known for his *Lives of the Poets* written, and published (1779–81), towards the end of his life, but he had begun to write biographies much earlier, and this collection represents his less well-known essays in the *genre*. Most were hack jobs, but they usually reveal the qualities of mind and style for which he later became famous, and one at least has become a classic.

The purpose of this collection has not been primarily to publish material for a critical edition, but rather to make available versions of these biographies which are either textually interesting because overlooked in the more generally known collections, or which are to be found only in out-of-the-way or rare publications.

In some instances the exigencies of legible photographic reproduction of books of different sizes have led to the rearrangement of the original typographical lay-out of the texts.

The earliest of his biographies was that of Father Paul Sarpi, published in the *GM* viii (Nov. 1738) 581–3. It was probably intended as an introduction to his projected but abortive translation of Sarpi's *History of the Council of Trent*. The Life of Sarpi was never revised and the text here reproduced is from the original version in the *GM*. An account of the sources from which Johnson derived his Life is given by E. L. McAdam in *PMLA* lviii (1943) 466–76; a study of its composition by J. L. Abbott is in *BJRL* xlviii (1966) 255–67, and a detailed survey of the whole venture of which this biography was only a part, by J. A. V. Chapple, is in *BJRL* xlv (1963) 340–69.

Herman Boerhaave died in 1738 and from January to April 1739 the *GM* published Johnson's Life of him in four parts. The principal source was Albert Schultens' commemorative eulogy. The Life was later added, in a slightly abbreviated version, to Dr Robert James's *Medicinal Dictionary* 1743–45 (below), together with a briefly annotated list of Boerhaave's works. This list has been denied to Johnson (*Life* iii. 473 &c.), and since the second version is influenced by the special interests of the *Dictionary*, it has not been adopted and the version in the *GM* is here reproduced. Later reprintings are not revised.

In August 1740 Johnson began to contribute a biography of Sir Francis Drake to the *GM* which was published in six monthly parts and not completed until January 1741. This Life, together with that of Blake (below), was in 1767 added to the third edition of the Life of Savage (below), but although a few misprints were corrected a similar number was introduced, and there is no conclusive evidence that Johnson revised his first version which is accordingly here reproduced. The sources of this Life are discussed by Bergen B. Evans in his Harvard dissertation *Dr. Johnson as a Biographer* (1932), and by E. L. McAdam (*PMLA* loc. cit. sup.).

The Life of Admiral Robert Blake was published in the *GM* for June 1740 with an introductory paragraph designed, like the Life of Drake, to recall the glories of Elizabethan wars against Spain and to relate to the then current War of Jenkins' Ear. That paragraph was removed when the Life was published later in the same year as a small octavo pamphlet (see E. L. McAdam in *TLS* 14 March 1936, 228), though there are no other unequivocal signs that Johnson revised it. The text of the *GM* is followed in all editions of Johnson's *Works*, but because it is likely that Johnson was responsible for the rare pamphlet, it is here reproduced. Accounts of the sources are given by Bergen B. Evans (op. cit.) and E. L. McAdam (*PMLA* loc. cit. sup.).

In 1741 in the July number of the *GM* Johnson published a translation of Fontenelle's *Eloge* (1731) on Dr Lewis Morin. This is the only authentic text and is here reproduced. See J. L. Abbott in *Romance Notes* viii (1966) 1–3.

Peter Burman, a classical scholar, died in March 1714. In the *GM* for April 1742, appeared Johnson's biography of him. It is the only authentic text and is here reproduced.

In the *GM* for July 1742, in a review of Jean Baptiste Du Halde's *Description of China*, there is a biographical account of Confucius. J. Leed in *BNYPL* lxx (1966) 189–99 gives strong reasons for attributing this Life to Johnson and it is therefore here reproduced from the *GM*.

In 1743 Johnson's old schoolfellow, Dr Robert James, began publishing in parts his great *Medicinal Dictionary* (1743–45). Johnson supplied him with a Dedication addressed to Dr Richard Mead, and with several biographies of medical worthies, notably under the letter 'A': Actuarius, Aegineta, Aesculapius, Aetius, Alexander, Archagathus, Aretaeus, Asclepiades, Oribasius, Ruysch (under 'Anatome') and Tournefort (under 'Botany'). His earlier Life of Boerhaave (see above) was also added. See A. T. Hazen in *BIHM* iv (1936) 455–65, viii (1939) 324–34, and L. C. McHenry in *JHMAS* xiv (1959) 298–310. J. L. Abbott discusses some sources in *MP* lxiii (1965) 121–7.

The young genius John Philip Barretier died in October 1740 and Johnson's Life of him, based on an account by Barretier's father, was published in *GM* x (Dec. 1740) 612, and xi (Feb. 1741) 87–8, 93. In December 1742 in the *GM* some further details were published in an 'Additional Account'. The three inchoate pieces were brought together by Johnson in a separate octavo pamphlet published in 1744. This finished version has been neglected by his editors who have usually reprinted the pieces from the *GM*. Johnson's own copy of the pamphlet in Glasgow University Library was too fragile to reproduce, but it bears a revision in his own handwriting on p. 26, where he inserted the word 'whole' between 'spent Days' in line 2.

Little is known of John Swan, M.D., who translated the medical works of Dr Thomas Sydenham from Latin into English and published *The Entire Works of Dr. Thomas Sydenham* in 1742. He was a contributor to the *GM* in 1739 about the time Johnson came up to London; he seems to have been a Staffordshire man, and perhaps Dr James was a common friend. To Swan's edition, Johnson prefixed a Life of Sydenham which was extensively revised for the second edition of 1749: four paragraphs were removed and replaced by that on p. ix, beginning 'The same attention to the benefit . . .' to '. . . Mr. *Havers* of *Cambridge*'. The first version of this biography was reprinted in the *GM* xii (Dec. 1742) 633–5 and Johnson's editors have generally followed that text, ignoring the revision of 1749 which is reproduced here.

Richard Savage died in August 1743 and shortly afterwards Johnson began writing his Life, of which the first edition appeared in February 1744. A revised second edition was published in 1748, and this revision, slight in substance but stylistically significant, is here reproduced. To the third edition of 1767 were added the Lives of Blake and Drake (above), but that and later editions are unrevised by Johnson. When the Life of Savage was added to the *Lives of the Poets* Johnson revised the text, but began with a version which derived directly from the first edition of 1744 and so bypassed the revisions of 1748.

In the *GM* xviii (May 1748) 214–17, Johnson published a biography of Wentworth Dillon, Earl of Roscommon. His Life of Roscommon in the *Lives of the Poets* derives in part from the early account, but is so largely re-written that it amounts to a new article. Alexander Chalmers was the first editor to point out (1806) that the *GM* contained the germ of the later biography, and it is here reproduced to illustrate the progress of Johnson's composition of a Life.

In 1751 Johnson contributed to *The Student, or the Oxford and Cambridge Monthly Miscellany* ii (1751) 260–9, 290–4, 331–4 a Life of Dr Francis Cheynel, parliamentary divine and scourge of Oxford University. The subject was naturally of local interest, but Johnson's contribution to the 7th, 8th and 9th numbers could not revive the dying publication which closed with the 10th. If, as in the first volume (1750), the numbers correspond to months, then Johnson was writing this Life in the summer of 1751 for publication in July to September. At the same time he was writing two *Ramblers* a week and working on the *Dictionary*. The Life of Cheynel was reprinted in the *GM* in March and April 1775, but without revisions. The *GM* version served as the basis of all subsequent editions. Here the original text is reproduced from *The Student*.

Edward Cave, founder, proprietor, printer and publisher of *The Gentleman's Magazine*, the first 'Magazine', was known to Johnson since his early days in London, and was Johnson's first major literary employer. Cave's death in 1753 was the second occasion for Johnson's writing the Life of a personal acquaintance. The biography first appeared in the *GM* xxiv (Feb. 1754) 55–8, but was revised for inclusion in the second edition by Dr Kippis, of *Biographia Britannica*, iii (1784) 313–15. According to John Nichols, Cave's successor as proprietor of the *GM*, the revisions were made by Johnson at his particular request (*Lit. Anec.* v (1812) 9n). The hitherto neglected revised version is here reproduced.

Sir Thomas Browne, a favourite author much quoted in the *Dictionary*, was the subject of Johnson's next biography prefixed to his edition of Browne's *Christian Morals*, 1756. It is called the 'Second' edition (the first was published in 1716) but is the first to contain Johnson's Life and notes; the 'Third' edition of 1761 is in fact a reissue of the sheets of 1756 with a cancel title. The biography is here reproduced from the edition of 1756.

In 1756 Johnson seems to have been the promoter and editor of a new venture, *The Literary Magazine*, a monthly periodical in which he published an account of Frederick the Great, King of Prussia. The Life appeared in instalments in no. VII (Nov. 1756) 327–33, no. VIII (Dec. 1756) 383–90, and no. IX (Jan. 1757) 439–42. 1756 was the first year of the Seven Years' War and so Frederick's character and actions were of considerable topical interest. When the Emperor died in August 1786, Johnson's Life was reprinted by James Harrison with a continuation of Frederick's life supplied by William Mavor (see D. Nichol Smith in *BQR* vi (1931) 259–60). The same year and month also saw the publication of Johnson's Life of Frederick from *The Literary Magazine* in a small sixpenny duodecimo pamphlet of which only one copy is known. Other contemporary biographies of Frederick drew upon Johnson's Life, though usually without acknowledgement. Neither of the versions of 1786 presents a revised text, and accordingly the original version is here reproduced from *The Literary Magazine*.

James Bennet, a schoolmaster at Hoddesdon, published an edition of the *English Works of Roger Ascham* in 1761. Johnson had encouraged the undertaking as early as December 1757 when the *Proposals* were published bearing an 'Advertisement' by him. To the *Works* themselves he contributed a biography of Ascham, and he seems also to have given considerable editorial assistance to Bennet. The edition did not sell well and was reissued with an undated title in 1767. Johnson's Life was unrevised and is here reproduced from the first issue of 1761.

Johnson met William Collins the poet, perhaps through the Wartons, although Collins had contributed to the *GM* in 1739 and to Dodsley's *Museum* in 1747 and so could have become known to Johnson through either Cave or Dodsley. Collins died in 1759, and in 1763 Johnson contributed a memoir of him to *The Poetical Calendar* edited by Francis Fawkes and William Woty. The Life was reprinted in the *GM* xxxiv (Jan. 1764) 23–24 and in the second edition of *The Poetical Calendar*, 1764, but was not revised until, with slight modifications, it was included in the *Lives of the Poets* (1781). As this later version is well known and commonly available, the original version of 1763 is here reproduced to illustrate the progress of the composition of a Life.

The Rev. Zachariah Mudge met Johnson when the latter visited Plymouth with Joshua Reynolds in 1762. Mudge preached a sermon for Johnson who became a friendly admirer. On Mudge's death in 1769, he drew up an obituary character which was published in the *London Chronicle* 29 April–2 May 1769, p. 410, col. 3. The original manuscript, dated '24 April 1769' and annotated by Thomas Percy, has not been recorded since 1870. The version in the *London Chronicle* is here reproduced.

Styan Thirlby was a theologian and literary critic some of whose Shakespearian emendations and readings were adopted by Johnson in his edition of 1765. Johnson's brief account of Thirlby was drawn up, apparently at the request of John Nichols who published it in a larger account in the *GM* liv (April and Dec. 1784) 260–2, 893n, which is here reproduced. The original manuscript draft by Johnson is now in the Hyde Collection.

Abbreviations, and short references

BIHM	*Bulletin of the Institute of the History of Medicine* (Johns Hopkins)
BJRL	*Bulletin of the John Rylands Library*, Manchester
BNYPL	*Bulletin of the New York Public Library*, New York
BQR	*The Bodleian Quarterly Record*, Oxford
GM	*The Gentleman's Magazine*
JHMAS	*Journal of the History of Medicine and Allied Sciences*
Life	*Boswell's Life of Johnson*, ed. G. B. Hill, revised L. F. Powell, 6 vols., Oxford 1934–64
Lit. Anec.	*Literary Anecdotes of the Eighteenth Century*, by John Nichols, 9 vols., 1812–15
MP	*Modern Philology*
PMLA	*Publications of the Modern Language Association*
TLS	*The Times Literary Supplement*

Acknowledgements

The editor and publishers wish to thank the following libraries for the use of works in their possession: the University of Aberdeen Library, for the Life of Mudge; Bath Municipal Libraries, for the *Life of Savage*; Birmingham Public Libraries, for the Life of Browne; the Curators of the Bodleian Library, for the Lives of Oribasius and Frederick the Great; Bristol Public Libraries, for the Lives of Boerhaave, Drake, Morin, Burman, Confucius, Roscommon and Thirlby; the Trustees of the British Museum, for extracts from *The Rambler* and *The Idler*, and the Lives of Barretier, Sydenham, Cave, Ascham and Collins; the Wellcome Institute of the History of Medicine, for Lives of Actuarius, Aegineta, Aesculapius, Aetius, Alexander, Archagathus, Aretaeus, Asclepiades, Ruysch and Tournefort; Yale University Library, for the *Life of Blake*.

T H E

R A M B L E R.

NUMB. 60.	Price 2 *d*.

To be continued on TUESDAYS *and* SATURDAYS.

S A T U R D A Y, *October* 13, 1750.

—*Quid fit pulchrum, quid turpe, quid utile, quid non,*
Plenius *et* **melius** Chryſippo *et* Crantore *dicit.*   HOR.

LL Joy or Sorrow for the Happineſs or Calamities of others is produced by an Act of the Imagination, that reali-ſes the Event however fictitious, or approximates it however remote, by placing us, for a Time, in the Conditi-on of him whoſe Fortune we contemplate; ſo that we feel, while the Deception laſts, whatever Motions would be excited by the ſame Good or Evil happening to our-ſelves.

OUR Paſſions are therefore more ſtrongly moved, in proportion as we can more readily adopt the Pains or Plea-ſures propoſed to our Minds, by recogniſing them as once our own, or conſidering them as naturally incident to

our

13

our State of Life. It is not eafy for the moft artful Writer to give us an Intereft in Happinefs or Mifery, which
we think ourfelves never likely to feel, and with which
we have never yet been made acquainted. Hiftories of the
Downfall of Kingdoms, and Revolutions of Empires are
read with great Tranquillity ; the imperial Tragedy pleafes common Auditors only by its Pomp of Ornament,
and Grandeur of Ideas ; and the Man whofe Faculties have
been engroffed by Bufinefs, and whofe Heart never flut-
tered but at the Rife or Fall of Stocks, wonders how the
Attention can be feized, or the Affections agitated by a
Tale of Love.

THOSE parallel Circumftances, and kindred Images to
which we readily conform our Minds, are, above all o-
ther Writings, to be found in Narratives of the Lives of
particular Perfons ; and there feems therefore no Species of
Writing more worthy of Cultivation than Biography,
fince none can be more delightful, or more ufeful, none
can more certainly enchain the Heart by irrefiftible Intereft, or more widely diffufe Inftruction to every Diverfity
of Condition.

THE general and rapid Narratives of Hiftory, which
involve a thoufand Fortunes in the Bufinefs of a Day, and
complicate innumerable Incidents in one great Tranfaction, afford few Leffons applicable to private Life, which
derives its Comforts and its Wretchednefs from the right
or wrong Management of Things, that nothing but
their Frequency makes confiderable, *Parva fi non fiunt
quotidie*, fays *Pliny*, and which can have no Place in
thofe Relations which never defcend below the Confultation of Senates, the Motions of Armies, and the Schemes
of Confpirators.

I HAVE often thought that there has rarely paffed a
Life of which a judicious and faithful Narrative would not
be

be ufeful. For, not only every Man has in the mighty
Mafs of the World great Numbers in the fame Condition with himfelf, to whom his Miftakes and Mifcarriages,
Efcapes and Expedients would be of immediate and apparent Ufe; but there is fuch an Uniformity in the Life
of Man, if it be confidered apart from adventitious and fe-
parable Decorations and Difguifes, that there is fcarce any
Poffibility of Good or Ill, but is common to Humankind.
A great Part of the Time of thofe who are placed at the
greateft Diftance by Fortune, or by Temper, muft unavoidably pafs in the fame Manner; and though, when the
Claims of Nature are fatisfied, Caprice, and Vanity, and
Accident, begin to produce Difcriminations, and Peculiarities, yet the Eye is not very heedful, or quick, which
cannot difcover the fame Caufes ftill terminating their Influence in the fame Effects, though fometimes accelerated,
fometimes retarded, or perplexed by multiplied Combinations. We are all prompted by the fame Motives, all deceived by the fame Fallacies, all animated by Hope, obftructed by Danger, entangled by Defire, and feduced by Pleafure.

It is frequently objected to Relations of particular
Lives, that they are not diftinguifhed by any ftriking or
wonderful Viciffitudes. The Scholar who paffes his Life
among his Books, the Merchant who conducted only his
own Affairs, the Prieft whofe Sphere of Action was not
extended beyond that of his Duty, are confidered as no
proper Objects of publick Regard, however they might
have excelled in their feveral Stations, whatever
might have been their Learning, Integrity, and Piety.
But this Notion arifes from falfe Meafures of Excellence
and Dignity, and muft be eradicated by confidering, that,
in the Eye of uncorrupted Reafon, what is of moft Ufe is
of moft Value.

It is, indeed, not improper to take honeft Advantages
of Prejudice, and to gain Attention by a great Name;
but

but the Bufinefs of the Biographer is often to pafs flightly over thofe Performances and Incidents, which produce vulgar Greatnefs, to lead the Thoughts into domeftick Privacies, and difplay the minute Details of daily Life, where exterior Appendages are caft afide, and Men excel each other only by Prudence, and by Virtue. The Life of *Thuanus* is, with great Propriety, faid by its Author to have been written, that it might lay open to Pofterity the private and familiar Character of that Man, *cujus Ingenium et Candorem ex ipfius Scriptis funt olim femper miraturi*, whofe Candour and Genius his Writings will to the End of Time preferve in Admiration.

THERE are many invifible Circumftances, which whether we read as Enquirers after natural or moral Knowledge, whether we intend to enlarge our Science, or encreafe our Virtue, are more important than publick Occurrences. Thus *Saluft*, the great Mafter, has not forgot, in his Account of *Catiline*, to remark that *his Walk was now quick, and again flow*, as an Indication of a Mind revolving fomething with violent Commotion. Thus the Story of *Melancthon* affords a ftriking Lecture on the Value of Time, by informing us that when he made an Appointment, he expected not only the Hour, but the Minute to be fixed, that Life might not run out in the Idlenefs of Sufpenfe ; and all the Plans and Enterprizes of *De Wit* are now of lefs Importance to the World, than that Part of his perfonal Character which reprefents him as careful of his Health, and negligent of his Life.

BUT Biography has often been allotted to Writers who feem very little acquainted with the Nature of their Tafk, or very negligent about the Performance. They rarely afford any other Account than might be collected from publick Papers, and imagine themfelves writing a Life when they exhibit a chronological Series of Actions or Preferments; and fo little regard the Manners or Behaviour

of

of their Heroes, that more Knowledge may be gained of a Man's real Character, by a fhort Converfation with one of his Servants, than from a formal and ftudied Narrative, begun with his Pedigree, and ended with his Funeral.

If now and then they condefcend to inform the World of particular Facts, they are not always fo happy as to felect thofe which are of moft Importance. I know not well what Advantage Pofterity can receive from the only Circumftance by which *Tickell* has diftinguifhed *Addifon* from the Reft of Mankind, the Irregularity of his Pulfe : nor can I think myfelf overpaid for the Time fpent in reading the Life of *Malherb*, by being enabled to relate, after the learned Biographer, that *Malherb* had two predominant Opinions ; one, that the Loofenefs of a fingle Woman might deftroy all the Boaft of ancient Defcent ; the other, that the *French* Beggers made ufe very improperly and barbaroufly of the Phrafe *noble Gentleman*, becaufe either Word included the Senfe of both.

There are, indeed, fome natural Reafons why thefe Narratives are often written by fuch as were not likely to give much Inftruction or Delight, and why moft Accounts of particular Perfons are barren and ufelefs. If a Life be delayed till all Intereft and Envy are at an End, and all Motives to Calumny or Flattery are fuppreffed, we may hope for Impartiality, but muft expect little Intelligence ; for the Incidents which give Excellence to Biography are of a volatile and evanefcent Kind, fuch as foon efcape the Memory, and are rarely tranfmitted by Tradition. We know how few can portray a living Acquaintance, except by his moft prominent and obfervable Particularities, and the groffer Features of his Mind ; and it may be eafily imagined how much of this little Knowledge may be loft in imparting it, and how foon a Succeffion of Copies will lofe all Refemblance of the Original.

If

IF the Biographer writes from perfonal Knowledge, and makes hafte to gratify the publick Curiofity, there is Danger left his Intereft, his Fear, his Gratitude, or his Tendernefs, overpower his Fidelity, and tempt him to conceal, if not to invent. There are many who think it an Act of Piety to hide the Faults or Failings of their Friends, even when they can no longer fuffer by their Detection; we therefore fee whole Ranks of Characters adorned with uniform Panegyrick, and not to be known from one another, but by extrinfick and cafual Circumftances. " Let me remember, fays *Hale*, when I find myfelf inclined to pity a Criminal, that there is likewife a " Pity due to the Country." If there is a Regard due to the Memory of the Dead, there is yet more Refpect to be paid to Knowledge, to Virtue, and to Truth.

The Univerſal Chronicle,

.NUMB. 86.

O R

WEEKLY GAZETTE.

To be Publiſhed every SATURDAY. Price Two-PENCE HALF-PENNY.

From SATURDAY, NOVEMBER 17, to SATURDAY, NOVEMBER 24, 1759.

The IDLER. No. 85.

IOGRAPHY is of the various kinds of narrative writing, that which is moſt eagerly read, and moſt eaſily applied to the Purpoſes of Life.

In Romances, when the wide Field of Poſſibility lies open to Invention, the Incidents may eaſily be made more numerous, the Viciſſitudes more ſudden, and the Events more wonderful; but from the Time of Life when Fancy begins to be overruled by Reaſon, and correĉted by Experience, the moſt artful Tale raiſes little Curioſity when it is known to be falſe; it may, perhaps, be ſometimes read as a Model of a plain or elegant Stile, not for the ſake of knowing what it contains, but how it is written; or thoſe that are weary of themſelves may have Recourſe to it as a pleaſing Dream, of which, when they awake, they voluntarily diſmiſs the Images from their Minds.

The Examples and Events of Hiſtory preſs, indeed, upon the Mind with the Weight of Truth; but when they are repoſited in the Memory, they are oftener employed for Shew than Uſe, and rather diverſify Converſation than regulate Life; few are engaged in ſuch Scenes as give them Opportunities of growing wiſer by the Downfal of Stateſmen or the Defeat of Generals. The Stratagems of War, and the Intrigues of Courts, are read by far the greater Part of Mankind with the ſame Indifference as the Adventures of fabled Heroes, or the Revolutions of a Fairy Region. Between Falſehood and uſeleſs Truth there is little difference; as Gold which he cannot ſpend will make no Man rich, ſo Knowledge which he cannot apply will make no Man wiſe.

The miſchievous Conſequences of Vice and Folly, of irregular Deſires and predominant Paſſions, are beſt diſcovered by thoſe Relations which are levelled with the general Surface of Life, which tell not how any Man became great, but how he was made happy; not how he loſt the Favour of his Prince, but how he became diſcontented with himſelf.

Thoſe Relations are therefore commonly of moſt Value in which the Writer tells his own Story. He that recounts the Life of another, commonly dwells moſt upon conſpicuous Events, leſſens the Familiarity of his Tale to increaſe its Dignity, ſhews his Favourite at a diſtance decorated and magnified like the ancient Aĉtors in their tragick Dreſs, and endeavours to hide the Man that he may produce a Hero.

But if it be true which was ſaid by a *French* Prince, *that no Man was a Hero to the Servants of his Chamber*, it is equally true that every Man is yet leſs a Hero to himſelf. He that is moſt elevated above the Croud by the Importance of his Employments or the Reputation of his Genius, feels himſelf affeĉted by Fame or Buſineſs but as they influence his domeſtick Life. The High and Low, as they have the ſame Faculties and the ſame Senſes, have no leſs Similitude in their Pains and Pleaſures. The Senſations are the ſame in all, tho' produced by very different Occaſions. The Prince feels the ſame Pain when an Invader ſeizes a Province, as the Farmer when a Thief drives away his Cow. Men thus equal in themſelves will appear equal in honeſt and impartial Biography; and thoſe whom Fortune or Nature place at the greateſt Diſtance may afford Inſtruĉtion to each other.

The Writer of his own Life has at leaſt the firſt Qualification of an Hiſtorian, the Knowledge of the Truth; and though it may be plauſibly objeĉted that his Temptations to diſguiſe it are equal to his Opportunities of knowing it, yet I cannot but think that Impartiality may be expected with equal Confidence from him that relates the Paſſages of his own Life, as from him that delivers the Tranſactions of another.

Certainty of Knowledge not only excludes Miſtake, but fortifies Veracity. What we collect by Conjecture, and by Conjecture only can one Man judge of another's Motives, or Sentiments, is eaſily modified by Fancy or by Deſire; as Objects imperfectly diſcerned, take Forms from the Hope or Fear of the Beholder. But that which is fully known cannot be falſified but with Reluctance of Underſtanding, and Alarm of Conſcience; of Underſtanding the Lover of Truth, of Conſcience the Sentinel of Virtue.

He that writes the Life of another is either his Friend or his Enemy, and wiſhes either to exalt his Praiſe or aggravate his Infamy; to him many Temptations to Falſehood will occur in the Diſguiſe of Paſſions, too ſpecious to fear much Reſiſtance. Love of Virtue will animate Panegyrick, and Hatred of Wickedneſs imbitter Cenſure. The Zeal of Gratitude, the Ardour of Patriotiſm, Fondneſs for an Opinion, or Fidelity to a Party, may eaſily overpower the Vigilance of a Mind habitually well diſpoſed, and prevail over unaſſiſted and unfriended Veracity.

But he that ſpeaks of himſelf has no Motive to Falſehood or Partiality except Self-love, by which all have ſo often been betrayed, that all are on the watch againſt it's Artifices. He that writes an Apology for a ſingle Action, to confute an Accuſation, or recommend himſelf to Favour is indeed always to be ſuſpected of favouring his own Cauſe; but he that ſits down calmly and voluntarily to review his Life for the Admonition of Poſterity, or to amuſe himſelf, and leaves this Account unpubliſhed, may be commonly preſumed to tell Truth, ſince Falſhood cannot appeaſe his own Mind, and Fame will not be heard beneath the Tomb.

The Life of Father PAUL SARPI, *Author of the History of the* COUNCIL *of* TRENT: *For printing a new Translation of which, by* S. JOHNSON, *we have publish'd Proposals.*

FATHER *Paul*, whose Name, before he entered into the monastic Life, was *Peter Sarpi*, was born at *Venice*, *August* 14, 1552. His Father follow'd Merchandise, but with so little Success, that, at his Death, he left his Family very ill provided for, but under the Care of a Mother, whose Piety was likely to bring the blessing of Providence upon them, and whose wise Conduct supplied the want of Fortune by Advantages of greater Value.

Happily for young *Sarpi*, she had a Brother, Master of a celebrated School, under whose Direction he was placed by her. Here he lost no Time, but cultiva- ted his Abilities, naturally of the first Rate, with unwearied Application. He was born for Study, having a natural Aversion to Pleasure and Gaiety, and a Memory so tenacious, that he could repeat thirty Verses upon once hearing them.

Proportionable to his Capacity was his Progress in Literature: At thirteen, having made himself Master of School-Learning, he turn'd his Studies to Philosophy and the Mathematicks, and entered upon Logick under *Capella* of *Cremona*, who, tho' a celebrated Master of that Science, confess'd himself in a very little Time unable to give his Pupil any farther Instructions.

As *Capella* was of the Order of the *Servites*, his Scholar was induced by his Acquaintance with him, to engage in the same Profession, tho' his Uncle and his Mother, represented to him the Hardships and Austerities of that kind of Life, and advis'd him with great Zeal against it. But he was steady in his Resolutions, and in 1566 took the Habit of the Order, being then only in his 14th Year, a Time of Life in most Persons very improper for such Engagements, but in him attended with such Maturity of Thought, and such a settled Temper, that he never seem'd to regret the Choice he then made, and which he confirm'd by a solemn publick Profession, in 1572.

At a general Chapter of the *Servites* held at *Mantua*, *Paul* (for so we shall now call him) being then only twenty Years old, distinguished himself so much in a publick Disputation by his Genius and Learning, that *William*, Duke of *Mantua*, a great Patron of Letters, solicited the Consent of his Superiors to retain him at his Court, and not only made him publick Professor of Divinity in the Cathedral, but honoured him with many Proofs of his Esteem.

But F. *Paul* finding a Court Life not agreeable to his Temper, quitted it two Years afterwards, and retired to his beloved Privacies, being then not only acquainted with the *Latin*, *Greek*, *Hebrew* and *Chaldee* Languages, but with Philosophy, the Mathematicks, Canon and Civil Law, all Parts of natural Philosophy, and Chemistry itself; for his Application was unintermitted, his Head clear, his Apprehension quick, and his Memory retentive.

Being made a Priest at twenty-two, he was distinguish'd by the illustrious Cardinal *Borromeo* with his Confidence, and employed by him on many Occasions, not without the Envy of Persons of less Merit, who were so far exasperated as to lay

Dddd

21

a Charge against him before the Inquisition, for denying that the Trinity could be proved from the first Chapter of *Genesis* ; but the Accusation was too ridiculous to be taken Notice of.

After this he passed successively thro' the Dignities of his Order, and in the Intervals of his Employment applied himself to his Studies with so extensive a Capacity, as left no Branch of Knowledge untouch'd. By him *Acquapendente*, the great Anatomist, confesses that he was informed how Vision is perform'd, and there are Proofs that he was not a Stranger to the Circulation of the Blood. He frequently convers'd upon Astronomy with Mathematicians, upon Anatomy with Surgeons, upon Medicine with Physicians, and with Chemists upon the Analysis of Metals, not as a superficial Enquirer, but as a complete Master.

But the Hours of Repose, that he employ'd so well, were interrupted by a new Information in the Inquisition, where a former Acquaintance produced a Letter written by him in Cyphers, in which he said, *that he detested the Court of* Rome, *and that no Preferment was obtained there but by dishonest Means*. This Accusation, however dangerous, was passed over on account of his great Reputation, but made such Impressions on that Court, that he was afterwards denied a Bishoprick by *Clement* VIII. After these Difficulties were surmounted, F. *Paul* again retired to his Solitude, where he appears, by some Writings drawn up by him at that Time, to have turn'd his Attention more to Improvements in Piety than Learning. Such was the Care with which he read the Scriptures, that, it being his Custom to draw a Line under any Passage which he intended more nicely to consider, there was not a single Word in his New Testament but was underlined; the same Marks of Attention appeared in his Old Testament, Psalter, and Breviary.

But the most active Scene of his Life began about the Year 1615, when Pope *Paul* Vth, exasperated by some Decrees of the Senate of *Venice* that interfered with the pretended Rights of the Church, laid the whole State under an Interdict.

The Senate, fill'd with Indignation at this Treatment, forbad the Bishops to receive or publish the Pope's Bull, and convening the Rectors of the Churches, commanded them to celebrate divine Service in the accustom'd Manner, with which most of them readily complied; but the Jesuits and some others refusing, were by a solemn Edict expell'd the State. Both Parties having proceeded to Ex-

tremities, employed their ablest Writers to defend their Measures : On the Pope's Side, among others, Cardinal *Bellarmine* entered the Lists, and with his confederate Authors defended the Papal Claims with great Scurrility of Expression, and very sophistical Reasonings, which were confuted by the *Venetian* Apologists in much more decent Language, and with much greater Solidity of Argument.

On this Occasion F. *Paul* was most eminently distinguish'd, by his *Defence of the Rights of the supreme Magistrate*, his *Treatise of Excommunication* translated from *Gerson*, with an *Apology*, and other Writings, for which he was cited before the Inquisition at *Rome*; but it may be easily imagin'd that he did not obey the Summons.

The *Venetian* Writers, whatever might be the Abilities of their Adversaries, were at least superior to them in the Justice of their Cause. The Propositions maintain'd on the Side of *Rome* were these : That the Pope is invested with all the Authority of Heaven and Earth. That all Princes are his Vassals, and that he may annul their Laws at pleasure. That Kings may appeal to him, as he is temporal Monarch of the whole Earth. That he can discharge Subjects from their Oaths of Allegiance, and make it their Duty to take up Arms against their Sovereign. That he may depose Kings without any Fault committed by them, if the Good of the Church requires it : That the Clergy are exempt from all Tribute to Kings, and are not accountable to them even in Cases of high-Treason. That the Pope cannot err . That his Decisions are to be received and obeyed on pain of Sin, tho' all the World should judge them to be false : That the Pope is God upon Earth, that his Sentence and that of God are the same, and that to call his Power in Question, is to call in Question the Power of God : Maxims equally shocking, weak, pernicious, and absurd! which did not require the Abilities or Learning of F. *Paul* to demonstrate their Falshood, and destructive Tendency.

It may be easily imagined that such Principles were quickly overthrown, and that no Court but that of *Rome* thought it for its Interest to favour them. The Pope therefore finding his Authors confuted, and his Cause abandon'd, was willing to conclude the Affair by Treaty which, by the Mediation of *Henry* IV. of *France*, was accommodated upon Terms very much to the Honour of the *Venetians*. But the Defenders of the *Venetian* Rights, were, tho' comprehended in the

Treaty,

The LIFE of Father PAUL.

Treaty, excluded by the *Romans* from the Benefit of it; some upon different Pretences were imprisoned, some sent to the Galleys, and all debarr'd from Preferment. But their Malice was chiefly aimed against F. *Paul*, who soon found the Effects of it, for as he was going one Night to his Convent, about six Months after the Accommodation, he was attack'd by five Ruffians armed with Stilettoes, who gave him no less than fifteen Stabs, three of which wounded him in such a manner that he was left for dead. The Murderers fled for Refuge to the Nuncio, and were afterwards received into the Pope's Dominions, but were pursued by divine Justice, and all, except one Man who dyed in Prison, perished by violent Deaths.

This, and other Attempts upon his Life obliged him to confine himself to his Convent, where he engage in writing the History of the Council of *Trent*, a Work unequal'd for the judicious Disposition of the Matter, and artful Texture of the Narration, commended by Dr *Burnet* as the compleatest Model of Historical Writing, and celebrated by Mr *Wotton* as equivalent to any Production of Antiquity; in which the Reader finds *Liberty without Licentiousness, Piety without Hypocrisy, Freedom of Speech without Neglect of Decency, Severity without Rigour, and extensive Learning without Ostentation.*

In this, and other Works of less Consequence, he spent the remaining Part of his Life, to the Beginning of the Year 1622, when he was seiz'd with a Cold and Fever, which he neglected till it became incurable. He languish'd more than 12 Months, which he spent almost wholly in a Preparation for his Passage into Eternity; and among his Prayers and Aspirations was often heard to repeat, *Lord! now let thy Servant depart in Peace.*

On Sunday the eighth of *January* of the next Year, he rose, weak as he was, to Mass, and went to take his Repast with the rest, but on Monday was seized with a Weakness that threatened immediate Death, and on Thursday prepared for his Change by receiving the *Viaticum* with such Marks of Devotion, as equally melted and edified the Beholders.

Through the whole Course of his Illness to the last Hour of his Life, he was consulted by the Senate in publick Affairs, and return'd Answers in his greatest Weakness, with such Presence of Mind, as could only arise from the Consciousness of Innocence.

On Saturday, the Day of his Death, he had the Passion of our blessed Saviour read to him out of St *John's* Gospel, as on every other Day of that Week, and spoke of the Mercy of his Redeemer, and his Confidence in his Merits.

As his End evidently approached, the Brethren of the Convent came to pronounce the last Prayers, with which he could only join in his Thoughts, being able to pronounce no more than these Words, *Esto perpetua, Mayst thou last for ever*; which was understood to be a Prayer for the Prosperity of his Country.

Thus dyed F. *Paul*, in the 71st Year of his Age: Hated by the *Romans* as their most formidable Enemy, and honour'd by all the Learned for his Abilities, and by the Good for his Integrity. His Detestation of the Corruption of the *Roman* Church appears in all his Writings, but particularly in this memorable Passage of one of his Letters. *There is nothing more essential than to ruin the Reputation of the Jesuits: By the Ruin of the Jesuits, Rome will be ruin'd ;and if Rome is ruin'd, Religion will reform of itself.*

He appears by many Passages of his Life to have had a high Esteem of the Church of *England*; and his Friend, F, *Fulgentio,* who had adopted all his Notions, made no Scruple of administring to Dr *Duncomb,* an *English* Gentleman that fell sick at *Venice,* the Communion in both Kinds, according to the Common Prayer which he had with him in *Italian.*

He was buried with great Pomp at the publick Charge, and a magnificent Monument was erected to his Memorial.

S. J.

The LIFE of Dr BOERHAAVE.

The following ACCOUNT *of the late Dr* BOERHAAVE, *so loudly celebrated, and so universally lamented thro' the whole learned World, will, we hope, be not unacceptable to our Readers: We could have made it much larger, by adopting flying Reports, and inserting unattested Facts; a close Adherence to Certainty has contracted our Narrative, and hindred it from swelling to that Bulk, at which modern Histories generally arrive.*

The LIFE *of Dr* HERMAN BOERHAAVE, *late Professor of Physick in the University of* Leyden *in* Holland.

DR *Herman Boerhaave* was born on ʃ last Day of *December*, 1668, ab ut One in the Morning, at *Voerhout*, a Village two Miles distant from *Leyden:* His Father, *James Boerhaave*, was Minister of *Voorhout*, of whom his Son, in a small Account of his own Life, has given a very amiable Character, for the Simplicity and Openness of his Behaviour, for his exact Frugality in the Management of a narrow Fortune, and the Prudence, Tenderness and Diligence, with which he educated a numerous Family of nine Children. He was eminently skill'd in History and Genealogy, and versed in the *Latin, Greek* and *Hebrew* Languages.

His Mother was *Hagar Daeldcr*, a Tradesman's Daughter of *Amsterdam*, from whom he might, perhaps, derive an hereditary Inclination to the Study of Physick, in which she was very inquisitive, and had obtained a Knowledge of it not common in Female Students.

This Knowledge, however, she did not live to communicate to her Son, for she died in 1673, ten Years after her Marriage.

His Father, finding himself encumber'd with the Care of seven Children, thought it necessary to take a second Wife, and in *July*, 1674, was married to *Eva du Bois*, Daughter of a Minister of *Leyden*, who, by her prudent and impartial Conduct, so endear'd herself to her Husband's Children, that they all regarded her as their own Mother.

Herman Boerhaave was always design'd by his Father for the Ministry, and with that View instructed by him in Grammatical Learning, and the first Elements of Languages; in which he made such a

---

* *Erat Hermanni Genitor Latinæ, Græcæ, Hebraicæ scientiæ: peritus valde historiarum & genealogiarum. Vir apertus, candidus, simplex: pater familias optimus amans, cura, diligentia, frugalitate, prudentia. Qui non magnus in re, sed plenus virtutis, novem liberis educandis exemplum præbuit singulare, quid exacta parsimonia polleat, & frugalitas.*

Proficiency, that he was, at the Age of eleven Years, not only Master of the Rules of Grammar, but capable of translating with tolerable Accuracy, and not wholly ignorant of critical Niceties.

At Intervals, to recreate his Mind and strengthen his Constitution, it was his Father's Custom to send him into the Fields, and employ him in Agriculture, and such kind of rural Occupations, which he continued thro' all his Life to love and practise; and by this Vicissitude of Study and Exercise, preserv'd himself, in a great Measure, from those Distempers and Depressions which are frequently the Consequences of indiscreet Diligence, and uninterrupted Application; and from which, Students, not well acquainted with the Constitution of the human Body, sometimes fly for Relief to Wine instead of Exercise, and purchase temporary Ease by the Hazard of the most dreadful Consequences.

The Studies of young *Boerhaave* were, about this time, interrupted by an Accident, which deserves a particular Mention, as it first inclin'd him to that Science, to which he was by Nature so well adapted, and which he afterwards carried to so great Perfection.

In the twelfth Year of his Age a stubborn, painful, and malignant Ulcer, broke out upon his left Thigh; which, for near five Years, defeated all the Art of the Surgeons and Physicians, and not only afflicted him with most excruciating Pains, but exposed him to such sharp and tormenting Applications, that the Disease and Remedies were equally insufferable. Then it was that his own Pain taught him to compassionate others, and his Experience of the Inefficacy of the Methods then in Use incited him to attempt the Discovery of others more certain.

He began to practise at least honestly, for he began upon himself; and his first Essay was a Prelude to his future Success, for, having laid aside all the Prescriptions of his Physicians, and all the Applications of his Surgeons, he, at last, by fomenting the Part with Salt and Urine, effected a Cure.

That he might, on this Occasion, obtain the Assistance of Surgeons with less Inconvenience and Expence, he was brought, by his Father, at Fourteen, to *Leyden*, and placed in the fourth Class of the publick School, after being examined by the Master: Here his Application and Abilities were equally conspicuous. In six Months, by gaining the first Prize in the fourth Class, he was raised to the fifth; and in six Months more, upon the same Proof of the Superiority of his Genius,
rewarded

rewarded with another Prize, and tranſlated to the ſixth ; trom whence it is uſual in ſix Months more to be removed to the Univerſity.

Thus did our young Student advance in Learning and Reputation, when, as he was within View of the Univerſity, a ſudden and unexpected Blow threaten'd to defeat all his Expectations.

On the 12th of *November*, in 1682, his Father died, and left behind him a very ſlender Proviſion for his Widow and nine Children, of which the Eldeſt was not yet ſeventeen Years old.

This was a moſt afflicting Loſs to the young Scholar, whoſe Fortune was by no means ſufficient to bear the Expences of a learned Education, and who therefore ſeem'd to be now ſummon'd by Neceſſity to ſome Way of Life more immediately and certainly lucrative; but with a Reſolution equal to his Abilities, and a Spirit not ſo depreſs'd or ſhaken, he determined to break thro' the Obſtacles of Poverty, and ſupply, by Diligence, § Want of Fortune.

He therefore ask'd and obtained the Conſent of his Guardians to proſecute his Studies as long as his Patrimony would ſupport him, and continuing his wonted Induſtry gained another Prize.

He was now to quit the School for the Univerſity, but on Account of the Weakneſs yet remaining in his Thigh, at his own Entreaty continued ſix Months longer under the Care of his Maſter, the learned *Wynſchotan*, where he once more was honoured with the Prize.

At his Removal to the Univerſity, the ſame Genius and Induſtry met with the ſame Encouragement and Applauſe. The learned *Triglandius*, one of his Father's Friends, made ſoon after Profeſſor of Divinity at *Leiden*, diſtinguiſhed him in a particular Manner and recommended him to the Friendſhip of Mr *Van Aphen*, in whom he found a generous and conſtant Patron.

He became now a diligent Hearer of the moſt celebrated Profeſſors, and made great Advances in all the Sciences, ſtill regulating his Studies with a View principally to Divinity, for which he was originally intended by his Father, and for that Reaſon exerted his utmoſt Application to attain an exact Knowledge of the *Hebrew* Tongue.

Being convinced of the Neceſſity of Mathematical Learning, he began to ſtudy thoſe Sciences in 1687, but without that intenſe Induſtry with which the Pleaſure he found in that Kind of Knowledge induced him afterwards to cultivate them.

In 1690, having perform'd the Exerciſes of the Univerſity with uncommon Reputation, he took his Degree in Philoſophy; and on that Occaſion diſcuſs'd the important and arduous Subject of the diſtinct Natures of the Soul and Body, with ſuch Accuracy, Perſpicuity and Subtilty, that he entirely confuted all the Sophiſtry of *Epicurus*, *Hobbes* and *Spinoſa*, and equally raiſed the Characters of his Piety and Erudition.

Divinity was ſtill his great Employment, and the chief Aim of all his Studies. He read the Scriptures in their original Languages, and when Difficulties occur'd, conſulted the Interpretations of the moſt antient Fathers, whom he read in order of Time, beginning with *Clemens Romanus*.

* In the Peruſal of theſe early Writers, he was ſtruck with the profoundeſt Veneration of the Simplicity and Purity of their Doctrine, the Holineſs of their Lives, and the Sanctity of the Diſcipline practiſed by them; but as he deſcended to the lower Ages, found the Peace of Chriſtianity broken by uſeleſs Controverſies, and its Doctrines ſophiſticated by the Subtilties of the Schools. He found the holy Writers interpreted according to the Notions of Philoſophers, and the Chimera's of Metaphyſicians adopted as Articles of Faith. He found Difficulties raiſed by Niceties, and fomented to Bitterneſs and Rancour. He ſaw the Simplicity of the Chriſtian Doctrine corrupted by the private Fancies of particular Parties, while each adhered to its own Philoſophy and Orthodoxy was confined to the Sect in Power.

(*More of this* Great Man, *next Month.*)

---

* *Jungebat his exercitiis quotidianam Patrum lectionem, ſecundum Chronologiam, a Clemente Romano exorſus, & juxta ſeriem ſeculorum deſcendens: ut Jeſu Chriſti Doctrinam in N. T. traditam, primis Patribus interpretantibus addiſceret. Horum ſimplicitatem ſinceræ Doctrinæ, diſciplinæ ſanctitatem, Vitæ Deo dicatæ integritatem adorabat. Subtilitatem Scholarum Divina poſtmodum inquinaſſe dolebat. Ægerrime tulit, Sacrorum interpretationem ex ſectis Sophiſtarum peti ; & Platonis, Ariſtotelis, Thomæ Aquinatis, Scoti; ſuoque tempore Carteſii, cogitata Metaphyſica adhiberi pro legibus, ad quas caſtigarentur ſacrorum Scriptorum de Deo ſententiæ. Experiebatur acerba diſſidia, ingeniorumque ſubtiliſſimorum acerrima certamina, odia, ambitiones, inde cæri, furri: adeo contraria paci cum Deo & Homine. Nihil hic magis illi obſtabat ; quam quod omnes aſſerat a ſacram Scripturam a biorotabe, loquentem, Soumpavos expoſcendam ; & Souplvu- ſinguli deſinant ex placitis ſua Metaphyſices. Horrebat, inde Dominantis ſectæ prævalentem opinionem, Orthodoxiæ medium, & regula, unice dare juxta dictata Metaphyſicorum, non ſacrarum Literarum ; unde tam variæ ſententiæ de doctrinæ ſimpliciſſima.*

a diligent Perufal *of Vefalius, Bartholin* and *Fallopius*, and to acquaint himſelf more fully with the Structure of Bodies, was a conſtant Attendant upon *Nuck*'s publick Diſſections in the Theatre, and himſelf very accurately inſpected the Bodies of different Animals.

Having furniſh'd himſelf with this preparatory Knowledge, he began to read the ancient Phyſicians in the order of Time, purſuing his Enquiries downwards from *Hippocrates* thro' all the *Greek* and *Latin* Writers.

Finding, as he tells us himſelf, that *Hippocrates* was the original Source of all Medical Knowledge, and that all the later Writers were little more than Tranſcribers from him, he returned to him with more Attention, and ſpent much Time in making Extracts from him, digeſting his Treatiſes into Method, and fixing them in his Memory.

He then deſcended to the Moderns, among whom none engaged him longer, or improved him more, than *Sydenham*, to whoſe Merit he has left this Atteſtation, *that he frequently peruſed him, and always with greater Eagerneſs.*

His inſatiable Curioſity after Knowledge engaged him now in the Practice of Chymiſtry, which he proſecuted with all the Ardour of a Philoſopher, whoſe Induſtry was not to be wearied, and whoſe Love of Truth was too ſtrong to ſuffer him to acquieſce in the Reports of others.

Yet did he not ſuffer one Branch of Science to withdraw his Attention from others: Anatomy did not withhold him from Chymiſtry, nor Chymiſtry, enchanting as it is, from the Study of *Botany*, in which he was no leſs ſkilled than in other Parts of Phyſick. He was not only a careful Examiner of all the Plants in the Garden of the Univerſity, but made Excurſions for his farther Improvement, ſon the Woods and Fields, and left no Place unviſited where any Increaſe of Botanical Knowledge could be reaſonably hoped for.

In conjunction with all theſe Enquiries he ſtill purſued his Theological ſtudies, and ſtill, as we are informed by himſelf, propoſed, when he had made himſelf Maſter of the whole Art of Phyſick, and obtained the Honour of a Degree in that Science, to petition regularly for a Licence to preach, and to engage in the Care of Souls, and intended in his Theological Exerciſe to diſcuſs this Queſtion, *Why ſo many were formerly converted to Chriſtianity by illiterate Perſons, and ſo few at preſent by Men of Learning.*

Continuation of the Life of D*r* BOER-HAAVE, *from p. 37.*

HAVING now exhauſted his Fortune in the Purſuit of his Studies, he found the Neceſſity of applying to ſome Profeſſion, that, without engroſſing all his Time, might enable him to ſupport himſelf, and having obtained a very uncommon Knowledge of the Mathematick, he read Lectures in thoſe Sciences to a ſelect Number of young Gentlemen in the Univerſity.

At length, his Propenſion to the Study of Phyſick grew too violent to be reſiſted, and, though he ſtill intended to make Divinity the great Employment of his Life, he could not deny himſelf the Satisfaction of ſpending ſome Time upon the Medical Writers, for the Peruſal of which he was ſo well qualified by his Acquaintance with the Mathematicks and Philoſophy.

But this Science correſponded ſo much with his natural Genius, that he could not forbear making that his Buſineſs which he intended only as his Diverſion, and ſtill growing more eager, as he advanced further, he at length determined wholly to maſter that Profeſſion, and to take his Degree in Phyſick, before he engaged in the Duties of the Miniſtry.

It is, I believe, a very juſt Obſervation, that Men's Ambition is generally proportioned to their Capacity. Providence ſeldom ſends any into the World with an Inclination to attempt great Things, who have not Abilities likewiſe to perform them. To have formed the Deſign of gaining a compleat Knowledge of Medicine by way of digreſſion from Theological Studies, would have been little leſs than Madneſs in moſt Men, and would have only expoſed them to Ridicule and Contemp. But *Boerhaave* was one of thoſe mighty Genius's, to whom ſcarce any thing appears impoſſible, and who think nothing worthy of their Efforts but what appears inſurmountable to common Underſtandings.

He began this new Courſe of Study by

27

In purſuance of this Plan, he went to *Hardewich*, in order to take the Degree of Doctor in Phyſick, which he obtained in *July* 1693, having performed a publick Diſputation, *de utilitate explorandorum excrementorum in ægris, ut ſignorum.*

Then returning to *Leiden*, full of his pious Deſign of undertaking the Miniſtry, he found to his ſurpriſe unexpected Obſtacles thrown in his Way, and an Inſinuation diſperſed through the Univerſity, that made him ſuſpected, not of any ſlight Deviation from received Opinions, not of any pertinacious Adherence to his own Notions in doubtful and diſputable Matters, but of no leſs than *Spinoſiſm*, or in plainer Terms of Atheiſm itſelf.

How ſo injurious a Report came to be raiſed, circulated and credited will be doubtleſs very eagerly inquired : We ſhall therefore give the Relation, not only to ſatisfy the Curioſity of Mankind, but to ſhew that no Merit, however exalted, is exempt from being not only attacked but wounded by the moſt contemptible Whiſpers. Thoſe who cannot ſtrike with Force, can however poyſon their Weapon, and, weak as they are, give mortal Wounds, and bring a Hero to the Grave : So true is that Obſervation, that many are able to do hurt, but few to do good.

This detestable Calumny owed its Riſe to an Incident from which no Conſequence of Importance could be poſſibly apprehended. As *Boerhaave* was ſitting in a common Boat, there aroſe a Converſation among the Paſſengers upon the impious and pernicious Doctrine of *Spinoſa*, which, as they all agreed, tends to the utter Overthrow of all Religion. *Boerhaave* ſat, and attended ſilently to this Diſcourſe for ſome time, till one of the Company, willing to diſtinguiſh himſelf by his Zeal, inſtead of confuting ÿ Poſitions of *Spinoſa* by Argument, begun to give a looſe to contumelious Language, and virulent Invectives, which *Boerhaave* was ſo little pleaſed with, that at laſt he could not forbear aſking him, whether he had ever read the Author he declaimed againſt.

The Orator, not being able to make much Anſwer, was checked in the midſt of his Invectives, but not without feeling a ſecret Reſentment againſt the Perſon who had at once interrupted his Harangue, and expoſed his Ignorance.

This was obſerved by a Stranger who was in the Boat with them; he enquired of his Neighbour the Name of the young Man, whoſe Queſtion had put an End to the Diſcourſe, and having learned it, ſet it down in his Pocket-book, as it appears, with a malicious Deſign, for in a few

Days, it was the common Converſation at *Leiden*, that *Boerhaave* had revolted to *Spinoſa*.

It was in vain that his Advocates and Friends pleaded his learned and unanſwerable Confutation of all atheiſtical Opinions, and particularly of the Syſtem of *Spinoſa*, in his Diſcourſe of the Diſtinction between Soul and Body. Such Calumnies are not eaſily ſuppreſs'd, when they are once become general. They are kept alive and ſupported by the Malice of bad, and ſometimes by the Zeal of good Men, who, though they do not abſolutely believe them, think it yet the ſecureſt Method to keep not only guilty but ſuſpected Men out of publick Employments, upon this Principle, That the Safety of Many is to be preferred before the Advantage of Few.

Boerhaave finding this formidable Oppoſition raiſed againſt his Pretenſions to Eccleſiaſtical Honours or Preferments, and even againſt his Deſign of aſſuming the Character of a Divine, thought it neither neceſſary nor prudent to ſtruggle with the Torrent of popular Prejudice, as he was equally qualified for a Profeſſion, not indeed of equal Dignity or Importance, but which muſt undoubtedly claim the ſecond Place among thoſe which are of the greateſt Benefit to Mankind.

He therefore applied himſelf to his Medical Studies with new Ardour and Alacrity, reviewed all his former Obſervations and Enquiries, and was continually employed in making new Acquiſitions.

(*To be continued.*)

28

The GENTLEMAN's MAGAZINE, Vol. IX.

neſs was, at firſt, not great, and his Circumſtances by no means eaſy; but ſtill ſuperiour to any Diſcouragement, he continued his Search after Knowledge, and determined that Proſperity, if ever he was to enjoy it, ſhould be the Conſequence, not of mean Art, or diſingenuous Solicitations, but of real Merit, and ſolid Learning.

His ſteady Adherence to his Reſolutions appears yet more plainly from this Circumſtance: He was, while he yet remained in this unpleaſing Situation, invi... .y one of the firſt Favourites of K. *William* III. to ſettle at the *Hague*, upon very advantageous Conditions; but declined the Offer. For having no Ambition but after Knowledge, he was deſirous of living at liberty, without any Reſtraint upon his Looks, his Thoughts, or his Tongue, and at the utmoſt Diſtance from all Contentions, and State-Parties. His Time was wholly taken up in viſiting the Sick, Studying, making Chymical Experiments, ſearching into every part of Medicine with the utmoſt Diligence, teaching the Mathematicks, and reading the Scriptures, and thoſe Authors who profeſs to teach a certain Method of loving God. *

This was his Method of living to the Year 1701, when he was recommended by Mr *Van Berg* to the Univerſity, as a proper Perſon to ſucceed *Drelincurtius* in the Profeſſorſhip of Phyſick, and elected without any Solicitation on his part, and almoſt without his Conſent, on the 18th of *May*.

On this Occaſion, having obſerved, with Grief, that *Hippocrates*, whom he regarded not only as the Father but as the Prince of Phyſicians, was not ſufficiently read or eſteemed by young Students, he pronounced an Oration, *de commendando Studio Hippocratico*; by which he reſtored that great Author to his juſt and antient Reputation.

He now began to read publick Lectures

Continuation of the Life of Dr BOERHAAVE, *from p.* 73.

HAVING now qualified himſelf for the Practice of Phyſick, he began to viſit Patients, but without that Encouragement & others, not equally deſerving, have ſometimes met with. His Buſi-

---

* Circa hoc tempus, ſumtis conſiliariis, interioris promiſſi, invitatus, plus vice ſimplici, a Viro primariis dynaſtiis, ad gratia ſignificatione favorem Regis Guilielmi III, ut Hagam Comitum ſedes caperet Profeſſoriam, declinavit oblatam. Conatus cohibitus eius libera, vanus in orbis, ſuadiſſet parvo peculando unice impendit, ubi nec ...orum alio labore & ſundore, alio ſavore & diſtendere; ſpatium ſuatis ...s; ... Sic hunc vitae curſu, aegros viſens, ſtudens dans in Muſeo ſe condere, chymicas Tabulatas quaerens; doctu Medicinae ſortes exercitus colligit; Mathematicas artes alias tradens; Sacra literas, & Auctores ſi profeſſolas docere volunteſtis deum amandi Deum.

with

with great Applause, and was prevailed upon by his Audience to enlarge his original Design, and instruct them in Chymistry.

This he undertook, not only to the great Advantage of his Pupils, but to the great Improvement of the Art itself, which had been hitherto treated only in a confused and irregular Manner, and was little more than a History of particular Experiments, nor reduced to certain Principles, nor connected one to another: this vast Chaos he reduced to Order, and made that clear and easy, which was before to the last degree difficult and obscure.

His Reputation began now to bear some Proportion to his Merit, and extended itself to distant Universities; so that in 1703, the Professorship of Physick being vacant at *Groningen*, he was invited thither; but he refused to leave *Leiden*, and chose to continue his present Course of Life.

This Invitation and Refusal being related to the Governors of the University of *Leiden*, they had so grateful a Sense of his Regard for them, that they immediately voted an Honorary Increase of his Salary, and promised him the first Professorship that should be vacant.

On this Occasion he pronounced an Oration upon *the Use of Mechanicks in the Science of Physick*, in which he endeavour'd to recommend a rational and mathematical Enquiry into the Causes of Diseases, and the Structure of Bodies; and to shew the Follies and Weaknesses of the Jargon introduced by *Paracelsus, Helmont*, and other chymical Enthusiasts, who have obtruded upon the World the most airy Dreams, and instead of enlightening their Readers with Explications of Nature have darken'd the plainest Appearances, and bewilder'd Mankind in Error and Obscurity.

Boerhaave had now for nine Years read physical Lectures, but without the Title or Dignity of a Professor, when by the Death of Professor *Hotton*, the Professorship of Physick and Botany fell to him of course.

On this Occasion he asserted the Simplicity and Facility of the Science of Physick, in opposition to those that think Obscurity contributes to the Dignity of Learning, and that to be admired it is necessary not to be understood.

His Profession of Botany made it part of his Duty to superintend the physical Garden, which improved so much by the immense Number of new Plants which he procured, that it was enlarged to twice its original Extent.

In 1714 he was deservedly advanced to the highest Dignities of the University, and in the same Year made Physician of St *Augustin*'s Hospital in *Leiden*, into which the Students are admitted twice a Week to learn the Practice of Physick.

This was of equal Advantage to the Sick and to the Students, for the Success of his Practice was the best Demonstration of the Soundness of his Principles.

When he laid down his Office of Governor of the University in 1715, he made an Oration upon the Subject of *attaining to Certainty in natural Philosophy*; in which he declares, in the strongest Terms, in favour of Experimental Knowledge, and reflects with just Severity upon those arrogant Philosophers, who are too easily disgusted with the slow Methods of obtaining true Notions by frequent Experiments, and who, possest with too high an Opinion of their own Abilities, rather chuse to consult their own Imaginations, than enquire into Nature, and are better pleased with the charming Amusement of forming Hypotheses, than the tuilsome Drudgery of making Observations.

The Emptiness and Uncertainty of all those Systems, whether venerable for their Antiquity, or agreeable for their Novelty, he has evidently shown; and not only declared, but proved, that we are entirely ignorant of the Principles of Things, and that all the Knowledge we have is of such Qualities alone as are discoverable by Experience, or such as may be deduced from them by Mathematical Demonstration.

This Discourse, filled as it was with Piety, and a true Sense of the Greatness of the Supreme Being, and the Incomprehensibility of his Works, gave such Offence to a Professor of *Francker*, who professed the utmost Esteem for Des *Cartes*, and considered his Principles as the Bulwark of Orthodoxy, that he appeared in vindication of his darling Author, and spoke of the Injury done him with the utmost Vehemence, declaring little less than that the *Cartesian* System and the Christian must inevitably stand and fall together, and that to say we were ignorant of the Principles of Things, was not only to enlist among the Sceptics but sink into Atheism itself.

So far can Prejudice darken the Understanding, as to make it consider precarious Systems as the chief Support of sacred and unvariable Truth.

This Treatment of *Boerhaave* was so far resented by the Governors of his University, that they procured from *Francker neker* a Recantation of the Invective that had been thrown out against him; this was not only complied with, but Offers were made him of more ample Satisfaction; to which he return'd an Answer not less to his Honour than the Victory he gain'd, " That he should think himself sufficiently compensated, if his Adversary received no farther Molestation on his Account."

[*To be continued in our next*]

CONCLUSION *of the* LIFE *of Dr* BOERHAAVE, *from p.* 114.

SO far was this weak and injudicious Attack from shaking a Reputation, not casually raised by Fashion or Caprice, but founded upon solid Merit, that the same Year his Correspondence was desired upon Botany and Natural Philosophy by the Academy of Sciences at *Paris*, of which he was, upon the Death of Count *Marsigli*, in the Year 1728, elected a Member.

Nor were the *French* the only Nation by which this great Man was courted and distinguished, for two Years after he was elected Fellow of our Royal Society.

It cannot be doubted, but thus caress'd, and honoured with the highest and most publick Marks of Esteem by other Nations, he became more celebrated in the University; for *Boerhaave* was not one of those learned Men, of whom the World has seen too many, that disgrace their Studies by their Vices, and by unaccountable Weaknesses make themselves ridiculous at home, while their Writings procure them the Veneration of distant Countries, where their Learning is known, but not their Follies.

Not that his Countrymen can be charged with being insensible of his Excellencies till other Nations taught them

to admire him; for in 1718 he was chosen to succeed *Le Mort* in the Professorship of *Chemistry*, on which Occasion he pronounced an Oration De *Chemia erroes sues uxurgante*, in which he treated that Science with an Elegance of Stile not often to be found in chemical Writers, who seem general'y to have affected not only a barbarous, but unintelligible Phrase, and to have, like the *Pythagoreans* of old, wrapt up their Secrets in Symbols and Ænigmatical Expressions, either because they believed that Mankind would reverence most what they least understood, or because they wrote not from Benevolence but Vanity, and were desirous to be praised for their Knowledge, though they could not prevail upon themselves to communicate it.

In 1722, his Course both of Lectures and Practice was interrupted by the Gout, which, as he relates it in his Speech after his Recovery, he brought upon himself, by an imprudent Confidence in the Strength of his own Constitution, and by transgressing those Rules which he had a thousand times inculcated to his Pupils and Acquaintance. Rising in the Morning before Day, he went immediately, hot and sweating, from his Bed into the open Air, and exposed himself to the cold Dews.

The History of his Illness can hardly be read without Horror: He was for five Months confined to his Bed, where he lay upon his Back without daring to attempt the least Motion, because any Effort renewed his Torments, which were so exquisite, that he was at length not only deprived of Motion but of Sense. Here Art was at a stand, nothing could be attempted, because nothing could be proposed with the least Prospect of Success. At length having, in the sixth Month of his Illness, obtained some Remission, he took simple Medicines * in large Quantities, and at length wonderfully recovered.

His Recovery, so much desired, and so unexpected, was celebrated on *Jan.* 11, 1723, when he open'd his School again with general Joy and publick Illuminations.

It would be an Injury to the Memory of *Boerhaave* not to mention what was related by himself to one of his Friends, That when he lay whole Days and Nights without Sleep, he found no Method of diverting

* Succos praefao bibit *Nigdr herbarum* Cichoreae, Endiviae, Eymariae, Nasturtii aquatici, Veronicae aquaticae latifoliae, copia ingenti : Simul deglutiens abundantissime gummi scrabten Arabic.

diverting his Thoughts so effectual as Meditation upon his Studies, and that he often relieved and mitigated the Sense of his Torments, by the Recollection of what he had read, and by reviewing those Stores of Knowledge which he had reposited in his Memory.

This is perhaps an Instance of Fortitude and steady Composure of Mind, which would have been for ever the Boast of the Stoick Schools, and increased the Reputation of *Seneca* or *Cato*. The Patience of *Boerhaave*, as it was more rational, was more lasting than theirs; it was that *Patientia Christiana* which *Lipsius*, the great Master of the Stoical Philosophy, begged of God in his last Hours; it was founded on Religion, not Vanity, not on vain Reasonings, but on Confidence in God.

In 1727 he was seized with a violent Burning Fever, which continued so long that he was once more given up by his Friends.

From this time he was frequently afflicted with Returns of his Distemper, which yet did not so far subdue him, as to make him lay aside his Studies or his Lectures, till in 1726 he found himself so worn out, that it was improper for him to continue any longer the Professorships of Botany and Chymistry, which he therefore resigned *April* 28, and upon his Resignation spoke a *Sermo Academicus*, or Oration, in which he asserts the Power and Wisdom of the Creator from the wonderful Fabric of the Human Body; and confutes all those idle Reasoners who pretend to explain the Formation of Parts, or the animal Operations, to which he proves that Art can produce nothing equal, nor any thing parallel. One Instance I shall mention, which is produced by him, of the Vanity of any Attempt to rival the Work of God. Nothing is more boasted by the Admirers of Chymistry, than that they can, by artificial Heats and Digestion, imitate the Productions of Nature. *Let all these Heroes of Science meet together,* says Boerhaave, *let them take Bread and Wine, the Food that forms the Blood of Man, and by Assimilation contributes to the Growth of the Body: Let them try all their Arts, they shall not be able from these Materials to produce a single Drop of Blood.* So much is the most common Act of Nature beyond the utmost Efforts of the most extended Science!

From this Time *Boerhaave* lived with less publick Employment indeed, but not an idle or an useless Life; for, besides his Hours spent in instructing his Scho-

lars, a great Part of his Time was taken up by Patients which came, when the Distemper would admit it, from all Parts of *Europe* to consult him, or by Letters which, in more urgent Cases, were continually sent to enquire his Opinion, and ask his Advice.

Of his Sagacity, and the wonderful Penetration with which he often discover'd and describ'd, at the first Sight of a Patient, such Distempers as betray themselves by no Symptoms to common Eyes, such wonderful Relations have been spread over ý World, as, though attested beyond doubt, can scarcely be credited. I mention none of them, because I have no Opportunity of collecting Testimonies, or distinguishing between those Accounts which are well proved, and those which owe their Rise to Fiction and Credulity.

Yet I cannot but implore, with the greatest Earnestness, such as have been conversant with this great Man, that they will not so far neglect the common Interest of Mankind, as to suffer any of these Circumstances to be lost to Posterity. Men are generally idle, and ready to satisfy themselves, and intimidate the Industry of others, by calling that impossible which is only difficult. The Skill to which *Boerhaave* attained, by a long and unwearied Observation of Nature, ought therefore to be transmitted in all its Particulars to future Ages, that his Successors may be ashamed to fall below him, and that none may hereafter excuse his Ignorance by pleading the Impossibility of clearer Knowledge.

Yet so far was this great Master from presumptuous Confidence in his Abilities, that in his Examinations of the Sick he was remarkably circumstantial and particular. He well knew that the Originals of Distempers are often at a Distance from their visible Effects, that to conjecture where Certainty may be obtained, is either Vanity or Negligence, and that Life is not to be sacrificed, either to an Affectation of quick Discernment, or of crowded Practice, but may be required, if trifled away, at the Hand of the Physician.

About the Middle of the Year 1737, he felt the first Approaches of that fatal Illness that brought him to the Grave, of which we have inserted an Account written by himself *Sept.* 8, 1738, to a Friend at *London* *; which deserves not only

* Aetas, labor, corporisque opima pinguedo, effecerunt, ante annum, ut inertibus refertum, grave, hebes, plenitudine turgens corpus, suboluæ ad motus minimos, cum sensu suffocationis, præsertim

only to be preferved as an Hiftorical Relation of the Difeafe which deprived us of fo great a Man, but as a Proof of his Piety and Refignation to the divine Will.

In this laft Illnefs, which was to the laft degree lingering, painful and afflictive, his Conftancy and Firmnefs did not forfake him. He neither intermitted the neceffary Cares of Life, nor forgot the proper Preparations for Death. Tho' Dejection and Lownefs of Spirit was, as he himfelf tells us, Part of his Diftemper, yet even this, in fome meafure, gave way to that Vigour which the Soul receives from a Confciousnefs of Innocence.

About three Weeks before his Death he received a Vifit at his Country Houfe from the Rev. Mr *Schultens*, his intimate Friend, who found him fitting without Door, with his Wife, Sifter, and Daughter. After the Compliments of Form, the Ladies withdrew, and left them to private Converfation; when *Boerhaave* took Occafion to tell him what had been, during his Illnefs, the chief Subject of his Thoughts. He had never doubted of the Spiritual and immaterial Nature of the Soul, but declared that he had lately had a kind of experimental Certainty of the Diftinction between Corporeal and Thinking Subftances, which mere Reafon and Philofophy cannot afford, and Opportunities of contemplating the wonderful and inexplicable Union of Soul and Body, which nothing but long Sicknefs can give. This he illuftrated by a Defcription of the Effects which the Infirmities of his Body had upon his Faculties, which yet they did not fo opprefs or vanquifh, but his Soul was always Mafter of itfelf, and always refigned to the Pleafure of its Maker.

He related, with great Concern, that once his Patience fo far gave way to Extremity of Pain, that, after having lain fifteen Hours in exquifite Tortures, he prayed to God that he might be fet free by Death.

Mr *Schultens*, by way of Confolation, anfwered, That he thought fuch Wifhes,

pulfa mœſtitiæ ſpeculo, ineptam evaderet ad ullam metem. Urgebat præcipue ſubſiſtens profus & intercepta reſpiratio ad prima ſomni initia: Unde ſomnus prorſus prohibebatur, cum ſomnulentii ſtrangulationis moleſtia. Hinc Hydrops pedum, crurum, femorum, ſcroti, præputii, & abdominis. Quæ tamen omnia fublata. Sed dolor manet in abdomine, cum anxietate ſumma, anhelitu fuffocante, & debilitate incredibili: Somnus paucus, eoque vago, per ſomnia turbatifſimo; Animus vero rebus agendis ſim pie. Cum his hactenus ſeſſus nec enetjo: Extimam expectans Dei juſti, quibus reſigno datu, quæ ſibi amo, & honore unice.

when forced by continued and exceffive Torments, unavoidable in the prefent State of human Nature; that the beft Men, even *Job* himfelf, were not able to refrain from fuch Starts of Impatience. This he did not deny, but faid, "He that loves God, ought to think nothing defirable but what is moft pleafing to the fupreme Goodnefs."

Such were his Sentiments, and fuch his Conduct in this State of Weaknefs and Pain: As Death approached nearer, he was fo far from Terror or Confufion, that he feemed even lefs fenfible of Pain, and more chearful under his Torments, which continued till the 23d Day of *September* 1738, on which he died, between Four and Five in the Morning, in the 70th Year of his Age.

Thus died *Boerhaave*, a Man formed by Nature for great Defigns, and guided by Religion in the Exertion of his Abilities. He was of a robuft and athletic Conftitution of Body, fo harden'd by early Severities, and wholefome Fatigue, that he was infenfible of any Sharpnefs of Air, or Inclemency of Weather. He was tall, and remarkable for extraordinary Strength. There was in his Air and Motion fomething rough and artlefs, but fo majeftick and great at the fame time, that no Man ever looked upon him without Veneration, and a kind of tacit Submiffion to the Superiority of his Genius.

The Vigour and Activity of his Mind fparkled vifibly in his Eyes, nor was it ever obferved, that any Change of his Fortune, or Alteration in his Affairs, whether happy or unfortunate, affected his Countenance.

He was always chearful, and defirous of promoting Mirth by a facetious and humourous Converfation; he was never foured by Calumny and Detraction, nor ever thought it neceffary to confute them; for *they are Sparks*, faid he, *which, if you do not blow them, will go out of themfelves.*

Yet he took Care never to provoke Enemies by Severity of Cenfure, for he never dwelt on the Faults or Defects of others, and was fo far from inflaming the Envy of his Rivals by dwelling on his own Excellencies, that he rarely mentioned himfelf or his Writings.

He was not to be over-aw'd or depref'd by the Prefence, Frowns, or Infolence of Great Men, but perfifted on all Occafions in the Right, with a Refolution always prefent and always calm. He was modeft, but not timorous, and firm without Rudenefs.

He could, with uncommon Readinefs and Certainty, make a Conjecture of Mens

33

Mens Inclinations and Capacity by their Aspect.

His Method of Life was, to study in the Morning and Evening, and to allot the middle of the Day to his publick Business. His usual Exercise was Riding, till, in his latter Years, his Distempers made it more proper for him to walk; when he was weary, he amused himself with playing on the Violin.

His greatest Pleasure was to retire to his House in the Country, where he had a Garden stored with all the Herbs and Trees which the Climate would bear; here he used to enjoy his Hours unmolested, and prosecute his Studies without Interruption.

The Diligence with which he pursued his Studies, is sufficiently evident from his success. Statesmen and Generals may grow great by unexpected Accidents, and a fortunate Concurrence of Circumstances, neither procured, nor foreseen by themselves: But Reputation in the Learned World must be the effect of Industry and Capacity. *Boerhaave* lost none of his Hours, but when he had attained one Science, attempted another: He added Physic to Divinity, Chemistry to the Mathematicks, and Anatomy to Botany. He examined Systems by Experiments, and formed Experiments into Systems. He neither neglected the Observations of others, nor blindly submitted to celebrated Names. He neither thought so highly of himself as to imagine he could receive no Light from Books, nor so meanly as to believe he could discover nothing but what was to be learned from them. He examined the Observations of other Men, but trusted only to his own.

Nor was he unacquainted with the Art of recommending Truth by Elegance, and embellishing the Philosopher with polite Literature: he knew that but a small part of Mankind will sacrifice their Pleasure to their Improvement, and those Authors, who would find many Readers, must endeavour to please while they instruct.

He knew the Importance of his own Writings to Mankind, and lest he might by a Roughness and Barbarity of Stile, too frequent among Men of great Learning, disappoint his own Intentions, and make his Labours less useful, he did not neglect the politer Arts of Eloquence and Poetry. Thus was his Learning at once various and exact, profound and agreeable.

But his Knowledge, however uncommon, holds, in his Character, but the second Place; his Virtue was yet much more uncommon than his Learning. He was an admirable Example of Temperance, Fortitude, Humility and Devotion. His Piety, and a religious Sense of his Dependance on God, was the Basis of all his Virtues, and the Principle of his whole Conduct. He was too sensible of his Weakness to ascribe any thing to himself, or to conceive that he could subdue Passion, or withstand Temptation by his own natural Power; he attributed every good Thought, and every laudable Action to the Father of Goodness. Being once asked by a Friend, who had often admired his Patience under great Provocations, whether he knew what it was to be angry, and by what means he had so entirely suppressed that impetuous and ungovernable Passion? He answer'd, with the utmost Frankness and Sincerity, that he was naturally quick of Resentment, but that he had, by daily Prayer and Meditation, at length attained to this Mastery over himself.

As soon as he rose in the Morning, it, was throughout his whole Life, his daily Practice to retire for an Hour to private Prayer and Meditation; this, he often told his Friends, gave him Spirit and Vigour in the Business of the Day, and this he therefore commended as the best Rule of Life; for nothing, he knew, could support the Soul in all Distresses but a Confidence in the Supreme Being, nor can a steady and rational Magnanimity flow from any other Source than a Consciousness of the divine Favour.

He asserted on all Occasions the divine Authority, and sacred Efficacy of the Holy Scriptures, and maintained that they alone taught the Way of Salvation, and that they only could give Peace of Mind. The Excellency of the Christian Religion was the frequent Subject of his Conversation. A strict Obedience to the Doctrine, and a diligent Imitation of the Example of our blessed Saviour he often declared to be the Foundation of true Tranquillity. He recommended to his Friends a careful Observation of the Precept of *Moses* concerning the Love of God and Man. He worshipped God as he is in himself, without attempting to enquire into his Nature. He desired only to think of God, what God knows of himself. There he stopped, lest by indulging his own Ideas, he should form a Deity from his own Imagination, and sin by falling down before him. To the Will of God he paid an absolute Submission, without endeavouring to discover the Reason of his Determinations; and this he accounted the first and most inviolable Duty of a Christian. When he heard of a Criminal condemned to die, dio, he used to think, Who can tell whether this Man is not better than I? Or, if I am better, it is not to be ascribed to myself but to the Goodness of God.

Such were the Sentiments of *Boerhaave,* whose Words we have added in) *Note.**
So far was this Man from being made A impious by Philosophy, or vain by Knowledge, or by Virtue, that he ascribed all his Abilities to the Bounty, and all his Goodness to the Grace of God. May his Example extend its Influence to his Admirers and Followers! May those who study his Writings imitate his Life, and those who endeavour after his Knowledge B aspire likewise to his Piety!

He married, *September* 17, 1710, *Mary Drolenveaux,* the only Daughter of a Burgo-master of *Leyden,* by whom he had *Joanna Maria,* who survives her Father, and three other Children who died in their Infancy. C

The Works of this great Writer are so generally known, and so highly esteemed, that, though it may not be improper to enumerate them in the Order of Time in which they were published, it is wholly unnecessary to give any other Account of them.

He published in 1707 *Institutiones Medica,* to which he added in 1708 *Aphorismi de cognoscendis & curandis morbis.* D

1710, *Index Stirpium in Horto Academico.*

1719, *De Materia Medica, & Remediorum formulis Liber;* and in 1727 a second Edition. E

1720, *Alter Index Stirpium,* &c. adorned with Plates, and containing twice the number of Plants as the former.

1722, *Epistola ad Cl. Ruischium, qua*

sententiam Malpighianam de glandulis defendit.

1724, *Atrocis nec prius descripti Morbi Historia Illustrissimi Baronis Wassenariae.*

1725, *Opera Anatomica & Chirurgica Andrea Vesalii,* with the Life of *Vesalius.*

1728, *Altera atrocis rarissimique Morbi Marchionis de Sancto Albano Historia.*

Auctores de lue Aphrodisiaca, cum tractatu praefixo.

1731, *Aretaei Cappadocis nova Editio.*

1732, *Elementa Chemia.*

1734, *Observata de Argento vivo, ad Reg. Soc. & Acad. Scient.*

These are the Writings of the great *Boerhaave,* which have made all Encomiums useless and vain, since no Man can attentively peruse them without admiring the Abilities, and reverencing the Virtue of the Author.

* Doctrinam sacris Literis Hebraicae & Graecae traditam, solam animae salutarem & agnovit & fuit. Omni opportunitate profitebatur disciplinam, quam Jesus Christus ore & vita profert, unice tranquillitatem dare menti. Saepe-saepe dicit Amicis, pacem animi haud reperiundam nisi in magno Messiae praecepto de amore Amicae Dei & hominis bene observato. Neque enim, Scena monumenta nisi sum invenit, quod mentem humet. Deum plus adesse, qui ... intelligere de Deo unice voluit id, quod Deus de se indicavit. Eo contentus ultra nihil inquisivit, ne ... erraret. In voluntate Dei sic acquiescebat, ut illam pullam omnino rationem independens putaret. Hanc unice supremam aequalem legem & aequabilem, destinatam conducere perfectionem coelestem. De ... a Deo statuebat: Ut quavis eriundus ... ad proximi bonum demensus esset, semper ... explicuit, saepe diceret; "Quicquid quis me fiat audivus? Utique, si luce audiat, id nem nihil audivi tribuendum esse prius excusatus; sed ita loquantur Deo."

HAving the Satisfaction to find that the Account of Admiral BLAKE in our last *Magazine* was not disagreeable to the Publick, we propose in our next to entertain our Readers with the Life and Actions of Sir FRANCIS DRAKE, including many of the most memorable Transactions of the Reign of Queen *Elizabeth*, in which our long continued Wars with the *Spaniards* laid the Foundation of that settled Animosity which yet continues between the two Nations. The Importance of DRAKE's Expeditions, and the Greatness of his Reputation sufficiently appear from the foregoing *Memorial*, which though more strictly belonging to our Narration, we thought it not proper to delay. But it is not only to his Military Virtues that his Country owes Reverence and Gratitude. His Fortitude in surmounting Difficulties and encountering Dangers of a different Kind, his Spirit in forming great Designs, and his Resolution in prosecuting them, deserve to be proposed to the Imitation of every Age; and we are more indebted to the Discoverer than the Soldier, as the Nation owes less of its Wealth and Power to its Arms than to its Navigation.

The LIFE of Sir FRANCIS DRAKE.

FRANCIS DRAKE was the Son of a Clergyman in *Devonshire*, who being inclined to the Doctrine of the Protestants, at that Time much opposed by *Henry* VIII. was obliged to fly from his Place of Residence into *Kent* for Refuge, from the Persecution raised against him, and those of the same Opinion, by the Law of the Six Articles.

How long he lived there, or how he was supported, was not known, nor have we any Account of the first Years of Sir *Francis Drake's* Life, if any Disposition to Hazards and Adventures which might have been discovered in his Childhood, or of the Education which qualified him for such wonderful Attempts.

We are only informed, that he was put Apprentice by his Father to the Master of a small Vessel that traded to *France* and the *Low Countries*, under whom he probably learned the Rudiments of Navigation, and familiarised himself to the Dangers and Hardships of the Sea.

But how few Opportunities soever he might have in this Part of his Life for the Exercise of his Courage, he gave so many Proofs of his Diligence and Fidelity, that his Master dying unmarried left him his little Vessel in reward of his Service; a Circumstance that deserves to be remembered, not only as it may illustrate the private Character of this brave Man, but as it may hint to all those who may hereafter propose his Conduct for their Imitation, That Virtue is the surest Foundation both of Reputation and Fortune, and that the first Step to Greatness is to be honest.

If it were not improper to dwell longer on an Incident at the first View so inconsiderable, it might be added, That it deserves the Reflection of those, who, when they are engaged in Affairs not adequate to their Abilities, pass them over with a contemptuous Neglect, and while they amuse themselves with chimerical Schemes, and Plans of future Undertakings, suffer every Opportunity of smaller Advantage to slip away as unworthy their Regard. They may learn from the Example of Drake, that Diligence in Employments of less Consequence is the most successful Introduction to greater Enterprizes.

After having followed for some time his Master's Profession, he grew weary of so narrow a Province, and having sold his little Vessel, ventured his Effects in the new Trade to the *West-Indies*, which having not been long discovered, and very little frequented by the *English* till that Time, were conceived so much to abound in Wealth, that no Voyage thither could

fail of being recompensed by great Advantages. Nothing was talked of among the mercantile or adventurous Part of Mankind, but the Beauty and Riches of this New World. Fresh Discoveries were frequently made, new Countries and Nations never heard of before were daily described, and it may easily be concluded that the Relaters did not diminish the Merit of their Attempts, by suppressing or diminishing any Circumstance that might produce Wonder, or excite Curiosity. Nor was their Vanity only engaged in raising Admirers, but their Interest likewise in procuring Adventurers, who were indeed easily gained by the Hopes which naturally arise from new Prospects, though thro' Ignorance of the *American* Seas, and by the Malice of the *Spaniards*, who from the first Discovery of those Countries considered every other Nation that attempted to follow them, as Invaders of their Rights, the best concerted Designs often miscarried.

Among those who suffered most from the *Spanish* Injustice, was Capt. *John Hawkins*, who having been admitted by the Viceroy to traffic in the Bay of *Mexico*, was, contrary to the Stipulation then made between them, and in Violation of the Peace between *Spain* and *England*, attacked without any Declaration of Hostilities, and obliged, after an obstinate Resistance, to retire with the Loss of four Ships, and a great Number of his Men, who were either destroyed or carried into Slavery.

In this Voyage *Drake* had adventured almost all his Fortune, which he in vain endeavoured to recover, both by his own private Interest, and by obtaining Letters from Q. *Elizabeth*; for the *Spaniards* deaf to all Remonstrances either vindicated the Injustice of the Viceroy, or at least forbore to redress it.

Drake thus oppress'd and impoverish'd, retain'd at least his Courage and his Industry, that ardent Spirit that prompted him to Adventures, and that indefatigable Patience that enab'ed him to surmount Difficulties. He did not sit down idly to lament Misfortunes which Heaven had put it in his Power to remedy, or to repine at Poverty while the Wealth of his Enemies was to be gained. But having made two Voyages to *America* for the Sake of gaining Intelligence of the State of the *Spanish* Settlements, and acquainted himself with the Seas and Coasts, he determined on a third Expedition of more Importance, by which the *Spaniards* should find how imprudently they always act, who injure and insult a brave Man.

4

On the 24th of *May*, 1572, *Francis Drake* set sail from *Plimouth* in the *Pascha* of seventy Tons, accompanied by the *Swan* of Twenty five Tons, commanded by his Brother *John Drake*, having in both the Vessels seventy three Men and Boys, with a Year's Provision, and such Artillery and Ammunition as was necessary for his Undertaking, which, however incredible it may appear to such as consider rather his Force than his Fortitude, was no less than to make Reprisals upon the most powerful Nation in the World.

The Wind continuing favourable they entered *June* 20, between *Guadalape* and *Dominica*, and on *July* 6th saw the Highland of *Santa Martha*, then continuing their Course, after having been becalm'd for some time, they arriv'd at Port *Pheasant*, so named by *Drake* in a former Voyage, to the East of *Nombre de Dios*. Here he proposed to build his Pinnaces, D he had brought in Pieces ready framed from *Plimouth*, and was going ashore with a few Men unarmed, but discovering a Smoke at a Distance, ordered the other Boat to follow him with a greater Force.

Then marching towards the Fire, he found was in the Top of a high Tree, he found a Plate of Lead nailed to another Tree, with an Inscription engraved upon it by one *Garret* an *Englishman*, who had left that Place but five Days before, and had taken this Method of informing him that the *Spaniards* had been advertised of his Intention to anchor at that Place, and that it therefore would be prudent to make a very short Stay there.

But *Drake* knowing how convenient this Place was for his Design, and considering that the Hazard and Waste of Time, which could not be avoided in seeking another Station, was equivalent to any other Danger which was to be apprehended from the *Spaniards*, determined to follow his first Resolution; only, for his greater Security, he ordered a kind of Palisade, or Fortification, to be made, by felling large Trees, and laying the Trunks and Branches one upon another by the Side of the River.

On *July* 20, having built their Pinnaces, and being joined by one Capt. *Rouse*, who happened to touch at the same Place with a Bark of 50 Men, they set sail towards *Nombre de Dios*, and taking two Frigates at the Island of *Pines*, were informed by the Negroes which they found in them, that the Inhabitants of that Place were in Expectation of some Soldiers, which the Governor of *Panama* had promised, to defend them from the *Symerons*, or fugitive Negroes, who having escaped from the Tyranny of their Masters in great Numbers, had settled themselves under two Kings, or Leaders, on each Side of the Way between *Nombre de Dios* and *Panama*, and not only asserted their natural Right to Liberty and Independence, but endeavoured to revenge the Cruelties they had suffer'd, and had lately put the Inhabitants of *Nombre de Dios* into the utmost Consternation.

These Negroes the Captain set on Shore on the main Land, so that they might, by joining the *Symerons*, recover their Liberty, or at least might not have it in their Power to give the People of *Nombre de Dios* any speedy Information of his Intention to invade them.

Then selecting fifty three Men from his own Company, and twenty from the Crew of his new Associate Captain *Rouse*, he embarked with them in his Pinnaces, and set sail for *Nombre de Dios*.

On *July* the 28th, at Night, he approached the Town undiscovered, and dropt his Anchors under the Shore, intending after his Men were refreshed, to begin the Attack; but finding that they were terrifying each other with formidable Accounts of the Strength of the Place, and the Multitude of the Inhabitants, he determined to hinder the Panic from spreading farther, by leading them immediately to Action; and therefore ordering them to their Oars, he landed without any Opposition, there being only one Gunner upon the Bay, tho' it was secur'd with six Brass Cannons of the largest Size ready mounted. But the Gunner, while they were throwing the Cannons from their Carriages, alarmed the Town, as they soon discovered by the Bell, the Drums, and the Noise of the People.

Drake leaving twelve Men to guard the Pinnaces, marched round the Town with no great Opposition, the Men being more hurt by treading on the Weapons left on the Ground by the flying Enemy, than by the Resistance which they encountered.

At length having taken some of the *Spaniards*, *Drake* commanded them to shew him the Governor's House, where the Mules that bring the Silver from *Panama* were unloaded; there they found the Door open, and entering the Room where the Silver was reposited, found it heaped up in Bars in such Quantities as almost exceed Belief, the Pile being, they conjectur'd, seventy Feet in Length, ten in Breadth, and twelve in Height, each Bar weighing between thirty and forty-five Pounds.

It

It is easy to imagine that at the Sight of this Treasure, nothing was thought on by the English, but by what means they might best convey it to their Boats; and doubtless it was not easy for Drake, who, considering their Distance from the Shore, and the Numbers of their Enemy, was afraid of being intercepted in his Retreat, to hinder his Men from encumbering themselves with so much Silver as might have retarded their March, and obstructed the Use of their Weapons; however, by promising to lead them to the King's Treasure-house, where there was Gold and Jewels to a far greater Value, and where the Treasure was not only more portable, but nearer the Coast, he persuaded them to follow him, and rejoin the main Body of his Men then drawn up under the Command of his Brother in the Market-place.

Here he found his little Troop much discouraged by the Imagination, that if they stayed any longer the Enemy would gain Possession of their Pinnaces, and that they should then, without any Means of Safety, be left to stand alone against the whole Power of that Country; Drake, not indeed easily terrified, but sufficiently cautious, sent to the Coast to enquire the Truth, and see if the same Terror had taken possession of the Men whom he had left to guard his Boats; but finding no Foundation for these dreadful Apprehensions, he persisted in his first Design, and led the Troop forward to the Treasure-house. In their Way there fell a violent Shower of Rain, which wet some of their Bow-strings, and extinguish'd many of their Matches; a Misfortune which which might soon have been repaired, and which perhaps the Enemy might suffer in common with them, but which however on this Occasion very much embarrass'd them, as the Delay produced by it repressed that Ardour which sometimes is only to be kept up by continued Action, and gave time to the Timorous and Slothful to spread their Insinuations, and propagate their Cowardice. Some, whose Fear was their predominant Passion, were continually magnifying the Numbers and Courage of their Enemies, and represented whole Nations as ready to rush upon them; others, whose Avarice mingled with their Concern for their own Safety, were more solicitous to preserve what they had already gained, than to acquire more; and others, brave in themselves, and resolute, began to doubt of Success in an Undertaking in which they were associated with such cowardly Companions. So that scarcely

any Man appeared to proceed in their Enterprize with that Spirit and Alacrity which could give Drake a Prospect of Success.

This he perceived, and with some Emotion told them, that if, after having had the chief Treasure of the World within their Reach, they should go home and languish in Poverty, they could blame nothing but their own Cowardice; that he had perform'd his Part, and was still desirous to lead them on to Riches and to Honour.

Then finding that either Shame or Conviction made them willing to follow him, he ordered the Treasure-house to be forced, and commanding his Brother, and Oxenham of Plymouth, a Man known afterwards for his bold Adventures in the same Parts, to take charge of the Treasure, he commanded the other Body to follow him to the Market-place, that he might be ready to oppose any scatter'd Troops of the Spaniards, and hinder them from uniting into one Body.

But as he stepp'd forward, his Strength fail'd him on a sudden, and he fell down speechless. Then it was that his Companions perceived a Wound in his Leg, which he had received in the first Encounter, but hitherto concealed, lest his Men, easily discouraged, should make their Concern for his Life a Pretence for returning to their Boats. Such had been his Loss of Blood, as was discovered upon nearer Observation, that it had filled the Prints of his Footsteps, and it appear'd scarce credible that after such Effusion of Blood Life should remain.

The Bravest were now willing to retire, neither the Desire of Honour nor of Riches was thought enough to prevail in any Man over his Regard for his Leader. Drake, whom Cordials had now restored to his Speech, was the only Man who could not be prevailed on to leave the Enterprize unfinish'd. It was to no Purpose that they advised him to submit to go on board to have his Wound dressed, and promised to return with him and compleat their Design; he well knew how impracticable it was to regain the Opportunity when it was once lost, and could easily foresee that a Respite, of but a few Hours, would enable the Spaniards to recover from their Consternation, to assemble their Forces, refit their Batteries, and remove their Treasure. What he had undergone so much Danger to obtain was now in his Hands, and the Thoughts of leaving it untouch'd was too mortifying to be patiently born.

However, as there was little Time for
Consultatio

39

Confultation, and the fame Danger attended their Stay in that Perplexity and Confufion, as their Return, they bound up his Wound with his Scarf, and partly by Force, partly by Entreaty, carried him to the Boats. In which they all embark'd by Break of Day.

Then taking with them, out of the Harbour, a Ship loaded with Wines, they went to the *Baftimentes*, an Ifland about a League from the Town, where they ftayed two Days to repofe the wounded Men, and to regale themfelves with the Fruits which grew in great Plenty in the Gardens of that Ifland.

During their Stay here there came over from the Main Land a *Spanifh* Gentleman, fent by the Governor with Inftructions to enquire whether the Captain was that *Drake* who had been before on their Coaft, whether the Arrows with which many of their Men were wounded were not poifon'd, and whether they wanted Provifions or other Neceffaries. The Meffenger likewife extoll'd their Courage with the higheft Encomiums, and expreffed his Admiration of their daring Undertaking. *Drake*, tho' he knew the Civilities of an Enemy are always to be fufpected, and that the Meffenger, amidft all his Proteffions of Regard, was no other than a Spy, yet knowing that he had nothing to apprehend, treated him with the higheft Honours that his Condition admitted of; in anfwer to his Enquiries, he affured him that he was the fame *Drake* with whofe Character they were before acquainted, that he was a rigid Obferver of the Laws of War, and never permitted his Arrows to be poifon'd; he then difmiffed him with confiderable Prefents, and told him that, tho' he had unfortunately fail'd in this Attempt, he would never defift from his Defign, till he had fhared with *Spain* the Treafures of *America*.

They then refolved to return to the Ifle of *Pines*, where they had left their Ships, and confult about the Meafures they were now to take, and having arrived, *Auguft* 1, at their former Station, they difmiffed Captain *Roufe*, who judging it unfafe to ftay any longer on the Coaft, defired to be no longer engaged in their Defigns.

But *Drake*, not to be difcouraged from his Purpofe by a fingle Difappointment, after having enquir'd of a Negro, whom he took aboard at *Nombre de Dios*, the moft wealthy Settlements, and weakeft Parts of the Coaft, refolved to attack *Carthagena*; and fetting fail without Lofs

of Time, came to anchor, *Auguft* 13, between *Charefha* and *St. Barnard's*, two Iflands at a little Diftance from the Harbour of *Carthagena*; then paffing with his Boats round the Ifland he entered the Harbour, and in the Mouth of it found a Frigate with only an old Man in it, who voluntarily inform'd them, that about an Hour before a Pinnace had paffed by with Sails and Oars, and all the Appearance of Expedition and Importance, that as fhe paffed the Crew on board her bid them take care of themfelves, and that as foon as fhe touched the Shore, they heard the Noife of Cannon fired as a Warning, and faw the Shipping in the Port drawn up under the Guns of the Caftle.

The Captain, who had himfelf heard the Difcharge of the Artillery, was foon convinced that he was difcover'd, and that therefore nothing could be attempted with any Probability of Succefs. He therefore contented himfelf with taking a Ship of *Seville*, of two hundred and forty Tons, which the Relater of this Voyage mentions as a very large Ship, and two fmall Frigates, in which he found Letters of Advice from *Nombre de Dios*, intended to alarm that Part of the Coaft.

Drake now finding his Pinnaces of great Ufe, and not having a fufficient Number of Sailors for all his Veffels, was defirous of deftroying one of his Ships, that his Pinnaces might be better mann'd: This, neceffary as it was, could not eafily be done without difgufting his Company, who having made feveral profperous Voyages in that Veffel, would be unwilling to have it deftroyed. *Drake* well knew that nothing but the Love of their Leaders could animate his Followers to encounter fuch Hardfhips as he was about to expofe them to, and therefore rather chofe to bring his Defigns to pafs by Artifice than Authority. He fent for the Carpenter of the *Swan*, took him into his Cabin, and having firft engaged him to Secrecy, ordered him in the middle of the Night to go down into the Well of the Ship, and bore three Holes through the Bottom, laying fomething againft them that might hinder the Bubbling of the Water from being heard. To this, the Carpenter, after fome Expoftulation, confented, and the next Night performed his Promife.

In the Morning, *Aug*. 15, *Drake* going out with his Pinnace a fifhing rowed up to the *Swan*, and having invited his Brother to partake of his Diverfion, enquired, with a negligent Air, why their Bark was so deep in the Water; upon which, the Steward going down returned immediately with an Account that the Ship was leaky, and in Danger of sinking in a little Time. They had Recourse immediately to the Pump, but having laboured till three in the Afternoon, and gained very little upon the Water, they willingly, according to *Drake's* Advice, set the Vessel on Fire, and went on Board the Pinnaces.

Finding it now necessary to lie conceal'd for some Time, till the *Spaniards* should forget their Danger, and remit their Vigilance, they set sail for the Sound of *Darien*, and without approaching the Coast, that their Course might not be observed, they arrived there in six Days.

This being a convenient Place for their Reception, both on Account of Privacy, as it was out of the Road of all Trade, and as it was well supplied with Wood, Water, wild Fowl, Hogs, Deer, and all Kinds of Provisions, he stayed here 15 Days to clean his Vessels, and refresh his Men, who worked interchangeably, on one Day the one half, and on the next the other.

On the fifth Day of *September*, *Drake* left his Brother with the Ship at *Darien*, and set out with two Pinnaces towards the *Rio Grande*, which it reached in three Days, and on the ninth were discovered by a *Spaniard* from the Bank, who believing them to be his Countrymen, made a Signal to them to come on Shore, with which they very readily complied; but he soon finding his Mistake abandoned his Plantation, where they found great Plenty of Provisions, with which having laden their Vessels, they departed. So great was the Quantity of Provisions which they amassed here and in other Places, that in different Parts of the Coast they built four Magazines or Storehouses, which they filled with Necessaries for the Prosecution of their Voyage. These they placed at such a Distance from each other, that the Enemy, if he should surprise one, might yet not discover the rest.

In the mean time, his Brother, Captain *John Drake*, went, according to the Instructions that had been left him, in search of the *Symerons* or fugitive Negroes, from whose Assistance alone they had now any Prospect of a successful Voyage, and touching upon the main Land, by means of the Negro whom they had taken from *Nombre de Dios*, engaged two of them to come on Board his Pinnace, leaving two of their own Men as Hostages for their returning. These Men, having assured *Drake* of the Affection of their

Nation, appointed an Interview between him and their Leaders. So leaving Port *Plenty*, in the Isle of *Pines*, so named by the *English* from the great Stores of Provisions which they had amassed at that Place, they came, by the Direction of the *Symerons*, into a secret Bay among beautiful Islands covered with Trees, which concealed their Ship from Observation, and where the Channel was so narrow and rocky, that it was impossible to enter it by Night, so that there was no Danger of a sudden Attack.

Here they met and entered into Engagements, which common Enemies and common Dangers preserved from Violation. But the first Conversation informed the *English* that their Expectations were not immediately to be gratified, for up n their Enquiries after the most probable Means of gaining Gold and Silver, the *Symerons* told them, that had they known sooner the chief End of their Expedition, they could easily have gratified them, but that during the rainy Season, which was now begun, and which continues six Months, they could not recover the Treasure, which they had taken from the *Spaniards*, out of the Rivers in which they had concealed it.

Drake, therefore, proposing to wait in this Place till the Rains were past, built, with the Assistance of the *Symerons*, a Fort of Earth and Timber, and leaving Part of his Company with the *Symerons*, set out with three Pinnaces towards *Carthagena*, being of a Spirit too active to lie still patiently, even in a State of Plenty and Security, and with the most probable Expectations of immense Riches.

On the 16th of *October*, he anchor'd within Sight of *Carthagena* without landing, and on the 17th, going out to Sea took a *Spanish* Bark, with which they enter'd the Harbour, where they were accosted by a *Spanish Gentleman*, whom they had some time before taken, and set at Liberty, who coming to them in a Boat, as he pretended, without the Knowledge of the Governor, made them great Promises of Refreshment and Professions of Esteem; but *Drake* having waited till the next Morning without receiving the Provisions he had been prevail'd upon to expect, found that all this pretended Kindness was no more than a Stratagem to amuse him, while the Governor was raising Forces for his Destruction.

October 20, they took two Frigates coming out of *Carthagena* without Lading. Why the *Spaniards*, knowing *Drake* to lie at the Mouth of the Harbour, sent out their Vessels on purpose to be taken, does not

41

not appear. Perhaps they thought that, in order to keep Possession of his Prizes, he would divide his Company, and by that Division be more easily destroyed.

In a few Hours afterwards, they sent out two Frigates well mann'd, which *Drake* soon forced to retire, and having sunk one of his Prizes, and burnt the other in their Sight, leaped afterwards ashore, single, in Defiance of their Troops, which hover'd at a Distance in the Woods and on the Hills, without ever venturing to approach within Reach of the Shot from the Pinnaces.

To leap upon an Enemy's Coast in Sight of a superiour Force, only to show how little they were feared, was an Act that would in these Times meet with little Applause, nor can the General be seriously commended, or rationally vindicated, who exposes his Person to Destruction, and, by consequence, his Expedition to Miscarriage, only for the Pleasure of an idle Insult, an insignificant Bravado. All that can be urged in his Defence, is, that, perhaps it might contribute to heighten the Esteem of his Followers, as few Men, especially of that Class, are philosophical enough to state the exact Limits of Prudence and Bravery, or not to be dazzled with an Intrepidity how improperly soever exerted. It may be added, that perhaps the *Spaniards*, whose Notions of Courage are sufficiently romantic, might look upon him as a more formidable Enemy, and yield more easily to a Hero of whose Fortitude they had so high an Idea.

However, finding the whole Country advertised of his Attempts, and in Arms to oppose him, he thought it not proper to stay longer where there was no Probability of Success, and where he might in time be overpowered by Multitudes, and therefore determined to go forwards to *Rio de Hcha.*

This Resolution, when it was known by his Followers, threw them into Astonishment, and the Company of one of his Pinnaces remonstrated to him, that they placed the highest Confidence in his Conduct, they could not think of undertaking such a Voyage without Provisions, having only a Gammon of Bacon, and a small Quantity of Bread for seventeen Men: *Drake* answered them, that there was on Board his Vessel even a greater Scarcity; but yet, if they would adventure to share his Fortune, he did not doubt of extricating them from all their Difficulties.

Such was the Heroic Spirit of *Drake*, that he never suffered himself to be diverted from his Designs by any Difficul-

ties, nor ever thought of relieving his Exigencies, but at the Expence of his Enemies.

Resolution and Success reciprocally produce each other. He had not sailed more than three Leagues, before they discover'd a large Ship, which they attack'd with all the Intrepidity that Necessity inspires, and happily found it laden with excellent Provisions.

But finding his Crew growing faint and sickly with their Manner of Living in the Pinnaces, which was less commodious than on Board the Ships, he determined to go back to the *Symerons*, with whom he left his Brother and Part of his Force, and attempt by their Conduct to make his Way over, and invade the *Spaniards* in the Inland Parts, where they would probably never dream of an Enemy.

When they arrived at Port *Diego*, so named from the Negro who had procured them their Intercourse with the *Symerons*, they found Capt. *John Drake*, and one of his Company dead, being killed, in attempting, almost unarmed, to board a Frigate well provided with all Things necessary for its Defence. The Captain was unwilling to attack it, and represented to them the Madness of their Proposal, but being overborn by their Clamours and Importunities, to avoid the Imputation of Cowardice, complied to his Destruction. So dangerous is it for the chief Commander to be absent!

Nor was this their only Misfortune, for, in a very short Time, many of them were attacked by the *Calenture*, a malignant Fever, very frequent in the hot Climates, which carried away, among several others, *Joseph Drake*, another Brother of the Commander.

While *Drake* was employed in taking Care of the sick Men, the *Symerons*, who ranged the Country for Intelligence, brought him an Account, that the *Spanish* Fleet was arrived at *Nombre de Dios*, the Truth of which was confirmed by a Pinnace, which he sent out to make Observations.

This, therefore, was the Time for their Journey, when the Treasures of the *American* Mines were to be transported from *Panama*, over Land, to *Nombre de Dios*. He therefore, by the Direction of the *Symerons*, furnished himself with all Things necessary, and on *Feb.* 3, set out from Port *Diego*.

Having lost already 28 of his Company, and being under a Necessity of leaving some to guard his Ship, he took with him only 18 *English*, and 30 *Symerons*, who, not only served as Guides to show the Way, but

The LIFE of Admiral D R A K E.

be as Parveyors to procure Provisions. They carryed not only Arrows for War, but for Hunting and Fowling; the Heads of which are proportioned in Size to the Game which they are pursuing; A for Oxen, Stags, or wild Boars, they have Arrows, or Javelins, with Heads weighing a Pound and half, which they discharge near Hand, and which scarcely ever fail of being mortal. The second Sort are about half as heavy as the other, and are generally shot from their Bows; B these are intended for smaller Beasts. With the third Sort, of which the Heads are an Ounce in Weight, they kill Birds. As this Nation is in a State, that does not set them above continual Cares for the immediate Necessaries of Life, he that can temper Iron best, is among them C most esteemed, and, perhaps, it would be happy for every Nation, if Honours and Applauses were as justly distributed, and he were most distinguished whose Abilities were most useful to Society. How many chimerical Titles to Precedence, how many false Pretences to Respect, would this Rule bring to the Ground! D Every Day, by Sun-rising, they began to march, and having travelled till ten, rested near some River till twelve, then travelling again till four, they reposed all Night in Houses, which the Symerons had either left standing in their former Marches, or very readily erected for them, by set- E ting up three or four Posts in the Ground, and laying Poles from one to another in Form of a Roof, which they thatched with Palmetto Boughs and Plantane Leaves. In the Valleys, where they were shelter'd from the Winds, they left three or four Foot below open; but on the Hills, F where they were more exposed to the chill Blasts of the Night, they thatched them close to the Ground, leaving only a Door for Entrance, and a Vent in the middle of the Room, for the Smoke of three Fires, which they made in every House.

In their March they met not only with G Plenty of Fruits upon the Banks of the Rivers, but with wild Swine in great Abundance, of which the Symerons, without Difficulty, killed, for the most Part, as much as was wanted. One Day, however, they found an Otter, and were about to dress it; at which Drake expressing H his Wonder, was asked by Pedro, the chief Symeron, Are you a Man of War, and in Want, and yet doubt whether this be Meat that hath Blood in it? For which Drake in private rebuked him, says the Relator, whether justly or not, it is not very important to determine. There seems to be in Drake's Scruple somewhat

of Superstition, perhaps not easily to be justified; and the Negroe's Answer was, at least, martial, and will I believe be generally acknowledged to be rational.

On the third Day of their March, Feb. 6, they came to a Town of the Symerons, situated on the Side of a Hill, and encompassed with a Ditch and a Mud Wall, to secure it from any sudden Surprize; here they lived with great Neatness and Plenty, and some Observation of Religion, paying great Reverence to the Cross; a Practice, which Drake prevailed upon them to change for the Use of the Lord's Prayer. Here they importuned Drake to stay for a few Days, promising to double his Strength; but he either thinking greater Numbers unnecessary, or fearing that if any Difference should arise, he should be overborn by the Number of the Symerons, or that they would demand to share the Plunder, that should be taken, in common, or for some other Reason, that might easily occur, refused any Addition to his Troop, endeavouring to express his Refusal in such Terms as might heighten their Opinion of his Bravery.

He then proceeded on his Journey through cool Shades, and lofty Woods, which sheltered them so effectually from the Sun, that their March was less toilsome than if they had travel'd in England during the Heat of the Summer. Four of the Symerons, that were acquainted with the Way, went about a Mile before the Troop, and scatter'd Branches to direct them; then followed twelve Symerons, after whom came the English, with the two Leaders, and the other Symerons closed the Rear.

On Feb. 11. they arrived at the Top of a very high Hill, on the Summit of which grew a Tree of wonderful Greatness, in which they had cut Steps for the more easy Ascent to the Top, where there was a Kind of Tower, to which they invited Drake, and from thence shew'd him not only the North Sea, from whence they came, but the great South Sea, on which no English Vessel had ever sailed. This Prospect exciting his natural Curiosity and Ardour for Adventures and Discoveries, he lifted up his Hands to God, and implor'd his Blessing upon the Resolution, which he then form-ed, of sailing in an English Ship on that Sea.

Then continuing their March, they came, after two Days, into an open, level Country, where their Passage was somewhat incommoded with the Grass, which is of a peculiar Kind, consisting of a Stalk

43

Stalk like that of Wheat, and a Blade, on which the Oxen and other Cattle feed, till it grows too high for them to reach; then the Inhabitants set it on fire, and in three Days it springs up again; this they are obliged to do thrice a Year, so great is the Fertility of the Soil.

At length, being within view of *Pa-* **A** *nama*, they left all frequented Roads, for fear of being discover'd, and posted themselves in a Grove near the Way between *Panama* and *Nombre de Dios*; then they sent a *Symeron*, in the Habit of a Negro of *Panama*, to enquire on what Night the *Recoes*, or Drivers of Mules, on **B** which the Treasure is carried, were to set forth. The Messenger was so well qualified for his Undertaking, and so industrious in the Prosecution of it, that he soon returned with an Account that the Treasurer of *Lima*, intending to return to *Europe*, would pass that Night, with eight **C** Mules laden with Gold, and one with Jewels.

Having received this Information, they immediately marched towards *Venta Cruz*, the first Town on the Way to *Nombre de Dios*, sending, for Security, two *Symerons* before, who, as they went, perceived, by the Scent of a Match, that some *Spa-* **D** *niard* was before them, and going silently forwards surprised a Solder asleep upon the Ground. They immediately bound him, and brought him to *Drake*, who, upon Enquiry, found that their Spy had not deceived them in his Intelligence. The Soldier having inform'd himself of **E** the Captain's Name, conceived such a Confidence in his well-known Clemency, that after having made an ample Discovery of the Treasure that was now at hand, he petitioned n t only that he would command the *Symerons* to spare his Life, but that when the Treasure shou'd fall into his Hands, he would allow him **F** as much as might maintain him and his Mistress, since they were about to gain more than their whole Company could carry away.

Drake then ordered his Men to lie down in the long Grass, about fifty Paces from the Road, Half on one Side, with **G** himself, and Half on the other, with Oxenham and the Captain of the *Symerons*, so much behind, that one Company might seize the foremost *Recoe*, and the other the hindermost, for the Mules of these *Recoes*, or Drivers, being tied together, travel on a Line, and are all guided by leading the first. **H**

N. B. In the Next we shall conclude the Account of this Expedition, and enter upon the Account of Drake's celebrated Voyage round the Globe.

44

rise up till the Signal should be given. But one *Robert Pike*, heated with strong Liquor, left his Company, and prevailed upon one of the *Symerons* to creep with him to the Way Side, that they might signalize themselves by seizing the first Mule, and hearing the Trampling of a Horse, as he lay, could not be restrained by the *Symeron* from rising up to observe who was passing by. This he did so imprudently, that he was discovered by the Passenger, for by *Drake's* Order, the *English* had put their Shirts on over their Coats, that the Night and the Tumult might not hinder them from knowing one another.

The Gentleman was immediately observed by *Drake* to change his Trot into a Gallop, but the Reason of it not appearing, it was imputed to his Fear of the Robbers that usually infest that Road, and the *English* still continued to expect the Treasure.

In a short Time one of the *Recoes* that were passing towards *Venta Cruz*, came up, and was eagerly seized by the *English*, who expected nothing less than half the Revenue of the *Indies*, nor is it easy to imagine their Mortification and Perplexity when they found only two Mules laden with Silver, the rest having no other Burthen than Provisions.

The Driver was brought immediately to the Captain, and informed him that the Horseman whom he had observed pass by with so much Precipitation, had informed the Treasurer of what he had observed, and advised him to send back the Mules that carried his Gold and Jewels, and suffer only the rest to proceed, that he might by that cheap Experiment discover whether there was any Ambush on the Way.

That *Drake* was not less disgusted than his Followers at the Disappointment, cannot be doubted; but there was now no Time to be spent in Complaints. The whole Country was alarmed, and all the Force of the *Spaniards* was summoned to overwhelm him. He had no Fortress to retire to, every Man was his Enemy, and every Retreat better known to the *Spaniards* than to himself.

This was an Occasion that demanded all the Qualities of an Hero, an Intrepidity never to be shaken, and a Judgment never to be perplexed. He immediately considered all the Circumstances of his present Situation, and found that it afforded him only the Choice of marching back by the same Way through which he came, or of forcing his Passage to *Venta Cruz*.

Continuation of the LIFE *of* Sir FRANCIS DRAKE, *from* p. 396.

When they had lain about an Hour in this Place, they began to hear the Bells of the Mules on each Hand, upon which Orders were given, that the Drivers which came from *Venta Cruz*, should pass unmolested, because they carried nothing of great Value, and those only be intercepted which were travelling thither, and that none of the Men should

To

To march back was to confefs the Superiority of his Enemies, and to animate them to the Purfuit; the Woods would afford Opportunities of Ambufh, and his Followers muft often difperfe themfelves in fearch of Provifions, who would become an eafy Prey, difpirited by their Difappointment, and fatigued by their March. On the Way to *Venta Cruz* he fhould have nothing to fear but from open Attacks, and expected Enemies.

Determining therefore to pafs forward to *Venta Cruz*, he asked *Pedro*, the Leader of the *Symerons*, whether he was refolv'd to follow him; and having received from him the ftrongeft Affurances that nothing fhould feparate them, commanded his Men to refrefh themfelves, and prepare to fet forward.

When they came within a Mile of the Town, they difmiffed the Mules which they had made ufe of for their more eafy and fpeedy Paffage, and continued their March along a Road cut through thick Woods, in which a Company of Soldiers, who were quartered in the Place to defend it againft the *Symerons*, had pofted themfelves, together with a Convent of Friars hea led by one of the Brethren, whofe Zeal againft the Northern Herefy had incited him to hazard his Perfon, and affume the Province of a General.

Drake, who was advertifed by two *Symerons*, whom he fent before, of the Approach of the *Spaniards*, commanded his Followers to receive the firft Volley without firing.

In a fhort Time he heard himfelf fummoned by the *Spanifh* Captain to yield, with a Promife of Protection and kind Treatment; to which he anfwered with Defiance, Contempt, and the Difcharge of his Piftol.

Immediately the *Spaniards* poured in their Shot, by which only one Man was killed, and *Drake*, with fome others, flightly wounded; upon which the Signal was given by *Drake's* Whiftle to fall upon them. The *Englifh*, after difcharging their Arrows and Shot, preffed furioufly forward, and drove the *Spaniards* before them, which the *Symerons*, whom the Terror of the Shot had driven to fome Diftance, obferved, and recalling their Courage, animated each other Songs in their own Language, and rufhed forward with fuch Impetuofity, that they overtook them near the Town, and, fupported by the *Englifh*, difperfed them with the Lofs of only one Man, who, after he had received his Wound, had Strength and Refolution left to kill his Affailant.

They purfued the Enemy into the Town, in which they met with fome Plunder, which was given to the *Symerons*, and treated the Inhabitants with great Clemency, *Drake* himfelf going to the *Spanifh* Ladies, to affure them that no Injuries fhould be offered them; fo infeparable is Humanity from true Courage.

Having thus broken the Spirits, and fcattered the Forces of the *Spaniards*, he purfued his March to his Ship, without any Apprehenfion of Danger, yet with great Speed, being very folicitous about the State of the Crew; fo that he allowed his Men, harraffed as they were, but little Time for Sleep or Refrefhment, but by kind Exhortations, gentle Authority, and a chearful Participation of all their Hardfhips, prevailed upon them to bear, without Murmurs, not only the Toil of Travelling, but on fome Days the Pain of Hunger.

In this March he owed much of his Expedition to the Affiftance of *Symerons*, who being accuftomed to the Climate, and naturally robuft, not only brought him Intelligence, and fhewed the Way, but carried Neceffaries, provided Victuals, and built Lodgings, and when any of the *Englifh* fainted in the Way, two of them would carry him between them for two Miles together; nor was their Valour lefs than their Induftry, after they had learned, from their *Englifh* Companions, to defpife the Fire-arms of the *Spaniards*.

When they were within five Leagues of the Ships, they found a Town built in their Abfence by the *Symerons*, at which *Drake* confented to halt, fending a *Symeron* to the Ship with his Gold Toothpick as a Token, which, though the Mafter knew it, was not fufficient to gain the Meffenger Credit, till upon Examination he found that the Captain, having ordered him to regard no Meffage without his Handwriting, had engraven his Name upon it with the Point of his Knife. He then fent the Pinnace up the River, which they met, and afterwards fent to Town for thofe whofe Wearinefs had made them unable to march farther. On *Feb.* 23. the whole Company was reunited, and *Drake*, whofe good or ill Succefs never prevailed over his Piety, celebrated their Meeting with Thanks to God.

Drake, not yet difcouraged, now turned his Thoughts to new Profpects, and without languifhing in melancholy Reflections upon his paft Mifcarriages, employed himfelf in forming Schemes for repairing them. Eager of Action, and acquainted with Man's Nature, he never fuf-

suffered Idleness to infect his Followers
Cowardice, but kept them from sink-
ing under any Disappointment by diverting
their Attention to some new Enterprize.

Upon Consultation with his own Men
and the *Symerons* he found them divided in
their Opinions : Some declaring that before they engaged in any new Attempt it
was necessary to increase their Stores of
Provisions, and others urging, that the
Ships in which the Treasure was conveyed should be immediately attack'd. The
Symerons proposed a third Plan, and advised him to undertake another March
over Land to the House of one *Pezoro*
near *Veregua,* whose Slaves brought him
every Day more than two hundred
Pounds Sterling from the Mines, which
he heaped together in a strong Stone-
house, which might by the help of the
English be easily forced.

Drake, being unwilling to fatigue his
Followers with another Journey, determined to comply with both the other
Opinions, and manning his two Pinnaces
the *Bear* and the *Minion,* he sent *John
Oxenham* in the *Bear* towards *Tolm,* to
seize upon Provisions, and went himself
in the *Minion* to the *Cabezas,* to intercept the Treasure that was to be transported from *Veragua,* and that Coast to
the Fleet at *Nombre de Dios,* first dismissing with Presents those *Symerons* that desired to return to their Wives, and ordering those that chose to remain to be entertained in the Ship.

Drake took at the *Cabezas* a Frigate
of *Nicaragua,* the Pilot of which informed him that there was in the Harbour of *Veragua,* a Ship freighted with
more than a Million of Gold, to which he
offered to conduct him (being we'l acquainted with the Soundings) if he might
be allowed his Share of the Prize ; so
much was his Avarice superiour to his
Honesty.

Drake, after some Deliberation, complying with the Pilot's Importunities,
sailed towards the Harbour, but had no
sooner entered the Mouth of it than he
heard the Report of Artillery, which was
answered by others at a greater Distance,
upon which the Pilot told him that they
were discovered, this being the Signal
appointed by the Governor to alarm the
Coast.

Drake now thought it convenient to
return to the Ship, that he might enquire
the Success of the other Pinnace, which
he found with a Frigate, that she had
taken with twenty-eight fat Hogs, two
hundred Hens, and great Store of *Maiz,*

or *Indian* Corn. The Vessel itself was
so strong, and well built, that he fitted
it out for War, determining to attack the
Fleet at *Nombre de Dios.*

On *March* the 21st he set sail with the
new Frigate and the *Bear* towards the
Cabezas, at which he arrived in about
two Days, and found there *Tetu,* a Frenchman, with a Ship of War, who after
having received from him a Supply of
Water, and other Necessaries, intreated
that he might join with him in his Attempt, which *Drake* consenting to, admitted him to accompany him with 20 of
his Men, stipulating to allow them an e-
qual Share of whatever Booty they
should gain. Yet were they not with out
some Suspicions of Danger from this new
Ally, he having eighty Men, and they
being now reduced to thirty-one.

Then manning the Frigate and two
Pinnaces, they set sail for the *Cabezas,*
where they left the Frigate, which was
too large for the Shallows over which
they were to pass, and proceeded to *Rio
Francisco.* Here they landed, and having
ordered the Pinnaces to return to the
same Place on the *4th* Day following,
travelled through the Woods towards
Numbre de Dios, with such Silence and
Regularity, as surprised the *French,* who
did not imagine the *Symerons* so discreet
or obedient as they appeared, and were
therefore in perpetual Anxiety about the
Fidelity of their Guides, and the Probability of their Return. Nor did the *Symerons* treat them with that Submission and
Regard which they paid to the *English,*
whose Bravery and Conduct they had already tried.

At length, after a laborious March of
more than seven Leagues, they began to
hear the Hammers of the Carpenters in
the Bay, it being the Custom in that hot
Season to work in § Night, and in a short
time they perceived the Approach of the
Recoes, or Droves of Mules, from *Panama.*
They now no longer doubted that their
Labours would be rewarded, and every
Man imagined himself secure from Poverty and Labour for the remaining Part
of his Life. They, therefore, when the
Mules came up, rushed out and seized
them, with an Alacrity proportioned to
their Expectations. The three Droves
consisted of one hundred and nine Mules,
each of which carried three hundred
Pounds Weight of Silver. It was to little purpose that the Solders, ordered to
guard the Treasure, attempted Resistance.
After a short Combat, in which the *French*
Captain, and one of the *Symerons* were

K k k   wounded,

47

wounded, it appeared with how much greater Ardour Men are animated by Interest than Fidelity.

As it was poſſible for them to carry away but a ſmall Part of this Treaſure, after having wearied themſelves with hiding it in Holes and ſhallow Waters, they determined to return by the ſame Way, and without being perſued entered the Woods, where the *French* Captain, being diſabled by his Wound, was obliged to ſtay, two of his Company continuing with him.

When they had gone forward about two Leagues, the *Frenchmen* miſſed another of their Company, who upon Enquiry was known to be intoxicated with Wine, and ſuppoſed to have loſt himſelf in the Woods, by neglecting to obſerve the Guides.

But common Prudence not allowing them to hazard the whole Company by too much Solicitude for a ſingle Life, they travelled on towards *Rio Franciſco*, at which they arrived *April* the 3d; but looking out for their Pinnaces, were ſurprized with the Sight of ſeven *Spaniſh* Shallops, and immediately concluded that ſome Intelligence of their Motions had been carried to *Nombre de Dios*, and that theſe Veſſels had been fitted out to purſue them, which might undoubtedly have overpower'd the Pinnaces and their feeble Crew: Nor did their Suſpicion ſtop here, but immediately it occur'd to them, that their Men had been compeli'd by Torture to diſcover where their Frigate and Ship were ſtationed, which being weakly manned, and without the Preſence of the chief Commanders, would fall into their Hands, almoſt without Reſiſtance, and all Poſſibility of eſcaping be entirely cut off.

Theſe Reflections ſunk the whole Company into Deſpair, and every one, inſtead of endeavouring to break thro' the Difficulties ſurrounded him, reſigned up himſelf to his Ill-Fortune; when *Drake*, whoſe Intrepidity was never to be ſhaken, and whoſe Reaſon was never to be ſurprized, or embarraſſed, repreſented to them that, though the *Spaniards* ſhould have made themſelves Maſters of their Pinnaces, they might yet be hindred from diſcovering the Ships. He put them in mind that the Pinnaces could not be taken, the Men examined, their Examinations compared, the Reſolutions formed, their Veſſels ſent out, and ſ Ships taken in an Inſtant. Some Time muſt neceſſarily be ſpent before the laſt Blow could be ſtruck, and if that Time were not negligently loſt, it might be poſſible for ſome of them to reach the Ships before the Enemy, and direct them to change their Station.

They were animated with this Diſcourſe, by which they diſcovered that their Leader was not without Hope; but when they came to look more nearly into their Situation, they were unable to conceive upon what it was founded. To paſs by Land was impoſſible, as the Way lay over high Mountains, thro' thick Woods, and deep Rivers, and they had not a ſingle Boat in their Power, ſo that a Paſſage by Water ſeemed equally impracticable. But *Drake*, whoſe Penetration immediately diſcovered all the Circumſtances and Inconveniencies of every Scheme, ſoon determined upon the only Means of Succeſs which their Condition afforded them; and ordering his Men to make a Raft out of the Trees that were then floating on the River, offered himſelf to put off to Sea upon it, and chearfully asked who would accompany him. *John Owen, John Smith* and two *Frenchmen*, who were willing to ſhare his Fortune, embarked with him on the Raft, which was fitted out with a Sail made of a Bisket-ſack, and an Oar to direct its Courſe inſtead of a Rudder.

Then having comforted the reſt with Aſſurances of his Regard for them, and Reſolution to leave nothing unattempted for their Deliverance, he put off, and after having, with much Difficulty, ſailed 3 Leagues, deſcried two Pinnaces haſting towards him, which, upon a nearer Approach, he diſcovered to be his own, and perceiving that they anchored behind a Point that jutted out into the Sea, he put to Shore, and croſſing the Land on Foot, was received by his Company with that Satisfaction which is only known to thoſe that have been acquainted with Dangers and Diſtreſſes.

The ſame Night they rowed to *Rio Franciſco*, where they took in the reſt, with what Treaſure they had been able to carry with them thro' the Woods; then ſailing back with the utmoſt Expedition, they returned to their Frigate, and ſoon after to their Ship, where *Drake* divided the Gold and Silver equally between the *French* and the *Engliſh*.

Here they ſpent about 14 Days in fitting out their Frigate more compleatly, and the diſmiſſing the *Spaniards* with their Ship, lay a few Days among the *Cabezas*, while twelve *Engliſh* and ſixteen *Symerons* travelled once more into the Country, as well to recover the *French* Captain, whom they had left wounded, as to bring away the Treaſure which they had hid in the Sands. *Drake*, whom his

his Company would not suffer to hazard his Person in another Land Expedition, went to them to *Rio Francisco*, where he found one of the *Frenchmen* who had stay'd to attend their Captain, and was informed by him, upon his Enquiries after his Fortune, that half an Hour after their Separation, the *Spaniards* came upon them, and easily seized upon the wounded Captain ; but that his Companion might have escaped with him, had he not preferred Money to Life ; for seeing him throw down a Box of Jewels that retarded him, he could not forbear taking it up, and with that, and the Gold which he had already, was so loaded that he could not escape. With regard to the Bars of Gold and Silver, which they had concealed in the Ground, he informed them that two thousand Men had been employed in digging for them.

The Men, however, either mistrusting the Informer's Veracity, or confident that what they had hidden could not be found, pursued their Journey ; but upon their Arrival at the Place, found the Ground turned up for two Miles round, and were able to recover no more than thirteen Bars of Silver, and a small Quantity of Gold. They discovered afterwards that the *Frenchman* who was left in the Woods, falling afterwards into the Hands of the *Spaniards*, was tortured by them till he confessed where *Drake* had concealed his Plunder. So fatal to *Drake's* Expedition was the Drunkenness of his Followers.

Then dismissing the *French*, they passed by *Carthagena* with their Colours flying, and soon after took a Frigate laden with Provisions and Honey, which they valued, as a great Restorative, and then sailed away to the *Cabezas*.

Here they stayed about a Week to clean their Vessels, and fit them for a long Voyage, determining to set sail for *England*. And that the faithful *Symerons* might not go away unrewarded, broke up their Pinnaces, and gave them the Iron, the most valuable Present in the World to a Nation whose only Employments were War and Hunting, and amongst whom Show and Luxury had no Place.

Pedro, their Captain, being desired by *Drake* to go through the Ship, and to choose what he must desired, fixed his Eye upon a Scymeter set with Diamonds, which the *French* Captain had presented to *Drake* ; and being unwilling to ask for so valuable a Present, offered for it four large Quoits, or thick Plates of Gold, which he had hitherto concealed ; but *Drake*, desirous to show him that Fidelity

seldom is without a Recompense, gave it him with the highest Professions of Satisfaction and Esteem, *Pedro* receiving it with the utmost Gratitude, informed him, that by bestowing it, he had conferred Greatness and Honour upon him ; for by presenting it to his King, he doubted not of obtaining the highest Rank amongst the *Symerons*. He then persisted in his Resolution of leaving the Gold, which was generously thrown by *Drake* into the common Stock ; for he said, that those at whose Expences he had been sent out, ought to share in all the Gain of the Expedition, whatever Pretence Cavil and Chicanery might supply for the Appropriation of any Part of it. Thus was *Drake's* Character confident with itself ; he was equally superior to Avarice and Fear, and through whatever Danger he might go in quest of Gold, he thought it not valuable enough to be obtain'd by Artifice or Dishonesty.

They now forsook the Coast of *America*, which for many Months they had kept in perpetual Alarms, having taken more than two hundred Ships of all Sizes between *Carthagena* and *Nombre de Dios*, of which they never destroyed any, unless they were fitted out against them, nor ever detained the Prisoners longer than was necessary for their own Security or Concealment, providing for them in the same Manner as for themselves, and protecting them from the Malice of the *Symerons* : A Behaviour, which Humanity dictates, and which, perhaps, even Policy cannot disapprove. He must certainly meet with obstinate Opposition, who makes it equally dangerous to yield as to resist, and who leaves his Enemies no Hopes but from Victory.

What Riches they acquired, is not particularly related; but it is not to be doubted, that the Plunder of so many Vessels, together with the Silver which they seized at *Nombre de Dios*, must amount to a very large Sum. tho' the Part that was allotted to *Drake* was not sufficient to lull him in Effeminacy, or to repress his natural Inclination to Adventures.

They arrived at *Plymouth* on the 9th of *August*, 1573, on *Sunday* in the Afternoon ; and so much were the People delighted with the News of their Arrival, that they left the Preacher, and ran in Crouds to the Key with Shouts and Congratulations.

An Account of Sir FRANCIS DRAKE's *VOYAGE round the World will be in our next.*

The LIFE of Sir FRANCIS DRAKE.

Continuation of the LIFE of Sir FRANCIS DRAKE, from p. 447.

DRAKE having, in his former Expedition, had a View of the South-Sea, and formed a Resolution to sail upon it, did not suffer himself to be diverted from his Design by the Prospect of any Difficulties that might obstruct the Attempt, nor any Dangers that might attend the Execution; Obstacles, which brave Men often find it much more easy to overcome, than secret Envy, and domestic Treachery.

Drake's Reputation was now sufficiently advanced to incite Detraction and Opposition; and it is easy to imagine that a Man by Nature superiour to mean Artifices, and bred, from his earliest Years, to the Labour and Hardships of a Sea-Life, was very little acquainted with Policy and Intrigue, very little versed in the Methods of Application to the Powerful and Great, and unable to obviate the Practices of those whom his Merit had made his Enemies.

Nor are such the only Opponents of great Enterprises: There are some Men of narrow Views, and grovelling Conceptions, who, without the Instigation of personal Malice, treat every new Attempt as wild and chimerical, and look upon every Endeavour to depart from the beaten Track, as the rash Effort of a warm Imagination, or the glittering Speculation of an exalted Mind, that may please and dazzle for a Time, but can produce no real or lasting Advantage.

These Men value themselves upon a perpetual Scepticism, upon believing nothing but their own Senses, upon calling for Demonstration where it cannot possibly be obtained, and sometimes upon holding out against it when it is laid before them; upon inventing Arguments against the Success of any new Undertaking, and, where Arguments cannot be found, upon treating it with Contempt and Ridicule.

Such have been the most formidable Enemies of the great Benefactors to Mankind, and to these we can hardly doubt but that much of the Opposition which Drake met with is to be attributed; for their Notions and Discourse are so agreeable to the Lazy, the Envious, and the Timorous, that they seldom fail of becoming popular, and directing the Opinions of Mankind.

Whatsoever were his Obstacles, and whatsoever were the Motives that produced them, it was not till the Year 1577, that he was able to assemble a Force proportioned to his Design, and to obtain a Commission from the Queen, by which he was constituted Captain General of a Fleet consisting of 5 Vessels, of which the Pellican Admiral, of an hundred Tuns, was commanded by himself; the Elizabeth, Vice-Admiral, of 80 Tuns, by John Winter; the Marigold, of 30 Tuns, by John Thomas; the Swan, 50 Tuns, by John Chester; the Christopher of 15 Tuns, by Thomas Moche, the same, as it seems, who was Carpenter in the former Voyage, and destroyed one of the Ships by Drake's Direction.

These Ships, equipped partly by himself, and partly by other private Adventurers, he mann'd with 164 stout Sailors, and furnished with such Provisions as he judged, necessary for the long Voyage in which he was engaged. Nor did he confine his Concern to naval Stores, or military Preparations, but carried with him whatever he thought might contribute to raise in those Nations, with which he should have any Intercourse, the highest Ideas of the Politeness and Magnificence of his native Country. He therefore not only procured a compleat Service of Silver for his own Table, and furnished the Cook-room with many Vessels of the same Metal, but engaged several Musicians to accompany him; rightly judging that nothing would more excite the Admiration of any savage and uncivilised People.

Having been driven back by a Tempest in their first Attempt, and obliged to return to Plymouth, to repair the Damages which they had suffered, they set sail again from thence on the 13th of December, 1577, and on the 25th had sight of Cape Cantire in Barbary, from whence they coasted on Southward to the Island of Mogadore, which Drake had appointed for the first Place of Rendezvous, and on the 27th brought the whole Fleet to anchor in a Harbour on the main Land.

They were soon after their Arrival discovered by the Moors that inhabited those Coasts, who sent two of the principal Men amongst them on board Drake's Ship, receiving at the same time two of his Company as Hostages. These Men he not only treated in the most splendid Manner, but presented with such Things as they appeared most to admire; it being with him an established Maxim, to endeavour to secure in every Country a kind Reception to such Englishmen as might come after him, by treating the Inhabitants with Kindness and Generosity; a Conduct at once just and politick, to the Neglect of which may be attributed many of the Injuries suffered by our Sailors in distant Countries, which are generally ascribed,

S f f   rather

50

rather to the Effects of Wickedness and Folly of our own Commanders, than the Barbarity of the Natives, who feed on fall upon any unless they have been first plundered or insulted; and in revenging the Ravages of one Crew upon another of the same Nation, are guilty of nothing but what in countenanced by the Example of the *Europeans* themselves.

But this friendly Intercourse was in appearance so n broken, for on the next Day observing the *Moors* making Signals from the Land, they sent out their Boat, as before, to fetch them to the Ship, and one *John Fry* leaped ashore, intending to become an Hostage as on the former Day, when immediately he was seized by the *Moors*, and the Crew observing great Numbers to start up from behind the Rock with Weapons in their Hands, found it Madness to attempt his Rescue, and therefore provided for their own Security by returning to the Ship.

Fry was immediately carried to the King, who being then in continual Expectation of an Invasion from *Portugal*, suspected that these Ships were sent only to observe the Coast, and discover a proper Harbour for the main Fleet; but being informed who they were, and whither they were bound, not only dismissed his Captive, but made large Offers of Friendship and Assistance, which *Drake*, however, did not stay to receive, but being disgusted at this Breach of the Laws of Commerce, and afraid of farther Violence, after having spent some Days in searching for his Man, in which he met with no Resistance, left the Coast on *Dec.* 3L same time before *Fry's* Return, who being obliged by this Accident to somewhat a longer Residence among the *Moors*, was afterwards sent home in a Merchant's Ship.

On *Jan.* 16, they arrived at *Cape Blanc*, having in their Passage taken several *Spanish* Vessels. Here while *Drake* was employing his Men in catching Fish, of which this Coast affords great Plenty, and various Kinds, the Inhabitants came down to the Sea-side with their *Alforges*, or Leather Bottles, to traffick for Water, which they were willing to purchase with Amber-grise, and other Gums. But *Drake* compassionating the Misery of their Condition, gave them Water whenever they asked for it, and left them their Commodities to traffick with, when they should be again reduced to the same Distress, without finding the same Generosity to relieve them.

Here having discharged some *Spanish* Ships, 0 the had taken, to-

wards the *Isles of Cape Verd*, and on *Jan.* 28, came to anchor, before *Mayo*, hoping to furnish themselves with fresh Water; but having landed they found the Town by the Water's Side entirely deserted, and marching farther up the Country, saw the Vallies extremely fruitful, and abounding with ripe Figs, Cocoes and Plantains, but could by no means prevail upon the Inhabitants to converse or traffick with them: However they were suffered by them to range the Country without Molestation, but found no Water, except at such a Distance from the Sea that the Labour of conveying it to their Ships was greater than it was at that time necessary for them to undergo. Salt, had they wanted it, might have been obtained with less Trouble, being left by the Sea upon the Sand, and harden'd by the Sun, during the Ebb, in such Quantities, that the chief Traffick of their Island is carried on with it.

Jan. 3L they passed by *St Jago*, an Island at that time divided between the Natives and the *Portuguese*, who first entering these Islands under the Show of Traffick, by degrees established themselves, claimed a Superiority over the original Inhabitants, and harrassed them with such Cruelty, that they obliged them either to fly to the Woods and Mountains, and perish with Hunger, or to take Arms against their Oppressors, and under the insuperable Disadvantages with which they contended, to die almost without a Battle in defence of their natural Rights, and antient Possessions.

Such Treatment had the Natives of *St Jago* received, which had driven them into the rocky Parts of the Island, from whence they made Incursions into the Plantations of the *Portuguese*, sometimes with Loss, but generally with that Success which Desperation naturally procures; so that the *Possessors* were in continual Alarms, and lived with the natural Consequences of Guilt, Terror and Anxiety. They were wealthy, but not happy, and possessed the Island, but not enjoyed it.

They then sailed on within sight of *Fogo*, an Island so called from a Mountain, about the middle of it, continually burning, and like the rest inhabited by the *Portuguese*, two Leagues to the South of which lies *Brava*, which has received its Name from its Fertility, abounding, tho' uninhabited, with all Kinds of Fruits, and watered with great Numbers of Springs and Brooks, which would easily invite the Possessors of the adjacent Islands to settle in it, but that it affords neither Harbour nor Anchorage. *Drake* after

having

51

having sent out his Boats with Plummers, was not able to find any Ground about it, and it is reported that many Experiments have been made with the same Success; however, he took in Water sufficient, and on the 2d of *Feb.* set sail for the Straits of *Magellan.*

On *Feb.* 17, they passed the Equator, and continued their Voyage, with sometimes Calms, and sometimes contrary Winds, but without any memorable Accident, to *March* 28, when one of their Vessels, with 28 Men, and the greatest Part of their fresh Water on board, was to their great Discouragement, separated from them; but their Perplexity lasted not long, for on the next Day they discovered and rejoined their Associates.

In their long Course, which gave them Opportunities of observing several Animals, both in the Air and Water, at that Time very little known, nothing entertained, or surprized them more, than the *Flying Fish,* which is near of the same Size with a Herring, and has Fins of the Length of his whole Body, by the Help of which, when he is pursued by the *Bonito,* or Great Mackerel, as soon as he finds himself upon the Point of being taken, he springs up into the Air, and flies forward as long as his Wings continue wet; Moisture being, as it seems, necessary to make them pliant and moveable; and when they become dry and stiff, he falls down into the Water, unless some Bark or Ship intercept him, and dips them again for a second Flight. This unhappy Animal is not only pursued by Fishes in his natural Element, but attacked in the Air, where he hopes for Security, by the *Don,* or *Sparhite,* a great Bird that preys upon Fish; and their Species must surely be destroy'd, were not their Increase so great, that the young Fry, in one Part of the Year, covers the Sea.

There is another Fish, named the *Cuttil.* of which whole Shoals will sometimes rise at once out of the Water, and of which a great Multitude fell into their Ship.

At length, having sailed without Sight of Land for 63 Days, they arrived, *April* 5, at the Coasts of *Brasil,* where, on the 7th, the *Christopher* was separated again from them by a Storm, after which they sailed near the Land to the Southward, and on the 14th anchored under a Cape, which they afterwards called *Cape Joy,* because in two Days the Vessel which they had lost, returned to them.

Having spent a Fortnight in the River of *Plate,* to refresh his Men after their

long Voyage, and then standing out to Sea, he was again surprized by a sudden Storm, in which they lost Sight of the *Swan.* This Accident determined *Drake* to contract the Number of his Fleet, that he might not only avoid the Inconvenience of such frequent Separations, but ease the Labour of his Men, by having more Hands in each Vessel.

For this Purpose he sailed along the Coast in quest of a commodious Harbour, and, on *May* 13, discovered a Bay, which seemed not improper for their Purpose, but which they durst not enter till it was examined; an Employment in which *Drake* never trusted any, whatever might be his Confidence in his Followers on other Occasions. He well knew how fatal one Moment's Inattention might be, and how easily almost every Man suffers himself to be surprized by Indolence and Security. He knew that the same Credulity that might prevail upon him to trust another, might induce another to commit the same Office to a third; and it must be, at length, that some of them would be deceived. He therefore, as at other Times, ordered the Boat to be hoisted out, and taking the Line into his Hand, went on sounding the Passage till he was three Leagues from his Ship; when, on a sudden, the Weather changed, the Skies blackened, the Winds whistled, and all the usual Forerunners of a Storm began to threaten them: Nothing was now desired but to return to the Ship, but the Thickness of the Fog intercepting it from their Sight, made the Attempt little other than desperate. By so many unforeseen Accidents is Prudence itself liable to be embarrassed! So difficult is it sometimes for the quickest Sagacity, and most enlightened Experience, to judge what Measures ought to be taken! To trust another to found an unknown Coast, appeared to *Drake* Folly and Presumption; to be absent from his Fleet, tho' but for an Hour, proved nothing less than to hazard the Success of all their Labours, Hardships and Dangers.

In this Perplexity, which *Drake* was not more sensible of than those whom he had left in the Ships, nothing was to be omitted, however dangerous, that might contribute to extricate them from it. As they could venture nothing of equal Value with the Life of their General. Capt. *Thomas,* therefore, having the lightest Vessel, steered boldly into the Bay, and taking the General aboard, dropp'd Anchor, and lay out of Danger, while the rest that were in the open Sea, suffered much from the Tempest, and the *Mary,* a *Portugueze* Prize, was driven away before

52

fore the Wind; the others, as foon as the Tempeft was over, difcovering by the Fires which were made on Shore, where *Drake* was, repaired to him.

Here going on fhore they met with no Inhabitants, though there were feveral Houfes or Huts ftanding, in which they found a good Quantity of dry'd Fowls, and among them a great Number of O-ftriches, of which the Thighs were as large as thofe of a Sheep. Thefe Birds are too heavy and unwieldy to rife from the Ground, but with the help of their Wings run fo fwiftly, that the *Englifh* could never come near enough to fhoot at them. The *Indians*, commonly, by hold-ing a large Plume of Feathers before them, and walking gently forward, drive the Oftriches into fome narrow Neck, or Point of Land, then fpreading a ftrong Net from one Side to the other, to hinder them from returning back to the open Fields, fet their Dogs upon them, thus confined between the Net and the Water, and when they are thrown on their Backs, rufh in and take them.

Not finding this Harbour convenient, or well ftored with Wood and Water, they left it on the 15th of *May*, and on the 18th entered another much fafer, and more commodious, which they no fooner arrived at, than *Drake*, whofe reftlefs Application never remitted, fent *Winter* to the Southward, in queft of thofe Ships which were abfent, and im-mediately after failed himfelf to the Northward, and happily meeting with the *Swan*, conducted it to the reft of the Fleet; after which, in Purfuance of his former Refolution, he ordered it to be broken up, referving the Iron Work for a future Supply. The other Veffel which they loft in the late Storm could not be difcovered.

While they were thus employed upon an Ifland about a Mile from the main Land, to which, at low Water, there was a Paffage on Foot, they were difco vered by the Natives, who appeared upon a Hill at a Diftance, dancing, and hold-ing up their Hands, as beckoning the *Englifh* to them; which *Drake* obferving, fent out a Boat with Knives, Bells, and Bugles, and fuch Things as, by their Ufe-fulnefs or Novelty, he imagined would be agreeable. As foon as the *Englifh* land-ed, they obferved two Men running to-wards them, as deputed by the Compa-ny, who came within a little Diftance, and then ftanding ftill, could not be pre-vailed upon to come nearer. The *Englifh* therefore tied their Prefents to a Pole, which they fixed in the Ground, and

then retiring, faw the *Indians* advance, who taking what they found upon the Pole, left, in Return, fuch Feathers as they wear upon their Heads, with a fmall Bone about fix Inches in length, carved round the Top, and burnifhed.

Drake obferving their Inclination to Friendfhip and Traffic, advanced with fome of his Company towards the Hill, upon Sight of whom the *Indians* ranged themfelves in a Line from Eaft to Weft, and one of them running from one End of the Rank to the other, backwards and forwards, bowed himfelf towards the Rifing and Setting of the Sun, hold-ing his Hands over his Head, and fre-quently ftopping in the Middle of the Rank, leaped up towards the Moon, which then fhone directly over their Heads; thus calling the Sun and Moon, the Deities they worfhip, to witnefs the Sincerity of their Profeffions of Peace and Friendfhip. While this Ceremony was performed, *Drake* and his Company a-fcended the Hill, to the apparent Terror of the *Indians*, whofe Apprehenfions when the *Englifh* perceived, they peacea-bly retired; which gave the Natives fo much Encouragement, that they came forward immediately, and exchanged their Arrows, Feathers, and Bones, for fuch Trifles as were offered them.

Thus they traded for fome Time, but by frequent Intercourfe finding that no Violence was intended, they became familiar, and mingled with the *Englifh* without the leaft Diftruft.

They go quite naked, except a Skin of fome Animal, which they throw over their Shoulders when they lie in the open Air. They knit up their Hair, which is very long, with a Roll of Oftrich Fea-thers, and ufually carry their Arrows wrapp'd up in it, that they may not en-cumber them, they being made with Reeds, headed with Flint, and therefore not heavy. Their Bows are about an Ell long.

Their chief Ornament is Paint, which they ufe of feveral Kinds, delineating ge-nerally upon their Bodies the Figures of the Sun and Moon, in Honour of their Deities.

It is obfervable, that moft Nations, a-mongft whom the Ufe of Cloaths is un-known, paint their Bodies. Such was the Practice of the firft Inhabitants of our own Country. From this Cuftom did our earlieft Enemies, the *Picts*, owe their Denomination. As it is not probable that Caprice or Fancy fhould be uniform, there muft be, doubtlefs, fome Reafon for a Practice fo general and prevailing in diftant distant Parts of the World, which have no Communication with each other. The original End of painting their Bodies was, probably, to exclude the Cold ; an End, which, if we believe some Relations, is so effectually produced by it, that the Men thus painted never shiver at the most piercing Blasts. But doubtless any People so hardened by continual Severities would, even without Paint, be less sensible of the Cold than the civilized Inhabitants of the same Climate. However this Practice may contribute, in some Degree, to defend them from the Injuries of Winter, and in those Climates where little evaporates by the Pores, may be used with no great Inconvenience ; but in hot Countries, where Perspiration in greater Degree is necessary, the Natives only use Unction to preserve them from the other Extream of Weather : So well do either Reason or Experience supply the Place of Science in Savage Countires !

They had no Canoes like the other *Indians*, nor any Method of crossing the Water, which was probably the Reason why the Birds in the adjacent Islands were so tame, that they might be taken with the Hand, having never been before frighted or molested. The great Plenty of Fowls and Seals, which crowded the Shallows in such Numbers, that they killed at their first Arrival two Hundred of them in an Hour, contributed much to the Refreshment of the *English*, who named the Place *Seal Bay* from that Animal.

These Seals seem to be the chief Food of the Natives, for the *English* often found raw Pieces of their Flesh half-eaten, and left, as they supposed, after a full Meal by the *Indians*, whom they never knew to make use of Fire, or any Art, in dressing or preparing their Victuals.

Nor were their other Customs less wild or uncouth, than their Way of feeding ; one of them having received a Cap off the General's Head, and being extremely pleased as well with the Honour as the Gift, to express his Gratitude, and confirm the Alliance between them, retired to a little Distance, and thrusting an Arrow into his Leg, let the Blood run upon the Ground, testifying, as it is probable, that he valued *Drake*'s Friendship above Life.

Having staid fifteen Days among these friendly Savages in 47 Deg. 30 Min. S. Lat. on *June* 3. they set sail towards the South Sea, and six Days afterwards stopp'd at another little Bay to break up the *Christopher*. Then passing on, they cast An-

chor in another Bay, not more than 20 Leagues distant from the Straits of *Magellan*.

It was now time seriously to deliberate in what Manner they should act with regard to the *Portugueze* Prize, which having been separated from them by the Storm, had not yet rejoined them. To return in Search of it was sufficiently mortifying ; to proceed without it, was not only to deprive themselves of a considerable Part of their Force, but to expose their Friends and Companions, whom common Hardships and Dangers had endeared to them, to certain Death or Captivity. This Consideration prevailed, and therefore on the 18th, after Prayers to God, with which *Drake* never forgot to begin an Enterprize, he put to Sea, and the next Day, near Port *Julian*, discovered their Associates, whose Ship was now grown leaky, having suffered much both in the first Storm by which they were dispersed, and afterwards in fruitless Attempts to regain the Fleet.

Drake therefore being desirous to relieve their Fatigues, entered Port *Julian*, and as it was his Custom always to attend in Person when any important Business was in hand, went ashore with some of the chief of his Company, to seek for Water, where he was immediately accosted by two Natives, of whom *Magellan* left a very terrible Account, having described them as a Nation of Giants and Monsters ; nor is his Narrative entirely without Foundation, for they are of the largest Size, tho' not taller than some *Englishmen*; their Strength is proportioned to their Bulk, and their Voice loud, boisterous, and terrible. What were their Manners before the Arrival of the *Spaniards*, it is not possible to discover ; but the Slaughter made of their Countrymen, perhaps without Provocation, by these cruel Intruders, and the general Massacre with which that Part of the World had been depopulated, might have raised in them a Suspicion of all Strangers, and by Consequence made them inhospitable, treacherous and bloody.

The two who associated themselves with the *English*, appeared much pleased with their new Guests, received willingly what was given them, and very exactly observed every thing that passed, seeming more particularly delighted with seeing *Oliver*, the Master Gunner, shoot an *English* Arrow. They shot themselves likewise in Emulation, but their Arrows always fell to the Ground far short of his.

Soon after this friendly Contest came another, who observing the Familiarity of

his

his Countrymen with the Strangers, appeared much displeased, and, as the Englishmen perceived, endeavoured to dissuade them from such an Intercourse. What Effect his Arguments had, was soon after apparent, for another of Drake's Companions being desirous to show the third Indian a Specimen of the English Valour and Dexterity, attempted likewise to shoot an Arrow but drawing it with his full Force, burst the Bow-string; upon which the Indians, who were unacquainted with their other Weapons, imagining him disarmed, followed the Company, as they were walking negligently down towards their Boat, and let fly their Arrows, aiming particularly at Winter, who had the Bow in his Hand. He finding himself wounded in the Shoulder, endeavoured to resit his Bow, and turning about, was pierced with a second Arrow in the Breast; Oliver, the Gunner, immediately presented his Piece at the insidious Assailants, which failing to take fire, gave them time to level another Flight of Arrows, by which he was killed; nor, perhaps, had any of them escaped, surprized and perplexed as they were, had not Drake, with his usual Presence of Mind, animated their Courage, and directed their Motions, ordering them, by perpetually changing their Places, to elude, as much as they could, the Aim of their Enemies, and to defend their Bodies with their Targets, and instructing them, by his own Example, to pick up, and break the Arrows as they fell; which they did with so much Diligence, that the Indians were soon in Danger of being disarmed. Then Drake himself taking the Gun, which Oliver had so unsuccessfully attempted to make use of, discharged it at the Indian that first began the Fray, and had killed the Gunner, aiming it so happily, that the Hail Shot, with which it was loaded, tore open his Belly, and forced him to such terrible Outcries, that the Indians, tho' their Numbers increased, and many of their Countrymen showed themselves from different Parts of the adjoining Wood, were too much terrified to renew the Assault, and suffered Drake, without Molestation, to withdraw his wounded Friend, who being hurt in his Lungs, languished two Days, and then dying, was interred with his Companion, with the usual Ceremony of a military Funeral.

They stayed here two Months afterwards, without receiving any other Injuries from the Natives, who finding the Danger to which they exposed themselves by open Hostilities, and not being able

any more to surprize the Vigilance of Drake, preferred their Safety to Revenge.

But Drake had other Enemies to conquer or escape, far more formidable than these Barbarians, and insidious Practices to obviate, more artful and dangerous than the Ambushes of the Indians; for in this Place was laid open a Design formed by one of the Gentlemen of the Fleet, not only to defeat the Voyage, but to murder the General.

This Transaction is related in so obscure and confused a Manner, that it is difficult to form any Judgment upon it. The Writer who gives the largest Account of it, has suppressed the Name of the Criminal, which we learn from a more succinct Narrative published in a Collection of Travels near that Time, to have been Thomas Doughtie. What were his Inducements to attempt the Destruction of his Leader, and the Ruin of the Expedition, or what were his Views if his Designs had succeeded, what Measures he had hitherto taken, whom he had endeavoured to corrupt, with what Arts, or what Success, we are no where told.

The Plot, as the Narrative assures us, was laid before their Departure from England, and discovered, in its whole Extent, to Drake himself in his Garden at Plymouth, who nevertheless not only entertained the Person so accused as one of his Company, but, this Writer very particularly relates, treated him with remarkable Kindness and Regard, setting him always at his own Table; and lodging him in the same Cabbin with himself. Nor did he ever discover the least Suspicion of his Intentions, till they arrived at this Place; but appeared, by the Authority with which he invested him, to consider him as one to whom, in his Absence, he could most securely intrust the Direction of his Affairs. At length, in this remote Corner of the World, he found out a Design formed against his Life, called together all his Officers, laid before them the Evidence on which he grounded the Accusation, and summoned the Criminal, who, full of all the Horrors of Guilt, and confounded at so clear a Detection of his whole Scheme, immediately confess'd his Crimes, and acknowledged himself unworthy of longer Life: Upon which the whole Assembly, consisting of thirty Persons, after having considered the Affair with the Attention which it required, and heard all that could be urged in Extenuation of his Offence, unanimously signed the Sentence by which he was condemned to suffer Death. Drake, however, unwilling, as it seemed, to proceed

to

to extreme Severities; offered him his Choice, either of being executed on the Island, or set ashore on the Main Land, or being sent to *England* to be tried before the Council; of which, after a Day's Consideration, he chose the first, alledging the Improbability of persuading any to leave the Expedition for the Sake of transporting a Criminal to *England*, and the Danger of his future State among Savages and Infidels. His Choice, I believe, few will approve: To be set ashore on the Main Land, was indeed only to be executed in a different Manner, for what Mercy could be expected from ý Natives so incensed, but ý most cruel and lingering Death? But why he should not rather have requested to be sent to *England* it is not so easy to conceive. In so long a Voyage he might have found a thousand Opportunities of escaping, perhaps with the Connivance of his Keepers, whose Resentment must probably in Time have given way to Compassion, or at least by their Negligence, as it is easy to believe, they would, in Times of Ease and Refreshment, have remitted their Vigilance, at least he would have gained longer Life, and to make Death desirable seems not one of the Effects of Guilt. However, he was, as 'tis related, obstinately deaf to all Persuasions, and adhering to his first Choice, after having received the Communion, and dined cheerfully with the General, was executed in the Afternoon, with many Proofs of Remorse, but none of Fear.

How far it is probable that *Drake*, after having been acquainted with this Man's Designs, should admit him into his Fleet, and afterwards caress, respect, and trust him; or that *Doughtie*, who is represented as a Man of eminent Abilities, should engage in so long and hazardous a Voyage with no other View than that of defeating it, is left to the Determination of the Reader. What Designs he could have formed with any Hope of Success, or to what Actions worthy of Death he could have proceeded without Accomplices, for none are mentioned, is equally difficult to imagine. Nor, on the other Hand, tho' the Obscurity of the Account, and the remote Place chosen for the Discovery of this wicked Project, seem to give some Reason for Suspicion, does there appear any Temptation, from either Hope, Fear, or Interest, that might induce *Drake*, or any Commander in his State, to put to death an innocent Man upon false Pretences.

(*To be continued.*)

Continuation of the Life of Sir FRANCIS DRAKE, *from p.* 515.

AFter ý Execution of this Man, ý whole Company, either convinced of ý Justice of the Proceeding, or awed by the Severity, applied themselves without any Murmurs, or Appearance of Discontent, to the Prosecution of the Voyage, and having broken up another Vessel, and reduced the Number of their Ships to three, they left the Port, and on *August* the 20th entered the Straits of *Magellan*, in which they struggled with contrary Winds, and the various Dangers to which the Intricacy of that winding Passage exposed them till Night, and then entered a more open Sea, in which they discovered an Island with a burning Mountain. On the 24th they fell in with three more Islands to which *Drake* gave Names, and, landing to take Possession of them in the Name of his Sovereign, found in the largest so prodigious a Number of Birds, that they killed three thousand of them in one Day. This Bird, of which they knew not the Name, was somewhat less than a Wild-Goose, without Feathers and covered with a kind of Down, unable to fly or rise from the Ground, but capable of running and swimming with amazing Celerity ; they feed on the Sea, and come to Land only to rest at Night or lay their Eggs, which they deposite in Holes like those of Conies.

From these Islands to the *South-Sea*, the Strait becomes very crooked and narrow, so that sometimes, by the Interposition of Headlands, the Passage seems shut up, and the Voyage entirely stopped. To double these Capes is very difficult, on Account of the frequent Alterations to be made in the Course. There are, indeed, as *Magellan* observes, many Harbours, but in most of them no Bottom is to be found.

The Land on both Sides rises into innumerable Mountains, the Tops of them are encircled with Clouds and Vapours, which being congealed fall down in Snow, and increase their Height by hardening into Ice, which is never dissolved ; but the Valleys are, nevertheless, green, fruitful, and pleasant.

Here *Drake* finding the Strait in Appearance shut up, went in his Boat to make farther Discoveries, and having found a Passage towards the North, was returning to his Ships, but Curiosity soon prevailed upon him to stop, for the Sake of observing a Canoe or Boat, with several Natives of the Country in it. He could not at a Distance forbear admiring the Form of this little Vessel, which seemed inclining to a Semicircle, the Stern and Prow standing up, and the Body sinking inward, but much greater was his Wonder, when, upon a nearer Inspection, he found it made only of the Barks of Trees sewed together with Thongs of Seal-skin, so artificially, that scarcely any Water entered the Seams. The People were well-shaped and painted, like those which have been already described. On the Land they had a Hut built with Poles and covered with Skins, in which they had Water Vessels and

other Utensils, made likewise of the Barks of Trees.

Among these People they had an Opportunity of remarking, what is frequently observable in savage Countries, how natural Sagacity, and unwearied Industry may supply the Want of such Manufactures, or natural Productions as appear to us absolutely necessary for the Support of Life. The Inhabitants of these Islands are wholly Strangers to Iron and its Use, but instead of it make Use of the Shell of a Muscle of prodigious Size, found upon their Coasts ; This they grind upon a Stone to an Edge, which is so firm and solid, that neither Wood nor Stone is able to resist it.

Sept. 6, they entered the *Great South-Sea*, on which no *English* Vessel had ever been navigated before, and proposed to have directed their Course towards the Line, that their Men, who had suffered by the Severity of the Climate, might recover their Strength in a warmer Latitude. But their Designs were scarce formed before they were frustrated ; for on *Sept.* 7. after an Eclipse of the Moon, a Storm arose, so violent, that it left them little Hopes of surviving it ; nor was its Fury so dreadful as its Continuance, for it lasted with little Intermission, till *Oct.* 28, Fifty-two Days, during which Time they were tossed incessantly from one Part of the Ocean to another, without any Power of spreading their Sails, or lying upon their Anchors, amidst shelving Shores, scattered Rocks, and unknown Islands, the Tempest continually roaring, and the Waves dashing over them.

In this Storm, on the 30th of *Sept.* the *Marigold*, commanded by Captain *Thomas*, was separated from them. On the 7th of *October* having entered a Harbour, where they hoped for some Intermission of their Fatigues, they were in a few Hours forced out to Sea by a violent Gust, which broke the Cable, at which Time they lost Sight of the *Elizabeth*, the Vice-Admiral, whose Crew, as was afterwards discovered, wearied with Labour, and discouraged by the Prospect of future Dangers, recovered the Straits on the next Day, and returning by the same Passage through which they came, sailed along the Coast of *Brasil*, and on the 2d of *June* in the Year following arrived at *England*.

From this Bay they were driven Southward to 55 Degrees, where, among some Islands, they stayed two Days to the great Refreshment of the Crew ; but being again forced into the main Sea, they were tossed about with perpetual

Expectations of perishing, till soon after they came again to anchor near the same Place, where they found the Natives whom the Continuance of the Storm had probably reduced to equal Distress, rowing from one Island to another and providing the Necessaries of Life.

It is, perhaps, a just Observation, that, with regard to outward Circumstances, Happiness and Misery are very equally diffused thro' all States of human Life. In civilized Countries where regular Policies have secured the Necessaries of Life, Ambition, Avarice, and Luxury, find the Mind at Leisure for their Reception, and soon engage it in new Pursuits; Pursuits that are to be carried on by incessant Labour, and whether vain or successful, produce Anxiety and Contention. Among Savage Nations, imaginary Wants find, indeed, no Place, but their Strength is exhausted by necessary Toils, and their Passions agitated not by Contests about Superiority, Affluence, or Precedence, but by perpetual Care for the present Day, and by fear of perishing for want of Food.

But for such Reflections as these they had no Time, for having spent 3 Days in supplying themselves with Wood and Water, they were by a new Storm driven to the Latitude of 56 Degrees, where they beheld the Extremities of the *American* Coast, and the Confluence of the Atlantic and Southern Ocean.

Here they arrived on the 28th of *Oct.* and at last were blessed with the Sight of a Calm Sea, having for almost two Months endured such a Storm as no Traveller has given an Account of; and such as in that Part of the World, tho' accustomed to Hurricanes, they were before unacquainted with.

On the 30th of *October*, they steered away towards the Place appointed for the Rendezvous of the Fleet, which was in 30 Degrees, and on 4 next Day discovered two Islands so well stocked with Fowls, that they victualled their Ships with them, and then sailed forwards, along the Coast of *Peru*, till they came to 37 Degrees, where finding neither their Ships, nor any convenient Port, they came to Anchor *November* the 25th, at *Macho*, an Island inhabited by such Indians as the Cruelty of their *Spanish* Conquerors had driven from the Continent, to whom they applied for Water and Provisions, offering them in return, such Things as they imagined most likely to please them. The *Indians* seemed willing to traffick, and having presented them with Fruits and two fat Sheep

shewed them a Place whither they should come for Water.

The next Morning, according to Agreement, the *English* landed to their Watervessels, and sent 2 Men forward towards 4 Place appointed, who, about the middle of the Way, were suddenly attacked by the *Indians*, and immediately slain. Nor were the rest of the Company out of Danger; for behind the Rocks was lodged an Ambush of five hundred Men, who, starting up from their Retreat, discharged their Arrows into 4 Boat, with such Dexterity, that every one of the Crew was wounded by them, the Sea being then high and hindering them from either retiring, or making use of their Weapons. *Drake* himself received an Arrow under his Eye, which pierced him almost to the Brain, and another in his Head. The Danger of these Wounds was much encreased by the Absence of their Surgeon, who was in the Vice-Admiral, so that they had none to assist them but a Boy, whose Age did not admit of much Experience or Skill, yet so much were they favoured by Providence, that they all recovered.

No Reason could be assigned for which the *Indians* should attack them with so furious a Spirit of Malignity, but that they mistook them for *Spaniards*, whose Cruelties might very reasonably incite them to Revenge, whom they had driven by incessant Persecution from their Country, wasting immense Tracks of Land, by Massacre and Devastation.

On the Afternoon, of the same Day, they set Sail, and on the 30th of *November* dropped Anchor in *Philips* Bay, where their Boat having been sent out to discover the Country, returned with an *Indian* in his Canoe, whom they had intercepted. He was of a graceful Stature, dressed in a white Coat or Gown, reaching almost to his Knees, very mild, humble and docile, such as perhaps, were all the *Indians*, till the *Spaniards* taught them Revenge, Treachery and Cruelty. This *Indian*, having been kindly treated, was dismissed with Presents, and informed, as far as the *English* could make him understand what they chiefly wanted, and what they were willing to give in return, *Drake* ordering his Boat to attend him in his Canoe and to set him safe on the Land.

When he was ashore, he directed them to wait till his Return, and meeting some of his Countrymen, gave them such an Account of his Reception, that, within a few Hours, several of them repaired with him to the Boat with Fowls, Eggs and a

Hog, and with them one of their Captains, who willingly came into the Boat, and defired to be conveyed by the *Englifh* to their Ship.

By this Man *Drake* was Informed, that no Supplies were to be expected here, but that fouthward in a Place to which he offered to be his Pilot, there was great Plenty. This Propofal was accepted and on the 5th of *December*, under the Direction of the good-natured *Indian*, they came to Anchor in the Harbour called by the *Spaniards Valparizo* near the Town of *St James* of *Chili* where they met not only with fufficient Stores of Provifion, and with Store-houfes full of the Wines of *Chili*, but with a Ship called the *Captain of Morial*, richly laden, having together with large Quantities of the fame Wines, fome of the fine Gold of *Baldivia*, and a great Crofs of Gold fet with Emeralds.

Having fpent three Days in ftoring their Ships with all kinds of Provifion in the utmoft Plenty, they departed and landed their *Indian* Pilot, where they firft received him, after having rewarded him much above his Expectations or Defires.

They had now little other Anxiety than for their Friends who had been feparated from them, and whom they now determined to feek, but confidering that by entering every Creek and Harbour with their Ship, they expofed themfelves to unneceffary Dangers, and that their Boat would not contain fuch a Number as might defend themfelves againft the *Spaniards*, they determined to ftation their Ship at fome Place, where they might commodioufly build a Pinnace, which being of light Burthen, might eafily fail where the Ship was in Danger of being ftranded, and at the fame time might carry a fufficient Force to refift the Enemy, and afford better Accommodation, than could be expected in the Boat.

To this End on the 19th of *December*, they entered a Bay near *Cippo* a Town inhabited by *Spaniards*, who difcovering them, immediately iffued out to the Number of an hundred Horfemen, with about two hundred naked *Indians* running by their Sides. The *Englifh* obferving their Approach, retired to their Boat without any Lofs, except of one Man whom no Perfuafions or Entreaties could move to retire with the reft, and who, therefore, was flain by the *Spaniards*, who exulting at the Victory, commanded the *Indians* to draw the dead Carcafe from the Rock on which he fell, and in the Sight of the *Englifh* beheaded it, then cut off the

right Hand, and tore out the Heart, which they carried away, having firft commanded the *Indians* to fhoot their Arrows all over the Body. The Arrows of the *Indians* were made of green Wood, for the immediate Service of the Day, the *Spaniards*, with the Fear that always harraffes Oppreffors, forbidding them to have any Weapons, when they do not want their prefent Affiftance.

Leaving this Place, they foon found a Harbour more fecure and convenient, where they built their Pinnace, in which *Drake* went to feek his Companions, but finding the Wind contrary, he was obliged to return in two Days.

Leaving this Place foon after, they failed along the Coaft, in fearch of frefh Water, and landing at *Tarapaca*, they found a *Spaniard* afleep, with Silver bars lying by him to the Value of three thoufand Ducats; not all the Infults which they had received from his Countrymen, could provoke them to offer any Violence to his Perfon, and therefore, they carried away his Treafure, without doing him any farther Harm.

Landing in another Place, they found a *Spaniard* driving eight *Peruvian* Sheep, which are the Beafts of Burthen in that Country, each laden with an hundred Pounds weight of Silver, which they feized likewife, and drove to their Boats. Further along the Coaft, lay fome *Indian* Towns, from which the Inhabitants repaired to the Ship, on Floats made of Seal-fkins, blown full of Wind, two of which they faften together, and fitting between them, row with great Swiftnefs and carry confiderable Burthens. They very readily traded for Glafs and fuch Trifles, with O the Old and the Young feemed equally delighted.

Arriving at *Mormorao* on the 26th of *January*, *Drake* invited the *Spaniards* to traffick with him, which they agreed to, and fupplied him with Neceffaries, felling to him among other Provifions fome of thofe Sheep, which have been mentioned, whofe Bulk is equal to that of a Cow, and whofe Strength is fuch, that one of them can carry three tall Men upon his Back, their Necks are like a Camels, and their Heads like thofe of our Sheep. They are the moft ufeful Animals of this Country, not only affording excellent Fleeces, and wholefome Flefh, but ferving as Carriages over Rocks and Mountains where no other Beaft can travel, for their Foot is of a peculiar Form which enables them to tread firm in the moft fteep and flippery Places.

On all this Coaft, the whole Soil is fo

impregnated with Silver, that five Ounces
may be separated from an hundred Po un
weight of common Earth.

Still coasting in Hopes of meeting their
Friends, they anchored on the 7th of
February before *Aria*, where they took
two Barks with about eight hundred
Pound weight of Silver, and persuing their
Course, seized an other Vessel laden with
Linens.

[*To be continued.*]

Continuation of the LIFE *of Sir* FRANCIS
DRAKE, *from* VOL. X. p. 603.

ON the 15 of *Feb.* 1578, they arrived
at *Lima*, and entered the Harbour
without Resistance, though thirty Ships
were stationed there, of which seventeen
were equipp'd for their Voyage, and many
of them are represented in the Narrative as Vessels of considerable Force ; so
that their Security seems to have consisted
not in their Strength, but in their Reputation, which had so intimidated the
Spaniards, that the Sight of their own
Superiority could not rouse them to Opposition. Instances of such panick Ter-

rours are to be met with in other Relations, but as they are, for the most Part,
quickly dissipated by Reason and Reflection, a wise Commander will rarely
found his Hopes of Success on them ;
and, perhaps, on this Occasion, the *Spaniards* scarcely deserve a severer Censure
for their Cowardice, than *Drake* for his
Temerity.

In one of these Ships they found fifteen hundred Bars of Silver, in another
a Chest of Money, and very rich Lading in many of the rest, of which the
Spaniards tamely suffered them to carry
the most valuable Part away, and would
have permitted them no less peaceably to
burn their Ships ; but *Drake* never made
War with a Spirit of Cruelty or Revenge, or carried Hostilities further than
was necessary for his own Advantage or
Defence.

They set Sail the next Morning towards
Panama, in quest of the *Caca Fuego*, a
very rich Ship, which had sailed fourteen
Days before bound thither from *Lima*,
which they overtook on the first ot *March*,
near Cape *Francisco*, and, boarding it,
found not only a Quantity of *Jewels*, and
12 Chests of Ryals of Plate, but eighty
Pounds Weight of Gold, and twenty-six
Tuns of uncoined Silver, with Pieces of
wrought Plate to a great Value. In un-
lading this Prize, they spent six Days,
and then dismissing the *Spaniards*, stood
off to Sea.

Being now sufficiently enriched, and
having lost all Hopes of finding their Associates, and perhaps beginning to be infected with that Desire of Ease and Pleasure which is the natural Consequence of
Wealth obtained by Dangers and Fatigues, they began to consult about their
Return Home, and in Pursuance of *Drake's*
Advice, resolved first to find out some
convenient Harbour, where they might
supply themselves with Wood and Water, and then endeavour to discover a
Passage from the *South Sea* into the *Atlantic* Ocean ; a Discovery which would not
only enable them to return home with
less Danger, and in a shorter Time, but
would much facilitate the Navigation in
those Parts of the World.

For this Purpose they had Recourse
to a Port in the Island of *Canes*, where
they met with Fish, Wood, and fresh
Water, and in their Course took a Ship
laden with Silk and Linnen, which was
the last that they met with on the Coast
of *America*.

But being desirous of storing them-
selves for a long Course, they touched
April the 15th, at *Guatulco*, a *Spanish*
Island

LIFE of Admiral DRAKE.

Island, where they supplied themselves with Provisions, and seized a Bushel of Ryals of Silver.

From *Guatulco*, which lies in 15 Deg. 40 Min. they stood out to Sea, and without approaching any Land, sailed forward, till on the Night following, the 3d of *June*, being then in the Lat. of 38 Deg. they were suddenly benum'd with such cold Blasts, that they were scarcely able to handle the Ropes. This Cold increased upon them, as they proceeded, to such a Degree, that the Sailors were discouraged from mounting upon the Deck; nor were the Effects of the Climate to be imputed to the Warmth of the Regions to which they had been lately accustomed, for the Ropes were stiff with Frost, and the Meat could scarcely be conveyed warm to the Table.

On *June* 17th they came to Anchor in 38 Deg. 30 Min. where they Law the Land naked, and the Trees without Leaves, and in a short Time had Opportunities of observing, that the Natives of that Country were not less sensible of the Cold than themselves; for the next Day came a Man rowing in his Canoe towards the Ship, and at a Distance from it, made a long Oration, with very extraordinary Gesticulations, and great Appearance of Vehemence, and a little Time afterwards made a second Visit in the same Manner, and then returning a third Time, he presented them, after his Harangue was finished, with a Kind of Crown of black Feathers, such as their Kings wear upon their Heads, and a Basket of Rushes filled with a particular Herb, both which he fastened to a short Stick, and threw into the Boat; nor could he be prevailed upon to receive any thing in return, though pushed towards him upon a Board; only he took up a Hat, which was flung into the Water.

Three Days afterwards, their Ship having received some Damage at Sea, was brought nearer to Land, that the Lading might be taken out. In order to which the *English*, who had now learned not too negligently to commit their Lives to the Mercy of savage Nations, raised a kind of Fortification with Stones, and built their Tents within it. All this was not beheld by the Inhabitants without the utmost Astonishment, which incited them to come down in Crowds to the Coast, with no other View, as it appeared, than to worship the new Divinities that had condescended to touch upon their Country.

Drake was far from countenancing their Errors, or taking Advantage of

their Weakness to injure or molest them, and therefore having directed them to lay aside their Bows and Arrows, he presented them with Linnen, and other Necessaries, of which he shewed them the Use. They then returned to their Habitations, about three Quarters of a Mile from the *English* Camp, where they made such loud and violent Outcries, that they were heard by the *English*, who found that they still persisted in their first Notions, and were paying them their kind of melancholy Adoration.

Two Days afterwards they perceived the Approach of a far more numerous Company, who stopped at the Top of a Hill which overlooked the *English* Settlement, while one of them made a long Oration, at the End of which all the Assembly bowed their Bodies, and pronounced the Syllable *Oh* with a solemn Tone, as by Way of Confirmation of what had been said by the Orator. Then the Men laying down their Bows, and leaving the Women and Children on the Top of the Hill, came down towards the Tents, and seemed transported in the highest Degree, at the Kindness of the General, who received their Gifts, and admitted them to his Presence. The Women at a Distance appeared seized with a Kind of Frenzy, such as that of old among the *Pagans* in some of their religious Ceremonies, and in Honour, as it seemed, of their Guests, tore their Cheeks and Bosoms with their Nails, and threw themselves upon the Stones with their naked Bodies till they were covered with Blood.

These cruel Rites, and mistaken Honours, were by no Means agreeable to *Drake*, whose predominant Sentiments were Notions of Piety; and therefore not to make that criminal in himself by his Concurrence, which, perhaps, Ignorance might make guiltless in them, he ordered his whole Company to fall upon their Knees, and with their Eyes lifted up to Heaven, that the Savages might observe that their Worship was addressed to a Being residing there, they all joined in praying that this harmless and deluded People might be brought to the Knowledge of the true Religion, and the Doctrines of our blessed Saviour; after which they sung Psalms, a Performance so pleasing to their wild Audience, that in all their Visits they generally first accosted them with a Request that they would sing. They then returned all the Presents which they had received, and retired.

Three Days after this, on *June* 25. 1579.

61

1779, our General received two Embassadors from the *Hioh*, or King of the Country, who intending to visit the Camp, required that some Token might be sent him of Friendship and Peace; this Request was readily complied with, and soon after came the King, attended by a Guard of about an hundred tall Men, and preceeded by an Officer of State, who carried a Scepter made of black Wood, adorned with Chains of a Kind of Bone or Horn, which are Marks of the highest Honour among them, and having two Crowns, made as before, with Feathers fastened to it, with a Bag of the same Herb which was presented to *Drake* at his first Arrival.

Behind him was the King himself, dressed in a Coat of Coney-Skins, with a Cawl woven with Feathers upon his Head, an Ornament so much in Estimation there, that none but the Domesticks of the King are allowed to wear it; his Attendants followed him, adorned nearly in the same Manner, and after them came the common People, with Baskets plaited so artificially, that they held Water, in which, by Way of Sacrifice, they brought Roots and Fish.

Drake, not lulled into Security, ranged his Men in Order of Battle and waited their Approach, who coming nearer, stood still while the Scepter-bearer made an Oration, at the Conclusion of which they again came forward to the Foot of the Hill, and then the Scepter-bearer began a Song, which he accompanied with a Dance, in both which the Men joined but the Women danced without singing.

Drake now distrusting them no longer, admitted them into his Fortification, where they continued their Song and Dance a short Time, and then both the King, and some others of the Company, made long Harangues, in which it appeared, by the rest of their Behaviour, that they entreated him to accept of their Country, and to take the Government of it into his own Hands; for the King, with the apparent Concurrence of the rest, placed the Crown upon his Head, graced him with the Chains, and other Signs of Authority, and saluted him by the Title of *Hioh*.

The Kingdom thus offered, tho' of no farther Value to him than as it furnished him with present Necessaries, *Drake* thought it not prudent to refuse, and therefore took Possession of it in the Name of Queen *Elizabeth* not without ancient Wishes that this Acquisition might have been of Use to his native Country, and that its mild and innocent People

might have been united to the Church of Christ.

The Kingdom being thus consigned, and the grand Affair at an End, the common People left their King and his Domesticks with *Drake*, and dispersed themselves over the Camp, and when they saw any one that pleased them by his Appearance more than the rest, they tore their Flesh, and vented their Outcries as before, in Token of Reverence and Admiration.

They then proceeded to shew them their Wounds and Diseases, in Hopes of a miraculous and instantaneous Cure, to which the *English*, to benefit and undeceive them at the same Time, applied such Remedies as they used on the like Occasions.

They were now grown confident and familiar, and came down to the Camp, every Day repeating their Ceremonies and Sacrifices, till they were more fully informed how disagreeable they were to those whose Favour they were so studious of obtaining: They then visited them without Adoration, indeed, but with a Curiosity so ardent, that it left them no Leisure to provide the Necessaries of Life, with which the *English* were therefore obliged to supply them.

They had then sufficient Opportunity to remark the Customs and Dispositions of these new Allies, whom they found tractable and benevolent, strong of Body, far beyond the *English*, yet unfurnished with Weapons, either for Assault or Defence, their Bows being too weak for any thing but Sport. Their Dexterity in taking Fish was such, that if they saw them so near the Shore that they could come to them without swimming, they never missed them.

The same Curiosity that had brought them in such Crowds to the Shore, now induced *Drake*, and some of his Company, to travel up into the Country, which they found, at some Distance from the Coast, very fruitful, filled with large Deer, and abounding with a peculiar Kind of Conies smaller than ours, with Tails like that of a Rat, and Paws such as those of a Mole, they have Bags under their Chin, in which they carry Provisions to their Young.

The Houses of the Inhabitants are round Holes dug in the Ground, from the Brink of which they raise Rafters, or Piles shelving towards the Middle, where they all meet, and are cramped together; they lie upon Rushes, with the Fire in the Midst, and let the Smoak fly out at the Door.

The Men are generally naked, but the Women make a kind of Petticoat of Bulrushes, which they comb like Hemp, and throw the Skin of a Deer over their Shoulders. They are very modest, tractable and obedient to their Husbands.

Such is the Condition of this People, and not very different is, perhaps, the State of the greatest Part of Mankind. Whether more enlightened Nations ought to look upon them with Pity, as less happy than themselves, some Sceptics have made, very unnecessarily, a Difficulty of determining. More, they say, is lost by the Perplexities than gained by the Instructions of Science; we enlarge our Vices with our Knowledge, and multiply our Wants with our Attainments, and the Happiness of Life is better secured by the Ignorance of Vice than by the Knowledge of Virtue.

The Fallacy by which such Reasoners have imposed upon themselves, seems to arise from the Comparison which they make, not between two Men equally inclined to apply the Means of Happiness in their Power, to the End for which Providence conferred them, but furnished in unequal Proportions with the Means of Happiness, which is the true State of savage and polished Nations, but between two Men, of which he to whom Providence has been most bountiful, destroys the Blessings by Negligence, or obstinate Misuse; while the other, steady, diligent, and virtuous, employs his Abilities and Conveniences to their proper End. The Question is not whether a good Indian, or bad Englishman be most happy, but which State is most desirable, imposing Virtue and Reason the same in both.

Nor is this the only Mistake which is generally admitted in this Controversy, for these Reasoners frequently confound Innocence with the mere Incapacity of Guilt. He that never saw, or heard, or thought of strong Liquors, cannot be proposed as a Pattern of Sobriety.

This Land was named by Drake, *Albion*, from its white Cliffs, in which it bore some Resemblance to his Native Country, and the whole History of the Resolution of it to the *English*, was engraven on a piece of Brass, then nailed on a Post, and set up before their Departure, which being now discovered by the People to be near at hand, they could not forbear perpetual Lamentations. When the *English* on the end of July weighed Anchor, they saw them climbing to the Tops of Hills, that they might keep them in sight, and observed them kindled up in many parts of

the Country, on which, as they supposed Sacrifices were offered.

Near this Harbour they touched at some Islands, where they found great Numbers of Seals, and despairing now to find any Passage through the Northern Parts, he after a general Consultation determined to steer away to the *Moluccas*, and setting Sail *July* 25th, he sail'd for sixty eight Days without Sight of Land; and on *September* 30th, arrived within View of some Islands, situate about eight Degrees Northward from the Line, from whence the Inhabitants resorted to them in Canoes, hollowed out of the solid Trunk of a Tree, and raised at both ends so high above the Water, that they seemed almost a Simicircle; they were burnished in such a Manner, that they shone like Ebony, and were kept steady by a piece of Timber, fixed on each side of them, with strong Canes, that were fastened at one End to the Boat, and at the other to the End of the Timber.

The first Company that came brought Fruits, Potatoes, and other things of no great Value, with an appearance of Traffick, and exchanged their Lading for other Commodities, with great shew of Honesty and Friendship, but having as they imagined, laid all Suspicion asleep, they soon sent another Fleet of Canoes, of which the Crews behaved with all the Insolence of Tyrants, and all the Rapacity of Thieves, for whatever was suffered to come into their Hands, they seemed to consider as their own, and would neither pay for it nor restore it, and at length finding the *English* resolved to admit them no longer, they discharged a Shower of Stones from their Boats, which Insult. Drake prudently and generously returned by ordering a Piece of Ordnance to be fired without hurting them, at which they were so terrify'd, that they leaped into the Water, and hid themselves under the Canoes.

Having for some Time but little Wind, they did not arrive at the *Moluccas* till the 3d of *November*, and then designing to touch at *Tidore*, they were visited, as they sailed by a little Island, belonging to the King of *Ternate*, by the Viceroy of the Place, who informed them, that it would be more Advantageous for them to have recourse to his Master for Supplies and Assistance than to the King of *Ternate*, who was in some Degree dependent on the Portuguese, and that he would himself carry the News of their Arrival, and prepare their Reception.

Drake was by the Arguments of the Viceroy prevailed upon to alter his Resolution,

tion, and on *November* 5, cast Anchor before *Ternate*, and scarce was he arrived, before the Viceroy with others of the chief Nobles, came out in three large Boats, rowed by sixty Men on each side, to conduct the Ship into a safe Harbour, and soon after the King himself having A received a Velvet Cloak by a Messenger from *Drake*, as a Token of Peace, came with such a Retinue and Dignity of Appearance as was not expected in those remote Parts of the World. He was received with Discharges of Cannon and every kind of Musick, with which he was B so much delighted, that desiring the Musicians to come down into the Boat, he was towed along in it at the Stern of the Ship.

The King was of a graceful Stature, and regal Carriage, of a mild Aspect, and low Voice, his Attendants were dressed in white Cotton or Calico of whom some C whose Age gave them a venerable Appearance, seemed his Counsellors, and the rest Officers or Nobles; his Guards were not ignorant of Fire-Arms, but had not many among them, being equipped for the most Part with Bows and Darts.

The King having spent some Time in D admiring the Multitude of New Objects that presented themselves, retired as soon as the Ship was brought to Anchor, and promised to return on the Day following, and in the mean Time, the Inhabitants having leave to traffick, brought down Provisions in great Abundance.

At the Time when the King was expected his Brother came aboard, to request of *Drake* that he would come to the Castle, proposing to stay himself as a Hostage for his return; *Drake* refused to go but sent some Gentlemen, detaining the King's Brother in the mean Time.

These Gentlemen were received by another of the King's Brothers, who conducted them to the Council-house near the Castle, in which they were directed to walk, there they found threescore Old Men, Privy Counsellors to the King, and on each side of the Door without, stood four old Men of foreign Countries, who G served as Interpreters in Commerce.

In a short Time the King came from the Castle, dressed in Cloth of Gold, with his Hair woven into gold Rings, a Chain of Gold upon his Neck, and on his Hands Rings very artificially set with Diamonds and Jewels of great Value; over his Head was born a rich Canopy, and by his Chair of State, on which he sat down H when he had entered the House, stood a Page with a Fann set with Sapphires, to moderate the Excess of the Heat. Here

he received the Compliments of the English, and then honourably dismissed them.

The Castle which they had some Opportunity of observing, seem'd of no great Force; it was built by the *Portuguese*, who attempting to reduce this Kingdom into absolute Subjection, murdered the King and intended to pursue their Scheme by the Destruction of all his Sons; but this general Abhorrence, which Cruelty and Perfidy naturally excites, armed all the Nation against them: and procured their total Expulsion from all the Dominions of *Ternate*, which from that Time increasing in Power, continued to make new Conquests, and to deprive them of other Acquisitions.

While they lay before *Ternate*, a Gentleman came on board attended by his Interpreter. He was dressed somewhat in the *European* Manner, and soon distinguished himself from the Natives of *Ternate*, or any Country that they had seen, by his Civility and Apprehension. Such a Visitant may easily be imagined to excite their Curiosity, which he gratified by informing them that he was a Native of *China*, of the Family of the D King then reigning, and that being accused of a capital Crime, of which, tho' he was innocent, he had not Evidence to clear himself, he had petitioned the King that he might not be exposed to a Tryal, but that his Cause might be referred to divine Providence, and that he might be allowed to leave his Country, E with a Prohibition against returning, unless Heaven, in Attestation of his Innocence, should enable him to bring back to the King some Intelligence, that might be to the Honour and Advantage of the Empire of *China*. In Search of such Information he had now spent three Years, F and had left *Tidore* for the Sake of conversing with the *English* General, from whom he hoped to receive such Accounts as would enable him to return with Honour and Safety.

Drake willingly recounted all his Adventures and Observations, to which the *Chinese* Exile listened with the utmost Attention and Delight, and having fixed them in his Mind, thanked God for the Knowledge he had gained. He then proposed to the *English* General to conduct him to *China*, recounting, by Way of Invitation, the Wealth, Extent, and Felicity of that Empire; but *Drake* could not H be induced to prolong his Voyage.

He therefore set sail on the 9th of *Nov.* in quest of some convenient Harbour, in a desart Island to refit his Ship, not being willing, as it seems, to admit the Gene-

...sity of the King of *Ternate*. Five Days afterwards he found a very commodious Harbour in an Island overgrown with Wood, where he repaired his Vessel and refreshed his Men without Danger or Interruption.

Leaving this Place the 12th of *December*, they sailed towards the *Celebes*; but having a Wind not very favourable, they were detained among a Multitude of Islands, mingled with dangerous Shallows, till *Jan.* 9, 1580. When they thought themselves clear, and were sailing forwards with a strong Gale, they were at the Beginning of the Night surprised in their Course by a sudden Shock, of which the Cause was easily discovered, for they were thrown upon a Shoal, and by the Speed of their Course, fixed too fast for any Hope of escaping. Here even the Intrepidity of *Drake* was shaken, and his Dexterity baffled, but his Piety, however, remained still the same, and what he could not now promise himself from his own Ability, he hoped from the Assistance of Providence. The Pump was plied, and the Ship found free from new Leaks.

The next Attempt was to discover towards the Sea some Place where they might fix their Boat, and from thence drag the Ship into deep Water; but upon Examination it appeared that the Rock on which they had struck, rose perpendicularly from the Water, and that there was no Anchorage, nor any Bottom to be found a Boat's Length from the Ship. But this Discovery, with its Consequences, was by *Drake* wisely concealed from the common Sailors, lest they should abandon themselves to Despair, for which there was, indeed, Cause; there being no Prospect left but that they must either sink with the Ship, which would undoubtedly be soon dashed to Pieces; or perish in attempting to reach the Shore in their Boat; or be cut in Pieces by Barbarians, if they should arrive at Land.

In the Midst of this Perplexity and Distress *Drake* directed that the Sacrament should be administered, and his Men, fortified with all the Consolation which Religion affords, then persuaded them to lighten the Vessel by throwing into the Sea Part of their Lading, which was cheerfully submitted to, but without Effect. At length, when their Hopes had forsaken them, and no new Struggles could be made, they were on a sudden delivered by a Remission of the Wind, which having hitherto blown strongly against the Side of the Ship which lay towards the Sea, held it upright against the Rock; but when the Blast slackened

(being then low Water) the Ship lying higher with that Part which rested on the Rock than with the other, and being born up no longer by the Wind, reeled into the deep Water, to the Surprize and Joy of *Drake* and his Companions.

This was the greatest, and most inextricable Distress which they had ever suffered, and made such an Impression upon their Minds, that for some Time afterwards they durst not adventure to spread their Sails, but went slowly forward with the utmost Circumspection.

They thus continued their Course without any observable Occurrence, till on the 11th of *March* they came to Anchor before the Island *Jour*, and sending to the King a present of Cloath and Silks, received from him, in Return, a large Quantity of Provisions, and the Day following *Drake* went himself on Shore, and entertained the King with his Musick, and obtained Leave to store his Ship with Provisions.

The Island is governed by a great Number of petty Kings, or Rulers, subordinate to one Chief; of these Princes three came on board together a few Days after their Arrival, and having upon their Return recounted the Wonders which they had seen, and the Civility with which they had been treated, inclined others to satisfy their Curiosity in the same Manner, and *Raia Donan*, the Chief King, came himself to view the Ship with the warlike Armaments and Instruments of Navigation.

This Intercourse of Civilities somewhat retarded the Business for which they came; but at length they not only victualled their Ship, but cleansed the Bottom, which, in the long Course, was overgrown with a Kind of Shell-fish that impeded her Passage.

Leaving *Java* on the twenty-sixth they sailed homewards by the Cape of *Good Hope* which they saw on *June* the fifth, on the fifteenth of *August* passed the Tropick, and on the 26th of *September* arrived at *Plimouth*, where they found that by passing through so many different Climates, they had lost a Day in their Account of Time, it being *Sunday* by their Journals, but *Monday* by the general Computation.

In this hazardous Voyage they had spent two Years ten Months and some odd Days, but were recompensed for their Toils by great Riches, and the universal Applause of their Countrymen, *Drake* afterwards brought his Ship up to *Deptford*, where Queen *Elizabeth* visited him on board his Ship, and conferred the

the Honour of Knighthood upon him; an Honour in that illustrious Reign not made cheap by Prostitution, nor even bestowed without uncommon Merit.

It is not necessary to give an Account equally particular of the remaining Part of his Life, as he was no longer a private Man, but engaged in public Affairs, and associated in his Expeditions with other Generals, whose Attempts, and the Success of them, are related in the Histories of those Times.

In 1585, on the 12th of *September*, Sir *Francis Drake* set sail from *Plimouth* with a Fleet of five and twenty Ships and Pinnaces, of which himself was Admiral, Captain *Martin Forbisher* Vice-Admiral, and Captain *Francis Knollis* Rear-Admiral; they were fitted out to cruise upon the *Spaniards*, and having touched at the Isle of *Bayonne*, and plundered *Vigo*, put to Sea again, and on the 16th of *Nov.* arrived before St *Jago*, which they entered without Resistance, and rested there fourteen Days, visiting in the mean Time, *San Domingo*, a Town within the Land, which they found likewise deserted; and carrying off what they pleased of the Produce of the Island, they at their Departure destroy'd the Town and Villages, in Revenge of the Murder of one of their Boys, whose Body they found mangled in a most inhuman Manner.

From this Island they persued their Voyage to the *West-Indies*, determining to attack *St Domingo* in *Hispaniola*, as the richest Place in that Part of the World, they therefore landed a thousand Men, and with small Loss entered the Town, of which they kept Possession for a Month without Interruption or Alarm; during which Time a remarkable Accident happened, which deserves to be related.

Drake having some Intention of treating with the *Spaniards*, sent to them a Negro-Boy with a Flag of Truce, which one of the *Spaniards* so little regarded, that he stabb'd him through the Body with a Lance. The Boy, notwithstanding his Wound, came back to the General, related the Treatment which he had found, and died in his Sight. *Drake* was so incensed, at this Outrage, that he ordered two Friers, then his Prisoners, to be conveyed with a Guard to the Place where the Crime was committed, and hang'd up in the Sight of the *Spaniards*, declaring that two *Spanish* Prisoners should undergo the same Death every Day, till the Offender should be delivered up by them: They were too well acquainted with the Character of *Drake* not to bring him on the Day following, when, to impress the Shame of such Actions

more effectually upon them, he compelled them to execute him with their own Hands. Of this Town, at their Departure, they demolished Part, and admitted the rest to be ransomed for five and twenty thousand Ducats.

From thence they sailed to *Carthagena*, where the Enemy having received Intelligence of the Fate of *St Domingo*, had strengthened their Fortifications, and prepared to defend themselves with great Obstinacy, but the *English* landing in the Night, came upon them by a Way they did not suspect, and being better armed, partly by Surprise, and partly by Superiority of Order and Valour, became Masters of the Place, where they stayed without Fear or Danger fix Weeks, and at their Departure received an hundred and ten thousand Ducats for the Ransom of the Town.

They afterwards took *St Augustine*, and touching at *Virginia*, took on board the Governor, Mr *Lane*, with the *English* that had been left there the Year before by Sir *Walter Raleigh*, and arrived at *Portsmouth* on *July* 28, 1586, having lost in the Voyage 750 Men. The Gain of this Expedition amounted to sixty thousand Pounds, of which forty were the Share of the Adventurers, who fitted out the Ships, and the rest distributed among the several Crews, amounted to fix Pounds each Man. So cheaply is Life sometimes hazarded.

The Transactions against *Armada*, 1588 are in themselves, far more memorable, but less necessary to be recited in this Succinct Narrative; only let it be remembered, that the Post of Vice-Admiral of *England*, to which Sir *Francis Drake* was then raised, is a sufficient Proof, that no Obscurity of Birth, or Meanness of Fortune, is unsurmountable to Bravery and Diligence.

In 1595 Sir *Francis Drake*, and Sir *John Hawkins*, went out with a Fleet to the *West Indies*, which Expedition was only memorable for the Destruction of *Nombre de Dios*, and the Death of the two Commanders, of whom Sir *Francis Drake* died *Jan.* 9, 1597, and was thrown into the Sea in a Leaden Coffin, with all the Pomp of naval Obsequies. It is reported by some, that the ill Success of this Voyage hastened his Death. Upon what this Conjecture is grounded does not appear, and we may be allowed to hope, for the Honour of so great a Man, that it is without Foundation, and that he whom no Series of Success could ever betray to Vanity, or Negligence, could have supported a Change of Fortune without Impatience or Dejection,

THE
LIFE
OF
Admiral *BLAKE.*

CONTAINING

An ACCOUNT of the gallant Actions of that
Brave Commander, in the several Expeditions wherein he served against the *Dutch,*
Spaniards, &c. Together with his Character in private Life, and during his being
a Member of the Celebrated Parliament
1640.

LONDON.

Printed for E. CAVE at *St John's Gate.*
MDCCXL.

THE
PREFACE.

AT a Time when the Nation is engaged in a War with an Enemy, whose Insults, Ravages and Barbarities have long called for Vengeance, an Account of such English Commanders as have merited the Acknowledgments of Posterity, by extending the Power, and raising the Honour of their Country, seem to be no improper Entertainment for our Readers. We shall therefore attempt a succinct Narrative of the Life and Actions of Admiral BLAKE, *in which we have nothing further in View than to do Justice to his Bravery and Conduct, without intending any Parallel between his Atchievments and those of our present Admirals.*

A

THE

LIFE

OF

Admiral *BLAKE*.

ROBERT BLAKE was born at *Bridgewater*, in *Somersetshire*, in *August* 1598, his Father being a Merchant of that Place, who had acquired a confiderable Fortune by the *Spanish* Trade. Of his earliest Years we have no Account, and therefore can amufe the Reader with none of thofe Prognofticks of his future Actions, fo often met with in Memoirs.

In 1615 he entred into the Univerfity of *Oxford*, where he continued till 1623, though without being much countenanced or carreffed by his Superiors; for he was more than once difappointed in his Endeavours after Academical Preferments. It is obfervable, that Mr. *Wood* (in his

his *Athenæ Oxonienses*) afcribes the Repulfe he met with at *Wadham* College, where he was Competitor for a Fellowfhip, either to want of Learning, or of Stature. With regard to the firft Objection, the fame Writer had before informed us, that he was an *early Rifer*, and *ftudious*, tho' he fometimes relieved his Attention by the Amufements of Fowling and Fifhing. As it is highly probable that he did not want Capacity, we may therefore conclude, upon this Confeffion of his Diligence, that he could not fail of being learned, at leaft in the Degree requifite to the Enjoyment of a Fellowfhip ; and may fafely afcribe his Difappointment to his want of Stature, it being the Cuftom of Sir *Henry Saville*, then Warden of that College, to pay much regard to the outward Appearance of thofe who folicited Preferment in that Society. So much do the greateft Events owe fometimes to Accident or Folly !

He afterwards retired to his native Place, where *he lived* (fays *Clarendon*) *without any Appearance of Ambition to be a greater Man than he was, but inveighed with great Freedom againft the Licence of the Times, and Power of the Court.*

In 1640 he was chofen Burgefs for *Bridgewater* by the Puritan Party, to whom he had recommended himfelf by his Difapprobation of Bifhop *Laud's* Violence and Severity, and his Non-compliance with thofe new Ceremonies which he was then endeavouring to introduce.

When the Civil War broke out, *Blake*, in conformity with his avowed Principles, declared for the Parliament ; and, thinking a bare Declaration for Right not all the Duty of a good Man, raifed a Troop of Dragoons for his Party, and appeared in the Field with fo much Bravery, that he was in a fhort Time advanced, without meeting any of thofe Obftructions which he had encountred in the Univerfity.

In 1645 he was Governor of *Taunton*, when the Lord *Goring* came before it with an Army of 10,000 Men. The Town was ill fortified, and unfupplied with almoft every Thing neceffary for fupporting a Siege. The State of this Garifon encouraged Colonel *Windham*, who was acquainted with *Blake*, to propofe a Capitulation, which was rejected by *Blake* with Indignation and Contempt : Nor were either Menaces or Perfuafions of any Effect ; for he maintained the

Place

Place, under all its Difadvantages, till the Siege was raifed by the Parliament's Army.

He continued, on many other Occafions, to give Proofs of an infuperable Courage, and a Steadinefs of Refolution not to be fhaken ; and, as a Proof of his firm Adherence to the Parliament, joined with the Borough of *Taunton* in returning Thanks for their Refolution to make no more Addreffes to the King. Yet was he fo far from approving the Death of *Charles* I. that he made no Scruple of declaring, that he would venture his Life to fave him, as willingly as he had done to ferve the Parliament.

In *February* 1648-9, he was made a Commiffioner of the Navy, and appointed to ferve on that Element, for which he feems by Nature to have been defigned. He was foon afterwards fent in Purfuit of Prince *Rupert*, whom he fhut up in the Harbour of *Kingfale* in *Ireland* for feveral Months, till want of Provifions, and Defpair of Relief, excited the Prince to make a daring Effort for his Efcape, by forcing thro' the Parliament's Fleet : This Defign he executed with his ufual Intrepidity, and fucceeded in it, tho' with the Lofs of three Ships. He was purfued by *Blake* to the Coaft of *Portugal*, where he was received into the *Tagus*, and treated with great Diftinction by the *Portuguefe*.

Blake coming to the Mouth of that River, fent to the King a Meffenger to inform him, that the Fleet in his Port belonging to the publick Enemies of the Common-wealth of *England*, he demanded Leave to fall upon it. This being refufed, tho' the Refufal was in very foft Terms, and accompanied with Declarations of Efteem, and a Prefent of Provifions, fo exafperated the Admiral, that, without any Hefitation, he fell upon the *Portuguefe* Fleet, then returning from *Brafil*, of which he took 17 Ships, and burnt 3. It was to no Purpofe that the King of *Portugal*, alarmed at fo unexpected a Deftruction, ordered Prince *Rupert* to attack them, and retake the *Brafil* Ships *Blake* carried home his Prizes without Moleftation, the Prince not having Force enough to purfue him, and well pleafed with the Opportunity of quitting a Port where he could no longer be protected.

Blake foon fupplied his Fleet with Provifions, and received Orders to make Reprifals upon the *French*, who had
fuffered.

suffered their Privateers to moleft the *Englifh* Trade; an Injury which, in thofe Days, was always immediately refented, and, if not repaired, certainly punifhed. Sailing with this Commiffion he took in his Way a *French* Man of War valued at a Million. How this Ship happened to be fo rich we are not informed, but as it was a Cruifer, it is probable the rich Lading was the accumulated Plunder of many Prizes. Then following the unfortunate *Rupert*, whofe Fleets by Storms and Battles was now reduced to 5 Ships, into *Carthagena*, he demanded Leave of the *Spanifh* Governor to attack him in the Harbour; but received the fame Anfwer which had been returned by the *Portuguefe*: That they had a Right to protect all Ships that came into their Dominions; that if the Admiral were forced in thither, he fhould find the fame Security; and that he required him not to violate the Peace of a neutral Port. *Blake* withdrew upon this Anfwer into the *Mediterranean*, and *Rupert* then leaving *Carthagena* entred the Port of *Malaga*, where he burnt and funk feveral *Englifh* Merchant Ships. *Blake* judging this to be an Infringement of the Neutrality profeffed by the *Spaniards*, now made no Scruple to fall upon *Rupert*'s Fleet in the Harbour of *Malaga*, and having deftroyed 3 of his Ships, obliged him to quit the Sea, and take Sanctuary at the *Spanifh* Court.

In *February* 1650-1, *Blake*, ftill continuing to cruife in the *Mediterranean*, met with a *French* Ship of confiderable Force, and commanded the Captain to come on board, there being no War declared between the two Nations. The Captain, when he came, was asked by him, whether *he was willing to lay down his Sword, and yield*; which he gallantly refufed though in his Enemy's Power: *Blake*, fcorning to take advantage of an Artifice, and detefting the Appearance of Treachery, told him that *he was at liberty to go back to his Ship, and defend it as long as he could* The Captain willingly accepted his Offer, and after a Fight of two Hours confeffed himfelf conquered, kiffed his Sword, and furrendred it.

In 1652 broke out the memorable War between the two Commonwealths of *England* and *Holland*; a War, in which the greateft Admirals, that perhaps any Age has produced, were engaged on each Side, in which nothing lefs was contefted than the Dominion of the Sea, and which was carried

on

on with Vigour, Animofity and Refolution, proportioned to the Importance of the Difpute. The chief Commanders of the *Dutch* Fleets where *Van Trump*, *de Ruyter* and *de Witt*, the moft celebrated Names of their own Nation, and who had been perhaps more renowned, had they been oppofed by any other Enemies. The States of *Holland* having carried on their Trade without Oppofition, and almoft without Competition, not only during the unactive Reign of *James* I. but during the Commotions of *England*, had arrived to that Height of Naval Power, and that Affluence of Wealth, that, with the Arrogance which a long-continued Profperity naturally produces, they began to invent new Claims, and to treat other Nations with Infolence, which nothing can defend but Superiority of Force. They had for fome Time made uncommon Preparations at a vaft Expence, and had equipped a large Fleet, without any apparent Danger threatning them, or any avowed Defign of attacking their Neighbours. This unufual Armament was not beheld by the *Englifh* without fome Jealoufy, and care was taken to fit out fuch a Fleet, as might fecure the Trade from Interruption, and the Coafts from Infults; of this *Blake* was conftituted Admiral for 9 Months. In this Situation the two Nations remained, keeping a watchful Eye upon each other, without actual Hoftilities on either Side, till the 18th of *May*, 1652, when *Van Trump* appeared in the *Downs* with a Fleet of 45 Men of War. *Blake*, who had then but 20 Ships, upon the Approach of the *Dutch* Admiral, faluted him with 3 fingle Shots, to require that he fhould, by ftriking his Flag, fhew that Refpect to the *Englifh*, which is due to every Nation in their own Dominions: To which the *Dutchman* anfwered with a Broadfide; and *Blake*, perceiving that he intended to difpute the Point of Honour, advanced with his own Ship before the reft of his Fleet, that, if it were poffible, a general Battle might be prevented. But the *Dutch*, inftead of admitting him to treat, fired upon him from their whole Fleet, without any regard to the Cuftoms of War, or the Law of Nations. *Blake* for fome time ftood alone againft their whole Force, till the reft of his Squadron coming up, the Fight was continued from between 4 and 5 in the Afternoon till 9 at Night, when the *Dutch* retired with the Lofs of 2 Ships, having not deftroyed a
fingle

fingle Veffel, nor more than 15 Men, moft of which were
on board the Admiral, who, as he wrote to the Parliament,
was himfelf engaged for 4 Hours with the main Body of the
Dutch Fleet, being the Mark at which they aimed ; and, as
Whitlock relates, received above a thoufand Shot. *Blake* in
his Letter acknowledges the particular Bleffing and Prefervation of God, and afcribes his Succefs to the Juftice of his
Caufe, the *Dutch* having firft attacked him upon the *Englifh*
Coaft. It is indeed little lefs than miraculous, that a thoufand great Shot fhould do no more Execution, and thofe
who will not admit the Interpofition of Providence, may
draw at leaft this Inference from it, that *the braveft Man is
not always in the moft Danger.*

In *July* he met the *Dutch* Fifhery Fleet with a Convoy of
12 Men of War, all which he took, with 100 of their Herring Buffes. And in *September*, being ftationed in the *Downs*
with about 60 Sail, he difcovered the *Dutch* Admirals *de Witt*
and *de Ruyter* with near the fame Number, and advanced towards them ; but the *Dutch* being obliged, by the Nature of
their Coaft, and Shallownefs of their Rivers, to build their
Ships in fuch a Manner that they require lefs Depth of Water
than the *Englifh* Veffels, took Advantage of the Form of their
Shipping, and fheltered themfelves behind a *Flat* called *Ken-
tifh-knock* ; fo that the *Englifh* finding fome of their Ships a-
ground, were obliged to alter their Courfe ; but perceiving
early the next Morning that the *Hollanders* had forfaken their
Station, they purfued them with all the Speed that the
Wind, which was weak and uncertain, allowed ; but found
themfeves unable to reach them with the Bulk of their Fleet,
and therefore detached fome of the lighteft Frigates to chafe
them. Thefe came fo near as to fire upon them about three
in the Afternoon ; but the *Dutch*, inftead of tacking a-
bout, hoifted their Sails, fteered toward their own Coaft,
and finding themfelves the next Day followed by the whole
Englifh Fleet, retired into *Goree*. The Sailors were eager to
attack them in their own Harbours, but a Council of War
being convened, it was judged imprudent to hazard the
Fleet upon the Shoals, or to engage in any important Enterprize without a frefh Supply of Provifions.

That in this Engagement the Victory belonged to the *En-
lifh* is beyond Difpute, fince without the Lofs of one Ship,
and with no more than 40 Men killed, they drove the Enemy

lay into his own Ports, took the Rear Admiral, and another Vessel, and so discouraged the *Dutch* Admirals, who had not agreed in their Measures, that *de Ruyter*, who had declared against hazarding a Battle, desired to resign his Commission, and *de Witt*, who had insisted upon Fighting, fell sick, as it was supposed, with Vexation. But how great the Loss of the *Dutch* is not certainly known; that two were taken they are too wise to deny; but affirm that those two were all that were destroyed The *English*, on the other Side, affirm that 3 of their Vessels were disabled at the first Encounter, that their Numbers on the second Day were visibly diminished, and that on the last Day they saw 3 or 4 Ships sink in their Flight.

De Witt being now discharged by the *Hollanders* as unfortunate, and the chief Command restored to *Van Trump*, great Preparations were made for retrieving their Reputation, and repairing their Losses. Their Endeavours were assisted by the *English*, themselves, now made factious by Success, the Men who who were intrusted with the civil Administration, being jealous of those whose military Commands had procured so much Honour, lest they who raised them should be eclipsed by them. Such is generally the Revolution of Affairs in every State; Danger and Distress produce Unanimity and Bravery, Virtues which are seldom unattended with Success; but Success is the Parent of Pride, and Pride of Jealousy and Faction; Faction makes Way for Calamity, and happy is that Nation whose Calamities renew their Unanimity. Such is the Rotation of Interests, that equally tend to hinder the total Destruction of a People, and to obstruct an exorbitant Increase of Power.

Blake had weakn'd his Fleet by many Detachments, and lay with no more than 40 Sail in the *Downs*, very ill provided both with Men and Ammunition, and expecting new Supplies from those whose Animosity hinder'd them from providing them, and who chose rather to see the Trade of their Country distress'd, than the Sea-officers exalted by a new Acquisition of Honour and Influence.

Van Trump, desirous of distinguishing himself at the Resumption of his Command, by some remarkable Action, had assembled 80 Ships of War, and 10 Fire-ships, and steered towards the *Downs*, where *Blake*, with whose Condition and Strength he was probably acquainted, was then stationed.

H   *Blake*

Blake not able to reſtrain his natural Ardour, or perhaps not fully informed of the Superiority of his Enemies, put out to encounter them, tho' his Fleet was ſo weakly man'd, that half of his Ships were obliged to lie idle without engaging for want of Sailors: The Force of the whole *Dutch* Fleet was therefore ſuſtained by about 22 Ships. Two of the *Engliſh* Frigates, named the *Vanguard* and *Victory*, after having for a long time ſtood engaged amidſt the whole *Dutch* Fleet, broke thro' without much Injury, nor did the *Engliſh* loſe any Ships till the Evening, when the *Garland* carrying 40 Guns was boarded at once by two great Ships, which were oppoſed by the *Engliſh* till they had ſcarcely any Men left to defend the Decks, then retiring into the lower Part of the Veſſel they blew up their Decks, which were now poſſeſſed by the Enemy, and at length were overpowered and taken. The *Bonaventure*, a ſtout well built Merchant-ſhip, going to relieve the *Garland*, was attacked by a Man of War, and, after a ſtout Reſiſtance, in which the Captain, who defended her with the utmoſt Bravery, was killed, was likewiſe carried off by the *Dutch*. *Blake* in the *Triumph*, ſeeing the *Garland* in diſtreſs, preſſed forward to relieve her, but in his way had his Foremaſt ſhatter'd, and was himſelf boarded, but beating off the Enemies he diſengaged himſelf, and retired into the *Thames* with the Loſs only of two Ships of Force, and 4 ſmall Frigates, but with his whole Fleet much ſhattered. Nor was the Victory gained at a cheap Rate, notwithſtanding the unuſual Diſproportion of Strength, for of the *Dutch* Flagſhips one was blown up, and the other two diſabled. A Proof of the *Engliſh* Bravery; which ſhould have induced *Van Trump* to have ſpared the Inſolence of carrying a Broom at his Topmaſt in his triumphant Paſſage thro' the Channel, which he intended as a Declaration that he would ſweep the Seas of the *Engliſh* Shipping; this, which he had little Reaſon to think of accompliſhing, he ſoon after periſhed in attempting.

There are ſomtimes Obſervations and Enquiries, which all Hiſtorians ſeem to decline by Agreement, of which this Action may afford us an Example: Nothing appears at the firſt View more to demand our Curioſity, or afford Matter for Examination, than this wild Encounter of 22 Ships with a Force, a Force, according to their Accounts who favour the *Dutch,* three times fuperior ; nothing can juftify a Commander in fighting under fuch Difadvantages, but the Impoffibility of retreating. But what hindred *Blake* from retiring as well before the Fight as after it ? To fay he was ignorant of the Strength of the *Dutch* Fleet, is to impute to him a very criminal Degree of Negligence, and, at leaft, it muft be confeffed that, from the time he faw them, he could not but know that they were too powerful to be oppofed by him, and even then there was Time for retreat. To urge the Ardour of his Sailors is to diveft him of the Authority of a Commander, and to charge him with the moft reproachful Weaknefs that can enter into the Character of a General. To mention the Impetuofity of his own Courage, is to make the Blame of his Temerity equal to the Praife of his Valour; which feems indeed to be the moft gentle Cenfure that the Truth of Hiftory will allow. We muft then admit, amidft our Elogies and Applaufes, that the great, the wife, and the valiant *Blake* was once betrayed to an inconfiderate and defperate Enterprife, by the refiftlefs Ardour of his own Spirit, and a noble Jealoufy of the Honour of his Country.

It was not long before he had an Opportunity of revenging his Lofs, and reftraining the Infolence of the *Dutch.* On the 18th of *February* 1652-3 *Blake* being at the Head of 80 Sail, and affifted, at his own Requeft, by Cols. *Monk* and *Dean,* efpied *Van Trump* with a Fleet of above 100 Men of War, as *Clarendon* relates, of 70 by their own publick Accounts, and 300 Merchant Ships under his Convoy. The *Englifh,* with their ufual Intrepidity, advanced towards them, and *Blake* in the *Triumph,* in which he always led his Fleet, with 12 Ships more, came to an Engagement with the main Body of the *Dutch* Fleet, and by the Difparity of their Force was reduced to the laft Extremity, having received in his Hull no fewer than 700 Shots, when *Lawfon* in the *Fairfax* came to his Affiftance. The reft of the *Englifh* Fleet now came in, and the Fight was continued with the utmoft Degree of Vigour and Refolution, till the Night gave the *Dutch* an Opportunity of retiring with the Lofs of one Flagfhip, and 6 other Men of War. The *Englifh* had many Veffels damaged, but none loft. On board *Lawfons* Ship were kill'd 100 Men, and as many on board *Blake*'s, who loft his Captain and Secretary, and himfelf received a Wound in the Thigh.

Blake

Blake having fet afhore his wounded Men, failed in Purfuit of *Van Trump*, who fent his Convoy before, and himfelf
retired fighting towards *Bulloign*. *Blake* ordering his light
Frigates to follow the Merchants, ftill continued to harrafs
Van Trump; and, on the third, the 20th of *February*, the
two Fleets came to another Battle, in which *Van Trump* once
more retired before the *Englifh*, and making Ufe of the
peculiar Form of his Shipping fecured himfelf in the Shoals.
The Accounts of this Fight, as of all the others, are various; but the *Dutch* Writers themfelves confefs that they
loft 8 Men of War, and more than 20 Merchant-fhips;
and it is probable that they fuffered much more than they
are willing to allow, for thefe repeated Defeats provoked
the common People to Riots and Infurrections, and obliged
the States to ask, tho' ineffectually, for Peace.

In *April* following the Form of Government in *England*
was changed, and the Supreme Authority affumed by *Cromwell*;
upon which Occafion *Blake*, with his Affociates, declared
that, notwithftanding the Change of the Adminiftration,
they fhould ftill be ready to difcharge their Truft, and to
defend the Nation from Infults, Injuries, and Encroachments; "It is not, fays *Blake*, the Bufinefs of a Seaman to
" mind State-Affairs, but to hinder Foreigners from fool-
" ing us." This was the Principle from which he never
deviated, and which he always endeavoured to inculcate in
the Fleet, as the fureft Foundation of Unanimity and Steadinefs. "Difturb not one another with domeftick Difputes,
" but remember that we are *Englifh*, and our Enemies are
" Foreigners. Enemies! which let what Party foever prevail,
" it is equally the Intereft of our Country to humble and
" reftrain."

After the 30th of *April* 1653, *Blake*, *Monk*, and *Dean* failed out of the *Englifh* Harbours with 100 Men of War, and
finding the *Dutch* with 70 Sail on their own Coafts, drove
them to the *Texel*, and took 50 Doggers. Then they failed
northward in purfuit of *Van Trump*, who having a Fleet of
Merchants under his Convoy, durft not enter the Channel,
but fteering towards the *Sound*, and by great Dexterity and
Addrefs efcaped the three *Englifh* Admirals, and brought all
his Ships into their Harbour : then knowing that *Blake* was
ftill in the North, came before *Dover*, and fired upon the
Town, but was driven off by the Caftle.

Monk and *Dean* ftationed themfelves again at the Mouth
of

of the *Texel*, and block'd up the *Dutch* in their own Ports with 80 Sail ; but hearing that *Van Trump* was at *Goree* with 120 Men of War, they ordered all Ships of Force in the River and Ports to repair to them.

On *June* 3d, the two Fleets came to an Engagement, in the beginning of which *Dean* was carried off by a Cannon Ball, yet the Fight continued from about 12 to 6 in the Afternoon, when the *Dutch* gave way, and retreated fighting.

On the 4th, in the Afternoon, *Blake* came up with 18 fresh Ships, and procured the *English* a compleat Victory ; nor could the *Dutch* any otherwise preserve their Ships than by retiring once more into the Flats and Shallows, where the largest of the *English* Vessels could not approach.

In this Battle *Van Trump* boarded Vice-Admiral *Pen*, but was beaten off, and himself boarded, and reduced to blow up his Decks, of which the *English* had gotten Possession. He was then entred at once by *Pen* and another, nor could possibly have escaped had not *de Ruyter* and *de Witt* arrived at that instant and rescued him.

However the *Dutch* may endeavour to extenuate their Loss in this battle, by admitting no more than 8 Ships to have been taken or destroy'd, it is evident that they must have received much greater Damages, not only by the Accounts of more impartial Historians, but by the Remonstrances and Exclamations of their Admirals themselves, *Van Trump* declaring before the *States*, that *without a numerous Reinforcement of large Men of War he could serve them no more*, and *de Witt* crying out before them, with the natural Warmth of his Character, *Why should I be silent before my Lords and Masters? The* English *are our Masters, and by consequence Masters of the Sea.*

In *November*, 1654, *Blake* was sent by *Cromwell* into the *Mediterranean* with a powerful Fleet, and may be said to have received the Homage of all that Part of the World : Being equally courted by the haughty *Spaniards*, the surly *Dutch*, and the lawless *Algerines*.

In *March*, 1666, having forced *Algiers* to Submission, he entred the Harbour of *Tunis*, and demanded Reparation for the Robberies practised upon the *English* by the Pirates of that Place, and insisted that the Captives of his Nation should be set at liberty. The Governour having planted Batteries along the Shore, and drawn up his Ships under the Castles, sent *Blake* an haughty and insolent Answer,

There

There are our *Castles* of *Goletta* and Porto Ferino, said he, upon which you may do your worst; adding other Menaces and Insults, and mentioning in Terms of Ridicule the Inequality of a Fight between Ships and Castles. *Blake* had likewise demanded leave to take in Water, which was refused him. Fired with this inhuman and insolent Treatment, he curled his Whiskers, as was his Custom when he was angry, and entering *Porto Ferino* with his great Ships discharged his shot so fast upon the Batteries and Castles, that in two Hours the Guns were dismounted, and the Works forsaken, though he was at first exposed to the Fire of 60 Cannon. He then ordered his Officers to send out their Long Boats well man'd to seize 9 of the Piratical Ships lying in the Road, himself continued to fire upon the Castle. This was so bravely executed, that with the Loss of only 25 Men killed, and 48 wounded, all the Ships were fired in the sight of *Tunis*. Thence sailing to *Tripoli* he concluded a Peace with that Nation, then returning to *Tunis* he found nothing but Submission: And such indeed was his Reputation, that he met with no farther Opposition, but collected a kind of Tribute from the Princes of those Countries his Business being to demand Reparation for all the Injuries offered to the *English* during the Civil Wars. He exacted from the Duke of *Tuscany* 60,000 *l.* and, as it is said, sent home 16 Ships laden with the Effects which he had received from the several States.

The Respect with which he obliged all Foreigners to treat his Countrymen appears from a Story related by Bishop *Burnet*. When he lay before *Malaga*, in a time of Peace with *Spain*, some of his Sailors went ashore, and meeting a Procession of the *Host*, not only refused to pay any Respect to it, but laughing at those that did. The People being put, by one of the Priests, upon resenting this Indignity, fell upon them, and beat them severely. When they returned to their Ship, they complained of their ill Treatment; upon which *Blake* sent to demand the Priest who had procured it. The Viceroy answered that, having no Authority over the Priests, he could not send him; to which *Blake* replied, *that he did not enquire into the Extent of the Viceroy's Authority, but that if the Priest were not sent within 3 Hours, he would burn the Town.* The Viceroy then sent the Priest to him, who pleaded the Provocation given by the Seamen. *Blake* bravely and rationally

onally anfwered, that if he had complained to him, he would have punifhed them feverely, for he would not have his Men affront the eftablifhed Religion of any Place; but that he was angry that the *Spaniards* fhould affume that Power, for he would have all the World know, *that an En*glifhman *was only to be punifhed by an* Englilhman. So having ufed the Prieft civilly, he fent him back, being fatisfied that he was in his Power. This Conduct fo much pleafed *Cromwell*, that he read the Letter with great Satisfaction, and faid, *He hoped to make the Name of an* Englifhman *as great as ever that of a* Roman *had been*.

In 1656, the Protector, having declared War againft *Spain*, difpatched *Blake* with 25 Men of War, to infeft their Coafts, and intercept their Shipping. In purfuance of thefe Orders he cruifed all Winter about the *Streights*, and then lay at the Mouth of the Harbour of *Cales*, where he received Intelligence that the *Spanifh* Plate-Fleet lay at Anchor in the Bay of *Santa Cruz*, in the Ifle of *Teneriffe*. On the 13th of *April* 1657, he departed from *Cales*, and on the 20th arrived at *Santa Cruz*, where he found 16 *Spanifh* Veffels. The Bay was defended on the northfide by a Caftle well mounted with Cannon; and in other Parts with 7 Forts, with Cannon proportioned to the Bignefs, all united by a Line of Communication manned with Mufqueteers. The *Spanifh* Admiral drew up his fmall Ships under the Cannon of the Caftle, and ftationed 6 great Galleons with their Broad-fides to the Sea: An advantageous and prudent Difpofition, but of little Effect againft the *Englifh* Commander; who determining to attack them, ordered *Stanyer* to enter the Bay with his Squadron; then pofting fome of his largeft Ships to play upon the Fortifications, himfelf attacked the Galleons, which, after a gallant Refiftance, were at length abandoned by the *Spaniards*, tho' the leaft of them was bigger than the biggeft of *Blake*'s Ships. The Forts and fmaller Veffels being now fhattered and forfaken, the whole Fleet was fet on fire, the Galleons by *Blake*, and the fmalleft Veffels by *Stanyer*, the *Englifh* Veffels being too much fhattered in the Fight to bring them away. Thus was the whole Plate-Fleet deftroyed, *and the* Spaniards, *according to* Rapin's Remark, *fuftained a great Lofs of Ships, Money, Men and Merchandife, while the* Englifh *gained nothing but Glory*. As if he that increafes the military Reputation of a People did not increafe their Power, er, and he that weakens his Enemy in effect strengthen himself.

The whole Action, says Clarendon, *was so incredible, that all Men, who knew the Place, wondered that any sober Man, with what Courage soever endued, would ever have undertaken it, and they could hardly persuade themselves to believe what they had done. While the* Spaniards *comforted themselves with the Belief, that they were Devils and not Men who had destroyed them in such a Manner. So much a strong Resolution of bold and courageous Men can bring to pass, that no Resistance or Advantage of Ground can disappoint them; and it can hardly be imagined how small a Loss the* English *sustained in this unparallel'd Action, not one Ship being left behind, and the Killed and Wounded not exceeding* 200 *Men, when the Slaughter on board the* Spanish *Ships and on Shore was incredible.* The General cruised for some time afterwards with his victorious Fleet at the Mouth of *Cales,* to intercept the *Spanish* Shipping; but finding his Constitution broken by the Fatigue of the last 3 Years, determined to return home, and dyed before he came to Land.

His Body was embalmed, and having lain some time in State at *Greenwich* House, was buried in *Henry* VII's Chapel, with all the funeral Solemnity due to the Remains of a Man so famed for his Bravery, and so spotless in his Integrity; nor is it without Regret that I am obliged to relate the Treatment his Body met a Year after the *Restoration,* when it was taken up by express Command, and buried in a Pit in *St. Margaret's* Church-yard. Had he been guilty of the Murder of *Charles* I. to insult his Body had been a mean Revenge; but as he was innocent, it was, at least, Inhumanity, and, perhaps, Ingratitude. *Let no Man,* says the oriental Proverb, *pull a dead Lyon by the Beard.*

But that Regard which was denied his Body has been paid to his better Remains, his Name and his Memory. Nor has any Writer dared to deny him the Praise of his Intrepidity, Honesty, Contempt of Wealth, and Love of his Country. *He was the first Man,* says Clarendon, *that declined the old Track, and made it apparent that the Sciences might be attained in less Time than was imagined.* ――――― *He was the first Man that brought Ships to contemn Castles on Shore, which had ever been thought very formidable, but were discovered by him to make a Noise only, and to fright those, who could rarely be hurt by them. He was the first that infused that Proportion of Courage into Seamen,*

by

by making them see, by *Experience*, what mighty *Things they could do if they were refolved, and taught them to fight in Fire as well as upon the Water* ; *and though he has been very well imitated and followed, was the firft that gave the Example of that kind of naval Courage, and bold and refolute Atchievements.*

To this Atteftation of his military Excellence, may be proper to fubjoin an Account of his moral Charaƈter from the Author of *Lives* Englifh *and* Foreign. *He was jealous, says that Writer, of the Liberty of the Subjeƈt, and the Glory of his Nation* ; *and as he made ufe of no mean Artifices to raife himfelf to the higheft Command at Sea, fo he needed no Intereft but his Merit to fupport him in it. He fcorned nothing more than Money, which, as faft as it came in, was laid out by him in the Service of the State* ; *and to fhew that he was animated by that brave, publick Spirit, which has fince been reckoned rather romantick than heroick, he was fo difinterefted, that though no Man had more Opportunities to enrich himfelf than he, who had taken fo many Millions from the Enemies of* England, *yet he threw it all into the publick Treafury, and did not die* 500 l. *richer than his Father left him : Which the Author avers from his perfonal Knowledge of his Family and their Circumftances, having been bred up in it, and often heard his Brother give this Account of him. He was religious according to the pretended Purity of thefe Times, but would frequently allow himfelf to be merry with his Officers, and by his Tendernefs and Generofity to the Seamen had fo endeared himfelf to them, that when he dyed they lamented his Lofs as that of a common Father.*

Inftead of more Teftimonies, his Charaƈter may be properly concluded with one incident of his Life, by which it appears how much the Spirit of *Blake* was fuperior to all private Views. His Brother, in the laft Aƈtion with the *Spaniards,* having not done his Duty, was, at *Blake's* Defire difcarded, and the Ship was given to another ; yet was he not lefs regardful of him as a Brother : For when he died he left him his Eftate, knowing him well qualified to adorn or enjoy a private Fortune, though he had found him unfit to ferve his Country in a publick Charaƈter ; and had therefore not fuffered him to rob it.

F I N I S.

A Panegyric on Dr MORIN,

By Mr FONTENELLE.

B LEWIS *Morin* was born at *Mans*, on the 11th of *July*, 1635, of Parents eminent for their Piety. He was the eldest of sixteen Children, a Family to which their Estate bore no Proportion, and which in Persons less resigned to Providence, would have caused great Uneasiness and Anxiety.

C His Parents omitted nothing in his Education, which Religion requires, and which their Fortune could supply. Botany was the Study that appeared to have taken Possession of his Inclination, as soon as the Bent of his Genius could be discovered. A Countryman, who supplied the Apothecaries of the Place, was his first D Master, and was paid by him for his Instructions with the little Money that he could procure, or that which was given him to buy something to eat after dinner. Thus Abstinence and Generosity discovered themselves with his Passion for Botany, and the Gratification of a Desire indifferent in itself, was procured by the E Exercise of two Virtues.

He was soon Master of all his Instructor's Knowledge, and was obliged to enlarge his Acquaintance with Plants, by observing them himself in the Neighbourhood of *Mans*. Having finished his grammatical Studies, he was sent to learn F Philosophy at *Paris*. Whither he travelled on Foot like a Student in Botany, and was careful not to lose such an Opportunity of Improvement.

When his Course of Philosophy was compleated, he was determined by his Love of Botany, to the Profession of Physic, and from that time engaged in a G sic, and from that time engaged in a Course of Life, which was never exceeded either by the Ostentation of a Philosopher, or the Severity of an Anchoret ; for he confined himself to Bread and Water, and at most allowed himself no Indulgence beyond Fruits. By this Method, he preserved a constant Freedom and Se- H renity of Spirits, always equally proper for Study ; for his Soul had no Pretences to complain of being overwhelmed with Matter.

This

87

This Regimen, extraordinary as it was, had many Advantages; for it preserved his Health, an Advantage which very few sufficiently regard; it gave him an Authority to preach Diet and Abstinence to his Patients; and it made him rich without the Assistance of Fortune, rich, not for himself, but for the Poor, who were the only Persons benefited by that artificial Affluence, which, of all others, is most difficult to acquire. It is easy to imagine that while he practised in the midst of *Paris* the severe Temperance of a Hermit, *Paris* differed no otherwise with regard to him, from a Hermitage, than as it supplied him with Books, and the Conversation of learned Men.

In 1662 he was admitted Doctor of Physic. About that time Dr *Fagon*, Dr *Longeot*, and Dr *Galois*, all eminent for their Skill in Botany, were employed in drawing up a Catalogue of the Plants in the *Royal Garden*, which was publish'd in 1665, under the Name of Dr *Vallot*, then first Physician; during the Prosecution of this Work, Dr *Morin* was often consulted, and from those Conversations it was that Dr *Fagon* conceived a particular Esteem of him, which he always continued to retain.

After having practised Physic some years, he was admitted *Expectant* at the *Hotel Dieu*, where he was regularly to have been made *Pensionary* Physician upon the first Vacancy; but mere unassisted Merit advances slowly, if, what is not very common, it advances at all. *Morin* had no Acquaintance with the Arts necessary to carry on Schemes of Preferment; the Moderation of his Desires preserved him from the Necessity of studying them, and the Privacy of his Life debar'd him from any Opportunity.

At last, however, Justice was done him in spite of Artifice and Partiality; but his Advancement added nothing to his Condition, except the Power of more extensive Charity, for all the Money which he received as a Salary, he put into the Chest of the Hospital, always, as he imagined, without being observed. Not content with serving the Poor for nothing, he paid them for being serv'd.

His Reputation rose so high in *Paris*, that Mademoiselle *de Guise* was desirous to make him her Physician, but it was not without difficulty that he was prevailed upon by his Friend, Dr *Dodart*, to accept the Place. He was by this new Advancement laid under the Necessity of keeping a Chariot, an Equipage very unsuitable to his Temper; but while he complied with those

exterior Appearances which the Publick had a Right to demand from him, he remitted nothing of his former Austerity in the more private and essential Parts of his Life, which he had always the Power of regulating according to his own Disposition.

In two Years and a half the Princess fell sick, and was despaired of by *Morin* who was a great Master of Prognosticks; at the time when she thought herself in no Danger, he pronounced her Death inevitable, a Declaration to the highest Degree disagreeable, but which was made more easy to him than to any other by his Piety, and artless Simplicity. Nor did his Sincerity produce any ill Consequences to himself; for the Princess affected by his Zeal, taking a Ring from her Finger, gave it him, as the last Pledge of her Affection, and rewarded him still more in his Satisfaction, by preparing for Death with a true Christian Piety. She left him by Will an yearly Pension of two thousand Livres, which was always regularly paid him.

No sooner was the Princess dead, but he freed himself from the Incumbrance of his Chariot, and retired to *St Victor* without a Servant, having, however, augmented his daily Allowance with a little Rice boiled in Water.

Dodart, who had undertaken the Charge of being ambitious on his Account, procured him, at the Restoration of the Academy in 1699, to be nominated *Associate Botanist*; not knowing, what he would doubtless have been pleased with the Knowledge of, that he introduced into that Assembly the Man that was to succeed him in his Place of Pensionary.

Dr *Morin* was not one who had upon his Hands the Labour of adapting himself to the Duties of his Condition, but always found himself naturally adapted to them. He had, therefore, no Difficulty in being constant at the Assemblies of the Academy notwithstanding the Distance of Places, while he had Strength enough to support the Journey. But his Regimen was not equally effectual to produce Vigour as to prevent Distempers; and being 64 Years old at his Admission, he could not continue his Assiduity more than a Year after the Death of *Dodart*, whom he succeeded in 1707.

When *Mr Tournefort* went to pursue his Botanical Enquiries in the *Levant*, he desired Dr *Morin* to supply his Place of Demonstrator of the Plants in the *Royal Garden*, and rewarded him for the Trouble, by inscribing to him a new Plant which he he brought from this East, by the Name of *Herba Orientalis*, as he named others the *Dodarto*, the *Fagonnea*, the *Bignonne*, the *Phillipeo*. These are Compliments proper to be made by the Botanists, not only to those of their own Rank, but to the greatest Persons; for a Plant is a Monument of a more durable Nature than a Medal or an Obelisk; and yet, as a Proof that even these Vehicles are not always sufficient to transmit to Futurity the Name conjoined with them, the *Nicotiana* is now scarcely known by any other Term than that of *Tobacco*.

Dr *Morin* advancing far in Age, was now forced to take a Servant, and what was yet a more essential Alteration, prevailed upon himself to take an Ounce of Wine a Day, @ he measured with the same Exactness as a Medicine, bordering up n Poison. He quitted at the same time all his Practice in the City, and confined it to the Poor of his Neighbourhood, and his Visits at the *Hotel Dieu*; but his Weakness encreasing, he was forced to encrease his Quantity of Wine, which yet he always continued to adjust by Weight.*

At 78 his Legs could carry him no longer, and he scarcely left his Bed, but his Intellects continued unimpaired, except in the last six Months of his Life. He expired, or to use a more proper Term, *went out*, on the first of *March* 1714, at the Age of 80 Years, without any Distemper, and merely for want of Strength, having enjoyed by the Benefit of his Regimen, a long and healthy Life, and a gentle and easy Death.

This extraordinary Regimen was but part of the daily Regulation of his Life, of which all the Offices were carried on with a Regularity and Exactness nearly approaching to that of the planetary Motions.

He went to Bed at seven and rose at two throughout the Year. He spent in the Morning three Hours at his Devotions, and went to the *Hotel Dieu* in the Sum-

mer between five and six, and in the Winter between six and seven, hearing Mass for the most part at *Notre Dame*. After his Return he read the Holy Scripture, dined at eleven, and when it was fair Weather walked till two in the Royal Garden, where he examined the new Plants, and gratified his earliest and strongest Passion. For the remaining Part of the Day, if he had no Poor to visit, he shut himself up, and read Books of Literature or Physic, but chiefly Physic, as the Duty of his Profession required. This likewise was the time he received Visits, if any were paid him. He often used this Expression, *Those that come to see me do me Honour, and those that stay away do me a Favour.* It is easy to conceive that a Man of this Temper was not crouded with Salutations: There was only now and then an *Autony* that would pay *Paul* a Visit.

Among his Papers was found a *Greek* and *Latin* Index to *Hippocrates*, more copious and exact than that of *Pini*, which he had finish'd only a Year before his Death. Such a Work requir'd the Assiduity and Patience of an Hermit. *

There is likewise a Journal of the Weather, kept without Interruption, for more than forty Years, in which he has accurately set down the State of the Barometer and Thermometer, the Dryness and Moisture of the Air, the Variations of the Wind in the Course of the Day, the Rain, the Thunders, and even the sudden Storms, in a very commodious and concise Method, which exhibits, in a little Room, a great Train of different Observations. What Numbers of such Remarks had escaped a Man less uniform in his Life, and whose Attention had been extended to common Objects?

All the Estate which he left is a Collection of Medals, another of Heros, and a Library rated at two thousand Crowns. Which make it evident that he spent much more upon his Mind than upon his Body.

---

* *The Practice of Dr Morin is forbidden, I believe, by every Writer that has left Rules for the Preservation of Health, and is directly opposite to that of Cornaro, who, by his Regimen repaired a broken Constitution, and protracted his Life without any painful Infirmities, or any Decay of his intellectual Abilities, to more than a hundred Years; it is generally agreed, that as Man advances in Years, they ought to take lighter Sustenance, and in less Quantities; and Reason seems easily to discover that as the nutritive Powers grow weaker, they ought to labour less.*

* *This is an Instance of the Disposition generally found in Writers of Lives, to exalt every common Occurrence and Action into Wonders. Are not Indexes daily written by Men who neither receive nor expect very loud Applauses for their Labours?*

of *June*, 1668. The Family from which he defcended, has for feveral Generations produced Men of great Eminence for Piety and Learning, and his Father, who was Profeffor of Divinity in the Uni-

A verfity, and Paftor of the City of *Utretcht*, was equally celebrated for the Strictnefs of his Life, the Efficacy and Orthodoxy of his Sermons, and the Learning and Perfpicuity of his Academical Lectures.

From the Affiftance and Inftruction, which fuch a Father would doubtlefs have

B been encouraged by the Genius of his Son not to have omitted, *Burman* was unhap-pily cut off in the eleven Year of his Age, being at that Time by his Father's Death thrown entirely under the Care of his Mother, by whofe Diligence, Piety, and Prudence, his Education was fo regulated, that he had fcarcely any Reafon, but

C Filial Tendernefs, to regret the Lofs of his Father.

He was about this Time fent to the pub-lic School of *Utretcht*, to be inftructed in the learned Languages; and it will con-vey no common Idea of his Capacity and Induftry to relate, that he had pafs'd through the Claffes, and was admitted

D into the Univerfity, in his thirteenth Year.

This Account of the Rapidity of his Progrefs in the firft Part of his Studies, is fo ftupendous, that, though it is attef-ted by his Friend Dr *Ofterdyke*, of whom it cannot be reafonably fufpected, that he is himfelf deceived, or that he can defire to deceive others, it muft be allowed far

E to exceed the Limits of Probability, if it be confidered with regard to the Me-thods of Education practifed in our Coun-try, where it is not uncommon for the higheft Genius, and moft comprehenfive Capacity to be entangled for ten Years, in thofe thorny Paths of Literature, which

F *Burman* is reprefented to have pafs'd in lefs than two; and we muft doubtlefs con-fefs the moft Skilful of our Mafters, much excelled by the Addrefs of the *Dutch* Teachers, or the Abilities of our greateft Scholars, far furpaffed by thofe of *Burman*.

But to reduce this Narrative to Credi-bility, it is neceffary that Admiration

G fhould give Place to Inquiry, and that it be difcovered what Proficiency in Litera-ture is expected from a Student, requeft-ing to be admitted into a *Dutch* Univer-fity. It is to be obferved, that in the Univerfities of foreign Countries, they have Profeffors of Philology, or Humani-

H ty, whofe Employment it is, to inftruct the Younger Claffes in Grammar, Rhe-toric, and Languages; nor do they en-gage in the Study of Philofophy, 'till they have

An Account of the Life of Peter Burman *the late Profeffor of Hiftory, Poetry, &c. in the Univerfity of* Leiden.

*P*ETER BURMAN, was born at UTRETCHT, on the 26th Day

90

have paſſed through a Courſe of Philological Lectures and Exerciſes, to which
in ſome Places two Years are commonly
allotted.

The *Engliſh* Scheme of Education,
which, with regard to Academical Studies,
is more rigorous, and ſets literary Honours at a higher Price than that of any
other Country, exacts from the Youth,
who are initiated in our Colleges, a Degree of Philological Knowledge, ſufficient to qualify them for Lectures in Philoſophy, which are read to them in *Latin*,
and to enable them to proceed in other
Studies without Aſſiſtance, ſo that it may
be conjectured, that *Burman*, at his Entrance into the Univerſity, had no ſuch
Skill in Languages, nor ſuch Ability of
Compoſition, as are frequently to be met
with in the higher Claſſes of an *Engliſh*
School ; nor was perhaps more than mo-
derately skill'd in *Latin*, and taught the
firſt Rudiments of *Greek*.

In the Univerſity, he was committed
to the Care of the learned *Grævius*,
whoſe Regard for his Father inclined him
to ſuperintend his Studies with more than
common Attention, which was ſoon confirmed and encreaſed by his Diſcoveries of
the Genius of his Pupil, and his Obſervation of his Diligence.

One of the Qualities which contributed eminently to qualify *Grævius* for an
Inſtructor of Youth, was the Sagacity by
which he readily diſcover'd the predominant Faculty of each Pupil, and the peculiar Deſignation, by which Nature had
allotted him to any Species of Literature,
and by which he was ſoon able to determine, that *Burman* was remarkably a-
dapted to claſſical Studies, and predict
the great Advances that he would make,
by induſtriouſly purſuing the Direction of
his Genius.

Animated by the Encouragement of a
Tutor ſo celebrated, he continued the Vi-
gour of his Application, and for ſeveral
Years, not only attended the Lectures of
Grævius, but made uſe of every other
Opportunity of Improvement, with ſuch
Diligence, as might juſtly be expected to
produce an uncommon Proficiency.

Having thus attained a ſufficient Degree of claſſical Knowledge, to qualify
him for Enquiries into other Sciences,
he applied himſelf to the Study of the
Law, and publiſh'd a Diſſertation, *de Vi-
ceſimis Hæreditatum*, which he publickly
defended under the Profeſſor *Van Muyden*,
with ſuch Learning and Eloquence, as
procured him great Applauſe.

Imagining then, that the Converſation
of other Men of Learning might be of

Uſe towards his farther Improvement,
and rightly judging, that Notions formed
in any ſingle Seminary, are for the greateſt Part contracted and partial ; he went
to *Leiden*, where he ſtudied Philoſophy
for a Year, under M. *de Volder*, whoſe
Celebrity was ſo great that the Schools
aſſigned to the Sciences, which it was his
Province to teach, were not ſufficient,
though very ſpacious, to contain the Audience that crowded his Lectures from
all Parts of *Europe*.

Yet he did not ſuffer himſelf to be engroſſed by Philoſophical Diſquiſitions, to
the Neglect of thoſe Studies in which he
was more early engaged, and to which
he was perhaps by Nature better adapted ; for he attended, at the ſame Time
Ryckius's Explanations of *Tacitus* and
James Gronovius's Lectures on the *Greek*
Writers, and has often been heard to acknowledge, at an advanced Age, the Aſſiſtance which he received from both.

Having thus paſſed a Year at *Leiden*,
with great Advantage, he returned to
Utrecht, and once more applied himſelf
to Philological Studies, under the Direction
of *Grævius*, whoſe early Hopes of his
Genius, were now raiſed to a full Confidence of that Excellence at which he afterwards arrived.

At *Utrecht*, in *March* 1688, in the
twentieth Year of his Age, he was advanced to the Degree of Doctor of Laws,
on which Occaſion, he publiſhed a learned Diſſertation, *de Tranſactionibus*, and
defended it with his uſual Eloquence,
Learning and Succeſs.

The Attainment of this Honour, was
far from having upon *Burman* that Effect
which has been too often obſerved to be
produced in others, who having in their
own Opinion no higher Object of Ambition, have lapſed into Idleneſs and Security, and ſpent the reſt of their Lives in
a lazy Enjoyment of their Academical
Dignities. *Burman* aſpired to farther Improvements, and not ſatisfied with the
Opportunities of literary Converſation,
which *Utrecht* afforded, travelled into
Swiſſerland and *Germany*, where he gain'd
an Increaſe both of Fame and Learning.

At his Return from this Excurſion, he
engaged in the Practice of the Law, and
pleaded ſeveral Cauſes with ſuch Reputation, as might be hoped by a Man who
had joined to his Knowledge of the Law,
the Embelliſhments of polite Literature,
and the ſtrict Ratiocination of true Philoſophy, and who was able to employ on
every Occaſion, both the Graces of Eloquence and the Power of Argumentation.

While *Burman* was haſtening to high
Reputation

Reputation in the Courts of Justice, and to those Riches and Honours which always follow it, he was summoned in 1691, by the Magistrates of *Utrecht*, to undertake the Charge of *Collector of the Tenths*, an Office in that Place of great Honour, and which he accepted therefore, as a Proof of their Confidence and Esteem.

While he was engaged in this Employment, he married *Eve Clotterboke*, a young Lady of a good Family, and uncommon Genius and Beauty, by whom he had ten Children, of which eight died young, and only two Sons, *Francis* and *Casper* lived to console their Mother for their Father's Death.

Neither Publick Business, nor Domestick Cares, detained *Burman* from the Prosecution of his Literary Enquiries, by which he so much endeared himself to *Graevius*, that he was recommended by him to the Regard of the University of *Utrecht*, and accordingly, in 1696. was chosen Professor of *Eloquence* and *History*, to which was added, after some Time, the Professorship of the *Greek Language*, and afterwards that of *Politicks*; so various did they conceive his Abilities, and so extensive his Knowledge.

At his Entrance upon this new Province, he pronounced an Oration upon *Eloquence and Poetry.*

Having now more frequent Opportunities of displaying his Learning, he rose, in a short Time, to a high Reputation, of which the great Number of his Auditors was a sufficient Proof, and which the Proficiency of his Pupils shewed not to be accidental or undeserved.

In 1714 he formed a Resolution of visiting *Paris*, not only for the Sake of conferring in Person, upon Questions of Literature, with the learned Men of that Place, and of gratifying his Curiosity with a more familiar Knowledge of those Writers whose Works he admired, but with a View more important, of visiting the Libraries, and making those Enquiries which might be of Advantage to his Darling Study.

The Vacation of the University allowed him to stay at *Paris* but six Weeks which he employ'd with so much Dexterity and Industry, that he had searched the principal Libraries, collated a great Number of Manuscripts and printed Copies, and brought back a large Treasure of curious Observations.

In this Visit to *Paris* he contracted an Acquaintance, among other learned Men, with the celebrated Father *Montfaucon*, with whom he conversed, at his first Interview, under no other Character than that of a Traveller; but their Discourse turning upon ancient Learning, the Stranger soon gave such Proofs of his Attainments, that *Montfaucon* declar'd a Traveller of uncommon Knowledge, and confessed his Curiosity to know his Name; which he no sooner heard, than he sprung from his Seat, and embracing him with the utmost Ardour, expressed his Satisfaction at having seen the Man whose Productions, of various Kinds, he had so much praised, and, as a real Proof of his Regard, offered, not only to procure him an immediate Admission to all the Libraries of *Paris*, but to those in remoter Provinces, which are not generally open to Strangers, and undertook to ease the Expences of his Journey by procuring him Entertainment in all the Monastries of his Order.

This Favour *Burman* was hindered from accepting, by the Necessity of returning to *Utrecht* at the usual Time of beginning a new Course of Lectures to which there was always so great a Concourse of Students, as much encreated the Dignity and Fame of the University in which he taught.

He had already extended, to distant Parts, his Reputation for Knowledge of ancient History by a Treatise *de Vectigalibus Populi Romani*, on *the Revenues of the Romans*, and for his Skill in Greek Learning, and in ancient Coins, by a Tract called *Jupiter Fulgurator*; and after his Return from *Paris*, he published *Phaedrus*, first with the Notes of former Commentators, and afterwards with his own. He printed many Poems, made many Orations upon different Subjects, and procured an Impression of the Epistles of *Gudius* and *Sarravius*.

While he was thus employ'd, the Professorships of History, Eloquence, and the *Greek* Language, became vacant at *Leiden*, by the Death of *Perizonius*, which *Burman's* Reputation incited the Curators of the University to offer him upon very generous Terms, and which, after some Struggles with his Fondness for his native Place, his Friends, and his Colleagues, he was prevailed on to accept, finding the Solicitations from *Leiden* warm and urgent, and his Friends at *Utrecht*, though unwilling to be deprived of him, yet not zealous enough for the Honour and Advantage of their University, to endeavour to detain him by great Liberality.

At his Entrance upon this new Professorship, which was conferred upon him in 1715, he pronounced an Oration upon the *Duty and Office of a Professor of polite Literature. De Publici Humanioris Disciplinae*

... Professor's proper office et manners.
And shewed by the Usefulness and Perspicuity of his Lectures, that he was not confined to Speculative Notions on that Subject, having a very happy Method of accommodating his Instructions to the different Abilities and Attainments of his Pupils.

Nor did he suffer the publick Duties of his Station to hinder him from promoting Learning by Labours of a different Kind; for, besides many Poems and Orations which he recited on different Occasions, he wrote several Prefaces to the Works of others, and publish'd many useful Editions of the best Latin Writers, with large Collections of Notes from various Commentators.

He was twice Rector, or Chief Governor of the University, and discharged that important Office with equal Equity and Ability, and gained by his Conduct in every Station, so much Esteem, that when the Professorship of History of the United Provinces became vacant, it was conferred on him, as an Addition to his Honours and Revenues, which he might justly claim; and afterwards, as a Proof of the Continuance of their Regard, and a Testimony that his Reputation was still encreasing they made him Chief Librarian, an Office which was the more acceptable to him, as it united his Business with his Pleasure, and gave him an Opportunity at the same Time of superintending the Library, and carrying on his Studies.

Such was the Course of his Life, till, in his old Age, leaving off his Practice of Walking and other Exercises, he began to be afflicted with the Scurvy, which discovered itself by very tormenting Symptoms of various Kinds; sometimes disturbing his Head with Vertigos, sometimes causing Faintness in his Limbs, and sometimes attacking his Legs with Anguish so excruciating, that all his Vigour was destroyed, and the Power of Walking entirely taken away, till at Length his Left Foot became motionless. The Violence of his Pain produced Irregular Fevers, deprived him of Rest, and entirely debilitated his whole Frame.

This tormenting Disease he bore, tho' not without some Degree of Impatience, yet without any unbecoming or irrational Despondency, and applied himself in the Intermission of his Pains to seek for Comfort in the Duties of Religion.

While he lay in this State of Misery he received an Account of the Promotion of two of his Grandsons, and a Catalogue of the King of France's Library, presented to

him by the Command of the King himself, and expressed some Satisfaction on all these Occasions; but soon diverted his Thoughts to the more important Consideration of his eternal State, into which he passed on the 31st of March 1741, in the 73d Year of his Age.

He was a Man of moderate Stature, of great Strength and Activity, which he preserved by temperate Diet, without medical Exactness, and by allotting Proportions of his Time to Relaxation and Amusement, not suffering his Studies to exhaust his Strength, but relieving them by frequent Intermissions, a Practice consistent with the most exemplary Diligence, and which, he that omits will find at last, that Time may be lost, like Money, by unseasonable Avarice.

In his Hours of Relaxation he was gay, and sometimes gave Way so far to his Temper, naturally satirical, that he drew upon himself the Ill-will of those who had been unfortunate the Subjects of his Mirth; but Enemies so provoked he thought it beneath him to regard or to pacify, for he was fierce but not malicious, disdained Dissimulation, and in his gay or serious Hours preserved a settled Detestation of Falshood. So that he was an open and undisguised Friend or Enemy, entirely unacquainted with the Artifices of Flatterers, but so judicious in the Choice of Friends, and so constant in his Affection to them, that those with whom he had contracted Familiarity in his Youth, had for the greatest Part his Confidence in his old Age.

His Abilities, which would probably have enabled him to have excelled in any Kind of Learning, were chiefly employ'd, as his Station required, on polite Literature, in which he arrived at very uncommon Knowledge, which, however, appears rather from judicious Compilations than original Productions. His Stile is lively and masculine, but not without Harshness and Constraint, nor, perhaps, always polished to that Purity which some Writers have attained. He was at least Instrumental to the Instruction of Mankind, by the Publication of many valuable Performances, which lay neglected by the greatest Part of the learned World, and if Reputation be estimated by Usefulness, he may claim a higher Degree in the Ranks of Learning than some others of happier Elocution, or more vigorous Imagination.

The Malice or Suspicion of those, who either did not know, or did not love him, had given Rise to some Doubts about his Religion, which he took an Op-
D d   portunity

Portunity of removing on his Death-bed by a voluntary Declaration of his Faith, his Hope of everlasting Salvation from the revealed Promises of God, and his Confidence in the Merits of our Redeemer, of the Sincerity of which Declaration his whole Behaviour in his long Illness was an incontestable Proof; and he concluded his Life, which had been illustrious for many Virtues, by exhibiting an Example of true Piety.

Of his Works we have not been able to procure a compleat Catalogue ; he publish'd,

Quintilianus, 2 *Vols* 4to   } Cum
Valerius Flaccus   } Notis
Ovidius, 3 *Vols* 4to   } Vario-
Poetæ Latini Minores, 2 *Vols* 4to } rum.
Buchanani Opera, 2 *Vols* 4to.

Confucius was born 551 Years before CHRIST, his Father, was of an illustrious Family, and enjoy'd the highest Offices of the Kingdom, but dying while he was only three Years old, left him without any Inheritance.

He was in his Childhood eminently serious and thoughtful, negligent of Trifles, and without any Regard to the common Amusements of that Age ; at fifteen he applied himself to the Study of the ancient Books, and to the Collection of such Maxims and Principles as might most contribute to the Establishment and Propagation of Virtue, an Employment which was very little interrupted by Domestick Cares, tho' he married at the Age of nineteen.

At this Time the several Provinces of *China*, were Kingdoms govern'd by their own Monarchs, with absolute Authority, tho' with at least a nominal Subordination to the Emperors, whom they all acknowledged as chief Governor, but whose Commands they frequently rejected, and whose Authority they reverenc'd only when they were in no Condition to resist it ; so that the Desire of Independency on one Part, and a Resolution of maintaining Superiority on the other, gave Occasion to perpetual Contests and daily Disorders. It is related that the Courts of all these inferior Sovereigns were Seminaries of Corruption and Licentiousness ; whether the particular Laws of those Countries were not well adapted to the Regulation of Manners, or whether the King was obliged to overlook the Faults of his Subjects, that they might give no Information of his Conduct or Designs to the Emperor of *China*.

These Irregularities it was the Design of *Confucius* to redress, and to establish Temperance, Integrity, and Purity of Manners, which he therefore incessantly promoted both by his Precepts and Example, and became in a short Time so eminent by his exemplary Behaviour, that the highest Employments were offer'd him in the Kingdom where he lived and accepted by him as Means of facilitating the Progress of Virtue, by making it more awful and illustrious, and therefore quitted them afterwards without Reluctance, when he found them no longer useful to the End which he proposed.

In his 55th Year he engaged in one of the chief Offices of the Kingdom of *Lu*, now the Province of *Shan tong*, his Native Country, which he had not possessed more than three Months, without a visible Reformation of the whole People, and Improvement of the general State of the Kingdom; the Laws were no longer broken, or the Breach of them was regularly punished, Property was secure from
java-

diffusion, and was therefore by every Man diligently increased:

The Prosperity and Affluence produced in this Kingdom by the Maxims of *Confuci* soon excited the Envy of the neighbouring Princes, by whom it was imagined that they were in Danger from a Neighbour, whom, as he grew every Day more powerful, they should not long be able to resist.

The King of *Tsi* being more disturbed than any other, at this imaginary Danger, consulted with his Ministers upon the most probable Method of interrupting that Prosperity which he looked upon as the certain Parent of Ambition, and which therefore ought to be obstructed, and determined to make use of Means which have seldom failed of Success, and by which the greatest Monarchs have been destroyed, when neither Policy could circumvent, nor Armies oppose them.

A magnificent Embassy was in pursuance of this Consultation dispatched to the King of *Lu*, with a fatal Present of a great Number of young Maidens of exquisite Beauty, and finished Accomplishments, skilful in every Art of attracting the Eye, and alluring the Mind, of awakening the Affections, and lulling Reason. These Girls soon gained the Attention of their new Master, and his Counsellors, by their Airs, their Dances, and their Songs. Business and Politicks, Learning and Morality were banished from the Court, where nothing was now regarded, but Feasts, Revelry, and Diversions, Scenes of Pleasure, and Assemblies of Gaiety, and where the Amusement of these lovely Strangers was preferr'd to the Care of the Publick.

It is no small Addition to the Honour of *Confucius*, that he remained uninfected amidst so fatal a Contagion; a Contagion against which the Preservatives of Philosophy have been often found of very little Effect. He endeavoured not only to escape, but to stop the Infection, and animated the King with all the Force of his Eloquence and Reason, to resume his Dignity, and re-establish the Authority of the Laws; but finding his Persuasions unregarded, and his Arguments over-born by sensual Gratifications, he laid down his Employments, and retired in Search of Men less immersed in Luxury, and less hardned'd to habitual Vice.

With this View he travelled over several Kingdoms, where the Superiority of his Virtue and Abilities procured him more Enemies than Admirers, and the Ministers, instead of introducing to the Princes a Man capable of promoting the

Publick Happiness, endeavoured to suppress his Reputation, lest his Abilities should be brought into Comparison with their own.

Confucius therefore, after having visited several Princes, and offered his Instructions in Policy to the Magistrates and Kings, and his Precepts of Morality to Persons of every Condition, was so far from finding a Reception agreeable to the Merit of his Conduct, or the Benevolence of his Intentions, that he was reduced to the lowest State of Poverty, in which he was far from losing any Part of his Philosophical Dignity, and which he never endeavoured to relieve by any mean Action.

It was probably on this Occasion that he said what is recorded of him in one of the Classical Books; "I am reduced to extreme Indigence, having "nothing to live upon but a little Rice "and Water, with which, however "I am content, because I look upon "Dignity or Wealth unjustly acquired, "as upon Clouds driven by the Winds". This Constancy cannot raise our Admiration after his former Conquest of himself; for how easily may he support Pain, who has been able to resist Pleasure.

The several Passages of his Life are not related in Order of Time, or connected with any Circumstances which may contribute to fix their Dates, it is therefore impossible to discover when the following Adventure happened, which yet deserves to be related.

Confucius being once abandoned by the People, and without the Protection of the Prince, was in the Hands of a Mandarin of War, remarkably savage and licentious, and therefore implacably exasperated by a Man whose Lectures were continual Satires upon his Conduct. He therefore no sooner saw *Confucius* in his Power, but he accused him of some pretended Offence, and commanded him to be executed. Some of the Spectators, who saw the Injustice of the Mandarin, and the Illegality of the Proceeding, advised him to retire, after the Example of most of his Followers, whom the first Appearance of Danger had driven from him; but *Confucius*, though he saw the Sword drawn for his Destruction, remaining calm and unconcerned, answered without any Hesitation, *If we are protected by Heaven* [Tyen] *what have we to fear from this Man, though he be President of the Tribunal of the Army*.

We are not informed whether he escaped this Danger by the Veneration which his Intrepidity produced in the Officer, or
by

by the Interpofition of others, who had Courage to oppofe the Execution of an unjuft Sentence, and Regard for his Virtue fufficient to engage them in his Caufe; or whether the Mandarin defigned in reality only to try whether his Principles were fufficient to fupport him under Immediate Danger, and whether he would not forfeit that Reputation, which was fo much envied, by abandoning his Doctrines at the Sight of Death; That this was his Intention feems probable, becaufe it appears from the Relation, that when he threatened him moft nearly, he ftill left him an Opportunity of efcaping, which he was doubtlefs defirous that he fhould have ufed, for the Flight of *Confucius* would have gratified his Malice more than the Death.

That he did efcape is certain, for in his feventy fifth Year he died of a Lethargy, occafioned, as it was imagined, by a Dejection of Spirits, at the Sight of the difordered State of the Empire; for a few Days before his laft Sicknefs he told his Followers, that *The Mountain was fallen, the high Machine was deftroyed, and the Sages were no more to be feen.* After which he began to loofe his Strength, and the feventh Day before his Death, turning to his Scholars, *The Kings,* faid he, *refufe to obferve my Maxims, and it is fit I fhould leave the World in which I am no longer ufeful.* After thofe Words he fell into a Slumber, in which he continued feven Days, and then expired.

He was tall and well-proportioned, with broad Shoulders and Breaft, an Olive Complection, large Eyes, a Beard long and black, and a Nofe fomewhat flat, his Air was grave and Majeftick, and his Voice ftrong and piercing. On the Middle of his Forehead grew a Wen, which fomewhat difigured him.

Confucius, fay his Difciples, had three Contrarieties in his Character, which fcarcely any other Man has known how to reconcile. He had all the Graces of Politenefs with all the Awefulnefs of Gravity; uncommon Severity of Countenance, with great Benignity of Temper; and the moft exalted Dignity, with the moft engaging Modefty in his Air.

He left behind him three Books, of which the firft is called the *Grand Science;* the fecond the *Immutable Medium,* a Title correfpondent to the Μεσοτρισμος of *Cleobulus,* and to the common Maxim, *Virtus confiftit in Medio;* and the third, *Moral and concife Difcourfes;* to which is added a Fourth, of almoft equal Authority, written by his Scholar *Mencius.*

In the Firft Book he endeavours to

fhew, that the fovereign Good confifts in a Conformity of all our Actions with right Reafon, and that all the Science requifite for Princes confifts in the Improvement of that reafonable Nature which they have received from Heaven, to which End it is neceffary to enquire diligently into the Nature of Good and Evil, that Love and Hatred may be directed towards their proper Objects; and when a Man has thus reftored himfelf to his original Purity, it will be eafy, fays he, to reform the Corruption of others.

How this Doctrine was received by the *Chinefe* Princes, it is not related; but if it be true, that the fame Condition has a Tendency to produce the fame Manners and Difpofitions, we may judge from the Conduct of *European* Monarchs, that his Rules have never yet been reduced to Practice.

In his Second Book he teaches that every Man ought to adhere to the *Mean,* in which he affirms Virtue to confift, and beginning with a Definition of human Nature and Paffions, introduces Examples of Piety, Fortitude, Prudence, Filial Reverence, and other Virtues, and fhews that they all arife from the Obfervation of the *Mean,* which, he fays, is eafy to practife, though it be a difficult Subject of Speculation. He gives Examples of feveral Princes who have confined their Conduct to the happy *Mean,* and lays down Rules by which Kings may make themfelves and their Subjects happy.

The Third Book is a Collection of Sentences utter'd by *Confucius,* either on Occafion of particular Events, or in his cafual Converfation with his Scholars, and contains a great Number of Reflections and Precepts very affecting and important. One of his Obfervations is, *that he never found any Man, however good, fo ardent in the Purfuit of Virtue, as the Voluptuous in queft of Pleafure.* A Remark not lefs Striking by its Truth, than by its Severity.

One of his Scholars once afked him, by what means he fhould die well, but was anfwered by him, *You have not yet learned to live well, and yet think it neceffary to enquire after Death;* a Reply, in which the way to die well is very emphatically taught.

Life and Death, fays Confucius, *depend on the Law of Heaven* [Tyen] *which no Man can alter; Poverty and Riches are difpenfed by Heaven, whofe Providence is not fubject to Compulfion. From a fubmiffive Reverence of thefe Laws and Difpenfations the wife Man derives his Tranquility and Happinefs.*

There

There are other Maxims relating to Oeconomy, or the Conduct of a Private Life;
others to the Administration of publick
Affairs; a:d others which conta:n Rules
of general Conduct. *Three sorts of Friends
says Confucius, are useful; those that* A
*are Virtuous, those that are Open, and
those that are Learned. He that is of an
inconstant Temper,* says he, *will never en-
grosse the Number of the Sages. He that
easily promises will often deceive.*

His whole Doctrine tends to the Propa
gation of Virtue, and the Restitution of B
Human Nature to its original Perfection,
and it is related that his Precepts always
received Illustrati:n from his Example,
and that in all Conditions of Life, he took
Care to prove by his Conduct, that he required no more from others, than he
thought it his own Duty to perform

C

ACTUARIUS was not the Name, but the Title of John, the Son of Zacharias, a Greek Writer of the latter Ages; a Title, which, though commonly beftowed on the Phyficians of the Conftantinopolitan Court, has by fome Accident, of which it is not now poffible to difcover the Original, been appropriated to this Writer, who is now fcarcely known by any other Appellation.

That he obtained the Honour of this Title, is almoft the only Incident of his Life, of which any Knowledge has defcended to our Times; but his Works, which remain, afford fufficient Teftimony, that he was not exalted beyond his Merit, and his Dignity was not the Veil of Ignorance, but the Diftinction of Knowledge.

His fix Books of *Therapeutics*, which he compofed for the Ufe of the Lord Chamberlain, who went on an Ambaffy into the North, tho' written, as he informs us, with very little Study, and defigned only for the private Ufe of the Ambaffador, contain, as Dr. Friend obferves, not only a judicious Compilation of the Writings of his Predeceffors, but fome Obfervations not to be found in the earlier Authors, as in his Section on the *Palpitation of the Heart*, of which he mentions two Kinds, one proceeding from Plenitude or Heat of Blood, which is the moft frequent Kind; and the other from Vapours; and directs, how they may be diftinguifhed, by remarking that an Inequality of the Pulfe always attends that which is the Confequence of Plenitude, but not that which is produced by Vapours. For this Diftemper he directs to purge and bleed, in which he has been followed by many of the greateft Phyficians of later Times.

His two Books, concerning the *Spirits*, are obferved by Dr. Friend, to be abftracted from Galen, and to be of little Ufe in the Practice of Phyfic.

The Doctrine, relating to *Urine*, is very amply laid down by him in feven Treatifes, in which at leaft, if we believe his own Teftimony, he has made large Additions to the Obfervations of former Writers.

He is placed by Fabricius in the Time of Andronicus Palæologus, about the Year 1300, or, according to others, 1100. But, as he is not mentioned by any Writer of thofe Times, the Age, in which he lived, cannot be afcertained; nor have we any other Knowledge of his Education, Studies, or Morals, than that with which we are fupplied by his own Writings, from which we may, with great Certainty, learn his Sentiments at leaft, though we cannot tell how far they influenced his Conduct.

In the Conclufion of his Difcourfe upon *Urines*, he fpeaks with a juft Severity of thofe that engrofs Truth and Science, and are difpleafed with any Improvements made public for the Benefit of Mankind. The Slanders of thefe Men, fays he, are Infections, againft which it would be more for the Intereft of the World to find an Antidote, than againft any Contagion or Difeafe ; and perhaps a Remedy, of refiftlefs and never failing Efficacy, may always be found in a generous Confidence in God, a fteady Conduct, with Refpect to thofe with whom we converfe, and a vigilant Attention to our Words and Actions.

His Difcourfe, upon the *animal Spirits*, is perhaps neither more nor lefs intelligible than modern Treitifes on the fame Subject ; he confiders it as the Minifter of the Soul, and the Defign of his Book is, to prefcribe the Methods by which it may be enabled moft vigoroufly to execute the Commands of the fuperior and prefiding Power.

He had a great Propenfion to Theory and Ratiocination, but was not contented to form Syftems in his Clofet, but extended his Speculations to Diftempers and Symptoms with which he was only acquainted by the Means of Books, which have always been found fallacious and uncertain Guides. For he informs us in his laft Chapter on *Urines*, that, having fpent fome Time in the Study of Nature, he found himfelf ftrongly inclined to that of Medicine, and applied himfelf to the Theoretic Part, as moft clofely connected with natural Philofophy; but that he fhould have been totally difcouraged from the Practice, by the Difguft and Labour with which it is attended, had he not difcovered, that a juft and folid Theory of the Pathology was abfolutely neceffary to the Science of Phyfic. It was my Opinion, fays he, that Methods of Cure, not founded upon Reafoning, never could be relied on ; and that a juft Theory would make Phyfic not only a more eafy Study, but a more fuccefsful Profeffion.

As the Authority of *Actuarius* is not fufficiently eftablifhed, to miflead any of our Readers, it is not neceffary to feparate with great Accuracy his Errors from his juft Notions. I fhall only obferve, that Theory may make Phyfic eafy, but its Succefs muft arife from Experience.

The Works of ACTUARIUS are,

Seven Books upon URINES, never publifhed in Greek, but tranflated into Latin, by Ambrofius Leo Nolanus, whofe Verfion was revifed by Goupilus, and is printed both in Octavo and in Hen. Stephen's *Artis Medicæ Principes*.

Six Books of THERAPEUTICS, not yet printed in Greek, of which the Fifth and Sixth were tranflated into Latin by Ruellius, whofe Verfion was publifhed at Paris. Henricus Mathifius tranflated the whole Work: His Verfion is extant, in the *Artis Medicæ Principes*.

One Book of the Actions or Affections, and a fecond of the Nu-

trition of the ANIMAL SPIRITS, publifhed in Greek at Paris, by Goupilus, with the Title : Περὶ Ἐνεργειῶν κỳ Παθῶν τοῦ ψυχικῦ Πνεύματος, κỳ τῆς κατ' αὐτὸν Διαίτης.

A Latin Tranflation of this Treatife, written by Julius Alexandrinus Tridentinus, is printed both fingly and in the *Artis Medicæ Principes.*

His Treatife, *De Venæ Sectione, De Diæta,* his *Regales* and *Commentarii in Hippocratis Aphorifmos,* are faid to be remaining in Manufcript.

ÆGINETA (PAULUS) a Phyfician of the feventh Century, was fo called from Ægina, the Place of his Birth, as appears from two Lines prefixed to the firft Edition of his Works.

Πάυλῃ πόνον με γνῶθι, τῦ γῆς τὸ πλίον
ΔιαδʒαμόῃΘ·, φύλΘ· ἐκ γῆς 'Αιγίνης.

This is the Work of Paulus, a Native of Ægina, who had travelled over the greateft Part of the World.

This Circumftance of his Life is the greateft Part of what is known of him; and the Curiofity which the Mention of a Traveller naturally excites, muft remain unfatisfied, and we muft confine ourfelves to an Account of his Works.

That Reputation of every kind is capricioufly diftributed cannot but be frequently obferved; nor is it lefs ufual for Authors, than for Men of every other Clafs, to be recompenfed for their Endeavours in a Manner difproportioned to their Merit. *Paulus* is, in the Opinion of Dr. Freind, one of thofe unfortunate Writers who have been long rated below their Value, and been defpifed for want of being read.

He appears, upon a careful Examination, not to be fo implicite a Tranfcriber as he is generally reprefented; but to have confidered the Practice of the Ancients attentively, and to have admitted or rejected it upon juft Confideration. He fometimes diffents from Galen, and once ventures to hint his Difapprobation of the Doctrine eftablifhed by Hippocrates himfelf.

In his fixth Book, in which he profeffedly treats of chirurgical Operations, and which Freind efteems the beft Body of Surgery produced before the Reftoration of Learning, there are many Practices and Operations mentioned, which no preceding Author appears to have been acquainted with.

He defcribes the feveral Sorts of Hernia's with great Exactnefs; and very circumftantially lays down the Method of making the Incifion, when the Gut cannot be replaced without it.

The Operation of opening the Arteries behind the Ears by a tranfverfe Section, and the Application of a Cautery afterwards are very accurately laid down by him.

101

He has a very exact Account of Bronchotomy, which is tranflated by Dr. Freind, and will be given under the Article BRONCHOTOMY.

His Work in feven Books has been feveral times printed in Greek.

The firft Edition is that of Aldus 1528.

The fecond was publifhed at Bafil 1538, by Andreas Cratander, under the Care of Hieronymus Gemufæus, who made fome Emendations in the Text, and added fome Notes.

It has been tranflated into Latin by three different Hands, Albanus Torinus, Johannes Guniterius Andernacus, and Janus Cornarius, to whom the World is obliged for many ufeful Remarks upon this Author.

The Arabians call this Phyfician *Bulos Al Agianithi*.

Herbelot fays he lived in the time of the Emperor Heraclius, and in the Reign of Omar, the fecond Chalife of the Mufulmans, who died in the Year of the Hegira 23, which anfwers to the Year of Chrift 645. Honani, the Son of Ifaac, tranflated the nine Books of *Paulus Ægineta* into Arabic. I do not know whether he met with two more than are now extant in Greek, or whether thefe feven were divided in a different Manner, fo as to make nine. Fabricius is of Opinion, that the fixth and feventh Book, which are pretty long, were each divided by the Arabian into two.

It is efteemed the peculiar Excellence of this Author to have underftood the Diforders to which Women are fubject; he acquired the Name of *Al-Kavabeli*, that is, *Obftetricius*, becaufe he ufed to inftruct Midwives in the Duties of their Office, and teach them how to treat Women in Child-bed. *Fabricius. Herbelot.*

ÆSCULAPIUS. The Hiftory of this great Phyfician, for fuch he appears to have been, is fo involved in Fable and Romance, that it is impoffible to extricate the Truth with any Certainty. Tully fays, there were three of the Name. The firft was the Son of Apollo, and the fame that was held in great Veneration by the Arcadians: He was the Inventor of the Probe and Bandage.

The fecond *Æfculapius* was Brother to the fecond Mercury. This is he that is reported to have been ftruck with Thunder by Jupiter, and is faid to lie buried at Cynofura in Peloponnefus.

The third was the Son of Arfippus and Arfione. He invented Purging, and Drawing of Teeth.

Monfieur Le Clerc is of Opinion, however, that there never was more than one *Æfculapius*, and that he was a Phenician, or rather a Nephew of Chanaan, which laft he apprehends to be the fame as Hermes. Or at leaft, if there was an *Æfculapius* amongft the Greeks, that he borrowed not only the Name, but the Character of the Phenician.

102

The Egyptians relate, that *Æsculapius* was taught Medicine by Hermes, whom they reprefent as the Inventor of the Art. And if the Account given by Sanchoniathon is true (See *Eufebius*) *Æsculapius* and Hermes were nearly related, for Misor, the Father of Hermes, had a Brother, whofe Name was Siduc, or Sadoc. This laft had feven Sons, called *Diofcures, Cabires,* or *Corybantes,* and an eighth, which was *Æsculapius,* by one of the Daughters of Saturn and Aftarte. By this Genealogy, it appears, that Hermes and *Æsculapius* were firft Coufins, and it renders the Egyptian Account, that *Æsculapius* learned Medicine of Hermes, the more probable. Upon the Whole, the intire Family feems to have been concerned in making Improvements in, or inventing Medicine, for the Sons of the Cabyres or Corybantes are by the fame Sanchoniathon reprefented to have employed themfelves in difcovering the Virtues of Plants, and Remedies againft venomous Bites.

The Oriental Authors relate, that *Æsculapius* was a Difciple of Edris, who is the fame as Enoch ; and the Oriental Chriftians have a Tradition, that Enoch, or Edris, is the fame as the Hermes of the Egyptians, called TRISMEGISTUS.

This *Æsculapius,* according to the Accounts given of him by the Eaftern Writers, gave the firft Rife to Idolatry, in this Manner : After the Death of Edris, or Enoch, *Æsculapius,* by the Inftigation of the Devil, made a Statue in Honour of his Mafter and Patron, whom he reprefented, holding a Branch of Althæa, or Marfh-Mallows in his Hand, and, being conftantly before it, feemed to pay it extraordinary Honours. This was afterwards imitated by his fuperftitious Countrymen, till at laft it rofe to Idolatry.

This is the Sum of what is related, with refpect to the Egyptian, or Phenician *Æsculapius.* The Accounts we have of the Grecian *Æsculapius* are much more ample, but equally uncertain, and perhaps more fabulous, it having been the Cuftom amongft the Greeks, to rob the Egyptians of their Mythology, and to difguife the allegorical Meaning with Fictions of their own.

The Mother of this *Æsculapius* was Coronis, a Daughter of Phlegias, King of the Lapithæ in Theffaly ; or, according to fome, Arfinoe, Daughter to Leucippus of Meffenia. This Lady, being clandeftinely with Child by Apollo, was delivered of her Son on a Mountain in the Territory of Epidaurus, during a Journey with her Father into Peloponnefus, where the Child was left. A Peafant of thofe Parts, miffing a fhe Goat and his Dog, went in Search of them, and found the Goat giving Suck to the young *Æsculapius,* and the Dog mean While guarding them.

Others give a different Account of his miraculous Birth. They agree, that Coronis was with Child by Apollo ; but fay, that Apollo having difcovered that the Nymph granted the fame Kind of Favours to a young Arcadian, which fhe had beftowed on him, in a Fit of Jealousy, sent his Sister Latona, to spread a Plague in the City where his Mistress lived, of which she died. But, as she was on the Funeral Pile, the God came, and took his Son away, out of the Midst of the Flames, and conveyed him to Chiron the Centaur, who undertook the Charge of his Education. *Pindar.*

Other fabulous Accounts are given of the Birth of *Æsculapius,* and many Countries dispute for the Honour of producing him, as was usual amongst the Greeks, with respect to their eminent Men. But it is agreed on all Hands, that he was bred under the Tuition of Chiron the Centaur, and that, by his Instructions, and the Assistance of his Father Apollo, he arrived at a very extraordinary Knowledge in Physic, which gained him a Place amongst the heathen Divinities, after he had rendered himself agreeable to Mankind, by curing those who stood in Need of his Assistance, of Ulcers, Wounds, Fevers, and painful Disorders, by Means of Incantations, lenient Potions, Incisions, and external Applications. It was on Account of his extraordinary Skill in all Branches of Physic, that he was chosen by the Heroes concerned in the Argonautic Expedition, to accompany them in that hazardous Enterprize.

The Greeks, much used to Exaggeration, when the Honour of any of their Countrymen is in Question, relate, that *Æsculapius* could not only recover People from dangerous Distempers, but also knew a Way of restoring Life to those that were dead; and of this they give many Instances, among which, the last was Hippolytus. Upon this, they say, Pluto made a Remonstrance to Jupiter, that, if *Æsculapius* was suffered to proceed in this Manner, the Regions under his Jurisdiction would in Time become desolate. Upon this Complaint Jupiter struck *Æsculapius* with a Thunderbolt, and with him Hippolytus, whom he had raised from the Dead; but at the Request of Apollo he was afterwards placed among the Stars by the Name of *Ophiucus.*

He left two Sons Machaon and Podalirius; of whom Homer makes honourable Mention. The Wife of *Æsculapius* was called *Epione,* or according to others *Hygeia,* or *Lampetia.* His Daughters were *Ægle, Panacæa, Jaso, Reme,* and *Aceso.* He is also said to have had a Sister called *Eriopis.* All these are said to have been concerned in improving the medicinal Art.

After the Death of *Æsculapius,* a great Number of Temples were built in Honour of him in Greece, and the Grecian Colonies. Schulzius reckons up from Pausanias, and other Authors, sixty-three, to which People from all Parts resorted, in order to be cured of their Distempers, which were probably performed by common Means, but were attributed to the miraculous Influence of the God by the Address of his Priests.

The Romans did not fail to imitate the Greeks in every Species of Superstition and Idolatry. Accordingly they built a

Temple to *Æfculapius* in the Ifland of Tiber, upon the following extraordinary Occafion, according to the Account Aurelius Victor gives of it.

Rome, at that Time, and the adjacent Territories, were ravaged by a Plague. Upon this Occafion an Ambaffy, confifting of ten, with Q. Ogulnius at their Head, was difpatched to Epidaurus, in order to invite the God *Æfculapius* to Rome. When thefe Ambaffadors arrived at Epidaurus, as they were admiring the extraordinary Statue of *Æfculapius*, a large Serpent came from under the Altar, and paffing from the Temple to the Roman Ship, went into the Apartment of Ogulnius. The Ambaffadors rejoiced at this Prodigy, immediately fet Sail, and arrived fafe at Antium with their Charge, but being detained there fome Days by the Tempeftuoufnefs of the Seas, the Serpent got out of the Veffel, and lodged himfelf in a neighbouring Temple dedicated to *Æfculapius*, but as foon as it was calm, returned, and then the Ambaffadors purfued their Voyage; but when they arrived at the Ifland of Tiber, the God in the Shape of a Serpent quitted the Ship, and went on Shore, where they built him a Temple, and the Plague immediately ceafed.

Pliny fays, this Temple was built there out of fome Difrefpect which the Romans had for the Art over which *Æfculapius* prefided. A very childifh Reafon; as if that wife People would have been at the Trouble to have fent a folemn Ambaffy to Epidaurus for the God, in order to affront him.

Plutarch, in the Opinion of Le Clerc, has given a better Reafon. This Author feems to think, that both the Temple at Rome, and the other Temples in Greece, dedicated to *Æfculapius*, were built in open and high Situations, that the Sick which reforted to them might enjoy the Advantage of a good Air.

There can be no Doubt, but that the Romans built this Temple to *Æfculapius*, at a Diftance from the City, in Imitation of the Greeks. And there is a better and very obvious Reafon, why the latter chofe fuch Situations for thefe Temples, I mean, becaufe they intended to prevent contagious Diftempers from being brought into their Cities, by the Sick which reforted to the Priefts of *Æfculapius* for their Cure, and from being bred in the clofe Air of a populous Place by a Concourfe of difeafed People.

The Statue of *Æfculapius* at Epidaurus, made by Thrafymedes, the Statuary, was remarkable for the Size, the Workmanfhip, and the Materials, which were Gold and Ivory. In this he was reprefented fitting on a Throne, with a Staff in one Hand, and leaning with the other on the Head of a large Serpent, with a Dog at his Feet. Paufanias fays, the Dog was placed there, becaufe he guarded *Æfculapius* in his

Infancy. Le Clerc rather thinks this Animal an Emblem of that Sagacity which is neceſſary to a Profeſſor of the Art over which this God preſides.

From the ſame Pauſanias we learn, that he was ſometimes figured holding a Pine-cone in his Hand. And that a large brown Serpent, peculiar to the Country of Epidaurus, was ſacred to him. This Sort of Serpent was eſteemed harmleſs, and ſome of them were always kept in his Temple at Epidaurus. In moſt of his Figures this Serpent is drawn twiſted round the Staff he holds in his Hand.

Sometimes a Cock is placed at his Feet to repreſent Vigilance ; ſometimes an Eagle, an Emblem of Diſcernment or Longevity, on his right Side, and a Ram's Head on the left, which is ſaid to be expreſſive of Dreams and Divinations.

Upon ſome Medals *Æſculapius* is accompanied by a little Figure of a Youth, cloathed in a Habit which covers his Head ; this, Mr. Spon ſays, was the Emblem of Sickneſs, the Object of Medicine, becauſe amongſt the Antients the Sick covered their Heads, whereas thoſe that were in Health went bareheaded. This little Figure was called by the Names of *Teleſphorus, Acceſius, Evamerion*, or, as Mr. Le Clerc remarks, OB. What the laſt-mentioned Author adds upon this Occaſion, is too curious to be omitted. With that, therefore, I ſhall conclude the fabulous Accounts of *Æſculapius*.

Monſieur Patin gives an Account of a Medal ſtruck in Honour of the Emperor Adrian (perhaps on Account of his Knowledge in Phyſic) where on one Side *Æſculapius* is repreſented accompanied with Hygeia ; on the other Teleſphorus with this Inſcription round it :

ΠΕΡΓΑ. ΕΠΙ ΚΕΦΑΛΑΙΩΝΟΣ.

And juſt before Teleſphorus the Letters O B. Mr. Patin explains the firſt Words *Pergamenorum ſub Cephalione*, adding in Italics, *Teleſphorus*. He afterwards adds, from Pauſanias, that Teleſphorus was a Divinity of the Pergamenians, who was ſo called by the Directions of an Oracle, and that ſome tranſlate the Word by *Familiar Spirit* (Devin) or *Ventriloquus*. This, ſays Mr. Le Clerc. made me imagine that TELESPHORUS and OB were the ſame, having found OB in other Places alſo tranſlated *Familiar Spirit*, or *Ventriloquus*.

Selden tells us, that the Word OB was uſually tranſlated *Python*, or *Magician*. This OB was a Spirit, or Demon, that gave Anſwers which ſeemed to come from the Pudenda, the Head, or the Armpits, but in a Voice ſo low, that it appeared to proceed from ſome deep Cavity, as if a dead Perſon ſpoke in a Tomb, inſomuch that thoſe who conſulted it, ſometimes did not hear it at all, but formed in their Imaginations what Anſwers they thought proper. Selden adds, See the Hiſtory of *Samuel*, whoſe Figure was repreſented to Saul by a Woman,

106

from the Pudenda of whom O♭ either fpoke, or was imagined to fpeak. The Scripture, in the firft Book of *Samuel*,
Chapter 38. [a] calls this Woman *Pythonefs*, or *Ventriloqua*, as it
is tranflated, a Woman who had O♭; hence Saul ad-
dreffes her thus, *Prophefy to me, I pray you, by* O♭, which
the Septuagint tranflate, *Prophefy to me by* VENTRILO-
QUUS. O♭ therefore was a Spirit which was fuppofed to fpeak
from the Belly.

Thus far Mr. Le Clerc, and as the Hebrew Word is אוב,
OB, [b] which in the Septuagint is tranflated, ἰγγαϛρίμυθος, and
our Tranflators render *Familiar Spirit*, I think there can be
no Difpute of his being right.

Buxtorf renders the Hebrew Word OB by *Pytho*, one who, in
giving Anfwers by diabolical Arts, feduces Men from God,
Levit. XIX. 31. [c] XX. 27. [d] The Word alfo, as he obferves,
fignifies *Bottles*, Job XXXII. 19. [e] Hence *Pytho*, according to
Aben Efra, means one who uttered Oracles from a fwollen Belly, as from a Bottle, whence the Perfon was called ἰγγαϛρίμυθος.

I muft remark farther, that there have been People in our
Days, who were Mafters of the Art of managing their Voice
in fuch a Manner, as to make it in Appearance proceed from
any Part about them, or even near them, and that in much fuch
a Tone as that of O♭ defcribed by Selden. There was a Fellow about Town about twenty-five Years ago, called the fpeaking Smith, who was a great Mafter in this Way, and who, inftead of being ambitious of the Character of a Conjurer, employed this Talent in frighting Porters, Drawers, and other
People, who were not acquainted with the Trick, and whom
their Friends contrived to bring into the Smith's Company, on
Purpofe to be teazed and terrified. About ten Years ago there
was another who poffeffed this Art, though in a lefs Degree
of Perfection. I have been feveral Times in his Company in
the Country, where he ufed to travel as a Rider, fo far as I
remember, to a Tobacconift. And a Woman who begged
about the Country, was faid to excel them both in this Way,
being able to carry on a feeming Converfation betwixt feveral
People, whom, fhe told the Ignorant, were her Husband and
Children that had been long dead. It is not to be difputed, but
thefe would have had it in their Power, with a little Artifice, in the Days of Ignorance, to have been efteemed converfant with familiar Spirits; and they might even have fur-

---

[a] See the Paffage.   [b] See the Septuagint.   [c] Regard
not them that have *Familiar Spirits,* אבות, *Oboth.* neither feek after
Wizards.   [d] A Man alfo or Woman that hath a *Familiar
Spirit* אוב, or that is a Wizard, fhall furely be put to Death.
[e] Behold my Belly is as Wine that hath no Vent, it is ready to
burft like new Bottles באבות.

107

prifed a more enlightened Age, if they had been artful and defigning enough to have guarded the Secret.

As to the Hiftory of *Æfculapius*, without having any Regard to the fabulous Accounts of him in the Grecian Theology, I am inclined to think he was a Phœnician, who having made very fuccefsful Searches into Nature, efpecially that Part of it that related to Pharmacy and Medicine, had gained great Reputation and Honour among his Countrymen.

His true original Name, I imagine, is loft to us in that, which the People that had experienced his Skill and Abilities in Phyfic, had given him by Way of Eminence and Diftinction; for it was a Cuftom in the Eaftern Nations, when any Perfon appeared among them of fingular Talents, to honour him with an Appellation declarative of his Merit, after the Manner of the Agnomen among the Romans. Hence it was, that Hermes, the Reftorer of the Egyptian Learning, was called *Trifmegiftus,* or rather by the Egyptian Name that anfwered that Meaning, for Trifmegiftus was the Greek Tranflation of the Egyptian Original; this Man's true Name was *Siphoas,* as Sincellus informs us out of Manetho. Σιφωας ὁ κỳ Ερμῆς.

As the Egyptians diftinguifhed Hermes by the Name of Trifmegiftus for his great Learning, fo the Phœnicians, according to the Tafte of thofe Times (for *Æfculapius* is fuppofed to be cotemporary with Trifmegiftus) gave him likewife a Name of Diftinction, on Account of his Skill in Phyfic and Medicine. They called him אב חשכל, *Hafkel-ab,* the *Father of Knowledge or Skill,* which laft Word, by-the-by, feems to take its Original from the Hebrew or Phœnician Word שכל, *Sekel, Knowledge or Underftanding.*

It was an ufual Phrafe amongft the antient Orientals, where they would defcribe a Perfon that had been beneficial to Mankind, by fome ufeful Invention or Difcovery, to call him the *Father* of it. For Inftance, this Hebrew Idiom is ufed in Holy Writ, with Regard to Jubal, *Gen.* IV. 21. where he is called *The Father of all fuch as handle the Organ and Harp,* from his firft inventing Mufic. Tubalcain alfo, from his firft Invention of fabricating Iron by Fire, was called אב אשתא, *Ab Efta,* or *The Father of Fire*; from whence the Greek formed their Ἥφαιςος; as the Latins did their *Vulcan* from *Tubalcain*; in like Manner the Phœnicians from the Skill in Medicine, that they found in the Perfon the Subject of this Enquiry, called him *Afkel-ab,* the *Father of Skill* (in Medicine) which the Greeks afterwards corrupted into *Æfculapius.*

What Mr. Le Clerc in his *Hiftory of Phyfic* obferves, that *Æfculapius* was a Phœnician, and that the Original of his Name was to be fought for there, is undoubtedly true. But I am afraid that cannot be faid of the Etymology he gives of it; he derives it from Is CALAPHOT, *A Man of the Knife*; fuppof-

ing him to be so called from the Use of the *Knife* in chirurgical Operations, in which Case it is much to be suspected, if
the Use of the Knife was then so much known, as would be
necessary to support the Etymology of this learned Man.

By all the fabulous Accounts of the Grecian *Æsculapius* it
appears that he was a considerable Benefactor to Mankind. It
remains that we endeavour to come at the Reality of his Person and Character, and to extricate Truth out of a Multitude
of Fables. And in order to do this, it is reasonable to make
Use of the Testimony of medicinal Writers, who, it is to be
supposed, are best acquainted with what relates to the Patron
of their Art. Amongst these Celsus is the first, who in his
Preface says thus: As the End of Agriculture is to supply the
Body with Aliment, that of Medicine is to procure it Health.
No Part of the World has been without some Share of Knowledge in this Art, for the most barbarous Nations were acquainted with the Virtues of Herbs, and other obvious Remedies, for their Wounds and Diseases. However, it was cultivated in Greece more than in other Nations, not however
originally, but a few Ages before it flourished among us, for
Æsculapius is celebrated for being the first Inventor of it, who
was deified, because he reduced the Science, before his Time
rude and empirical, to a more regular Art.

We find something more particular with Respect to *Æsculapius* in Galen, who has in a great Measure avoided the Exaggerations usual amongst his Countrymen, though he speaks
of the national Divinity of the Place where he was born.

Æsculapius, the Deity of our Country, prescribed entertaining Songs, Buffoonery, and some Sorts of Music, for such as by
the too vehement Motion of the Mind had rendered the Temperament of their Body hotter than was consistent with Moderation: To others, and those not a few, he enjoined Hunting, Riding, and Exercises at Arms, and directed the Kind of
Motion they were to be employed in, and the Arms in which
they were to exercise. He did not think it enough to teach
in general, how the Mind, when sunk, might be raised, without ascertaining the Measure of it from the Idea of the Exercise. *Galen, de Sanit. tuenda, L. 2. C. 8.*

True Medicine forms Conjectures concerning the Nature or
Constitution of the Patient, which the Generality of Physicians call *Idiosyncrasy*. But this is by all confessed to be in-
comprehensible; therefore all ascribe the true Art of Medicine
to *Apollo* and *Æsculapius*. *Galen, Meth. Med. L. 3. C. 7.*

The Greeks ascribe the Invention of Arts to the Sons, or near
Kindred of the Gods, by whom they were communicated.
On this Account it appears, that *Æsculapius* was the Inventor
of Medicine, in the Knowledge of which he was first in-
stituted by his Father Apollo, and afterwards delivered the same
to Mankind. Before his Time the Art of Healing was un-

known, though the Antients had fome Infight into the Virtues of Medicines and Herbs ; fuch as Chiron, the Centaur, among the Greeks, and the Heroes under his Tuition. They had alfo, it feems, by what is afcribed to Ariftæus, Melampus, and Polyidus, made fome Experiment that Way. That the Egyptians had fome Notion of other Remedies befides Herbs, feems evident enough from Homer.

Befides, the firft Phyficians muft have learnt many Things in Surgery and manual Operation from the Opening of Carcafles, which it was the Cuftom to do, in order to embalm them. Some Inventions are imputed to Chance, as Couching for a Cataract to the cafual Obfervation of a certain Goat, who, labouring under that Defect, recovered its Sight by impreffing its Eye on a fharp-pointed Rufh. The Ufe of a Clyfter alfo, they fay, is derived from the Bird Ibis, who, making the Skin of her long Neck ferve inftead of a Bladder, fills it with the Water of the Nile, or Sea-water, and by the Help of her Beak introduces it into her Body through the Anus. And Herodotus, the Hiftorian, writes, that it was an antient Cuftom to bring out their Sick into the Street, and moft frequented Places, to receive the Advice and Prefcriptions of fuch Perfons, as had laboured under the fame Diftempers, and had been cured ; and fo, by this Means, was Medicine at length eftablifhed, being raifed into an Art from the Multitude of Facts and Experiments. But all this while Reafon was wanting to affift and perfect Experience, and *Æfculapius* alone was the firft Inventor of true and rational Medicine, and fuch as, on all Accounts, deferved that Name. His Succeffors, the Afclepiadæ, delivered it down to Pofterity, as it were, by hereditary Succeffion. Among them Hippocrates was the moft eminent by many Degrees, and was the firft among the Greeks who perfected the Art of Medicine. *Galen's Introduction.*

If we reflect upon the fabulous Accounts related of the Grecian *Æfculapius* above, and join with thefe what is faid by Celfus and Galen, we may perhaps have Reafon to believe the following Conjectures, in Regard to the true Hiftory of this *Æfculapius*, to be not very diftant from the Truth.

He appears therefore to have been the illegitimate Son of fome Lady of Diftinction, who expofed him on a Mountain in the Territory of Epidaurus, to avoid the Reproaches ufual on fuch Occafions. In this Situation he was probably found by the Means of the Dog of fome Shepherd, or Goatherd, for it is ufual with thefe fagacious Animals to apprize their Mafters of any Thing uncommon that occurs, by ftaying near it and barking ; and, if this was the Cafe, a very fmall Degree of Superftition, joined with a ftrong Imagination, would furnifh him with a Goat for his Nurfe, whilft under fuch a Diftrefs.

When he was once found, it is not unlikely that his Mo-

110

ther might privately take Care to have him delivered to Chiron, a Man in thofe Days eminent for the Education of Youth.

We may very reafonably fuppofe that the young *Æfculapius* had very extraordinary Parts, for which a great many natural Children, both amongft the Antients and Moderns, have been remarkable, and that upon this Account his Tutor Chiron took more than ordinary Pains in the Inftruction of his Pupil. Add to this that the Youth, finding he had nothing to depend on but his own Genius and Diligence, might be prompted by his Ambition to an extraordinary Application, that he might fometime make a Figure in the World, equal to that of his Fellow Students, who were Sons to People of Condition, thus fupplying the Difadvantages of Birth by Induftry. This Suppofition will appear lefs chimerical, if we reflect, that thofe who have in all Ages made very extraordinary Progreffes in Sciences, have generally been fuch whofe Circumftances have obliged them early to take uncommon Pains.

Æfculapius, thus furnifhed with a Capacity, would not fail to lay hold of the Opportunities of Improvement which prefented, and to purfue the Way to Eminence by the Road to which he was directed by his Genius. His favourite Study therefore being that of Phyfic, when he arrived at fuch a Degree of Knowledge in the Art, as to excel his Contemporaries in the Cure of Difeafes, his Countrymen, or perhaps Chiron himfelf, might give him the honorary Appellation of *Æfculapius*, a Name borrowed from the Phœnician Inventor of Phyfic, with the Hiftory and Character of whom the Greeks had at that Time been made acquainted.

The Circumftances of his Birth, added to his Eminence in Medicine, would give his fuperftitious Countrymen an obvious Hint to call him the Son of Apollo, and a national Vanity might at laft make him a God.

This appears to me the moft real and genuine Account of the Greek *Æfculapius*, for I can by no Means agree with thofe Authors who are of Opinion that there never was fuch a Perfon amongft the Greeks. Hippocrates is faid to be a Defcendant from him, and a regular Pedigree is produced, by which it appears that he was the eighteenth from *Æfculapius*, inclufive. Now if this was not real, the Afclepiadæ could never have been guilty of fo impudent a Fiction, attended with a great many Circumftances that might have been difproved, which, however, does not appear to have been ever attempted, even by the Phyficians of the Cnidian School, who, as it feems, were no great Friends to Hippocrates, and who maintained a Spirit of Emulation againft the Phyficians of Cos. This Pedigree will be given with the Life of Hippocrates; mean Time it may fuffice to remark that the Pofterity of *Æfculapius*, by Podalirius, reigned Kings of Caria, till the Time of Theodorus the Second of that Name, who was obliged by the Heraclidæ to retire from that Country, and settle in Cos, an Island not far from Caria.

I shall end this Account of *Æsculapius* with remarking, that if the Art of Healing had not been very much advanced before the Time of Hippocrates, it would have been impossible for any one Man to have made Observations sufficient to establish those universal Rules, laid down by that extraordinary Man ; Rules which, at the Distance of more than two thousand Years, are confirmed by every Case that occurs in the Practice of Physic, infomuch that it may be truly said, that if the Writings of Hippocrates had been lost so far, that later Writers in Physic could not have borrowed his Sentiments, Medicine which, though far from being perfect, is nevertheless beneficial to the World in an eminent Degree, would have been scarce worth regarding, and of little Importance to Mankind. This I venture to affirm, because I am certain that every Physician in Europe, who is acquainted with this Author, and knows his Profession, will agree to it.

AETIUS. There appears to have been three Physicians of this Name, who all made themselves enough known to be recorded by the Learned.

The first was *Aetius Sicanius*, out of whose Writings, together with others, the Book, *de Atra Bile*, ascribed to Galen, is said to be collected. *Fabricii Biblioth. Græc.*

The Second was *Aetius* of Antioch, a Man remarkable for changing his Profession several Times, and for being a great Patron of the Arian Heresy. He was originally bred to the Cultivation of Vines, which he quitted, and took up the Trade of a Gold and Silversmith. After this he got into the Service of one Sopolis a Physician, and then being supplied with Money by a certain Armenian, he applied himself to Letters, and, upon the Credit of having been a Servant to a Physician, set up for one himself; but changed once again his Way of Life, and entered into holy Orders, where he seems to have succeeded somewhat better than in Physic, for in or about the Year 361 we find he was made a Bishop.

This *Aetius* appears to have been extremely zealous in propagating the Arian Heresy, which he carried to a greater Length than even the Author of it himself; it is for this Reason that he has incurred the Scandal of being an Atheist, which however must be malicious, for it is not probable that a Man who was an Atheist, would be very follicitous in establishing any Modes of Belief with Respect to the Christian Religion.

Different from this, in the Opinion of the Learned, was *Aetius* of Amida, whofe Works are preferved. He is faid to have lived in the latter End of the fourth, or Beginning of the fifth Century. All that we know of him for certain is, that he travelled into Egypt, where he probably ftudied, and into Cœlo-Syria.

He was undoubtedly a Chriftian, as appears from two Paffages in his Works. One in *Tetrabiblos* 2. *Serm.* 4. *Cap.* 50. where he gives the Method of extracting any Thing that happens to ftick in the Throat. When other Ways fail, he advifes the following as the laft Refuge, and on which he feems to lay fome Strefs: Turn, fays he, to the Patient and bid him attend, then fay, Bone come out (if it happens to be a Bone) as Jefus Chrift brought Lazarus out of the Sepulchre, and as Jonas was brought out of the Belly of the Whale. Then, laying hold of the Throat, fay, Blafius the Martyr and Servant of Chrift fays, Either come up or go down.

The next Paffage I would bring for a Proof of his being Chriftian is in *Tetrabib.* 4. *Serm.* 1. *Chap.* 11. where fpeaking of the Stings of Wafps and Bees, he fays, that the venerable and vivifying Image of the Crofs, engraved upon an iron Seal and preffed upon the Part ftung, is of great Service, preventing all Manner of Inflammation. To this Prefcription of *Aetius*, I muft add, and I hope without Danger of any Imputation of Superftition, that the Remedy he advifes has great Effects in the Cafes he mentions, generally taking off the Pain and preventing Inflammation. But for Fear I fhould miflead my Readers, I muft remark, that an iron Seal without the Figure of the Crofs, or even the Blade of a Knife, will do as well.

Thefe Paffages prove *Aetius* a Chriftian, but at the fame Time fuch a one as brings very little Credit to the Faith he profeffed, fince a fmall Degree of Evidence was fufficient to influence his Belief; for, though the Truth of the Chriftian Religion admits of all the Proof that a reafonable Man could require, yet thefe Fooleries, the Effects of a miftaken Zeal, which he feems to give Credit to, are not in the leaft countenanced either by Reafon or Revelation.

Upon the Whole *Aetius* appears to have been a very credulous Man in many Inftances, and was far from giving the Compofition of Medicines which had acquired a Character, with a Defign to expofe them, as Dr. Friend thinks, for in the very Inftances that are brought to prove this, I mean the Collyrium of Danaus, and the Antidotum Ifotheos, the Author does not feem to difpute the Reality of the Virtues attributed to them, but mentions their great Price in all Appearance with a View to increafe his Readers Opinion of their Value.

Notwithftanding the Credulity of *Aetius*, he is a very valuable Author, and has preferved many Things confiderable with Respect to the Practice of Physic in his Collections from Authors whose Works are now lost. Of this frequent Instances will occur in the practical Part of this Work, for which Reason I shall omit taking Notice of them in this Place.

Fabricius and Friend relate, that in some Manuscripts he is stiles Κόμης ὀψίκιε, *Comes Obsequii*, which the last-mentioned Author explains, *The chief Officer of those who used to go before the Emperor as his Attendance and Harbingers.*

His Works are at present divided into four Tetrabibli, and each of them into four Sermones, which are again subdivided into Chapters. This Division appears not to have been made by *Aetius* himself, but was probably the Work of some Copyist, that transcribed his Writings since the Time of Photius, for in his Days they were divided into sixteen Books, the Number of Sermones which the four Tetrabibli contain.

Photius says, that *Aetius* did not only make his Collections from the same Authors that Oribasius extracted his from, which he dedicates to Julian, Euftathius, and Eunapius, but also from the Therapeutic Tracts of Galen, and from Archigenes, and Rufus, and besides these from Diofcorides, Soranus, Philagrius, Philomenus, Pofidonius, and some others who had made their Names famous for their Skill in Physic.

He begins his Works (says our Author) with the Virtues of simple Medicines and Aliments, which he abbreviates from Galen, and closes with the Sixteenth Book, which treats of the Diseases of Women ; to which he adds some Chapters containing Medicines to clear the Face, and cleanse the Skin, with the Preparation of Oinantharia [*Sweet Ointments made with Wine and Lilies*] and other Things of the like Kind. So the Work begins and ends ; but, to be more particular,

The First Book treats, in a summary Way, of the Nature of simple Medicines and Aliments. This is the first Sermo of the first Tetrabiblos, according to the present Division of his Works.

The Second speaks of the Virtues and Use of metallic Substances, and of Animals, both whole, and their Parts, in a compendious Manner. And this may be reckoned to contain no inconsiderable Part of the Materia Medica. This is the second Sermo of the first Tetrabiblos.

The Third Book treats of Gymnastics and its Preparatories. Then, after speaking of insensible Evacuations, he discourses largely on Phlebotomy, distinguishing the different Ways of Section, and directing the Form and Bigness of the Incision, with the Time and Measure of Evacuation. He goes on to the Section of an Artery, prescribes a Medicine to

114

stop the Bleeding of an Artery, fpeaks of Cupping, Scarification, and the Choice of Leeches. From thence he proceeds to treat of Cathartics, and the different Preparations of purging Wines, of purging Meads, and medicated purging Wines, of Abfinthaton, Rofaton, Honey of Rofes, and Oxymel, purging Garum, Honey, Metheglin, and Oxygarum, of emollient Broths, Milk, and purging Olives. Concerning all thefe he gives Directions ; and proceeds to compound Oxyporia, and different Sorts of Cathartics, to purging Loaves, and Troches. He defcribes the purging Medicines prepared of Aloes, and alfo of Salts ['Αλμηδάρια κ) ἁλικτα] with the five Hieras. He prefcribes Help for thofe who have taken Purgatives which will not work, or, on the Contrary, evacuate too much ; gives his Advice concerning Emetics, fhews the Virtues of Hellebore, and the Perfons for whom it is proper, and who are qualified to take it ; how to make Experiments of the Strength of Hellebore, and how the Patient is to prepare himfelf for the taking of it ; of the various Ufes of Hellebore, and the different Ways of adminiftring it, and the Care that ought to be taken of thofe who have drank it. He proceeds to purging Epithems, and takes Notice of thofe Parts of our Bodies which may be purged, as the Eyes, Ears, and the reft in Order. Of Suffumigations producing the fame Effect, and of Medicines evacuating the fmall Inteftines, and the concave Part of the Liver and its Appurtenances ; of the Air, Winds, and Significations of the Stars ; of Waters, of Baths natural and artificial ; of cold Bathing [ψυχρολυσίας] of Baths of Oil [τῆς ἰις ἴλαιον ιμβάσιως] of pouring Water on the Face [τῶ προσώπυ κλυσμάτων] of Perfufions, Infeffions, Irrigations, and dry Fomentations [πυριάσιως]. Moreover the Book treats of the various Kinds of Cataplafms; of the Dropax, Pication, Sinapifm, Rubification [φοινιγμῶ] and metafyncritical Remedies [μετασυγκριτικοῖς βοηθήμασιν]. This is the third Sermo of the firft Tetrabiblos.

In his Fourth Book he difcourfes on Regimen, or the Method of preferving Health. Here he begins with the Nature of Infants, defcribes their Difeafes, and gives Remedies. Then he prefcribes a proper Regimen for all Ages and Conditions of Life ; tells when we are to exchange Flefh for a thinner Diet ; treats of Laffitude from Exercife, and its different Kinds ; of Laffitude from Venery ; of that Species which arifes from no manifeft Caufe, and which they call *fpontaneous* ; of the Care we ought to take of Concoction ; of Perfpiration ftopped, and its Cure ; of burning Heats [ἰγκαύσιος] and feafonable Friction ; of Indigeftion, Crapula [κραιπάλης] and equal Dyfcrafies [ὁμαλῶς δυσκρασίας]. How to know the beft Temperament ; gives us the Characteriftics of a hot Temperament, and of others, both fimple and mixed, and that not only of the whole Body, but of the Head, Brain, Belly, Lungs, Heart, Liver, and

Testicles; and prescribes Remedies for all their Disorders. This is the fourth Sermo of the first Tetrabiblos.

The Fifth is a Treatise of Diseases. Here first he recommends the Study of Hippocrates, and discourses on Fevers, their Signs [σημείωσις] Prognostics and Diagnostics, with their Cures, and whatever else belongs to this Branch of Medicine, in a very exact Manner. What is to be accounted the Beginning of Distempers, and that the same is threefold; what we are to understand by Paroxysm [παροξυσμῦ] and Remission, the Height and Declension [ἀκμὴ κỳ παρακμὴ] of the Paroxysm, either affecting the whole Body, or some Part of it. What are the Signs of Death or Recovery to the Patient, and which of them portend quick or slow, or in a middle Way, Destruction or Delivery. Of the Signs of Pulses, and Diagnostics by Urines, and what is to be learnt by them; of the Marks of Excrements, with the Signs and Prognostics of Vomiting; of an Hæmorrhage from the Nose, and of the Catamenia; of the critical Signs of Sweats and Abscesses, and what may be gathered from the Spittle. That a skilful Physician will know when a Disease is past a Solution, and when it only seems to be so, and can foretel the Day and Hour when the Sick will die. He goes on to treat of general, epidemic, and pestilential Distempers, of such as, on some Occasions, are seized with Faintings, and of Lipothymies and their Causes; of Pain in the Head, Ears, and Eyes; Want of Sleep, and Dulness of Sight attending a Fever; of such as under a Fever are seized with an Hæmorrhage, and their Cure, and what Care ought to be taken of feverish Patients. Moreover, it treats of the Bladder, of Difficulty of Urine, Pains in the Loins, Exulceration of the Parts about the Os Sacrum, of the Testicles and Anus, Breakings out of Pustules [ἐξανθήματα] over the whole Body, or some Part thereof; of Tremors and Convulsions, and gives a Detail of Medicines which are both agreeable and effectual. This is the first Sermo of the second Tetrabiblos.

Aetius, in his Sixth Book, treats of the Disorders incident to the Head and Brain universally, and not only describes them, but shews a Way to cure them. He proceeds to speak of those who are bit by a mad Dog, of the Apoplexy and Palsy; of the Resolution of the Eye-brow, Eyelid, Tongue, vocal Instruments, and Oesophagus; and prescribes Cures for them all. Thence he goes on to the Spasmus Cynicus, and shews how to cure a Resolution of the Bladder, Penis, and Intestinum Rectum, the Leg, or any other Member; treats of a Tetanus [ττάυυ] and of the different Sorts of Headaches, from whatever Cause they arise, of a Cephalaia [an intense Pain in the Head] and a Hemicrania [a Pain confined to one Side of the Head]; prescribes a Cure for the Alopecia, and Defluxions of the Hair, and for bald Eyebrows; gives Receipts for dying, curling, eradicating Hair; to make it fine, and to prevent its shedding; and teaches the Making of Psilothra [Ointments to fetch off Hair]; speaks moreover, of the Pituriasis [a Sort of Scurf] Phthiriasis [lousy Disease] Achores, and those Pustules [ἰξανθήματα] which rise about the Head without any manifest Cause; for all these and the like Distempers he gives us a Cure; also for those various Indispositions from different Causes, to which the Ear is incident; for an Hæmorrhage from that Part, and for the Parotides. Thence he passes to the Nose, and its Distempers, when he treats of Sternutatories, and how to suppress immoderate Sneezing. This is the second Sermo of the second Tetrabiblos.

In the Seventh he proceeds to consider the Nature of the Eye, and those manifold Disorders to which it is subject, whether they proceed from an internal or external Cause. He instructs us in the Section of an Artery, in scarifying the Sinciput [πιρισκυφισμᾶ, the Edition of Photius's *Bibliotheca at Rouen*, 1653, has it πιρὶ σκυθισμᾶ, which Error has passed into the Latin Translation] and the Forehead, in the Method of Bleeding; among the rest he gives us Prescriptions for Ointments, Cataplasms, and various Sorts of Collyriums; and all this with no small Accuracy and Judgment. This is the third Sermo of the second Tetrabiblos.

In the Beginning of the Eighth he has something to say about adorning and setting off the Eyebrows; then speaks of a black Eye, how it comes, and how to cure it; teaches us to defend the Face from Burning, either by Sun or Wind, to preserve the same from Wrinkles, to alter a black Colour, with other additional Beautifyings, and to diffuse a good Scent over the Skin. Hence he passes to consider at large the Distempers incident to the Face, Mouth, and Tonsils, whether from an internal or external Cause. He treats of the various Maladies to which the Teeth are liable, and prescribes a Cure; also those of the Tongue, Uvula, and all that are comprised within the Compass of the Mouth. Among this Number are the Cynanche and the Synanche, which have their Seat in the Jaws; the Tonsils also have their Place among the rest. He shews a Way to revive those who are strangled, but not dead; discourses on the Diseases of the Arteries, and their Remedies; of Coughs also, and Catarrhs, where he prescribes Anodynes for the Cough, with Suffumigations and Epithems. After these he considers those who are afflicted with Asthmas, Difficulty of Breathing, and Palpitations of the Heart; and having first treated of the Diseases of the Breast and Lungs, he closes the Book with a Discourse on the Pleurify, the real and the reputed one, describes them both, and shews a Method of Cure. This is the fourth Sermo of the second Tetrabiblos.

The Ninth Book begins with the cardiac Passion, and pro-

117

ceeds to speak of those who have their Stomach affected with Atra Bilis, or the Mouth of the Ventricle any Way disordered, describing the Cataplasms, and other Remedies for the various Distempers of the Stomach. Here he considers the Case of those who suffer Convulsions of the Stomach, after the Manner of epileptic Patients; treats also of Want of Appetite, of the canine Appetite, of Indigestion, and their Cures. Then he shews how to cure a Surfeit, and prescribes a Remedy for Costiveness; treats moreover of Flatulencies, the iliac Passion, and the Colic, of Fluxes of the Belly, and what is called a Disposition to the Colic, of Colliquations, of Worms, round and broad, of those called Ascarides, and of the Affections of the Intestines. He prescribes a Remedy for those who have swallowed Gold, Brass, or any such Thing; as also for such as labour under a Dysentery, to be taken at the Mouth, or injected beneath, such as Pastils, Suppositories, Ointments, Epithems; and at last ends his Book with treating of a Lientery. This is the first Sermo of the third Tetrabiblos.

He begins his Tenth Book with the Liver, its Weakness, and other Disorders, and prescribes Medicines for them. Then proceeds to consider the Affections of the Spleen, and its various Disorders, such as Inflations, Inflammations, Scirrhosities, preternatural Tumors, and Hardness, and shews how to cure them; after these, of the Jaundice, Cachexy, and Dropsy; shews you whence every one of these Distempers proceeds, and puts you in a Way and Method how to cure them. This is the second Sermo of the third Tetrabiblos.

The Eleventh Book treats of a Diabetes, and the lax Tone of the Reins, of bloody Urine, of Stone in the Kidnies and Bladder, of Inflammation, Hardness, and Suppuration of the Kidnies; of Dysury, Strangury, and Ischury; of Resolution of the Bladder, of such as cannot hold their Water in Sleep, of the Inflammation, Hæmorrhage, Clots of Blood, Tubercles, and Ulcers in the Bladder; also of the Flux and Itch of the same Part; of a Satyriasis, Priapismus, Gonorrhœa, and venereal Dreams. To all these Distempers, as far as possible, he assigns proper Causes, and subjoins the necessary Cautions, and Cures. At the End of this Book he prescribes Exercises and Medicines for Impotency. This is the third Sermo of the third Tetrabiblos.

In his Twelfth Book he considers the Sciatica, and the Gout, and examines into the Causes, both general and particular, of these Distempers, and prescribes Variety of Remedies for them, and for other Disorders consequent upon them. He recounts the several Ways of Evacuation, the Chrisms, Emollients, Anointings, the Acopa, and the Ointments, as also the proper Cathartics, and Antidotes, and Abundance of other Things proper to give Relief under these Diseases. This is the fourth Sermo of the third Tetrabiblos.

118

His Thirteenth treats of the Bites of Animals, what Alterations and Symptoms they produce in the Subject bitten, and how to remove and cure them. He makes the like Obfervations on Animals that ejaculate their Poifon, and points out thofe Plants and Herbs which are venomous and deftructive, with fingular Care and Diligence. He difcourfes on Fungi, Bull's Blood, and Milk clotted in the Stomach; informs us what metalline Subftances are hurtful to an Animal, when taken inwardly; explains how drinking of cold Water or Wine may be hurtful; makes Obfervations on thofe who are ftrangled, drowned, or precipitated from fome high Place; of Precaution and Forefight in Brute Animals, efpecially domeftic ones. He then difcourfes of the Theriaca Andromachi, of Vipers, gives its Preparation, Ufes, Seafons of ufing it, Ways to try it, the Dofe, and the Diftempers in which it is properly adminiftered; alfo the other Theriacæ, particularly the Antidotus Mithridatica, or Mithridate, its Preparation, Ufe, and in what Cafes it is to be adminiftered. To this he fubjoins other Antidotes, and to them the two Cyphi [precious Ointments]. From thence he proceeds to write of the Elephantiafis, of pruriginous Eruptions [ἐπσμωδῶν ἐξανθημάτων] Pfydraces, and Puftules arifing from Sweat [ψυδρακῶν κὴ ἰδρωτίδων] ulcerous Eruptions [ἑλκωδῶν ἐκβρασμάτων] in the Legs, Scars from Ulcers which blacken and deform the Body. He proceeds to treat of the two Species of Alphus [Ἄλφος, a Kind of Leprofy] and of the Leuce [λεύκη, a white Sort of Leprofy] and laftly of the Leprofy; fhews their Original and Caufes, and prefcribes their Cures. This is the firft Sermo of the fourth Tetrabiblos.

In the Fourteenth Book *Aetius* treats with great Accuracy of the various Difeafes incident to the Anus, of Warts [θύμοι] and Fiffures in the Pudenda, of a Phlegmon, Carbuncle, phagedenic Ulcers, and fuch as have their Seat in the urinary Paffages; of a fcabbed Scrotum, of an Inflammation in that Part and the Tefticles, and the Species of Herniæ; of the Compofition of Plaifters, and the Way of preparing the Ingredients. He treats moreover of wounded and bruifed Nerves, of Buboes, and Phlegmons in general; alfo of Abfceffes, and hollow Ulcers, declaring their Nature, and prefcribing Remedies for all, and alfo for Worms bred in Ulcers, and againft the Spreading, Putrefying, and Bleeding of the fame. He carries on his Difcourfe to a Sinus, Fiftula, Gangrene, Sphacelus, cancerated Tumors, Carbuncles, Eryfipelas, Herpes, Terminthus, and Puftules, fpecifying their Caufes and Cures. He prefcribes healing Medicines for fuch as are burnt with Fire, fcalded with Water, or fcourged with Whips; for Abrafions, Galls, Contufions, where the Flefh is whole or broken [σαρκὸς θλασθέντος ἢ ῥαγείσης] for Convulfions, Contorfions, Luxations, and Chilblains, not omitting Excrefcences over the Nails, Whitlows [στεφυγίων, παρωνυχίας] Nails crufhed, bloody, loofe, or rotten; alfo to make freſh Nails grow out in the Room of thoſe which are fallen off, to get off Rings that are grown into the Fleſh, to cure Corns and Chaps in the Feet, and alſo Varices. The Book concludes with the Management and Cure of the Dracunculi in the Arms and Legs. This is the ſecond Sermo of the fourth Tetrabiblos.

The Fifteenth Book contains the Theory and Cure of œdematous, emphyſematous. indurated, and incyſted Tumors, of Strumæ, Bronchocele, Meliceridcs, Steatomata, Ganglia, Aneuriſms, Favi, and Hydrocephalus. Of all theſe you have the Origin, and Cauſes, with the chirurgical and other Methods of Cure, and the Preparation of many and various Sorts of Plaiſters. This is the third Sermo of the fourth Tetrabiblos.

In the Sixteenth, and laſt, the Author treats of the Situation, Structure, and Magnitude, of the Womb, with the Seaſons of its Purgation and Semination. Of Conception, of the Marks of Fœcundity, and having actually conceived, and of the Symptoms peculiar to pregnant Women. Of the great Care that is to be taken of them; who are qualified for eaſy Labour, and who are unhappy in that Reſpect. Of hard Labours, and preternatural Births, of the Cæſarean Section, and Extraction of the Secundines; what are the Cauſes of Infœcundity in Man or Woman. For all theſe fore-mentioned Evils, Remedies are provided in this Book; as, for Inſtance, Potions, Peſſaries, and Suſſumigations are preſcribed to promote Conception. · Hence he goes on to the Diſeaſes of Womens Breaſts, which he treats of in a ſkilful Manner, explaining their Origin, Eſſence, chirurgical and other Methods of Cure. After this, he enquires into the Cauſes of the Obſtruction of the Menſes, of their too plentiful Efflux; both the red, and the white; of Hyſterics, and a Fluor albus, with excellent Preſcriptions in theſe Caſes. He proceeds to treat of other Diſtempers of the Uterus; as Abſceſſes, œdematous Tumors, Moles, Dropſy, Ulcers, &c. and other Things of the like Kind, not forgetting to ſpeak of the Phimoſis, and Imperforation, and other like Incidents, with their proper Remedies; alſo of the Section of the Nymphæ, Cercoſis, the Hernia varicoſa, Thymi, and ſuch like; and how to cure them. To all theſe he ſubjoins ſome Smegmata [a Sort of Waſh-balls] for the Face, and other Parts of the Body, with Preſcriptions for the Compoſition of ſome precious Ointments, with which he cloſes his Treatiſe of the Art of Medicine. This is the fourth Sermo of the fourth Tetrabiblos.

This Work of *Aetius*, in my Opinion, excels the Synopſes of Oribaſius, I mean thoſe dedicated to Euſtathius and Eunapius, on all Accounts; for he does not only give us the Definitions, the Cauſes, the Diagnoſtics, and Prognoſtics, in a more perſpicuous Manner, but is more full and copious in the therapeutic Part. And he is not only his Superior in those Refpects, but even in what he has epitomifed from Galen, both in Perfpicuity, and Extenfivenefs, as comprehending more Difeafes. But, perhaps, there is no Comparifon between this Work and that of Oribafius, which takes up feventy Books, becaufe our Author has not only omitted Anatomy, which Oribafius has explained, but has faid nothing about the Ufe of the Parts, which indeed more properly comes under the Confideration of a Philofopher than a Phyfician. On thefe Accounts, perhaps, it will be thought inferior to the fore-mentioned Epitome of Galen's Works. But, to fpeak my Mind freely, in this negligent Age, which minds nothing lefs than the Sick, I would recommend this Collection above all other Works of that Kind, efpecially to thofe who do not care to fearch into the Depth of the Theory of Medicines, but have the Health of Mankind more at Heart. They will here find Remedies in Abundance, and an ample Recompence for all their Pains and Study on this valuable Piece of Medicine. *Photii Biblioth.*

This is the Character Photius beftows on *Aetius*, and Cornarius agrees with him fo exactly, that he feems to tranfcribe him.

Of the Works of *Aetius*, only the two firft Tetrabibli, or eight firft Books, have yet been printed in Greek, and thefe only once in Folio, at Venice, 1534. The reft are faid to remain in Manufcript in many Libraries.

Johannes Baptifta Montanus, a Phyfician of Verona, was the firft who publifhed a Latin Tranflation of all his Works, at Bafil, 1535, in Folio.

In 1542, Janus Cornarius publifhed his Tranflation of all the Works of *Aetius* at Bafil in Folio. This has been feveral Times reprinted, and is publifhed amongft the *Medica Artis Principes*, by H. Stevens.

ALEXANDER. A Phyfician of the fixth Century was named *Trallianus*, from *Tralles*, a City of Lydia where he was born. He was equally happy in all the Circumftances of his Birth, for Tralles was famous for the Purity of its Dialect, and his Father Stephanus was by Profeffion a Phyfician, whofe Tendernefs probably enforced his Inftructions, and contributed much to the Advancement of his Son's Studies.

Alexander having been fome Time taught by his Father, either after his Death, or in Hopes that as every Man of Eminence has fome Excellencies peculiar to himfelf, the Precepts of another Mafter might afford him new Light, became the Difciple of another Phyfician, the Father of that Cofmas at whofe Requeft he compiled his Book, and made fuch Advances in Phyfic, as procured him when he engaged in Practice the higheft Reputation ; a Reputation fo extenfive that not only at Rome, but wherever he travelled, he was confulted and applied to as the greateft Mafter of his Art, and became known by the Title of ALEXANDER THE PHYSICIAN.

His Claim to this honorary Appellation appears to have been founded not upon popular Caprice, or fome fingle Inftances of accidental Succefs, to one or other of which many have been indebted both for their Honours and their Riches, but to exten-five Knowledge, and judicious Practice. He is the only Writer of the later Ages who has ventured to form his own Plan, or who can claim the Character of an original Author.

His Method is accurate and perfpicuous ; he begins with the Diftempers of the Head, and defcends to all the Parts of the Bo-dy in their natural Order. His Account of the Diagnoftics is remarkably exact, and his Method of Cure for the moft Part ra-tional and falutary.

Without engaging in Difquifitions relating to the Materia Medica, Anatomy, or Surgery, he confines himfelf to the De-fcription of Difeafes, which feems to be his peculiar Excellency, and the Method of Cure, which the Multiplicity of his Practice enabled him to lay down with more Accuracy and Certainty, than thofe whofe Learning was lefs affifted by Experience. Of many Cafes he has left exact Hiftories, with a regular Detail of the Succeffion of the Symptoms, and the Application of his Medicines.

It is to be obferved to his Honour that his Omiffion of Sur-gery was not the Effect of his Ignorance of that Science, but of his Knowledge of the Art of Writing, and his Conviction of the Neceffity of one fimple uniform Plan. He had obferved how much Digreffions into remote Enquiries, and a Mixture of different Subjects, had contributed to the Obfcurity of Writings Intended to promote Science, and therefore propofed, as he in-forms us, to treat of Fractures and the Difeafes of Eyes in fepa-rate Books.

His intire Omiffion of the *Diftempers of Women,* is another Inftance of the Accuracy of his Method. As thofe Diforders proceed from the peculiar Structure and Functions of the Parts, he probably imagined, that they had no Place in a general Treatife of Phyfic, and that by enlarging his Scheme he fhould only perplex it.

Whether he intended another Treaife on Female Difeafes, or whether he lived to execute his other Defigns, it is now im-poffible to difcover ; but as he wrote the Books which now re-main in his old Age, when he could no longer fupport the Fa-tigue of Practice, it is more probable that he did not live to finifh his Defigns than that any of his Works could perifh.

He appears through his whole Works to have attended dili-gently not only the Inftructions of his Predeceffors, but to the Precepts of far greater Certainty, the Dictates of Reafon, and the Evidence of Experience. He seems to have adventured to use violent Methods in Extremities, yet not wantonly to have sported with Life. He frequently deviates from the received Practice, and perhaps the Introduction of *Steel in Substance* may be justly ascribed to him, since it is mentioned by no earlier Author.

Alexander's Learning and Judgment did not exempt him from some Weaknesses, from which it might be justly expected that either his Reason should have preserved him, or his Experience set him free.

He is strongly inclined to believe whatever has been told of the Efficacy of Medicines, and seems never to suspect either Weakness or Imposture. Nor is the Power of Medicines the only Object of his Credulity, which extends even to the Efficacy of Amulets and Charms, and he mentions some Remedies of this Sort for the Ague, Stone, Gout, and Colic. Those whose Reverence for Antiquity produces in them a Regard even for the Follies and Superstitions of antient Times, may here gratify their Curiosity with a Quotation from Ostanes, one of the old Persian Magi.

It is useless either to inquire into the Reasons of this Depravation of *Alexander*'s Understanding, or to extenuate his Error, by enumerating the learned and wise Men that have been misled by Superstition. The Causes of Error are innumerable, and therefore cannot be particularly pointed out, and to produce Testimonies in Favour of Folly, is at least to contribute very little to its Extirpation.

It is probable from some of these Charms, which consist of Passages from the Bible that *Alexander* was a Christian ; but if this Proof of his Religion be allowed, it evinces likewise, what is no Advancement of his Character, that he had learned his Religion with a very slight Attention.

Whatever might have been his Character as a Man, he has deserved as a Writer much more Applause than he commonly receives, and perhaps he is in Merit the next of the Greek Authors to Aretæus and Hippocrates.

The EDITIONS of ALEXANDER's WORKS are

In Greek, *Parisiis apud Robertum Stephanum*, 1548, *Fol. cum Castigationibus Jacobi Goupili.*

An old barbarous Latin Translation, in the Opinion of Fabricius, from some Arabic Translation, under the Title of *Alexandri Yatros Practica*, of which there have been many Editions, as *Lugduni*, 1504. 4to. *Papiæ*, 1512. 8vo. *Venetiis*, 1522. *Fol.*

Albanus Torinus afterwards put this into better Latin, but this was not a Translation from the Greek, but a Metaphrasis of the barbarous Translation above-mentioned. It was published, *Basil. apud Henricum Petri*, 1533. *Fol.* and 1541. *Fol.*

Johannes Guinterius Andernacus tranflated the Greek into Latin. Of this Tranflation there have been the following Editions :

Argentorati apud Remigium Guidonem, 1549. *8vo.*
Lugduni apud Antonium Vincentium, 1560. *12mo.*
Lugduni, 1575, *cum Johannis Molinæi Annotationibus.*

This Tranflation is alfo amongft the *Medicæ Artis Principes,* publifhed by Stevens.

Many detached Pieces have alfo been publifhed amongft Collections of Authors upon different Medicinal Subjects.

There is a fmall Treatife, Πιϛ ιλμίνθων, of Worms, which is afcribed to *Alexander* by Mercurialis, and is addreffed by *Alexander* to his Friend Theodorus. This is publifhed amongft fome of the Works of Mercurialis, and is inferted by Fabricius in his *Bibliotheca Græca,* in Greek and Latin, at the End of his Article of *Alexander.* It is not printed amongft his other Works.

There were many Phyficians of this Name before *Alexander Trallianus,* but we know of nothing remarkable relating to them.

ARCHAGATHUS. A celebrated Phyfician amongft the *Romans.*

'Tis by fome afferted, that before the Arrival of *Archagathus* at *Rome,* Phyfic was not fo much as known in that City ; and if we may believe *Pliny,* this ufeful Branch of Learning was unknown to the *Romans,* till after all the other liberal Arts and Sciences were eftablifhed among them : " The *Roman* People,
" fays he, [*Lib.* 29. *Cap.* 1.] were more than fix hun-
" dred Years without Phyficians, though they were very early
" in cultivating the other Arts, and even fond of *Phyfic* itfelf,
" till, becoming acquainted with it by Experience, they con-
" demn'd it. *Caffius Hemina* informs us, that *Archagathus*
" the Son of *Lyfanias* the *Peloponnefian* was the firft Phyfician
" who arrived at *Rome,* under the Confulfhip of *Marcus Au-*
" *relius* and *Marcus Livius,* in the Year of the City 535.
" adding, that he had the Freedom of the City beftowed upon
" him ; and that the Public had, at their own Charges, pur-
" chafed a Shop for him in the Street of *Accilius,* that he might
" exercife his Profeffion to the greater Advantage ; that at firft
" they gave him the Surname of *Vulnerarius,* or *The Healer*
" *of Wounds* ; that his Arrival was very agreeable to the People,
" but that foon after, his Practices of *Burning* and *Cutting* ap-
" pearing cruel and barbarous in the Eyes of the People, they
" exchanged his former Surname for that more infamous one
" of *Executioner* ; from which time they conceived an impla-
" cable Averfion to *Phyfic* and all its Profeffors."

It appears fomewhat furprifing, that a People fo polite as the *Romans* were, fhould be fo long without Phyficians. To the Authority of *Pliny* we shall oppose that of *Dionysius* of *Halicarnassus*, who in his tenth Book has these Words: " The " Plague beginning to appear in *Rome* in the Year of the City " 301. and happening to rage more violently than any other " Plague with which they had been afflicted in the Memory " of Man, it carried off almost all the Slaves, and half of the Ci- " tizens, the Physicians not being able to attend and take care " of such a large Number of Patients." There were then Phy- sicians in *Rome* at that time, that is, more than two hundred Years before the Period mentioned by *Pliny*, as indeed there have been Practisers of this Art in all Ages among all People. But, in order to reconcile these two Authors, we must suppose, that *Pliny* means only foreign Physicians, especially those of the *Greek* Nation ; and indeed he explains himself to that Purpose a little afterwards in these Words : " In order to be convinced " of the Aversion the *Romans* in those Days bore to Physic, " we need only hear the Sentiments of *Marcus Cato* upon that " Point, who lived seventy Years after *Archagathus*, and who " was a Man of whom we may say, that the Honour of a " Triumph decreed in his Favour, and the Dignity of the " Censorship, which Office he bore, are the least shining Parts " of his Character, since so many other Circumstances con- " curr'd in his Person to render him venerable and awful." These following are his own Words, taken from a Letter he wrote to his Son : " I will tell you, my Son *Marcus*, at a pro- " per Occasion, what Notion I entertain of these *Greeks*, and " what I think most valuable in *Athens*. It is not improper to " study their Learning and Sciences cursorily, but 'tis by no " means necessary to make one's self a complete Master of it. " I shall say no more at present of that wicked and arrogant " Race ; but persuade yourself of this, as much as if an Oracle " had spoken it, that as soon as this Nation has communicated " her Learning to us, she will spoil and corrupt *Rome* ; and " this dire Event will be still more easily brought about, if she " continue to send her Physicians to us. They have sworn " among themselves to kill all the *Barbarians*, by means of " their Art ; and still they exact a Fee for their Pains from " the Patients with whom they deal, that they may gain their " Confidence more effectually, and consequently have it in " their Power to destroy them with the less Danger of Suspi- " cion. They have such a Degree of Insolence as to call not " only other Nations, but *us*, *Barbarians* ; nay, they carry " their Arrogance farther, and style us ὀπικοὶ, rude, and " Strangers to true Politeness. In a Word, my Son, re- " member, that I have discharged you from having any thing " to do with Physicians."

'Tis plain from the Strain of *Cato's* Language, that he had only foreign Physic in his View ; and this *Pliny* acknowledges, by starting to himself the following Objection, which he makes use of as a Conclusion : " Must we then believe, that *Cato* con-

" demn'd a thing so useful and beneficial as Physic? Assuredly not;
" since he himself vouchsafes to informs us by the Use of what
" Medicines he himself and his Wife had arrived at such an
" advanced Age ; and that he had written a Book, in which he
" lays down the Method of his Practice, with regard to his Son,
" his Slaves, and even his Cattle, when they were indis-
" posed."

The *Romans* then were not absolutely without Physicians
in the earlier Ages of their Republic ; but in all Probability,
before the Arrival of *Archagathus*, they only used that *Natural
Physic*, or simple Empiricism; which we may well suppose to
have been practised by the Infant World, when Men made their
first Appearance upon it. This was the Physic relished by *Cato*,
and on which he wrote the first of all the *Romans*. He had
some Peculiarities in his Practice, which, if they will not inform
the Judgment, will, at least, excite the Laughter of every thinking Person; for 'tis well known, that he approved of superfti-
tious Remedies; and in that Part of his Works which has
reached our Hands, he has given us an inimitable *Formula* of
Words to be pronounced for the Cure of a Dislocation or
Fracture ; but because there is not a Possibility of translating
them, I shall give them as he himself gave them : " *Luxum si*
" *quod est, hac Cautione sanum fiet. Harundinem prende tibi*
" *viridem P. 4. aut 5. Longam. Mediam diffinde, & duo Ho-*
" *mines teneant ad Coccendices. Incipe Cantare in alio. S. F.*
" *Motas væta Daries Dardaries, Astataries Dissunapiter, usque*
" *dum coeant. Ferrum insuper jactato. Ubi coierint, & al-*
" *tera alteram tetigerit ; id Manu prende, & dextra sinistra*
" *præcide. Ad Luxum aut Fracturam alliga, sanum fiet, &*
" *tamen quotidie cantato in alio, S. F. vel Luxato, vel hoc*
" *modo, huat, hanat, huat, ista. Pista, sista, domiabo dam-*
" *naustra, & luxato. Vel hoc modo, huat, haut, haut, ista,*
" *sis tar sis ardannabon dunnaustra."* Cato de re rustic Cap.
160.

Pliny also informs us, that *Cato* in his Practice made a great
deal of Use of Cabbage, in which, as he observes, the whole
Materia Medica of the *Romans* consisted for six hundred Years.
This *Panacea* must undoubtedly appear ridiculous in our Days ;
but we shall be less surprised, that this People confided so much
in a common Plant, if we call to mind the uncommon Esteem
in which it was had among the most learned and skilful of the
first *Greek* Physicians.

Plutarch observes, with regard to the Practice of *Cato*, that
he did not approve of Abstinence for the Cure of Diseases, but
recommended Herbs, and the Flesh of Ducks, Pigeons, and
Hares. But this Author does not pay so profound a Veneration to the Physic of *Cato* as *Pliny* does ; he observes on the
contrary, that the Wife and Son of that *Roman* died before
himself; adding at the same time, that if *Cato* lived to so
great an Age, it was owing to the natural Goodness of his

Conftitution, and not the judicious and happy Choice of his Medicines. As *Plutarch* was a *Grecian*, he may poffibly be fufpeÉed of being animated with too keen a Defire of revenging the Caufe of the *Greek* Phyficians; though, at the fame time, what he afferts has very much the Air of Probability.

As for the Phyfic of the *Greeks*, 'tis not at all furprifing, that the *Romans* fhould be unacquainted with it till the Arrival of *Archagathus* amongft them, fince even in other Inftances they were very late in cultivating the Sciences and liberal Arts. And tho' *Pliny*, in the Paffage already quoted, affirms, that the *Romans* foon received the Arts; yet this is only to be under-ftood of thefe mechanical Arts, which are abfolutely neceffary to human Life: " *Cicero* [*Tufculanar. Quæft. Lib.* 1.] informs " us, that Poetry was not introduced among the *Romans* till " very late, and that even Philofophy had been in great Dif-" repute till his Days. *Suetonius* alfo [*De illuftrib. Gramma-*" *ticis*] affirms, that Grammar was not at all in Ufe among " the firft *Romans*, much lefs was it efteemed and valued, be-" caufe the People of thefe Days were as yet favage and unpo-" lite, and fo throughly addiÉted to the Bufinefs of War, that " none apply'd themfelves very much to the liberal Arts." But there cannot poffibly be a more convincing Proof, that Learn-ing made her Entrance into *Rome* very late, than *Cato*'s Dread, left fhe fhould make her Appearance in his Days, though he lived, as we have obferved, feventy Years after *Archagathus*. Though the greater Part of this Article may feem to be a kind of Digreffion, yet, upon a clofer View, the Whole will appear to have fome ConneÉtion with the Life and Hiftory of *Archagathus*. Befides, 'tis fraught with fo much Learn-ing, and has fuch a direÉt Tendency to acquaint us with the State of Phyfic in *Rome*, that it will fpeak for its own *Propriety*. *Le Clerc. Hiftoire de la Medicine.*

ARETÆUS. *Le Clerc*, an Author of profound Learning, and fingular Penetration, has fet the Sentiments and CharaÉter of *Aretæus* in a very juft Light.

Aretæus is an Author of fo uncommon a CharaÉter and Re-putation, that we fhould do a manifeft Injury both to him and to the World, if, on this Occafion, we fhould negleÉt to inquire into the SeÉt to which he belong'd, and the Time at which he lived; and this Tafk will at once prove curious and ufeful, fince, as we go along, we fhall have Occafion to mention fome Circumftances, that place the Sentiments and PraÉtice of *Aretæus* in a clearer Light, than poffibly moft People are able to view them in without this Affiftance.

As to the SeÉt, then, to which this Phyfician belonged, there is not perhaps a fingle Point in the whole Hiftory of Phyfic, that has been either more miftaken, or lefs adverted to; for *Caftellanus*, who writes a fmall Abridgment of the Lives of the antient Phyficians, exprefly affirms, that *Aretæus* was attached to no particular Sect whatever. Something more accurate and explicit might have been expected from *Henifchius*, a Phyfician of *Aufburg*, who wrote Commentaries upon *Aretæus*, but he declares himfelf of the fame Opinion with *Caftellanus*, and all along difcovers fuch a Fund of Prejudice and Partiality, that one would be tempted to think he had written his Commentaries with no other View than to mifreprefent *Aretæus*, and make him fay things he never fo much as thought of. Inftead of explaining the difficult Paffages of his Author, he endeavours to fupply the Defects of the Text in fuch a manner as to fpeak his own or *Galen*'s Sentiments, and not thofe of *Aretæus*. And, what is ftill more furprifing, *Hieronymus Mercurialis*, who was fo throughly acquainted with the Writings of the antient Phyficians, and who had undoubtedly read *Aretæus*, as appears from feveral Paffages in his Works, forgets to take Notice of the Sect to which this Phyfician belonged. But notwithftanding the Uncertainty this Point has hitherto laboured under, I fhall venture to pronounce, that *Aretæus* was an Abettor of the Pneumatic Sect; and, my Reafons for thinking fo, are thefe:

'Tis well known, that the Pneumatic Sect eftablifhed a fifth Element, which they called *Spirit*, the Changes and Alterations of which, according to them, laid the Foundations of various Difeafes. Now 'tis plain, that *Aretæus* means this *fame Spirit*, when he fays, that "there are two Sorts of Quinfeys, "the one caufed by an Inflammation of the Inftruments of "Refpiration, of the Amygdalæ, Epiglottis, Pharynx, Uvula, "and fuperior Part of the Afpera Arteria; and the other pro- "ceeding from a Diforder of the *Spirit*, which is itfelf the im- "mediate Caufe of this Diftemper. In the latter of thefe "Quinfeys, adds our Author, the Inftruments of Refpiration "are fo far from being diftended, that they are rather more "contracted than in their natural State; and yet the Suffoca- "tion and Difficulty of Breathing are far greater than in the "former; for which Reafon, thofe who labour under it, ima- "gine that they have a latent Inflammation in the very Mid- "dle of their Lungs, and in the Parts adjacent to their Heart. "As for my fhare, continues he, I am of Opinion, that it is "the Spirit alone which is affected, and which by an unhappy "Change is become very hot and dry, but that there is no "Phlegmon or Inflammation in any Part whatever." *Aretæus* confirms his Opinion, by an Example drawn from the Exhalations which arife from the *Charonian Pits*, which in a Moment fuffocate thofe who are expofed to them, though they fhould happen to be in a State of perfect Health immediately before. He alfo confirms it by an Inftance drawn from the Breath of mad Dogs, which, as he affirms, kills thofe who receive it, though they have not been bit by the Dogs them-

128

felves. From thefe Examples he concludes, " That a Change, " with regard to Refpiration, may be produced by internal " Caufes, which bear an Analogy and Refemblance to fuch as " are external; that, in like manner, there are fometimes Hu- " mours in our Bodies, which partake of the Nature of Poi- " fons, as much as external Subftances which come under that " Denomination; and that we may obferve natural Diftem- " pers accompanied with the fame Symptoms as thofe produced " by Poifons; and Patients vomit the fame kind of Matter in " Fevers, which others do upon taking Poifons: For which " Reafon, continues our Author, we ought not to be fur- " prifed, if the *Athenians*, who were ignorant of the Analogy " between the Effects of certain Poifons, and thofe of certain " peftilential Difeafes, imagined that they were afflicted with " Diftempers of that Nature, becaufe the Inhabitants of the " *Peloponnefus*, with whom they were at War, had poifoned " the Wells of the *Piræus*."

From thefe Paffages we may infer, that by the Word *Spirit*, *Aretæus* meant no more than the *Matter of Refpiration*; and he feems to confirm that Point in another Paffage, where he fays, that *the Coldnefs and Humidity of the Spirit are the Caufe of an Afthma :* But it is not in thefe Cafes alone, according to *Aretæus*, that the *Spirit* contributes to the Production of Dif- eafes; for the *Iliac Paffion* is, in his Opinion, produced by a cold and flow *Spirit*, which cannot eafily difcharge itfelf either upwards or downwards. In a Scirrhus of the Spleen, the Belly, fays he, is filled with a thick and dark *Spirit*, which feems to be humid, though it is not really fo. In a Dropfy called a *Tympanites*, our Author acknowledges a *Spirit* which does not change its Situation, though the Part which includes it, moves upwards and downwards; and adds, that if this Spirit is changed into Water or Vapour, the Tympanites is changed into an Afcites. He afferts in another Paffage, that the Smell or Vapour of the Poppy thickens the dry and fubtile *Spirit* of Phrenetic Patients. In fhort, *Aretæus* infifts fo much on the *Spirit* eftablifhed as a fifth Element by the Pneumatics, that we have no Reafon to doubt of his being a profeffed Abettor of that Sect.

And even though this fhould be denied, a great many other Circumftances concur to prove, that *Aretæus* was a real Pneu- matic; for 'tis paft all Difpute, that the Phyficians of that Sect afferted, that Fire, Air, Earth, and Water, were not real Elements; but that the Name of Element rather belonged to the Qualities of which thefe Bodies were poffeffed, or to Heat, Cold, Drynefs, and Humidity : Now, that *Aretæus* was of the fame Sentiment, is plain from a great Number of Paffages in his Works.

It muft be own'd, that in fome Cafes the Sentiments of *Are- tæus* coincided with thofe of the Methodic Sect; for though other Phyficians acknowledged a Difference between acute and chronical Diforders, yet thofe of the Methodic Sect firft wrote of them feparately and apart : Now, that *Aretæus* followed them in this Particular, is plain from his having written four Books upon acute, and as many upon chronical Diftempers.

This is not the only Point in which he feems to follow them; for, in Imitation of them, he gives very particular Directions with regard to the Chamber in which Patients, labouring under certain Diforders, fhould be lodged. He likewife fpecifies the Air the Patient ought to breathe, the Bed on which he fhould lie, and the Manner in which he is to be covered. He alfo imitates them in recommending all the different Exercifes they ufed to prefcribe towards the Termination of Difeafes, fuch as Walking, the different Manners of Geftation, the Exercife of the Voice in Vociferation, or talking loud, and the throwing of the Coit, or other weighty Machines, ufed for the fame Purpofe. He alfo orders a certain Gefticulation of the Hands, which he calls *Chironomia*. Now all thefe are the profeffed Tenets of the Methodic Sect. *Aretæus* indeed in one Inftance carries the Point of Exercife farther, and advifes thofe who are fubject to Vertigos to behave as Prize-fighters do, that is, to beat each other foundly with their Fifts. 'Tis no eafy matter to comprehend his Meaning by this Advice. *Mercurialis* fuppofes, that it is a Fault in the Text; which is not improbable, fince we can fcarce fuppofe fuch a Treatment proper for vertiginous People, who are incommoded and rendered worfe by the leaft Noife or Motion. Befides, *Aretæus* had this in common with the Methodic Sect, that he afcribed a great deal to Topics, or external Applications, fuch as Fomentations, Cataplafms, and Unctions.

Tho' *Aretæus* agreed with the Methodic Sect in the abovementioned Particulars, yet on other Occafions he argued from quite different Principles, and prefcribed Remedies that were openly difapproved of by *Theffalus* and *Soranus*, who were avowed Favourers of the Methodic Sect: For Inftance, he orders Purgations, and the Compofition called *Hiera*, was what he moft ufed, and moft confided in. He alfo on fome Occafions prefcribed fimple Purgatives, fuch as the Fecula of wild Cucumbers, Baftard Saffron, and Hellebore. He no lefs remarkably oppofed the Methodic Sect, in venturing on certain Occafions to prefcribe acrid and irritating Clyfters.

He alfo ufed Caftor on feveral Occafions, which the Methodic Sect never did ; and, in direct Oppofition to them, prefcribed Narcotic Medicines, fuch as Opium and the Poppy. But his Practice with regard to the Ufe of thefe was not rafh and unguarded, as appears from the important Caution he gives in thefe Words: " 'Tis fometimes neceffary, fays he, to ad-
" minifter *fomniferous Medicines* to fuch as labour under Peri-
" pneumonies, or are afflicted with long Watchings, left they
" fhould become furious, and in order to mitigate and allay
" their Diforder and Inquietude. But we muft beware of

" ufing Medicines of this Nature, when the Patients are in
" Danger of being fuffocated with a Defluxion of Humours,
" or are thought to be on the very Verge of Death, becaufe in
" thefe Cafes the Phyfician runs a Rifque of being cenfured
" for killing the Patient."

Our Author's Practice, with regard to letting Blood, was
alfo very different from that of the Methodic Sect; for in Apo-
plexies he obferved, that taking away too much Blood killed the
Patient, and that taking too fmall a Quantity produced no Effect
at all: He was neverthelefs of Opinion, that it was moft proper
to take little at a time, and to repeat the Operation frequently.
In a Quinfey, he ufed Venefection, and allowed the Blood to
flow till the Patient was ready to faint away. In Vomitings of
Blood proceeding from whatever Caufe, he univerfally recommended Venefection: " For, fays he, whether this Difcharge
" of Blood is the Confequence of a Veffel's being broken, or
" corroded by the acrid Quality of the Blood, Venefection is
" ftill very ufeful; and if this Accident proceeds from the
" Thinnefs of the Veffels, Phlebotomy prevents their being
" burft, in Confequence of their being over-full. We muft
" alfo take care, continues he, not to allow the Orifice made
" in the Vein of the Arm to agglutinate and clofe up, that we
" may the more commodioufly take away a little Blood at
" different times for feveral Days running; a fmall Quantity
" muft be taken at a time; but the Operation muft be repeat-
" ed the fame Day, the following, the third, and the fourth,
" if the Patient's Strength is not too much exhaufted." Some
Phyficians, in the Days of *Aretæus*, ufed in Vomitings of
Blood to open the Veins of the Hand; but he entirely difap-
proves of that Practice: " For, fays he, why would you rather
" open a Vein near the Fingers than in the Place where the
" Elbow bends, fince, in the latter, the Vein is larger, and
" better difpofed for an Evacuation of the Blood?" In that
Species of continued burning Fevers, called *Caufus*, from
a *Greek* Word which fignifies *to burn*, our Author alfo orders
to take away a great deal of Blood, though at different times,
and during feveral Days. We muft likewife obferve, that
he imagined Fevers of this Kind to proceed from a Phlegmon
or Inflammation, properly fo called, of the Trunk of the *Vena
Cava*, or that of the great Artery. But what is furprifing is,
that the People of his Age imagined, that Patients labouring
under that Species of Fever called *Caufus* predicted future
Events; and that they talked or carried on Correfpondences
with the Dead. *Aretæus* feems to have been convinced of this
himfelf, fince he endeavours to account for it by faying, that
the Heat of the Fever having confumed the thicker and more
grofs Parts of the Humours, the Soul is by that means render'd
more pure, and enabled to fee things it did not formerly perceive. This Opinion feems to have been originally broached
by fome weak and fuperftitious Trifler, who liftened to the

incoherent Reveries of Patients of this Kind, and endeavoured to find out a Senfe and Meaning in them. In acute Pains, and Inflammations of the Kidneys caufed by the Stone, *Arètæus* prefcribed the taking away a great Quantity of Blood, in order to relax the Paffage in which the Stone was lodged, and allay the Inflammation of the Parts, which, he faid, *were compreffed or bound up with a kind of Ligature, which could not be refolved by any other Means than by evacuating the Veins.*

Aretæus did not confine Venefection to the Arm alone ; for he ordered Bleeding in the Forehead, for fuch as laboured under violent Head-achs, and took about nine Ounces of Blood from that Part, having firft blooded the Patient in the Arms.

For the fame Diforder he prefcribed Bleeding in the Veins, that are fituated in the Infide of the Nofe, by means of certain Inftruments, one of which he calls καλεισάδιον, and the other σοϛύνη. If none of thofe Inftruments can be had, he orders the Barrel of a Goofe's Quill, cut at one End like the Teeth of a Saw, to be paffed into the Noftrils almoft as far as the *Os Ethmoides*, and to be moved in fuch a manner with the Hands, as to procure a Difcharge of Blood. In an *Elephantiafis*, of which he gives a very exact Defcription, he orders Venefection in both Arms, and both Feet, in one and the fame Day.

Aretæus in his Practice made ufe of Vomits, for which Purpofe he fometimes recommends the bulbous Part of a Species of *Narciffus* ; but confided more in the Efficacy of *White Hellebore*, of which he talks in this Strain : " *White Hellebore,*
" fays he, not only excites Vomitings, but is alfo the moft
" efficacious and powerful of all purgative Medicines, not with
" regard to the Quantity and Variety of the Excrements of
" which it occafions a Difcharge ; for in the Difeafe called
" *Cholera,* the Excrements come away in the fame manner :
" Neither is its Efficacy owing to the Efforts it occafions, or
" the Violence with which it excites Vomitings, fince Nau-
" feas, and Sailing on the Sea, operate with ftill greater Vio-
" lence ; but its Excellence is owing to a particular Virtue
" which cannot be fufficiently admired, fince, even in the
" Cafes where it purges very little, it neverthelefs cures the
" Patients who ufe it. Befides, in Difeafes of long ftanding,
" when other Medicines have proved too weak, it is the only
" one which operates with Effect. In a word, white Helle-
" bore refembles Fire ; for what Fire produces by burning or
" inflaming, white Hellebore produces more effectually, by
" penetrating into all the Parts of the human Body. It ren-
" ders Refpiration eafy to thofe who breathe with Difficulty ;
" it reftores a frefh Colour to thofe who were pale, and Fat-
" nefs to thofe who were lean and extenuated. "

The Manner in which *Aretæus* us'd *Cantharides*, ought not to be forgot. The Abettors of the Methodic Sect, and even moft of the antient Phyficians ufed Medicines, to which they gave the Name of *Metafyncritical*, in order to draw Humours from the Centre to the Circumference of the Body ; for this Purpose they employ'd *Muftard*, or the Plant called the *deadly Carrot*. This was alfo a Part of *Aretæus*'s Practice ; but he likewife ufed Cantharides, in order to attract more powerfully, and raife Blifters on the Skin, which might be full of an acrid and hot Water, and might, in due time, difcharge themfelves, to the no fmall Relief of the Patient. This Species of Remedy is in our Days call'd a *Veficatory* ; and I cannot find, that before his Time this Remedy was ufed by any of the Phyficians, or, at leaft, that Cantharides were employ'd for that Purpofe by any except *Archigenes*, who was of the fame Sect with *Aretæus*, and in all Probability liv'd fome time before him.

The Knowledge the Antients had of the Effects produced by Cantharides on the urinary Ducts, was probably the Reafon why they look'd upon that Infect or Fly as very venomous, and a Species of Poifon, which prevented their ufing them as a Medicine, except on fome particular Occafions. Thus, according to *Galen*, " they were mix'd with thofe Plaifters which were " defign'd for making diftemper'd Nails fall off ; and the Pow-" der of Cantharides was ufed in Medicines againft the Le-" profy and Itch, and in the Preparations defign'd for con-" fuming and rotting the Flefh. He adds, that Cantharides " were us'd internally, in order to provoke a Difcharge of " Urine ; but that great Precaution, both with regard to the " Quantity and Method of Preparation, was abfolutely necef-" fary, left they fhould prove hurtful. "

Aretæus, in Epilepfies, propofes Frictions of the Head with Cantharides ; and when treating of the Head-ach, he alfo mentions thofe Remedies which excite Blifters on the Skin, tho' in that Paffage he does not fpecify Cantharides. But as *Archigenes* employ'd them on thefe Occafions, 'tis not improbable but *Aretæus* might do the fame.

Archigenes is by *Aetius* reprefented as fpeaking in this manner : " We ufe, fays he, a Cataplafm, into whofe Compo-" fition Cantharides enter, and which produces wonderful " Effects, provided the little Ulcers it excites remain fuffici-" ently long open, and run fufficiently freely. But the Bladder " in the mean time muft be guarded and defended by the Ufe of " Milk, both internally and externally. "

Aretæus was no lefs remarkable for his fingular Modefty, than for the Extent of his Skill and Knowledge : Of this we have a remarkable Inftance, in what he fays concerning a particular Species of Dropfy, of which other Phyficians have made no Mention. " There is, fays he, a Species of Dropfy form'd by " a great Number of Bladders full of Water, and lodg'd in the " Place where the Dropfy Afcites has its Seat [that is, in the " lower Belly]. Each of thefe Veffels is very full ; and if " we pierce the lower Belly with an Inftrument proper for that " Purpofe, the firft of thefe Bladders which occurs difcharges

133

" its Contents, but afterwards contracts itself; and if we
" want, that more Water should be discharged, we must pass
" the Instrument deeper [*in order to pierce others of the Blad-*
" *ders*]. Some, says he, affirm, that these Bladders proceed
" from the Intestines; but for this I have not the Testimony of
" my own Eyes, and consequently can say nothing concern-
" ing it. "

Aretæus gives also an Account of another Disease, of a no less
singular and uncommon Nature. " There is, says he, a Spe-
" cies of Madness, in which the Patients, prompted by a Prin-
" ciple of Superstition, tear their Bodies, and cut their Flesh,
" imagining that by these means they render themselves dearer
" to the Gods they serve, and that these Gods exacted such
" Things at their Hands. This Species of Madness only takes
" Place with regard to this Opinion, or religious Sentiment,
" and the Patients are sensible enough in other respects : They
" are roused or restored to themselves by the Sound of the Flute,
" or other Amusements, or by being made drunk, or by Peo-
" ples making Remonstrances to them. This is a divine Fury,
" and, when the Patients are freed from it, they are of a gay
" and chearful Humour, believing themselves to be initiated in
" the Service of the particular God under whose Influence it
" was pretended they were. Besides, they are pale and ghastly,
" and their Bodies remain for a long time weaken'd by the
" Wounds they have inflicted on themselves. "

As this is not a proper Occasion for entering upon the Ana-
tomy of *Aretæus*, I shall only take Notice of one Instance of his
Conduct in this particular, which is, that he generally begins his
Chapters by a short Anatomical Description of the Parts whose
Disorders he intends to treat of in the Sequel of the Chapter.

Thus it appears, that *Aretæus* was a very exact and skilful Pra-
ctitioner, and his Remedies powerful and well-chosen, tho' at the
same time it must be own'd, that his Reasoning on Points of
Theory was sometimes none of the most conclusive : However,
as it does not appear, that it had any great Influence on his Practice, his Success, as a Physician, was not on that account the
less considerable.

It now remains, that we fix the particular Time at which
Aretæus liv'd; a Point which no one has hitherto clear'd up in a
satisfactory manner. Some Authors will have him to be after
Galen, and others will have him to be much more antient. The
Opinion of the former is supported on this, that *Galen* does
not quote *Aretæus*. But besides this Circumstance of our not
having all the Works of *Galen*, it may be answer'd, That it
is not possible he should quote all the Physicians who liv'd before
him. It was sufficient, that he mention'd the principal Men of
each Sect, and spoke, for Instance, of *Athenæus* and *Archigenes*,
who were the first and most celebrated of the Pneumatic Sect :
Besides, *Galen* might have possibly not cited *Aretæus*, because
they might have both liv'd at one and the same Time; so that
the Argument drawn from *Galen*'s Silence, with regard to *Are*

tæus, proves nothing either one way or the other.

Voſſius, who is among the Number of thoſe who believe *Aretæus* much more antient, ſupports his Conjecture upon this Circumſtance alone, That this Phyſician wrote in the *Ionic Dialect*, which, according to that learned Critic, was in Diſuſe as well as the *Doric*, long before the *Cæſars*; theſe two Dialects being never us'd, except when *Greece* flouriſh'd. But in this laſt Aſſertion, *Voſſius* is miſtaken, as Mr. *Menage* [*in Amœnitatibus Juris*] proves by one of the Books of *Arrian*, intituled *Indica*, which is written in the *Ionic* Dialect, and by two other Books written in the ſame Dialect; the one by an Author call'd *Cephalio* or *Cephalo*, who liv'd under *Adrian* as well as *Arrian*, and who is quoted by *Suidas*; the other by one *Dionyſius Mileſius*, contemporary with *Philoſtratus*, who liv'd under *Severus*, and who is alſo quoted by *Suidas*.

Theſe are Facts which cannot be contradicted; and beſides, we need only look into *Aretæus* himſelf, to be convinced, that he is not ſo antient. This, in all Probability, *Voſſius* had not done with that Leiſure and Attention he ought to have us'd on ſuch an Occaſion. If he had, he would have ſeen, that this Phyſician, far from living before the *Cæſars*, could not have liv'd at ſooneſt till under *Nero*. To be convinced of this, he had no more to do than caſt his Eyes upon thoſe Paſſages, in which *Aretæus* [*De Curat. Diuturnor. Lib.* 1. *Cap.* 5. & *ibid. Lib.* 2. *Cap.* 5.] talks of the Antidote compos'd of Vipers; ſince 'tis well known, that this Antidote is the Invention of *Andromachus* a Phyſician of *Nero*'s: *Aretæus*, in the above cited Paſſages, alſo makes mention of the *Antidote of Mithridates*, by which 'tis plain, that he liv'd after that King, and conſequently cannot have preceded the firſt Emperors; which ſingle Circumſtance is of itſelf ſufficient to deſtroy the Conjecture of *Voſſius*. I ſhall not here mention the Compoſitions of *Philon*, *Byſtinus*, and *Symphon*, which *Aretæus* likewiſe recommends, becauſe the Times in which theſe Phyſicians liv'd are uncertain.

From all theſe Circumſtances we conclude, that the preciſe Time in which *Aretæus* liv'd, cannot be determin'd, tho' the Knowledge we have of his Sect proves, that he could not live till after *Athenæus*, who is ſuppoſed to be contemporary with *Pliny*, who liv'd under *Veſpaſian*. We alſo know, that *Aretæus* wrote before *Paulus Ægineta* and *Aëtius*, becauſe theſe two Authors quote him. But from all this we cannot infer the preciſe Time in which *Aretæus* liv'd, becauſe the two laſt-mention'd Authors did not live till upwards of two Ages after *Pliny*: Neither can we certainly determine whether *Galen* or *Aretæus* wrote firſt. All we can lay hold of as certain is, that they both liv'd in the Interval between *Pliny*, and *Paulus Ægineta*, and *Aetius*; but this Interval is ſo long, that we cannot pretend to come very near the preciſe Time. It is not impoſſible, as we obſerv'd before, but *Aretæus* and *Galen* may have been Contemporaries; and it may likewiſe have happen'd, that the one follow'd a great many Years after the other.

Thus far *Le Clerc*. *Wigan* concludes, that *Aretæus* liv'd after the Beginning of *Nero*'s Reign, and before that of *Domitian*'s.

EDITIONS of ARETÆUS.

Junius Paulus Craſſus publiſh'd a *Latin* Tranſlation of *Aretæus* in 4to. *Venetiis*, 1552.

Jacobus Goupilus firſt publiſh'd *Aretæus* in *Greek*, and added five Chapters, which were wanting in the Tranſlation of *Craſſus*. This was accurately and correctly printed by *Turnebus* at *Paris*, 1554. in 8vo.

In 1554. alſo, at *Paris*, the *Latin* Verſion of *Craſſus* was reprinted by G. *Morelius*, and *J. Puteanus*, with Annotations, and the five Chapters which were omitted in the Verſion of *Craſſus*, by an anonymous Author, who is ſuppos'd to be *Goupilus*.

In 1567. *H. Stevens* publiſh'd the laſt-mention'd Tranſlation amongſt the *Medicæ Artis Principes*.

Petrus Perna publiſh'd the Verſion of *Craſſus*, together with the five Books which before were wanting, tranſlated by the ſame *Craſſus*. *Braſil*, 1581. 4to.

Georgius Heniſchius publiſh'd an Edition of *Aretæus* in *Greek* and *Latin*, *Auguſtæ Vindelicorum*, 1603.

Dr. *John Wigan* publiſh'd a pompous and accurate Edition of this Author, in *Greek* and *Latin*, Fol. *Oxon.* 1723.

Menage, *Le Clerc*, and *Wigan*, take notice of a Commentary of *Aretæus* written by Mr. *Petit*, a Phyſician at *Paris*; and ſeem to regret its not being publiſh'd.

It appears by *Boerhaave*'s Preface to the *Leyden* Edition of *Aretæus*, that he found means to procure the Manuſcript from which theſe Commentaries are printed in the Edition abovemention'd. It is intituled.

Aretæi Cappadocis de Cauſis & Signis acutorum & diuturnorum Morborum Libri Quatuor, de curatione acutorum & diuturnorum Morborum Libri Quatuor, cum Commentariis integris Petri Petiti Medici Pariſienſis, atque Clariſſimi Joannis Wigani doctis & laborioſis notis, & celeberrimi Mattairii opuſculis in eundem, tandemque eruditiſſimi atque celebratiſſimi Danielis Wilhelmi Trilleri Obſervationibus & Emendatis. Editionem curavit Hermannus Boerhaave, Lugd. Bat. 1735.

ASCLEPIADES.

Though the Deſcendants of *Æſculapius* were called the *Aſclepiadæ*, that is, the Children of *Aſclepius*, which is the *Greek* Name of *Æſculapius*; yet there was a Phyſician of the Name of *Aſclepiades*, who was not of that Family.

This Phyſician was in great Reputation at *Rome*, during the Life of *Mithridates*, that is, towards the Middle of the Thirty-ninth Century, according to the Teſtimony of *Pliny*, from

136

which I conclude, that this Author contradicts himself, when he says, in the same Chapter, that Phyfic was not known in *Rome*, till after *Pompey's* Victory over *Mithridates*. *Archagathus*, a *Greek* Phyfician, came to *Rome* about an hundred Years before; where, on his firft Appearance, he was well received; but his Profeffion was afterwards brought into Difgrace. Now in all Probability, this *Afclepiades* was one of the firft who reeftablifhed its Character and Reputation. This Phyfician [according to *Pliny, Lib.* 26. *Cap.* 3.] was a Native of *Prufa* in *Bithynia*, but happened at laft to fettle in *Rome*, in Imitation of a great many other *Greeks*, who had now begun to eftablifh themfelves in this Capital of the World, hoping there to acquire greater Riches than in their own Country. Upon his firft Appearance in *Rome*, he taught Rhetoric; but not finding his Expectations anfwered by that Profeffion, he refolved to try whether that of Phyfician would not be more fortunate to him; and though, according to *Pliny*, he had at that time no Knowledge of the Bufinefs, yet he imagined, that by the Brightnefs of his Genius, he fhould foon furmount the Difadvantages arifing from his not having been regularly bred to Medicine.

The Method this Phyfician ufed to eftablifh his Character was, to run directly counter to the Practice of *Archagathus*, who had been condemned for his Cruelty; and to decry not only his Method, but alfo a great Part of the Medicines daily recommended by other Phyficians. The Practice of *Afclepiades* confifted principally, [according to *Pliny, Lib.* 26. *Cap.* 3.] in throwing the Patient into a Sweat, by means of warm Coverings, or by expofing him to the Heat of the Fire, or the Rays of the Sun. *Afclepiades* alfo condemned the antient Manner of curing Quinfeys by thrufting an Inftrument forcibly down the Throat, in order to clear the Paffage. But of all other things, he made the higheft Remonftrances againft Vomits, which, in thefe Days, were frequently ufed; and even againft Purgatives, which he looked upon as hurtful to the Stomach.

At the fame time that *Afclepiades* condemned and decried the above Medicines, he fubftituted in their room very mild ones, faying, *Tuto, celeriter & jucunde, id Votum eft:* But adds *Celfus, Lib.* 3. *Cap.* 4. *Sed fere periculofa effe nimia & Feftinatio & Voluptas folet.* It were to be wifhed, that Difeafes could be cured furely, foon, and agreeably; but Attempts to cure too fuddenly, or by means of too agreeable Medicines, are generally attended with Danger.

The fuperftitious Methods of curing Difeafes, or the Magical Remedies, of which, before the Arrival of *Afclepiades*, they were fo fond, which *Cato* himfelf had on fome Occafions ufed, but which were beginning to be in Difcredit, contributed not a little to the favourable and ready Reception of this new Phyfic of *Afclepiades*. This Obfervation *Pliny* makes in the Beginning of his twenty-fixth Book, where he ufes thefe Words: *The Vanity of Magic was a Circumftance of more Ufe to him than any thing elfe.* One *Doringius*, a *German* Author,

de Medicina &: Medicis, not adverting that these Words of
Pliny had a Relation to what he had said in the Beginning of
the foregoing Chapter, explains this Passage, as if *Pliny* had
intended to say, that *Asclepiades had, in a particular manner,
used Magic in his Practice of Physic,* which is quite the Re-
verse of what *Pliny* thought, and inconsistent with the Character of *Asclepiades,* who was an *Epicurean.*

" 'Till the Days of *Asclepiades,* says *Pliny,* Antiquity stood
" it well out. In vain did *Herophilus* advance his refined Spe-
" culations; neither he, nor any of a like Character, were
" followed universally; and considerable Remains of antient
" Physic as yet supported themselves, with all the Authority
" they had ever acquired. But this second *Æsculapius,* having
" reduced all the Learning of a Physician to the Knowledge
" or Investigation of the Causes of Diseases, Physic, which
" at first was an Art founded on Experience, became *con-*
" *jectural,* and entirely changed its Face."

What easily gained a Party to *Asclepiades,* to the Prejudice
of antient Physic, and made People relish his Reasoning, was,
his using very mild and gentle Remedies, which *Pliny* reduces
to five: Abstinence from Food; Abstinence from Wine on
certain Occasions; Frictions; Walking; and Gestation. As
People saw, that they could easily submit themselves to these,
they judged the Physic of *Asclepiades* so much the better for its
being easily practised. Besides, being very eloquent, and a
great Philosopher, he attracted the Esteem almost of all Mankind, and was looked on as one sent from Heaven.

Pliny adds, that this Physician had the Art of gaining the
Affections of People by certain Stratagems peculiar to himself; such as promising his Patients Wine, and actually giving
them some on proper Occasions, and allowing them to drink
cold Water, in order to refresh themselves. And as he had
been among the first who used this Remedy, he took a certain
Pleasure in being called Δοσίψυχρὸς, or *The Giver of cold Water.*
Wine, in the mean time, contributed no less to the Establishment of his Reputation. *Apuleius* says, that *Asclepiades* was
the first of the Physicians, who prescribed Wine for the Relief
of his Patients; and the same Author afterwards tells a Story
of a Man being restored to Life by *Asclepiades,* after he was
thought dead, and ready to be interred. He does not indeed
mention his using Wine upon that Occasion; but from what
he had before said, one may infer, that the Miracle was
wrought by means of that Liquor, though the Author ascribes
the Recovery of the Man to certain Medicines which *Asclepiades*
gave him.

This Physician also contrived, almost every Day, some new
Invention to please and humour his Patients: He ordered them
to be laid in pensile Beds, which were a Species of Cradles
shaked, in order to lull the Patients to sleep, or mitigate their
Pains. He also invented an hundred new Sorts of Baths, some

of which were penfile.

This is, according to *Pliny*, the Character of *Afclepiades* ; but as that Author is fufpected of Partiality in characterifing, we fhall inquire what Sentiments others entertained concerning this Phyfician.

We find then, that almoft all the Antients give a favourable Character of *Afclepiades* : *Apuleius* ftyles him *The Prince*, or *Firft of Phyficians*, after *Hippocrates*. He is alfo by *Scribonius Largus* [in *Epiftol. ad Galliftum*] called, *A very great Author in Phyfic*. And *Sextus Empiricus, Adverfus Mathematicos, Lib.* 7. calls him *A Phyfician inferior to none. Celfus* alfo had him in great Efteem. Another Proof of the great Reputation he had acquired, was his being defired by *Mithridates* to affume the Character of his Phyfician. But a Circumftance of all others the moft advantageous to his Character is, his having been the Phyfician and intimate Friend of *Cicero*, as he himfelf teftifies, [*De Oratore, Lib.* 1.] and at the fame time feems to pay a great Deference to his Eloquence, which proves that this Phyfician did not quit the Profeffion of Rhetorician for want of a Capacity.

Galen, who declares himfelf againft the Practice of *Afclepiades*, yet owns him to be very eloquent, but upbraids him with being a Sophift, and having a Practice of contradicting every one he had any thing to do with. *Cælius Aurelianus, Acutor. Lib.* 1. *Cap.* 15. charges him with the fame Fault. When *Afclepiades*, fays he, was called to a Patient who had another Phyfician, he condemned all the Medicines that Phyfician had ordered, and approved of others which he had not mentioned, as if the fame Medicines, which, when ordered by others, were noxious, became fafe and falutary, when prefcribed by him. The Author laft quoted, draws this Confequence from a Paffage in one of the Books of *Afclepiades*, where, in fpeaking of the Cure of a Phrenfy, he fays, that if a Perfon labouring under that Diftemper fhould fall into his Hands, before having come through thofe of any other Phyfician, or ufed any other Medicine, that in that Cafe he would ufe external Applications of ftrong-fcented Subftances, fuch as Caftor, Hogs-fenel, Rue, and Vinegar, or the Liquor in which thefe Subftances had been infufed ; and that he would afterwards order him a Clyfter to relieve the obftructed Parts ; but, faid he, if another Phyfician has before dealt with the Patient, all Cataplafms, Oils, and ftrong-fcented Medicines, muft be difcharged in the very Beginning of the Cure, and the Patient muft be removed from a dark Place to a clear and open Light. 'Tis poffible, *Afclepiades* might not have followed this Practice from a Principle of Envy or Contradiction, as *Cælius Aurelianus* infinuates, but from a quite different Motive. As the fame Difeafe may fometimes be cured by different Methods, he might poffibly believe, that Succefs, on fome Occafions, might attend a Change of the Method of Cure, from what it was in the Infancy of the Difeafe, or the paffing from the Ufe of cold to hot Medicines, and from hot to cold. As a Proof, that *Afclepiades* entertained this Notion, he calls the Cure here mentioned, bold and extraordinary, not to be undertaken but in defperate Cafes.

Pieces of Practice like this undoubtedly made People who were ignorant of the true Principle upon which *Afclepiades* acted, conclude, that he was an errant Quack. This is the Idea which *Pliny* feems to entertain of this famous Phyfician, in what he has hitherto advanced concerning him ; and we can have no Reafon to doubt, that this was his real Sentiment, if we confider the finifhing Stroke of thefe Encomiums, which he pretends to beftow upon him [in *Lib.* 7. *Cap.* 37.]. " *Afclepiades*, fays he, having bid a Defiance to " Fortune, by faying, he confented not to be efteemed a Phy-" fician, if ever he was attacked by any Difeafe whatever, " remained victorious in this Point ; for he died in an extreme " old Age, and that by an accidental Fall from a Stair-cafe. " It is not probable, that a Man of fo philofophical a Turn as *Afclepiades* was, would have talked in fo ridiculous and foolifh a manner.

We fhould be better able to form a Judgment of the Sentiments of *Afclepiades*, if his Writings had reached our Hands ; but they are loft, as well as a great many other valuable Pieces of Antiquity, which would have undoubtedly given us Satisfaction with regard to a great many things, of which we muft now be contented to remain ignorant. Tho' *Afclepiades* might not, poffibly, have been a Model for the Direction of Practice, yet there would have been a certain Pleafure in reading his Works, fince 'tis to be prefumed they were beautifully written ; and if they had not been a Standard for Phyficians, they would have, at leaft, proved an Amufement for Philofophers, and ferved to illuftrate the Doctrines of *Epicurus*, *Lucretius*, and *Democritus*. As the Reputation of this *Afclepiades* was very great, both during his Life, and after his Death, fo he had a great Number of Difciples and Followers.

Among other antient Authors, who wrote on the Compofition of Medicines, there were two called *Afclepiades* ; but both different from the *Afclepiades* above-mentioned ; for they are both quoted by *Galen* ; and that Author obferves, that they both lived after *Andromachus*, who was Phyfician to *Nero*.

The *Afclepiades* moft frequently quoted by *Galen*, and whom he ordinarily calls by the fingle Name of *Afclepiades*, was more particularly diftinguifhed by the Surname of *Pharmacion*, as *Galen* informs us ; and this Surname denoted the principal Bufinefs of this Phyfician, which was the Compofition of Medicines, by the *Greeks* called *Pharmaca*.

This *Afclepiades*, whom the learned Mr. *Di Capoa* confounds with the firft-mentioned *Afclepiades*, wrote ten Books, five upon Medicines to be ufed externally ; and five other upon fuch as were to be ufed internally. *Galen* fays, he wrote very well, and ranks him among the beft Authors who had handled that Subject. He even praises him in a particular manner, for his Exactness in describing the *Modus Faciendi*, or the precise Method one ought to take in making the Compositions he described. He also commends him for his Exactness in determining the Qualities of these Medicines, and the particular Manner in which they were to be used. The following is an Example of the Exactness of *Asclepiades*, and of the Advantages attending it:

The PLAISTER of ASCLEPIADES for CHIRONIAN ULCERS, and others of difficult Cure.

" Take of Verdigrise, one Ounce; of Wax, half a Pound;
" of the Resin of the Larch-tree, [*Venice* Turpentine]
" half an Ounce. The Wax and Resin must be melted;
" and after pounding the Verdigrise, add it to them; then
" stir the Whole. "

The way of using it is this: Spread a little of this Plaister upon as much Leather as will cover the Ulcer; place round it some Medicine for preventing Inflammation, and let your Plaister lie on for three Days. Then wash the Part affected gently; wash also and soften the old Plaister, and apply it again to the Ulcer; continue this Method every three Days till the Cicatrix is formed.

Galen, who gives us an Account of this Method, after approving of it, tries to account for its Success, by a certain Relation the Plaister acquires to the Body of the Patient, by means of its long Stay upon the Ulcer. But this may be the more rationally accounted for in another way, which is, that by rarely raising the Plaister, or allowing it to remain on the Ulcer for three Days, the Cicatrix has more Time to form itself, and the Flesh is more commodiously nourished, because the Ulcer is by that means less frequently exposed to the Air, which, by introducing some foreign Substance into the Wound, breaks the Fibres which began to unite themselves, and form Flesh and Skin. Besides, the Motion excited in the Ulcer, or Part affected, by the taking away, and again applying, the Plaister, interrupts the Formation of the Cicatrix, by breaking and putting out of Order the Fibres, which, in such a Case, are very tender. In short, the renewing the Plaister, for the same Reason, retards the Cicatrix, because a fresh Plaister has always more Force and Penetration, than one which has been used before. There are a great many more *Asclepiades*; but as their Characters have nothing very remarkable in them, and as the Accounts we have of them, are involved in such Obscurity and Perplexity, as can never be surmounted by the greatest Industry, we shall say no more concerning them. *Le Clerc.*

ORIBASIUS. This Phyfician, though commonly reckon'd a *Sardian*, was born at *Pergamus*, and bred up, together with *Magnus* and *Ionicus*, in the School of *Zeno* the *Cyprian*, who taught then, I fuppofe, at *Sardis*; though afterwards he removed to *Alexandria*, where he became a famous Profeffor. *Eunapius*, who had good Knowledge in Phyfic, and is the fame Perfon, probably, to whom the four Books *de Euporiftis*, &c. are infcribed, reprefents *Oribafius* as the greateft Scholar and Phyfician of his Time, and a very engaging and agreeable Man in Converfation. He defcribes him as no lefs confiderable in his Intereft, than in his Learning. According to his Account, he contributed very much to the Advancement of *Julian* to the Empire, who, in Return, made him Quæftor of *Conftantinople*; and who, as appears by one of his Letters, had an entire Confidence in him. In the fucceeding Emperor's Time, through the Envy of his Enemies, he fell into Difgrace, had all his Eftate confifcated, was banifhed, and delivered into the Hands of Barbarians; among whom, in a little Time, by his Courage and Skill, he gained fo much Love and Reverence, that they, feeing what great Cures he perform'd, adored him as a God. At laft, he was recal'd by the *Roman* Emperor, and flourifhed in Reputation and Riches, at the very Time when *Eunapius* wrote this Account, which muft be near the Year 400; for *Eunapius* was then, as it fhould feem, in the firft Rank of Phyficians, and was but twelve Years old at the Death of *Julian*, in 363.

Oribafius wrote feventy (according to *Photius*) or (according to *Suidas*) feventy-two Books of Collections, which he compiled not only from *Galen*, but from all the preceding Phyficians, and his own Experience, at the Defire of *Julian*; the fifteen firft of which are only remaining, and two others, treating of Anatomy, which are called by the Tranflator, *Rafarius*, the twenty-fourth and twenty-fifth of that Collection. Afterwards he made na Epitome of this great Work, and reduced it into nine Books, for the Ufe of his Son *Euftathius*. He alfo wrote four Books about Medicines and Diftempers, as was before obferved, to his Friend *Eunapius*. Befides thefe, *Photius* gives an Account of two other Pieces, extant in his Time; one confifting of four, the other of feven Books, which were merely an Epitome of *Galen's* Works, and dedicated likewife to *Julian*. *Paulus* mentions this Epitome; but it is now loft, as are fome other Tracts, which *Suidas* takes notice of. There are feveral Receipts of *Oribafius*, quoted by *Aetius*. The Commentaries upon the Aphorifms of *Hippocrates*, put out by *Guinther* under his Name, are, without doubt, fpurious.

Dr. *Freind* obferves, that *Oribafius* ufes a great Variety of Expreffion, of which we have this Advantage, that often one Place, or one Author, explains another; and this Juftice ought to be done to him, that he helps us the better to underftand feveral Paffages in *Galen*, relating both to Anatomy and Medicine. He was, by all Accounts, a Man, not only of a great Genius, but of great Bufinefs and Experience: And, accordingly, if we perufe him with Attention, which, I believe, has fcarce ever been done by thofe who have pretended to give a Character of him, we fhall find very juft Rules of Practice laid down in feveral Cafes.

The Works of *Oribafius*, mentioned by *Photius* and *Suidas*, are;

1. *Four Books of Medicinal Commentaries*, contracted from the Writings of *Galen*, by the Command of the Emperor *Julian* the Apoftate, and dedicated to him. Thefe are mention'd by *Oribafius* himfelf, in the Preface to his *Synopfis*, but have long fince been loft; at leaft, were never publifhed.

2. His *Synopfis*, compiled not only from *Galen*, but other Phyficians, by Command of the fame Emperor, who had approved the former Work. Of this *Synopfis*, which confifted, according to *Suidas*, of feventy-two Books, there are extant the firft fifteen, with the twenty-fourth and twenty-fifth, tranflated into *Latin* by *J. Baptifta Rafarius*, a Phyfician of *Novara*, with *Oribafius's* Preface to the Emperor *Julian*.

3. A *Synopfis* of the former feventy-two Books, written after the Death of the Emperor *Julian* to his Son *Euftathius*, and contracted into nine Books. This, alfo, is extant in the *Latin* Verfion of *Rafarius* above-mention'd.

4. *Euporifta*, or Medicines eafily prepared, in four Books, to *Eunapius*; or, as it is in fome Copies, according to *Photius*, to *Eugenius*; but the Copies, made ufe of by both the *Latin* Tranflators, read *Eunapius*. For thefe four Books were tranflated into *Latin* by an *Anonymus*, and publifhed by *J. Sichard*, together with *Cœlius Aurelianus*, of chronic Difeafes at *Bafil*, 1529. in Folio, (not printed in Octavo, as it is faid in *Merklin's Lindenius renovatus*) and afterwards printed with a new Verfion, by the above-mention'd *Rafarius*, together with the reft of the Works of *Oribafius*, at *Bafil*, 1557. Octavo; and alfo with the *Medici Principes* of *Henricus Stephanus*, at *Paris*, 1567. Fol. There was an old Manufcript *Latin* Verfion of *Oribafius's* Works, very different from that publifhed, both with refpect to the Order of the Books, and the Matters treated of in them, in the Library of *René Moreau*, as we are told by *Labbeus*, *Bibl. novæ Manuscrip. p. 214.* There is, alfo, an Epitome of the Writings of *Oribafius*, compofed at the Command of the Emperor *Conftantinus Porphyrogenitus*, by one *Theophanes*, in *Greek*, which lies, fomewhere or other, in Manufcript, in the Emperor's Library. *Fabricii Bibl. Vol. 9. p. 451.*

To this Account we are to add, that the fix firft Chapters of the fifth Book of the *Synopfis*, and the fourteenth Chapter of the firft Book to *Eunapius*, on Waters, in *Greek*; together with the Fragments of *Galen*, *Rufus*, *Diocles*, and *Athenæus*, on the fame Subject, with a *Latin* Verfion of them feparately fubjoined, was publifhed at *Rome*, *An.* 1543. Quarto, by the Care of *Aug. Ricius*, a Phyfician of *Luca*. In the Catalogue of the *Bibliotheca Bigotiana*, are mentioned fome of *Oribafius's Medicinal Collections*, printed in *Greek*, at *Paris*, 1556. in Octavo, which Book I never yet had the Fortune to fee. *Antonius Verderius*, in his *Bibliotheca Gallica*, fays, that he faw a *French* Manufcript Verfion of *Oribafius's* Works, by one *Adam de la Vallée.* The two Books of Chirurgical Bandages and Machines, from *Heracles,* or *Heraclides Ephefius, Soranus,* and *Heliodorus,* are alfo extant in *Latin,* tranflated by *Vietus Vidius,* in *Gefner's* Collection of Chirurgical Treatifes, publifhed at *Zurich,* 1555. in Folio. The *Synopfis Medica,* to his Son *Euftathius,* in nine Books, tranflated by *Rafarius,* was printed at *Venice,* 1555. Octavo; and all that remains extant of the feventy Books of his *Synopfis,* tranflated, alfo, by *Rafarius,* printed at *Paris,* 1555. Octavo. The Commentaries on the Aphorifms of *Hippocrates,* printed firft in *Latin,* by *J. Guinter Andernac,* at *Paris,* 1553. Octavo, for *Simon Colinæus,* were reprinted at *Bafil,* 1535. at *Venice,* 1553. and at *Padua,* 1658. Octavo. It is eafier to fay, they were not written by *Oribafius,* than to affign their true Author; but they feem to be compofed in *Latin,* and by fome Chriftian. The Fragment of *Oribafius,* concerning Diet proper for all Seafons of the Year, was publifhed in *Latin,* with *Plinius Valerianus,* by *Albanus Torinus,* at *Bafil,* 1528. Folio. *Oribafius of Simples,* with four Books of the *Euporifta* of *Octavius Horatianus;* the Phyfics of *Hildegardes;* the Regimen of *Theodorus* the Naturalift; and *Æfculapius* of the Caufes, Defcription, and Cure of Difeafes, were printed at *Strasburg,* 1533, and 1544. Folio. Extracts from the Works of *Oribafius,* on Waters and Baths, tranflated by *Aug. Gadaldinus,* of *Modena,* were printed in a *Venetian* Work, which treated of Baths, *An.* 1553. Folio. *Fabricii Bibliotheca Græca.*

RUYSCH (FREDERIC)

Was born at the *Hague,* on the 23d of *March* 1638. He was the Son of *Henry Ruyfch,* Secretary to the States General, and to *Anne Van Berghem.* The Family from which he was defcended, was originally of *Amfterdam,* where from the Year 1365. his Anceftors had, without Interruption, bore the moft honourable Offices of the State, till the Year 1576. when a War happening betwixt *Spain* and the States, occafioned a Revolution in the Fortunes of the Family.

But Mr. *Ruyfch* is far lefs confiderable on account of his Extraction, than his diftinguifhed Merit as a Member of Society, a Phyfician, and an Anatomift.

This Gentleman, from his Infancy, devoted himfelf to Phyfic, and began his firft Refearches with the Materia Medica. The Virtues of Plants, the Structures of Animals, the Qualities of Mineral Bodies, Chymical Operations, and Anatomical Diffections, were the Objects that firft ftruck his Fancy, and called for his improving Hand. He was none of thofe fuperficial Inquirers, who either thro' Prejudice, or Indolence, reft fatisfied on this Side of Truth; for he had ftripp'd his Mind of all thofe unreafonable Attachments, which are inconfiftent with the Temper of a Philofopher; and acquir'd fuch an indefatigable Turn, that his hardeft Labours in Purfuit of Truth became his higheſt Pleaſures, and his only Recreations. And even when he married in 1661. it was in a great meaſure with a View to render his Circumſtances eaſy, that he might purſue Truth to the greater Advantage.

About this Time, the famous *Bilſius*, being appointed Profeſſor of Anatomy at *Louvain*, made his Appearance at *Leyden*. This Phyſician bore it with a high Hand; undervalued thoſe who were juſtly eſteemed the Ornaments of their Profeſſion, and, with all the haughty and ſupercilious Airs of a *Spaniard*, extoll'd his own Diſcoveries above theirs, eſpecially with regard to the Motion of the Bile, the Lymph, the Chyle, and Fat. But as Inſolence ſeldom fails to be chaſtiſed by real Merit, ſo *Deleboe, Sylvius*, and *Van Horne*, then Profeſſors at *Leyden*, had a mind to check the exorbitant Vanity of this Stranger. For this Purpoſe they courted the Aſſiſtance of young *Ruyſch*, who had been more converſant in minute and delicate Diſſections, than they themſelves. Mr. *Ruyſch* came from the *Hague*, where he lived, to *Leyden*, by Night, preſented them with Materials proper for encountering and confounding *Bilſius*, and returned home directly, to make new Preparations for the ſame Purpoſe.

After having thus fought in Secret againſt *Bilſius*, the two Combatants came at laſt to an open Engagement; for *Sylvius* and *Van Horne*, to whom he had lent ſo ſeaſonable an Aid, had no mind to aſſume the Reſults of his Induſtry as their own Diſcoveries. Mr. *Ruyſch*, in the Courſe of the Debate, had aſſerted, that the Reſiſtance he felt upon blowing into the Lymphatic Veſſels, gave him Reaſon to believe, that theſe Veſſels were furniſhed with Valves, which, he confeſs'd, he had not ſeen, but ſaid, he was not ſingular in his Judgment as to that Particular. *Bilſius* not only denied the Fact with uncommon Aſſurance, but even teſtified a ſtrong Contempt for thoſe who pronounced the thing poſſible. *Ruyſch*, who was bleſs'd at once with a clear Head, and an accurate Hand, actually found thoſe Valves, to the Number of above two thouſand, and gave inconteſtable Proofs of the Reality of that, which he had before advanced as a Conjecture only. This Accident gave unſpeakable Satisfaction to Men of Senſe, who always rejoice to ſee Merit triumph over Arrogance and Ignorance. *Bilſius*, who regarded Reputation more than Truth, promiſed to yield the Point as ſoon as he himſelf ſhould ſee theſe Valves: But when the Evidence of his own Senſes reduced him to a Neceſſity of acknowledging their Exiſtence, he added Arrogance to his Ignorance, and confidently aſſerted, That he knew theſe Valves, tho', for Reaſons of his own, he did not chuſe to diſcover his Knowledge in that Particular. *Ruyſch*, in a ſmall Volume, publiſhed in 1665. which, by the way, was the firſt Work of his that ſaw the Light, has given us a particular Account of this Conteſt; in which *Bilſius*, inſenſible of the

Advantages of Modefty, renders himfelf famous, or rather in-famous, for the oppofite Vice.

Mr. *Ruyfch* was in the Year 1664. created Doctor of Phyfic in the Univerfity of *Leyden*, and had very foon after a very fine, but at the fame time, a very deplorable Opportunity put into his Hand, of convincing the World with how great Juftice that Dignity was conferr'd upon him; for the Plague began to rage all over *Holland*, and Mr. *Ruyfch* had the Care of thofe that were infected at the *Hague*, committed to him. This Office, whatever Share of Glory it might procure him, was nevertheless far from being defirable in itfelf: But it is no uncommon thing for Merit and Learning to fubject their Pof-feffors to Inconveniencies, from which the Ignorant and Illite-rate are entirely free.

But his principal Bufinefs, and the Employment which en-grofs'd moft of his Time, confifted in carrying Anatomy to that noble Height of Perfection, at which it had never before arrived. Anatomifts had long contented themfelves with fuch Inftruments as were judged neceffary for feparating thofe folid Parts, the particular Structures, or mutual Relations, of which they wanted to difcover. *Regnier de Graaf,* an entire Friend, and an intimate Acquaintance of Mr. *Ruyfch's*, was the firft, who, in order to difcover the Motion of the Blood in the Veffels, and the feveral Roads it took during Life, invented a new Spe-cies of Syringe, by means of which, he filled the Veffels with fome high-coloured Subftance, which fufficiently difcovered the Road taken by itfelf, and confequently that taken by the Blood in a living Animal. This Invention was at firft approved of; but the Practice was foon after difcountenanced, becaufe the Matter gradually made its Efcape, and left the Preparation good for nothing.

John Swammerdam endeavour'd to fupply this Defect in *de Graaf's* Invention, and happily concluded, that there was a Neceffity for ufing fome warm Subftance, which becoming gradually cool, in Proportion as it flow'd into the Veffels, might at laft, when arrived at their Extremities, lofe the Nature of a Fluid, and by that means become capable of being retain'd in the Veffels. This, no doubt, required a very nice and difcern-ing Judgment, both with regard to the particular Quality of the injected Matter, its due Degree of Heat, and the juft Momen-tum, or Proportion of Force, with which it was to be impell'd. By this means *Swammerdam* firft render'd the Capillary Arteries and Veins of the Face vifible; but he did not long perfift either in the Ufe or Improvement of his new Invention; for an Ex-cefs of Piety foon after fpoil'd his Anatomical Turn, and made him look upon fuch Practices as impious. The devout *Swam-merdam* was, no doubt, afraid of rivalling the Almighty in the Perfection of his Works; but his Fears in this Particular were ill-founded. But as the moft exalted Degrees of Devotion rare-ly extinguifh all the Motions of Vanity in the Heart, fo *Swam-merdam* was tempted to communicate his Invention to his Friend

Mr. *Ruyfch*; who was not only fond of it, but afterwards practifed it without any Fear of offending God.

Upon his firft Trial he found the Experiment to hold, and, in all Probability, produced a more perfect Preparation than *Swammerdam* himfelf had done: The Veffels were fo curioufly injected, that the remoteft Parts of their Ramifications, which were as flender as the Threads of a Spider's Web, became vifible; and, which is ftill more furprifing, fometimes were not fo, without the Affiftance of a Microfcope. What then muft the Nature of that Subftance be, which is, at once, fo fine as to enter the imperceptible Cavities of thefe Canals, and at the fame time is poffefs'd of fuch a Quality as to indurate itfelf there?

Small Ramifications were difcover'd, which were neither obfervable in the Living, nor to be feen in diffecting the Bodies of thofe that were newly dead.

The entire Carcafes of Children were injected; for the Operation was thought very difficult, if not entirely impoffible, in Adults. Neverthelefs, in the Year 1666. by the Order of the States General, he undertook to inject the Body of the *Englifh* Admiral *Bercley*, who was killed on the 11th of *June*, in the Engagement betwixt the *Dutch* and *Englifh* Fleets: This Body, tho' very much fpoil'd, before *Ruyfch* put his artful Hand to it, was yet fent over to *England* as curioufly prepar'd as if it had been the frefh Carcafe of an Infant; and the States General beftow'd a Recompence which was at once proportion'd to their Grandeur, and the Artift's Merit.

Every Part of the injected Matter preferved its Confiftence, its Softnefs, its Flexibility, and even gradually acquir'd frefh Degrees of Beauty with Time.

Carcafes, with all their Vifcera, were fo far from having a naufeous Smell, that they even acquired an agreeable one, and that too in Cafes where they fmell'd very ftrong before the Operation.

Every Part was preferved from Corruption by Mr. *Ruyfch's* Secret. A long Life afforded him the Pleafure of feeing, that his Preparations had, till then, been Proof againft the Shocks of Time, and even put it out of his Power to afcertain the Length of their future Duration. All his injected Carcafes glow with the ftriking Luftre and Bloom of Youth; they appear like fo many living Perfons faft afleep; and their pliant Limbs pronounce them ready to walk: In fhort, the Mummies of Mr. *Ruyfch* were fo many Prolongations of Life; whereas thofe of the antient *Egyptians* were only fo many deplorable Continuations of Death.

When Mr. *Ruyfch* began to produce fuch furprifing Preparations, abundance of incredulous People pronounced the Facts impoffible; but he gently oppofed their Obftinacy with thefe Words, *Come and fee*. His Mufeum was not only always open, but richly ftor'd, if I may be allow'd the Expreffion, with liv-

147

ing Monuments of his Art, who were ready to pronounce in his Favour, and give the Lye to his Oppofers. A certain Profeffor of Phyfic very ferioufly advifed him to renounce thefe Novelties, and tread in the fafe and beaten Paths of his Predeceffors; but as Mr. *Ruyfch* defpifed the foolifh Admonition, the Doctor redoubled his Letters, and at laft told him, that his Conduct in that Particular was inconfiftent with the Dignity of a Profeffor; to all which *Ruyfch* replied, in a noble and truly Laconic Strain, COME AND SEE.

Mr. *Ruyfch* conceals the Name of the Profeffor, who was fo friendly, or rather fo foolifh, as to give him this Advice; but he has acted otherwife with regard to Meff. *Raw* and *Bidloo*, who were both famous for their Skill in Anatomy, and had openly declared themfelves againft him; efpecially *Bidloo*, who confidently boafted, that he knew the Secret of preparing and preferving Carcafes better than Mr. *Ruyfch* himfelf. Upon this Mr. *Ruyfch* afked him, Why, fince it was fo, he had not difcover'd fuch and fuch Parts? And why he had mangled his Anatomical Tables, by committing notorious Blunders? which he fpecifies and points out to him. Thus far the Conduct of Mr. *Ruyfch* was unexceptionable, and hitherto he appears with all the Advantages that a good Caufe, and Candour in Difpute, can give him: But foon after he lofes the Temper of the Philofopher, and the Gentleman; for, upon *Bidloo's* calling him a *fubtile Butcher*, he falls into perfonal Reflections, and fays, that he rather chofe to be *Lanio fubtilis, quam Leno famofus,* " a " fubtile Butcher, than an infamous Pimp." The Play of Words, and the imagin'd Antithefis, betwixt *Lanio* and *Leno*, may poffibly have induced him to tranfgrefs fo far againft the Laws of Decorum, and true Politenefs: But what had he to do with the Morals of his Antagonift, when the Extent of his Knowledge was the Subject in Difpute? True it is, that *Bidloo's* Conduct was fo provoking as not to admit of an Apology, when he call'd him *miferrimus Anatomicorum,* " the moft " miferable of Anatomifts." But the Extravagance of one Man ought never to unhinge the Mind, or authorize the Rafhnefs of another.

But tho' Falfhood may fometimes have refolute Champions, yet Truth never fails to come off victorious in the End. The Beauties of Mr. *Ruyfch's* Art were feen, and the Advantages of it felt. The Subjects neceffary for Diffection, which the reigning Superftition of the Times render'd very few, foon fpoil'd in the Hands of other Anatomifts; but Mr. *Ruyfch* had the incomparable Secret of rendering them of eternal Ufe. Diffections were now no more accompanied with thofe Ideas of Horror and Averfion, which before had proved fatal to Anatomy: Hitherto Anatomical Demonftrations could only be made in the Winter Seafon, but now the moft fcorching Heats were equally proper for that Purpofe, provided the Days were equally clear.

Now, confidering the Advantages of this Secret, and the

ſtrong Curioſity that naturally reign'd in Mr. *Ruyſch*'s Breaſt, we need not be ſurpriſed, if he diſcover'd things that had eſcap'd the Notice of all that went before him, ſuch as the Bronchial Artery, which ſupplies the Lungs with Nouriſhment, before unknown to the moſt minute and accurate Anatomiſts; the Perioſteum of the *Oſſicula Auditus*, which were formerly look'd upon as bare; the Ligaments belonging to the Articulations of theſe *Oſſicula*. He likewiſe found, that the Cortical Subſtance of the Brain was not glandular, as was commonly thought, but conſiſted of Veſſels infinitely ramified; and that ſeveral other Parts, which were falſly look'd upon as glandular Bodies, were no more than ſo many Congeries of ſimple Veſſels, which only differ'd in their reſpective Lengths, their Diameters, the Curves they deſcribed in their Courſes, and the Diſtance of their Extremities *from the Heart*, Circumſtances on which the various Secretions or Filtrations depend. *Frederic Schreiber*, who writes his Life, when talking of the Extent and Importance of his Diſcoveries, ſeems animated with a kind of Enthuſiaſm, and expoſtulates the Matter in this warm Strain: *Who before him obſerv'd the Veſſels running thro' the Tunica Aranea, the Patella, and the Acetabulum Coxæ? Who diſcovered the Veſſels diffuſed in that Membrane which ſurrounds the Marrow of the Vertebræ? Or who found out the Veſſels in the Meditullium of the Bones, and in thoſe Tendons and Ligaments which are deſtitute of Blood?*

Ruyſch, beſides his Practice of Phyſic, and Profeſſorſhip of Anatomy, was, by the Burgo-maſters of *Amſterdam*, appointed Inſpector of all thoſe who were either kill'd or wounded in perſonal Quarrels. He was likewiſe, for the general Good of the State, created *Maſter of the Midwives*, who, generally ſpeaking, were very ignorant of their Buſineſs; they were too haſty, for Inſtance, in forcibly extracting the *Placenta*, when it came not away; and were often raſh enough to tear it, which frequently cauſed unavoidable Death: But Mr. *Ruyſch* taught them, tho' with ſome Difficulty, to wait with Patience for its coming away, or at leaſt only gently to aſſiſt its Expulſion; becauſe an orbicular Muſcle, which he had diſcover'd in the Bottom of the Uterus, naturally thruſt it outwards, and was even ſufficient to expel it intirely.

At laſt *Ruyſch* was created Profeſſor of Botany, in the Exerciſe of which Office he gave the ſame Scope to his natural Genius, which he had formerly done in Anatomy. The extenſive Commerce of the *Hollanders* ſupplied him with many exotic Plants, which he diſſected and preſerved with incomparable Art: He dexterouſly ſeparated their Veſſels from their Parenchyma, and by that means plainly ſhew'd wherein their Life conſiſted. Thus Animals and Plants were equally embalmed, and equally ſure of Duration, by the ſkilful Touches of Mr. *Ruyſch*'s Hand.

His Muſeum, or Repoſitory of Curioſities, contain'd ſuch a rich and magnificent Variety, that one would have rather taken it for the Collection of a King than the Property of a private Man : But not satisfied with the Store and Variety it afforded, he would beautify the Scene, and join an additional Lustre to the curious Prospect. He mingled Groves of Plants, and Designs of Shell-work, with Skeletons, and dismember'd Limbs ; and, that nothing might be wanting, he animated, if I may so speak, the Whole with apposite Inscriptions, taken from the best *Latin* Poets. This Museum was the Admiration of Foreigners : Generals of Armies, Embassadors, Electors, and even Princes and Kings, were fond to visit it. When *Peter* the First, of *Muscovy*, came into *Holland*, in the Year 1695. he was so struck with the View of Mr. *Ruysch*'s Collection, that he tenderly kiss'd a little Infant, which sparkled with all the Graces of real Life, and seem'd to smile upon him. On his second coming over, in 1714. he purchased the Collection, and sent it to *Petersburg* ; but the Industry and long Experience of Mr. *Ruysch* soon supplied him with another.

In the Year 1727. he was chosen Honorary Associate of the University of *Petersburg*. He was also a Member of the *Leopoldine* Academy in *Germany*, and of the Royal Society in *England*.

He died of a Fever in the 92d Year of his Age in 1731. and had this peculiar Advantage over most other learned Men, that he lived to see all that Opposition, which Malice and Envy made to his Merit, hush'd and laid to sleep.

Mr. *Ruysch* has publish'd a great many Pieces at different Times, which were at last reduced into a very confused and unaccountable Order, and printed, as the Title-page of the first Volume imports, *Amstelodami, apud Jassonio-Waesbergios,* 1737.

There is a Peculiarity in one Work of Mr. *Ruysch*'s, which deserves to be taken Notice of, which is, that some Passages of his *Adversaria*, which he publish'd in *Latin* and *Dutch*, are left untranslated into the *Dutch*. What influenced this Author in this Case, every one must judge for himself, from the Nature of the Passages untranslated.

We hope the vast Variety both of entertaining and instructing Incidents that occur in the Life of Mr. *Ruysch*, will sufficiently apologize for its Length, and account for our spending more Time upon him than some of the rest.

LIFE *of* TOURNEFORT.

When we observe any Man distinguish'd by a superior Knowledge, or Skill of any Kind, it is natural for the Mind to be solicitous and inquisitive about the several Circumstances which have concurr'd to render him thus conspicuous. When, for Example, we hear of *Alexander*'s Skill in all the Arts of War and Conqueſt; when we view the brave and heroic Actions of *Cæſar*, *Scipio*, and *Hannibal*; when we reflect on the extenſive Knowledge, the deep Reſearches, the accurate Deductions, and important Diſcoveries, of the incomparable Sir *Iſaac Newton*; our Minds are indeed ſtruck with certain Ideas of Grandeur and Surprize; but a ſecret Diſſatisfaction is ſtill lodged in the Breaſt, and the labouring Soul remains, as it were, on the Rack, till we know ſomething more about the Men, and have diſcovered their Turns of Mind, and the ſeveral Steps by which they have gradually advanced to Honour, and paved their Way to immortal Glory. Now, as Mr. *Tournefort* is univerſally allow'd to have carried Botany to a higher Degree of Perfection than any who went before him, by enriching it with numberleſs Diſcoveries, advancing it into a Science, giving it an Air of Accuracy, which it formerly wanted, and ſmoothing all its Difficulties; it muſt, of courſe, be an uncommon Satisfaction to become acquainted with the Education, the Genius, the Diſpoſition, and Studies of this celebrated Botaniſt.

Joſeph Pitton de Tournefort, then, was born at *Aix* in *Provence*, on the Fifth of *June*, 1656. He was the Son of *Peter Pitton de Tournefort*, and *Aimare de Fagone*, the Deſcendant of a Family of Note in *Paris*.

Their Son *Joſeph* was put to the Jeſuits College in *Aix*, with a View to learn *Latin*, as the other Scholars did. But, as ſoon as he ſaw any Plants, the Bent of his Genius diſcover'd the future *Botaniſt*; for he was anxious and uneaſy, till he found out their Names: He carefully remark'd their Differences, and ſometimes neglected to attend his Claſs, in order to diſcover Herbs, and ſtudy Nature in the Fields, inſtead of the Language of the antient *Romans* in the Schools. And as it is no uncommon thing to ſee ſome People excel in an Art, by the mere Force of Genius, without the Aſſiſtance of a Maſter, this young Botaniſt had, by his own Induſtry, acquir'd a Knowledge of all the Plants produced about the Village where he was born.

When he enter'd upon his Philoſcphical Studies, he diſcover'd no great Reliſh for what was taught him. In Diſquiſitions of this Kind, inſtead of Nature, with whoſe Contemplation he was ſo highly charm'd, he found only vague and abſtracted Ideas, which decoy and amuſe the Mind, without enriching it with any thing that is ſolid and ſatisfactory. During this Period of his Education, he accidentally found the Philoſophy of *Deſcartes* in his Father's Study, and ſoon diſcover'd it to be the very Thing he wanted. Tho' he could only read the Productions of this Author privately, and, as it were, by Stealth, yet he read them with Care and Accuracy; and the Father, who violently oppoſed ſo uſeful a Study, afforded him, without being ſenſible of it, the Advantages of a fine Education.

As he deſtin'd his young Son for the Church, he made him apply to the Study of Theology, and for that Purpoſe enter'd him in a Seminary. But in his Breaſt *Botany* could not endure a Rival, and the Bent of Nature was too powerful to be balanced by any Views, or overcome by any Byas.

Notwithſtanding the Intentions of the Father, the Son muſt neceſſarily ſee Plants ; and for this End he retired to proſecute his darling Study, either to a curious Garden belonging to an Apothecary of *Aix*, or to the neighbouring Fields, or to the Summits of Rocks, which had been inacceſſible to others, fir'd with a leſs ardent Deſire of Knowledge than he. Either by Stratagem or Preſents he found Acceſs to the moſt cloſe and conceal'd Places, where he ſuſpected there were Plants not to be found elſewhere ; and when theſe Means fail'd, ſo undaunted was his Reſolution, that he would make his Way into them in an unlawful and clandeſtine manner, rather than not ſatisfy his Curioſity ; and, indeed, for an Attempt of this Kind, he once ran a Riſque of being ſtoned to Death by the Country-people, who took him for a Robber. But what Hardſhips will not a Mind, actuated with an ardent and inſatiable Deſire of Knowledge, undergo for Satisfaction ?

Mr. *Tournefort* was almoſt as fond of Anatomy and Chymiſtry as he was of *Botany* ; and at laſt Phyſic and Medicine ſo engroſs'd his Affections, as to gain a thorough Victory over his Inclinations to Theology, which he now reſolved to drop. In this Reſolution he was encouraged by an Uncle on his Father's Side, who was a Phyſician of great Skill and Reputation. Soon after, the Death of his Father in the Year 1677. left him at his own Diſpoſal, and Maſter of his own Inclinations.

He quickly improv'd this Revolution made in his Fortune by his Father's Death; for, in the Year 1678. he carefully ranged the Mountains of *Dauphiny* and *Savoy*, from which he return'd with a large Quantity of beautiful dry Plants, which were the Beginnings of his celebrated Collection of Herbs.

Botany is not an unactive and ſedentary Science, which, like Geometry or Hiſtory, may be acquir'd by a recluſe and ſolitary Application within the narrow Precincts of a Cloſet; or which, like Chymiſtry, Anatomy, and Aſtronomy, demands only ſuch Operations as may be perform'd without a great deal of Exerciſe, Toil, and Fatigue. The Botaniſt muſt wander thro' Mountains and Valleys, range the gloomy Foreſts, climb the ſteepeſt Rocks, and expoſe his Life on the Brinks of hideous Precipices, in Queſt of Knowledge. The only Books capable of inſtructing us thoroughly in this Science, are, with a rich and liberal Hand, ſcatter'd up and down the whole Surface of our Globe. But Reſolution and Patience, Induſtry, and Contempt of Danger, are neceſſary to collect and gather them. This is the Reaſon why ſo few excel in this Science : That Degree of Ardor which is capable of rendering a Man ſkill'd in other Branches of Literature, is by no means ſufficient for forming a complete Botaniſt ; who, beſides the inſurmountable Ardour of his Soul, muſt have an uncommon Strength of Body, and Soundneſs of Conſtitution, to bear him up under the Toils and Fatigues he muſt neceſſarily undergo. Now, Mr. *Tourne-fort* had a briſk laborious Turn of Mind, a robuſt Conſtitution, and a large Fund of natural Gaiety in his Temper, to ſupport him under his painful Reſearches ; ſo that both the Make of his Body, and the Turn of his Mind, joined their united Force to qualify him for a Botaniſt.

In the Year 1679. he went from *Aix* to *Montpelier*, where he perfected himſelf in Anatomy and Phyſic. The Garden of Plants eſtabliſhed in that City by *Henry* IV. rich as it was, could not ſatisfy his unbounded Curioſity. He ranſack'd all the Tracts of Ground within more than ten Leagues of *Mont-pelier*, and, as a Recompence for his Labour, found Plants un-known and unheard of by the Inhabitants of the Country themſelves. But as he thought himſelf ſtill confin'd within too narrow Bounds, he quitted *Montpelier*, and went to *Bar-celona*, in the Month of *April* 1681. He proceeded as far as *St. John*, in the Mountains of *Catalonia*, where he was follow'd about from one Place to another by the Phyſicians and young Students of Medicine, to whom he deſcrib'd the ſeveral Plants which occur'd ; and one would have thought, that in this he reſembled the antient *Gymnoſophiſts*, who led their Diſciples in-to the Deſarts, in order to inſtruct them.

The *Pyrenean* Mountains, which were now not far of, could not fail tempting him to make them a Viſit; and before he under-took this Expedition, he knew that in theſe forbidding Soli-tudes he ſhould have no other Suſtenance than what the moſt auſtere Hermits are accuſtom'd to ; and that the miſerable In-habitants, who could ſupply him with it, were not more nu-merous than the Robbers, to whoſe Violence he was ſure to be expoſed. Accordingly he was ſeveral times robb'd by the *Spaniſh* Miquelets. In order to prevent the like Misfortunes for the future, he bethought himſelf of a happy Expedient ; for he incloſed his Money in ſome Bread, which was ſo black and hard, that the *Spaniſh* Robbers, undoubtedly the greedieſt in the World, did not think it a Prize worth the taking. The unconquerable Force of his Inclinations ſur-mounted all Difficulties ; and the dreadful and almoſt inaccef-ſible Rocks, which ſurrounded him on every Side, had to him transform'd themſelves into a magnificent and well ſtor'd Li-brary, where he paſſed the Time with Pleaſure, and fully ſatif-fied the Ardour of his Soul. One Day a ruinous Cottage, in which he had the Misfortune to lodge, fell all on a ſudden ; and Mr. *Tournefort*, being buried under its Ruins for two Hours, had undoubtedly periſh'd, had not a ſeaſonable Relief been afforded him. But this Accident, which of itſelf would have ſtruck Terror into the Braveſt, did not interrupt the Courſe of his painful Inquiries, nor fright him from a Scene in other reſpects ſo agreeable to him.

At laſt, in 1681. he return'd to *Montpelier*, and thence to *Aix*, the Place of his Nativity, where he ranged in his Repofitory of Herbs all the Plants he had collected about *Provence*, *Languedoc*, *Dauphiné*, and *Catalonia*, and thofe lefs known produc'd by the *Alps* and *Pyrenean* Mountains; and whatever People, whofe Minds and Studies are turned another way, may think, the Pleafure of feeing fuch a large Number of Plants, entire, well preferved, and difpofed in a beautiful Order in large Paper Books, was a fufficient Recompence for the Toil and Pains they had coft him.

The Fame of Mr. *Tournefort*'s extenfive Skill in Botany had by this time reach'd the Ears of Mr. *Fagon*, who was himfelf a curious Botanift, and firft Phyfician to the Queen; and, as he had receiv'd a very advantageous Character of *Tournefort* from all Quarters, he conceived a Defign of alluring him to *Paris*, the general Rendezvous of all the Literati of *France*. For this Purpofe he apply'd to Madam *de Venelle*, who was fecond Governefs to the Daughters of the Royal Family, and who was intimately acquainted with Mr. *Tournefort*, and his Relations. Accordingly, this Lady, prevailing on him to come to *Paris* in 1683. prefented him to Mr. *Fagon*, who, before that Year was expir'd, procured him the Place of Profeffor of *Botany* in the Royal Garden of Plants eftablifhed at *Paris* by *Lewis* XIII. for the Inftruction of the young Students of Phyfic.

This Employment did not hinder him from undertaking feveral other Voyages; for he went back to *Spain*, and thence to *Portugal*, where he faw new Plants, but found no Botanifts. When he was in *Andalufia*, a Country fertile in Silk-worms, he endeavour'd to find out the Truth of the Reports fo long ago handed down to us, concerning the Amours between the Male and Female of thefe Infects; but he could difcover nothing certain with regard to this Particular; and thefe Amours, if real, are hitherto myfterious. He travelled alfo into *Holland* and *England*, where he had an Opportunity of feeing Plants he had never feen before, and converfing with fome of the greateft Botanifts of the Age, whofe Efteem and Friendfhip he eafily gained. As a Proof of this, no other Circumftance is neceffary to be mentioned, than his being folicited by friendly and importunate Letters from Mr. *Herman*, the celebrated Profeffor of Botany at *Leyden*, to accept of his Place, which, as he was too old and infirm, he offer'd to refign in favour of Mr. *Tournefort*. This Gentleman's Zeal for the Intereft of Botany made him choofe *Tournefort* for his Succeffor, tho' he was not only a Foreigner, but belonged to a Nation then engaged in an open War with his own Country. Mr. *Herman* promifed him four thoufand Livres in the Name of the States-General, and gave him Reafon to think, that his Salary would be augmented, when his Merit came to be better known. But tho' the Income affixed to his Place in the Royal Garden was very moderate, yet the Love of his Country prevailed upon him to reject fo fair and advantageous an Offer. He also gave his Friends an additional Reason for his Refusal of this Place, which was, that the Sciences were at least in as flourishing a State at *Paris*, as in any other Part of the World ; for the native Country of a genuine and unfeign'd Virtuoso would be but a dull and uncomfortable Scene to him, if the Sciences did not thrive and prosper in it.

His Country did not prove ungrateful for the Love he had shewn her in rejecting Preferment in a distant Nation; for, in the Year 1691. the Academy of Sciences being put under the Inspection of the Abbé *Bignon*, that Gentleman exerted his Authority, two Months after he was vested with it, by taking into the Society Mr. *Tournefort*, and Mr. *Homberg*, neither of whom he was personally acquainted with, tho' he was no Stranger to the Fame and Reputation they justly acquir'd.

In 1694. Mr. *Tournefort*'s Elements of Botany, or the Method of knowing Plants, was printed at the *Louvre*, in three Octavo Volumes. This Work, tho' generally approv'd, found some very powerful Opposers ; for its Author was attack'd upon some Points by Mr. *Ray*, a celebrated Botanist in *England*. And in 1697. Mr. *Tournefort* answered the Charge in a *Latin* Dissertation addressed to Mr. *Sherrard*, another *English* Gentleman, who was a skilful Botanist. The Dispute on both Sides was manag'd not only without Bitterness, but even with a certain graceful Air of Decorum and Politeness, which bespeak Candour, and a Love of Truth. It may possibly be said, that the Subject was not of sufficient Moment to ruffle their Spirits, or inflame their Passions, since the Question in Dispute was only, whether the Flowers and the Fruits of Plants were sufficient to establish their Genuses ; and whether certain Plants were of one Genus, or another. But this Circumstance does not at all detract from the Merit of these two Disputants, since 'tis natural for Men, especially of Learning, to become enrag'd at each other, on account of the most arrant Trifles in the World. Mr. *Tournefort*, in a Work posterior to the Date of this Dispute, passes very high Encomiums on Mr. *Ray* and his System ; an exalted Instance of a candid and generous Soul !

Mr. *Tournefort* was created Doctor of Physic, of the Faculty of *Paris*; and in 1698. he published his *History of the Plants which grow about* Paris, *together with an Account of their Use in Medicine*. Now we cannot readily suppose, that the Man who had made his Way to the Summits of the *Alps* and *Pyrenean* Mountains, in Quest of Plants, could be a careless Observer of those produced about *Paris*, where he had resided so long. Botany would only be an Amusement to the Mind, if it had no Relation to Medicine ; but Mr. *Tournefort* has in this Work shewn the Subserviency of the former to the latter.

We may also reckon among the Works of *Tournefort*, a

Book, or at leaſt a Part of a Book, which yet was not printed by his Orders, intituled *Schola Botanica, ſive Catalogus Plantarum, quas ab aliquot annis in Horto Regio Pariſienſi, ſtudioſis indigitavit Vir clariſſimus Joſephus Pitton de Tournefort Doctor Medicus; ut & Pauli Hermanni Paradiſi Batavi, Prodromus, &c. Amſtelædami,* 1699. One Mr. *Simon Wharton,* an *Engliſh* Gentleman, who had ſtudied Botany for three Years in the Royal Garden under Mr. *Tournefort,* made this Catalogue of the Plants he had there an Opportunity of ſeeing.

As *the Elements of Botany* had met with as favourable a Reception as the Author himſelf could have deſired, in the Year 1700. for the ſake of Foreigners he gave a *Latin* Tranſlation of it conſiderably inlarg'd, under the Title of *Inſtitutiones Rei Herbariæ,* in three Quarto Volumes; the firſt of which contains the Names of the Plants diſtributed according to his own Syſtem, and the other two their Figures very accurately engraved. To this Work he has prefixed a large Preface or Introduction to Botany, containing the Principles of his own Syſtem, ingeniouſly and ſolidly eſtabliſh'd, and a Hiſtory of Botany and Botaniſts collected with uncommon Care, and written with an agreeable Spirit. We may eaſily ſuppoſe, that he employ'd himſelf with Pleaſure on every Object that had the leaſt relation to Botany, his darling Study.

But his Curioſity was not entirely confin'd to Plants and Herbs; for he was almoſt equally fond of all other natural Rarities, ſuch as figur'd Stones, uncommon Marcaſites, extraordinary Petrifications, and Cryſtallizations, and Shells of all Kinds. 'Tis true, he looked upon Stones to be Plants which vegetated, and had their reſpective Seeds; he was alſo pretty much inclin'd to extend this Syſtem to Metals, and ſeem'd inclin'd to transform every Object into the Nature of Vegetables, the Contemplation of which afforded him ſo ecſtatic and ſuperlative a Delight. He alſo collected the Garments, the Arms and Inſtruments of diſtant Nations, another Species of Curioſities, which, tho' not coming immediately from the Hands of Nature, may yet afford proper Occaſions of philoſophizing to thoſe happy Souls who have the Art of doing it. With all theſe Objects he had furniſhed a Muſeum, ſurpriſingly magnificent for a private Perſon, and juſtly famous in *Paris.* The Virtuoſi valued it at forty-five or fifty thouſand Livres, an Expence which would have thrown an indelible Blot on the Character of a Philoſopher, had the Money been laid but for leſs curious and inſtructive Purpoſes. This Circumſtance however proves, that Mr. *Tournefort,* conſidering his moderate Incomes, could not lay out a great deal of Money on other Pleaſures more frivolous in themſelves, tho' more eagerly purſued by the Generality of Mankind.

When we take a View of the fine Qualities of which Mr. *Tournefort* was poſſeſſed, we muſt readily perceive how well he was calculated for making an excellent Traveller; by which Word I do not mean the Man who runs from one Country to another, without knowing what he is about, or entertaining the leaft Thought of rendering himfelf wifer and better; but the Man who attentively views Nature in all her Variety of Shapes, with a View to become ufeful to his fellow Creatures, and treafure up a grateful Store of Knowledge in his own Mind; fo that the faithful Accounts of the Travels of a real Philofopher may be look'd upon as facred Archives of ineftimable Value. We may therefore account it an Advantage to the Sciences, that in 1700. Mr. *Tournefort* received an Order from the King to travel into *Greece*, *Afia*, and *Africa*, not only to take a View of the Plants mention'd by the Antients, and perhaps to difcover others unknown to them, but alfo to make Obfervations upon Natural Hiftory in general, upon antient and modern Geography, and even upon the Cuftoms, the Religion, and the Commerce, of the People. He had Orders to write, as often as he had Opportunities, to Mr. *de Pontchartrain*, and to give him a Detail of his Difcoveries and Adventures. Accordingly Mr. *Tournefort*, accompanied by Mr. *Gundelſheimer*, a *German*, and an excellent Phyfician, and Mr. *Aubriet*, a fkilful Painter, went as far as the Frontiers of *Perfia*, collecting and making Obfervations on Herbs. Other Travellers convey themfelves by Sea from one Part to another, if they poffibly can; and, when that cannot be done, they take the moft beaten and patent Roads by Land. But Mr. *Tournefort* with his Affociates were as little at Sea as was poffible, difdained the common Roads, and bravely ftruck out new ones before untrod by Mortals. A Pleafure, blended with Gloom and Horror, rifes in the Mind upon reading an Account of their Defcent into the Grotto of *Antiparos*, which confifts of three or four hideous Abyffes, one after another. Mr. *Tournefort* had here the fenfible Pleafure of beholding a new Species of Garden, in which the Plants were different Shoots of Marble, as yet young and fpringing, and which, according to the Circumftances with which their Formation was accompanied, muft neceffarily vegetate. In vain did Nature endeavour to conceal the Vegetation of Stones in thefe profound and inacceffible Caverns, from fo bold and curious Virtuofi.

Africa was comprehended in the original Defign of Mr. *Tournefort's* Voyage; but the Plague, which rag'd in *Egypt*, determin'd him to return from *Smyrna* to *France* in 1702. This was the firft Accident that put a Stop to the Execution of his vaft and extenfive Defign: However, he return'd, loaded with the Spoils of the *Eaft*; for, befides the numberlefs different Obfervations he had made, he brought along with him one thoufand three hundred and fifty-fix new Species of Plants, moft of which ranged themfelves, as it were, of their own Accord, under fome one or other of the fix hundred and feventy three Genufes he had already eftablifhed; and, for all the reft, he had only twenty-five Genuſes to create, without being obliged to augment the Number of Claſſes. A Circumſtance which ſufficiently proves the Advantage and Commodiouſneſs of a Syſtem to which ſo many foreign and unexpected Plants were eaſily reducible. Of theſe he compoſed his *Corollarium Inſtitutionum Rei Herbariæ* printed in 1703.

When he return'd to *Paris*, he thought of reſuming the Practice of Phyſic, which he had ſacrificed to his *Levant* Voyage, at a time when he began to be well employed. Experience ſhews us, that in every thing depending on the Taſte of the Public, eſpecially Affairs of this Nature, Delays are dangerous. The Approbation of Men is ſomething forc'd, and ſoon comes to an End. Mr. *Tournefort* then found a Difficulty in getting into the Buſineſs he had left. Beſides, he was obliged to go through his former Exerciſes in the Royal Garden, and thoſe of the Royal College, in which he was one of the Profeſſors of Medicine. The Functions of the Academy alſo took up ſome Part of his Time ; and, beſides theſe, he wanted to reviſe and poliſh the Relation of his laſt Voyage, of which he had only the ſimple Memoirs roughly drawn up, and intelligible only by himſelf. This Multiplicity of Buſineſs put him upon ſtudying in the Night-time, a Circumſtance which ſoon broke his Health ; and, when he was in this un-comfortable State, he accidentally receiv'd a Blow on the Breaſt, which he thought would very ſoon prove mortal to him. Accordingly he languiſh'd for ſome Months, and died on the twenty-eighth of *December* 1708.

He made a laſt Will, in which he left his Muſeum of Ra-rities to the King, for the Uſe of the Literati, and his botani-cal Books to the Abbé *Bignon*. This ſecond Article was no leſs a Proof of his Love to the Sciences than the former, con-ſidering the Character of the *Abbé*.

One Volume of Mr. *Tournefort's* Travels was printed in the Author's Life-time at the *Louvre :* And the ſecond is, ſince his Death, printed from his own Manuſcript, which was found perfect and finiſhed. This Work, in which the original Form of Letters addreſſed to Mr. *de Pontchartrain* is retain'd, contains two hundred Plates of Plants, and other Antiquities, well engraved. Beſides the Branches of Knowledge, of which we have already ſhewn Mr. *Tournefort* to be poſſeſſed, he in this Work diſcovers an uncommon Degree of Learning, and a very extenſive Knowledge of antient and modern Hiſtory. But one Quality, when poſſeſſed in an eminent Degree, is often the Reaſon why we overlook others, which however, de-ſerve our Attention. *Hiſt. de l'Acad. des Sciences, A.* 1708.

A N

ACCOUNT

OF THE

LIFE

OF

John Philip Barretier,

Who was Mafter of Five LANGUAGES at
the Age of Nine YEARS.

Compiled from his Father's L E T T E R S, &c.

L O N D O N:
Printed for *J. Roberts* in *Warwick lane.* 1744,
[Price Sixpence.]

A N

ACCOUNT

OF THE

LIFE

OF

JOHN PHILIP BARRETIER,

Compiled from his Father's L E T T E R S, &c.

OHN PHILIP BARRETIER
was born at *Schwabach*, *Jan.* 19,
1720-21.

His Father was *Francis Bar-
retier*, Paſtor of the *Calviniſt* Church of
that Place, who took upon himſelf the
Care of his Education, for which he formed
a Scheme, that ſeems to be ſufficiently vindicated by its Succeſs from the
Cenſures to which new Attempts are generally
expoſed , and therefore requires a very particular Account ; for if M. *Le Fevre* thought

B   the

the Method in which he taught his Children, worthy to be communicated to the learned World, how juftly may M. *Barretier* claim the univerfal Attention of Mankind to this new Scheme that has produced fuch a ftupendous Progrefs! The Authors, who have endeavoured to teach Rules for obtaining a long Life, however they have failed in their Attempts, are univerfally confeffed to have, at leaft, the Merit of a great and noble Defign, and to have deferved Gratitude and Honour. How much more then is due to M. *Barretier*, who has fucceeded in what they have only attempted? For to prolong Life, and improve it, are nearly the fame. If to have all that Riches can purchafe is to be rich, to do all that can be done in a long Time, is to live long, and he is equally a Benefactor to Mankind, who teaches them to protract the Duration, or fhorten the Bufinefs of Life.

That there are therefore few Things more worthy our Curiofity than this Method, by which the Father affifted the Genius of the Son, every Man will be convinced, who fhall hear the early Proficiency at which it enabled him to arrive, fuch as no one has yet reached at the fame Age, and to which it is therefore probable that every advantageous Circumftance concurred.

French

French, which was the native Language of his Mother, was that which he learned firft, mixed, by living in *Germany,* with fome Words of the Language of the Country. After fome Time his Father took Care to introduce, in his Converfation with him, fome Words of *Latin,* in fuch a Manner that he might difcover the Meaning of them by the Connexion of the Sentence, or the Occafion on which they were ufed, without obferving, that he had any Intention of inftructing him, or that any new Attainment was propofed.

By this Method of Converfation, in which new Words were every Day introduced, when his Ear had been fomewhat accuftomed to the Inflections and Variations of the *Latin* Tongue, he began to attempt to fpeak like his Father, and was in a fhort Time drawn on by imperceptible Degrees to fpeak *Latin,* intermixed with any other Language.

Thus, when he was but four Years old, he fpoke, every Day, *French* to his Mother, *Latin* to his Father, and *High Dutch* to the Maid, without any Perplexity to himfelf, or any Confufion of one Language with another.

While he was thus learning Languages without Study, and almoft without perceiving that he was learning, his Father took care to teach him to read and write, of which he performed

B 2   formed

form'd one without Books, and the other without Paper; but by what Methods we are not informed. It is indeed eafy to conceive many that might be ufed, nor does it feem, with refpect to the Art of Writing, of any Importance, whether he made his firft Effays with Paper, or any other Materials, as the Operation muft be nearly the fame. Thefe Methods, whatever they were, fucceeded fo well, that he was able to read currently at the Age of three Years, and foon after was taught to write.

When he had thus learned to read, his Father put fome Books into his Hands, chiefly fuch as were filled with Pictures accompanied with Explanations. With thefe the young Student was wonderfully delighted, when he perceived, fays the Author of his Life, that they talked and reafoned like himfelf, and from that Time might be dated his wonderful Fondnefs for Books which became greater every Day.

The other Languages of which he was Mafter, he learned by a Method yet more uncommon. The only Book that he made ufe of was the Bible, which his Father laid before him in the Language he then propofed to learn, accompanied with a Tranflation, being taught by Degrees the Inflections of Nouns and Verbs. This Method, fays his
Father,

Father, made the *Latin* more familiar to him in his fourth Year than any other Language.

When he was near the End of his fixth Year, he entered upon the Study of the Old Teftament in its original Language, beginning with the Book of *Genefis*, to which his Father confined him for fix Months, after which he read curforily over the reft of the Hiftorical Books in which he found very little Difficulty, and then applied himfelf to the Study of the poetical Writers, and the Prophets, which he read over fo often, with fo clofe an Attention, and fo happy a Memory, that he could not only tranflate them without a Moment's Hefitation into *Latin* or *French*, but turn, with the fame Facility, the Tranflations into the original Language in his tenth Year.

When he was only eight Years old, he could repeat not only all the Pfalms in *Hebrew*, but all that Collection of Texts which *Henricus Opitius* has publifhed under the Title of *Biblia Parva*; this Collection he tranfcribed, and added to it a new Tranflation. He drew up likewife in 400 Pages in *Quarto*, a Dictionary of the moft rare and difficult Words of the *Hebrew* Language, in which be interfperfed a great Number of curious Remarks and critical Obfervations.

Having

Having now gained such a Degree of Skill in the *Hebrew* Language as to be able to compose in it both in Prose and Verse, he was extremely desirous of reading the *Rabbins*; and having borrowed of the neighbouring Clergy, and the Jews of *Schwabach*, all the Books with which they could supply him, he prevailed on his Father to buy him the great *Rabinical* Bible, published at *Amsterdam* in 4 *Tomes*, Folio, 1728, and read it with that Accuracy and Attention which appears by the Account of it written by him to his Favourite M. *Le Maitre*, inserted in the Beginning of the 26th Volume of the *Bibliotheque Germanique.*

These Writers were read by him, as other young Persons peruse Romances or Novels, only from a puerile Desire of Amusement; for he had so little Veneration for them, even while he studied them with most Eagerness, that he often diverted his Parents with recounting their Fables and Chimeras.

At the Age of nine Years, he not only was Master of five Languages, an Attainment in itself almost incredible, but understood, says his * Father, the holy Writers, better in their original Tongues, than in his own. If he means by this Assertion, that he knew the Sense of many Passages in the Original, which were obscure

* In a Letter which was communicated to the Author of this Account.

166

obſcure in the Tranſlation, the Account, however wonderful, may be admitted ; but if he
intends to tell his Correſpondent, that his Son
was better acquainted with the two Languages
of the Bible, than with his own, he muſt be
ſuppoſed to ſpeak hyperbolically, or to admit
that his Son had ſomewhat neglected the Study of his native Language : Or we muſt own,
that the Fondneſs of a Parent has tranſported
him into ſome natural Exaggerations.

Part of this Letter I am tempted to ſuppreſs, being unwilling to demand the Belief
of others to that which appears incredible to
myſelf; but as my Incredulity may, perhaps,
be the Product rather of Prejudice than Reaſon, as Envy may beget a Diſinclination to
admit ſo immenſe a Superiority, and as an
Account is not to be immediately cenſured as
falſe, merely becauſe it is wonderful, I ſhall
proceed to give the reſt of his Father's Relation, from his Letter of the 3d of *March*,
1729-30. He ſpeaks, continues he, *German*,
Latin and *French* equally well. He, can by
laying before him a Tranſlation, read any of
the Books of the Old or New Teſtament in
its original Language, without Heſitation or
Perplexity. He is no Stranger to Biblical
Criticiſm or Philoſophy, nor unacquainted
with antient or modern Geography, and is
qua-

qualified to support a Conversation with learned Men, who frequently visit and correspond with him.

In his eleventh Year, he not only published a learned Letter in *Latin*, but translated the Travels of *Rabbi Benjamin* from the *Hebrew* into *French*, which he illustrated with Notes, and accompanied with Differtations; a Work in which his Father, as he himself declares, could give him little Affiftance, as he did not understand the Rabbinical Dialect.

The Reafon for which his Father engaged him in this Work, was only to prevail upon him to write a fairer Hand than he had hitherto accuftomed himself to do, by giving him Hopes, that if he fhould tranflate fome little Author, and offer a fair Copy of his Verfion to fome Bookfeller, he might in Return for it, have other Books which he wanted and could not afford to purchafe.

Incited by this Expectation, he fixed upon the *Travels of Rabbi Benjamin*, as moft proper for his Purpofe, being a Book neither bulky nor common, and in one Month compleated his Tranflation, applying only one or two Hours a Day to that particular Task. In another Month, he drew up the principal Notes; and in the third, wrote fome Differtations

tations upon particular Paſſages which ſeemed to require a larger Examination.

Theſe Notes contain ſo many curious Remarks, and Enquiries out of the common Road of Learning, and afford ſo many Inſtances of Penetration, Judgment, and Accuracy, that the Reader finds in every Page ſome Reaſon to perſuade him that they cannot poſſibly be the Work of a Child, but of a Man long accuſtomed to theſe Studies, enlightened by Reflection, and dextrous, by long Practice, in the Uſe of Books. Yet, that it is the Performance of a Boy thus young, is not only proved by the Teſtimony of his Father, but by the concurrent Evidence of M. *LeMaitre*, his Aſſociate in the Church of *Schwobach*, who not only aſſerts his Claim to this Work, but affirms, that he heard him, at ſix Years of Age, explain the *Hebrew* Text as if it had been his native Language; ſo that the Fact is not to be doubted, without a Degree of Incredulity which it will not be very eaſy to defend.

This Copy was however far from being written with the Neatneſs which his Father deſired, nor did the Bookſellers, to whom it was offered, make Propoſals agreeable to the Expectation of the young Tranſlator; but after having examined the Performance in their

C   Manner, and determined to print it upon Conditions not very advantageous, returned it to be tranfcribed, that the Printers might not be embarraffed with a Copy fo difficult to read.

Barretier was now advanced to the latter End of his twelfth Year, and had made great Advances in his Studies, notwithftanding an obftinate Tumour in his left Hand, which gave him great Pain, and obliged him to a tedious and troublefome Method of Cure; and reading over his Performance, was fo far from contenting himfelf with barely tranfcribing it, that he altered the greateft Part of the Notes, new-modelled the Differtations, and augmented the Book to twice its former Bulk.

What Applaufes are due to an old Age, wafted in a fcrupulous Attention to Particles, Accents and Etymologies, may appear, fays his Father, by feeing how little Time is required to arrive at fuch an Eminence in thefe Studies as many even of thefe venerable Doctors, have not attained, for want of rational Methods and regular Application.

This Cenfure is doubtlefs juft, upon thofe who fpend too much of their Lives upon ufelefs Niceties, or who appear to labour without making any Progrefs. But as the Knowledge of Languages is neceffary, and a minute Accuracy fometimes requifite, they are by no Means to be blamed, who, in Compliance

pliance with the particular Benefit of their own Minds, make the Difficulties of dead Languages their chief Study, and arrive at Excellence proportionate to their Application, since it was to the Labour of such Men that his Son was indebted for his own Learning.

Thus he continued his Studies, neither drawn aside by Pleasures, nor discouraged by Difficulties. The greatest Obstacle to his Improvement was want of Books, with which his narrow Fortune could not liberally supply him ; so that he was obliged to borrow the greatest Part of those which his Studies required, and to return them when he had read them, without being able to consult them occasionally, or to recur to them, when his Memory should fail him.

It is observable, that neither his Diligence, unintermitted as it was, nor his Want of Books, a Want of which he was in the highest Degree sensible, ever produced in him that Asperity, which a long and recluse Life, without any Circumstance of Disquiet, frequently create. He was always gay, lively, and facetious, a Temper which contributed much to recommend his Learning, and of which some Students much superior in Age would consult their Ease, their Reputation and their Interest by copying from him.

C 2

His

171

His Father being somewhat uneasy to observe so much Time spent by him on Rabinical Trifles, thought it necessary now to recall him to the Study of the *Greek* Language, which he had of late neglected; but to which he returned with so much Ardour, that in a short Time he was able to read *Greek* with the same Facility as *French* or *Latin*.

In his twelfth Year he applied more particularly to the Study of the Fathers and Councils of the first six Centuries, and began to make a regular Collection of their Canons. He read every Author in the Original, having discovered so much Negligence or Ignorance in most Translations, that he paid no Regard to their Authority.

Soon after he undertook, at his Father's Desire, to confute a Treatise of *Samuel Crellius*, in which, under the Name of *Artemonius*, he has endeavoured to substitute in the Beginning of St *John*'s Gospel, a Reading different from that which is at present received, and less favourable to the orthodox Doctrine of the Divinity of our Saviour.

This Task was undertaken by *Barretier* with great Ardour, and prosecuted by him with suitable Application, for he not only drew up a formal Confutation of *Artemonius*, but made large Collections from the earliest Writers,

Writers, relating to the History of Herefies, which he propofed at firft to have publifhed as Preliminaries to his Book; but finding the Introduction grew at laft to a greater Bulk than the Book itfelf, he determined to print it apart.

While he was engroffed by thefe Enquiries, Accident threw a Pair of Globes into his Hands, in *Oct.* 1734. by which his Curiofity was fo much exalted, that he laid afide his *Artemonius*, and applied himfelf to Geography and Aftronomy. In ten Days he was able to folve all the Problems in the Doctrine of the Globes, and had attained Ideas fo clear and ftrong of all the Syftems, as well ancient as modern, that he began to think of making new Difcoveries; and for that Purpofe, laying afide for a Time all Searches into Antiquity, he employed his utmoft Intereft to procure Books of Aftronomy and of Mathematicks, and made fuch a Progrefs in three or four Months, that he feemed to have fpent his whole Life upon that Study; for he not only made an Aftrolabe, and drew up aftronomical Tables; but invented new Methods of Calculation, or fuch at leaft as appeared new to him, becaufe they were not mentioned in the Books which he had then an Opportunity of Reading, and it is a fufficient Proof both of

the

the Rapidity of his Progreſs, and the Extent of his Views, that in three Months after his firſt Sight of a Pair of Globes, he formed Schemes for finding the Longitude, which he ſent, in *Jan.* 1735, to the Royal Society at *London.*

His Scheme, being recommended to the Society by the Queen, was confidered by them with a Degree of Attention which, perhaps, would not have been beſtowed upon the Attempt of a Mathematician ſo young, had he not been dignified with ſo illuſtrious a Patronage. But it was ſoon found, that for want of Books, he had imagined himſelf the Inventor of Methods already in common Uſe, and that he propoſed no Means of diſcovering the Longitude, but ſuch as had been already tried and found inſufficient. Such will be very frequently the Fate of thoſe whoſe Fortune either condemns them to ſtudy, without the neceſſary Aſſiſtance from Libraries, or who, in too much Haſte, publiſh their Diſcoveries.

This Attempt exhibited, however, ſuch a Specimen of his Capacity for mathematical Learning, and ſuch a Proof of an early Proficiency, that, in 1735, the Royal Society of *Berlin* admitted him as one of their Members.

Not-

Notwithſtanding theſe Avocations and Amuſements, he publiſhed, in 1735, Anti-Artemonius, *ſeu Initium Evangelii S. Johannis Apoſtoli, adverſus iniquiſſimam* L. M. Artemonij *Neo-Photiniani Criticam vindicatum atq, illuſtratum, quâ Occaſione etiam multa alia S. Scripturæ Veterumque Loca vindicantur, et multis Antiquitatis Monumentis Lux affunditur, cui in Fine accedit Diſſertatio de Dialogis tribus* Theodoreto *vulgo tributis.* Auctore *J. P. Barreterio, SS. Theologiæ* aliarumque bonarum Artium Cultore. *Norimbergæ.* 8vo.

This Work is divided into five Parts. In the firſt of which *Barretier* proves, that the Text was always read as it now ſtands. In the Second he ſhews, that *Artemonius's* Notion of the Method by which it was changed, is groundleſs. In the Third, he examines the internal Evidence brought by *Artemonius* to prove that St *John* could not write the Words as they are now read. In the Fourth, he refutes the Opinion of *Socinus*, that St *John* ſaying, that *by the Word all Things were made,* ſpeaks of a new Creation. In the Fifth, he proves the Divinity of our Saviour from other Parts of the holy Writings, and concludes with a Paraphraſe of the firſt Verſes of St *John's* Goſpel. To the whole is added an

Eſſay

Effay to prove, that the Dialogues afcribed to *Theodoret*, are the Work of another Writer.

He had now attained fuch a Degree of Reputation, that not only the Public, but Princes, who are commonly the laft by whom Merit is diftinguifhed, began to intereft themfelves in his Succefs; for the fame Year the King of *Pruffia*, who had heard of his early Advances in Literature, on Account of a Scheme for difcovering the Longitude, which had been fent to the Royal Society of *Berlin*, and which was tranfmitted afterwards by him to *Paris* and *London*, engaged to take care of his Fortune, having received further Proofs of his Abilities at his own Court, to which he was introduced in the following Manner.

M. *Barretier*, being promoted to the Cure of the Church of *Stetin*, was obliged to travel with his Son thither from *Schwobach*, thro' *Leipfic* and *Berlin*, a Journey very agreaable to his Son, as it would furnifh him with new Opportunities of improving his Knowledge, and extending his Acquaintance among Men of Letters. For this Purpofe they ftaid fome time at *Leipfic*, and then travelled to *Hall*, where young *Barretier* fo diftinguifhed himfelf in his Converfation with the Profeffors of the Univerfity, that they offered him his Degree of Doctor in Philofophy, a Dignity correfponrefpondent to that of Mafter of Arts among us. *Barretier* drew up that Night fourteen Pofitions in Philofophy and the Mathematicks, which he fent immediately to the Prefs, and defended the next Day in a crowded Auditory, with fo much Wit, Spirit, Prefence of Thought, and Strength of Reafon, that the whole Univerfity was delighted and amaz'd; he was then admitted to his Degree, and attended by the whole Concourfe to his Lodgings, with Compliments and Acclamations.

His *Thefes*, or philofophical Pofitions, which he printed in Compliance with the Practice of that Univerfity, ran through feveral Editions in a few Weeks, and no Teftimony of Regard was wanting that could contribute to animate him in his Progrefs.

When they arrived at *Berlin*, the King ordered him to be brought into his Prefence, and was fo much pleafed with his Converfation, that he fent for him almoft every Day, during his ftay at *Berlin*; and diverted himfelf with engaging him in Converfations on a Multitude of Subjects, and in Difputes with learned Men, on all which Occafions he acquitted himfelf fo happily, that the King formed the higheft Ideas of his Capacity and future Eminence. And thinking perhaps with Reafon, that active Life was the nobleft

D   Sphere

Sphere of a great Genius, he recommended to him the Study of Modern History, the Customs of Nations, and those Parts of Learning, that are of Use in publick Transactions and civil Employments, declaring that such Abilities properly cultivated, might exalt him, in ten Years, to be the greatest Minister of State in *Europe*. *Barretier*, whether we attribute it to his Moderation or Inexperience, was not dazzled by the Prospect of such high Promotion, but answered, that he was too much pleased with Science and Quiet, to leave them for such inextricable Studies, or such harrassing Fatigues. A Resolution so unpleasing to the King, that his Father attributes to it, the Delay of those Favours which they had Hopes of receiving, the King having, as he observes, determined to employ him in the Ministry.

The Science that withheld him from complying with such flattering Proposals, was Astronomy, which was always his Favourite Study, and so much engrossed his Thoughts that he did not willingly converse on any other Subject; nor was he so well pleased with the Civilities of the greatest Persons, as with the Conversation of the Mathematicians. An Astronomical Observation was sufficient to with-hold him from

Court,

Court, or to call him away abruptly from the moſt illuſtrious Aſſemblies; none could hope to enjoy his Company long without inviting ſome Profeſſor to keep him in Temper, and engage him in Diſcourſe; nor was it poſſible, without this Expedient, to prevail upon him to ſit for his Picture.

It is not unlikely, that paternal Affection might ſuggeſt to M. *Barretier* ſome falſe Conceptions of the King's Deſigns; for he infers from the Introduction of his Son to the young Princes, and the Careſſes which he received from them, that the King intended him for their Preceptor, a Scheme, ſays he, which ſome other Reſolution happily deſtroyed.

Whatever was originally intended, and by whatever Means theſe Intentions were fruſtrated; *Barretier*, after having been treated with the higheſt Regard by the whole Royal Family, was diſmiſſed with a Preſent of two hundred Crowns, and his Father, inſtead of being fixed at *Stetin*, was made Paſtor of the *French* Church at *Hall*; a Place more commodious for Study, to which they retired; *Barretier* being recommended by the King to the Univerſity.

D 2 As

As the Scene of M. *Barretier's* Life was now changed, it feems not improper to recur to fome of the former Parts of it, and to recount fome Honours conferred upon him, which, if Diftinctions are to be rated by the Knowledge of thofe who beftow them, may be confidered as more valuable than thofe which he received from Princes.

In *June* 1731, He was initiated in the Univerfity of *Altdorft*, and at the End of the Year 1732, the Synod of the Reformed Churches, held at *Chriftian Erlang*, admitted him to be prefent at their Confultations, and, to preferve the Memory of fo extraordinary a Tranfaction, as the Reception of a Boy of eleven Years into an Ecclefiaftical Council, recorded it in a particular Article of the Acts of the Synod.

Barretier had been diftinguifhed much more early by the Margravine of *Anfpach*, who in 1726, fent for his Father and Mother to the Court, where their Son, whom they carried with them, prefented her with a Letter in *French*, and addreffed another in *Latin* to the young Prince; who afterwards, in 1743, granted him the Privilege of borrowing Books from the Libraries of *Anfpach*, together with an annual Penfion of fifty Florins, which he enjoyed for four Years.

M.

M. *Barretier* returned on the 28th of *April*, 1735, to *Hall*, where he continued the remaining Part of his Life, of which it may not be improper to give a more particular Account.

At his Settlement in the Univerſity, he determined to exert his Privileges as Maſter of Arts, and to read publick Lectures to the Students, a Deſign from which his Father could not diſſuade him, tho' he did not approve it ; ſo certainly do Honours or Preferments, too ſoon conferred, infatuate the greateſt Capacities. He publiſhed an Invitation to three Lectures, one Critical on the Book of *Job*, another on Aſtronomy, and a third upon ancient Eccleſiaſtical Hiſtory. But of this Employment he was ſoon made weary by the Petulance of his Auditors, the Fatigue which it occaſioned, and the Interruption of his Studies which it produced ; and therefore, in a Fortnight, he deſiſted wholly from his Lectures, and never afterwards reſumed them.

He then applied himſelf to the Study of the Law, almoſt againſt his own Inclination, which, however, he conquered ſo far as to become a regular Attendant on the Lectures in that Faculty, but ſpent all his other Time upon different Studies.

The

The firſt Year of his Reſidence at *Hall* was ſpent upon Natural Philoſophy and Mathematicks; and ſcarcely any Author, ancient or modern, that has treated on thoſe Parts of Learning was neglected by him, nor was he ſatisfied with the Knowledge of what had been diſcovered by others, but made new Obſervations, and drew up immenſe Calculations for his own Uſe.

He then returned to Eccleſiaſtical Hiſtory, and began to retouch his *Account of Hereſies,* which he had begun at *Schwobach*; on this Occaſion he read the Primitive Writers with great Accuracy, and formed a Project of regulating the Chronology of thoſe Ages; which produced a *Chronological Diſſertation on the Succeſſion of the Biſhops of* Rome, *from St* Peter *to* Victor; printed in *Latin* at *Utrecht,* 1740.

He afterwards was wholly abſorbed in Application to polite Literature, and read not only a Multitude of Writers in the *Greek* and *Latin,* but in the *German, Dutch, French, Italian, Engliſh,* and *Arabick* Languages, and, in the laſt Year of his Life, he was engroſſed by the Study of Inſcriptions, Medals, and Antiquities of all Nations.

In

In 1737, he refumed his Defign of finding a certain Method of difcovering the Longitude, which he imagined himfelf to have attained by exact Obfervations of the Declination and Inclination of the Needle, and fent to the Academy of Sciences, and to the Royal Society of *London* at the fame Time, an Account of his Schemes; to which it was firft anfwered by the Royal Society, that it appear'd the fame with one that Mr. *Whifton* had laid before them; and afterwards by the Academy of Sciences, that his Method was but very little different from one that had been propofed by M. *de la Croix*, and which was ingenious, but ineffectual.

M. *Barretier* finding his Invention already in the Poffeffion of two Men eminent for mathematical Knowledge, defifted from all Enquiries after the Longitude, and engaged in an Examination of the *Egyptian* Antiquities, which he propofed to free from their prefent Obfcurity, by deciphering their Hierogliphicks, and explaining their Aftronomy, but this Defign was interrupted by his Death.

This Defign he had propofed to himfelf, to execute in fuch a Manner, as fhould eftablifh his Reputation; and, indeed, it appears from the Scheme which he fent to M. *Le Maitre*,

Maitre, * that the Work was not unworthy
of fuch Abilities, and it is to be lamented
that, fince he could not finifh it, he has not
left fuch Materials as might enable others to
per-

' * De Doctrina Temporum fecundum Rationes prifcorum
' Ægyptiorum Libri V.
' Primus, De Anni forma apud Ægyptios agit. Ibi de variis
' eorum annis, de anno Ægyptiaco vago, proprie fic dicto,
' cujus natura fufe expenditur; De magna Periodo caniculari,
' quâ revolutio iftius anni peragitur; De Caniculæ principio
' fcil. hujus anni & de ejus motibus; De Oris, & quid fint; De
' menfibus Ægyptiorum; De quatuor anni cardinibus, & Feftis
' tunc celebratis; De tribus anni tempeftatibus & Feftis tunc
' quoque actis; De Feftorum revolutionibus; De characteribus
' Anni Ægyptiaci, &c. Multa alia digrediendo paffim illu-
' ftrantur.
' Secundus, Cœlum Ægyptiacum fiftit. De Planetarum
' nominibus & ordine; De Hebdomadibus; De Sphæra Ægy-
' ptiaca ejufque figuris; De Hypothefibus Ægyptiorum circa
' motus tam errantium quam fixarum; De Aftrologiæ ortu
' ex Aftronomia Ægyptiaca; De Decanis, Periodis Pla-
' netarum, Climacteribus, aliifque Aftrologiæ inventis,
' quorum verus fenfus eruitur. Ex hifce omnibus demon-
' ftrantur Epochæ primarum obfervationum apud Ægyptios,
' aliarumque quas deinde paulatim addiderunt, quod primum &
' certiffimum fundamentum eft Chronologiæ Ægyptiacæ. Agi-
' tur hic quoque de Cyclis Ægyptiorum, eorum Calenda-
' riis, &c.
' Tertius, Periodos Ægyptiorum exponit. Non unica Perio-
' dus Canicularis. Aliæ natæ e Feftorum annuorum revolutione.
' Earum recenfio. Sphingis allegoria pleniffime enucleata. E-
' pochæ illæ celebres Nabonaffari aliæque Ægyptiis debitæ.
' Aftronomi Alexandrini & Cyclographi Chriftiani ab Ægyptiis
' hauferunt. Canon Aftronomicus Regum iifdem debitus. Eorum
' annales, Annalium forma, Characteres Chronolcgici, ἀκρίβεια
' Iidem Annales continuati diu poft mortem Chrifti, res queque
exoticas

184

perfue his Ideas. It is indeed not to be related
without fome Degree of Wonder, that there
were found in his Collections but a few Sheets
relating to this great Work ; for which he informs his Friend that he has collected all the
Materials, and declares that the greatest Part
of the Labour being performed, he shall be
able to write it without any Impediment.

He continued to add new Acquifitions to
his Learning, and to encreafe his Reputation
by new Performances, till in the Beginning
of his nineteenth Year, his Health began to
decline, and his Indifpofition, which being
not alarming, or violent, was perhaps not at
first sufficiently regarded, increased by flow

E

De-

' exoticas referebant. Methodus in numerandis Principum an_
' nis; unde lux affunditur Numis Ægyptiacis Ptolomæorum &
' Imperatorum. Hiftoria anni Ægyptiaci & Periodi Canicularis
' ex præcedentibus colligitur.

' Quartus, Fundamenta generalia Hiftoriæ Ægyptiacæ firmi_
' ter collocat, tum ex charaƈteribus Aftronomicis, tum ex Epo-
' chis hiftoricis indubiis.

' Quintus, eandem Hiftoriam explet, & appendicis loco Canon
' Chronologicus fubjungitur. In hifce duobus ultimis, mole fu_
' perioribus multa hiftorica monumenta illuftrantur, Synchronifmi
' vicinarum gentium, præcipue rerum Græcarum antiquiffima_
' rum ante Bellum Trojanum recenfentur, Mythologiæ Ægyp
' tiorum fax accenditur ; De immanibus annorum Summis, quas
' Ægyptii jaƈtabant, differitur, ut & de Diis, Semideis, Heroi-
' bus, &c. Regum feries exhibetur, quamvis non plena, quo-
' niam nihil nifi certum & indubitatum in hoc opere admittitur.
' Ubi igitur monumenta deficiunt, lacunæ apparent ; at maxima
' pars vacuo caret, & ea quidem quæ noftra maxime intereft ut
' integra habeatur'.

Degrees for eighteen Months, during which he spent Days among his Books, and neither neglected his Studies, nor lost his Gaiety, till his Distemper, ten Days before his Death, deprived him of the Use of his Limbs, he then prepared himself for his End, without Fear or Emotion, and on the 5th of *October*, 1740, resigned his Soul into the Hands of his Saviour, with Confidence and Tranquillity.

Thus died *Barretier*, in the 20th Year of his Age, having given a Proof how much may be performed in so short a Time by indefatigable Diligence. He was not only Master of many Languages, but skilled almost in every Science, and capable of distinguishing himself in every Profession, except that of Physick, from which he had been discouraged by remarking the Diversity of Opinions among those who had been consulted concerning his own Disorders.

His Learning, however vast, had not depressed or over-burthen'd his natural Faculties, for his Genius appeared always predominant; and when he enquired into the various Opinions of the Writers of all Ages, he reasoned and determined for himself, having a Mind at once comprehensive and delicate, active and attentive. He was able to reason with the Metaphysicians on the most abstruse

ſtruſe Queſtions, or to enliven the moſt unpleaſing Subjects by the Gaiety of his Fancy. He
wrote with great Elegance and Dignity of
Stile, and had the peculiar Felicity of Readi-
neſs and Facility in every Thing that he undertook, being able without Premeditation to
tranſlate one Language into another. He was
no Imitator, but ſtruck out new Tracts, and
formed original Syſtems. He had a Quickneſs
of Apprehenſion, and Firmneſs of Memory,
which enabled him to read with incredible Rapidity, and at the ſame Time to retain what he
had read, ſo as to be able to recollect and apply it. He turned over Volumes in an Inſtant,
and ſelected what was uſeful for his Purpoſe.
He ſeldom made Extracts, except of Books
which he could not procure, when he might
want them a ſecond Time, being always able to
find in any Author, with great Expedition,
what he had once read. He read over, in one
Winter, twenty vaſt Folio's; and the Catalogue
of Books which he had borrow'd, compriſed 41
Pages in Quarto, the Writing cloſe, and the
Titles abridged. He was a conſtant Reader of
Literary Journals.

With regard to common Life, he had ſome
Peculiarities. He could not bear Muſick, and
if he was ever engaged at Play, could not attend to it. He neither loved Wine nor Enter-
tain-

tainments, nor Dancing, nor the Sports of the Field, nor relieved his Studies with any other Diverfion than that of Walking and Conversation. He eat little Flefh, and lived almoft wholly upon Milk, Tea, Bread, Fruits, and Sweetmeats.

He had great Vivacity in his Imagination, and Ardour in his Defires, which the eafy Method of his Education had never repreffed, he therefore converfed among thofe who had gained his Confidence with great Freedom; but his Favourites were not numerous, and to others he was always referved and filent, without the leaft Inclination to difcover his Sentiments, or difplay his Learning. He never fixed his Choice upon any Employment, nor confined his Views to any Profeffion, being defirous of nothing but Knowledge, and entirely untainted with Avarice or Ambition. He preferved himfelf always independent, and was never known to be guilty of a Lie. His conftant Application to Learning fuppreffed thofe Paffions which betray others of his Age to Irregularities, and excluded all thofe Temptations to which Men are expofed by Idlenefs, or common Amufements.

F I N I S.

The LIFE of

Dr *SYDENHAM.*

THOMAS SYDENHAM was born in the year 1624, at *Winford Eagle* in *Dorsetshire*, where his father *William Sydenham* Esq; had a large fortune. Under whose care he was educated, or in what manner he passed his childhood, whether he made any early discoveries of a genius peculiarly adapted to the study of nature, or gave any presages of his future eminence in medicine, no information is to be obtained. We must therefore repress that curiosity which would naturally incline us to watch the first attempts of so vigorous a mind, to persue it in its childish enquiries, and see it struggling with rustic prejudices, breaking on trifling occasions the shackles of credulity, and giving proofs in its casual excursions, that it was formed to shake off the yoke of prescription, and dispel the phantoms of hypothesis.

That the strength of SYDENHAM's understanding, the accuracy of his discernment, and ardour of his curiosity might have been remarked from his infancy by a diligent observer, there is no reason to doubt. For there is no instance of a man whose history has been minutely related, that did not in every part of life discover the same proportion of intellectual vigour; but it has been the lot of the greatest part of those who have excelled in science, to be known only by their own writings, and to have left behind them no remembrance of their domestic life, or private transactions, or only such memorials of particular passages as are, on certain occasions, necessarily recorded in publick registers.

From these it is discovered, that at the age of eighteen, in 1642, he commenced a commoner of *Magdalen-Hall* in *Oxford*, where it is not probable that he continued long; he informs us himself, that he was

was withheld from the univerfity by the commencement of the war; nor is it known in what ftate of life he engaged, or where he refided during that long feries of publick commotion. It is indeed reported, that he had a commiffion in the king's army, but no particular account is given of his military conduct; nor are we told what rank he obtained when he entered into the army, or when, or on what occafion he retired from it.

It is, however, certain, that if ever he took upon him the profeffion of arms, he fpent but few years in the camp; for in 1648 he obtained at *Oxford*, the degree of batchelor of phyfick, for which, as fome medicinal knowledge is neceffary, it may be imagined that he fpent fome time in qualifying himfelf.

His application to the ftudy of phyfick was, as he himfelf relates, produced by an accidental acquaintance with Dr *Cox*, a phyfician eminent at that time in *London*, who in fome ficknefs prefcribed to his brother, and attending him frequently on that occafion, enquired of him what profeffion he intended to follow. The young man telling him that he was undetermined, the doctor recommended phyfick to him, on what account, or with what arguments, it is not related; but his perfuafions were fo effectual, that SYDENHAM determined to follow his advice, and retired to *Oxford* for leifure and opportunity to perfue his ftudies.

It is evident that this converfation muft have happened before his promotion to any degree in phyfick, becaufe he himfelf fixes it in the interval of his abfence from the univerfity, a circumftance which will enable us to confute many falfe reports relating to Dr SYDENHAM, which have been confidently inculcated, and implicitely believed.

It is the general opinion, that he was made a phyfician by accident and neceffity, and Sir *Richard Blackmore* reports in plain terms, [*preface to his treatife on the fmall-pox*] that he engaged in practice without any preparatory ftudy, or previous knowledge, of the medicinal fciences; and affirms, that when he was confulted by
him

him what books he fhould read to qualify him for the fame profeffion, he recommended *Don Quixote.*

That he recommended *Don Quixote* to *Blackmore,* we are not allowed to doubt; but the relater is hindered by that felf-love which dazzles all mankind, from difcovering that he might intend a fatire very different from a general cenfure of all the antient and modern writers on medicine, fince he might perhaps mean either ferioufly, or in jeft, to infinuate, that *Blackmore* was not adapted by nature to the ftudy of phyfick, and that, whether he fhould read *Cervantes* or *Hippocrates,* he would be equally unqualified for practice, and equally unfuccefsful in it.

Whatfoever was his meaning, nothing is more evident, than that it was a tranfient fally of an inclination warmed with gaiety, or the negligent effufion of a mind intent on fome other employment, and in hafte to difmifs a troublefome intruder; for it is certain that SYDENHAM did not think it impoffible to write ufefully on medicine, becaufe he has himfelf written upon it; and it is not probable that he carried his vanity fo far, as to imagine that no man had ever acquired the fame qualifications befides himfelf. He could not but know that he rather reftored than invented moft of his principles, and therefore could not but acknowledge the value of thofe writers whofe doctrines he adopted and enforced.

That he engaged in the practice of phyfick without any acquaintance with the theory, or knowledge of the opinions or precepts of former writers, is undoubtedly falfe; for he declares, that after he had, in perfuance of his converfation with Dr *Cox,* determined upon the profeffion of phyfick, he *applied himfelf in earneft to it,* and *fpent feveral years in the univerfity* [aliquot annos in academicâ palæftrâ] before he began to practife in *London.*

Nor was he fatisfied with the opportunities of knowledge which *Oxford* afforded, but travelled to *Montpellier,* as *Default* relates [*differtation on confumptions*] in queft of farther information; *Montpellier* being at that time
the

the moſt celebrated ſchool of phyſick : So far was SY-
DENHAM from any contempt of academical inſtitutions, and ſo far from thinking it reaſonable to learn phyſick by experiments alone, which muſt neceſſarily be
made at the hazard of life.

What can be demanded beyond this by the moſt
zealous advocate for regular education ? What can be
expected from the moſt cautious and moſt induſtrious
ſtudent, than that he ſhould dedicate *ſeveral years* to
the rudiments of his art, and travel for further inſtruc-
tions from one univerſity to another ?

It is likewiſe a common opinion, that SYDENHAM
was thirty years old before he formed his reſolution of
ſtudying phyſick, for which I can diſcover no other foundation than one expreſſion in his dedication to Dr *Maple-*
toft, which ſeems to have given riſe to it by a groſs miſ-
interpretation ; for he only obſerves, that from his converſation with Dr *Cox* to the publication of that treatiſe *thirty years* had intervened.

Whatever may have produced this notion, or how
long ſoever it may have prevailed, it is now proved beyond controverſy to be falſe, ſince it appears that
SYDENHAM having been for ſome time abſent from
the univerſity, returned to it in order to perſue his
phyſical enquiries before he was twenty four years old,
for in 1648 he was admitted to the degree of batchelor
of phyſick.

That ſuch reports ſhould be confidently ſpread, even
among the cotemporaries of the author to whom they
relate, and obtain in a few years ſuch credit as to require a regular confutation ; that it ſhould be imagined
that the greateſt phyſician of the age arrived at ſo high
a degree of ſkill, without any aſſiſtance from his predeceſ-
ſors ; and that a man, eminent for integrity, practiſed
medicine by chance, and grew wiſe only by murder, is
not to be conſidered without aſtoniſhment.

But if it be on the other part remembered, how
much this opinion favours the lazineſs of ſome, and
the pride of others ; how readily ſome men confide in
natural

natural sagacity, and how willingly most would spare
themselves the labour of accurate reading and tedious
enquiry, it will be easily discovered how much the interest of multitudes was engaged in the production and
continuance of this opinion, and how cheaply those of
whom it was known that they practised physick before
they studied it, might satisfy themselves and others
with the example of the illustrious SYDENHAM.

It is therefore in an uncommon degree useful to
publish a true account of this memorable man, that
pride, temerity, and idleness may be deprived of that
patronage which they have enjoyed too long ; that life
may be secured from the dangerous experiments of the
ignorant and presumptuous ; and that those who shall
hereafter assume the important province of superintending the health of others, may learn from this great
master of the art, that the only means of arriving at
eminence and success are labour and study.

About the same time that he became batchelor
of physick, he obtained, by the interest of a relation,
a fellowship of *All Souls* college, having submitted to
the subscription required to the authority of the vi-
sitors appointed by the parliament, upon what principles,
or how consistently with his former conduct, it is now
impossible to discover.

When he thought himself qualified for practice, he
fixed his residence in *Westminster*, became doctor of
physick at *Cambridge*, received a licence from the
college of physicians, and lived in the first degree of reputation, and the greatest affluence of practice, for
many years, without any other enemies than those
which he raised by the superior merit of his conduct,
the brighter lustre of his abilities, or his improvements
of his science, and his contempt of pernicious methods
supported only by authority, in opposition to sound
reason and indubitable experience. These men are indebted to him for concealing their names, when he records their malice, since they have thereby escaped the
contempt and detestation of posterity.

The same attention to the benefit of mankind, which
animated

animated him in the perfuit of a more falutary practice
of medicine, may be fuppofed to have incited him to
declare the refult of his enquiries, and communicate
thofe methods of which his fagacity had firft conjectured, his experience afterwards confirmed the fuccefs;
he therefore drew up thofe writings which have been
from his time the chief guides of phyfic, and that they
might be ufeful to a greater extent, procured them to
be put into latin, partly by Dr *Mapletoft*, to whom part
is dedicated, and partly by Mr *Havers* of *Cambridge*.

It is a melancholy reflection, that they who have
obtained the higheft reputation, by preferving or re-
ftoring the health of others, have often been hurried
away before the natural decline of life, or have paffed
many of their years under the torments of thofe diftempers, which they profefs to relieve. In this number was SYDENHAM, whofe health began to fail in
the fifty fecond year of his age, by the frequent attacks
of the gout, to which he was fubject for a great part of
his life, and which was afterwards accompanied with
the ftone in the kidneys, and, its natural confequence,
bloody urine.

Thefe were diftempers which even the art of SY-
DENHAM could only palliate, without hope of a perfect
cure, but which, if he has not been able by his precepts
to inftruct us to remove, he has, at leaft, by his example, taught us to bear; for he never betray'd any
indecent impatience, or unmanly dejection, under his
torments, but fupported himfelf by the reflections of
philofophy, and the confolations of religion, and in every
interval of eafe, applied himfelf to the affiftance of o-
thers with his ufual affiduity.

After a life thus ufefully employed, he died at his
houfe in *Pall-mall*, on the 29th of *December*, in the
year 1689, and was buried in the ifle, near the fouth
door, of the church of *St. James* in *Weftminfter*.

What was his character, as a phyfician, appears from
the treatifes which he has left, which it is not neceffary to epitomife or tranfcribe; and from them it may
likewife be collected, that his fkill in phyfick was not
his

his higheft excellence; that his whole character was amiable; that his chief view was the benefit of mankind, and the chief motive of his actions the will of GOD, whom he mentions with reverence, well becoming the moft enlightened and moft penetrating mind. He was benevolent, candid, and communicative, fincere and religious; qualities, which it were happy if they would copy from him, who emulate his knowledge, and imitate his methods.

A N

ACCOUNT

OF THE

LIFE

OF

Mr *Richard Savage,*

Son of the Earl RIVERS.

By Samuel Johnson.

The SECOND EDITION.

L O N D O N:

Printed for E. CAVE at *St John's Gate.*
M.DCC.XLVIII.

AN

ACCOUNT

OF THE

LIFE

OF

Mr RICHARD SAVAGE.

IT has been obſerved in all Ages, that
the Advantages of Nature or of Fortune have contributed very little to the
Promotion of Happineſs ; and that thoſe
whom the Splendor of their Rank, or the
Extent of their Capacity, havé placed upon
the Summits of human Life, have not often
given any juſt Occaſion to Envy in thoſe
who look up to them from a lower Station.
Whether it be that apparent Superiority incites
great Deſigns, and great Deſigns are naturally
liable to fatal Miſcariages, or that the general
Lot of Mankind is Miſery, and the Misfortunes
of thoſe whoſe Eminence drew upon them an

B   uni-

univerfal Attention, have been more carefully recorded, becaufe they were more generally obferved, and have in reality been only more confpicuous than thofe of others, not more frequent, or more fevere.

That Affluence and Power, Advantages ex- trinfic and adventitious, and therefore eafily fe- parable from thofe by whom they are poffeffed, fhould very often flatter the Mind with Ex- pectation of Felicity which they cannot give, raifes no Aftonifhment; but it feems rational to hope, that intellectual Greatnefs fhould pro- duce better Effects, that Minds qualified for great Attainments fhould firft endeavour their own Benefit, and that they who are moft able to teach others the Way to Happinefs, fhould with moft Certainty follow it themfelves.

But this Expectation, however plaufible, has been very frequently difappointed. The Heroes of literary as well as civil Hiftory have been very often no lefs remarkable for what they have fuffered, than for what they have atchieved; and Volumes have been written only to enume- rate the Miferies of the Learned, and relate their unhappy Lives, and untimely Deaths.

To thefe mournful Narratives, I am about to add the Life of *Richard Savage*, a Man whofe Writings entitle him to an eminent Rank in the Claffes of Learning, and whofe Mis- fortunes claim a Degree of Compaffion, not al- ways

ways due to the Unhappy, as they were often the Confequences of the Crimes of others, rather than his own.

In the Year 1697, *Anne* Countefs of *Macclesfield*, having lived for fome time upon very uneafy Terms with her Hufband, thought a public Confeffion of Adultery the moft obvious and expeditious Method of obtaining her Liberty, and therefore declared, that the Child, with which fhe was then great, was begotten by the Earl *Rivers*. Her Hufband, as may be eafily imagined, being thus made no lefs defirous of a Separation than herfelf, profecuted his Defign in the moft effectual Manner; for he applied not to the Ecclefiaftical Courts for a Divorce, but to the Parliament for an Act, by which his Marriage might be diffolved, the nuptial Contract totally annulled, and the Child of his Wife illegitimated. This Act, after the ufual Deliberation, he obtained, tho' without the Approbation of fome, who confidered Marriage as an Affair only cognizable by Ecclefiaftical Judges *; and on *March* 3d was feparated from his Wife,

* This Year was made remarkable by the Diffolution of a Marriage folemnifed in the Face of the Church. *Salmon's Review.*

The following Proteft is regiftered in the Books of the Houfe of Lords.

Diffentient.

Becaufe we conceive that this is the firft Bill of that Nature that hath paffed, where there was not a Divorce firft obtained

Wife, whose Fortune, which was very great, was repaid her; and who having as well as her Husband the Liberty of making another Choice, was in a short Time married to Colonel *Bret*.

While the Earl of *Macclesfield* was prosecuting this Affair, his Wife was, on the tenth of *January* 1697-8, delivered of a Son, and the Earl *Rivers*, by appearing to consider him as his own, left none any Reason to doubt of the Sincerity of her Declaration; for he was his Godfather, and gave him his own Name, which was by his Direction inserted in the Register of *St Andrew*'s Parish in *Holbourn*, but unfortunately left him to the Care of his Mother, whom, as she was now set free from her Husband, he probably imagined likely to treat with great Tenderness the Child that had contributed to so pleasing an Event. It is not indeed easy to discover what Motives could be found to over-balance that natural Affection of a Parent, or what Interest could be promoted by Neglect or Cruelty. The Dread of Shame or of Poverty, by which some Wretches have been incited to abandon or to murder their Children, cannot be supposed to have affected a Woman who had proclaimed her Crimes

tained in the Spiritual Court; which we look upon as an ill Precedent, and may be of dangerous Consequence in the future,

Halifax.   *Rochester.*

Crimes and folicited Reproach, and on whom the Clemency of the Legiflature had undefervedly beftowed a Fortune, that would have been very little diminifhed by the Expences which the Care of her Child could have brought upon her. It was therefore not likely that fhe would be wicked without Temptation, that fhe would look upon her Son from his Birth with a kind of Refentment and Abhorrence ; and inftead of fupporting, affifting, and defending him, delight to fee him ftruggling with Mifery, that fhe would take every Opportunity of aggravating his Misfortunes, and obftructing his Refources, and with an implacable and reftlefs Cruelty continue her Perfecution from the firft Hour of his Life to the laft.

But whatever were her Motives, no fooner was her Son born, than fhe difcovered a Refolution of difowning him ; and in a very fhort Time removed him from her Sight, by committing him to the Care of a poor Woman, whom fhe directed to educate him as her own, and enjoined never to inform him of his true Parents.

Such was the Beginning of the Life of *Richard Savage :* Born with a legal Claim to Honour and to Riches, he was in two Months illegitimated by the Parliament, and difowned by his Mother, doomed to Poverty and Obfcurity, and launched upon the Ocean of Life,

only

only that he might be swallowed by its Quick-sands, or dashed upon its Rocks.

His Mother could not indeed infect others with the same Cruelty. As it was impossible to avoid the Inquiries which the Curiosity or Tenderness of her Relations made after her Child, she was obliged to give some Account of the Measures that she had taken; and her Mother, the Lady *Mason*, whether in Approbation of her Design, or to prevent more criminal Contrivances, engaged to transact with his Nurse, pay her for her Care, and superintend his Education.

In this charitable Office she was assisted by his Godmother Mrs *Loyd*, who while she lived always looked upon him with that Tenderness, which the Barbarity of his Mother made peculiarly necessary; but her Death, which happened in his tenth Year, was another of the Misfortunes of his Childhood; for though she kindly endeavoured to alleviate his Loss by a Legacy of three hundred Pounds, yet as he had none to prosecute his Claim, to shelter him from Oppression, or call in Law to the Assistance of Justice, her Will was eluded by the Executors, and no part of the Money was ever paid.

He was however not yet wholly abandoned. The Lady *Mason* still continued her Care, and directed him to be placed at a small Grammar School

School near St. *Alban's*, where he was called by the Name of his Nurfe, without the leaft Intimation that he had a Claim to any other.

Here he was initiated in Literature, and paffed through feveral of the Claffes, with what Rapidity or what Applaufe cannot now be known. As he always fpoke with Refpect of his Mafter, it is probable that the mean Rank, in which he then appeared, did not hinder his Genius from being diftinguifhed, or his Induftry from being rewarded, and if in fo low a State he obtained Diftinction and Rewards, it is not likely that they were gained but by Genius and Induftry.

It is very reafonable to conjecture, that his Application was equal to his Abilities, becaufe his Improvement was more than proportioned to the Opportunities which he enjoyed; nor can it be doubted, that if his earlieft Productions had been preferved, like thofe of happier Students, we might in fome have found vigorous Sallies of that fprightly Humour, which diftinguifhes the *Author to be let*, and in others, ftrong Touches of that ardent Imagination which painted the folemn Scenes of *the Wanderer*.

While he was thus cultivating his Genius, his Father the Earl *Rivers* was feized with a Diftemper, which in a fhort Time put an End to his Life. He had frequently inquired after his

his Son, and had always been amufed with fallacious and evafive Anfwers; but being now in
his own Opinion on his Death-bed, he thought
it his Duty to provide for him among his other
natural Children, and therefore demanded a pofitive Account of him, with an Importunity not
to be diverted or denied. His Mother, who could
no longer refufe an Anfwer, determined at leaft
to give fuch as fhould cut him off for ever from
that Happinefs which Competence affords, and
therefore declared that he was dead; which is
perhaps the firft Inftance of a Lye invented by a
Mother to deprive her Son of a Provifion which
was defigned him by another, and which fhe
could not expect herfelf, though he fhould lofe it.

This was therefore an Act of Wickednefs
which could not be defeated, becaufe it could
not be fufpected; the Earl did not imagine,
that there could exift in a human Form a Mother that would ruin her Son without enriching
herfelf, and therefore beftowed upon fome other
Perfon fix thoufand Pounds, which he had in
his Will bequeathed to *Savage.*

The fame Cruelty which incited his Mother
to intercept this Provifion which had been intended him, prompted her in a fhort Time to
another Project, a Project worthy of fuch a
Difpofition. She endeavoured to rid herfelf
from the Danger of being at any Time made
known

known to him, by sending him secretly to the *American* Plantations *.

By whose Kindness this Scheme was counteracted, or by what Interposition she was induced to lay aside her Design, I know not; it is not improbable that the Lady *Mason* might persuade or compel her to desist, or perhaps she could not easily find Accomplices wicked enough to concur in so cruel an Action; for it may be conceived, that even those who had by a long Gradation of Guilt hardened their Hearts against the Sense of common Wickedness, would yet be shocked at the Design of a Mother to expose her Son to Slavery and Want, to expose him without Interest, and without Provocation; and *Savage* might on this Occasion find Protectors and Advocates among those who had long traded in Crimes, and whom Compassion had never touched before.

Being hindered, by whatever Means, from banishing him into another Country, she formed soon after a Scheme for burying him in Poverty and Obscurity in his own; and that his Station of Life, if not the Place of his Residence, might keep him for ever at a Distance from her, she ordered him to be placed with a Shoemaker in *Holbourn*, that after the usual Time of Trial, he might become his Apprentice†.

C   It

* † *Savage's* Preface to his Miscellany.

It is generally reported, that this Project was for some time succesful, and that *Savage* was employed at the Awl longer than he was willing to confess ; nor was it perhaps any great Advantage to him, that an unexpected Disco-very determined him to quit his Occupation.

About this Time his Nurse, who had al-ways treated him as her own Son, died, and it was natural for him to take Care of those Effects which by her Death were, as he ima-gined, become his own ; he therefore went to her House, opened her Boxes, and exami-ned her Papers, among which he found some Letters written to her by the Lady *Mason*, which informed him of his Birth, and the Reasons for which it was concealed.

He was now no longer satisfied with the Employment which had been allotted him, but thought he had a Right to share the Af-fluence of his Mother, and therefore without Scruple applied to her as her Son, and made use of every Art to awaken her Tenderness, and attract her Regard. But neither his Let-ters, nor the Interposition of those Friends which his Merit or his Distress procured him, made any Impression upon her: She still resolved to neglect, though she could no longer disown him.

It was to no Purpose that he frequently so-licited her to admit him to see her ; she avoided him

him with the moſt vigilant Precaution, and ordered him to be excluded from her Houſe, by whomſoever he might be introduced, and whatReaſon ſoever he might give for entering it.

Savage was at the ſame Time ſo touched with the Diſcovery of his real Mother, that it was his frequent Practice to walk in the dark Evenings * for ſeveral Hours before her Door, in Hopes of ſeeing her as ſhe might come by Accident to the Window, or croſs her Apartment with a Candle in her Hand.

But all his Aſſiduity and Tenderneſs were without Effect, for he could neither ſoften her Heart, nor open her Hand, and was reduced to the utmoſt Miſeries of Want, while he was endeavouring to awaken the Affection of a Mother: He was therefore obliged to ſeek ſome other Means of Support, and having no Profeſſion, became, by Neceſſity, an Author.

At this Time the Attention of all the literary World was engroſſed by the *Bangorian* Controverſy, which filled the Preſs with Pamphlets, and the Coffee-houſes with Diſputants. Of this Subject, as moſt popular, he made Choice for his firſt Attempt, and without any other Knowledge of the Queſtion, than he had caſually collected from Converſation, publiſhed a Poem againſt the Biſhop.

C 2   What

---

* *Plain Dealer.*

What was the Succefs or Merit of this Performance I know not, it was probably loft a-
mong the innumerable Pamphlets to which
that Difpute gave Occafion. Mr *Savage* was
himfelf in a little time afhamed of it, and endeavoured to fupprefs it, by deftroying all the
Copies that he could collect.

He then attempted a more gainful Kind of
Writing †, and in his eighteenth Year offered
to the Stage a Comedy borrowed from a *Spanifh* Plot, which was refufed by the Players,
and was therefore given by him to Mr *Bullock*,
who having more Intereft, made fome flight
Alterations, and brought it upon the Stage,
under the Title of * *Woman's a Riddle*, but
allowed the unhappy Author no Part of the
Profit.

Not difcouraged however at this Repulfe,
he wrote two Years afterwards *Love in a Veil*,
another Comedy, borrowed likewife from the
Spanifh, but with little better Succefs than
before ; for though it was received and acted,
yet it appeared fo late in the Year, that the
Author obtained no other Advantage from it,
than the Acquaintance of Sir *Richard Steele*,
and Mr *Wilks*; by whom he was pitied, ca-
refled, and relieved.

Sir

---

† *Jacob's* Lives of Dramatick Poets.
  * This Play was printed firft in 8vo, and afterwards
in 12mo, the fifth Edition.

Sir *Richard Steele* having declared in his Favour with all the Ardour of Benevolence which conftituted his Character, promoted his Intereft with the utmoft Zeal, related his Mif-fortunes, applauded his Merit, took all Oppor-tunities of recommending him, and afferted * that *the Inhumanity of his Mother had given him a Right to find every good Man his Father.*

Nor was Mr *Savage* admitted to his Ac-quaintance only, but to his Confidence, of which he fometimes related an Inftance too extraordinary to be omitted, as it affords a very juft Idea of his Patron's Character.

He was once defired by Sir *Richard*, with an Air of the utmoft Importance, to come very early to his Houfe the next Morning. Mr *Savage* came as he had promifed,. found the Chariot at the Door, and Sir *Richard* waiting for him, and ready to go out. What was in-tended, and whither they were to go, *Savage* could not conjecture, and was not willing to enquire, but immediately feated himfelf with his Friend, the Coachman was ordered to drive, and they hurried with the utmoft Ex-pedition to *Hyde-Park Corner*, where they ftopped at a petty Tavern, and retired to a private Room. Sir *Richard* then informed him, that he intended to publifh a Pamphlet, and that he had defired him to come thither that he might write for him. They foon fat down

* *Plain Dealer.*

down to the Work, Sir *Richard* dictated, and *Savage* wrote, till the Dinner that had been ordered was put upon the Table. *Savage* was surprised at the Meanness of the Entertainment, and after some Hesitation, ventured to ask for Wine, which Sir *Richard*, not without Reluctance, ordered to be brought. They then finished their Dinner, and proceeded in their Pamphlet, which they concluded in the Afternoon.

Mr *Savage* then imagined his Task over, and expected that Sir *Richard* would call for the Reckoning, and return home ; but his Expectations deceived him, for Sir *Richard* told him, that he was without Money, and that the Pamphlet must be sold before the Dinner could be paid for ; and *Savage* was therefore obliged to go and offer their new Production to Sale for two Guineas, which with some Difficulty he obtained. Sir *Richard* then returned home, having retired that Day only to avoid his Creditors, and composed the Pamphlet only to discharge his Reckoning.

Mr *Savage* related another Fact equally uncommon, which, though it has no Relation to his Life, ought to be preserved. Sir *Richard Steele* having one Day invited to his House a great Number of Persons of the first Quality, they were surprised at the Number of Liveries which surrounded the Table ; and after

ter Dinner, when Wine and Mirth had fet them free from the Obfervation of rigid Ceremony, one of them enquired of Sir *Richard,* how fuch an expenfive Train of Domeftics could be confiftent with his Fortune. He with great Franknefs confeffed, that they were Fellows of whom he would very willingly be rid. And being then afked, why he did not difcharge them, declared that they were Bailiffs who had introduced themfelves with an Execution, and whom, fince he could not fend them away, he had thought it convenient to embellifh with Liveries, that they might do him Credit while they ftaid.

His Friends were diverted with the Expedient, and by paying the Debt difcharged their Attendance, having obliged Sir *Richard* to promife that they fhould never again find him graced with a Retinue of the fame Kind.

Under fuch a Tutor, Mr *Savage* was not likely to learn Prudence or Frugality, and perhaps many of the Misfortunes which the Want of thofe Virtues brought upon him in the following Parts of his Life, might be juftly imputed to fo unimproving an Example.

Nor did the Kindnefs of Sir *Richard* end in common Favours. He propofed to have eftablifhed him in fome fettled Scheme of Life, and to have contracted a Kind of Alliance with him, by marrying him to a natural Daughter,
on

on whom he intended to beſtow a thouſand
Pounds. But though he was always laviſh of
future Bounties, he conducted his Affairs in
ſuch a Manner, that he was very ſeldom able
to keep his Promiſes, or execute his own Intentions; and as he was never able to raiſe the
Sum which he had offered, the Marriage was
delayed. In the mean Time he was offici-
ouſly informed that Mr *Savage* had ridiculed
him; by which he was ſo much exaſperated,
that he withdrew the Allowance which he
had paid him, and never afterwards admitted
him to his Houſe.

It is not indeed unlikely that *Savage* might
by his Imprudence expoſe himſelf to the Malice of a Tale-bearer; for his Patron had many Follies, which as his Diſcernment eaſily
diſcovered, his Imagination might ſometimes
incite him to mention too ludicrouſly. A little
Knowledge of the World is ſufficient to diſcover
that ſuch Weakneſs is very common, and that
there are few who do not ſometimes in the
Wantonneſs of thoughtleſs Mirth, or the Heat
of tranſient Reſentment, ſpeak of their Friends
and Benefactors with Levity and Contempt,
though in their cooler Moments, they want
neither Senſe of their Kindneſs, nor Reverence
for their Virtue. The Fault therefore of Mr
Savage was rather Negligence than Ingratitude; but Sir *Richard* muſt likewiſe be acquitted

quitted of Severity, for who is there that can patiently bear Contempt from one whom he has relieved and supported, whose Establishment he has laboured, and whose Interest he has promoted?

He was now again abandoned to Fortune, without any other Friend than Mr *Wilks*; a Man, who, whatever were his Abilities or Skill as an Actor, deserves at least to be remembered for his Virtues*, which are not often to be

D   found

---

* As it is a Loss to Mankind, when any good Action is forgotten, I shall insert another Instance of Mr *Wilks's* Generosity, very little known. Mr *Smith*, a Gentleman educated at *Dublin*, being hindred by an Impediment in his Pronunciation from engaging in Orders, for which his Friends designed him, left his own Country, and came to *London* in Quest of Employment, but found his Solicitations fruitless, and his Necessities every Day more pressing. In this Distress he wrote a Tragedy, and offered it to the Players, by whom it was rejected. Thus were his last Hopes defeated, and he had no other Prospect than of the most deplorable Poverty. But Mr *Wilks* thought his Performance, though not perfect, at least worthy of some Reward, and therefore offered him a Benefit. This Favour he improved with so much Diligence, that the House afforded him a considerable Sum, with which he went to *Leyden*, applied himself to the Study of Physic, and prosecuted his Design with so much Diligence and Success, that when Dr *Boerhaave* was desired by the Czarina to recommend proper Persons to introduce into *Russia* the Practice and Study of Physic, Dr *Smith* was one of those whom he selected. He had a considerable Pension settled on him at his Arrival, and is now one of the chief Physicians at the *Russian* Court.

found in the World, and perhaps lefs often in his Profeffion than in others. To be humane, generous and candid, is a very high Degree of Merit in any State; but thofe Qualities deferve ftill greater Praife, when they are found in that Condition, which makes almoft every other Man, for whatever Reafon, contemptuous, infolent, petulant, felfifh, and brutal.

As Mr *Wilks* was one of thofe to whom Calamity feldom complained without Relief, he naturally took an unfortunate Wit into his Protection, and not only affifted him in any cafual Diftreffes, but continued an equal and fteady Kindnefs to the Time of his Death.

By his Interpofition Mr *Savage* once obtained from his Mother † fifty Pounds, and a Promife of one hundred and fifty more; but it was the Fate of this unhappy Man, that few Promifes of any Advantage to him were performed. His Mother was infected among others with the general Madnefs of the *South-Sea* Traffick, and having been difappointed in her Expectations, refufed to pay what perhaps nothing but the Profpect of fudden Affluence prompted her to promife.

Being thus obliged to depend upon the Friendfhip of Mr *Wilks*, he was confequently an affiduous Frequenter of the Theatres, and in a fhort

† This I write upon the Credit of the Author of his Life, which was publifhed 1727.

a fhort Time the Amufements of the Stage took fuch Poffeffion of his Mind, that he never was abfent from a Play in feveral Years.

This conftant Attendance naturally procured him the Acquaintance of the Players, and among others, of Mrs *Oldfield*, who was fo much pleafed with his Converfation, and touched with his Misfortunes, that fhe allowed him a fettled Penfion of fifty Pounds a Year, which was during her Life regularly paid.

That this Act of Generofity may receive its due Praife, and that the good Actions of Mrs *Oldfield* may not be fullied by her general Character, it is proper to mention, what Mr *Savage* often declared in the ftrongeft Terms, that he never faw her alone, or in any other Place than behind the Scenes.

At her Death, he endeavoured to fhew his Gratitude in the moft decent Manner, by wearing Mourning as for a Mother, but did not celebrate her in Elegies, becaufe he knew that too great Profufion of Praife would only have revived thofe Faults which his natural Equity did not allow him to think lefs, becaufe they were committed by one who favoured him; but of which, though his Virtue would not endeavour to palliate them, his Gratitude would not fuffer him to prolong the Memory, or diffufe the Cenfure.

In

In his *Wanderer*, he has indeed taken an Opportunity of mentioning her, but celebrates her not for her Virtue, but her Beauty, an Excellence which none ever denied her: This is the only Encomium with which he has rewarded her Liberality, and perhaps he has even in this been too lavish of his Praise. He seems to have thought that never to mention his Benefactress, would have an Appearance of Ingratitude, though to have dedicated any particular Performance to her Memory, would have only betrayed an officious Partiality, that, without exalting her Character, would have depressed his own.

He had sometimes, by the Kindness of Mr *Wilks*, the Advantage of a Benefit, on which Occasions he often received uncommon Marks of Regard and Compassion; and was once told by the Duke of *Dorset*, that it was just to consider him as an injured Nobleman, and that in his Opinion the Nobility ought to think themselves obliged without Solicitation to take every Opportunity of supporting him by their Countenance and Patronage. But he had generally the Mortification to hear that the whole Interest of his Mother was employed to frustrate his Applications, and that she never left any Expedient untried, by which he might be cut off from the Possibility of supporting Life. The same Disposition she endeavoured to diffuse a-

mong

mong all thofe over whom Nature or Fortune gave her any Influence, and indeed fucceeded too well in her Defign, but could not always propagate her Effrontery with her Cruelty, for fome of thofe whom fhe incited againft him, were afhamed of their own Conduct, and boafted of that Relief which they never gave him.

In this Cenfure I do not indifcriminately involve all his Relations; for he has mentioned with Gratitude the Humanity of one Lady, whofe Name I am now unable to recollect, and to whom therefore I cannot pay the Praifes which fhe deferves for having acted well in Oppofition to Influence, Precept and Example.

The Punifhment which our Laws inflict upon thofe Parents who murder their Infants, is well known, nor has its Juftice ever been contefted; but if they deferve Death who deftroy a Child in its Birth, what Pains can be fevere enough for her who forbears to deftroy him only to inflict fharper Miferies upon him; who prolongs his Life only to make it miferable; and who expofes him without Care and without Pity, to the Malice of Oppreffion, the Caprices of Chance, and the Temptations of Poverty; who rejoices to fee him overwhelmed with Calamities; and when his own Induftry, or the Charity of others, has enabled him to rife for a fhort Time above his Miferies, plunges him again into his former Diftrefs?

The

The Kindnefs of his Friends not affording him any conftant Supply, and the Profpect of improving his Fortune, by enlarging his Acquaintance, neceffarily leading him to Places of Expence, he found it neceffary * to endeavour once more at dramatic Poetry, for which he was now better qualified by a more extenfive Knowledge, and longer Obfervation. But having been unfuccefsful in Comedy, though rather for Want of Opportunities than Genius, he refolved now to try whether he fhould not be more fortunate in exhibiting a Tragedy.

The Story which he chofe for the Subject, was that of Sir *Thomas Overbury*, a Story well adapted to the Stage, though perhaps not far enough removed from the prefent Age, to admit properly the Fictions neceffary to complete the Plan ; for the Mind which naturally loves Truth is always moft offended with the Violation of thofe Truths of which we are moft certain, and we of courfe conceive thofe Facts moft certain which approach neareft to our own Time.

Out of this Story he formed a Tragedy, which, if the Circumftances in which he wrote it be confidered, will afford at once an uncommon Proof of Strength of Genius, and Evennefs of Mind, of a Serenity not to be ruffled, and an Imagination not to be fuppreffed.

During

* In 1724.

During a confiderable Part of the Time, in which he was employed upon this Performance, he was without Lodging, and often without Meat; nor had he any other Conveniences for Study than the Fields or the Streets allowed him, there he ufed to walk and form his Speeches, and afterwards ftep into a Shop, beg for a few Moments the Ufe of the Pen and Ink, and write down what he had compofed upon Paper which he had picked up by Accident.

If the Performance of a Writer thus dif-treffed is not perfect, its Faults ought furely to be imputed to a Caufe very different from Want of Genius, and muft rather excite Pity than provoke Cenfure.

But when under thefe Difcouragements the Tragedy was finifhed, there yet remained the Labour of introducing it on the Stage, an Un-dertaking which to an ingenuous Mind was in a very high Degree vexatious and difgufting; for having little Intereft or Reputation, he was obliged to fubmit himfelf wholly to the Players, and admit, with whatever Reluctance, the E-mendations of Mr *Cibber*, which he always confidered as the Difgrace of his Performance.

He had indeed in Mr *Hill* another Critic of a very different Clafs, from whofe Friendfhip he received great Affiftance on many Occafions, and whom he never mentioned but with the utmoft

utmoft Tendernefs and Regard*. He had been
for fome Time diftinguifhed by him with very particular Kindnefs, and on this Occafion it
was natural to apply to him as an Author of an
eftablifhed Character.   He therefore fent this
Tragedy to him with a fhort Copy of Verfes†,

in

---

* He infcribed to him a fhort Poem, called *The Friend,*
printed in his Mifcellanies, in which he addreffes him with
the utmoft Ardour of Affection.

> O lov'd *Hillarius !* thou by Heav'n defign'd
> To charm, to mend, and to inftruct Mankind :
> To whom my Hopes, Fears, Joys, and Sorrows tend,
> Thou Brother, Father, nearer yet—thou Friend——
> —Kind are my Wrongs, I thence thy Friendfhip own,
> What State could blefs, were I to thee unknown ?
> —While fhun'd, obfcur'd, or thwarted and expos'd,
> By Friends abandon'd, and by Foes enclos'd,
> Thy Guardian Counfel foftens ev'ry Care,
> To Eafe fooths Anguifh, and to Hope, Defpair.

† *To* A. HILL, *Efq; with the Tragedy of Sir*
THOMAS OVERBURY.

> As the Soul ftrip'd of mortal Clay
>   Shews all divinely fair,
> And boundlefs roves the Milky Way,
>   And views fweet Profpects there :
> This Hero clog'd with droffy Lines
>   By thee new Vigour tries ;
> As thy correcting Hand refines
>   Bright Scenes around him rife.
> Thy Touch brings the wifh'd Stone to pafs,
>   So fought, fo long foretold ;
> It turns polluted Lead and Brafs
>   At once to pureft Gold.

in which he defired his Correction. Mr *Hill*, whofe Humanity and Politenefs are generally known, readily complied with his Requeft ; but as he is remarkable for Singularity of Sentiment, and bold Experiments in Language, Mr *Savage* did not think his Play much improved by his Innovation, and had even at that Time the Courage to reject feveral Paffages which he could not approve; and, what is ftill more laudable, Mr *Hill* had the Generofity not to refent the Neglect of his Alterations, but wrote the Prologue and Epilogue, in which he touches on the Circumftances of the Author with great Tendernefs.*

After all thefe Obftructions and Compliances, he was only able to bring his Play upon the Stage in the Summer, when the chief Actors had retired, and the reft were in Poffeffion of the Houfe for their own Advantage. Among thefe Mr *Savage* was admitted to play the Part of Sir *Thomas Overbury*, by which he gained no great Reputation, the Theatre being a Province for which Nature feemed not to have defigned him; for neither his Voice, Look, nor Gefture, were fuch as are

E   expected

---

* In a full World our Author lives alone,
 Unhappy, and by Confequence unknown ;
 Yet amidft Sorrow he difdains Complaint,
 Nor languid in the Race of Life grows faint :
 He fwims, unyielding, againft Fortune's Stream,
 Nor to his private Sufferings ftoops his Theme.

expected on the Stage, and he was himself fo much afhamed of having been reduced to appear as a Player, that he always blotted out his Name from the Lift, when a Copy of his Tragedy was to be fhown to his Friends.

In the Publication of his Performance he was more fuccefsful, for the Rays of Genius that glimmered in it, that glimmered through all the Mifts which Poverty had been able to fpread over it, procured him the Notice and Efteem of many Perfons eminent for their Rank, their Virtue, and their Wit.

Of this Play, acted, printed, and dedicated, the accumulated Profits arofe to an hundred Pounds, which he thought at that Time a very large Sum, having been never Mafter of fo much before.

In the Dedication*, for which he received ten Guineas, there is nothing remarkable. The Preface contains a very liberal Encomium on the blooming Excellencies of Mr *Theophilus Cibber*; which Mr *Savage* could not in the latter Part of his Life fee his Friends about to read, without fnatching the Play out of their Hands.

The Generofity of Mr *Hill* did not end on this Occafion; for afterwards, when Mr *Savage*'s Neceffities returned, he encouraged a Subfcription to a Mifcellany of Poems in a very extraordinary Manner, by publifhing his Story

* To —— *Tryfte*, Efq; of *Herefordfhire*.

Story in the *Plain Dealer* *, with some affecting Lines†, which he asserts to have been
written

* The *Plain Dealer* was a periodical Paper written by
Mr *Hill* and Mr *Bond*, whom Mr *Savage* called the two
contending Powers of Light and Darkness. They wrote
by Turns, each six Essays, and the Character of the Work
was observed regularly to rise in Mr *Hill*'s Weeks, and
fall in Mr *Bond*'s.

† Hopeless, abandon'd, aimless, and opprefs'd,
Lost to Delight, and, ev'ry Way, distrefs'd ;
Crofs his cold Bed, in wild Diforder, thrown,
Thus figh'd *Alexis*, friendless, and alone——
    Why do I breathe ?—What Joy can Being give ?
When she, who gave me Life, forgets I live !
Feels not thefe wintry Blasts ;—nor heeds my Smart;
But shuts me from the Shelter of her Heart !
Saw me expos'd to Want ! to Shame ! to Scorn !
To Ills !——which make it *Mifery*, to be *born* !
Caft me, regardlefs, on the World's bleak Wild;
And bade me be a Wretch, while yet a Child !
    Where can he hope for Pity, Peace, or Reft,
Who moves no Softnefs in a Mother's Breaft ?
Cuftom, Law, Reafon, *all* ! my Caufe forfake,
And *Nature fleeps*, to keep my Woes *awake* !
Crimes, which the *Cruel* fcarce believe can be,
The *Kind* are guilty of, to ruin *me*.
Ev'n she, who bore me, blafts me with her Hate,
And, *meant* my *Fortune*, makes herfelf my *Fate*.
    Yet has this fweet Neglecter of my Woes,
The fofteft, tend'reft Breaft, that *Pity* knows !
Her Eyes shed Mercy, wherefoe'er they shine ;
And her Soul *melts* at ev'ry Woe——but *mine*.
Sure then ! fome fecret Fate, for Guilt unwill'd,
Some Sentence pre-ordain'd to be fulfill'd !

written by Mr *Savage* upon the Treatment received by him from his Mother, but of which he was himself the Author, as Mr *Savage* afterwards declared. These Lines, and the Paper in which they were inserted, had a very powerful Effect upon all but his Mother, whom, by making her Cruelty more publick, they only hardened in her Aversion.

Mr *Hill* not only promoted the Subscription to the Miscellany, but furnished likewise the greatest Part of the Poems of which it is composed, and particularly *the Happy Man,* which he published as a Specimen.

The Subscriptions of those whom these Papers should influence to patronise Merit in Distress, without any other Solicitation, were directed to be left at *Button*'s Coffee-house; and Mr *Savage* going thither a few Days afterwards, without Expectation of any Effect from his Proposal, found to his Surprise seventy Guineas†, which had been sent him
in

Plung'd me, thus deep, in Sorrow's searching Flood;
And wash'd me from the Mem'ry of her Blood.
    But, Oh ! whatever Cause has mov'd her Hate,
Let me but sigh, in Silence, at my Fate;
The God, *within,* perhaps may touch her Breast;
And, when she *pities,* who can be distress'd ?

† The Names of those who so generously contributed to his Relief, having been mentioned in a former Account, ought not to be omitted here. They were the Dutchess of
Cleveland,

in Confequence of the Compaffion excited by Mr *Hill*'s pathetic Reprefentation.

To this Mifcellany he publifh'd a Preface*, in which he gives an Account of his Mother's Cruelty

Cleveland, Lady *Cheyney*, Lady *Caftlemain*, Lady *Gower*, Lady *Lechmere*, the Dutchefs Dowager, and Dutchefs of *Rutland*, Lady *Strafford*, the Countefs Dowager of *Warwick*, Mrs *Mary Floyer*, Mrs *Sofuel Noel*, Duke of *Rutland*, Lord *Gainfborough*, Lord *Milfington*, Mr *John Savage*.

---

* This Preface is as follows :

> *Crudelis Mater magis, an Puer improbus ille ?*
> *Improbus ille Puer, crudelis tu quoque Mater.* Virg.

My Readers, I am afraid, when they obferve *Richard Savage* join'd fo clofe, and fo conftantly, *to Son of the late Earl* Rivers, will impute to a ridiculous Vanity, what is the Effect of an unhappy Neceffity, which my hard Fortune has thrown me under——I am to be pardoned for adhering a little tenacioufly to my Father, becaufe my Mother will allow me to be No-body; and has almoft reduced me, among heavier Afflictions, to that uncommon Kind of Want, which the *Indians* of *America* complained of at our firft fettling among them ; when they came to beg *Names* of the *Englifh*, becaufe (faid they) we are poor Men of ourfelves, and have none we can lay Claim to.

The good Nature of thofe, to whom I have not the Honour to be known, would forgive me the ludicrous Turn of this Beginning, if they knew but how little Reafon I have to be merry——It was my Misfortune to be Son of the above-mentioned Earl, by the late Countefs of *Macclesfield*, (now Widow of Colonel *Henry Bret*) whofe Divorce, on Occafion of the Amour which I was a Confequence of, has left fomething on Record, which I take to be very remarkable ; and it is this : Certain of our great Judges, in their *temporal* Decifions, act with a *fpiritual* Regard

Cruelty in a very uncommon Strain of Humour, and with a Gaiety of Imagination,
which

Regard to *Levitical Divinity*; and in particular to the Ten
Commandments: Two of which seem in my Cafe, to
have vifibly influenced their Opinions——*Thou shalt not
commit Adultery*, pointed fulleft on my Mother: But, as to
The Lord's vifiting the Sins of the Fathers upon the Children,
it was confidered as what could regard *me* only: And for
that Reafon, I fuppofe, it had been inconfiftent with the
Rules of Sanctity, to affign Provifion out of my Mother's
return'd Eftate, for Support of an Infant Sinner.

Thus, while *legally* the Son of one Earl, and *naturally*
of another, I am, *nominally*, No-body's Son at all: For
the Lady having given me *too much Father*, thought it but
an equivalent Deduction, to leave me *no Mother*, by Way
of Balance——So I am fported into the World, a Kind
of Shuttlecock, between Law and Nature——If Law had
not beaten me back, by the Stroke of an Act, on purpofe,
I had not been *above Wit*, by the Privilege of a Man of
Quality: Nay, I might have preferved into the Bargain,
the Lives of *Duke Hamilton* and *Lord Mohun*, whofe Difpute arofe from the Eftate of that Earl of *Macclesfield*, whom
(but for the mentioned Act) I muft have *called Father*—
And, if Nature had not ftruck me off, with a ftronger
Blow than Law did, the other Earl, who was moft *emphatically* my Father, could never have been told, I was
dead, when he was about to enable me, by his *Will*, to
have lived to fome Purpofe. An unaccountable Severity
of a Mother! whom I was then not old enough to have
deferved it from: And by which I am a fingle unhappy
Inftance, among that Nobleman's natural Children; and
thrown, friendlefs on the World, without Means of fupporting *myfelf*; and without Authority to apply to thofe,
whofe Duty I know it is to fupport me.

Thus

which the Succefs of his Subfcription probably produced.

The

Thus however ill qualified I am to *live by my Wits*, I
have the beft Plea in the World for attempting it; fince
it is too apparent, that I was *born to it*—Having wearied
my Judgment with fruitlefs Endeavours to be happy, I gave
the Reins to my Fancy, that I might learn, at leaft, to be
eafy.

But I ceafe a while to fpeak of *myfelf*, that I may fay
fomething of my Mifcellany——I was furnifhed, by the
Verfes of my Friends, with *Wit* enough to deferve a Subfcription; but I wanted another much more profitable
Quality, which fhould have emboldened me to folicit it,
(another of my Wants, that, I hope, may be imputed to
my Mother!) I had met with little Encouragement, but
for the Endeavours of fome few Gentlemen, in my Be-
half, who were generous enough to confider my ill Fortune, as a Merit that intitled me to their Notice.

Among thefe I am particularly indebted to the Author
of the *Plain Dealers*, who was pleafed, in two of his Papers (which I intreat his Pardon, for reprinting before my
Mifcellany) to point out my unhappy Story to the World,
with fo touching a Humanity, and fo good an Effect,
that many Perfons of Quality, of all Ranks, and of both
Sexes, diftinguifhed themfelves with the Promptnefs he
had hinted to the noble-minded; and not ftaying till they
were applied to, fent me the Honour of their Subfcriptions, in the moft liberal and handfome Manner, for Encouragement of my Undertaking.

I ought here to acknowledge feveral Favours from Mr
Hill, whofe Writings are a fhining Ornament of this Mifcellany; but I wave detaining my Readers, and beg Leave
to refer them to a Copy of Verfes called the *Friend,* which
I have taken the Liberty to addrefs to that Gentleman.

To

The Dedication is addreſſed to the Lady *Mary Wortley Montague*, whom he flåtters with-

To return to the Lady, my Mother—Had the celebrated Mr *Locke* been acquainted with her Example, it had certainly appeared in his *Chapter* againſt innate practical Principles ; becauſe it would have completed his Inſtances of Enormities : Some of which, though not exactly in the Order that he mentions them, are as follow—*Have there not been* (ſays he) *whole Nations, and thoſe of the moſt civilized People, amongſt whom, the expoſing their Children, to periſh by Want or wild Beaſts, has been a Practice as little condemned or ſcrupled as the begetting them?* Were I inclinable to be ſerious, I could eaſily prove that I have not been more gently dealt with by Mrs *Bret* ; but if this is any way foreign to my Caſe, I ſhall find a nearer Example in the whimſical one that enſues.

It is familiar (ſays the afore-cited Author) *among the* Mengrelians, *a People profeſſing Chriſtianity, to bury their Children alive without Scruple*——There are indeed ſundry Sects of Chriſtians, and I have often wondered which could be my *Mamma's,* but now I find ſhe piouſly profeſſes and practiſes Chriſtianity after the Manner of the *Mengrelians* ; ſhe induſtriouſly obſcured me, when my Fortune depended on my being known, and, in that Senſe, ſhe may be ſaid to have buried me alive ; and ſure, like a *Mengrelian,* ſhe muſt have committed the Action without Scruple ; for ſhe is a Woman of Spirit, and can ſee the Conſequence without Remorſe——*The* Caribees (continues my Author) *were wont to caſtrate their Children in order to fat and eat them*—— Here indeed I can draw no Parallel ; for to ſpeak Juſtice of the Lady, ſhe never contributed ought to have me pampered, but always promoted my being ſtarved : Nor did ſhe, even in my Infancy, betray Fondneſs enough to be ſuſpected of a Deſign to devour me ; but, on the contrary, not enduring

230

without Reserve, and, to confefs the Truth, with very little * Art. The fame Obfervation
may

during me ever to approach her, offered a Bribe to have me fhipp'd off, in an odd Manner, to one of the Plantations—When I was about fifteen her Affection began to awake, and had I but known my Intereft, I had been handfomly provided for. In fhort, I was folicited to be bound Apprentice to a very honeft and reputable Occupation——a *Shoemaker*; an Offer which I undutifully rejected. I was, in fine, unwilling to underftand her in a literal Senfe, and hoped, that, like the Prophets of old, fhe might have hinted her Mind in a Kind of Parable, or proverbial Way of fpeaking; as thus—That one Time or other I might, on due Application, have the Honour of *taking the Length of her Foot.*

Mr *Locke* mentions another Set of People that difpatch their Children, if a pretended Aftrologer declares them to have unhappy Stars——Perhaps my *Mamma* has procured fome *cunning Man* to calculate my Nativity; or having had fome ominous Dream, which preceded my Birth, the dire Event may have appeared to her in the dark and dreary Bottom of a *China* Cup, where Coffee-Stains are often confulted for Prophecies, and held as infallible as were the Leaves of the ancient *Sybils*—To be partly ferious: I am rather willing to wrong her Judgment, by fufpecting it to be tainted a little with the Tenets of Superftition, than fuppofe fhe can be Miftrefs of a feared Confcience, and act on no Principle at all.

* This the following Extract from it will prove.
——" Since our Country has been honoured with the Glory of your Wit, as elevated and immortal as your Soul, it no longer remains a Doubt whether your Sex have Strength of Mind in Proportion to their Sweetnefs. There is fomething in your Verfes as diftinguifhed as your Air—They

F   are

231

may be extended to all his Dedications : His Compliments are conftrained and violent, heaped together without the Grace of Order, or the Decency of Introduction : He feems to have written his Panegyrics for the Perufal only of his Patrons, and to have imagined that he had no other Tafk than to pamper them with Praifes however grofs, and that Flattery would make its Way to the Heart, without the Affiftance of Elegance or Invention.

Soon afterwards the Death of the King furnifhed a general Subject for a poetical Conteft, in which Mr *Savage* engaged, and is allowed to have carried the Prize of Honour from his Competitors; but I know not whether he gained by his Performance any other Advantage than the Increafe of his Reputation ; though it muft certainly have been with farther Views that he prevailed upon himfelf to attempt a Species of Writing, of which all the

are as ftrong as Truth, as deep as Reafon, as clear as Innocence, and as fmooth as Beauty——They contain a namelefs and peculiar Mixture of Force and Grace, which is at once fo movingly ferene, and fo majeftically lovely, that it is too amiable to appear any where but in your Eyes, and in your Writings."

" As Fortune is not more my Enemy than I am the Enemy of Flattery, I know not how I can forbear this Application to your Ladyfhip, becaufe there is fcarce a Poffibility that I fhould fay more than I believe, when I am fpeaking of your Excellence."——

the Topics had been long before exhaufted, and which was made at once difficult by the Multitudes that had failed in it, and thofe that had fucceeded.

He was now advancing in Reputation, and though frequently involved in very diftrefs-ful Perplexities, appeared however to be gaining upon Mankind, when both his Fame and his Life were endangered by an Event, of which it is not yet determined, whether it ought to be mentioned as a Crime or a Calamity.

On the 20th of *November* 1727. Mr *Savage* came from *Richmond*, where he then lodged that he might perfue his Studies with lefs Interruption, with an Intent to difcharge another Lodging which he had in *Weftminfter*; and accidentally meeting two Gentlemen his Acquaintances, whofe Names were *Merchant* and *Gregory*, he went in with them to a neighbouring Coffee-houfe, and fat drinking till it was late, it being in no Time of Mr *Savage*'s Life any Part of his Character to be the firft of the Company that defired to feparate. He would willingly have gone to Bed in the fame Houfe, but there was not Room for the whole Company, and therefore they agreed to ramble about the Streets, and divert themfelves with fuch A-

mufements

mufements as fhould offer themfelves till Morning.

In their Walk they happened unluckily to difcover Light in *Robinfon's* Coffee-houfe, near *Charing-Crofs*, and therefore went in. *Merchant*, with fome Rudenefs, demanded a Room, and was told that there was a good Fire in the next Parlour, which the Company were about to leave, being then paying their Reckoning. *Merchant* not fatisfied with this Anfwer, rufhed into the Room, and was followed by his Companions. He then petulantly placed himfelf between the Company and the Fire, and foon after kicked down the Table. This produced a Quarrel, Swords were drawn on both Sides, and one Mr. *James Sinclair* was killed. *Savage* having wounded likewife a Maid that held him, forced his Way with *Merchant* out of the Houfe; but being intimidated and confufed, without Refolution either to fly or ftay, they were taken in a back Court by one of the Company and fome Soldiers, whom he had called to his Affiftance.

Being fecured and guarded that Night, they were in the Morning carried before three Juftices, who committed them to the *Gate-houfe*, from whence, upon the Death of Mr *Sinclair*, which happened the fame Day, they

they were removed in the Night to *Newgate,* where they were however treated with some Distinction, exempted from the Ignominy of Chains, and confined, not among the common Criminals, but in the *Press-Yard.*

When the Day of Trial came, the Court was crouded in a very unusual Manner, and the Publick appeared to interest itself as in a Cause of general Concern. The Witnesses against Mr *Savage* and his Friends were, the Woman who kept the House, which was a House of ill Fame, and her Maid, the Men who were in the Room with Mr *Sinclair*, and a Woman of the Town, who had been drinking with them, and with whom one of them had been seen in Bed. They swore in general, that *Merchant* gave the Provocation, which *Savage* and *Gregory* drew their Swords to justify; that *Savage* drew first, and that he stabbed *Sinclair* when he was not in a Posture of Defence, or while *Gregory* commanded his Sword; that after he had given the Thrust he turned pale, and would have retired, but that the Maid clung round him, and one of the Company endeavoured to detain him, from whom he broke, by cutting the Maid on the Head, but was afterwards taken in a Court.

There was some Difference in their Depositions; one did not see *Savage* give the Wound, another saw it given when *Sinclair* held his

Point

Point towards the Ground ; and the Woman of the Town afferted, that fhe did not fee *Sinclair*'s Sword at all : This Difference however was very far from amounting to Inconfiftency, but it was fufficient to fhew, that the Hurry of the Quarrel was fuch, that it was not eafy to difcover the Truth with relation to particular Circumftances, and that therefore fome Deductions were to be made from the Credibility of the Teftimonies.

Sinclair had declared feveral times before his Death, that he received his Wound from *Savage* ; nor did *Savage* at his Trial deny the Fact, but endeavoured partly to extenuate it by urging the Suddennefs of the whole Action, and the Impoffibility of any ill Defign, or premeditated Malice, and partly to juftify it by the Neceffity of Self-Defence, and the Hazard of his own Life, if he had loft that Opportunity of giving the Thruft : He obferved, that neither Reafon nor Law obliged a Man to wait for the Blow which was threatned, and which, if he fhould fuffer it, he might never be able to return ; that it was always allowable to prevent an Affault, and to preferve Life by taking away that of the Adverfary, by whom it was endangered.

With regard to the Violence with which he endeavoured his Efcape, he declared, that it was not his Defign to fly from Juftice, or decline

decline a Trial, but to avoid the Expences and Severities of a Prifon, and that he intended to have appeared at the Bar without Compulfion.

This Defence, which took up more than an Hour, was heard by the Multitude that thronged the Court with the moft attentive and refpectful Silence : Thofe who thought he ought not to be acquitted owned that Applaufe could not be refufed him ; and thofe who before pitied his Misfortunes, now reverenced his Abilities.

The Witneffes which appeared againft him were proved to be Perfons of Characters which did not entitle them to much Credit; a common Strumpet, a Woman by whom Strumpets were entertained, and a Man by whom they were fupported; and the Character of *Savage* was by feveral Perfons of Diftinction afferted, to be that of a modeft inoffenfive Man, not inclined to Broils, or to Infolence, and who had, to that Time, been only known for his Misfortunes and his Wit.

Had his Audience been his Judges, he had undoubtedly been acquitted ; but Mr *Page*, who was then upon the Bench, treated him with his ufual Infolence and Severity, and when he had fummed up the Evidence, endeavoured to exafperate the Jury, as Mr *Savage* ufed to relate it, with this eloquent Harangue.

" Gentlemen

" Gentlemen of the Jury, you are to con-
" fider, that Mr *Savage* is a very great Man,
" a much greater Man than you or I, Gentle-
" men of the Jury; that he wears very fine
" Clothes, much finer Clothes than you or I,
" Gentlemen of the Jury; that he has abun-
" dance of Money in his Pocket, much more
" Money than you or I, Gentlemen of the
" Jury; but, Gentlemen of the Jury, is it
" not a very hard Cafe, Gentlemen of the
" Jury, that Mr *Savage* fhould therefore kill
" you or me, Gentlemen of the Jury?"

Mr *Savage* hearing his Defence thus mif-
reprefented, and the Men who were to decide
his Fate incited againft him by invidious
Comparifons, refolutely afferted, that his Caufe
was not candidly explained, and began to re-
capitulate what he had before faid with regard to his Condition, and the Neceffity of
endeavouring to efcape the Expences of Imprifonment; but the Judge having ordered
him to be filent, and repeated his Orders
without Effect, commanded that he fhould
be taken from the Bar by Force.

The Jury then heard the Opinion of the
Judge, that good Characters were of no
Weight againft pofitive Evidence, though they
might turn the Scale, where it was doubtful;
and that though when two Men attack each
other,

other, the Death of either is only Manflaughter; but where one is the Aggreffor, as
in the Cafe before them, and in Purfuance
of his firft Attack, kills the other, the Law
fuppofes the Action, however fudden, to be
malicious. They then deliberated upon their
Verdict, and determined that Mr *Savage* and
Mr *Gregory* were guilty of Murder, and
Mr *Merchant*, who had no Sword, only of
Manflaughter.

Thus ended this memorable Trial, which
lafted eight Hours. Mr *Savage* and Mr *Gregory* were conducted back to Prifon, where
they were more clofely confined, and loaded
with Irons of fifty Pounds Weight: Four
Days afterwards they were fent back to the
Court to receive Sentence; on which Occafion Mr *Savage* made, as far as it could be
retained in Memory, the following Speech.

"It is now, my Lord, too late to offer
" any Thing by way of Defence, or Vindi-
" cation; nor can we expect ought from your
" Lordfhips, in this Court, but the Sentence
" which the Law requires you, as Judges, to
" pronounce againft Men of our calamitous
" Condition.---But we are alfo perfuaded,
" that as mere Men, and out of this Seat of
" rigorous Juftice, you are fufceptive of the
" tender Paffions, and too humane, not to
G " com-

" commiferate the unhappy Situation of thofe
" whom the Law fometimes perhaps————
" exacts————from you to pronounce upon.
" No doubt you diftinguifh between Offences,
" which arife out of Premeditation, and a
" Difpofition habituated to Vice or Immo-
" rality, and Tranfgreffions, which are the
" unhappy and unforefeen Effects of a cafual
" Abfence of Reafon, and fudden Impulfe of
" Paffion : We therefore hope you will con-
" tribute all you can to an Extenfion of that
" Mercy, which the Gentlemen of the Jury
" have been pleafed to fhew Mr *Merchant*,
" who (allowing Facts as fworn againft us by
" the Evidence) has led us into this our Ca-
" lamity. I hope, this will not be conftrued
" as if we meant to reflect upon that Gentle-
" man, or remove any Thing from us upon
" him, or that we repine the more at our
" Fate, becaufe he has no Participation of it:
" No, my Lord ! For my Part, I declare
" nothing could more foften my Grief, than
" to be without any Companion in fo great
" a Misfortune*."

Mr *Savage* had now no Hopes of Life, but
from the Mercy of the Crown, which was
very earneftly folicited by his Friends, and
which,

* Mr *Savage's* Life.

240

which, with whatever Difficulty the Story may obtain Belief, was obstructed only by his Mother.

To prejudice the Queen against him, she made use of an Incident, which was omitted in the order of Time, that it might be mentioned together with the Purpose which it was made to serve. Mr *Savage*, when he had discovered his Birth, had an incessant Desire to speak to his Mother, who always avoided him in publick, and refused him Admission into her House. One Evening walking, as it was his Custom, in the Street that she inhabited, he saw the Door of her House by Accident open; he entered it, and finding none in the Passage, to hinder him, went up Stairs to salute her. She discovered him before he could enter her Chamber, alarmed the Family with the most distressful Outcries, and when she had by her Screams gathered them about her, ordered them to drive out of the House that Villain, who had forced himself in upon her, and endeavoured to murder her. *Savage*, who had attempted with the most submissive Tenderness to soften her Rage, hearing her utter so detestable an Accusation, thought it prudent to retire, and, I believe, never attempted afterwards to speak to her.

But shocked as he was with her Falshood and her Cruelty, he imagined that she intend-

G 2   ed

ed no other Ufe of her Lye, than to fet herfelf free from his Embraces and Solicitations,
and was very far from fufpecting that fhe
would treafure it in her Memory, as an Inftrument of future Wickednefs, or that fhe
would endeavour for this fictitious Affault to
deprive him of his Life.

But when the Queen was folicited for his
Pardon, and informed of the fevere Treat-
ments which he had fuffered from his Judge,
fhe anfwered, that however unjuftifiable might
be the Manner of his Trial, or whatever Extenuation the Action for which he was condemned might admit, fhe could not think
that Man a proper Object of the King's Mercy, who had been capable of entering his
Mother's Houfe in the Night, with an Intent
to murder her.

By whom this atrocious Calumny had been
tranfmitted to the Queen, whether fhe that
invented, had the Front to relate it; whether
fhe found any one weak enough to credit it,
or corrupt enough to concur with her in her
hateful Defign, I know not; but Methods
had been taken to perfuade the Queen fo
ftrongly of the Truth of it, that fhe for a
long Time refufed to hear any of thofe who
petitioned for his Life.

Thus had *Savage* perifhed by the Evidence
of a Bawd, a Strumpet, and his Mother, had
not

not Juſtice and Compaſſion procured him an Advocate of Rank too great to be rejected unheard, and of Virtue too eminent to be heard without being believed. His Merit and his Calamities happened to reach the Ear of the Counteſs of *Hertford,* who engaged in his Support with all the Tenderneſs that is excited by Pity, and all the Zeal which is kindled by Generoſity, and demanding an Audience of the Queen, laid before her the whole Series of his Mother's Cruelty, expoſed the Improbability of an Accuſation by which he was charged with an Intent to commit a Murder, that could produce no Advantage, and ſoon convinced her how little his former Conduct could deſerve to be mentioned as a Reaſon for extraordinary Severity.

The Interpoſition of this Lady was ſo ſuccefsful, that he was ſoon after admitted to Bail, and on the 9th of *March,* 1728, pleaded the King's Pardon.

It is natural to enquire upon what Motives his Mother could proſecute him in a Manner ſo outrageous and implacable; for what Reaſon ſhe could employ all the Acts of Malice, and all the Snares of Calumny, to take away the Life of her own Son, of a Son who never injured her, who was never ſupported by her Expence, nor obſtructed any Proſpect of Pleaſure or Advantage; why ſhe ſhould endeavour

to

to deftroy him by a Lye; a Lye which could not gain Credit, but muft vanifh of itfelf at the firft Moment of Examination, and of which only this can be faid to make it probable, that it may be obferved from her Conduct, that the moft execrable Crimes are fometimes committed without apparent Temptation.

This Mother is ftill alive, and may perhaps even yet, though her Malice was fo often defeated, enjoy the Pleafure of reflecting, that the Life which fhe often endeavoured to deftroy, was at leaft fhortened by her maternal Offices; that though fhe could not tranfport her Son to the Plantations, bury him in the Shop of a Mechanick, or haften the Hand of the publick Executioner, fhe has yet had the Satisfaction of imbittering all his Hours, and forcing him into Exigences, that hurried on his Death.

It is by no Means neceffary to aggravate the Enormity of this Woman's Conduct, by placing it in Oppofition to that of the Countefs of *Hertford*; no one can fail to obferve how much more amiable it is to relieve, than to opprefs, and to refcue Innocence from Deftruction, than to deftroy without an Injury.

Mr *Savage*, during his Imprifonment, his Trial, and the Time in which he lay under Sentence of Death, behaved with great Firmnefs and Equality of Mind, and confirmed by

his

his Fortitude the Efteem of thofe, who before admired him for his Abilities. The peculiar Circumftances of his Life were made more generally known by a fhort Account*, which was then publifhed, and of which feveral thoufands were in a few Weeks difperfed over the Nation ; and the Compaffion of Mankind operated fo powerfully in his Favour, that he was enabled, by frequent Prefents, not only to fupport himfelf, but to affift Mr *Gregory* in Prifon ; and when he was pardoned and releafed, he found the Number of his Friends not leffened.

The Nature of the Act for which he had been tried was in itfelf doubtful ; of the Evidences which appeared againft him, the Character of the Man was not unexceptionable, that of the Women notorioufly infamous ; fhe whofe Teftimony chiefly influenced the Jury to condemn him, afterwards retracted her Affertions. He always himfelf denied that he was drunk, as had been generally reported. Mr *Gregory*, who is now Collector of *Antigua*, is faid to declare him far lefs criminal than he was imagined even by fome who favoured him : And *Page* himfelf afterwards confeffed, that he had treated him with uncommon Rigour. When all thefe Particulars are rated together, perhaps the Memory of *Savage* may not be much fullied by his Trial.

Some

* Written by Mr *Beckingham* and another Gentleman.

Some Time after he had obtained his Liberty, he met in the Street the Woman that had fworn with fo much Malignity againft him. She informed him, that fhe was in Diftrefs, and, with a Degree of Confidence not eafily attainable, defired him to relieve her. He, inftead of infulting her Mifery, and taking Pleafure in the Calamities of one who had brought his Life into Danger, reproved her gently for her Perjury, and changing the only Guinea that he had, divided it equally between her and himfelf.

This is an Action which in fome Ages would have made a Saint, and perhaps in others a Hero, and which, without any hyperbolical Encomiums, muft be allowed to be an Inftance of uncommon Generofity, an Act of complicated Virtue; by which he at once relieved the Poor, corrected the Vicious, and forgave an Enemy; by which he at once remitted the ftrongeft Provocations, and exercifed the moft ardent Charity.

Compaffion was indeed the diftinguifhing Quality of *Savage*; he never appeared inclined to take Advantage of Weaknefs, to attack the defencelefs, or to prefs upon the falling; whoever was diftreffed was certain at leaft of his Good-Wifhes; and when he could give no Affiftance, to extricate them from Misfortunes, he endeavoured to footh them by Sympathy and Tendernefs. But

But when his Heart was not foftened by the Sight of Mifery, he was fometimes obftinate in his Refentment, and did not quickly lofe the Remembrance of an Injury. He always continued to fpeak with Anger of the Infolence and Partiality of *Page*, and a fhort Time before his Death revenged it by a Satire*.

It

* The Satire from which the following Lines are extracted was called by Mr *Savage*, *An Epiftle on Authors :* It was never printed intire, but feveral Fragments were inferted by him in the *Magazine*, after his Retirement into the Country.

Were all like YORKE of delicate Addrefs,
Strength to difcern, and Sweetnefs to exprefs ;
Learn'd, juft, polite, born ev'ry Heart to gain ;
Like *Cummins* mild, like a *Fortefcue* humane;
All eloquent of Truth, divinely known ;
So deep, fo clear, all Science is his own.
How far unlike fuch Worthies, once a Drudge,
From flound'ring in low Caufes, rofe a JUDGE.
Form'd to make Pleaders laugh, his *Nonfenfe* thunders,
And, on low Juries, breathes contagious Blunders.
His Brothers blufh, becaufe no Blufh he knows,
Nor e'er b *one uncorrupted Finger fhows.*
See, drunk with Power, the *Circuit Lord* expreft !
Full, in his Eye, his Betters ftand confeft ;
Whofe Wealth, Birth, Virtue, from a Tongue fo loofe,
'Scape not provincial, vile, buffoon Abufe.
Still to what Circuit is affign'd his Name,
There, fwift before him, flies the Warner *Fame.*

H   Conteft

a The Hon. *William Fortefcue*, Efq; now Mafter of the Rolls.
b When *Page* one uncorrupted Finger fhows.
D. of *Wharton* .

It is natural to enquire in what Terms Mr *Savage* fpoke of this fatal Action, when the Danger was over, and he was under no Neceffity of ufing any Art to fet his Conduct in the faireft Light. He was not willing to dwell upon it, and if he tranfiently mentioned it, appeared neither to confider himfelf as a Murderer, nor as a Man wholly free from the Guilt of Blood*. How much and how long he regretted it, appeared in a † Poem which he

Conteft ftops fhort, Confent yields every Caufe
To Coft, Delay, endures them and withdraws.
But how 'fcape *Pris'ners?* To their Trial chain'd,
All, all fhall ftand condemn'd, who ftand arraign'd.
Dire *Guilt,* which elfe would Deteftation caufe,
Pre-judg'd with Infult, wond'rous Pity draws.
But 'fcapes ev'n *Innocence* his harfh Harangue?
Alas —— ev'n Innocence itfelf muft hang;
Muft hang to pleafe him, when of Spleen poffeft:
Muft hang to bring forth an abortive Jeft.
　Why liv'd he not ere *Star-Chambers* had fail'd,
When Fine, Tax, Cenfure, all, but Law, prevail'd;
Or Law, fubfervient to fome murd'rous Will,
Became a Precedent to Murder ftill?
Yet ev'n when Patriots did for Traytors bleed,
Was e'er the Jobb to fuch a Slave decreed;
Whofe favage Mind wants fophift Art to draw,
O'er murder'd Virtue, fpecious Veils of Law?

Gentleman's Magazine, Sept. 1741.

* In one of his Letters he ftiles it, a *fatal Quarrel, but too well known.*
† Is Chance a Guilt, that my difaft'rous Heart,
　For Mifchief never meant, muft ever fmart?

Can

he publifhed many Years afterwards. On Occafion of a Copy of Verfes in which the Failings of good Men were recounted, and in which the Author had endeavoured to illuftrate his Pofition, that *the beft may fometimes deviate from Virtue*, by an Inftance of Murder committed by *Savage* in the Heat of Wine, *Savage* remarked, that it was no very juft Reprefentation of a good Man, to fuppofe him liable to Drunkennefs, and difpofed in his Riots to cut Throats.

He was now indeed at Liberty, but was, as before, without any other Support than accidental Favours and uncertain Patronage afforded him; Sources by which he was sometimes

H 2

Can Self-Defence be Sin ?—Ah ! plead no more ;
What though no purpos'd Malice ftain'd thee o'er ;
Had Heav'n befriended thy unhappy Side,
Thou hadft not been provok'd, or then hadft dy'd.
Far be the Guilt of Home-fhed Blood from all
On whom, unfought, embroiling Dangers fall.
Still the pale *Dead* revives and lives to me,
To me, through Pity's Eye, condemn'd to fee.
Remembrance veils his Rage, but fwells his Fate,
Griev'd I forgive, and am grown cool too late.
Young and unthoughtful then, who knows one Day,
What rip'ning Virtues might have made their Way ?
He might one Day his Country's Friend have prov'd,
Been gen'rous, happy, candid and belov'd ;
He might have fav'd fome Worth now doom'd to fall,
And I perchance in him have *murder'd* all.   *Baftard.*

times very liberally fupplied, and which at other Times were fuddenly ftopped; fo that he fpent his Life between Want and Plenty, or, what was yet worfe, between Beggary and Extravagance; for as whatever he received was the Gift of Chance, which might as well favour him at one Time as another, he was tempted to fquander what he had, becaufe he always hoped to be immediately fupplied.

Another Caufe of his Profufion was the abfurd Kindnefs of his Friends, who at once rewarded and enjoyed his Abilities, by treating him at Taverns, and habituated him to Pleafures which he could not afford to enjoy, and which he was not able to deny himfelf, though he purchafed the Luxury of a fingle Night by the Anguifh of Cold and Hunger for a Week.

The Experience of thefe Inconveniences determined him to endeavour after fome fettled Income, which, having long found Submiffion and Intreaties fruitlefs, he attempted to extort from his Mother by rougher Methods. He had now, as he acknowledged, loft that Tendernefs for her, which the whole Series of her Cruelty had not been able wholly to reprefs, till he found, by the Efforts which fhe made for his Deftruction, that fhe was not content with refufing to affift him, and being neutral in his Struggles with Poverty, but was as ready to fnatch

fnatch every Opportunity of adding to his Misfortunes, and that fhe was to be confidered as an Enemy implacably malicious, whom nothing but his Blood could fatisfy. He therefore threatned to harafs her with Lampoons, and to publifh a copious Narrative of her Conduct, unlefs fhe confented to purchafe an Exemption from Infamy, by allowing him a Penfion.

This Expedient proved fuccefsful. Whether Shame ftill furvived, though Virtue was extinct, or whether her Relations had more delicacy than herfelf, and imagined that fome of the Darts which Satire might point at her would glance upon them: Lord *Tyrconnel*, whatever were his Motives, upon his Promife to lay afide his Defign of expofing the Cruelty of his Mother, received him into his Family, treated him as his Equal, and engaged to allow him a Penfion of two hundred Pounds a Year.

This was the Golden Part of Mr *Savage*'s Life; and for fome Time he had no Reafon to complain of Fortune; his Appearance was fplendid, his Expences large, and his Acquaintance extenfive. He was courted by all who endeavoured to be thought Men of Genius, and careffed by all who valued themfelves upon a refined Tafte. To admire Mr *Savage* was a Proof of Difcernment, and to be acquainted with him was a Title to poetical Reputation.

Reputation. His Prefence was fufficient to make any Place of publick Entertainment popular; and his Approbation and Example conftituted the Fafhion. So powerful is Genius, when it is invefted with the Glitter of Affluence; Men willingly pay to Fortune that Regard which they owe to Merit, and are pleafed when they have an Opportunity at once of gratifying their Vanity, and practifing their Duty.

This Interval of Profperity furnifhed him with Opportunities of enlarging his Knowledge of human Nature, by contemplating Life from its higheft Gradations to its loweft; and had he afterwards applied to Dramatic Poetry, he would perhaps not have had many Superiors; for as he never fuffered any Scene to pafs before his Eyes without Notice, he had treafured in his Mind all the different Combinations of Paffions, and the innumerable Mixtures of Vice and Virtue, which diftinguifh one Character from another; and as his Conception was ftrong, his Expreffions were clear, he eafily received Impreffions from Objects, and very forcibly tranfmitted them to others.

Of his exact Obfervations on human Life he has left a Proof, which would do Honour to the greateft Names, in a fmall Pamphlet, called, *The Author to be let*, where he introduces

duces

duces *Iſcariot Hackney*, a proſtitute Scribler, giving an Account of his Birth, his Education, his Diſpoſition and Morals, Habits of Life, and Maxims of Conduct. In the Introduction are related many ſecret Hiſtories of the petty Writers of that Time, but ſometimes mixed with ungenerous Reflections on their Birth, their Circumſtances, or thoſe of their Relations; nor can it be denied, that ſome Paſſages are ſuch as *Iſcariot Hackney* might himſelf have produced.

He was accuſed likewiſe of living in an Appearance of Friendſhip with ſome whom he ſatiriſed, and of making uſe of the Confidence which he gained by a ſeeming Kindneſs to diſcover Failings and expoſe them ; it muſt be confeſſed, that Mr *Savage's* Eſteem was no very certain Poſſeſſion, and that he would lampoon at one Time thoſe whom he had praiſed at another.

It may be alledged, that the ſame Man may change his Principles, and that he who was once deſervedly commended, may be afterwards ſatiriſed with equal Juſtice ; or that the Poet was dazzled with the Appearance of Virtue, and found the Man whom he had celebrated, when he had an Opportunity of examining him more nearly, unworthy of the Panegyric which he had too haſtily beſtowed ; and that as a falſe Satire ought to be recanted, for

for the fake of him whofe Reputation may be injured, falfe Praife ought likewife to be obviated, left the Diftinction between Vice and Virtue fhould be loft, left a bad Man fhould be trufted upon the Credit of his Encomiaft, or left others fhould endeavour to obtain the like Praifes by the fame Means.

But though thefe Excufes may be often plaufible, and fometimes juft, they are very feldom fatisfactory to Mankind ; and the Writer, who is not conftant to his Subject, quickly finks into Contempt, his Satire lofes its Force, and his Panegyric its Value, and he is only confidered at one Time as a Flatterer, and as a Calumniator at another.

To avoid thefe Imputations, it is only neceffary to follow the Rules of Virtue, and to preferve an unvaried Regard to Truth. For though it is undoubtedly poffible, that a Man, however cautious, may be fometimes deceived by an artful Appearance of Virtue, or by falfe Evidences of Guilt, fuch Errors will not be frequent; and it will be allowed, that the Name of an Author would never have been made contemptible, had no Man ever faid what he did not think, or mifled others, but when he was himfelf deceived.

If the *Author to be let* was firft publifhed in a fingle Pamphlet, and afterwards inferted in a Collection of Pieces relating to the *Dunciad,*

ciad, which were addreſſed by Mr *Savage* to the Earl of *Middleſex*, in a * Dedication, which he was prevailed upon to ſign, though he did not write it, and in which there are
ſome

* *To the Right Hon. the Earl of* Middleſex.

My Lord,

That elegant Taſte in Poetry, which is hereditary to your Lordſhip, together with that particular Regard, with which you honour the Author to whom theſe Papers relate, make me imagine this Collection will not be unpleaſing to you. And I may preſume to ſay, the Pieces themſelves are ſuch as are not unworthy your Lordſhip's Patronage, my own Part in it excepted. I ſpeak only of the *Author to be let*, having no Title to any other, not even the ſmall ones out of the Journals. May I be permitted to declare (to the End I may ſeem not quite ſo unworthy of your Lordſhip's Favour, as ſome Writers of my *Age* and Circumſtances) that I never was concerned in any Journals. I ever thought the exorbitant Liberty, which moſt of thoſe Papers take with their Superiors, unjuſtifiable in any Rank of Men; but deteſtable in ſuch who do it merely for Hire, and without even the bad Excuſe of *Paſſion* and *Reſentment*. On the contrary, being once inclined, upon ſome advantageous Propoſals, to enter into a †Paper of another Kind, I immediately deſiſted, on finding admitted into it (though as the Publiſher told me purely by an Accident) two or three Lines reflecting on a *great Miniſter*. Were my Life ever ſo unhappy, it ſhall not be ſtain'd with a Conduct, which my Birth at leaſt (though neither my *Education* nor *good Fortune*) ſhould ſet me
I   above,

† The Paper here meant, was probably the *Grubſtreet-Journal*, which Mr *Savage* was once invited to undertake, but which he declined, whether for the Reaſon here mentioned is not certain.

ſome Poſitions, that the true Author would
perhaps

above, much leſs with any Ingratitude to that noble Perſon, to whoſe Interceſſion (next to his Majeſty's Good-
neſs) I owe in a great Meaſure that *Life itſelf*.

> ——*Nec ſi miſerum Fortuna Sinonem*
> *Finxit, vanum etiam mendacemque improba finget.*

I believe your Lordſhip will pardon this Digreſſion, or
any other which keeps me from the Stile, you ſo much
hate, of Dedication.

I will not pretend to diſplay thoſe riſing Virtues in your
Lordſhip, which the next Age will certainly know without
my Help, but rather relate (what elſe it will as certainly be
ignorant of) the Hiſtory of theſe Papers, and the Occaſion which produced the *War of the Dunces*, (for ſo it has
been commonly called) which begun in the Year 1727,
and ended in 1730.

When Dr *Swift* and Mr *Pope* thought it proper, for
Reaſons ſpecified in the Preface to their Miſcellanies, to
publiſh ſuch little Pieces of theirs as had caſually got abroad,
there was added to them the Treatiſe of the *Bathos, or the
Art of Sinking in Poetry*. It happened that in one Chapter
of this Piece, the ſeveral Species of bad Poets were ranged
in Claſſes, to which were prefixed almoſt all the Letters of
the Alphabet (the greateſt Part of them at Random) but
ſuch was the Number of Poets eminent in *that Art*, that
ſome one or other took every Letter to himſelf : All fell
into ſo violent a Fury, that for half a Year, or more, the
common *News-Papers* (in moſt of which they had ſome
Property, as being *hired Writers*) were filled with the moſt
abuſive Falſhoods and Scurrilities they could poſſibly deviſe.
A Liberty no way to be wonder'd at in thoſe People, and
in thoſe Papers, that, for many Years during the uncon-
rolled Liberty of the Preſs, had aſperſed almoſt all the
great

perhaps not have publiſhed under his own
Name ;

great *Characters* of the Age; and this with Impunity, their
own *Perſons* and *Names* being utterly ſecret and obſcure.

This gave Mr *Pope* the Thought, that he had now ſome
Opportunity of doing Good, by detecting and dragging
into Light theſe common Enemies of Mankind ; ſince to
invalidate this univerſal Slander, it ſufficed to ſhew what
contemptible Men were the Authors of it. He was not
without Hopes, that by manifeſting the Dulneſs of thoſe
who had only Malice to recommend them, either the Bookſellers would not find their Account in employing them, or
the Men themſelves, when diſcovered, want Courage to
proceed in ſo unlawful an Occupation. This it was that
gave Birth to the *Dunciad*, and he thought it an Happineſs, that by the late Flood of Slander on himſelf, he had
acquired ſuch a peculiar Right over their *Names* as was neceſſary to this Deſign.

On the 12th of *March* 1729, at St *James's*, that Poem
was preſented to the KING and QUEEN (who had before
been pleaſed to read it) by the Right Honourable Sir *Robert
Walpole*: And ſome Days after the whole Impreſſion was
taken and diſperſed by ſeveral Noblemen and Perſons of
the firſt Diſtinction.

It is certainly a true Obſervation, that no People are ſo
impatient of Cenſure as thoſe who are the greateſt Slander-
ers : Which was wonderfully exemplified on this Occaſion.
On the Day the Book was firſt vended, a Crowd of Authors
beſieged the Shop ; Entreaties, Advices, Threats of Law,
and Battery, nay Cries of Treaſon were all employed to
hinder the coming out of the *Dunciad*: On the other ſide
the Bookſellers and Hawkers made as great Efforts to procure it : What could a few poor Authors do againſt ſo great
a Majority as the Publick ? There was no ſtopping a Torrent with a Finger, ſo out it came.

I 2   Many

Name; and on which Mr *Savage* afterwards reflected with no great Satisfaction.

The Enumeration of the bad Effects of the *uncontrolled Freedom of the Press,* and the Affertion that the *Liberties taken by the Writers of Journals with their Superiors were exorbitant and unjuftifiable,* very ill became Men, who

Many ludicrous Circumftances attended it : The Dunces (for by this Name they were called) held weekly Clubs, to confult of Hoftilities againft the Author; one wrote a Letter to a great Minifter, affuring him Mr *Pope* was the greateft Enemy the Government had; and another brought his Image in Clay, to execute him in Effigy; with which fad Sort of Satisfactions the Gentlemen were a little comforted.

Some falfe Editions of the Book having an Owl in their Frontifpiece, the true one, to diftinguifh it, fixed in its ftead an Afs laden with Authors. Then another furreptitious one being printed with the fame Afs, the new Edition in Octavo returned for Diftinction to the Owl again. Hence arofe a great Conteft of Bookfellers againft Bookfellers, and Advertifements againft Advertifements; fome recommending the *Edition of the Owl,* and others the *Edition of the Afs;* by which Names they came to be diftinguifhed, to the great Honour of the Gentlemen of the *Dunciad.*

Your Lordfhip will not think thefe Particulars altogether unentertaining; nor are they impertinent, fince they clear fome Paffages in the following Collection. The whole cannot but be of fome Ufe, to fhew the *different Spirit* with which good and bad Authors have ever *acted,* as well as *written;* and to evince a Truth, a greater than which was never advanced, that————

" *Each bad Author is as bad a Friend.*"

How-

258

who have themfelves not always fhewn the exacteft Regard to the Laws of Subordination in their Writings, and who have often fatirifed thofe that at leaft thought themfelves their Superiors, as they were eminent for their hereditary Rank, and employed in the higheft Offices of the Kingdom. But this is only an Inftance of that Partiality which almoft every Man indulges with Regard to himfelf; the Liberty of the Prefs is a Blefling when we are inclined to write againft others, and a Calamity when we find ourfelves overborn by the Multitude of our Affailants; as the Power of the Crown is always thought too great by thofe who fuffer by its Influence, and too little by thofe in whofe Favour it is exerted; and a Standing Army is generally accounted neceffary by thofe who command, and dangerous and oppreffive by thofe who fupport it.

Mr

However, the Imperfection of this Collection cannot but be owned, as long as it wants that Poem with which you, my Lord, have honoured the Author of the *Dunciad*, but which I durft not prefume to add in your Abfence. As it is, may it pleafe your Lordfhip to accept of it, as a diftant Teftimony, with what Refpect and Zeal I am,

My LORD,
your moft obedient
and devoted Servant,
R. SAVAGE.

Mr *Savage* was likewife very far from believing, that the Letters annexed to each
Species of bad Poets in the *Bathos*, were, as
he was directed to affert, *fet down at Random*;
for when he was charged by one of his
Friends with putting his Name to fuch an
Improbability, he had no other Anfwer to
make, than that *he did not think of it*, and his
Friend had too much Tendernefs to reply,
that next to the Crime of writing contrary to
what he thought, was that of writing without thinking.

After having remarked what is falfe in this
Dedication, it is proper that I obferve the Impartiality which I recommend, by declaring,
what *Savage* afferted, that the Account of the
Circumftances which attended the Publication
of the *Dunciad*, however ftrange and improbable, was exactly true.

The Publication of this Piece at this Time
raifed Mr *Savage* a great Number of Enemies among thofe that were attacked by Mr
Pope, with whom he was confidered as a
Kind of Confederate, and whom he was fufpected of fupplying with private Intelligence
and fecret Incidents: fo that the Ignominy of
an Informer was added to the Terror of a
Satirift.

That he was not altogether free from literary
Hypocrify, and that he fometimes fpoke one
thing,

thing, and wrote another, cannot be denied, becaufe he himfelf confeffed, that when he lived in great Familiarity with *Dennis*, he wrote an Epigram * againft him.

Mr *Savage* however fet all the Malice of all the pigmy Writers at Defiance, and thought the Friendfhip of Mr *Pope* cheaply purchafed by being expofed to their Cenfure and their Hatred; nor had he any Reafon to repent of the Preference, for he found Mr *Pope* a fteady and unalienable Friend almoft to the End of his Life.

About this Time, notwithftanding his a-vowed Neutrality with regard to Party, he publifhed a Panegyric on Sir *Robert Walpole*, for which he was rewarded by him with twenty Guineas; a Sum not very large, if ei-ther the Excellence of the Performance, or the Wealth of the Patron be confidered; but greater than he afterwards obtained from a Perfon of yet higher Rank, and more de-firous in Appearance of being diftinguifhed as a Patron of Literature.

As

* *This Epigram was, I believe, never publifhed.*
Should *Dennis* publifh you had ftabb'd your Brother,
Lampoon'd your Monarch, or debauch'd your Mother,
Say what Revenge on *Dennis* can be had,
Too dull for Laughter, for Reply too mad?
On one fo poor you cannot take the Law,
On one fo old your Sword you fcorn to draw:
Uncag'd, then let the harmlefs Monfter rage,
Secure in Dulnefs, Madnefs, Want, and Age.

As he was very far from approving the Conduct of Sir *Robert Walpole*, and in Conversation mentioned him sometimes with Acrimony, and generally with Contempt, as he was one of those who were always zealous in their Assertions of the Justice of the late Opposition, jealous of the Rights of the People, and alarmed by the long continued Triumph of the Court; it was natural to ask him what could induce him to employ his Poetry in Praise of that Man, who was, in his Opinion, an Enemy to Liberty, and an Oppressor of his Country? He alleged, that he was then dependent upon the Lord *Tyrconnel*, who was an implicit Follower of the Ministry, and that being enjoined by him, not without Menaces, to write in Praise of his Leader, he had not Resolution sufficient to sacrifice the Pleasure of Affluence to that of Integrity.

On this and on many other Occasions he was ready to lament the Misery of living at the Tables of other Men, which was his Fate from the Beginning to the End of his Life; for I know not whether he ever had, for three Months together, a settled Habitation, in which he could claim a Right of Residence.

To this unhappy State it is just to impute much of the Inconstancy of his Conduct; for though

though a Readinefs to comply with the Inclination of others was no Part of his natural
Chara&er, yet he was fometimes obliged to
relax his Obftinacy, and fubmit his own
Judgment and even his Virtue to the Government of thofe by whom he was fupported :
So that if his Miferies were fometimes the
Confequence of his Faults, he ought not yet
to be wholly excluded from Compaffion, becaufe his Faults were very often the Effe&ts
of his Misfortunes.

In this gay Period * of his Life, while he
was fupported by Affluence and Pleafure, he
publifhed *the Wanderer*, a moral Poem, of
which the Defign is comprifed in thefe Lines :

I fly all public Care, all venal Strife,
To try the *ftill* compar'd with *active Life* ;
To prove by thefe, the Sons of Men may owe
The Fruits of Blifs to burfting Clouds of Woe;
That even Calamity, by Thought refin'd,
Infpirits and adorns the thinking Mind.

And more diftin&ly in the following Paffage;

By Woe the Soul to daring A&ion fwells,
By Woe in plaintlefs Patience it excels ;
FromPatience prudent, clearExperience fprings,
And traces Knowledge through the Courfe of
    Things.
                        K   Thence
    * 1729.

263

Thence Hope is form'd, thence Fortitude, Succefs,
Renown—whate'er Men covet and carefs.

This Performance was always confidered
by himfelf as his Mafter-piece, and Mr *Pope*
when he afked his Opinion of it, told him,
that he read it once over, and was not difpleafed with it, that it gave him more Pleafure at the fecond Perufal, and delighted him
ftill more at the third.

It has been generally objected to *the Wan-*
derer, that the Difpofition of the Parts is irregular, that the Defign is obfcure, and the
Plan perplexed; that the Images, however
beautiful, fucceed each other without Order;
and that the whole Performance is not fo
much a regular Fabric, as a Heap of fhining
Materials, thrown together by Accident,
which ftrikes rather with the folemn Magnificence of a ftupendous Ruin, than the elegant Grandeur of a finifhed Pile.

This Criticifm is univerfal, and therefore
it is reafonable to believe it at leaft in a great
Degree juft; but Mr *Savage* was always of
a contrary Opinion; he thought his Drift
could only be miffed by Negligence or Stupi-
dity, and that the whole Plan was regular,
and the Parts diftinct.

It was never denied to abound with ftrong
Reprefentations of Nature, and juft Obfervations

tions upon Life, and it may eafily be obferved,
that moſt of his Pictures have an evident Tendency to illuſtrate his firſt great Poſition,
that Good is the Confequence of Evil. The
Sun that burns up the Mountains, fructifies
the Vales; the Deluge that rufhes down the
broken Rocks with dreadful Impetuofity, is
feparated into purling Brooks; and the Rage
of the Hurricane purifies the Air.

Even in this Poem he has not been able to
forbear one Touch upon the Cruelty of his
Mother*, which, though remarkably delicate
and tender, is a Proof how deep an Impref-
ficn it had made upon his Mind.

This muſt be at leaſt acknowledged, which
ought to be thought equivalent to many other
Excellencies, that this Poem can promote no
other Purpofes than thofe of Virtue, and that
it is written with a very ftrong Senfe of the
Efficacy of Religion.

K 2 But

* Falfe Pride! what Vices on our Conduct fteal,
From the World's Eye one Frailty to conceal!
Ye cruel Mothers—foft! thefe Words command—
So near fhould *Cruelty* and *Mother* ftand?
Can the fond Goat, or tender fleecy Dam
Howl like the Wolf to tear the Kid or Lamb?
Yes, there are Mothers——there I fear'd his Aim,
And confcious trembled at the coming Name:
Then with a Sigh his iffuing Words oppos'd,
Straight with a falling Tear his Speech he clos'd;
That Tendernefs which Ties of Blood deny,
Nature repaid me from a Stranger's Eye.
Pale grow my Cheeks——

But my Province is rather to give the History of Mr *Savage*'s Performances, than to display their Beauties, or to obviate the Criticisms, which they have occasioned, and therefore I shall not dwell upon the particular Passages which deserve Applause : I shall neither show the Excellence of his Descriptions*,

nor

* *Of his Descriptions this Specimen may be offered.*

Now, from yon Range of Rocks, strong Rays rebound,
Doubling the Day on flow'ry Plains around :
Kingcups beneath far-striking Colours glance,
Bright as th' etherial glows the green Expanse.
Gems of the Field !—The Topaz charms the Sight,
Like these, effulging yellow Streams of Light.
From the same Rocks fall Rills with soften'd Force,
Meet in yon Mead, and swell a River's Source.
Through her clear Channel shine her finny Shoals,
O'er Sands like Gold the liquid Cryftal rolls.
Dim'd in yon coarfer Moor her Charms decay,
And shape through ruftling Reeds a ruffled Way:
Near Willows short and bushy Shadows throw :
Now lost she seems through nether Tracts to flow ;
Yet at yon Point winds out in Silver State,
Like Virtue from a Labyrinth of Fate.
In length'ning Rows prone from the Mountains run
The Flocks :—their Fleeces glift'ning in the Sun ;
Her Streams they seek, and, 'twixt her neighb'ring Trees,
Recline in various Attitudes of Ease:
Where the Herds sip, the little scaly Fry,
Swift from the Shore, in scatt'ring Myriads fly.
Each liv'ried Cloud, that round th' Horizon glows,
Shifts in odd Scenes, like Earth from whence it rose.
The Bee hums wanton in yon Jefs'mine Bower,
And circling settles, and despoils the Flower.

Melodious

nor expatiate on the terrific Portrait of *Suicide**,

nor

Melodious there the plumy Songſters meet,
And call charm'd Echo from her arch'd Retreat.
Neat, poliſh'd Manſions riſe in Proſpects gay ;
Time-batter'd Tow'rs frown awful in Decay :
The Sun plays glitt'ring on the Rocks and Spires,
And the Lawn lightens with reflected Fires.

     * Who in the ſecond Canto is thus introduced.

   Now Grief and Rage, by gath'ring Sighs ſuppreſt,
Swell my full Heart, and heave my lab'ring Breaſt !
With ſtruggling Starts each vital String they ſtrain,
And ſtrike the tott'ring Fabric of my Brain !
O'er my ſunk Spirits frowns a vap'ry Scene,
Woe's dark Retreat ! the madding Maze of Spleen !
A deep, damp Gloom o'erſpreads the murky Cell ;
Here pining Thoughts, and ſecret Terrors dwell !
Here learn the Great unreal Wants to feign !
Unpleaſing Truths here mortify the Vain !
Here Learning, blinded firſt, and then beguil'd,
Looks dark as Ignorance, as Frenzy wild !
Here firſt Credulity on Reaſon won !
And here *falſe Zeal* myſterious Rants begun !
Here *Love* impearls each Moment with a Tear,
And *Superſtition* owes to *Spleen* her Fear !
—Here the lone Hour, a Blank of Life, diſplays,
Till now bad Thoughts a Fiend more active raiſe ;
A Fiend in evil Moments ever nigh !
Death in her Hand, and Frenzy in her Eye !
Her Eye all red, and ſunk ! A Robe ſhe wore,
With Life's Calamities embroider'd o'er.
A Mirror in one Hand collective ſhows,
Varied, and multiplied, that Group of Woes.
This endleſs Foe to gen'rous Toil and Pain
Lolls on a Couch for Eaſe ; but lolls in vain ;
She muſes o'er her Woe-embroider'd Veſt,
And Self-abhorence heightens in her Breaſt.

To

nor point out the artful Touches*, by which he

To fhun her Care, the Force of Sleep fhe tries,
Still wakes her Mind, tho' Slumbers doze her Eyes:
She dreams, ftarts, rifes, ftalks from Place to Place,
With reftlefs, thoughtful, interrupted Pace:
Now eyes the Sun, and curfes ev'ry Ray,
Now the green Ground, where Colour fades away:
Dim Spe&tres dance! Again her Eyes fhe rears;
Then from the Blood-fhot Ball wipes purpled Tears;
She preffes hard her Brow, with Mifchief fraught,
Her Brow half burfts with Agony of Thought!
From me (fhe cries) pale Wretch thy Comfort claim,
Born of Defpair, and *Suicide* my Name!

* His three Rebels are thus defcribed.
Of thefe were three by different Motives fir'd,
Ambition one, and one Revenge infpir'd.
The third, O *Mammon*, was thy meaner Slave;
Thou Idol, feldom of the Great and Brave.

Florio, whofe Life was one continued Feaft,
His Wealth diminifh'd, and his Debts encreas'd,
Vain Pomp and Equipage his low Defires,
Who ne'er to intelle&tual Blifs afpires;
He, to repair by Vice what Vice has broke,
Durft with bold Treafons Judgment's Rod provoke.
His Strength of Mind, by Lux'ry half diffolv'd,
Ill brooks the Woe where deep he ftands involv'd.
—His Genius flies; refle&ts he now on Prayer?
Alas! bad Spirits turn thofe Thoughts to Air.
What fhall he next? What? ftrait relinquifh Breath,
To bar a public, juft and fhameful Death?
Rafh, horrid Thought! yet now afraid to live,
Murd'rous he ftrikes; may Heav'n the Deed forgive!
—Why had he thus falfe Spirit to rebel?
And why not Fortitude to fuffer well?
—Where no kind Lips the hallow'd Dirge refound,
Far from the Compafs of yon facred Ground;

Full

Full in the Center of three meeting Ways,
Stak'd through he lies——Warn'd let the Wicked gaze !
Near yonder Fane where Mis'ry fleeps in Peace,
Whofe Spire faft-leffens, as thefe Shades encreafe,
Left to the North, whence oft brew'd Tempefts roll,
Tempefts, dire Emblems, *Cofmo*, of thy Soul !
There ! mark that *Cofmo* much for Guile renown'd !
His Grave by unbid Plants of Poifon crown'd.
When out of Pow'r, through him the public Good,
So ftrong his factious Tribe, fufpended ftood.
In Power, vindictive Actions were his Aim,
And Patriots perifh'd by th' ungenerous Flame.
If the beft Caufe he in the Senate chofe,
Ev'n Right in him from fome wrong Motive rofe.
The Bad he loath'd, and would the Weak defpife !
Yet courted for dark Ends, and fhun'd the Wife.
When ill his Purpofe, eloquent his Strain,
His Malice had a Look and Voice humane :
His Smile the Signal of fome vile Intent,
A private Ponyard, or empoifon'd Scent ;
Proud, yet to popular Applaufe a Slave ;
No Friend he honour'd, and no Foe forgave.
His Boons unfrequent, or unjuft to Need,
The Hire of Guilt, of Infamy the Meed ;
But if they chanc'd on learned Worth to fall,
Bounty in him was Oftentation all.
No true Benevolence his Thought fublimes,
His nobleft Actions are illuftrious Crimes.
——*Cofmo*, as Death draws nigh, no more conceals
That Storm of Paffions, which his Nature feels ;
He feels much Fear, more Anger, and moft Pride ;
But Pride and Anger make all Fear fubfide.
Dauntlefs he meets at length untimely Fate ;
A defp'rate Spirit ! rather fierce, than great.
Darkling he glides along the dreary Çoaft,
A fullen, wand'ring, felf-tormenting Ghoft.
————Where

269

of the Rebels, who suffer Death in his laſt
Canto.

——Where veiny Marble dignifies the Ground,
With Emblem fair in Sculpture riſing round,
Juſt where a croſſing, length'ning Iſle we find,
Full Eaſt; whence God returns to judge Mankind,
Once lov'd *Horatio* ſleeps, a Mind elate!
Lamented Shade, Ambition was thy Fate!
Ev'n Angels, wond'ring, oft his Worth ſurvey'd;
Behold a Man like one of us! they ſaid.
Straight heard the Furies, and with Envy glar'd,
And to precipitate his Fall prepar'd:
Firſt *Av'rice* came. In vain Self-love ſhe preſs'd;
The Poor he pitied ſtill, and ſtill redreſs'd:
Learning was his, and Knowledge to commend,
Of Arts a Patron, and of Want a Friend.
Next came *Revenge*: But her Eſſay, how vain!
Nor Hate nor Envy in his Heart remain:
No previous Malice could his Mind engage,
Malice the Mother of vindictive Rage.
No—from his Life his Foes might learn to live;
He held it ſtill a Triumph to forgive.
At length *Ambition* urg'd his Country's Weal,
Aſſuming the fair Look of public *Zeal*;
Still in his Breaſt ſo gen'rous glow'd the Flame,
The Vice, when there, a Virtue half became.
His pitying Eye ſaw Millions in Diſtreſs,
He deem'd it God-like to have Pow'r to bleſs;
Thus, when unguarded, Treaſon ſtain'd him o'er;
And Virtue and Content were then no more.
    But when to Death by rig'rous Juſtice doom'd,
His genuine Spirit Saint-like State reſum'd.
Oft from ſoft Penitence diſtill'd a Tear;
Oft Hope in heav'nly Mercy lighten'd Fear;
Oft would a Drop from ſtruggling Nature fall,
And then a Smile of Patience brighten all.
                                    CANTO V.

Canto. It is, however, proper to obferve, that *Savage* always declared the Characters wholly fictitious, and without the leaft Allufion to any real Perfons or Actions.

From a Poem fo diligently laboured, and fo fuccefsfully finifhed, it might be reafonably expected that he fhould have gained confiderable Advantage; nor can it without fome Degree of Indignation and Concern be told that he fold the Copy for ten Guineas, of which he afterwards returned two, that the two laft Sheets of the Work might be reprinted, of which he had in his Abfence intrufted the Correction to a Friend, who was too indolent to perform it with Accuracy.

A fuperftitious Regard to the Correction of his Sheets was one of Mr *Savage's* Peculiarities; he often altered, revifed, recurred to his firft Reading or Punctuation, and again adopted the Alteration; he was dubious and irrefolute without End, as on a Queftion of the laft Importance, and at laft was feldom fatisfied; the Intrufion or Omiffion of a Comma was fufficient to difcompofe him, and he would lament an Error of a fingle Letter as a heavy Calamity. In one of his Letters relating to an Impreffion of fome Verfes, he remarks, that he had with regard to the Correction of the Proof *a Spell upon him*; and indeed the Anxiety, with which he dwelt upon the minuteft and moft trifling Niceties, de-

L   ferved

ferved no other Name than that of Fafcination.

That he fold fo valuable a Performance for fo fmall a Price, was not to be imputed either to Neceffity, by which the Learned and Ingenious are often obliged to fubmit to very hard Conditions, or to Avarice, by which the Bookfellers are frequently incited to opprefs that Genius by which they are fupported, but to that intemperate Defire of Pleafure, and habitual Slavery to his Paffions, which involved him in many Perplexities; he happened at that Time to be engaged in the Purfuit of fome trifling Gratification, and being without Money for the prefent Occafion, fold his Poem to the firft Bidder, perhaps for the firft Price that was propofed, and would probably have been content with lefs, if lefs had been offered him.

This Poem was addreffed to the Lord *Tyrconnel* not only in the firft Lines *, but in a formal Dedication filled with the higheft Strains of Panegyric, and the warmeft Profeffions

* Fain would my Verfe, *Tyrconnel*, boaft thy Name,
  Brownlow at once my Subject, and my Fame :
  O could that Spirit which thy Bofom warms,
  Whofe Strength furprifes, and whofe Goodnefs charms,
  Thy various Worth—could that infpire my Lays,
  Envy fhould fmile, and Cenfure learn to praife :
  Yet though unequal to a Soul like thine,
  A gen'rous Soul approaching to divine ;
  While blefs'd beneath fuch Patronage I write,
  Great my Attempt, though hazardous my Flight.

feſſions of Gratitude, but by no means remarkable for Delicacy of Connection, or Elegance of Stile.

Theſe Praiſes in a ſhort Time he found
himſelf inclined to retract, being diſcarded by
the Man on whom he had beſtowed them, and
whom he then immediately diſcovered not to
have deſerved them. Of this Quarrel, which
every Day made more bitter, Lord *Tyrconnel*
and Mr *Savage* aſſigned very different Reaſons,
which might perhaps all in Reality concur,
though they were not all convenient to be alleged by either Party. Lord *Tyrconnel* affirmed,
that it was the conſtant Practice of Mr *Savage*, to enter a Tavern with any Company
that propoſed it, drink the moſt expenſive
Wines, with great Profuſion, and when the
Reckoning was demanded, to be without
Money : If, as it often happened, his Companions were willing to defray his Part, the Affair ended without any ill Conſequences ; but
if they were refractory, and expected that the
Wine ſhould be paid for by him that drank it,
his Method of Compoſition was, to take them
with him to his own Apartment, aſſume the
Government of the Houſe, and order the
Butler in an imperious Manner to ſet the beſt
Wine in the Cellar before his Company, who
often drank till they forgot the Reſpect due to
the Houſe in which they were entertained,

indulged

indulged themselves in the utmost Extravagance of Merriment, practised the most licentious Frolics, and committed all the Outrages of Drunkenness.

Nor was this the only Charge which Lord *Tyrconnel* brought against him: Having given him a Collection of valuable Books, stamped with his own Arms, he had the Mortification to see them in a short Time exposed to Sale upon the Stalls, it being usual with Mr *Savage*, when he wanted a small Sum, to take his Books to the Pawnbroker.

Whoever was acquainted with Mr *Savage*, easily credited both these Accusations; for having been obliged from his first Entrance into the World to subsist upon Expedients, Affluence was not able to exalt him above them; and so much was he delighted with Wine and Conversation, and so long had he been accustomed to live by Chance, that he would at any time go to the Tavern, without Scruple, and trust for his Reckoning to the Liberality of his Company, and frequently of Company to whom he was very little known. This Conduct indeed very seldom drew upon him those Inconveniences that might be feared by any other Person, for his Conversation was so entertaining, and his Address so pleasing, that few thought the Pleasure which they received from him dearly purchased by paying
for

for his Wine. It was his peculiar Happineſs, that he ſcarcely ever found a Stranger, whom he did not leave a Friend; but it muſt likewiſe be added, that he had not often a Friend long, without obliging him to become a Stranger.

Mr *Savage*, on the other Hand, declared, that Lord *Tyrconnel* * quarrelled with him, becauſe he would not ſubtract from his own Luxury and Extravagance what he had promiſed to allow him, and that his Reſentment was only a Plea for the Violation of his Promiſe: He aſſerted that he had done nothing that ought to exclude him from that Subſiſtence which he thought not ſo much a Favour, as a Debt, ſince it was offered him upon Conditions, which he had never broken; and that his only Fault was, that he could not be ſupported with nothing.

He acknowledged, that Lord *Tyrconnel* often exhorted him to regulate his Method of Life, and not to ſpend all his Nights in Taverns, and that he appeared very deſirous, that he would paſs thoſe Hours with him which he ſo freely beſtowed upon others. This Demand Mr *Savage* conſidered as a Cenſure of his Conduct, which he could never patiently bear; and

* His Expreſſion in one of his Letters, was, that Ld *T——l* *had involved his Eſtate, and therefore poorly ſought an Occaſion to quarrel with him.*

and which even in the latter and cooler Part of his Life was so offensive to him, tha the declared it as his Resolution, *to spurn that Friend who should presume to dictate to him*; and it is not likely, that in his earlier Years he received Admonitions with more Calmness.

He was likewise inclined to resent such Expectations, as tending to infringe his Liberty, of which he was very jealous when it was necessary to the Gratification of his Passions, and declared, that the Request was still more unreasonable, as the Company to which he was to have been confined was insupportably disagreeable. This Assertion affords another Instance of that Inconsistency of his Writings with his Conversation, which was so often to be observed. He forgot how lavishly he had, in his * Dedication to *the* WANDERER, extolled the Delicacy and Penetration

---

* Part of this Poem had the Honour of your Lordship's Perusal when in Manuscript, and it was no small Pride to me when it met with Approbation.—My Intention is to embrace this Opportunity of throwing out Sentiments that relate to your Lordship's Goodness and Generosity, which give me leave to say I have lately experienced.

That *I live*, my Lord, is a Proof, that Dependance upon your Lordship and the present Ministry is an Assurance of Success. I am persuaded Distress in many other Instances affects your Soul with a Compassion that always shews itself in a Manner most humane and active, that to forgive Injuries, and confer Benefits, is your Delight, and that to deserve

netration, the Humanity and Generofity, the Candour and Politenefs of the Man, whom, when he no longer loved him, he declared to be a Wretch without Underftanding, without Good-Nature, and without Juftice; of whofe Name he thought himfelf obliged to leave no Trace in any future Edition of his Writings; and accordingly blotted it out of that Copy of *the Wanderer* which was in his Hands.

During his Continuance with the Lord *Tyrconnel* he wrote *The * Triumph of Health and Mirth*, on the Recovery of Lady *Tyrconnel*

deferve your Friendfhip is to deferve the Countenance of the beft of Men. To be admitted to the Honour of your Lordfhip's Converfation (permit me to fpeak but Juftice) is to be elegantly introduced into the moft inftructive as well as entertaining Parts of Literature: It is to be furnifhed with the fineft Obfervations upon human Nature, and to receive from the moft unaffuming, fweet, and winning Candour, the worthieft and moft polite Maxims—fuch as are always inforced by the Actions of your own Life.—If my future Morals and Writings fhould gain any Approbation from Men of Parts and Probity, I muft acknowledge all to be the Product of your Lordfhip's Goodnefs.—

* *Of the Numbers and Sentiments the following Lines will afford a Specimen*

Where *Thames* with Pride beholds *Augufta's* Charms,
And either *India* pours into her Arms,—
High thron'd appears the laughter-loving Dame—
Goddefs of Mirth—

O'er the gay World the fweet Infpirer reigns,
Spleen flies, and Elegance her Pomp fuftains;
Thee, Goddefs, thee the Fair and Young obey,
Wealth, Wit, and Mufic, all confefs thy Sway.—

The

nel from a languishing Illness. This Performance is remarkable, not only for the Gayety of the Ideas, and the Melody of the Numbers, but for the agreeable Fiction upon which it is formed *. *Mirth* overwhelmed with Sorrow, for the Sickness of her Favourite, takes a Flight in Quest of her Sister *Health,*

The Goddess summons each illustrious Name,
Bids the gay Talk, and forms th' amusive Game,
She whose fair Throne is fix'd in human Souls,
From Joy to Joy her Eye delighted rolls:
But where, she cry'd, is she, my fav'rite she,
Of all my Race the dearest far to me——
Whose Life's the Source of each refin'd Delight?
She said, but no *Belinda* glads her Sight——
In kind low Murmurs all the Loss deplore,
Belinda droops, and Pleasure is no more.
The Goddess silent paus'd in museful Air,
But Mirth, like Virtue, cannot long despair,——
Strait wafted on the tepid Breeze she flies,
Where *Bath*'s ascending Turrets meet her Eyes,
She flies, her elder Sister Health to find,
She finds her on a Mountain's Brow reclin'd,
Around her Birds in earliest Consort sing,
Her Cheek the Semblance of the kindling Spring.——
Loose to the Wind her verdant Vestments flow,
Her Limbs yet recent from the Springs below:
Thereof she bathes, then peaceful sits secure,
Where ev'ry Breath is fragrant, fresh and pure.——
Hail, Sister, hail, the kindred Goddess cries,
No common Suppliant stands before your Eyes——
Strength, Vigour, Wit, depriv'd of thee decline,
Each finer Sense that forms Delight is thine——

Bright

* See the whole Poem, *Gent. Mag.* Vol. VII. *p.* 243.

Health, whom fhe finds reclined upon the Brow of a lofty Mountain, amidſt the Fragrance of perpetual Spring, with the Breezes of the Morning ſporting about her. Being ſolicited by her Siſter *Mirth*, ſhe readily promiſes her Aſſiſtance, flies away in a Cloud, and impregnates the Waters of *Bath* with new Virtues, by which the Sickneſs of *Belinda* is relieved.

As the Reputation of his Abilities, the particular Circumſtances of his Birth and Life, the Splendor of his Appearance, and the Diſtinction which was for ſome Time paid him by Lord *Tyrconnel*, intitled him to Familiarity with Perſons of higher Rank, than thoſe to whoſe Converſation he had been before admitted, he did not fail to gratify that Curioſity, which induced him to take a nearer View of thoſe whom their Birth, their Employments, or their Fortunes, neceſſarily place at a Diſtance from the greateſt Part of Mankind, and to examine, whether their Merit was magnified or diminiſhed by the Medium through which it was contemplated ; whe-

M   ther

Bright Suns by thee diffuſe a brighter Blaze,
And the freſh Green a freſher Green diſplays—
Such thy vaſt Pow'r—The Deity replies,
Mirth never aſks a Boon which Health denies ;
Our mingled Gifts tranſcend imperial Wealth,
Health ſtrengthens Mirth, and Mirth inſpirits Health.

ther the Splendor with which they dazzled their Admirers, was inherent in themfelves, or only reflected on them by the Objects that furrounded them; and whether great Men were felected for high Stations, or high Stations made great Men.

For this Purpofe, he took all Opportunities of converfing familiarly with thofe who were moft confpicuous at that Time, for their Power, or their Influence; he watched their loofer Moments, and examined their domeftic Behaviour, with that Acutenefs which Nature had given him, and which the uncommon Variety of his Life had contributed to increafe, and that Inquifitivenefs which muft always be produced in a vigorous Mind by an abfolute Freedom from all preffing or domeftic Engagements. His Difcernment was quick, and therefore he foon found in every Perfon, and in every Affair, fomething that deferved Attention; he was fupported by others, without any Care for himfelf, and was therefore at Leifure to purfue his Obfervations.

More Circumftances to conftitute a Critic on human Life could not eafily concur, nor indeed could any Man who affumed from accidental Advantages more Praife than he could juftly claim from his real Merit, admit an Acquaintance more dangerous than that of *Savage*; of whom likewife it muft be confeffed, feſſed, that Abilities really exalted above the common Level, or Virtue refined from Paſſion, or Proof againſt Corruption could not eaſily find an abler Judge, or a warmer Advocate.

What was the Reſult of Mr *Savage*'s Enquiry, though he was not much accuſtomed to conceal his Diſcoveries, it may not be entirely ſafe to relate, becauſe the Perſons whoſe Characters he criticiſed are powerful; and Power and Reſentment are ſeldom Strangers; nor would it perhaps be wholly juſt, becauſe what he aſſerted in Converſation might, though true in general, be heightened by ſome momentary Ardour of Imagination, and as it can be delivered only from Memory, may be imperfectly repreſented; ſo that the Picture at firſt aggravated, and then unſkilfully copied, may be juſtly ſuſpected to retain no great Reſemblance of the Original.

It may, however, be obſerved, that he did not appear to have formed very elevated Ideas of thoſe to whom the Adminiſtration of Affairs, or the Conduct of Parties, has been intruſted; who have been conſidered as the Advocates of the Crown, or the Guardians of the People, and who have obtained the moſt implicit Confidence, and the loudeſt Applauſes. Of one particular Perſon, who has been at one Time ſo popular as to be generally eſteemed, and at another ſo formidable as to

M 2 be

be univerfally detefted, he obferved, that his Acquifitions had been fmall, or that his Capacity was narrow, and that the whole Range of his Mind was from Obfcenity to Politics, and from Politics to Obfcenity.

But the Opportunity of indulging his Speculations on great Characters was now at an End. He was banifhed from the Table of Lord *Tyrconnel*, and turned again adrift upon the World, without Profpect of finding quickly any other Harbour. As Prudence was not one of the Virtues by which he was diftinguifhed, he had made no Provifion againft a Misfortune like this. And though it is not to be imagined, but that the Separation muft for fome Time have been preceded by Coldnefs, Peevifhnefs, or Neglect, though it was undoubtedly the Confequence of accumulated Provocations on both Sides, yet every one that knew *Savage* will readily believe, that to him it was fudden as a Stroke of Thunder; that though he might have tranfiently fufpected it, he had never fuffered any Thought fo unpleafing to fink into his Mind, but that he had driven it away by Amufements, or Dreams of future Felicity and Affluence, and had never taken any Meafures by which he might prevent a Precipitation from Plenty to Indigence.

This Quarrel and Separation, and the Difficulties to which Mr *Savage* was expofed by
them

them, were foon known both to his Friends and Enemies; nor was it long before he perceived, from the Behaviour of both, how much is added to the Luftre of Genius, by the Ornaments of Wealth.

His Condition did not appear to excite much Compaffion; for he had not always been careful to ufe the Advantages which he enjoyed with that Moderation, which ought to have been with more than ufual Caution preferved by him, who knew, if he had reflected, that he was only a Dependant on the Bounty of another, whom he could expect to fupport him no longer than he endeavoured to preferve his Favour, by complying with his Inclinations, and whom he neverthelefs fet at Defiance, and was continually irritating by Negligence or Encroachments.

Examples need not be fought at any great Diftance to prove that Superiority of Fortune has a natural Tendency to kindle Pride, and that Pride feldom fails to exert itfelf in Contempt and Infult; and if this is often the Effect of hereditary Wealth, and of Honours enjoyed only by the Merit of others, it is fome Extenuation of any indecent Triumphs to which this unhappy Man may have been betrayed that his Profperity was heightened by the Force of Novelty, and made more intoxicating by a Senfe of the Mifery in which he had fo
long

long languished, and perhaps of the Insults which he had formerly borne, and which he might now think himself entitled to revenge. It is too common for those, who have unjustly suffered Pain, to inflict it likewise in their Turn, with the same Injustice, and to imagine that they have a Right to treat others as they have themselves been treated.

That Mr *Savage* was too much elevated by any good Fortune is generally known; and some Passages of his Introduction to the *Author to be let* sufficiently shew, that he did not wholly refrain from such Satire as he afterwards thought very unjust, when he was exposed to it himself; for when he was afterwards ridiculed in the Character of a distressed Poet, he very easily discovered, that Distress was not a proper Subject for Merriment, or Topic of Invective. He was then able to discern that if Misery be the Effect of Virtue, it ought to be reverenced; if of Ill-Fortune, to be pitied; and if of Vice, not to be insulted, because it is perhaps itself a Punishment adequate to the Crime by which it was produced. And the Humanity of that Man can deserve no Panegyric, who is capable of reproaching a Criminal in the Hands of the Executioner.

But these Reflections, though they readily occurred to him in the first and last Parts of
his

his Life, were, I am afraid, for a long Time forgotten; at leaft they were, like many other Maxims, treafured up in his Mind, rather for Show than Ufe, and operated very little upon his Conduct, however elegantly he might fometimes explain, or however forcibly he might inculcate them.

His Degradation therefore from the Condition which he had enjoyed with fuch wanton Thoughtlefnefs, was confidered by many as an Occafion of Triumph. Thofe who had before paid their Court to him, without Succefs, foon returned the Contempt which they had fuffered, and they who had received Favours from him, for of fuch Favours as he could beftow he was very liberal, did not always remember them. So much more certain are the Effects of Refentment than of Gratitude: It is not only to many more pleafing to recollect thofe Faults which place others below them, than thofe Virtues by which they are themfelves comparatively depreffed; but it is likewife more eafy to neglect, than to recompenfe; and though there are few who will practife a laborious Virtue, there will never be wanting Multitudes that will indulge an eafy Vice.

Savage however was very little difturbed at the Marks of Contempt which his Ill-Fortune brought upon him, from thofe whom he never efteemed,

esteemed, and with whom he never considered himself as levelled by any Calamities; and
though it was not without some Uneasiness
that he saw some, whose Friendship he valued,
change their Behaviour; he yet observed their
Coldness without much Emotion, considered
them as the Slaves of Fortune, and the Wor-
shippers of Prosperity; and was more inclined
to despise them, than to lament himself.

It does not appear, that after this Return of
his Wants, he found Mankind equally favourable to him, as at his first Appearance in the
World. His Story, though in Reality not
less melancholy, was less affecting, because it
was no longer new; it therefore procured him
no new Friends, and those that had formerly
relieved him thought they might now consign
him to others. He was now likewise considered by many rather as criminal, than as unhappy; for the Friends of Lord *Tyrconnel* and
of his Mother were sufficiently industrious to
publish his Weaknesses, which were indeed
very numerous, and nothing was forgotten,
that might make him either hateful or ridiculous.

It cannot but be imagined, that such Repre-
sentations of his Faults must make great Numbers less sensible of his Distress; many who
had only an Opportunity to hear one Part
made no scruple to propagate the Account
which

which they received; many affisted their Circulation from Malice or Revenge, and perhaps
many pretended to credit them, that they
might with a better Grace withdraw their
Regard, or withhold their Affistance.

Savage however was not one of thofe who
fuffer themfelves to be injured without Refiftance, nor was lefs diligent in expofing the
Faults of Lord *Tyrconnel*, over whom he obtained at leaft this Advantage, that he drove
him firft to the Practice of Outrage and Violence; for he was fo much provoked by the
Wit and Virulence of *Savage*, that he came
with a Number of Attendants, that did no
Honour to hisCourage, to beat him at a Coffee-
Houfe. But it happened that he had left the
Place a few Minutes, and his Lordfhip had
without Danger the Pleafure of boafting how
he would have treated him. Mr *Savage* went
next Day to repay his Vifit at his own Houfe,
but was prevailed on, by his Domeftics, to retire without infifting upon feeing him.

Lord *Tyrconnel* was accufed by Mr *Savage*
of fome Actions, which fcarcely any Provocations will be thought fufficient to juftify,
fuch as feizing what he had in his Lodgings,
and other Inftances of wanton Cruelty, by
which he increafed the Diftrefs of *Savage*
without any Advantage to himfelf.

N　　　　　Thefe

These mutual Accusations were retorted on both Sides for many Years, with the utmost Degree of Virulence and Rage, and Time seemed rather to augment than diminish their Resentment; that the Anger of Mr *Savage* should be kept alive is not strange, because he felt every Day the Consequences of the Quarrel; but it might reasonably have been hoped, that Lord *Tyrconnel* might have relented, and at length have forgot those Provocations, which, however they might have once inflamed him, had not in Reality much hurt him.

The Spirit of Mr *Savage* indeed never suffered him to solicit a Reconciliation; he returned Reproach for Reproach, and Insult for Insult: his Superiority of Wit supplied the Disadvantages of his Fortune, and inabled him to form a Party, and prejudice great Numbers in his Favour.

But though this might be some Gratification of his Vanity, it afforded very little Relief to his Necessities, and he was very frequently reduced to uncommon Hardships, of which, however, he never made any mean or importunate Complaints, being formed rather to bear Misery with Fortitude, than enjoy Prosperity with Moderation.

He now thought himself again at Liberty to expose the Cruelty of his Mother, and therefore, I believe, about this Time, published *The*

The Baftard, a Poem remarkable for the vivacious Sallies of Thought in the Beginning*, where he makes a pompous Enumeration of the imaginary Advantages of bafe Birth, and the pathetic Sentiments at the End, where he recounts the real Calamities which he fuffered by the Crime of his Parents.

The Vigour and Spirit of the Verfes, the peculiar Circumftances of the Author, the Novelty of the Subjeдt, and the Notoriety of the Story, to which the Allufions are made,
procured

---

* In gayer Hours, when high my Fancy ran,
The Mufe, exulting, thus her Lay began.
 Bleft be the Baftard's Birth ! thro' wondrous Ways,
He fhines eccentrick like a Comet's Blaze.
No fickly Fruit of faint Compliance he;
He ! ftampt in Nature's Mint with Extafy!
He lives to build, not boaft, a gen'rous Race :
No tenth Tranfmitter of a foolifh Face.
His daring Hope, no Sire's Example bounds ;
His firft-born Lights no Prejudice confounds.
He, kindling, from within, requires no Flame,
He glories in a Baftard's glowing Name.
 ――Loos'd to the World's wide Range――enjoin'd no Aim;
Prefcrib'd no Duty, and affign'd no Name :
Nature's unbounded Son he ftands alone,
His Heart unbiafs'd, and his Mind his own.
 ――O Mother, yet no Mother !―'tis to you,
My Thanks for fuch diftinguifh'd Claims are due.
 ――What had I loft, if conjugally kind,
By Nature hating, yet by Vows confin'd,

N 2
――You

289

procured this Performance a very favourable
Reception ; great Numbers were immediately
difperfed, and Editions were multiplied with
unufual Rapidity.

One Circumftance attended the Publication,
which *Savage* ufed to relate with great Satif-
faction. His Mother, to whom the Poem
was *with due Reverence* infcribed, happened
then to be at *Bath*, where fhe could not con-
veniently retire from Cenfure, or conceal herfelf from Obfervation ; and no fooner did the
Reputation

——You had *faint-drawn* me with a Form alone,
A lawful Lump of Life by Force your own !
——I had been born your dull domeftick Heir ;
Load of your Life, and Motive of your Care ;
Perhaps been poorly Rich, and meanly Great ;
The Slave of Pomp, a Cypher in the State ;
Lordly negleᵭful of a Worth unknown,
And flumb'ring in a *Seat*, by *Chance* my own.
——Thus unprophetic, lately uninfpir'd,
I fung ; gay, flatt'ring Hope my Fancy fir'd ;
Inly fecure, thro' confcious Scorn of Ill ;
Nor taught by Wifdom how to balance Will.
——But now expos'd and fhrinking from Diftrefs,
I fly to Shelter while the Tempefts prefs.

After the Mention of the Death of Sinclair, *he goes on thus* :

——Where fhall my Hope find Reft ?—No Mother's Care
Shielded my infant Innocence with Pray'r :
No Father's guardian Hand my Youth maintain'd,
Call'd forth my Virtues, and from Vice reftrain'd.

Reputation of the Poem begin to fpread, than fhe heard it repeated in all Places of Concourfe, nor could fhe enter the Affembly Rooms, or crofs the Walks, without being faluted with fome Lines from *The Baftard.*

This was perhaps the firft Time that ever fhe difcovered a Senfe of Shame, and on this Occafion the Power of Wit was very confpicuous ; the Wretch who had, without Scruple, proclaimed herfelf an Adulterefs, and who had firft endeavoured to ftarve her Son, then to tranfport him, and afterwards to hang him, was not able to bear the Reprefentation of her own Conduct, but fled from Reproach, though fhe felt no Pain from Guilt, and left *Bath* with the utmoft Hafte, to fhelter herfelf among the Crouds of *London.*

Thus *Savage* had the Satisfaction of finding, that though he could not reform his Mother, he could punifh her, and that he did not always fuffer alone.

The Pleafure which he received from this Increafe of his poetical Reputation, was fufficient for fome Time to over-balance the Miferies of Want, which this Performance did not much alleviate, for it was fold for a very trivial Sum to a Bookfeller, who, though the Succefs was fo uncommon, that five Impreffions were fold, of which many were undoubtedly very numerous, had not Generofity fufficient

cient

cient to admit the unhappy Writer to any Part of the Profit.

The Sale of this Poem was always mentioned by Mr *Savage* with the utmoſt Elevation of Heart, and referred to by him as an inconteſtable Proof of a general Acknowledgement of his Abilities. It was indeed the only Production of which he could juſtly boaſt a general Reception.

But though he did not loſe the Opportunity which Succeſs gave him of ſetting a high Rate on his Abilities, but paid due Deference to the Suffrages of Mankind when they were given in his Favour, he did not ſuffer his Eſteem of himſelf to depend upon others, nor found any thing ſacred in the Voice of the People when they were inclined to cenſure him; he then readily ſhewed the Folly of expecting that the Publick ſhould judge right, obſerved how ſlowly poetical Merit had often forced its Way into the World, he contented himſelf with the Applauſe of Men of Judgment; and was ſomewhat diſpoſed to exclude all thoſe from the Character of Men of Judgment, who did not applaud him.

But he was at other Times more favourable to Mankind, than to think them blind to the Beauties of his Works, and imputed the Slowneſs of their Sale to other Cauſes; either they were publiſhed at a Time when the Town was empty,

empty, or when the Attention of the Public was engroffed by fome Struggle in the Parliament, or fome other Object of general Concern; or they were by the Neglect of the Publifher not diligently difperfed, or by his Avarice not advertifed with fufficient Frequency. Addrefs, or Induftry, or Liberality, was always wanting; and the Blame was laid rather on any other Perfon than the Author.

By Arts like thefe, Arts which every Man practifes in fome Degree, and to which too much of the little Tranquillity of Life is to be afcribed, *Savage* was always able to live at Peace with himfelf. Had he indeed only made ufe of thefe Expedients to alleviate the Lofs or Want of Fortune or Reputation, or any other Advantage, which it is not in Man's Power to beftow upon himfelf, they might have been juftly mentioned as Inftances of a philofophical Mind, and very properly propofed to the Imitation of Multitudes, who, for want of diverting their Imaginations with the fame Dexterity, languifh under Afflictions which might be eafily removed.

It were doubtlefs to be wifhed, that Truth and Reafon were univerfally prevalent; that every Thing were efteemed according to its real Value; and that Men would fecure themfelves from being difappointed in their Endeavours after Happinefs, by placing it only in
Virtue,

Virtue, which is always to be obtained; but if adventitious and foreign Pleasures must be persued, it would be perhaps of some Benefit, since that Persuit must frequently be fruitless, if the Practice of *Savage* could be taught, that Folly might be an Antidote to Folly, and one Fallacy be obviated by another.

But the Danger of this pleasing Intoxication must not be concealed; nor indeed can any one, after having observed the Life of *Savage*, need to be cautioned against it. By imputing none of his Miseries to himself, he continued to act upon the same Principles, and follow the same Path ; was never made wiser by his Sufferings, nor preserved by one Misfortune from falling into another. He proceeded throughout his Life to tread the same Steps on the same Circle; always applauding his past Conduct, or at least forgetting it, to amuse himself with Phantoms of Happiness, which were dancing before him ; and willingly turned his Eyes from the Light of Reason, when it would have discovered the Illusion, and shewn him, what he never wished to see, his real State.

He is even accused, after having lulled his Imagination with those ideal Opiates, of having tried the same Experiment upon his Conscience ; and having accustomed himself to impute all Deviations from the right to foreign Causes,

Caufes, it is certain that he was upon every Occafion too eafily reconciled to himfelf, and that he appeared very little to regret thofe Practices which had impaired his Reputation. The reigning Error of his Life was, that he miftook the Love for the Practice of Virtue, and was indeed not fo much a good Man as the Friend of Goodnefs.

This at leaft muft be allowed him that he always preferved a ftrong Senfe of the Dignity, the Beauty, and the Neceffity of Virtue, and that he never contributed deliberately to fpread Corruption amongft Mankind ; his Actions, which were generally precipitate, were often blameable, but his Writings, being the Productions of Study, uniformly tended to the Exaltation of the Mind, and the Propagation of Morality and Piety.

Thefe Writings may improve Mankind, when his Failings fhall be forgotten, and therefore he muft be confidered upon the whole as a Benefactor to the World ; nor can his perfonal Example do any Hurt, fince who-ever hears of his Faults, will hear of the Miferies which they brought upon him, and which would deferve lefs Pity, had not his Condition been fuch as made his Faults pardonable. He may be confidered as a Child *expofed* to all the Temptations of Indigence, at an Age when Refolution was not yet ftrengthen-

O   ed

ed by Conviction, nor Virtue confirmed by Habit; a Circumstance which in his *Bastard* he laments in a very affecting Manner.

——No Mother's Care
Shielded my Infant Innocence with Prayer:
No Father's guardian Hand my Youth maintain'd,
Call'd forth my Virtues, and from Vice restrain'd.

The *Bastard*, however it might provoke or mortify his Mother, could not be expected to melt her to Compassion, so that he was still under the same Want of the Necessaries of Life, and he therefore exerted all the Interest, which his Wit, or his Birth, or his Misfortunes could procure, to obtain upon the Death of *Eusden* the Place of Poet Laureat, and prosecuted his Application with so much Diligence, that the King publickly declared it his Intention to bestow it upon him; but such was the Fate of *Savage*, that even the King, when he intended his Advantage, was disappointed in his Schemes; for the Lord Chamberlain, who has the Disposal of the Laurel as one of the Appendages of his Office, either did not know the King's Design, or did not approve it, or thought the Nomination of the Laureat an Encroachment upon his Rights, and therefore bestowed the Laurel upon *Colly Cibber*.

Mr *Savage* thus disappointed took a Resolution

folution of applying to the Queen, that having once given him Life, fhe would enable him to fupport it, and therefore publifhed a fhort Poem on her Birth-Day, to which he gave the odd Title of *Volunteer Laureat.* The Event of this Effay he has himfelf related in the following Letter, which he prefixed to the Poem, when he afterwards reprinted it in the *Gentleman's Magazine,* from whence I have copied it intire, as this was one of the few Attempts in which Mr *Savage* fucceeded.

' Mr *Urban,*

' In your Magazine for *February* you
' publifhed the laft *Volunteer Laureat,* writ-
' ten on a very melancholy Occafion, the
' Death of the Royal Patronefs of Arts and
' Literature in general, and of the Author
' of that Poem in particular ; I now fend
' you the firft that Mr *Savage* wrote under
' that Title.———This Gentleman, notwith-
' ftanding a very confiderable Intereft, being,
' on the Death of Mr *Eufden,* difappointed
' of the Laureat's Place, wrote the follow-
' ing Verfes; which were no fooner pub-
' lifhed, but the late Queen fent to a Book-
' feller for them: The Author had not at
' that Time a Friend either to get him in-
' troduced, or his Poem prefented at Court;
' yet fuch was the unfpeakable Goodnefs of

' that

' that Princefs, that, notwithftanding this
' Act of Ceremony was wanting, in a few
' Days after Publication, Mr *Savage* re-
' ceived a Bank-Bill of fifty Pounds, and
' a gracious Meffage from her Majefty, by
' the Lord *North* and *Guilford*, to this Effect:
" That her Majefty was highly pleafed with
" the Verfes; that fhe took particularly kind
" his Lines there relating to the King; that
" he had Permiffion to write annually on the
" fame Subject; and that he fhould yearly
" receive the like Prefent, till fomething bet-
" ter (which was her Majefty's Intention)
" could be done for him." ' After this he was
' permitted to prefent one of his annual
' Poems to her Majefty, had the Honour of
' kiffing her Hand, and met with the moft
' gracious Reception,

' Your's, &c.'

The VOLUNTEER LAUREAT.

A Poem : On the *Queen's Birth-Day*. Hum-
bly addreffed to her MAJESTY,

Twice twenty tedious Moons have roll'd away,
Since Hope kind Flatt'rer tun'd my penfive Lay,
Whifp'ring, that you, who rais'd me from Defpair,
Meant, by your Smiles, to make Life worth my Care ;
With pitying Hand an Orphan's Tears to fcreen,
And 'o'er the Motherlefs extend the Queen.

Twill

'Twill be---the Prophet guides the Poet's Strain!
Grief never touch'd a Heart like your's in vain:
Heav'n gave you Power, becaufe you love to blefs;
And Pity, when you feel it, is Redrefs.

Two Fathers join'd to rob my Claim of one!
My Mother too thought fit to have no Son!
The Senate next, whofe Aid the Helplefs own,
Forgot my Infant Wrongs, and mine alone!
Yet Parents pitilefs, nor Peers unkind,
Nor Titles loft, nor Woes myfterious join'd,
Strip me of Hope--- by Heav'n thus lowly laid,
To find a *Pharaoh's* Daughter in the Shade.

You cannot hear unmov'd, when Wrongs im-
plore,
Your Heart is Woman, though your Mind be more;
Kind, like the Pow'r who gave you to our Pray'rs,
You would not lengthen Life to fharpen Cares:
They who a barren Leave to live beftow,
Snatch but from Death to facrifice to Woe.
Hated by her, from whom my Life I drew,
Whence fhould I hope, if not from Heav'n and you,
Nor dare I groan beneath Affliction's Rod,
My Queen, my Mother; and my Father, God.

The pitying Mufes faw me Wit purfue,
A *Baftard Son*, alas! on that Side too,
Did not your Eyes exalt the Poet's Fire,
And what the Mufe denies, the Queen infpire;
While rifing thus your heav'nly Soul to view,
I learn how Angels think, by copying you.

Great Princefs! 'tis decreed---once ev'ry Year
I march uncall'd your Laureat Volunteer;

Thus

Thus fhall your Poet his low Genius raife,
And charm the World with Truths too vaft for Praife.
Nor need I dwell on Glories all your own,
Since furer Means to tempt your Smiles are known;
Your Poet fhall allot your Lord his Part,
And paint him in his noblest Throne, your Heart.

   Is there a Greatnefs that adorns him beft,
A rifing Wifh that ripens in his Breaft?
Has he fore-meant fome diftant Age to blefs,
Difarm Oppreffion, or expel Diftrefs?
Plans he fome Scheme to reconcile Mankind,
People the Seas, and bufy ev'ry Wind?
Would he, by Pity, the Deceiv'd reclaim,
And fmile contending Factions into Shame?
Would his Example lend his Laws a Weight,
And breathe his own foft Morals o'er his State?
The Mufe fhall find it all, fhall make it feen,
And teach the World his Praife, to charm his Queen.

   Such be the annual Truths my Verfe imparts,
Nor frown, fair *Fav'rite* of a People's Hearts!
Happy if plac'd, perchance, beneath your Eye,
My Mufe unpenfion'd might her Pinions try,
Fearlefs to fail, while you indulge her Flame,
And bid me proudly boaft your Laureat's Name;
Renobled thus by Wreaths my Queen beftows,
I lofe all Memory of Wrongs and Woes.

   Such was the Performance, and fuch its
Reception; a Reception which, though by
no means unkind, was yet not in the higheft
Degree generous: To chain down the Genius
of a Writer to an annual Panegyric, fhewed
                                          in

in the Queen too much Defire of hearing her own Praifes, and a greater Regard to herfelf than to him on whom her Bounty was conferred. It was a kind of avaricious Generofity, by which Flattery was rather pur-chafed than Genius rewarded.

Mrs *Oldfield* had formerly given him the fame Allowance with much more he-roic Intention; fhe had no other View than to enable him to profecute his Studies, and to fet himfelf above the Want of Affiftance, and was contented with doing good without fti-pulating for Encomiums.

Mr *Savage* however was not at Liberty to make Exceptions, but was ravifhed with the Favours which he had received, and probably yet more with thofe which he was promifed; he confidered himfelf now as a Favourite of the Queen, and did not doubt but a few an-nual Poems would eftablifh him in fome pro-fitable Employment.

He therefore affumed the Title of *Volun-teer Laureat*, not without fome Reprehenfions from *Cibber*, who informed him, that the Title of *Laureat* was a Mark of Honour conferred by the King, from whom all Honour is derived, and which therefore no Man has a Right to beftow upon himfelf; and added, that he might with equal Propriety ftile him-felf a Volunteer Lord, or Volunteer Baronet.

It

It cannot be denied that the Remark was juft, but *Savage* did not think any Title, which was conferred upon Mr *Cibber*, fo honourable as that the Ufurpation of it could be imputed to him as an Inftance of very exorbitant Vanity, and therefore continued to write under the fame Title, and received every Year the fame Reward.

He did not appear to confider thefe Enco-miums as Tefts of his Abilities, or as any thing more than annual Hints to the Queen of her Promife, or Acts of Ceremony, by the Performance of which he was intitled to his Penfion, and therefore did not labour them with great Diligence, or print more than fifty each Year, except that for fome of the laft Years he regularly inferted them in the *Gen-tleman's Magazine*, by which they were dif-perfed over the Kingdom.

Of fome of them he had himfelf fo low an Opinion, that he intended to omit them in the Collection of Poems, for which he printed Propofals, and folicited Subfcriptions; nor can it feem ftrange, that being confined to the fame Subject, he fhould be at fome times indolent, and at others unfuccefsful; that he fhould fometimes delay a difagreeable Tafk, till it was too late to perform it well; or that he fhould fometimes repeat the fame Sentiment on the fame Occafion, or at others

be

be mifled by an Attempt after Novelty to forced Conceptions, and far-fetched Images.

He wrote indeed with a double Intention, which fupplied him with fome Variety; for his Bufinefs was to praife the Queen for the Favours which he had received, and to complain to her of the Delay of thofe which fhe had promifed: In fome of his Pieces, therefore, Gratitude is predominant, and in fome Difcontent; in fome he reprefents himfelf as happy in her Patronage, and in others as difconfolate to find himfelf neglected.

Her Promife, like other Promifes made to this unfortunate Man, was never performed, though he took fufficient Care that it fhould not be forgotten. The Publication of his *Volunteer Laureat* procured him no other Reward than a regular Remittance of fifty Pounds.

He was not fo depreffed by his Difappointments as to neglect any Opportunity that was offered of advancing his Intereft. When the Princefs *Anne* was married, he wrote a Poem upon her Departure, only, as he declared, *becaufe it was expected from him*, and he was not willing to bar his own Profpects by any Appearance of Neglect.

He never mentioned any Advantage gain'd by this Poem, or any Regard that was paid to it, and therefore it is likely that it was
P   confidered

confidered at Court as an Act of Duty, to which he was obliged by his Dependence, and which it was therefore not neceffary to reward by any new Favour : Or perhaps the Queen really intended his Advancement, and therefore thought it fuperfluous to lavifh Prefents upon a Man whom fhe intended to eftablifh for Life.

About this Time not only his Hopes were in Danger of being fruftrated, but his Penfion likewife of being obftructed by an accidental Calumny. The Writer of the *Daily Courant*, a Paper then publifhed under the Direction of the Miniftry, charged him with a Crime, which, though not very great in itfelf, would have been remarkably invidious in him, and might very juftly have incenfed the Queen 1-gainft him. He was accufed by Name of influencing Elections againft the Court, by appearing at the Head of a Tory Mob; nor did the Accufer fail to aggravate his Crime, by reprefenting it as the Effect of the moft atrocious Ingratitude, and a kind of Rebellion a-gainft the Queen, who had firft preferved him from an infamous Death, and afterwards dif-tinguifhed him by her Favour, and fupported him by her Charity. The Charge, as it was open and confident, was likewife by good Fortune very particular. The Place of the Tranfaction was mentioned, and the whole Series

Series of the Rioter's Conduct related. This
Exactnefs made Mr *Savage'* s Vindication eafy,
for he never had in his Life feen the Place
which was declared to be the Scene of his
Wickednefs, nor ever had been prefent in
any Town when its Reprefentatives were chofen. This Anfwer he therefore made hafte
to publifh, with all the Circumftances neceffary
to make it credible, and very reafonably demanded, that the Accufation fhould be retracted in the fame Paper, that he might
no longer fuffer the Imputation of Sedi-
tion and Ingratitude. This Demand was likewife preffed by him in a private Letter to the
Author of the Paper, who either trufting to
the Protection of thofe whofe Defence he had
undertaken, or having entertained fome perfonal Malice againft Mr *Savage*, or fearing
left by retracting fo confident an Affertion, he
fhould impair the Credit of his Paper, refufed
to give him that Satisfaction.

Mr *Savage* therefore thought it neceffary,
to his own Vindication, to profecute him in
the King's Bench ; but as he did not find any
ill Effects from the Accufation, having fufficiently cleared his Innocence, he thought any
farther Procedure would have the Appearance
of Revenge, and therefore willingly dropped it.

He faw foon afterwards a Procefs commenced in the fame Court againft himfelf, on

P 2 an

an Information in which he was accufed of writing and publifhing an obfcene Pamphlet.

It was always Mr *Savage*'s Defire to be diftinguifhed, and when any Controverfy became popular, he never wanted fome Reafon for engaging in it with great Ardour, and appearing at the Head of the Party which he had chofen. As he was never celebrated for his Prudence, he had no fooner taken his Side, and informed himfelf of the chief Topics of the Difpute, than he took all Opportunities of afferting and propagating his Principles, without much Regard to his own Intereft, or any other vifible Defign than that of drawing upon himfelf the Attention of Mankind.

The Difpute between the Bifhop of *London* and the Chancellor is well known to have been for fome Time the chief Topic of political Converfation, and therefore Mr *Savage*, in purfuance of his Character, endeavoured to become confpicuous among the Controvertifts with which every Coffee-Houfe was filled on that Occafion. He was an indefatigable Oppofer of all the Claims of Ecclefiaftical Power, though he did not know on what they were founded, and was therefore no Friend to the Bifhop of *London*. But he had another Reafon for appearing as a warm Advocate for Dr *Rundle*, for he was the Friend of Mr

Mr *Foſter* and Mr *Thompſon*, who were the Friends of Mr *Savage*.

Thus remote was his Intereſt in the Queſtion, which however, as he imagined, concerned him ſo nearly, that it was not ſufficient to harangue and diſpute, but neceſſary likewiſe to write upon it.

He therefore engaged with great Ardour in a new Poem, called by him, *The Progreſs of a Divine*, in which he conducts a profligate Prieſt, by all the Gradations of Wickedneſs, from a poor Curacy in the Country, to the higheſt Preferments of the Church, and deſcribes, with that Humour which was natural to him, and that Knowledge which was extended to all the Diverſities of human Life, his Behaviour in every Station, and inſinuates that this Prieſt thus accompliſhed found at laſt a Patron in the Biſhop of *London*.

When he was aſked by one of his Friends, on what Pretence he could charge the Biſhop with ſuch an Action, he had no more to ſay than that he had only inverted the Accuſation, and that he thought it reaſonable to believe, that he, who obſtructed the Riſe of a good Man without Reaſon, would for bad Reaſons promote the Exaltation of a Villain.

The Clergy were univerſally provoked by this Satire, and *Savage*, who, as was his conſtant Practice, had ſet his Name to his Performance,

formance, was cenfured in the *Weekly Mif-cellany* * with a Severity, which he did not feem inclined to forget.

But

* *A fhort Satire was likewife publifhed in the fame Paper, in which were the following Lines :*

For cruel Murder doom'd to Hempen Death,
Savage, by Royal Grace, prolong'd his Breath.
Well might you think, he fpent his *future* Years
In Prayer, and Fafting, and repentant Tears.
----But, O vain Hope !----the truly *Savage* cries,
" Priefts, and their flavifh Doctrines, I defpife.
" Shall I ------
" Who, by free Thinking to free Action fir'd,
" In midnight Brawls a deathlefs Name acquir'd,
" Now ftoop to *learn* of *Ecclefiaftic Men ?*----
" ----No, arm'd with Rhime, at Priefts I'll take my Aim,
" Though Prudence bids me murder but their Fame.
                                        Weekly Mifcellany.

An Anfwer was publifhed in the Gentleman's *Magazine, written by an unknown Hand, from which the following Lines are felected :*

Transform'd by thoughtlefs Rage, and midnight Wine,
From Malice free, and pufh'd without *Defign,*
In equal Brawl if *Savage* lung'd a Thruft,
And brought the Youth a Victim to the Duft :
So ftrong the Hand of Accident appears,
The royal Hand from Guilt and Vengeance clears.
    Inftead of wafting " *all thy future Years,*
" *Savage, in Pray'r and vain repentant Tears,* "
Exert thy Pen to mend a vicious Age,
To curb the Prieft, and fink his High-Church Rage;
                                        To

But a Return of Invective was not thought a fufficient Punifhment. The Court of *King's Bench* was therefore moved againft him, and he was obliged to return an Anfwer to a Charge of Obfcenity. It was urged in his Defence, that Obfcenity was criminal when it was intended to promote the Practice of Vice, but that Mr *Savage* had only introduced obfcene Ideas with the View of expofing them to Deteftation, and of amending the Age by fhewing the Deformity of Wickednefs. This Plea was admitted, and Sir *Philip Yorke*, who then prefided in that Court, difmiffed the Information with Encomiums upon the Purity and Excellence of Mr *Savage*'s Writings.

The

To fhew what Frauds the holy Veftments hide;
The Nefts of Av'rice, Luft, and pedant Pride.
Then change the Scene, let Merit brightly fhine,
And round the Patriot twift the Wreath divine ;
The heav'nly Guide deliver down to Fame ;
In well-tun'd Lays tranfmit a *Fofter*'s Name.
Touch every Paffion with harmonious Art,
Exalt the Genius, and correct the Heart.
Thus future Times fhall royal Grace extol ;
Thus polifh'd Lines thy prefent Fame enrol.
——But grant————
——Malicioufly that *Savage* plung'd the *Steel*,
And made the Youth its fhining Vengeance feel ;
My Soul abhors the Act, the Man detefts,
But more the Bigotry in prieftly Breafts.
                    Gentleman's Magazine, May 1735.

The Profecution however anfwered in fome
meafure the Purpofe of thofe by whom it
was fet on Foot, for Mr *Savage* was fo far
intimidated by it, that when the Edition of
his Poem was fold, he did not venture to reprint it, fo that it was in a fhort Time forgotten, or forgotten by all but thofe whom
it offended.

It is faid, that fome Endeavours were ufed
to incenfe the Queen againft him, but he
found Advocates to obviate at leaft Part of
their Effect ; for though he was never advanced, he ftill continued to receive his Penfion.

This Poem drew more Infamy upon him
than any Incident of his Life, and as his Conduct cannot be vindicated, it is proper to fecure his Memory from Reproach, by informing thofe whom he made his Enemies, that
he never intended to repeat the Provocation ;
and that, though when ever he thought he had
any Reafon to complain of the Clergy, he
ufed to threaten them with a new Edition of
The Progrefs of a Divine, it was his calm and
fettled Refolution to fupprefs it for ever.

He once intended to have made a better
Reparation for the Folly or Injuftice with
which he might be charged, by writing another Poem, called, *The Progrefs of a Free-
Thinker,* whom he intended to lead through
all

all the Stages of Vice and Folly, to convert him from Virtue to Wickedneſs, and from Religion to Infidelity by all the modiſh Sophiſtry uſed for that Purpoſe ; and at laſt to diſmiſs him by his own Hand into the other World.

That he did not execute this Deſign is a real Loſs to Mankind, for he was too well acquainted with all the Scenes of Debauchery to have failed in his Repreſentations of them, and too zealous for Virtue not to have repreſented them in ſuch a Manner as ſhould expoſe them either to Ridicule or Deteſtation.

But this Plan was, like others, formed and laid aſide, till the Vigour of his Imagination was ſpent, and the Efferveſcence of Invention had ſubſided, but ſoon gave Way to ſome other Deſign, which pleaſed by its Novelty for a while, and then was neglected like the former.

He was ſtill in his uſual Exigencies, having no certain Support but the Penſion allowed him by the Queen, which though it might have kept an exact Oeconomiſt from Want, was very far from being ſufficient for Mr *Savage*, who had never been accuſtomed to diſmiſs any of his Appetites without the Gratification which they ſolicited, and whom nothing but Want of Money withheld from partaking of every Pleaſure that fell within his View.

Q His

His Conduct with regard to his Penſion was very particular. No ſooner had he changed the Bill, than he vaniſhed from the Sight of all his Acquaintances, and lay for ſome Time out of the Reach of all the Enquiries that Friendſhip or Curioſity could make after him; at length he appeared again pennyleſs as before, but never informed even thoſe whom he ſeemed to regard moſt, where he had been, nor was his Retreat ever diſcovered.

This was his conſtant Practice during the whole Time that he received the Penſion from the Queen: He regularly diſappeared and returned. He indeed affirmed, that he retired to ſtudy, and that the Money ſupported him in Solitude for many Months; but his Friends declared, that the ſhort Time in whieh it was ſpent ſufficiently confuted his own Account of his Conduct.

His Politeneſs and his Wit ſtill raiſed him Friends, who were deſirous of ſetting him at length free from that Indigence by which he had been hitherto oppreſſed, and therefore ſolicited Sir *Robert Walpole* in his Favour with ſo much Earneſtneſs, that they obtained a Promiſe of the next Place that ſhould become vacant, not exceeding two hundred Pounds a Year. This Promiſe was made with an uncommon Declaration, *that it was not the Promiſe*

Promiſe of a Miniſter to a Petitioner, but of a Friend to his Friend.

Mr *Savage* now concluded himſelf ſet at Eaſe for ever, and, as he obſerves in a Poem *
written

* *The Poet's Dependence on a Stateſman; which was publiſhed in the* Gentleman's Magazine (Vol. VI. p. 225.) *and contained among others the following Paſſages.*

Some ſeem to hint, and others Proof will bring,
That, from Neglect, my num'rous Hardſhips ſpring.
" Seek the *great Man,*" they cry——'tis then decreed
In *him* if I court *Fortune,* I ſucceed.
What Friends to ſecond ? Who, for *me,* ſhould ſue,
Have Int'reſts, partial to *themſelves,* in View.
They own my matchleſs Fate Compaſſion draws,
They all wiſh well, lament, but drop my Cauſe.
——Say, ſhall I turn where *Lucre* points my Views ;
At firſt deſert my Friends, at length abuſe ?
But, on leſs Terms, in *Promiſe* he complies ;
Years bury Years, and Hopes on Hopes ariſe ;
I truſt, am truſted on my fairy Gain ;
And Woes on Woes attend, an endleſs Train.
 Be Poſts diſpos'd at Will !——I have, for theſe,
No Gold to plead, no Impudence to teaze.
All Secret Service from my Soul I hate ;
All dark Intrigues of Pleaſure, or of State.
 ——Where theſe are not, what Claim to me belongs ;
Though mine the *Muſe* and *Virtue, Birth* and *Wrongs?*
Where lives the *Stateſman,* ſo in *Honour* clear,
To give where he has nought to hope, nor fear ?
No ! —there to ſeek, is but to find freſh Pain :
The Promiſe broke, renew'd and broke again ;
To be, as Humour deigns, receiv'd, refus'd ;
By turns affronted, and by turns amus'd ;

Q 2
To

written on that Incident of his Life, *trusted* and *was trusted*, but soon found that his Confidence was ill-grounded, and this *friendly* Promise was not inviolable. He spent a long Time in Solicitations, and at last despaired and desisted.

He did not indeed deny that he had given the Minister some Reason to believe that he should not strengthen his own Interest by advancing him; for he had taken Care to distinguish himself in Coffee-Houses as an Advocate for the Ministry of the last Years of Queen *Anne*, and was always ready to justify the Conduct, and exalt the Character of Lord *Bolingbroke*, whom he mentions with great Regard in an Epistle upon Authors, which he wrote about that Time, but was too wise to publish, and of which only some Fragments * have appeared, inserted by him in the Magazine after his Retirement.

To

To lose that Time, which worthier Thoughts require,
To lose that Health, which should those Thoughts inspire;
To starve on Hope ; or, like Camelions, fare
On *ministerial Faith,* which means but Air.
—A Scene *will* shew —(all-righteous Vision haste)
The Meek exalted, and the Proud debas'd !——
Oh! to be there! —to tread that friendly Shore ;
Where *Falsehood,* **Pride** and *Statesmen* are no more !

* *From these the following Lines are selected as an Instance rather of his Impartiality than Genius.*

Materials which Belief in Gazettes claim,
Loose strung, run gingling into Hist'ry's Name.

Thick

To defpair was not, however, the Cha-
                                        racter

Thick as Egyptian Clouds of raining Flies ;
As thick as Worms where Man corrupting lies ;
As Pefts obfcene that haunt the ruin'd Pile ;
As Monfters flound'ring in the muddy Nile ;
Minutes Memoirs, Views, and Reviews appear,
Where Slander darkens each recorded Year.
In a paft Reign is fam'd fome am'rous League ;
Some Ring, or Letter, now reveals th' Intrigue ;
Queens with their Minions work unfeemly Things,
And Boys grow Dukes, when Catamites to Kings.
Does a Prince die ? What Poifons they furmife !
No Royal Mortal fure by Nature dies.
Is a Prince born ? What Birth more bafe believ'd ?
Or, what's more ftrange. his Mother ne'er conceiv'd !
Thus Slander popular o'er Truth prevails,
And eafy Minds imbibe romantic Tales.
    Some ufurp Names ——an *Englifh Garretteer*,
From *Minutes* forg'd, is *Monfieur Menager*.
——Where *hear-fay Knowledge* fits on public Names,
And bold *Conjeƈure* or extols, or blames,
Spring *Party Libels* ; from whofe Afhes dead,
A *Monfter*, mifnam'd *Hift'ry*, lifts its Head.
Contending Faƈtions croud to hear its Roar !
But when once heard, it dies to noife no more.
From thefe no Anfwer, no Applaufe from thofe,
O'er half they fimper, and o'er half they doze.
So when in Senate, with egregious Pate,
Perks up Sir ——in fome deep Debate ;
He hems, looks wife, tunes then his lab'ring Throat,
To prove Black White, poftpone or palm the Vote ,
In fly Contempt, fome, *hear him ! hear him !* cry ;
Some yawn, fome fneer; none fecond, none reply.
    But dare fuch Mifcreants now rufh abroad,
By Blanket, Cane, Pump, Pillory, unaw'd ?
                                        Dare

racter of *Savage*, when one Patronage failed, he had recourfe to another. The Prince was now extremely popular, and had very liberally rewarded the Merit of fome Writers whom Mr *Savage* did not think fuperior to himfelf, and therefore he refolved to addrefs a Poem to him.

For this Purpofe he made Choice of a Subject, which could regard only Perfons of the higheft Rank and greateft Affluence, and which was therefore proper for a Poem intended

Dare they imp Falfhood thus, and plume her Wings,
From prefent Characters, and recent Things?
Yes, what Untruths! or Truths in what Difguife!
What *Boyers*, and what *Oldmixons* arife!
What *Facts*, from all but *them* and *Slander* fcreen'd!
Here meets a Council, no where elfe conven'd;
There, from *Originals*, come, thick as Spawn,
Letters ne'er wrote, Memorials never drawn;
To *fecret Conf'rence*, never held, they yoke
Treaties ne'er plann'd, and Speeches never fpoke.
From, *Oldmixon*, thy Brow, too well we know,
Like *Sin* from *Satan*'s, far and wide they go.
In vain may *St John* fafe in Confcience fit,
In vain with Truth confute, contemn with Wit:
Confute, contemn, amid felected Friends;
There finks the Juftice, there the Satire ends.
Here through a *Cent'ry* fcarce fuch Leaves unclofe,
From Mold and Duft the Slander facred grows.
Now none reply where all defpife the Page;
But will dumb Scorn deceive no future Age?
　　　　　　　　Gentleman's Magazine, Sept. 1741.

tended to procure the Patronage of a Prince; and having retired for some Time to *Rich_mond*, that he might profecute his Defign in full Tranquillity, without the Temptations of Pleafure, or the Solicitations of Creditors, by which his Meditations were in equal Danger of being difconcerted, he produced a Poem *On public Spirit, with regard to public Works*.

The Plan of this Poem is very extenfive, and comprifes a Multitude of Topics, each of which might furnifh Matter fufficient for a long Performance, and of which fome have already employed more eminent Writers; but as he was perhaps not fully acquainted with the whole Extent of his own Defign, and was writing to obtain a Supply of Wants too prefling to admit of long or accurate Enquiries, he paffes negligently over many public Works, which, even in his own Opinion, deferved to be more elaborately treated.

But though he may fometimes difappoint his Reader by tranfient Touches upon thefe Subjects, which have often been confidered, and therefore naturally raife Expectations, he muft be allowed amply to compenfate his Omiffions by expatiating in the Conclufion of his Work upon a Kind of Beneficence not yet celebrated by any eminent Poet, though it now appears more fufceptible of Embellifhments, more adapted to exalt the Ideas,

317

Ideas, and affect the Paffions, than many of thofe which have hitherto been thought moft worthy of the Ornaments of Verfe. The Settlement of Colonies in uninhabited Countries, the Eftablifhment of thofe in Security whofe Misfortunes have made their own Country no longer pleafing or fafe, the Acquifition of Property without Injury to any, the Appropriation of the wafte and luxuriant Bounties of Nature, and the Enjoyment of thofe Gifts which Heaven has fcattered upon Regions uncultivated and unoccupied, cannot be confidered without giving Rife to a great Number of pleafing Ideas, and bewildering the Imagination in delightful Profpects; and, therefore, whatever Speculations they may produce in thofe who have confined themfelves to political Studies, naturally fixed the Attention, and excited the Applaufe of a Poet. The Politician, when he confiders Men driven into other Countries for Shelter, and obliged to retire to Forefts and Deferts, and pafs their Lives and fix their Pofterity in the remoteft Corners of the World, to avoid thofe Hardfhips which they fuffer or fear in their native Place, may very properly enquire why the Legiflature does not provide a Remedy for thefe Miferies, rather than encourage an Efcape from them. He may conclude, that the Flight of every honeft Man is a Lofs to the

the Community, that thofe who are unhappy without Guilt ought to be relieved, and the Life which is overburthened by accidental Calamities, fet at Eafe by the Care of the Publick, and that thofe, who have by Mifconduct forfeited their Claim to Favour, ought rather to be made ufeful to the Society which they have injured, than be driven from it. But the Poet is employed in a more pleafing Undertaking than that of propofing Laws, which, however juft or expedient, will never be made, or endeavouring to reduce to rational Schemes of Government Societies which were formed by Chance, and are conducted by the private Paffions of thofe who prefide in them. He guides the unhappy Fugitive from Want and Perfecution, to Plenty, Quiet, and Security, and feats him in Scenes of peaceful Solitude, and undifturbed Repofe.

Savage has not forgotten, amidft the pleafing Sentiments which this Profpect of Retirement fuggefted to him, to cenfure thofe Crimes which have been generally committed by the Difcoverers of new Regions, and to expofe the enormous Wickednefs of making War upon barbarous Nations becaufe they cannot refift, and of invading Countries becaufe they are fruitful; of extending Navigation only to propagate Vice, and of vifiting diftant Lands only to lay them wafte.

R   He

He has afferted the natural Equality of Mankind, and endeavoured to fupprefs that Pride
which inclines Men to imagine that Right is
the Confequence of Power*.

His Defcription of the various Miferies
which force Men to feek for Refuge in diftant
Countries, affords another Inftance of his Proficiency in the important and extenfive Study
of human Life; and the Tendernefs with
which he recounts them, another Proof of his
Humanity and Benevolence.

It is obfervable, that the Clofe of this Poem
difcovers a Change which Experience had
made

* Learn, future Natives of this promis'd Land,
  What your Fore-fathers ow'd my faving Hand !
  Learn, when *Defpair* fuch fuden Blifs fhall fee,
  Such Blifs muft fhine from OGLETHORPE or †Me !
  Do you the neighb'ring, blamelefs *Indian* aid,
  Culture what he neglects, not his invade ;
  Dare not, oh ! dare not, with ambitious View,
  Force or demand Subjection, never due.
  Let by *my* fpecious Name no *Tyrants* rife,
  And cry, while they enflave, they civilize !
  Why muft I *Afric*'s fable Children fee
  Vended for Slaves, though form'd by Nature free ?
  The namelefs Tortures cruel Minds invent,
  Thofe to fubject, whom Nature equal meant ?
  If thefe you dare, albeit unjuft Succefs
  Empow'rs you now unpunifh'd to opprefs,
  Revolving Empire you and yours may doom ;
  Rome all fubdu'd, yet *Vandals* vanquifh'd *Rome :*
  Yes, Empire may revolve, give them the Day,
  And Yoke may Yoke, and Blood may Blood repay.
          * *Publick Spirit.*

made in Mr *Savage*'s Opinions. In a Poem
written by him in his Youth, and publifhed in
his Mifcellanies, he declares his Contempt of
the contracted Views and narrow Profpects
of the middle State of Life, and declares his
Refolution either to tower like the Cedar, or
be trampled like the Shrub; but in this Poem,
though addreffed to a Prince, he mentions this
State of Life as comprifing thofe who ought
moft to attract Reward, thofe who merit
moft the Confidence of Power, and the Familiarity of Greatnefs; and accidentally mentioning this Paffage to one of his Friends, declared that in his Opinion all the Virtue of
Mankind was comprehended in that State.

In defcribing Villas and Gardens, he did
not omit to condemn that abfurd Cuftom,
which prevails among the *English*, of per-
mitting Servants to receive Money from Strangers for the Entertainment that they receive;
and therefore inferted in his Poem thefe Lines:

But what's the flow'ring Pride of Gardens rare,
However royal, or however fair,
If Gates, which to Accefs fhould ftill give way,
Ope but, like *Peter*'s Paradife, for Pay?
If perquifited Varlets frequent ftand,
And each new Walk muft a new Tax demand?
What foreing Eye but with Contempt furveys?
What Mufe fhall from Oblivion fnatch their Praife?

But before the Publication of his Performance he recollected, that the Queen allowed her Garden and Cave at *Richmond* to be fhewn for Money, and that fhe fo openly countenanced the Practice, that fhe had beftowed the Privilege of fhewing them as a Place of Profit on a Man whofe Merit fhe valued herfelf upon rewarding, though fhe gave him only the Liberty of difgracing his Country.

He therefore thought, with more Prudence than was often exerted by him, that the Publication of thefe Lines might be officioufly reprefented as an Infult upon the Queen to whom he owed his Life and his Subfiftence, and that the Propriety of his Obfervation would be no Security againft the Cenfures which the Unfeafonablenefs of it might draw upon him ; he therefore fuppreffed the Paffage in the firft Edition, but after the Queen's Death thought the fame Caution no longer neceffary, and reftored it to the proper Place.

The Poem was therefore publifhed without any political Faults, and infcribed to the Prince ; but Mr *Savage* having no Friend upon whom he could prevail to prefent it to him, had no other Method of attracting his Obfervation than the Publication of frequent Advertifements, and therefore received no Reward from his Patron, however generous on other Occafions

This

This Difappointment he never mentioned without Indignation, being by fome means or other confident that the Prince was not ignorant of his Addrefs to him, and infinuated, that if any Advances in Popularity could have been made by diftinguifhing him, he had not written without Notice, or without Reward.

He was once inclined to have prefented his Poem in Perfon, and fent to the Printer for a Copy with that Defign; but either his Opinion changed, or his Refolution deferted him, and he continued to refent Neglect without attempting to force himfelf into Regard.

Nor was the Public much more favourable than his Patron, for only feventy-two were fold, though the Performance was much commended by fome whofe Judgment in that Kind of Writing is generally allowed. But *Savage* eafily reconciled himfelf to Mankind without imputing any Defect to his Work, by obferving that his Poem was unluckily publifhed two Days after the Prorogation of the Parliament, and by confequence at a Time when all thofe who could be expected to regard it were in the Hurry of preparing for their Departure, or engaged in taking Leave of others upon their Difmiffion from Public Affairs.

It muft be however allowed, in Juftification of the Public, that this Performance is

not

not the moft excellent of Mr *Savage's* Works, and that though it cannot be denied to contain many ftriking Sentiments, majeftic Lines, and juft Obfervations, it is in general not fufficiently polifhed in the Language, or enlivened in the Imagery, or digefted in the Plan.

Thus his Poem contributed nothing to the Alleviation of his Poverty, which was fuch as very few could have fupported with equal Patience, but to which it muft likewife be confeffed, that few would have been expofed who receive punctually fifty Pounds a Year; a Salary which, though by no means equal to the Demands of Vanity and Luxury, is yet found fufficient to fupport Families above Want, and was undoubtedly more than the Neceffities of Life require.

But no fooner had he received his Penfion, than he withdrew to his darling Privacy, from which he return'd in a fhort Time to his former Diftrefs, and for fome Part of the Year, generally lived by Chance, eating only when he was invited to the Tables of his Acquaintances, from which the Meannefs of his Drefs often excluded him, when the Politenefs and Variety of his Converfation would have been thought a fufficient Recompence for his Entertainment.

He lodged as much by Accident as he dined, and paffed the Night fometimes in mean Houfes.

Houſes, which are ſet open at Night to any caſual Wanderers, ſometimes in Cellars among the Riot and Filth of the meaneſt and moſt profligate of the Rabble ; and ſometimes, when he had no Money to ſupport even the Expences of theſe Receptacles, walked about the Streets till he was weary, and lay down in the Summer upon a Bulk, or in the Winter, with his Aſſociates in Poverty, among the Aſhes of a Glaſs-houſe.

In this Manner were paſſed thoſe Days and thoſe Nights, which Nature had enabled him to have employed in elevated Speculations, uſeful Studies, or pleaſing Converſation. On a Bulk, in a Cellar, or in a Glaſs-houſe among Thieves and Beggars, was to be found the Author of the *Wanderer*, the Man of ex-alted Sentiments, extenſive Views, and curious Obſervations, the Man whoſe Remarks on Life might have aſſiſted the Stateſman, whoſe Ideas of Virtue might have enlightned the Mo-raliſt, whoſe Eloquence might have influenced Senates, and whoſe Delicacy might have po-liſhed Courts.

It cannot be imagined but that ſuch Neceſſities might ſometimes force him upon diſreputable Practices, and it is probable that theſe Lines in the *Wanderer* were occaſioned by his Re-flections on his own Conduct.

Though

Though Mis'ry leads to Fortitude and Truth,
Unequal to the Load this languid Youth,
(O! let none cenfure if untry'd by Grief,
Or amidft Woes untempted by Relief,)
He ftoop'd, reluctant, to mean Acts of Shame,
Which then, ev'n then, he fcorn'd, and blufh'd to
   name.

Whoever was acquainted with him, was certain to be folicited for fmall Sums, which the Frequency of the Requeft made in Time confiderable, and he was therefore quickly fhunned by thofe who were become familiar enough to be trufted with his Neceffities; but his rambling Manner of Life, and conftant Appearance at Houfes of public Refort, always procured hin a new Succeffion of Friends, whofe Kindnefs had not been exhaufted by repeated Requefts, fo that he was feldom abfolutely without Refources, but had in his utmoft Exigences this Comfort, that he always imagined himfelf fure of fpeedy Relief.

It was obferved that he always afked Favours of this Kind without the leaft Submiffion or apparent Confcioufnefs of Dependence, and that he did not feem to look upon a Compliance with his Requeft as an Obligation that deferved any extraordinary Acknowledgments, but a Refufal was refented by him as an Affront, or complained of as an Injury; nor
   did

did he readily reconcile himself to thofe who either denied to lend, or gave him afterwards any Intimation, that they expected to be repaid.

He was fometimes fo far compaffionated by thofe who knew both his Merit and his Diftreffes, that they received him into their Families, but they foon difcovered him to be a very incommodious Inmate; for being always accuftomed to an irregular Manner of Life, he could not confine himfelf to any ftated Hours, or pay any Regard to the Rules of a Family, but would prolong his Converfation till Midnight, without confidering that Bufinefs might require his Friend's Application in the Morning; nor when he had perfuaded himfelf to retire to Bed, was he without equal Difficulty, called up to Dinner; it was therefore impoffible to pay him any Diftinction without the entire Subverfion of all Oeconomy, a Kind of Eftablifhment which, wherever he went, he always appeared ambitious to overthrow.

It muft therefore be acknowledged, in Juftification of Mankind, that it was not always by the Negligence or Coldnefs of his Friends that *Savage* was diftreffed, but becaufe it was in reality very difficult to preferve him long in a State of Eafe. To fupply him with Money was a hopelefs Attempt, for no fooner did he fee himfelf Mafter of a Sum fufficient to fet

S him

him free from Care for a Day, than he became profuse and luxurious. When once he had entred a Tavern, or engaged in a Scheme of Pleasure, he never retired till Want of Money obliged him to some new Expedient. If he was entertained in a Family, nothing was any longer to be regarded there but Amusements and Jollity; wherever *Savage* entered he immediately expected that Order and Business should fly before him, that all should thenceforward be left to Hazard, and that no dull Principle of domestic Management should be opposed to his Inclination, or intrude upon his Gaiety.

His Distresses, however afflictive, never dejected him; in his lowest State he wanted not Spirit to assert the natural Dignity of Wit, and was always ready to repress that Insolence which Superiority of Fortune incited, and to trample the Reputation which rose upon any other Basis than that of Merit: He never admitted any gross Familiarities, or submitted to be treated otherwise than as an Equal. Once when he was without Lodging, Meat, or Cloaths, one of his Friends, a Man not indeed remarkable for Moderation in his Prosperity, left a Message, that he desired to see him about nine in the Morning. *Savage* knew that his Intention was to assist him, but was very much disgusted, that he
should

should presume to prescribe the Hour of his Attendance, and, I believe, refused to visit him, and rejected his Kindness.

The same invincible Temper, whether Firmness or Obstinacy, appeared in his Conduct to the Lord *Tyrconnel*, from whom he very frequently demanded that the Allowance which was once paid him should be restored, but with whom he never appeared to entertain for a Moment the Thought of soliciting a Reconciliation, and whom he treated at once with all the Haughtiness of Superiority, and all the Bitterness of Resentment. He wrote to him not in a Stile of Supplication or Respect, but of Reproach, Menace, and Contempt, and appeared determined, if he ever regained his Allowance, to hold it only by the Right of Conquest.

As many more can discover, that a Man is richer than that he is wiser than themselves, Superiority of Understanding is not so readily acknowledged as that of Condition; nor is that Haughtiness, which the Consciousness of great Abilities incites, borne with the same Submission as the Tyranny of Wealth; and therefore *Savage*, by asserting his Claim to Deference and Regard, and by treating those with Contempt whom better Fortune animated to rebel against him, did not fail to raise a great Number of Enemies in the different Classes of

Mankind.

Mankind. Thofe who thought themfelves raifed above him by the Advantages of Riches, hated him becaufe they found no Protection from the Petulance of his Wit. Thofe who were efteemed for their Writings feared him as a Critic, and maligned him as a Rival, and almoft all the fmaller Wits were his profeffed Enemies.

Among thefe Mr *Millar* fo far indulged his Refentment as to introduce him in a Farce, and direct him to be perfonated on the Stage in a Drefs like that which he then wore; a mean Infult which only infinuated, that *Savage* had but one Coat, and which was therefore defpifed by him rather than refented; for though he wrote a Lampoon againft *Millar*, he never printed it: and as no other Perfon ought to profecute that Revenge from which the Perfon who was injured defifted, I fhall not preferve what Mr *Savage* fuppreffed; of which the Publication would indeed have been a Punifhment too fevere for fo impotent an Affault.

The great Hardfhips of Poverty were to *Savage* not the Want of Lodging or of Food, but the Neglect and Contempt which it drew upon him. He complained that as his Affairs grew defperate he found his Reputation for Capacity vifibly decline, that his Opinion in Queftions of Criticifm was no longer regarded,

garded, when his Coat was out of Fashion;
and that those who in the Interval of his
Prosperity were always encouraging him to
great Undertakings by Encomiums on his Genius and Assurances of Success, now received
any Mention of his Designs with Coldness,
thought that the Subjects on which he proposed to write were very difficult ; and were
ready to inform him, that the Event of a
Poem was uncertain, that an Author ought to
employ much Time in the Confideration of
his Plan, and not presume to sit down to
write in Confidence of a few cursory Ideas,
and a superficial Knowledge ; Difficulties were
started on all Sides, and he was no longer
qualified for any Performance but the *Volunteer
Laureat*.

Yet even this Kind of Contempt never depressed him; for he always preserved a steady
Confidence in his own Capacity, and believed
nothing above his Reach which he should at
any Time earnestly endeavour to attain. He
formed Schemes of the same Kind with regard to Knowledge and to Fortune, and flat-
tered himself with Advances to be made in
Science, as with Riches to be enjoyed in
some distant Period of his Life. For the Acquisition of Knowledge he was indeed far
better qualified than for that of Riches; for
he was naturally inquisitive and desirous of
the

the Converfation of thofe from whom any Information was to be obtained, but by no Means folicitous to improve thofe Opportunities that were fometimes offered of raifing his Fortune; and was remarkably retentive of his Ideas, which, when once he was in Poffeffion of them, rarely forfook him; a Quality which could never be communicated to his Money.

While he was thus wearing out his Life in Expectation that the Queen would fome time recollect her Promife, he had Recourfe to the ufual Practice of Writers, and publifhed Propofals for printing his Works by Subfcription, to which he was encouraged by the Succefs of many who had not a better Right to the Favour of the Public; but whatever was the Reafon, he did not find the World equally inclined to favour him, and he obferved with fome Difcontent, that though he offered his Works at half a Guinea, he was able to procure but a fmall Number in Comparifon with thofe who fubfcribed twice as much to *Duck*.

Nor was it without Indignation that he faw his Propofals neglected by the Queen, who patronifed Mr *Duck*'s with uncommon Ardour, and incited a Competition among thofe who attended the Court, who fhould moft promote his Intereft, and who fhould firft offer a Subfcription. This was a Diftinction to which

which Mr *Savage* made no Scruple of afferting that his Birth, his Misfortunes, and his Genius gave him a fairer Title, than could be pleaded by him on whom it was conferred.

Savage's Applications were however not univerfally unfuccefsful; for fome of the Nobility countenanced his Defign, encouraged his Propofals, and fubfcribed with great Liberality. He related of the Duke of *Chandos* particularly, that, upon receiving his Propofals, he fent him ten Guineas.

But the Money which his Subfcriptions afforded him was not lefs volatile than that which he received from his other Schemes; whenever a Subfcription was paid him he went to a Tavern, and as Money fo collected is neceffarily received in fmall Sums, he never was able to fend his Poems to the Prefs, but for many Years continued his Solicitation, and fquandered whatever he obtained.

This Project of printing his Works was frequently revived, and as his Propofals grew obfolete, new ones were printed with frefher Dates. To form Schemes for the Publication was one of his favourite Amufements, nor was he ever more at Eafe than when with any Friend who readily fell in with his Schemes, he was adjufting the Print, forming the Advertifements, and regulating the Difperfion of his new Edition, which he really intended
some

some time to publish, and which, as long Experience had shewn him the Impossibility of printing the Volume together, he at last determined to divide into weekly or monthly Numbers, that the Profits of the first might supply the Expences of the next.

Thus he spent his Time in mean Expedients and tormenting Suspense, living for the greatest Part in Fear of Prosecutions from his Creditors, and consequently skulking in obscure Parts of the Town, of which he was no Stranger to the remotest Corners. But wherever he came his Address secured him Friends, whom his Necessities soon alienated, so that he had perhaps a more numerous Acquaintance than any Man ever before attained, there being scarcely any Person eminent on any Account to whom he was not known, or whose Character he was not in some Degree able to delineate.

To the Acquisition of this extensive Acquaintance every Circumstance of his Life contributed. He excelled in the Arts of Conversation, and therefore willingly practised them: He had seldom any Home, or even a Lodging in which he could be private, and therefore was driven into public Houses for the common Conveniences of Life, and Supports of Nature. He was always ready to comply with every Invitation, having no Employment

ployment to withhold him, and often no Money to provide for himſelf; and by dining with one Company, he never failed of obtaining an Introduction into another.

Thus diſſipated was his Life, and thus caſual his Subſiſtence; yet did not the Diſtraction of his Views hinder him from Reflection, nor the Uncertainty of his Condition depreſs his Gaiety. When he had wandered about without any fortunate Adventure, by which he was led into a Tavern, he ſometimes retired into the Fields, and was able to employ his Mind in Study to amuſe it with pleaſing Imaginations; and ſeldom appeared to be melancholy, but when ſom ſudden Misfortune had juſt fallen upon him, and even then in a few Moments he would diſentangle himſelf from his Perplexity, adopt the Subject of Converſation, and apply his Mind wholly to the Objects that others preſented to it.

This Life, unhappy as it may be already imagined, was yet imbitter'd in 1738, with new Calamities. The Death of the Queen deprived him of all the Proſpects of Preferment with which he had ſo long entertained his Imagination; and as Sir *Robert Walpole* had before given him Reaſon to believe that he never intended the Performance of his Pro-

T miſe,

mife, he was now abandoned again to Fortune.

He was, however, at that time, fupported by a Friend; and as it was not his Cuftom to look out for diftant Calamities, or to feel any other Pain than that which forced itfelf upon his Senfes, he was not much afflicted at his Lofs, and perhaps comforted himfelf that his Penfion would be now continued without the annual Tribute of a Panegyric.

Another Expectation contributed likewife to fupport him; he had taken a Refolution to write a fecond Tragedy upon the Story of Sir *Thomas Overbury*, in which he preferved a few Lines of his former Play; but made a total Alteration of the Plan, added new Incidents, and introduced new Characters; fo that it was a new Tragedy, not a Revival of the former.

Many of his Friends blamed him for not making Choice of another Subject; but in Vindication of himfelf, he afferted, that it was not eafy to find a better; and that he thought it his Intereft to extinguifh the Memory of the firft Tragedy, which he could only do by writing one lefs defective upon the fame Story; by which he fhould entirely defeat the Artifice of the Bookfellers, who after the Death of any Author of Reputation, are always induftrious

to

to fwell his Works, by uniting his worft Productions with his beft.

In the Execution of this Scheme, however,
he proceeded but flowly, and probably only
employed himfelf upon it when he could find
no other Amufement; but he pleafed himfelf
with counting the Profits, and perhaps imagined, that the theatrical Reputation which
he was about to acquire, would be equivalent
to all that he had loft by the Death of his Patronefs.

He did not in confidence of his approaching
Riches neglect the Meafures proper to fecure
theContinuance of his Penfion, though fome of
his Favourers thought him culpable for omitting to write on her Death; but on her Birth-
Day next Year he gave a Proof of the Solidity
of his Judgment, and the Power of his Genius.

He knew that the Track of Elegy had been
fo long beaten, that it was impoffible to travel
in it without treading in the Footfteps of thofe
who had gone before him ; and that therefore
it was neceffary, that he might diftinguifh himfelf from the Herd of Encomiafts, to find out
fome new Walk of funeral Panegyric.

This difficult Tafk he performed in fuch a
Manner, that his Poem may be juftly ranked
among the beft Pieces that the Death of
Princes has produced. By transferring the

T 2 Men-

Mention of her Death to her Birth-Day, he has formed a happy Combination of Topics, which any other Man would have thought it very difficult to connect in one View, but which he has united in such a Manner, that the Relation between them appears natural; and it may be juſtly ſaid, that what no other Man would have thought on, it now appears ſcarcely poſſible for any Man to miſs *.

The

* To exhibit a Specimen of the Beauties of this Poem, the following Paſſages are ſelected.

Oft has the Muſe, on this diſtinguiſh'd Day,
Tun'd to glad Harmony the vernal Lay;
But, O lamented Change! The Lay muſt flow
From grateful Rapture now to grateful Woe.
She, to this Day, who joyous Luſtre gave,
Deſcends for ever to the ſilent Grave.
She born at once to charm us and to mend,
Of human Race the Pattern and the Friend.
—-And, thou, bright Princeſs! ſeated now on high,
Next one, the faireſt Daughter of the Sky,
Whoſe warm-felt Love is to all Beings known,
Thy Siſter *Charity!* next her thy Throne;
See at thy Tomb the Virtues weeping lie!
There in dumb Sorrow ſeem the Arts to die.
So were the Sun o'er other Orbs to blaze,
And from our World, like thee, withdraw his Rays,
No more to viſit where he warm'd before,
All Life muſt ceaſe, and Nature be no more.
Yet ſhall the Muſe a heav'nly Height eſſay,
Beyond the Weakneſs mix'd with mortal Clay;
Beyond the Loſs, which, tho' ſhe bleeds to ſee,
Tho' ne'er to be redeem'd, the Loſs of thee;

Beyond

The Beauty of this peculiar Combination of Images is fo mafterly, that it is fufficient to fet this Poem above Cenfure; and therefore it is not neceffary to mention many other delicate Touches which may be found in it, and which would defervedly be admired in any other Performance.

To thefe Proofs of his Genius may be added, from the fame Poem, an Inftance of his Prudence, an Excellence for which he was not fo often diftinguifhed; he does not forget * to remind the King, in the moft delicate and artful Manner, of continuing his Penfion.

With

Beyond ev'n this, fhe hails, with joyous Lay,
Thy better Birth, thy firft true natal Day;
A Day, that fees Thee born, beyond the Tomb,
To endlefs Health, to Youth's eternal Bloom;
Born to the mighty Dead, the Souls fublime
Of ev'ry famous Age, and ev'ry Clime;
To Goodnefs fix'd, by Truth's unvarying Laws,
To Blifs that knows no Period, knows no Paufe——
Save when thine Eye, from yonder pure Serene,
Sheds a foft Ray on this our gloomy Scene.

* ————Deign one Look more! Ah! See thy Confort
dear!
Wifhing all Hearts, except his own, to cheer.
Lo! ftill he bids thy wonted Bounties flow
To weeping Families of Worth and Woe.
He ftops all Tears, however faft they rife,
Save thofe that ftill muft fall from grateful Eyes:
And fpite of Griefs, that fo ufurp his Mind,
Still watches o'er the Welfare of Mankind.

339

With regard to the Succefs of this Addrefs he was for fome Time in Sufpenfe, but
was in no great Degree follicitous about it,
and continued his Labour upon his new Tragedy with great Tranquillity, till the Friend,
who had for a confiderable time fupported
him, removing his Family to another Place,
took Occafion to difmifs him. It then became
neceffary to enquire more diligently what was
determined in his Affair, having Reafon to
fufpect that no great Favour was intended him,
becaufe he had not received his Penfion at the
ufual Time.

It is faid, that he did not take thofe Methods
of retrieving his Intereft which were moft likely
to fucceed; and fome of thofe who were employed in the Exchequer, cautioned him a-
gainft too much Violence in his Proceedings;
but Mr *Savage*, who feldom regulated his
Conduct by the Advice of others, gave way to
his Paffion, and demanded of Sir *Robert Walpole*, at his Levee, the Reafon of the Diftinction
that was made between him and the other
Penfioners of the Queen, with a Degree of
Roughnefs, which perhaps determined him to
withdraw what had been only delayed.

Whatever was the Crime of which he was
accufed or fufpected, and whatever Influence
was employed againft him, he received foon
after

after an Account that took from him all Hopes of regaining his Penſion; and he had now no Proſpect of Subſiſtence but from his Play, and he knew no Way of Living for the Time required to finiſh it.

So peculiar were the Misfortunes of this Man, deprived of an Eſtate and Title by a particular Law, expoſed and abandoned by a Mother, defrauded by a Mother of a Fortune which his Father had allotted him, he enter'd the World without a Friend; and though his Abilities forced themſelves into Eſteem and Reputation, he was never able to obtain any real Advantage, and whatever Proſpects aroſe, were always intercepted as he began to approach them. The King's Intentions in his Favour were fruſtrated; his Dedication to the Prince, whoſe Generoſity on every other Occaſion was eminent, procured him no Reward; Sir *Robert Walpole*, who valued himſelf upon keeping his Promiſe to others, broke it to him without Regret; and the Bounty of the Queen was, after her Death, withdrawn from him, and from him only.

Such were his Misfortunes, which yet he bore not only with Decency, but with Cheerfulneſs, nor was his Gaiety clouded even by his laſt Diſappointment, though he was in a ſhort Time reduced to the loweſt Degree of Diſtreſs,

ſtreſs, and often wanted both Lodging and Food. At this Time he gave another Inſtance of the inſurmountable Obſtinacy of his Spirit; his Cloaths were worn out, and he received Notice that at a Coffee-Houſe ſome Cloaths and Linen were left for him; the Perſon who ſent them, did not, I believe, inform him to whom he was to be obliged, that he might ſpare the Perplexity of acknowledging the Benefit; but though the Offer was ſo far generous, it was made with ſome Neglect of Ceremonies, which Mr *Savage* ſo much reſented, that he refuſed the Preſent, and declined to enter the Houſe, till the Cloaths that had been deſigned for him were taken away.

His Diſtreſs was now publickly known, and his Friends, therefore, thought it proper to concert ſome Meaſures for his Relief; and one of them wrote a Letter to him, in which he expreſſed his Concern *for the miſerable withdrawing of his Penſion*; and gave him Hopes that, in a ſhort Time, he ſhould find himſelf ſupplied with a Competence, *without any Dependence on thoſe little Creatures which we are pleaſed to call the Great*.

The Scheme propoſed for this happy and independent Subſiſtence, was, that he ſhould retire into *Wales*, and receive an Allowance of fifty Pounds a Year, to be raiſed by a Sub-ſcription,

ſcription, on which he was to live privately in a cheap Place, without aſpiring any more to Affluence, or having any farther Care of Reputation.

This Offer Mr *Savage* gladly accepted, tho' with Intentions very different from thoſe of his Friends; for they propoſed, that he ſhould continue an Exile from *London* for ever, and ſpend all the remaining Part of his Life at *Swanſea*; but he deſigned only to take the Opportunity, which their Scheme offered him, of retreating for a ſhort Time, that he might prepare his Play for the Stage, and his other Works for the Preſs, and then to return to *London* to exhibit his Tragedy, and live upon the Profits of his own Labour.

With regard to his Works, he propoſed very great Improvements, which would have required much Time, or great Application; and when he had finiſh'd them, he deſigned to do Juſtice to his Subſcribers, by publiſhing them according to his Propoſals.

As he was ready to entertain himſelf with future Pleaſures, he had planned out a Scheme of Life for the Country, of which he had no Knowledge but from Paſtorals and Songs. He imagined that he ſhould be tranſported to Scenes of flow'ry Felicity, like thoſe which one Poet has reflected to another, and had projected

U   a per-a perpetual Round of innocent Pleafures, of which he fufpected no Interruption from Pride, or Ignorance, or Brutality.

With thefe Expectations he was fo en-chanted, that when he was once gently re-proach'd by a Friend for fubmitting to live upon a Subfcription, and advifed rather by a refolute Exertion of his Abilities to fupport himfelf, he could not bear to debar himfelf from the Happinefs which was to be found in the Calm of a Cottage, or lofe the Opportunity of liftening, without Intermiffion, to the Melody of the Nightingale, which he believ'd was to be heard from every Bramble, and which he did not fail to mention as a very important Part of the Happinefs of a Country Life.

While this Scheme was ripening, his Friends directed him to take a Lodging in the Liberties of the Fleet, that he might be fecure from his Creditors, and fent him every Monday a Guinea, which he commonly fpent before the next Morning, and trufted, after his ufual Manner, the remaining Part of the Week to the Bounty of Fortune.

He now began very fenfibly to feel the Miferies of Dependence: Thofe by whom he was to be fupported, began to prefcribe to him with an Air of Authority, which he knew

knew not how decently to refent, nor patiently to bear; and he foon difcovered, from the
Conduct of moft of his Subfcribers, that he
was yet in the Hands of *Little Creatures*.

Of the Infolence that he was obliged to
fuffer, he gave many Inftances, of which none
appeared to raife his Indignation to a greater
Height, than the Method which was taken
of furnifhing him with Cloaths. Inftead of
confulting him, and allowing him to fend to
a Taylor his Orders for what they thought
proper to allow him, they propofed to fend
for a Taylor to take his Meafure, and then
to confult how they fhould equip him.

This Treatment was not very delicate, nor
was it fuch as *Savage*'s Humanity would
have fuggefted to him on a like Occafion; but
it had fcarcely deferved Mention, had it not,
by affecting him in an uncommon Degree,
fhewn the Peculiarity of his Character. Upon
hearing the Defign that was formed, he came
to the Lodging of a Friend with the moft violent Agonies of Rage; and being asked what
it could be that gave him fuch Difturbance,
he replied, with the utmoft Vehemence of
Indignation, " That they had fent for a
Taylor to meafure him."

How the Affair ended, was never enquired,
for fear of renewing his Uneafinefs. It is pro-

bable

bable that, upon Recollection, he submitted with a good Grace to what he could not avoid, and that he discovered no Resentment where he had no Power.

He was, however, not humbled to implicit and universal Compliance; for when the Gentleman, who had first informed him of the Design to support him by a Subscription, attempted to procure a Reconciliation with the Lord *Tyrconnel*, he could by no means be prevailed upon to comply with the Measures that were proposed.

A Letter was written for him to Sir *William Lemon*, to prevail upon him to interpose his good Offices with Lord *Tyrconnel*, in which he solicited Sir *William*'s Assistance, *for a Man who really needed it as much as any Man could well do*; and informed him that he was retiring *for ever to a Place where he should no more trouble his Relations, Friends, or Enemies*; he confessed, that his *Passion* had *betrayed* him to some Conduct, with regard to Lord *Tyrconnel*, *for which he could not but heartily ask his Pardon*; and as he imagined Lord *Tyrconnel*'s Passion might be yet so high, that he would not *receive a Letter from him*, begg'd that Sir *William* would endeavour to soften him; and expressed his

his Hopes, that he would comply with his Requeſt, and that *ſo ſmall a Relation would not harden his Heart againſt him.*

That any Man ſhould preſume to dictate a Letter to him, was not very agreeable to Mr *Savage*; and therefore he was, before he had opened it, not much inclined to approve it. But when he read it, he found it contained Sentiments entirely oppoſite to his own, and, as he aſſerted, to the Truth; and therefore inſtead of copying it, wrote his Friend a Letter full of maſculine Reſentment, and warm Expoſtulations. He very juſtly obſerved that the Style was too ſupplicatory, and the Repreſentation too abject, and that he ought at leaſt to have made him complain with *the Dignity of a Gentleman in Diſtreſs.* He declared that he would not write the Paragraph in which he was to ask Lord *Tyrconnel's* Pardon; for *he deſpiſed his Pardon, and therefore could not heartily, and would not hypocritically ask it.* He remarked, that his Friend made a very unreaſonable Diſtinction between himſelf and him; for, ſays he, when you mention Men of high Rank *in your own Character,* they are *thoſe little Creatures whom we are pleaſed to call the Great*; but when you addreſs them *in mine,* no Servility is ſufficiently humble. He then with great Propriety explained

plained the ill Confequences might be expected from fuch a Letter, which his Relations would print in their own Defence, and which would for ever be produced as a full Anfwer to all that he fhould allege againft them ; for he always intended to publifh a minute Account of the Treatment which he had received. It is to be remembered to the Honour of the Gentleman by whom this Letter was drawn up, that he yielded to Mr *Savage*'s Reafons, and agreed that it ought to be fuppreffed.

After many Alterations and Delays, a Sub-fcription was at length raifed, which did not amount to fifty Pounds a Year, though twenty were paid by one Gentleman ; fuch was the Generofity of Mankind, that what had been done by a Player without Solicitation, could not now be effected by Application and In-tereft ; and *Savage* had a great Number to court and to obey for a Penfion lefs than that which Mrs *Oldfield* paid him without exact-ing any Servilities.

Mr *Savage* however was fatisfied, and willing to retire, and was convinced that the Allow-ance, though fcanty, would be more than fufficient for him, being now determined to commence a rigid Oeconomift, and to live ac-cording to the exacteft Rules of Frugality ; for nothing was in his Opinion more contemptible than

than a Man, who, when he knew his Income, exceeded it; and yet he confeſſed that Inſtances of ſuch Folly were too common, and lamented, that ſome Men were not to be truſted with their own Money.

Full of theſe ſalutary Reſolutions, he left *London*, in *July* 1739, having taken Leave with great Tenderneſs of his Friends, and parted from the Author of this Narrative with Tears in his Eyes. He was furniſhed with fifteen Guineas, and informed, that they would be ſufficient, not only for the Expence of his Journey, but for his Support in *Wales* for ſome Time; and that there remained but little more of the firſt Collection. He promiſed a ſtrict Adherence to his Maxims of Parſimony, and went away in the Stage Coach; nor did his Friends expect to hear from him, till he informed them of his Arrival at *Swanſea*.

But when they leaſt expected, arrived a Letter dated the fourteenth Day after his Departure, in which he ſent them Word, that he was yet upon the Road, and without Money; and that he therefore could not proceed without a Remittance. They then ſent him all the Money that was in their Hands, with which he was enabled to reach *Briſtol*, from whence he was to go to *Swanſea* by Water.

At *Briſtol* he found an Embargo laid upon the Shipping, ſo that he could not immediately ob-

obtain a Paſſage ; and being therefore obliged
to ſtay there ſome Time, he, with his uſual
Felicity, ingratiated himſelf with many of the
principal Inhabitants, was invited to their
Houſes, diſtinguiſhed at their publick
Feaſts, and treated with a Regard that gratify'd his Vanity, and therefore eaſily engaged
his Affection.

He began very early after his Retirement
to complain of the Conduct of his Friends in
London, and irritated many of them ſo much
by his Letters, that they withdrew, however
honourably, their Contributions ; and it is believed, that little more was paid him than
the twenty Pounds a Year, which were allowed
him by the Gentleman who propoſed the Sub-
ſcription.

After ſome Stay at *Briſtol*, he retired to
Swanſea, the Place *originally* propoſed for
his Reſidence, where he lived about a Year,
very much diſſatisfied with the Diminution of
his Salary, but contracted, as in other Places,
Acquaintance with thoſe who were moſt diſtinguiſhed in that Country, among whom he
has celebrated Mr *Powel* and Mrs *Jones*,
by ſome Verſes which he inſerted in the
Gentleman's Magzine.

Here he completed his Tragedy, of which
two Acts were wanting when he left *London*,
and

and was defirous of coming to Town to bring it upon the Stage. This Defign was very warmly oppofed, and he was advifed by his chief Benefactor to put it into the Hands of Mr *Thompfon* and Mr *Mallet*, that it might be fitted for the Stage, and to allow his Friends to receive the Profits, out of which an annual Penfion fhould be paid him.

This Propofal he rejected with the utmoft Contempt. He was by no means convinced that the Judgment of thofe to whom he was required to fubmit, was fuperior to his own. He was now determined, as he expreffed it, to be *no longer ke t in Leading-ftrings*, and had no elevated Idea of *his Bounty*, who propofed to *penfion him out of the Profits of his own Labours*.

He attempted in *Wales* to promote a Sub-fcription for his Works, and had once Hopes of Succefs ; but in a fhort Time afterwards, formed a Refolution of leaving that Part of the Country, to which he thought it not reafonable to be confined, for the Gratifica-tion of thofe, who having promifed him a liberal Income, had no fooner banifhed him to a remote Corner, than they reduced his Allowance to a Salary fcarcely equal to the Neceffities of Life.

His Refentment of this Treatment, which, in his own Opinion, at leaft, he had not defer-

X   ved,

ved, was such that he broke off all Correspondence with most of his Contributors, and appeared to confider them as Persecutors and Oppressors, and in the latter Part of his Life declared, that their Conduct toward him, since his Departure from *London, had been Perfidiousness improving on Perfidiousness, and Inhumanity on Inhumanity.*

It is not to be supposed, that the Necessities of Mr *Savage* did not some times incite him to satirical Exaggerations of the Behaviour of those by whom he thought himself reduced to them. But it must be granted, that the Diminution of his Allowance was a great Hardship, and, that those who withdrew their Subscription from a Man, who, upon the Faith of their Promise, had gone into a Kind of Banishment, and abandoned all those by whom he had been before relieved in his Distresses, will find it no easy Task to vindicate their Conduct.

It may be alleged, and, perhaps, justly, that he was petulant and contemptuous, that he more frequently reproached his Subscribers for not giving him more, than thanked them for what he had received; but it is to be remembred, that this Conduct, and this is the worst Charge that can be drawn up against him, did them no real Injury; and that it, therefore, ought rather to have been pitied than

than refented, at leaft, the Refentment that it might provoke ought to have been generous and manly; Epithets which his Conduct will hardly deferve, that ftarves the Man whom he has perfuaded to put himfelf into his Power.

It might have been reafonably demanded by *Savage*, that they fhould, before they had taken away what they promifed, have replaced him in his former State, that they fhould have taken no Advantages from the Situation to which the Appearance of their Kindnefs had reduced him, and that he fhould have been re-called to *London*, before he was abandoned. He might juftly reprefent, that he ought to have been confidered as a Lion in the Toils, and demand to be releafed before the Dogs fhould be loofed upon him.

He endeavoured, indeed, to releafe himfelf, and with an Intent to return to *London*, went to *Briftol*, where a Repetition of the Kindnefs which he had formerly found, invited him to ftay. He was not only careffed and treated, but had a Collection made for him of about thirty Pounds, with which it had been happy if he had immediately departed for *London*; but his Negligence did not fuffer him to confider, that fuch Proofs of Kindnefs were not often to be expected, and that this Ardour of Benevolence was, in

X 2　　　　　a great

a great Degree, the Effect of Novelty, and might, probably, be every Day lefs; and therefore he took no Care to improve the happy Time, but was encouraged by one Favour to hope for another, till at length Generofity was exhaufted, and Officioufnefs wearied.

Another Part of his Mifconduct was the Practice of prolonging his Vifits, to unfeafonable Hours, and difconcerting all the Families into which he was admitted. This was an Error in a Place of Commerce, which all the Charms of his Converfation could not compenfate; for what Trader would purchafe fuch airy Satisfaction by the Lofs of folid Gain, which muft be the Confequence of Midnight Merriment, as thofe Hours which were gained at Night, were generally loft in the Morning?

Thus Mr *Savage*, after the Curiofity of the Inhabitants was gratified, found the Number of his Friends daily decreafing, perhaps without fufpecting for what Reafon their Conduct was altered, for he ftill continued to harrafs, with his nocturnal Intrufions, thofe that yet countenanced him, and admitted him to their Houfes.

But he did not fpend all the Time of his Refidence at *Briftol*, in Vifits or at Taverns; for he fometimes returned to his Studies, and be-

began feveral confiderable Defigns. When he felt an Inclination to write, he always retired from the Knowledge of his Friends, and lay hid in an obfcure Part of the Suburbs, till he found himfelf again defirous of Company, to which it is likely that Intervals of Abfence made him more welcome.

He was always full of his Defign of returning to *London* to bring his Tragedy upon the Stage; but having neglected to depart with the Money that was raifed for him, he could not afterwards procure a Sum fufficient to defray the Expences of his Journey; nor, perhaps, would a frefh Supply have had any other Effect, than, by putting immediate Pleafures in his Power, to have driven the Thoughts of his Journey out of his Mind.

While he was thus fpending the Day in contriving a Scheme for the Morrow, Diftrefs ftole upon him by imperceptible Degrees. His Conduct had already wearied fome of thofe who were at firft enamoured of his Converfation; but he might, perhaps, ftill have devolved to others, whom he might have entertained with equal Succefs, had not the Decay of his Cloaths made it no longer confiftent with their Vanity to admit him to their Tables, or to affociate with him in publick Places. He now began to find every Man from home at whofe Houfe he called; and was, therefore,

no

no longer able to procure the Neceſſaries of Life, but wandered about the Town ſlighted and neglected, in queſt of a Dinner, which he did not always obtain.

To complete his Miſery, he was perſued by the Officers for ſmall Debts which he had contracted; and was, therefore, obliged to withdraw from the ſmall Number of Friends from whom he had ſtill Reaſon to hope for Favours. His Cuſtom was to lie in Bed the greateſt Part of the Day, and to go out in the Dark with the utmoſt Privacy, and after having paid his Viſit, return again before Morning to his Lodging, which was in the Garret of an obſcure Inn.

Being thus excluded on one hand, and confined on the other, he ſuffered the utmoſt Extremities of Poverty, and often faſted ſo long that he was ſeized with Faintneſs, and had loſt his Appetite, not being able to bear the Smell of Meat, 'till the Action of his Stomach was reſtored by a Cordial.

In this Diſtreſs he received a Remittance of fifty Pounds from *London*, with which he provided himſelf a decent Coat, and determined to go to *London*, but unhappily ſpent his Money at a favourite Tavern. Thus was he again confined to *Briſtol*, where he was every Day hunted by Bailiffs. In this Exigence he once more found a Friend, who ſhel-

sheltered him in his House, though at the usual Inconveniences with which his Company was attended; for he could neither be persuaded to go to bed in the Night, nor to rise in the Day.

It is observable, that in these various Scenes of Misery, he was always disengaged and cheerful; he at some Times persued his Studies, and at others continued or enlarged his epistolary Correspondence, nor was he ever so far dejected as to endeavour to procure an Encrease of his Allowance, by any other Methods than Accusations and Reproaches.

He had now no longer any Hopes of Assistance from his Friends at *Bristol*, who as Merchants, and by Consequence sufficiently studious of Profit, cannot be supposed to have look'd with much Compassion upon Negligence and Extravagance, or to think any Excellence equivalent to a Fault of such Consequence as Neglect of Oeconomy. It is natural to imagine, that many of those who would have relieved his real Wants, were discouraged from the Exertion of their Benevolence, by Observation of the Use which was made of their Favours, and Conviction that Relief would only be momentary, and that the same Necessity would quickly return.

At last he quitted the House of his Friend, and returned to his Lodging at the Inn, still intending
tending

tending to set out in a few Days for *London*; but on the tenth of *January* 1742-3, having been at Supper with two of his Friends, he was at his Return to his Lodgings arrested for a Debt of about eight Pounds, which he owed at a Coffee-House, and conducted to the House of a Sheriff's Officer. The Account which he gives of this Misfortune in a Letter to one of the Gentlemen with whom he had supped, is too remarkable to be omitted.

" It was not a little unfortunate for me,
" that I spent yesterday's Evening with you;
" because the Hour hindered me from enter-
" ing on my new Lodging; however, I have
" now got one; but such an one, as I be-
" lieve Nobody would chuse.

" I was arrested at the Suit of Mrs *Read*,
" just as I was going up Stairs to Bed, at
" Mr *Bowyer*'s; but taken in so private a
" Manner, that I believe Nobody at the
" *White Lyon* is apprised of it. Tho' I let
" the Officers know the Strength (or rather
" Weakness of my Pocket) yet they treated
" me with the utmost Civility, and even when
" they conducted me to Confinement, 'twas in
" such a Manner, that I verily believe I could
" have escaped, which I would rather be
" ruined than have done; notwithstanding
" the whole Amount of my Finances was but
" three Pence halfpenny. In

" In the firſt Place I muſt inſiſt, that you
" will induſtriouſly conceal this from Mrs
" S——s; becauſe I would not have her
" good Nature ſuffer that Pain, which, I
" know, ſhe would be apt to feel on this Oc-
" caſion.

 " Next I conjure you, dear Sir, by all the
" Ties of Friendſhip, by no means to have
" one uneaſy Thought on my Account ; but
" to have the ſame Pleaſantry of Countenance,
" and unruffled Serenity of Mind, which
" (God be praiſed !) I have in this, and have
" had in a much ſeverer Calamity. Further-
" more, I charge you, if you value my Friend-
" ſhip as truly as I do yours, *not* to utter, or
" even harbour the leaſt Reſentment againſt
" Mrs *Read*. I believe ſhe has ruin'd me,
" but I freely forgive her; and (tho' I will
" never more have any Intimacy with her)
" would, at a due Diſtance, rather do her an
" Act of good than ill Will. Laſtly, (par-
" don the Expreſſion) I *abſolutely command*
" you not to offer me any pecuniary Aſſiſt-
" ance, nor to attempt getting me any from
" any one of your Friends. At another Time, or
" on any other Occaſion, you may, dear
" Friend, be well aſſured, I would rather
" write to you in the ſubmiſſive Stile of a Re-
" queſt, than that of a peremptory Command.
     Y   "How-

" However, that my truly valuable Friend
" may not think I am too proud to afk a Fa-
" vour, let me entreat you to let me have
" your Boy to attend me for this Day, not
" only for the Sake of faving me the Expence
" of Porters, but for the Delivery of fome
" Letters to People whofe Names I would
" not have known to Strangers.

" The civil Treatment I have thus far
" met from thofe, whofe Prifoner I am, makes
" me thankful to the Almighty, that tho'
" He has thought fit to vifit me (on my
" Birth-night) with Affliction; yet (fuch is
" his great Goodnefs!) my Affliction is not
" without alleviating Circumftances. I mur-
" mur not, but am all Refignation to the
" *divine Will.* As to the World, I hope
" that I fhall be endued by Heaven with
" that Prefence of Mind, that ferene Dignity
" in Misfortune, that conftitutes the Cha-
" racter of a true Nobleman; a Dignity far
" beyond that of Coronets; a Nobility arifing
" from the juft Principles of Philofophy,
" refined and exalted by thofe of Chriftianity.

He continued five Days at the Officer's, in
Hopes that he fhould be able to procure
Bail, and avoid the Neceffity of going to Prifon. The State in which he paffed his Time,
and the Treatment which he received, are
very juftly expreffed by him in a Letter
which

which he wrote to a Friend; " The whole
" Day, *fays he,* has been employed in vari-
" ous People's filling my Head with their
" foolifh chimerical Syftems, which has ob-
" liged me coolly (as far as Nature will ad-
" mit) to digeft, and accommodate myfelf to,
" every different Perfon's Way of thinking;
" hurried from one wild Syftem to another,
" 'till it has quite made a Chaos of my Ima-
" gination, and nothing done— promifed—
" difappointed—Order'd to fend every Hour,
" from one part of the Town to the o-
" ther."————

When his Friends, who had hitherto careffed and applauded, found that to give
Bail and pay the Debt was the fame, they
all refufed to preferve him from a Prifon, at
the Expence of eight Pounds; and therefore
after having been for fome Time at the Officer's Houfe, *at an immenfe Expence,* as he
obferves in his Letter, he was at length removed to *Newgate.*

This Expence he was enabled to fupport,
by the Generofity of Mr *Nafh* at *Bath,* who
upon receiving from him an Account of his
Condition, immediatly fent him five Guineas, and promifed to promote his Subfcription at *Bath,* with all his Intereft.

By his Removal to *Newgate,* he obtained
at leaft a Freedom from Sufpenfe, and Reft

from

from the difturbing Viciffitudes of Hope and
Difappointment; he now found that his
Friends were only Companions, who were willing to fhare his Gaiety, but not to partake
of his Misfortunes; and therefore he no longer
expected any Affiftance from them.

It muft however be obferved of one Gentleman, that he offered to releafe him by paying the Debt, but that Mr *Savage* would not
confent, I fuppofe, becaufe he thought he
had been before too burthenfome to him.

He was offered by fome of his Friends,
that a Collection fhould be made for his En-
largement, but he *treated the Propofal*, and
declared *, *that he fhould again treat it, with
Difdain. As to writing any mendicant Letters, he had too high a Spirit, and determined only to write to fome Minifters of State,
to try to regain his Penfion.*

He continued to complain † of thofe that
had fent him into the Country, and objected
to them that he had *loft the Profits of his
Play, which had been finifhed three Years*;
and in another Letter declares his Refolution
to publifh a Pamphlet, that the World might
know how *he had been ufed.*

This Pamphlet was never written, for he
in a very fhort Time recover'd his ufual Tranquillity,

* In a Letter after his Confinement.
† Letter *Jan.* 15.

quillity, and chearfully applied himfelf to more inoffenfive Studies. He indeed fteadily declared, that he was promifed an yearly Allowance of fifty Pounds, and never received half the Sum; but he feemed to refign himfelf to that as well as to other Misfortunes, and lofe the Remembrance of it in his Amufements and Employments.

The Chearfulnefs with which he bore his Confinement, appears from the following Letter, which he wrote, *Jan.* 30th, to one of his Friends in *London*.

I Now write to you from my Confinement in *Newgate*, where I have been ever fince Monday laft was Sev'n-night; and where I enjoy myfelf with much more Tranquillity than I have known for upwards of a twelvemonth paft; having a Room entirely to myfelf, and perfuing the Amufement of my poetical Studies, uninterrupted, and agreeable to my Mind. I thank the Almighty, I am now all collected in myfelf; and tho' my Perfon is in Confinement, my Mind can expatiate on ample and ufeful Subjects, with all the Freedom imaginable. I am now more converfant with the Nine than ever; and if, inftead of a *Newgate* Bird, I may be allowed to be a Bird of the Mufes, I affure you, Sir, I fing very freely in my Cage; fometimes indeed in the plaintive Notes of the

the Nightingale; but, at others, in the chearful Strains of the Lark——

In another Letter he observes, that he ranges from one Subject to another, without confining himself to any particular Task, and that he was employed one Week upon one Attempt, and the next upon another

Surely the Fortitude of this Man deserves, at least, to be mentioned with Applause; and whatever Faults may be imputed to him, the Virtue of *suffering well* cannot be denied him. The two Powers which, in the Opinion of *Epictetus*, constitute a wise Man, are those of *bearing* and *forbearing*, which cannot indeed be affirmed to have been equally possessed by *Savage*, but it was too manifest that the Want of one obliged him very *frequently* to practise the other.

He was treated by Mr *Dagg*, the Keeper of the Prison, with great Humanity; was supported by him at his own Table without any Certainty of Recompence, had a Room to himself, to which he could at any Time retire from all Disturbance, was allowed to stand at the Door of the Prison, and sometimes taken out into the Fields; so that he suffered fewer Hardships in the Prison, than he had been accustomed to undergo in the greatest part of his Life.

The

The Keeper did not confine his Benevolence to a gentle Execution of his Office, but made some Overtures to the Creditor for his Releafe, tho' without Effect; and continued, during the whole Time of his Imprisonment, to treat him with the utmost Tendernefs and Civility.

Virtue is undoubtedly moft laudable in that State which makes it moft difficult; and therefore the Humanity of a Goaler certainly deferves this public Atteftation; and the Man whofe Heart has not been hardened by fuch an Employment, may be juftly propofed as a Pattern of Benevolence. If an Infcription was once engraved to the *honeft Toll-gatherer*, lefs Honours ought not to be paid to the *tender Goaler*.

Mr *Savage* very frequently received Vifits, and fometimes Prefents from his Acquaintances, but they did not amount to a Subfiftence, for the greater Part of which he was indebted to the Generofity of this Keeper; but thefe Favours, however they might endear to him the particular Perfons from whom he received them, were very far from impreffing upon his Mind any advantageous Ideas of the People of *Briftol*; and therefore he thought he could not more properly employ himfelf in Prifon, than in writing the following Poem.

L O N-

TWO Sea-port Cities mark *Britannia*'s
    Fame,
And thefe from Commerce different Honours
    claim.
What different Honours fhall the Mufes pay,
While one infpires and one untunes the Lay?
  Now filver *Ifis* bright'ning flows along,
Echoing from *Oxford*'s Shore each claffic
    Song;
Then weds with *Tame*; and thefe, O *London*,
    fee
Swelling with naval Pride, the Pride of Thee!
Wide, deep, unfullied *Thames* meand'ring
    glides,
And bears thy Wealth on mild majeftic Tides.
Thy Ships, with glided Palaces that vie,
In glitt'ring Pomp, ftrike wond'ring *China*'s
    Eye;
And thence returning bear, in fplendid State,
To *Britain*'s Merchants, *India*'s eaftern
    Freight.
India, her Treafures from her weftern Shores,
Due at thy Feet, a willing Tribute pours;
Thy warring Navies diftant Nations awe,
And bid the World obey thy righteous Law.

                           Thus

---

* The Author preferr'd this Title to that of London
and Briftol *compared*; which, when he began the Piece,
he intended to prefix to it.

Thus fhine thy manly Sons of lib'ral Mind;
Thy Change deep-bufied, yet as Courts re-
    fin'd;
Councils like Senates that enforce Debate,
With fluent Eloquence, and Reafon's Weight :
Whofe Patriot Virtue, lawlefs Pow'r con-
    trouls;
Their *Britifh* emulating *Roman* Souls.
Of thefe the worthieft ftill felefted ftand,
Still lead the Senate, and ftill fave the Land.
Social, not felfifh, here, O Learning, trace
Thy Friends, the Lovers of all human Race !

In a dark Bottom funk, O *Brifol*, now,
With native Malice lift thy low'ring Brow !
Then as fome Hell-born Sprite, in mortal
    Guife,
Borrows the Shape of Goodnefs and belies,
All fair, all fmug to yon proud Hall invite,
To feaft all Strangers ape an Air polite !
From *Cambria* drain'd, or *England*'s weftern
    Coaft,
Not elegant yet coftly Banquets boaft!
Revere, or feem the Stranger to revere ;
Praife, fawn, profefs, be all things but fincere ;
Infidious now, our bofom Secrets fteal,
And thefe with fly farcaftic Sneer reveal.
Prefent we meet thy fneaking treach'rous
    Smiles ;
The harmlefs Abfent ftill thy Sneer reviles;
        Z   Such

Such as in Thee all Parts fuperior find ;
The Sneer that marks the Fool and Knave
     combin'd.
When melting Pity wou'd afford Relief,
The ruthlefs Sneer, that Infult adds to Grief.
What Friendfhip can'ft thou boaft? what
     Honours claim ?
To thee each Stranger owes an injur'd Name.
What Smiles thy Sons muft in their Foes ex-
     cite !
Thy Sons, to whom all Difcord is Delight ;
From whom eternal mutual Railing flows ;
Who in each others Crimes their own expofe :
Thy Sons, tho' crafty, deaf to Wifdom's
     Call ;
Defpifing all Men, and defpis'd by all :
Sons, while thy Cliffs a ditch-like River
     laves,
Rude as thy Rocks, and muddy as thy
     Waves ;
Of Thoughts as narrow, as of Words immenfe ;
As full of Turbulence, as void of Senfe.
Thee, Thee what Senatorial Souls adorn ?
Thy Natives fure wou'd prove a Senate's
     Scorn.
Do Strangers deign to ferve Thee ? what
     their Praife ?
Their gen'rous Services thy Murmurs raife.
What Fiend malign, that o'er thy Air prefides,
Around from Breaft to Breaft inherent glides,
             And,

And, as he glides, there fcatters in a Trice
The lurking Seeds of ev'ry rank Device?
Let foreign Youths to thy Indentures run !
Each, each will prove, in thy adopted Son,
Proud, pert and dull—Tho' brilliant once
      from Schools,
Will fcorn all Learning's as all Virtue's Rules ;
And, tho' by Nature friendly, honeft,
      brave,
Turn a fly, felfifh, fimp'ring, fharpingKnave.
Boaft petty Courts, where 'ftead of fluent
      Eafe ;
Of cited Precedents, and learned Pleas ;
'Stead of fage Counfel in the dubious Caufe,
Attorneys, chatt'ring wild, burlefque the
      Laws.
So fhamelefs Quacks, who Doctors' Rights
      invade,
Of Jargon and of Poifon form a Trade.
So canting Coblers, while from Tubs they
      teach,
Buffoon the Gofpel they pretend to preach.
Boaft petty Courts, whence Rules new Ri-
      gour draw,
Unknown to Nature's and to Statute Law ;
Quirks that explain all faving Rights away,
To give th' Attorney and the Catch-poll
      Prey.

Z 2

Is

369

Is there where Law too rig'rous may de-
    fcend?
Or Charity her kindly Hand extend?
Thy Courts, that fhut when Pity wou'd re-
    drefs,
Spontaneous open to inflict Diftrefs.
Try Mifdemeanours!---all thy Wiles em-
    ploy,
Not to chaftife th' Offender but deftroy.
Bid the large lawlefs Fine his Fate foretell;
Bid it beyond his Crime and Fortune fwell.
Cut off from Service due to kindred Blood,
To private Welfare and to public Good,
Pitied by all, but thee, he fentenc'd lies;
Imprifon'd languifhes, imprifon'd dies,

* * * * * * * * * * *
* * * * * * * * * * *
* * * * * * * * * * *
* * * * * * * * * * *
* * * * * * * * * * *
* * * * * * * * * * *

Boaft fwarming Veffels, whofe *Plebeian*
    State
Owes not to Merchants but Mechanics
    Freight.
Boaft nought but Pedlar Fleets—In War's
    Alarms,
Unknown to Glory, as unknown to Arms.

                      Boaft

Boaſt thy baſe * *Tolſey*, and thy turn-ſpit
    Dogs;
Thy † *Hallier's* Horſes, and thy humanHogs;
Upſtarts and Muſhrooms, proud, relentleſs
    Hearts;
Thou Blank of Sciences! Thou Dearth of
    Arts!
Such Foes as Learning once was doom'd to
    ſee;
Huns, *Goths* and *Vandals* were but Types
    of Thee.

Proceed, great *Briſtol*, in all-righteous
    Ways,
And let one Juſtice heighten yet thy Praiſe;
Still ſpare the Catamite, and ſwinge the
    Whore,
And be whate'er *Gomorrah* was before.

When he had brought this Poem to its
preſent State, which, without conſidering the
Chaſm, is not perfect, he wrote to *London* an
Account of his Deſign, and informed his
Friend, that he was determined to print it
with his Name; but enjoined him not to
                           com-

---

* A Place where the Merchants uſed to meet to tranſact
their Affairs before the Exchange was erected. *See Gen-*
tleman's Magazine. Vol. xiii. p. 496.

† *Halliers* are the Perſons who drive or own the
Sledges, which are here uſed inſtead of Carts.

communicate his Intention to his *Briſtol* Acquaintance. The Gentleman ſurpriſed at his Reſolution, endeavoured to diſſuade him from publiſhing it, at leaſt from prefixing hisName; and declared, that he could not reconcile the Injunction of Secrecy with his Reſolution to own it at its firſt Appearance. To this Mr *Savage* returned an Anſwer agreeable to his Character in the following Terms.

" I received yours this Morning, and not
" without a little Surprize at the Contents.
" To anſwer a Queſtion with a Queſtion,
" you ask me concerning *London* and *Briſtol*,
" *Why will I add* delineated ? Why did Mr
" *Woolaſton* add the ſame Word to his Reli-
" gion of Nature? I ſuppoſe that it was
" his Will and Pleaſure to add it in his Caſe;
" and it is mine to do ſo in my Own. You
" are pleaſed to tell me, that you underſtand
" not why Secrecy is injoined, and yet I in-
" tend to ſet my Name to it. My Anſwer
" is—I have my private Reaſons; which I
" am not obliged to explain to any One.
" You doubt, my Friend Mr *S·——— —*
" would not approve of it——And what is it
" to me whether he does or not? Do you
" imagine, that Mr *S———* is to dictate to
" me? If any Man, who calls himſelf my
" Friend, ſhould aſſume ſuch an Air, I
" would ſpurn at his Friendſhip with Con-
"tempt.

" tempt. You say, I feem to think fo by not
" letting him know it—And fuppofe I do,
" what then? Perhaps I can give Reafons
" for that Difapprobation, very foreign from
" what you would imagine. You go on in
" faying, fuppofe, I fhould not put my Name
" to it——My Anfwer is, that I will not fup-
" pofe any fuch Thing, being determined to
" the contrary; neither, Sir, would I have
" you fuppofe, that I applied to you for
" Want of another Prefs: Nor would I
" have you imagine, that I owe Mr S———
" Obligations which I do not."

Such was his Imprudence, and fuch his obftinate Adherence to his own Refolutions,
however abfurd. A Prifoner! fupported by
Charity! and, whatever Infults he might
have received during the latter Part of his
Stay in *Briftol*, once careffed, efteemed, and
prefented with a liberal Collection, he could
forget on a fudden his Danger, and his Obligations, to gratify the Petulance of his Wit, or
the Eagernefs of his Refentment, and publifh a Satire by which he might reafonably
expect, that he fhould alienate thofe who
then fupported him, and provoke thofe whom
he could neither refift nor efcape.

This Refolution, from the Execution of
which, it is probable, that only his Death
could have hindered him, is fufficient to fhew
how

how much he difregarded all Confiderations that oppofed his prefent Paffions, and how readily he hazarded all future Advantages for any immediate Gratifications. Whatever was his predominant Inclination, neither Hope nor Fear hinder'd him from complying with it, nor had Oppofition any other Effect than to heighten his Ardour, and irritate his Vehemence.

This Performance was however laid afide, while he was employed in folicitingAffiftances from feveral great Perfons; and one Interruption fucceeding another hinder'd him from fupplying the Chafm, and perhaps from retouching the other Parts, which he can hardly be imagined to have finifhed, in his own Opinion; for it is very unequal, and fome of the Lines are rather inferted to rhyme to others than to fupport or improve the Senfe; but the firft and laft Parts are worked up with great Spirit and Elegance.

His Time was fpent in the Prifon for the moft part in Study, or in receiving Vifits; but fometimes he defcended to lower Amufements, and diverted himfelf in the Kitchen with the Converfation of the Criminals; for it was not pleafing to him to be much without Company, and though he was very capable of a judicious Choice, he was often contented with the firft that offered; for this he was

fome-sometimes, reproved by his Friends who found him surrounded with Felons; but the Reproof was on that as on other Occasions thrown away; he continued to gratify himself, and to set very little Value on the Opinion of others.

But here, as in every other Scene of his Life, he made use of such Opportunities as occurr'd of benefiting those who were more miserable than himself, and was always ready to perform any Offices of Humanity to his fellow Prisoners.

He had now ceased from corresponding with any of his Subscribers except one, who yet continued to remit him the twenty Pounds a Year which he had promised him; and by whom it was expected, that he would have been in a very short Time enlarged, because he had directed the Keeper to enquire after the State of his Debts.

However he took care to enter his Name according to the Forms of the Court, that the Creditor might be obliged to make him some Allowance, if he was continued a Prisoner, and when on that Occasion he appeared in the Hall was treated with very unusual Respect

But the Resentment of the City was afterwards raised by some Accounts that had been spread of the Satire, and he was informed that

some

some of the Merchants intended to pay the Allowance which the Law required, and to detain him Prifoner at their own Expence. This he treated as an empty Menace, and perhaps might have haften'd the Publication, only to fhew how much he was fuperior to their Infults, had not all his Schemes been fuddenly deftroyed,

When he had been fix Months in Prifon he received from one of his Friends, in whofe Kindnefs he had the greateft Confidence, and on whofe Affiftance he chiefly depended, a Letter that contained a Charge of very a-trocious Ingratitude, drawn up in fuch Terms as fudden Refentment dictated. Mr *Savage* returned a very folemn Proteftation of his Innocence, but however appeared much di-fturbed at the Accufation. Some Days after-wards he was feized with a Pain in his Back and Side, which as it was not violent was not fufpected to be dangerous; but growing dai-ly more languid and dejected, on the 25th of *July* he confined himfelf to his Room, and a Fever feized his Spirits. The Symptoms grew every Day more formidable, but his Condi-tion did not enable him to procure any Af-fiftance. The laft Time that the Keeper faw him was on *July* the 31ft, when *Savage* feeing him at his Bed-fide faid, with an uncommon Earneftnefs, *I have fomething to fay to you,*

you, Sir; but after a Paufe moved his Hand in a melancholy Manner, and finding himfelf unable to recollect what he was going to communicate, faid *'Tis gone.* The Keeper fcon after left him, and the next Morning he died. He was buried in the Church-Yard of St *Peter,* at the Expence of the Keeper.

Such were the Life and Death of *Richard Savage,* a Man equally diftinguifhed by his Virtues and Vices, and at once remarkable for his Weakneffes and Abilities.

He was of a middle Stature, of a thin Habit of Body, a long Vifage, coarfe Features, and melancholy Afpect; of a grave and. manlyDeportment, a folemnDignity of Mien, but which upon a nearer Acquaintance foftened into an engaging Eafinefs of Manners. His Walk was flow, and his Voice tremulous and mournful. He was eafily excited to Smiles, but very feldom provoked to Laughter.

His Mind was in an uncommon Degree vigorous and active. His Judgment was accurate, his Apprehenfion quick, and his Memory fo tenacious, that he was frequently obferved to know what he had learned from others in a fhort Time better than thofe by whom he was informed, and could frequently recollect Incidents, with all their Combination of Circumftances, which few would have regarded at the prefent Time; but which the

A a 2 Quick-

Quickneſs of his Apprehenſion impreſſed upon him. He had the peculiar Felicity, that
his Attention never deſerted him; he was
preſent to every Object, and regardful of the
moſt trifling Occurrences. He had the Art
of eſcaping from his own Reflections, and
accommodating himſelf to every new Scene.

To this Quality is to be imputed the Extent of his Knowledge, compared with the
ſmall Time which he ſpent in viſible Endeavours to acquire it. He mingled in curſory
Converſation with the ſame Steadineſs of Attention as others apply to a Lecture, and, a-
midſt the Appearance of thoughtleſs Gayety,
loſt no new Idea that was ſtarted, nor any
Hint that could be improved. He had therefore
made in Coffee-Houſes the ſame Proficiency as
others in Studies; and it is remarkable, that
the Writings of a Man of little Education,
and little Reading, have an Air of Learning
ſcarcely to be found in any other Performances, but which perhaps as often obſcures as
embelliſhes them.

His Judgment was eminently exact, both
with regard to Writings and to Men. The
Knowledge of Life was indeed his chief Attainment, and it is not without ſome Satisfaction, that I can produce the Suffrage of *Savage*
in favour of human Nature, of which he never appeared to entertain ſuch odious Ideas,

as

as fome, who perhaps had neither his Judgment nor Experience, have publifhed, either in Oftentation of their Sagacity, Vindication of their Crimes, or Gratification of their Malice.

His Method of Life particularly qualified him for Converfation, of which he knew how to practife all the Graces. He was never vehement or loud, but at once modeft and eafy, open and refpectful; his Language was vivacious and elegant, and equally happy upon grave or humorous Subjects. He was generally cenfured for not knowing when to retire, but that was not the Defect of his Judgment, but of his Fortune; when he left his Company, he was frequently to fpend the remaining Part of the Night in the Street, or at leaft was abandoned to gloomy Reflections, which it is not ftrange that he delayed as long as he could, and fometimes forgot that he gave others Pain to avoid it himfelf.

It cannot be faid, that he made Ufe of his Abilities for the Direction of his own Conduct; an irregular and diffipated Manner of Life had made him the Slave of every Paffion that happened to be excited by the Prefence of its Object, and that Slavery to his Paffions reciprocally produced a Life irregular and diffipated. He was not Mafter of his own Motions,

Motions, nor could promife any thing for the next Day.

With regard to his Oeconomy, nothing can be added to the Relation of his Life: he appeared to think himfelf born to be fupported by others, and difpenfed from all Neceffity of providing for himfelf; he therefore never profecuted any Scheme of Advantage, nor endeavoured even to fecure the Profits which his Writings might have afforded him.

His Temper was, in confequence of the Dominion of hisPaffions, uncertain and capricious; he was eafily engaged, and eafily difgufted; but he is accufed of retaining his Hatred more tenacioufly than his Benevolence.

He was compaffionate both by Nature and Principle, and always ready to perform Offices of Humanity; but when he was provoked, and very fmall Offences were fufficient to provoke him, he would profecute his Revenge with the utmoft Acrimony till his Paffion had fubfided.

His Friendfhip was therefore of little Value; for though he was zealous in the Support or Vindication of thofe whom he loved, yet it was always dangerous to truft him, becaufe he confidered himfelf difcharged, by the firft Quarrel, from all Ties of Honour or Gratitude;

titude; and would betray thofe Secrets which in the Warmth of Confidence had been imparted to him. This Practice drew upon him an univerfal Accufation of Ingratitude; nor can it be denied that he was very ready to fet himfelf free from the Load of an Obligation; for he could not bear to conceive himfelf in a State of Dependence, his Pride being equally powerful with his other Paffions, and appearing in the Form of Infolence at one time, and of Vanity at another. Vanity, the moft innocent Species of Pride, was moft frequently predominant: he could not eafily leave off when he had once began to mention himfelf or his Works, nor ever read his Verfes without ftealing his Eyes from the Page, to difcover in the Faces of his Audience, how they were affected with any favourite Paffage.

A kinder Name than that of Vanity ought to be given to the Delicacy with which he was always careful to feparate his own Merit from every other Man's, and to reject that Praife to which he had no Claim. He did not forget, in mentioning his Performances, to mark every Line that had been fuggefted or amended, and was fo accurate as to relate that he owed *three Words* in *THE WANDERER*, to the Advice of his Friends.

His

His Veracity was queftioned, but with little Reafon; his Accounts, tho' not indeed always the fame, were generally confiftent. When he loved any Man, he fupprefs'd all his Faults, and when he had been offended by him, concealed all his Virtues: but his Characters were generally true, fo far as he proceeded; tho' it cannot be denied that his Partiality might have fometimes the Effect of Falfehood.

In Cafes indifferent he was zealous for Virtue, Truth and Juftice; he knew very well the Neceffity of Goodnefs to the prefent and future Happinefs of Mankind; nor is there perhaps any Writer, who has lefs endeavoured to pleafe, by flattering the Appetites, or perverting the Judgment.

As an Author, therefore, and he now ceafes to influence Mankind in any other Character, if one Piece, which he had refolved to fupprefs, be excepted, he has very little to fear from the ftricteft moral or religious Cenfure. And though he may not be altogether fecure againft the Objections of the Critic, it muft however be acknowledged, that his Works are the Productions of a Genius truly poetical; and, what many Writers, who have been more lavifhly applauded, cannot boaft, that they have an original Air, which has no Refemblance of any foregoing Writer; that the Verfification and Sentiments have

a Caft

a Caſt peculiar to themſelves, which no Man can imitate with Succeſs, becauſe what was Nature in *Savage* would in another be Affeſtation. It muſt be confeſſed that his Deſcriptions are ſtriking, his Images animated, his Fictions juſtly imagin'd, and his Allegories artfully perfued ; that his Diction is elevated, though ſometimes forced, and his Numbers ſonorous and majeſtick, though frequently ſluggiſh and encumbered. Of his Stile the general Fault is Harſhneſs, and the general Excellence is Dignity ; of his Sentiments the prevailing Beauty is Sublimity, and Uniformity the prevailing Defect.

For his Life, or for his Writings, none who candidly conſider his Fortune, will think an Apology either neceſſary or difficult. If he was not always ſufficiently inſtructed in his Subject, his Knowledge was at leaſt greater than could have been attained by others in the ſame State. If his Works were ſometimes unfiniſhed, Accuracy cannot reaſonably be exacted from a Man oppreſſed with Want, which he has no Hope of relieving but by a ſpeedy Publication. The Inſolence and Reſentment of which he is accuſed, were not eaſily to be avoided by a great Mind, irritated by perpetual Hardſhips, and conſtrained hourly to return the Spurns of Contempt, and repreſs the Inſolence of Proſperity ; and Vanity

B b

ſure-

surely may be readily pardoned in him, to whom Life afforded no other Comforts than barren Praises, and the Consciousness of deserving them.

Those are no proper Judges of his Conduct who have slumber'd away their Time on the Down of Abundance, nor will a wise Man easily presume to say, " Had I been in *Savage's* " Condition, I should have lived, or writ- " ten, better than *Savage.*"

This Relation will not be wholly without its Use, if those, who languish under any Part of his Sufferings, shall be enabled to fortify their Patience by reflecting that they feel only those Afflictions from which the Abilities of *Savage* did not exempt him; or if those, who, in confidence of superior Capacities or Attainments disregard the common Maxims of Life, shall be reminded that nothing will supply the Want of Prudence, and that Negligence and Irregularity, long continued, will make Knowledge useless, Wit ridiculous, and Genius contemptible.

F I N I S.

LIFE *of the* Earl *of* ROSCOMMON

DILLON [*Wentworth*,] Earl of *Roscommon*, an eminent poet, was born in * *Ireland*, in the lieutenancy of the Earl of *Strafford*,† who was his godfather, and named him by his own surname. He pass'd some of his first years in his native country, till the Earl of *Strafford*, imagining when the rebellion first broke out, that his father, who had been converted by Archbishop *Usher* to the protestant religion, would be exposed to great danger, and be unable to protect his family, sent for his godson and placed him at his own seat in *Yorkshire*, under the tuition of Dr *Hall* afterwards Bishop of *Norwich*. ‡ When the Earl of *Strafford*

* Though he was born in *Ireland*, yet as part of his life was spent in *England*, as he was distinguished by honours and employments at the *English* court, and is known or valued by posterity only as an *English* poet, our collections of *English* lives must be considered as imperfect, none of them having an account of him. Though every country imagines itself intitled to the reputation of those who happened to be born in it, this claim may be sometimes not unreasonably disputed; for that nation has at least as good a right to the honours paid to literary merit, which has given masters to him who obtains them, as that which has given parents.

† *Fenton's* notes on *Waller*.

‡ ' By him he was instructed in *Latin*; and without learning the common ' rules of grammar, which he could ' never retain in his memory, he attain

first was prosecuted, he went to *Caen* in *Normandy*, by the advice of Bishop *Usher*, to continue his studies under *Bochart*, ¶ where he is said to have had an extraordinary impulse on his father's death.¶ Some years after he travelled to *Rome*, and returned to *England* upon the restoration of King *Charles*, by whom he was made captain of the band of pensioners, an honour which tempted him to some extravagances.¶ A dispute about part of his estate obliging him to return to *Ireland*, he resign'd this post, and upon his arrival at *Dublin*, was made captain of the guards by the Duke of *Ormond*, but he generously resigned his commission to a gentleman, who saved his life when he was attacked by ruffians. * Having finish'd his affairs

---

' ed to write in that language with clas-
' sical elegance and propriety ; and
' with so much ease, that he chose it to
' correspond with those friends, who
' had learning sufficient to support the
' commerce.' *Fenton.*

§ ' The lord *Roscommon* being a boy
' of ten years of age, at *Caen* in *Norman-*
' *dy*, one day was, as it were, madly
' extravagant in playing, leaping, get-
' ting over the table, boards, &c. He
' was wont to be sober enough ; they
' said, God grant this bodes no ill luck
' to him. In the heat of this extrava-
' gant fit, he cries out, *My father is*
' *dead.* A fortnight after, news came
' from *Ireland*, that his father was dead.
' This account I had from Mr *Knolles*,
' who was his governor, and then with
' him, since secretary to the Earl of
' *Stafford* ; and I have heard his lord-
' ship's relations confirm the same.'
Aubrey's Miscellany.
The present age is very little inclined to
favour any accounts of this kind, nor
will the name of *Aubrey* much recommend it to credit; it ought not, however, to be omitted, because better evidence of a fact cannot easily be found,
than is here offered, and it must be by
perusing such relations that we may at
last judge how much they are to be regarded. If we stay to examine this account, we shall find difficulties on both
sides; here as a relation of a fact given
by a man who had no interest to deceive, and who could not be deceived
himself ; and here is, on the other
hand, a miracle which produces no effect, the order of nature is interrupted
to discover not a future, but only a distant event, the knowledge of which is
of no use to whom it is revealed.
Between these difficulties, what way
shall be found ? Is reason or testimony
to be rejected ? I believe what *Osborne*
says of an appearance of sanctity, may
be applied to such impulses or whisper-
ings of this : *Do not wholly slight them,*
because they may be true; but do not easily
trust them, because they may be false.

¶ ' After some years he travelled to
' *Rome*, where he grew familiar with
' the most valuable remains of antiqui-
' ty ; applying himself particularly to
' the knowledge of medals, which he
' gained in perfection : And spoke
' *Italian* with so much grace and fluen-
' cy, that he was frequently mistaken
' there for a native.'

¶ ' In the gaieties of that age, he
' was tempted to indulge a violent passi-
' on for gaming ; by which he fre-
' quently hazarded his life in duels, and
' exceeded the bounds of a moderate
' fortune.' *Fenton.* This was the fate
of many other men, whose genius was
of no other advantage to them, than that
it recommended them to employments,
or to distinction, by which the temptations to vice were multiplied, and their
parts became soon of no other use than
that of enabling them to succeed in
wickedness.

* " He was at *Dublin* as much as ever
distempered with the same fatal affection for play, which engaged him in one
adventure that well deserves to be related. As he returned to his lodgings
from a gaming table, he was attacked in
the dark by three ruffians, who were
employed to assassinate him : The Earl
defended himself with so much resolution, that he dispatch'd one of the aggressors ; whilst a gentleman, accidentally
passing that way, interpos'd, and disarmed another ; the third secured himself
by flight. This generous assistant was
a disbanded officer of a good family,
and fair reputation ; who, by what we
call the partiality of fortune, to avoid
censuring the iniquities of the times,
wanted even a plain suit of cloaths to
make a decent appearance at the castle.
But his lordship, on this occasion, presenting him to the Duke of *Ormond*,
with great importunity prevailed with
his grace, that he might not signify himself
of

fairs he returned to *London*, was made master of the horse to the dutchess of *York*, and married the lady *Frances*, eldest daughter of the E. of *Burlington*, and widow of Colonel *Courtney*. Here he formed a design of † instituting a society for the refinement of the *English* language, but upon the commotions which were produced by King *James*'s endeavours to introduce alterations in religion, he

of captain of the guards to his friend; which for about three years the gentleman enjoyed, and, upon his death, the Duke returned the commission to his generous benefactor." *Fenton.*

† ' He formed a design of instituting a society for the refinement of the *English* language.—About this time, in imitation of those learned and polite ' assemblies, with which he had been ' acquainted abroad, particularly, one ' at *Caen* (in which his tutor *Bochart* ' died suddenly whilst he was delivering an oration) he began to form a ' society for the refining and fixing the ' standard of our language. In this ' design, his great friend, Mr *Dryden*, ' was a principal assistant: A design, of ' which it is much easier to conceive an ' agreeable idea, than any rational ' hope ever to see it brought to per- ' fection.' *Fenton.*

This design was again set on foot, under the ministry of the Earl of *Oxford*, and was again defeated by a conflict of parties, and the necessity of attending only to political disquisitions, of defending the conduct of the administration, and forming parties in the parliament. " Since that time it has never been mentioned, either because it has been hitherto a sufficient objection, that it was one of the designs of the Earl of *Oxford*, the detestable Earl of *Oxford*, by whom *Godolphin* was defeated, or because the statesmen who succeeded him have not had more leisure for literary schemes. *See a letter written by Dr* Swift *to the Lord Treasurer.*

‡ ' The moment in which he expir'd, ' he cry'd out with a voice that express'd ' the most intense fervour of devotion, ' *My God, my father, and my friend,* ' *Do not forsake me at my end,* two lines of his own version of the hymn *Dies iræ, Dies illa.*' ‡ *Fenton.*

§ Mr *Fenton* has, in his notes upon *Waller*, given *Roscommon* a character too general to be critically just. ' In his

resolved to retire to *Rome*, alledging that *it was best to sit next to the chimney when the chamber smoked.* This journey was hindred by the gout, of which he was so impatient, that he admitted a repellent application from a *French* empiric, by which his distemper was driven up into his bowels; and an end put to his life in 1685, his character as a writer is eminent [...]

' writings, says he, we view the image ' of a mind, which was naturally great ' and bold; richly furnish'd, and a- ' dorned with all the ornaments of art ' and science; and those ornaments un- ' affectedly disposed in the most regular ' and elegant order. His imagination ' might have, probably, been more ' fruitful and sprightly, if his judgment ' had been less severe: But that seve- ' rity (deliver'd in a masculine, close, ' succinct stile) contributed to make ' him so eminent in the didactical man- ' ner, that no man with justice can affirm ' he was ever equalled by any of our ' nation, without confessing at the same ' time that he is inferior to none. In ' some other kinds of writing his geni- ' us seems to have wanted fire to attain ' the point of perfection; but who can ' attain it?' From this account of the riches of his mind, who would not imagine that they had been display'd in large volumes, and numerous perform ances? Who would not, after the perusal of this character, be surprised to find, that all the proofs of this genius, and knowledge, and judgment, are not sufficient to form a single book, or to appear otherwise than in conjunction with the works of some other writer of the same petty size? But thus it is that characters are written, we know somewhat, and we imagine the rest. The observation *that his imagination would probably have been more fruitful and sprightly, if his judgment had been less severe*, may be answer'd, by a remark somewhat inclined to cavil, by a contrary supposition, *that his judgment would probably have been less severe, if his imagination had been more fruitful.* It is ridiculous to oppose judgment and imagination; for it does not appear that men have necessarily less of one as they have more of the other.

We must allow of *Roscommon*, what *Fenton* has not mentioned, so distinctly as he ought, and, what is yet very much to

‖ … are, ‡ *An Essay on transla-*
tion, a translation of the *Art of*

… his honour, that he is, perhaps, the
only correct writer in verse before *Ad-*
dison; and that if there are not so many
or so great beauties in his composition,
… those of some contemporaries, there
are at least fewer faults. Nor is this
his highest praise; for Mr *Pope* has celebrated him as the only moral writer of
King *Charles's* reign.

… may Dryden'—in all Charles's days,
Roscommon only boasts unspotted lays.

'It was my Lord *Roscommon's*
'*Essay on translated Verse*, says *Dryden*,
'which made me uneasy, till I tried
'whether or no I was capable of follow-
'ing his rules, and of reducing the
'speculation into practice. For many
'a fair precept in poetry is like a seem-
'ing demonstration in mathematics;
'very specious in the diagram, but fail-
'ing in the mechanic operation. I
'think, I have generally observed his
'instructions; I am sure my reason is
'sufficiently convinc'd both of their
'truth and usefulness; which, in other
'words, is to confess no less a vanity
'than to pretend that I have, at least
'in some places, made examples to his
'rules.'

This declaration of *Dryden*, will, I
am afraid, be found little more than
one of those cursory civilities, which
one author pays to another; for when
the sum of Lord *Roscommon's* precepts
is collected, it will not be easy to discover, how they can qualify their reader for a better performance of translation, than might have been attained by
his own reflections. They are, however, here laid down, and disentangled
from the ornaments with which they are
embellished, and the digressions with
which they are diversify'd.

'To write, composing is the nobler part,
'But good translation is no easy art,
'For the materials have long since been found,
'Yet both your fancy and your hands are bound;
'And by improving what was writ before,
'Invention labours less, but judgment, more.—
'Each poet with a different talent writes,
'One praises, one instructs, another bites.
'Horace did ne'er aspire to *Epick* bays,
'Nor lofty *Maro* stoop to *Lyrick* lays.
'Examine how your humour is inclin'd,
'And which the ruling passion of your mind;
'Then, seek a poet who your way does bend,
'And chuse an author as you chuse a friend.
'United by this sympathetick bond,
'You grow familiar, intimate, and fond;
'Your thoughts, your words, your stiles, your souls agree,
'No longer his interpreter, but he.——

Poetry, and some little poems, and
translations.

'Take then a subject, proper to expound;
'But moral, great, and worth a poet's voice,
'For men of sense despise a trivial choice:
'And such applause it must expect to meet,
'As wou'd some painter, busy in a street,
'To copy bulls and bears, and ev'ry sign
'That calls the staring sots to nasty wine.——

'Take pains the genuine meaning to explore;
'There sweat, there strain, tug the laborious oar;
'Search ev'ry comment that your care can find,
'Some here, some there, may hit the poet's
'   mind;
'Yet be not blindly guided by the throng;
'The multitude is always in the wrong.
'When things appear unnatural or hard,
'Consult your author, with himself compar'd.
'Who knows what blessings *Phœbus* may be-
'And future ages to your labour owe?   [stow,
'Such secrets are not easily found out,
'But once discover'd, leave no room for doubt.
'Truth stamps conviction in your ravish'd breast,
'And peace and joy attend the glorious guest.
'Yet if the shadow of a scruple stay,
'Sure the most beaten is the safest way.——

'They who too faithfully on names insist,
'Rather create than dissipate the mist;
'And give us vulgar by being over nice,
'(For superstitious virtue turns to vice.)
'Let *Crassus'* ghost, and *Labienus'* tell
'How twice in *Parthian* plains their legions fell;
'Since *Rome* hath been so jealous of her fame,
'That we know *Pacorus* or *Monæses'* name.——

'And 'tis much safer to leave out than add.
'Abstruse and mystick thoughts you must express
'With painful care, but seeming easiness;   }
'For truth shines brightest thro' the plainest
'   dress.
'Your author always will the best advise,
'Fall when he falls, and when he rises, rise.

He that can abstract his mind from
the elegance of the poetry, and confine it to the sense of the precepts, will
find no other direction, than that the
author should be suitable to the transla-
tor's genius; that he should be such as
may deserve a translation; that he who
intends to translate him, should endeavour to understand him; that perspicuity should be studied, and uncouth or
uncouth names sparingly inserted,
and that the stile of the original should
be copied in its elevation and depression. These are the rules which are celebrated as so definite and so important,
and for the delivery of which so mankind, so much honour has been paid.
Roscommon has, indeed, deserved his
honours, had they been given with
discernment, and bestowed not on the
rules themselves, but the art with which
they are introduced, and the depressions with which they are adorned.
B e

The L I F E of

Dr. FRANCIS CHEYNEL.

THERE is always this advantage in contending with illuftrious adverfaries, that the combatant is equally immortalized by conqueft or defeat. He that dies by the fword of a hero, will always be mentioned, when the acts of his enemy are mentioned. The man, of whofe life the following account is offered to the public, was indeed eminent among his own party, and had qualities, which, employed in a good caufe, would have given him fome claim to diftinction; but no one is now fo much blinded with bigotry, as to imagine him equal, either to HAMMOND or CHILLINGWORTH, nor would his memory perhaps have been preferved, had he not, by being conjoined with fuch illuftrious names, become the object of public curiofity.

FRANCIS CHEYNEL was * born in 1608, at *Oxford,* where his father Dr. JOHN CHEYNEL, who had been fellow of *Corpus-Chrifti* College, practifed phyfic with great reputation. He was educated in one of the grammar fchools of his native city, and in the beginning of the year 1623, became a member of the Univerfity.

It is probable that he loft his father, when he was very young; for it appears, that before 1629, his mother had married Dr. ABBOT, bifhop of *Salifbury,* whom fhe had likewife buried. From this marriage he received great advantage; for his mother being now allied to Dr. BRENT then warden of *Merton* College, exerted her intereft fo vigoroufly, that he was admitted there a *Probationer,* and afterwards obtained a * fellowfhip.

* *Vide* WOOD'S Ath. Ox.

Having

Having taken the degree of mafter of arts, he was admitted to orders according to the rites of the *Church* of *England*, and held a curacy near *Oxford*, together with his Fellowfhip. He continued in his college 'till he was qualified by his years of refidence for the degree of batchelor of divinity, which he attempted to take in 1641, but was denied his *grace* * for difputing concerning predeftination, contrary to the king's injunctions.

This refufal of his degree he mentions in his dedication to his account of Mr. CHILLINGWORTH; " Do not " conceive that I fnatch up my pen in an angry mood, " that I might vent my dangerous wit, and eafe my over- " burden'd fpleen. No, no, I have almoft forgot the " *vifitation at* Merton *college, and the denial of my grace, the* " *plundering of my houfe, and little library:* I know when, " and where, and of whom, to demand fatisfaction for " all thefe injuries, and indignities. I have learnt *centum* " *plagas Spartana nobilitate concoquere.* I have not learnt " how to plunder others of goods, or living, and make " my felf amends, by force of arms. I will not take a " living which belonged to any civil, ftudious, learned " delinquent; unlefs it be the much neglected *commendam* " of fome lordly prelate, condemned by the known laws " of the land, and the higheft court of the kingdom, for " fome offence of the firft magnitude."

It is obfervable that he declares himfelf to have almoft forgot his injuries and indignities, tho' he recounts them with an appearance of acrimony, which is no proof that the impreffion is much weakened; and infinuates his defign of demanding, at a proper time, fatisfaction for them.

Thefe vexations were the confequence rather of the abufe of learning, than the want of it; no one that reads his works can doubt, that he was turbulent, obftinate and

* *Vide* WOOD's Hift. Univ. Ox.

petulant,

petulant, and ready to inftruct his fuperiors when he moft
needed information from them. Whatever he believ'd (and
the warmth of his imagination naturally made him precipitate in forming his opinions) he thought himfelf oblig'd
to profefs ; and what he profefs'd, he was ready to defend,
without that modefty which is always prudent, and generally neceffary; and which, tho' it was not agreeable to
Mr. CHEYNEL's temper, and therefore readily condemn'd
by him, is a very ufeful affociate to truth, and often introduces her by degrees, where fhe never could have
forced her way by argument, or declamation.

A temper of this kind is generally inconvenient and offenfive in any fociety; but in a place of education, is
leaft to be tolerated; for as authority is neceffary to inftruction, whoever endeavours to deftroy fubordination,
by weakening that reverence which is claimed by thofe
to whom the guardianfhip of youth is committed by their
country, defeats at once the inftitution; and may be juftly
driven from a fociety, by which he thinks himfelf too
wife to be governed, and in which he is too young to
teach, and too opinionative to learn.

This may be readily fuppos'd to have been the cafe of
CHEYNEL ; and I know not how thofe can be blamed
for cenfuring his conduct, or punifhing his difobedience,
who had a right to govern him, and who might certainly act with equal fincerity, and with greater knowledge.

With regard to the vifitation of *Merton* college, the account is equally obfcure; vifitors are well known to be
generally called to regulate the affairs of colleges, when
the members difagree with their head, or with one another; and the temper that Dr. CHEYNEL difcovers, will
eafily incline his readers to fufpect, that he could not
long live in any place without finding fome occafion for
debate ; nor debate any queftion without carrying his oppofition to fuch a length as might make a moderator neceffary.

céffary. Whether this was his conduct at *Merton*, or whether an appeal to the vifitor's authority was made by him, or his adverfaries, or any other member of the college, is not to be known; it appears only, that there was a vifitation; that he fuffered by it, and refented his punifhment.

He was afterwards prefented to a living of great value, near *Banbury*, where he had fome difpute with Archbifhop LAUD. Of this difpute I have found no particular account. CALAMY only fays, *he had a ruffle with Bifhop* LAUD, *while at his height*.

Had CHEYNEL been equal to his adverfary in greatnefs and learning, it had not been eafy to have found either a more proper oppofite; for they were both to the laft degree zealous, active and pertinacious, and would have afforded mankind a fpectacle of refolution, and boldnefs, not often to be feen. But the amufement of beholding the ftruggle, would hardly have been without danger, as they were too fiery not to have communicated their heat, tho' it fhould have produc'd a conflagration of their country.

About the year 1641, when the whole nation was engag'd in the controverfy about the rights of the church and neceffity of epifcopacy, he declared himfelf a prefbyterian, and an enemy to bifhops, liturgies, ceremonies, and was confider'd as one of the moft learned and acute of his party; for having fpent much of his life in a college, it cannot be doubted, that he had a confiderable knowledge of books, which the vehemence of his temper enabled him often to difplay when a more timorous man would have been filent, though in learning not his inferiour.

When the war broke out, Mr. CHEYNEL in confequence of his principles declared himfelf for the parliament, and as he appears to have held it, as a firft principle, that all great and noble fpirits abhor neutrality, there is no doubt, but that he exerted himfelf to gain profelytes and to promote the intereft of that party, which he had thought it his duty

to

to efpoufe. Thefe endeavours were fo much regarded by the parliament, that, having taken the covenant, he was no-minated one of the affembly of divines, who were to meet at *Weftminfter* for the fettlement of the new difcipline.

This diftinction drew neceffarily upon him the hatred of the cavaliers; and his living being not far diftant from the king's head quarters, he received a vifit from fome of the troops, who, as he affirms, plundered his houfe, and drove him from it. His living, which was, I fuppofe, confider'd as forfeited by his abfence, (though he was not fuffered to continue upon it) was given to a clergyman, of whom he fays, that he would become a ftage better than a pulpit, a cenfure, which I can neither confute, nor admit; becaufe I have not difcovered, who was his fucceffor. He then re-tir'd into *Suffex* to exercife his miniftry among his friends, *in a place where,* as he obferves, *there had been little of the power of religion either known, or practifed.* As no reafon can be given, why the inhabitants of *Suffex* fhould have lefs knowledge or virtue, than thofe of other places, it may be fufpected that he means nothing more than a place where the prefbyterian difcipline or principles had never been re-ceived. We now obferve, that the methodifts, where they fcatter their opinions, reprefent themfelves as preaching the gofpel to unconverted nations. And enthufiafts of all kinds have been inclined to difguife their particular tenets with pompous appellations, and to imagine themfelves the great inftruments of falvation. Yet it muft be confeffed that all places are not equally enlightned; that in the moft civilized nations there are many corners, which may yet be called barbarous, where neither politenefs, nor religion, nor the common arts of life have yet been cultivated; and it is like-wife certain, that the inhabitants of *Suffex* have been fome-times mentioned as remarkable for brutality.

From *Suffex* he went often to *London,* where, in 1643, he preached three times before the parliament, and re-turning in *November* to *Colchefter* to keep the monthly

faft

faft there, as was his cuftom, he obtained a convoy of fixteen foldiers, whofe bravery or good fortune was fuch, that they faced and put to flight more than two hundred of the king's forces.

In this journey, he found Mr. CHILLINGWORTH in the hands of the parliament's troops, of whofe ficknefs and death he gave the account which has been fufficiently made known to the learned world by Dr. MAIZEAUX; in his life of CHILLINGWORTH.

With regard to this relation, it may be obferved, that it is written with an air of fearlefs veracity, and with the fpirit of a man who thinks his caufe juft, and his behaviour without reproach ; nor does there appear any reafon for doubting, that CHEYNEL fpoke and acted as he relates For he does not publifh an apology, but a challenge; and writes not fo much to obviate calumnies, as to gain from others that applaufe, which he feems to have beftowed very liberally upon himfelf, for his behaviour on that occafion.

Since therefore, this relation is credible; a great part of it being fupported by evidence, which cannot be refufed; Dr. MAIZEAUX feems very juftly in his life of Mr. CHIL-LINGWORTH to oppofe the common report, that his life was fhortened by the inhumanity of thofe, to whom he was a prifoner ; for CHEYNEL appears to have preferved amidft all his deteftation of the opinions, which he imputed to him, a great kindnefs to his perfon, and veneration for his capacity ; nor does he appear to have been cruel to him otherwife than by that inceffant importunity of difoutation, to which he was doubtlefs incited, by a fincere belief of the danger of his foul, if he fhould die without renouncing fome of his opinions.

The fame kindnefs, which made him defirous to convert him before his death, would incline him to preferve him from dying before he was converted ; and accordingly we find, that, when the caftle was yielded, he took

Numb. VII. Vol. II.   L l   care

care to procure him a commodious lodging; when he was to have been unfeafonably removed, he attempted to fhorten a journey, which he knew would be dangerous; when the phyfician was difgufted by CHILLINGWORTH's diftruft, he prevail'd upon him, as the fymptoms grew more dangerous, to renew his vifits; and when death left no other act of kindnefs to be practifed, procured him the rites of burial which fome would have denied him.

Having done thus far juftice to the humanity of CHEY-NEL, it is proper to enquire, how far he deferves blame. He appears to have extended none of that kindnefs to the opinions of CHILLINGWORTH, which he fhewed to his perfon; for he interprets every word in the worft fenfe, and feems induftrious to difcover in every line herefies which might have efcaped for ever any other apprehenfion, he appears always fufpicious of fome latent malignity, and ready to perfecute what he only fufpects, with the fame violence, as if it had been openly avowed; in all his procedure he fhews himfelf fincere, but without candour.

About this time CHEYNEL, in purfuance of his natural ardour, attended the army under the command of the Earl of ESSEX, and added the praife of valour, to that of learning; for he diftinguifhed himfelf fo much by his perfonal bravery, and obtained fo much fkill in the fcience of war, that his commands were obeyed by the colonels with as much refpect, as thofe of the general. He feems indeed to have been born a foldier; for he had an intrepidity, which was never to be fhaken by any danger, and a fpirit of enterprize not to be difcouraged by difficulty; which were fupported by an unufual degree of bodily ftrength. His fervices of all kinds were thought of fo much importance by the parliament, that they beftowed upon him the living of *Petworth* in *Suffex*. This living was of the value of 700l. per annum, from which, they had ejected a man remarkable for his loyalty; and therefore, in their opinion, not worthy of fuch revenues. And it

may

395

may be enquir'd, whether in accepting this preferment, CHEYNEL did not violate the proteftation, which he makes in the paffage already recited, and whether, he did not fuffer his refolution to be overborn, by the temptations of wealth.

In 1646, when *Oxford* was taken by the forces of the Parliament, and the reformation of the Univerfity was refolved, Mr. CHEYNEL was fent with fix others, to prepare the way for a vifitation; being authorifed by the parliament to preach in any of the churches, without regard to the right of the members of the Univerfity, that their doctrine might prepare their hearers, for the changes which were intended.

When they arrived at *Oxford*, they began to execute their commiffion by poffeffing themfelves of the pulpits; but if the relation of WOOD * is to be regarded, were heard with very little veneration. Thofe, who had been accuftomed to the preachers of *Oxford*, and the liturgy of the church of *England*, were offended at the emptinefs of their difcourfes, which were noify and unmeaning; at the unufual geftures, the wild diftortions, and the uncouth tone with which they were delivered; at the coldnefs of their prayers for the king, and the vehemence and exuberance of thofe, which they did not fail to utter for *the bleffed councils*, and actions of the parliament, and army; and, at what was furely not to be remarked without indignation, their omiffion of the Lord's Prayer.

But power eafily fupplied the want of reverence, and they proceeded in their plan of reformation; and thinking fermons not fo efficacious to converfion as private interrogatories and exhortations, they eftablifhed a weekly meeting for *freeing tender confciences from fcruple*, at a houfe, that from the bufinefs to which it was appropriated, was called the *Scruple-fhop*.

* *Vide* WOOD's Hift. Antiq. Oxon.

L l 2   With

With this project they were so well pleased, that they sent to the parliament an account of it, which was afterwards printed and is ascribed by WOOD to Mr. CHEYNEL. They continued for some weeks to hold their meetings regularly, and to admit great numbers, whom curiosity, or a desire of conviction, or compliance with the prevailing party brought thither. But their tranquillity was quickly disturb'd by the turbulence of the independents, whose opinions then prevailed among the soldiers, and was very industriously propagated by the discourses of WILLIAM EARBURY, a preacher of great reputation among them, who one day gathering a considerable number of his most zealous followers went to the house appointed for the resolution of scruples, on a day which was set apart for a disquisition of the dignity and office of a minister, and began to dispute with great vehemence against the presbyterians, whom he denied to have any true ministers among them, and whose assemblies he affirmed not to be the true church. He was opposed with equal heat by the presbyterians, and at length they agreed to examine the point another day, in a regular disputation. Accordingly they appointed the twelfth of *November* for an enquiry, *whether in the christian church the office of minister is committed to any particular persons.*

On the day fixed the antagonists appeared, each attended by great numbers; but when the question was proposed, they began to wrangle, not about the doctrine, which they had engaged to examine, but about the terms of the proposition, which the independent alledged to be changed, since their agreement; and at length the soldiers insisted, that the question should be, *whether those who call themselves ministers have more right, or power to preach the gospel than any other man, that is a christian.* This question was debated for some time with great vehemence and confusion; but without any prospect of a conclusion. At length one of the soldiers, who thought they had an equal right with the rest to engage in the controversy, demanded of the presbyterians,
whence

whence they themfelves received their orders, whether from bifhops or any other perfons. This unexpected interrogatory put them to great difficulties ; for it happened that they were all ordain'd by the bifhops, which they durft not acknowledge, for fear of expofing themfelves to a general cenfure ; and being convicted from their own declarations, in which they had frequently condemned epifcopacy, as contrary to chriftianity ; nor durft they deny it, becaufe they might have been confuted, and muft at once have funk into contempt. The foldiers feeing their perplexity, infulted them ; and went away boafting of their victory : nor did the prefbyterians, for fometime, recover fpirit enough, to renew their meetings, or to proceed in the work of eafing confciences.

[*To be continued.*]

The LIFE of

Dr. FRANCIS CHEYNEL,

CONTINUED.

EARBURY exulting at the victory, which not his own abilities, but the fubtilty of the foldier had procured him, began to vent his notions of every kind without fcruple, and at length afferted, that *the Saints had an equal meafure of the divine nature with our Saviour, though not equally*

equally manifest. At the fame time he took upon him the dignity of a prophet, and began to utter predictions relating to the affairs of *England* and *Ireland*.

His prophecies were not much regarded, but his doctrine was cenfured by the Prefbyterians in their pulpits; and Mr. CHEYNEL challenged him to a difputation to which he he agreed, and at his firft appearance in St. *Mary's* church addreffed his audience in the following manner:

" Chriftian friends, kind fellow-foldiers, and worthy
" ftudents, I, the humble fervant of all mankind, am this
" day drawn, againft my will, out of my cell, into this
" public affembly, by the double chain of accufation and
" a challenge from the pulpit; I have been charged with
" herefy, I have been challenged to come hither in a letter
" written by Mr. FRANCIS CHEYNEL. Here then I
" ftand in defence of myfelf and my doctrine, which I fhall
" introduce with only this declaration, that I claim not
" the office of a minifter on account of any outward
" call, though I formerly received ordination, nor do I
" boaft of *illumination*, or the knowledge of our Saviour,
" though I have been held in efteem by others, and
" formerly by myfelf. For I now declare, that I know
" and am nothing, nothing, nor would I be thought of
" otherwife than as an enquirer and feeker."

He then advanced his former pofition in ftronger terms, and with additions equally deteftable, which CHEYNEL attacked with the vehemence, which, in fo warm a temper, fuch horrid affertions might naturally excite. The difpute, frequently interrupted by the clamours of the audience, and tumults raifed to difconcert CHEYNEL, who was very unpopular, continued about four hours, and then both the controvertifts grew weary and retired. The Prefbyterians afterwards thought they fhould more fpeedily put an end to the herefies of EARBURY by power than by argument; and, by folliciting General FAIRFAX, procured his removal.

O o 2

Mr.

Mr. CHEYNEL publifhed an account of this difpute under the title of *Faith triumphing over Error and Herefy in a Revelation,* &c. nor can it be doubted but he had the victory, where his caufe gave him fo great fuperiority.

Somewhat before this, his captious and petulant difpofition engaged him in a controverfy, from which he could not expect to gain equal reputation. Dr. HAMMOND had not long before publifhed his *Practical Catechifm,* in which Mr. CHEYNEL, according to his cuftom, found many errors implied; if not afferted, and therefore, as it was much read, thought it convenient to cenfure it in the pulpit. Of this Dr. HAMMOND being informed, defired him in a letter to communicate his objections; to which Mr. CHEYNEL returned an anfwer written with his ufual temper, and therefore fomewhat perverfe. The controverfy was drawn out to a confiderable length, and the papers on both fides were afterwards made public by Dr. HAMMOND.

In 1647. it was determined by Parliament, that the reformation of *Oxford* fhould be more vigoroufly carried on; and Mr. CHEYNEL was nominated one of the vifitors. The general procefs of the vifitation, the firmnefs and fidelity of the ftudents, the addrefs by which the enquiry was delayed, and the fteadinefs with which it was oppofed, which are very particularly related by WOOD, and after him by WALKER, it is not neceffary to mention here; as they relate not more to Dr. CHEYNEL's life than to thofe of his affociates.

There is indeed fome reafon to believe that he was more active and virulent than the reft, becaufe he appears to have been charged in a particular manner with fome of their moft unjuftifiable meafures. He was accufed of propofing, that the members of the Univerfity fhould be denied the affiftance of council, and was lampooned by name, as a madman, in a fatire written on the vifitation.

One

One action which fhews the violence of his temper, and his difregard both of humanity and decency, when they came into competition with his paffions, muft not be forgotten. The vifitors being offended at the obftinacy of Dr. FELL, Dean of *Chrift Church,* and Vice-chancellor of the Univerfity, having firft deprived him of the Vice-chancellorfhip, determined afterwards to difpoffefs him of his deanery; and, in the courfe of their proceedings, thought it proper to feize upon his chambers in the college. This was an act which moft men would willingly have referred to the officers to whom the law affigned it; but CHEYNEL's fury prompted him to a different conduct. He, and three more of the vifitors went and demanded admiffion; which, being fteadily refufed them, they obtained by the affiftance of a file of foldiers, who forced the doors with pick-axes. Then entring, they faw Mrs. FELL in the lodgings, Dr. FELL being in prifon at *London,* and ordered her to quit them; but found her not more obfequious than her hufband. They repeated their orders with menaces, but were not able to prevail upon her to remove. They then retired, and left her expofed to the brutality of the foldiers, whom they commanded to keep poffeffion; which Mrs. FELL however did not leave. About nine days afterwards fhe received another vifit of the fame kind from the new Chancellor, the Earl of PEMBROKE; who having, like the others, ordered her to depart without effect, treated her with reproachful language, and at laft commanded the foldiers to take her up in her chair, and carry her out of doors. Her daughters and fome other gentlewomen that were with her, were afterwards treated in the fame manner; one of whom predicted without dejection, that fhe fhould enter the houfe again with lefs difficulty, at fome other time; nor was fhe miftaken in her conjecture, for Dr. FELL lived to be reftored to his deanery.

At

401

At the reception of the Chancellor, Cheynel, as the moft accomplifhed of the vifitors, had the province of prefenting him with the enfigns of his office, fome of which were counterfeit, and addreffing him with a proper oration. Of this fpeech, which Wood has preferved, I fhall give fome paffages by which a judgment may be made of his oratory.

Of the ftaves of the beadles he obferves, that " fome " are ftained with double guilt, that fome are pale with " fear, and that others have been made ufe of as crutches, " for the fupport of bad caufes and defperate fortunes ;" and he remarks of the book of ftatutes, which he delivers, that " the ignorant may perhaps admire the fplendour of " the cover, but the learned knew that the real treafure is " within." Of thefe two fentences it is eafily difcovered, that the firft is forced and unnatural, and the fecond trivial and low.

Soon afterwards Mr. Cheynel was admitted to the degree of Batchelor of Divinity for which his grace had been denied him 1641. and as he then fuffered for an ill-timed affertion of the Prefbyterian doctrines, he obtained that his degree fhould be dated from the time at which he was refufed it ; an honour, which however did not fecure him from being foon after publicly reproached as a madman.

The LIFE of

Dr. FRANCIS CHEYNEL,

CONCLUDED.

BUT the vigour of Cheynel was thought by his companions to deferve profit as well as honour; and Dr. Bailey, the Prefident of St. *John's College*, being not more obedient to the authority of the Parliament than the reft, was deprived of his revenues and authority, with which Mr. Cheynel was immediately invefted; who,

T t 2

with

402

with his ufual coolnefs and modefty, took poffeffion of the lodgings foon after by breaking open the doors.

This preferment being not thought adequate to the deferts or abilities of Mr. CHEYNEL, it was therefore defired by the committee of parliament, that the vifitors would recommend him to the lecturefhip of divinity founded by the Lady MARGARET. To recommend him and to choofe was at that time the fame; and he had now the pleafure of propagating his darling doctrine of predeftination, without interruption and without danger.

Being thus flufhed with power and fuccefs, there is little reafon for doubting, that he gave way to his natural vehemence, and indulged himfelf in the utmoft exceffes of raging zeal, by which he was indeed fo much diftinguifhed, that, in a fatire mentioned by WOOD, he is dignified by the title of Arch-vifitor; an appellation which he feems to have been induftrious to deferve by feverity and inflexibility: For, not contented with the commiffion which he and his collegues had already received, he procured fix or feven of the members of parliament to meet privately in Mr. ROUSE's lodgings, and affume the ftile and authority of a committee, and from them obtained a more extenfive and tyranical power, by which the vifitors were enabled to force *the folemn League and Covenant*, and the *negative oath* upon all the members of the Univerfity, and to profecute thofe for a contempt who did not appear to a citation, at whatever diftance they might be, and whatever reafons they might affign for their abfence.

By this method he eafily drove great numbers from the Univerfity, whofe places he fupplied with men of his own opinion, whom he was very induftrious to draw from other parts, with promifes of making a liberal provifion for them out of the fpoils of heretics and malignants.

Having in time almoft extirpated thofe opinions which he found fo prevalent at his arrival, or at leaft obliged thofe, who would not recant, to an appearance of conformity,

formity, he was at leifure for employments which deferve to be recorded with greater commendation. About this time, many Socinian writers began to publifh their notions with great boldnefs, which the Prefbyterians confidering as heretical and impious, thought it neceffary to confute ; and therefore CHEYNEL, who had now obtained his Doctor's degree, was defired in 1649 to write a vindication of the doctrine of the Trinity, which he performed, and publifhed the next year.

He drew up likewife a confutation of fome Socinian tenets advanced by JOHN FRY, a man who fpent great part of his life in ranging from one religion to another, and who fat as one of the judges on the king; but was expelled afterwards from the houfe of commons, and difabled from fitting in parliament. Dr. CHEYNEL is faid to have fhewn himfelf evidently fuperior to him in the controverfy, and was anfwered by him only with an opprobrious book, againft the Prefbyterian clergy.

Of the remaining part of his life there is found only an obfcure and confufed account. He quitted the prefidentfhip of St. *John's*, and the profefforfhip in 1650, as CALAMY relates, becaufe he would not take the engagement; and gave a proof that he could fuffer as well as act in a caufe which he believed juft. We have indeed no reafon to queftion his refolution, whatever occafion might be given to exert it; nor is it probable, that he feared affliction more than danger, or that he would not have born perfecution himfelf for thofe opinions which inclined him to perfecute others.

He did not fuffer much on this occafion; for he retained the living of *Petworth*, to which he thence-forward confined his labours, and where he was very affiduous, and, as CALAMY affirms, very fuccefsful in the exercife of his miniftry; it being his peculiar character to be warm and zealous in all his undertakings.

This

This heat of his difpofition, increafed by the uncommon turbulence of the time in which he lived, and by the oppofition to which the unpopular nature of fome of his employments expofed him, was at laft heightened to diftraction, fo that he was for fome time difordered in his underftanding, as both WOOD and CALAMY relate, but with fuch difference, as might be expected from their oppofite principles. WOOD appears to think that a tendency to madnefs was difcoverable in a great part of his life; CALAMY, that it was only tranfient and accidental, though in his additions to his firft narrative, he pleads it as an extenuation of that fury with which his kindeft friends confefs him to have acted on fome occafions. WOOD declares that he died little better than diftracted; CALAMY, that he was perfectly recovered to a found mind before the reftoration, at which time he retired to *Prefton*, a fmall village in *Suffex*, being turned out of his living of *Petworth*.

It does not appear, that he kept his living till the general ejection of the Nonconformifts; and it is not unlikely, that the afperity of his carriage, and the known virulence of his temper might have raifed him enemies, who were willing to make him feel the effects of perfecution which he had fo furioufly incited againft others; but of this incident of his life there is no particular account.

After his deprivation he lived (till his death, which happened in 1665) at a fmall village near *Chichefter*, upon a paternal eftate, not augmented by the large preferments, wafted upon him in the triumphs of his party; having been remarkable throughout his life, for hofpitality and contempt of money.

S. J——N.

• This Life,
written by Dr.
Johnson in the
year 1754, is
here inserted by
his permiffion.

*** [CAVE (EDWARD),* was born at Newton in Warwickſhire, on the 29th day of February, in the year 1691. His father was the younger ſon of Mr. Edward Cave, of Cave's in the Hole, a lone houſe, on the Street-Road in the ſame County, which took its name from the occupier; but having concurred with his elder brother in cutting off the intail of a ſmall hereditary eſtate, by which act it was loſt from the family, he was reduced to follow in Rugby the trade of a ſhoemaker. He was a man of good reputation in his narrow circle, and remarkable for ſtrength and ruſtick intrepidity. He lived to a great age, and was in his latter years ſupported by his ſon.

It was fortunate for Edward Cave, that having a diſpoſition to literary attainments, he was not cut off by the poverty of his parents from opportunities of cultivating his faculties. The ſchool of Rugby, in which he had, by the rules of its foundation, a right to be inſtructed, was then in high reputation, under the Reverend Mr. Holyock, to whoſe care moſt of the neighbouring families, even of the higheſt rank, entruſted their ſons. He had judgment to diſcover, and, for ſome time, generoſity to encourage the genius of young Cave; and was ſo well pleaſed with his quick progreſs in the ſchool, that he declared his reſolution to breed him for the Univerſity, and recommend him as a Servitor to ſome of his ſcholars of high rank. But proſperity which depends upon the caprice of others, is of ſhort duration. Cave's ſuperiority in literature, exalted him to an invidious familiarity with boys who were far above him in rank and expectations; and, as in unequal aſſociations it always happens, whatever unlucky prank was played, was imputed to Cave. When any miſchief, great or ſmall, was done, though perhaps others boaſted of the ſtratagem when it was ſucceſsful, yet upon detection or miſcarriage, the fault was ſure to fall upon poor Cave.

At laſt, his miſtreſs by ſome inviſible means loſt a favourite cock; Cave was with little examination ſtigmatized as the thief or murderer; not becauſe he was more apparently criminal than others, but becauſe he was more eaſily reached by vindictive juſtice. From that time Mr. Holyock withdrew his kindneſs viſibly from him, and treated him with harſhneſs, which the crime, in its utmoſt aggravation, could ſcarcely deſerve; and which ſurely he would have forborn, had he conſidered how hardly the habitual influence of birth and fortune is reſiſted; and how frequently men, not wholly without ſenſe of virtue, are betrayed to acts more atrocious than the robbery of a hen-rooſt, by a deſire of pleaſing their ſuperiors.

Thoſe reflections his maſter never made, or made without effect; for under pretence that Cave obſtructed the diſcipline of the ſchool, by ſelling clandeſtine aſſiſtance, and ſupplying exerciſes to idlers, he was oppreſſed with unreaſonable taſks, that there might be an opportunity of quarrelling with his failure; and when his diligence had ſurmounted them, no regard was paid to the performance. Cave bore this perſecution a-while, and then left the ſchool, and the hope of a literary education, to ſeek ſome other means of gaining a livelihood.

He was firſt placed with a collector of the exciſe. He uſed to recount with ſome pleaſure a journey or two which he rode with him as his clerk, and relate the victories that he gained over the exciſemen in grammatical diſputations. But the inſolence of his miſtreſs, who employed him in ſervile drudgery, quickly diſguſted him, and he went up to London in queſt of more ſuitable employment.

He was recommended to a timber merchant at the Bank-ſide, and while he was there on liking, is ſaid to have given hopes of great mercantile abilities; but this place he ſoon left, I know not for what reaſon, and was bound apprentice to Mr. Collins, a printer of ſome reputation, and deputy Alderman.

This was a trade for which men were formerly qualified by a literary education, and which was pleasing to Cave, because it furnished some employment for his scholastick attainments. Here therefore he resolved to settle, though his master and mistress lived in perpetual discord, and their house was therefore no comfortable habitation. From the inconveniencies of these domestick tumults he was soon released, having in only two years attained so much skill in his art, and gained so much the confidence of his master, that he was sent without any superintendant to conduct a printing-house at Norwich, and publish a weekly paper. In this undertaking he met with some opposition, which produced a public controversy, and procured young Cave the reputation of a writer.

His master died before his apprenticeship was expired, and he was not able to bear the perversefness of his mistress. He therefore quitted her house upon a stipulated allowance, and married a young widow with whom he lived at Bow. When his apprenticeship was over, he worked as a journeyman at the printing-house of Mr. Barber, a man much distinguished and employed by the Tories, whose principles had at that time so much prevalence with Cave, that he was for some years a writer in Mist's Journal; which, though he afterwards obtained, by his wife's interest, a small place in the Post-office, he for some time continued. But as interest is powerful, and conversation, however mean, in time persuasive, he by degrees inclined to another party; in which, however, he was always moderate, though steady and determined.

When he was admitted into the Post-office he still continued, at his intervals of attendance, to exercise his trade, or to employ himself with some typographical businefs. He corrected the *Gradus ad Parnassum*; and was liberally rewarded by the Company of Stationers. He wrote an Account of the Criminals, which had for some time a considerable sale; and published many little pamphlets that accident brought into his hands, of which it would be very difficult to recover the memory. By the correspondence which his place in the Post-office facilitated, he procured country news-papers, and sold their intelligence to a Journalist in London, for a guinea a week.

He was afterwards raised to the office of clerk of the franks, in which he acted with great spirit and firmness; and often stopped franks, which were given by Members of Parliament to their friends; because he thought such extension of a peculiar right illegal. This raised many complaints, and having stopped, among others, a frank given to the old Dutchess of Marlborough by Mr. Walter Plummer, he was cited before the House, as for breach of privilege, and accused, I suppose very unjustly, of opening letters to detect them. He was treated with great harshness and severity, but declining their questions by pleading his oath of secrecy, was at last dismissed. And it must be recorded to his honour, that when he was ejected from his office, he did not think himself discharged from his trust, but continued to refuse to his nearest friends any information about the management of the office.

By this constancy of diligence and diversification of employment, he in time collected a sum sufficient for the purchase of a small printing-office, and began the Gentleman's Magazine, a periodical pamphlet, of which the scheme is known wherever the English language is spoken. To this undertaking he owed the affluence in which he passed the last twenty years of his life; and the fortune which he left behind him, which though large, had been yet larger, had he not rashly and wantonly impaired it by innumerable projects, of which I know not that ever one succeeded.

The Gentleman's Magazine, which has now subsisted fifty-one years †, and still continues to enjoy the favour of the world, is one of the most successful and lucrative pamphlets which literary history has upon record, and therefore deserves, in this narrative, particular notice.

Mr. Cave, when he formed the project, was far from expecting the success which he found; and others had so little prospect of its consequence, that though he had for several

† In the beginning of the year 1782.

408

years talked of his plan among Printers and Bookfellers, none of them thought it worth the trial. That they were not reftrained by their virtue from the execution of another man's defign, was fufficiently apparent as foon as that defign began to be gainful; for in a few years a multitude of magazines arofe, and perifhed; only the London Magazine, fupported by a powerful affociation of Bookfellers, and circulated with all the art, and all the cunning of trade, exempted itfelf from the general fate of Cave's invaders, and obtained, though not an equal, yet a confiderable fale.

Cave now began to afpire to popularity; and being a greater lover of Poetry than any other art, he fometimes offered fubjects for Poems, and propofed prizes for the beft performers. The firft prize was fifty pounds, for which, being but newly acquainted with wealth, and thinking the influence of fifty pounds extremely great, he expected the firft authors of the kingdom to appear as competitors; and offered the allotment of the prize to the Univerfities. But when the time came, no name was feen among the writers that had been ever feen before; the Univerfities and feveral private men rejected the province of affigning the prize *. At all this Mr. Cave wondered for a while; but his natural judgment, and a wider acquaintance with the world, foon cured him of his aftonifhment, as of many other prejudices and errors. Nor have many men been feen raifed by accident or induftry to fudden riches, that retained lefs of the meannefs of their former ftate.

He continued to improve his magazine, and had the fatisfaction of feeing its fuccefs proportionate to his diligence, till in the year 1751 his wife died of an afthma. He feemed not at firft much affected by her death, but in a few days loft his fleep and his appetite, which he never recovered; but after having lingered about two years, with many viciffitudes of amendment and relapfe, fell by drinking acid liquors into a diarrhœa, and afterwards into a kind of lethargick infenfibility, in which one of the laft acts of reafon which he exerted, was fondly to prefs the hand that is now writing this little narrative. He died on January 10, 1754, having juft concluded the twenty-third annual collection.

He was a man of a large ftature, not only tall but bulky, and was, when young, of remarkable ftrength and activity. He was generally healthful, and capable of much labour and long application; but in the latter years of his life was afflicted with the gout, which he endeavoured to cure or alleviate by a total abftinence both from ftrong liquors and animal food. From animal food he abftained about four years, and from ftrong liquors much longer; but the gout continued unconquered, perhaps unabated.

His refolution and perfeverance were very uncommon; in whatever he undertook, neither expence nor fatigue were able to reprefs him: but his conftancy was calm, and, to thofe who did not know him, appeared faint and languid, but he always went forward though he moved flowly.

The fame chilnefs of mind was obfervable in his converfation: he was watching the minuteft accent of thofe whom he difgufted by feeming inattention; and his vifitant was furprized when he came a fecond time, by preparations to execute the fcheme which he fuppofed never to have been heard.

He was, confiftently with this general tranquillity of mind, a tenacious maintainer, though not a clamorous demander of his right. In his youth having fummoned his fellow journeymen to concert meafures againft the oppreffion of their mafters, he mounted

* The determination was left to Dr. Cromwell Mortimer and Dr. Birch; and by the latter the award was made, which may be feen in Gent. Mag. vol. vi. p. 59.

a kind of roftrum, and harangued them fo efficacioufly, that they determined to refift all future invafions; and when the Stamp Officers demanded to ftamp the laft half fheet of the Magazines, Mr. Cave alone defeated their claim, to which the proprietors of the rival Magazines would meanly have fubmitted.

He was a friend rather eafy and conftant, than zealous and active; yet many inftances might be given, where both his money and his diligence were employed liberally for others. His enmity was in like manner cool and deliberate; but though cool it was not infidious, and though deliberate, not pertinacious.

His mental faculties were flow. He faw little at a time, but that little he faw with great exactnefs. He was long in finding the right, but feldom failed to find it at laft. His affections were not eafily gained, and his opinion not quickly difcovered. His referve, as it might hide his faults, concealed his virtues: but fuch he was, as they who beft knew him, have moft lamented (a).]

(a) Gentleman's Magazine, vol. xxiv. p. 55.

*** [Befides the pleafure we have in adorning our work with a life written by Dr. Johnfon, we think that Edward Cave was otherwife worthy of a place in the Biographia, as the inventor of a new fpecies of publication, which may be confidered as fomething of an epocha in the literary Hiftory of this Country. The periodical performances before that time were almoft wholly confined to political tranfactions, and to foreign and domeftic occurrences. But the monthly Magazines have opened a way for every kind of inquiry and information. The intelligence and difcuffion contained in them are very extenfive and various; and they have been the means of diffufing a general habit of reading through the nation, which, in a certain degree, hath enlarged the public underftanding. Many young authors, who have afterwards rifen to confiderable eminence in the literary world, have here made their firft attempts in compofition. Here, too, are preferved a multitude of curious and ufeful hints, obfervations, and facts, which otherwife might have never appeared; or, if they had appeared in a more evanefcent form, would have incurred the danger of being loft. If it were not an invidious tafk, the hiftory of them would be no incurious or unentertaining fubject. The Magazines that unite utility with entertainment, are undoubtedly preferable to thofe (*if there have been any fuch*) which have only a view to idle and frivolous amufement. It may be obferved, that two of them, " The Gentleman's" and " The London," which laft was begun the year after the former, have, amidft their numerous rivals, preferved their reputation to the prefent day. They have both of them, in general, joined inftruction with pleafure; and this, likewife, hath been the cafe with fome others of a later origin.]

410

CHRISTIAN MORALS:

BY

Sir THOMAS BROWNE,

Of NORWICH, M. D.

AND AUTHOR OF

RELIGIO MEDICI.

THE SECOND EDITION.

WITH

A LIFE OF THE AUTHOR,

BY

SAMUEL JOHNSON;

AND

EXPLANATORY NOTES.

LONDON:
Printed by RICHARD HETT,
For J. PAYNE, at POPE's HEAD, in
PATER-NOSTER ROW.

MDCCLVI.

THE

L I F E

O F

Sir THOMAS BROWNE.

THOUGH the writer of the following ESSAYS feems to have had the fortune common among men of letters, of raifing little curiofity after his private life, and has, therefore, few memorials preferved of his felicities or misfortunes; yet, becaufe an edition of a pofthumous work appears imperfect and neglected, without fome account of the author, it was thought neceffary to attempt the gratification of that curio-

fity

fity which naturally inquires, by what peculiarities of nature or fortune eminent men have been diftinguifhed, how uncommon attainments have been gained, and what influence learning has had on its poffeffors, or virtue on its teachers.

SIR THOMAS BROWNE was born at London, in the parifh of St. Michael in Cheapfide, on the 19th of October, MDCV. [a] His father was a merchant of an antient family at Upton in Chefhire. Of the name or family of his mother, I find no account.

OF his childhood or youth, there is little known; except that he loft his father very early; that he was, according to the common [b] fate of orphans, defrauded by one of his guardians; and that he was placed for his education at the fchool of Winchefter.

HIS mother, having taken [c] three thoufand pounds, as the third part of

[a] Life of Sir THOMAS BROWNE, prefixed to the antiquities of Norwich.
[b] Whitefoot's character of Sir THOMAS BROWNE in a marginal note.
[c] Life of Sir THOMAS BROWNE.

her

her hufband's property, left her fon, by confequence, fix thoufand; a large fortune for a man deftined to learning, at that time when commerce had not yet filled the nation with nominal riches. But it happened to him as to many others, to be made poorer by opulence; for his mother foon married Sir THOMAS DUTTON, probably by the inducement of her fortune; and he was left to the rapacity of his guardian, deprived now of both his parents, and therefore helplefs and unprotected.

HE was removed in the beginning of the year MDCXXIII from Winchefter to Oxford; [d] and entered a gentleman-commoner of Broadgate-Hall, which was foon afterwards endowed, and took the name of Pembroke-College, from the EARL OF PEMBROKE then chancellor of the Univerfity. He was admitted to the degree of bachelor of arts, January 31, MDCXXVI-VII; being, as WOOD remarks, the firft man of eminence graduated from the new college, to which the zeal or gratitude of thofe that love

[d] Wood's Athenæ Oxonienfes.

it

it moſt, can wiſh little better, than that
it may long proceed as it began.

HAVING afterwards taken his degree
of maſter of arts, he turned his ſtudies
to phyſick, [a] and practiſed it for ſome
time in Oxfordſhire; but ſoon afterwards, either induced by curioſity, or
invited by promiſes, he quitted his ſet-
tlement, and accompanied his [b] father-
in-law, who had ſome employment in
Ireland, in a viſitation of the forts and
caſtles, which the ſtate of Ireland then
made neceſſary.

HE that has once prevailed on himſelf to break his connexions of acquaintance, and begin a wandering life, very
eaſily continues it. Ireland had, at that
time, very little to offer to the obſervation of a man of letters: he, therefore, paſſed [c] into France and Italy;
made ſome ſtay at Montpellier and Padua, which were then the celebrated
ſchools of phyſick; and returning home
through Holland, procured himſelf to
be created Doctor of phyſick at Leyden.

[a] WOOD.   [b] Life of Sir THOMAS BROWNE.
[c] Ibid.

WHEN

416

WHEN he began his travels, or when he concluded them, there is no certain account; nor do there remain any obfervations made by him in his paſſage through thoſe countries which he viſited. To confider, therefore, what pleaſure or inſtruction might have been received from the remarks of a man ſo curious and diligent, would be voluntarily to indulge a painful reflection, and load the imagination with a wiſh, which, while it is formed, is known to be vain. It is, however, to be lamented, that thoſe who are moſt capable of improving mankind, very frequently neglect to communicate their knowledge; either becauſe it is more pleaſing to gather ideas than to impart them, or becauſe to minds naturally great, few things appear of ſo much importance as to deſerve the notice of the publick.

ABOUT the year MDCXXXIV, [d] he is ſuppoſed to have returned to London; and the next year to have written his celebrated treatiſe, called RELIGIO MEDICI, " The Religion of a Phyſi-

[d] Biographia Britannica.

a 3 " cian,"

" cian," [a] which he declares himfelf never to have intended for the prefs, having compofed it only for his own exercife
and entertainment.   It, indeed, contains
many paffages, which, relating merely
to his own perfon, can be of no great
importance to the publick : but when it
was written, it happened to him as to
others, he was too much pleafed with
his performance, not to think that it
might pleafe others as much ; he, therefore, communicated it to his friends,
and receiving, I fuppofe, that exube-
rant applaufe with which every man re-
pays the grant of perufing a manufcript,
he was not very diligent to obftruct his
own praife by recalling his papers, but
fuffered them to wander from hand to
hand, till at laft, without his own confent, they were in MDCXLII given to a
printer.

THIS has, perhaps, fometimes befallen others ; and this, I am willing to
believe, did really happen to Dr. BROWNE:
but there is, furely, fome reafon to

[a] Letter to Sir KENELM DIGBY, prefixed to the Religio Medici, folio edit.

doubt

doubt the truth of the complaint fo frequently made of furreptitious editions. A fong, or an epigram, may be eafily printed without the author's knowledge; becaufe it may be learned when it is repeated, or may be written out with very little trouble: but a long treatife, however elegant, is not often copied by mere zeal or curiofity, but may be worn out in paffing from hand to hand, before it is multiplied by a tranfcript. It is eafy to convey an imperfect book, by a diftant hand, to the prefs, and plead the circulation of a falfe copy as an excufe for publifhing the true, or to correct what is found faulty or offenfive, and charge the errors on the tranfcriber's depravations.

THIS is a ftratagem, by which an author panting for fame, and yet afraid of feeming to challenge it, may at once gratify his vanity, and preferve the appearance of modefty; may enter the lifts, and fecure a retreat: and this, candour might fuffer to pafs undetected as an innocent fraud, but that indeed no fraud is innocent; for the confidence

a 4   which

419

which makes the happiness of society, is in some degree diminished by every man, whose practice is at variance with his words.

THE RELIGIO MEDICI was no sooner published than it excited the attention of the publick, by the novelty of paradoxes, the dignity of sentiment, the quick succession of images, the multitude of abstrufe allusions, the subtlety of disquisition, and the strength of language.

WHAT is much read, will be much criticised. The EARL OF DORSET recommended this book to the perusal of Sir KENELM DIGBY, who returned his judgment upon it, not in a letter, but a book; in which, though mingled with some positions fabulous and uncertain, there are acute remarks, just censures, and profound speculations, yet its principal claim to admiration is, that ᵃ it was written in twenty-four hours, of which part was spent in procuring BROWNE's book, and part in reading it.

ᵃ DIGBY's letter to BROWNE, prefixed to the Religio Medici, folio edit.

OF

OF thefe animadverfions, when they were yet not all printed, either officioufnefs or malice informed Dr. BROWNE; who wrote to Sir KENELM with much foftnefs and ceremony, declaring the unworthinefs of his work to engage fuch notice, the intended privacy of the compofition, and the corruptions of the impreffion; and received an anfwer equally gentle and refpectful, containing high commendations of the piece, pompous profeffions of reverence, meek acknowledgments of inability, and anxious apologies for the haftinefs of his remarks.

THE reciprocal civility of authors is one of the moft rifible fcenes in the farce of life. Who would not have thought, that thefe two luminaries of their age had ceafed to endeavour to grow bright by the obfcuration of each other: yet the animadverfions thus weak, thus precipitate, upon a book thus injured in the tranfcription, quickly paffed the prefs; and RELIGIO MEDICI was more accurately publifhed, with an admonition prefixed " to thofe who have
" or

" or fhall perufe the obfervations upon
" a former corrupt copy;" in which
there is a fevere cenfure, not upon
DIGBY, who was to be ufed with ceremony, but upon the Obfervator who
had ufurped his name: nor was this invective written by Dr. BROWNE, who
was fuppofed to be fatisfied with his opponent's apology; but by fome officious
friend zealous for his honour, without
his confent.

BROWNE has, indeed, in his own preface, endeavoured to fecure himfelf
from rigorous examination, by alleging,
that " many things are delivered rheto-
" rically, many expreffions merely tro-
" pical, and therefore many things to
" be taken in a foft and flexible fenfe,
" and not to be called unto the rigid
" teft of reafon." The firft glance upon his book will indeed difcover examples of this liberty of thought and expreffion : " I could be content (fays he)
" to be nothing almoft to eternity, if I
" might enjoy my Saviour at the laft."
He has little acquaintance with the a-
cutenefs of BROWNE, who fufpects him
of

of a ferious opinion, that any thing can
be " almoft eternal," or that any time
beginning and ending is not infinitely
lefs than infinite duration.

IN this book, he fpeaks much, and,
in the opinion of DIGBY, too much of
himfelf; but with fuch generality and
concifenefs as affords very little light to
his biographer: he declares, that, befides the dialects of different provinces,
he underftood fix languages; that he
was no ftranger to aftronomy; and that
he had feen feveral countries: but what
moft awakens curiofity, is his folemn
affertion, that " His life has been a mi-
" racle of thirty years; which to relate,
" were not hiftory but a piece of poe-
" try, and would found like a fable."

THERE is, undoubtedly, a fenfe, in
which all life is miraculous; as it is an
union of powers of which we can image
no connexion, a fucceffion of motions
of which the firft caufe muft be fupernatural: but life, thus explained, whatever it may have of miracle, will have
nothing of fable; and, therefore, the
author undoubtedly had regard to fomething,

thing, by which he imagined himfelf
diftinguifhed from the reft of mankind.

OF thefe wonders, however, the view
that can be now taken of his life offers no appearance. The courfe of his
education was like that of others, fuch
as put him little in the way of extraordinary cafualties. A fcholaftick and
academical life is very uniform; and
has, indeed, more fafety than pleafure.
A traveller has greater opportunities of
adventure; but BROWNE traverfed no
unknown feas, or Arabian defarts: and,
furely, a man may vifit France and
Italy, refide at Montpellier and Padua,
and at laft take his degree at Leyden,
without any thing miraculous. What
it was, that would, if it was related,
found fo poetical and fabulous, we are
left to guefs; I believe, without hope of
gueffing rightly. The wonders probably were tranfacted in his own mind:
felf-love, co-operating with an imagination vigorous and fertile as that of
BROWNE, will find or make objects of
aftonifhment in every man's life: and,
perhaps, there is no human being, however

ever hid in the crowd from the obfervation of his fellow-mortals, who, if he
has leifure and difpofition to recollect his
own thoughts and actions, will not conclude his life in fome fort a miracle,
and imagine himfelf diftinguifhed from
all the reft of his fpecies by many difcriminations of nature or of fortune.

THE fuccefs of this performance was
fuch, as might naturally encourage the
author to new undertakings. A gentleman of Cambridge, a whofe name was
MERRYWEATHER, turned it not ine-
legantly into Latin; and from his verfion it was again tranflated into Italian,
German, Dutch, and French; and at
Strafburg the Latin tranflation was publifhed with large notes, by Lenuus
Nicolaus Moltfarius. Of the Englifh annotations, which in all the editions from
MDCXLIV accompany the book, the author is unknown.

OF MERRYWEATHER, to whofe
zeal BROWNE was fo much indebted
for the fudden extenfion of his renown,
I know nothing, but that he publifhed

a Life of Sir THOMAS BROWNE.

a

a fmall treatife for the inftruction of
young perfons in the attainment of
a Latin ftile. He printed his tranflation in Holland with fome difficulty [a].
The firft printer to whom he offered it,
carried it to SALMASIUS, " who laid it
" by (fays he) in ftate for three months,"
and then difcouraged its publication: it
was afterwards rejected by two other
printers, and at laft was received by
HACKIUS.

THE peculiarities of this book raifed
the author, as is ufual, many admirers
and many enemies; but we know not
of more than one profeffed anfwer,
written under [b] the title of " Medicus
" medicatus," by ALEXANDER ROSS,
which was univerfally neglected by the
world.

AT the time when this book was
publifhed, Dr. BROWNE refided at Norwich, where he had fettled in MDCXXXVI,
by [c] the perfuafion of Dr. LUSHINGTON

[a] MERRYWEATHER's letter, inferted in the life of
Sir THOMAS BROWNE.
[b] Life of Sir THOMAS BROWNE.
[c] WOOD's Athenæ Oxonienfes.

his

his tutor, who was then rector of Barn-
ham Weftgate in the neighbourhood.
It is recorded by WOOD, that his practice was very extenfive, and that many
patients reforted to him. In MDCXXXVII
d he was incorporated Doctor of phyfick
in Oxford.

HE married in MDCXLI e Mrs. MILE-
HAM, of a good family in Norfolk; " a
" lady (fays WHITEFOOT) of fuch
" fymmetrical proportion to her worthy
" hufband, both in the graces of her
" body and mind, that they feemed to
" come together by a kind of natural
" magnetifm."

THIS marriage could not but draw
the raillery of contemporary wits f upon
a man, who had juft been wifhing in his
new book, " that we might procreate,
" like trees, without conjunction ;" and
had g lately declared, that " the whole
" world was made for man, but only
" the twelfth part of man for woman ;"
and, that " man is the whole world,

d WOOD.   e WHITEFOOT.
f HOWEL's letters.   g RELIGIO MEDICI.

but

" but woman only the rib or crooked
" part of man."

WHETHER the lady had been yet
informed of thefe contemptuous pofitions, or whether fhe was pleafed with
the conqueft of fo formidable a rebel,
and confidered it as a double triumph,
to attraɗ fo much merit, and overcome
fo powerful prejudices; or whether,
like moft others, fhe married upon
mingled motives, between convenience
and inclination; fhe had, however, no
reafon to repent: for fhe lived happily
with him one and forty years; and bore
him ten children, of whom one fon and
three daughters outlived their parents:
fhe furvived him two years, and paffed
her widowhood in plenty, if not in opulence.

BROWNE having now entered the
world as an author, and experienced the
delights of praife and moleftations of
cenfure, probably found his dread of the
publick eye diminifhed; and, therefore,
was not long before he trufted his
name to the criticks a fecond time: for

in

in MDCXLVI [a] he printed ENQUIRIES IN-
TO VULGAR AND COMMON ERRORS;
a work, which as it arofe not from
fancy and invention, but from obfervation and books, and contained not a
fingle difcourfe of one continued tenor,
of which the latter part rofe from the
former, but an enumeration of many
unconnected particulars, muft have been
the collection of years, and the effect
of a defign early formed and long perfued, to which his remarks had been continually referred, and which arofe gradually to its prefent bulk by the daily
aggregation of new particles of knowledge. It is, indeed, to be wifhed, that
he had longer delayed the publication,
and added what the remaining part of
his life might have furnifhed: the
thirty-fix years which he fpent afterwards in ftudy and experience, would
doubtlefs have made large additions
to an " Enquiry into vulgar errors." He
publifhed in MDCLXXIII the fixth edition, with fome improvements; but

[a] Life of Sir THOMAS BROWNE.

b   I

I think rather with explications of what he had already written, than any new heads of difquifition. But with the work, fuch as the author, whether hindered from continuing it by eagernefs of praife, or wearinefs of labour, thought fit to give, we muft be content; and remember, that in all fublunary things, there is fomething to be wifhed, which we muft wifh in vain.

THIS book, like his former, was received with great applaufe, was anfwered by ALEXANDER ROSS, and tranflated into Dutch and German, and not many years ago into French. It might now be proper, had not the favour with which it was at firft received filled the kingdom with copies, to reprint it with notes partly fupplemental and partly emendatory, to fubjoin thofe difcoveries which the induftry of the laft age has made, and correct thofe miftakes which the author has committed not by idlenefs or negligence, but for want of BOYLE's and NEWTON's philofophy.

HE appears, indeed, to have been willing to pay labour for truth. Having
heard

heard a flying rumour of fympathetick needles, by which, fufpended over a circular alphabet, diftant friends or lovers might correfpond, he procured two fuch alphabets to be made, touched his needles with the fame magnet, and placed them upon proper fpindles: the refult was, that when he moved one of his needles, the other, inftead of taking by fympathy the fame direction, " ftood like the pillars of Hercules." That it continued motionlefs, will be eafily believed; and moft men would have been content to believe it, without the labour of fo hopelefs an experiment. BROWNE might himfelf have obtained the fame conviction by a method lefs operofe, if he had thruft his needles through corks, and then fet them afloat in two bafons of water.

NOTWITHSTANDING his zeal to detect old errors, he feems not very eafy to admit new pofitions; for he never mentions the motion of the earth but with contempt and ridicule, though the opinion, which admits it, was then growing popular, and was, furely, plau-

b 2   fible,

fible, even before it was confirmed by later obfervations.

THE reputation of BROWNE encouraged fome low writer to publifh, under his name, a book called ᵃ " Nature's ca-" binet unlocked," tranflated, according to WOOD, from the phyficks of MAGIRUS; of which BROWNE took care to clear himfelf, by modeftly advertifing, that " if any man ᵇ had been " benefited by it, he was not fo ambi-" tious as to challenge the honour " thereof, as having no hand in that " work."

IN MDCLVIII the difcovery of fome antient urns in Norfolk gave him occafion to write HYDRIOTAPHIA, URN-BURIAL, OR A DISCOURSE OF SEPULCHRAL URNS, in which he treats with his ufual learning on the funeral rites of the antient nations ; exhibits their various treatment of the dead ; and examines the fubftances found in his Norfolcian urns. There is, perhaps, none of his works which better exemplifies

ᵃ WOOD, and Life of THOMAS BROWNE.
ᵇ At the end of Hydriotaphia.

his

his reading or memory. It is fcarcely to be imagined, how many particulars he has amaffed together, in a treatife which feems to have been occafionally written; and for which, therefore, no materials could have been previoufly collected. It is, indeed, like other treatifes of antiquity, rather for curiofity than ufe; for it is of fmall importance to know which nation buried their dead in the ground, which threw them into the fea, or which gave them to birds and beafts; when the practice of cremation began, or when it was difufed; whether the bones of different perfons were mingled in the fame urn; what oblations were thrown into the pyre; or how the afhes of the body were diftinguifhed from thofe of other fubftances. Of the ufelefnefs of all thefe enquiries, BROWNE feems not to have been ignorant; and, therefore, concludes them with an obfervation which can never be too frequently recollected.

" ALL or moft apprehenfions refted
" in opinions of fome future being,
" which ignorantly or coldly believed,

" begat

" begat thofe perverted conceptions,
" ceremonies, fayings, which chriftians
" pity or laugh at. Happy are they,
" which live not in that difadvantage
" of time, when men could fay little
" for futurity, but from reafon; where-
" by the nobleft mind fell often upon
" doubtful deaths, and melancholy dif-
" folutions : with thefe hopes SOCRA-
" TES warmed his doubtful fpirits, a-
" gainft the cold potion ; and CATO,
" before he durft give the fatal ftroke,
" fpent part of the night in reading
" the Immortality of PLATO, thereby
" confirming his wavering hand unto
" the animofity of that attempt.

" IT is the heavieft ftone that me-
" lancholy can throw at man, to tell
" him he is at the end of his nature ;
" or that there is no further ftate to
" come, unto which this feems pro-
" greffional, and otherwife made in
" vain : without this accomplifhment,
" the natural expectation and defire of
" fuch a ftate, were but a fallacy in na-
" ture ; unfatisfied confiderators would
" quarrel the juftice of their conftitu-
" tion,

" tion, and reft content that ADAM
" had fallen lower, whereby, by know-
" ing no other original, and deeper ig-
" norance of themfelves, they might
" have enjoyed the happinefs of infe-
" rior creatures, who in tranquillity
" poffefs their conftitutions, as having
" not the apprehenfion to deplore their
" own natures; and being framed be-
" low the circumference of thefe hopes
" or cognition of better things, the
" wifdom of GOD hath neceffitated
" their contentment. But the fuperior
" ingredient and obfcured part of our-
" felves, whereto all prefent felicities
" afford no refting contentment, will
" be able at laft to tell us we are more
" than our prefent felves; and evacuate
" fuch hopes in the fruition of their
" own accomplifhments."

To his treatife on URNBURIAL was
added THE GARDEN OF CYRUS, OR THE
QUINCUNXIAL LOZENGE, OR NETWORK
PLANTATION OF THE ANTIENTS, AR-
TIFICIALLY, NATURALLY, MYSTICAL-
LY CONSIDERED. This difcourfe he
begins with the SACRED GARDEN, in
b 4   which

which the firſt man was placed; and
deduces the practice of horticulture
from the earlieſt accounts of antiquity
to the time of the Perſian Cyrus,
the firſt man whom we actually know
to have planted a Quincunx; which,
however, our author is inclined to believe of longer date, and not only diſcovers it in the deſcription of the hanging gardens of Babylon, but ſeems willing to believe, and to perſuade his reader, that it was practiſed by the feeders
on vegetables before the flood.

Some of the moſt pleaſing performances have been produced by learning
and genius exerciſed upon ſubjects of
little importance. It ſeems to have been,
in all ages, the pride of wit, to ſhew how
it could exalt the low, and amplify the
little. To ſpeak not inadequately of things
really and naturally great, is a taſk
not only difficult but diſagreeable; becauſe the writer is degraded in his own
eyes by ſtanding in compariſon with his
ſubject, to which he can hope to add
nothing from his imagination: but it is a
perpetu ; triumph of fancy to expand a
ſcanty

scanty theme, to raise glittering ideas
from obscure properties, and to produce
to the world an object of wonder to
which nature had contributed little.
To this ambition, perhaps, we owe the
Frogs of Homer, the Gnat and the Bees
of Virgil, the Butterfly of Spenser,
the Shadow of Wowerus, and the
Quincunx of Browne.

In the prosecution of this sport of
fancy, he considers every production of
art and nature, in which he could find
any decussation or approaches to the
form of a Quincunx; and as a man once
resolved upon ideal discoveries, seldom
searches long in vain, he finds his favourite
figure in almost every thing, whether
natural or invented, antient or modern,
rude or artificial, sacred and civil; so
that a reader, not watchful against the
power of his infusions, would imagine
that decussation was the great business of the world, and that nature and
art had no other purpose than to exem-
plify and imitate a Quincunx.

To shew the excellence of this figure, he enumerates all its properties;
and

and finds in it almoſt every thing of uſe
or pleaſure: and to ſhew how readily
he ſupplies what he cannot find, one
inſtance may be ſufficient; " though
" therein (ſays he) we meet not with
" right angles, yet every rhombus con-
" taining four angles equal unto two
" right, it virtually contains two right
" in every one."

THE fanciful ſports of great minds
are never without ſome advantage to
knowledge. BROWNE has interſperſed
many curious obſervations on the form
of plants, and the laws of vegetation;
and appears to have been a very accurate obſerver of the modes of germi-
nation, and to have watched with great
nicety the evolution of the parts of
plants from their ſeminal principles.

HE is then naturally led to treat of
the number five; and finds, that by
this number many things are circum-
ſcribed; that there are five kinds of ve-
getable productions, five ſections of a
cone, five orders of architecture, and five
acts of a play. And obſerving that five was
the antient conjugal or wedding number,
he

he proceeds to a fpeculation which I
fhall give in his own words; " The
" antient numerifts made out the con-
" jugal number by two and three, the
" firft parity and imparity, the active
" and paffive digits, the material and
" formal principles in generative focie-
" ties."

THESE are all the tracts which he
publifhed: but many papers were found
in his clofet, " Some of them, (fays
" WHITEFOOT) defigned for the prefs,
" were often tranfcribed and corrected
" by his own hand, after the fafhion of
" great and curious writers."

OF thefe, two collections have been
publifhed; one by Dr. TENNISON, the
other in MDCCXXII by a namelefs editor.
Whether the one or the other felected
thofe pieces which the author would
have preferred, cannot now be known:
but they have both the merit of giving
to mankind what was too valuable to be
fuppreffed; and what might, without
their interpofition, have, perhaps, perifhed among other innumerable labours of
learned men, or have been burnt in a
fcarcity

fcarcity of fuel like the papers of
Perefkius.

THE firft of thefe pofthumous treatifes contains " Obfervations upon feve-
" ral plants mentioned in Scripture."
Thefe remarks, though they do not
immediately either rectify the faith, or
refine the morals of the reader, yet are
by no means to be cenfured as fuperfluous niceties or ufelefs fpeculations; for
they often fhew fome propriety of defcription, or elegance of allufion, utterly
undifcoverable to readers not fkilled in
oriental botany; and are often of more
important ufe, as they remove fome difficulty from narratives, or fome obfcurity
from precepts.

THE next is " Of garlands, or cc-
" ronary and garland plants;" a fubject
merely of learned curiofity, without
any other end than the pleafure of reflecting on antient cuftoms, or on the
induftry with which ftudious men have
endeavoured to recover them.

THE next is a letter, " on the fifhes
" eaten by our SAVIOUR with his dif-
" ciples, after his refurrection from the
" dead ; "

440

" dead;" which contains no determinate refolution of the queſtion, what they were, for indeed it cannot be determined. All the information that diligence or learning could ſupply, conſiſts in an enumeration of the fiſhes produced in the waters of Judea.

THEN follow " Anſwers to certain " queries about fiſhes, birds, and in-
" ſects;" and " A letter of hawks and " falconry antient and modern:" in the firſt of which he gives the proper interpretation of ſome antient names of animals, commonly miſtaken; and in the other has ſome curious obſervations on the art of hawking, which he conſiders as a practice unknown to the antients. I believe all our ſports of the field are of Gothick original; the antients neither hunted by the ſcent, nor ſeem much to have practiſed horſemanſhip as an exerciſe; and though, in their works, there is mention of " au-
" cupium" and " piſcatio," they ſeem no more to have been conſidered as diverſions, than agriculture or any other manual labour.

IN

441

I N two more letters he fpeaks of " the cymbals of the Hebrews," but without any fatisfactory determination; and of " repalick or gradual verfes," that is, of verfes beginning with a word of one fyllable, and proceeding by words of which each has a fyllable more than the former; as,

" O Deus, æternæ ftationis conciliator.

AUSONIUS.

and, after his manner, purfuing the hint, he mentions many other reftrained methods of verfifying, to which induftrious ignorance has fometimes voluntarily fubjected itfelf.

H I s next attempt is " On languages, " and particularly the Saxon tongue." He difcourfes with great learning, and generally with great juftnefs, of the derivation and changes of languages; but, like other men of multifarious learning, he receives fome notions without examination. Thus he obferves, according to the popular opinion, that the Spaniards have retained fo much Latin, as to be able to compofe fentences that fhall be at once gramatically Latin and Caftilian:

Caſtilian: this will appear very unlikely to a man that conſiders the Spaniſh terminations; and HOWEL, who was eminently skilful in the three provincial languages, declares, that after many eſſays he never could effect it.

THE principal deſign of this letter, is to ſhew the affinity between the modern Engliſh and the antient Saxon; and he obſerves, very rightly, that " though " we have borrowed many ſubſtantives, " adjectives, and ſome verbs, from the " French; yet the great body of nu- " merals, auxiliary verbs, articles, pro- " nouns, adverbs, conjunctions, and " prepoſitions, which are the diſtin- " guiſhing and laſting parts of a lan- " guage, remain with us from the " Saxon."

To prove this poſition more evidently, he has drawn up a ſhort diſcourſe of ſix paragraphs, in Saxon and Engliſh; of which every word is the ſame in both languages, excepting the terminations and orthography. The words are, indeed, Saxon, but the phraſeology is Engliſh; and, I think, would not have been

been underſtood by Bede or Ælfric, notwithſtanding the confidence of our author. He has, however, ſufficiently proved his poſition, that the Engliſh reſembles its parental language, more than any modern European dialect.

There remain five tracts of this collection yet unmentioned; one " Of ar-
" tificial hills, mounts, or burrows, in
" England;" in reply to an interrogatory letter of E. D. whom the writers of Biographia Britannica ſuppoſe to be, if rightly printed, W. D. or Sir William Dugdale, one of Browne's correſpondents. Theſe are declared by Browne, in concurrence, I think, with all other antiquarians, to be for the moſt part funeral monuments. He proves, that both the Danes and Saxons buried their men of eminence under piles of earth, " which admitting (ſays he) nei-
" ther ornament, epitaph, nor inſcrip-
" tion, may, if earthquakes ſpare them,
" outlaſt other monuments: obeliſks
" have their term, and pyramids will
" tumble; but theſe mountainous mo-
" numents may ſtand, and are like
" to

" to have the fame period with the
" earth."

IN the next, he anfwers two geo-
graphical queſtions; one concerning
Troas, mentioned in the Acts and Epi-
ſtles of St. PAUL, which he determines
to be the city built near the antient
Ilium; and the other concerning the
dead fea, of which he gives the fame
account with other writers.

ANOTHER letter treats " Of the an-
" fwers of the oracle of Apollo at Del-
" phos, to Crœfus king of Lydia." In
this tract nothing deferves notice, more
than that BROWNE confiders the oracles
as evidently and indubitably fupernatural,
and founds all his difquifition upon that
poſtulate. He wonders why the phyfio-
logiſts of old, having fuch means of in-
ſtruction, did not inquire into the fe-
crets of nature: but judicioufly concludes, that fuch queſtions would probably have been vain ; " for, in matters
" cognofcible, and formed for our dif-
" quifition, our induſtry muſt be our
" oracle, and reafon our Apollo,"

T H E pieces that remain are, " A pro-
" phecy concerning the future ftate of
" feveral nations;" in which BROWNE
plainly difcovers his expectation to be
the fame with that entertained lately
with more confidence by Dr. BERKLEY,
" that America will be the feat of the
" fifth empire:" and " Mufeum clau-
" fum, five Bibliotheca abfcondita;"
in which the author amufes himfelf
with imagining the exiftence of books
and curiofities, either never in being, or
irrecoverably loft.

T H E S E pieces I have recounted as
they are ranged in TENNISON's collection, becaufe the editor has given no account of the time at which any of them
were written. Some of them are of
little value, more than as they gratify
the mind with the picture of a great
fcholar, turning his learning into amufement; or fhew, upon how great a variety
of enquiries the fame mind has been
fuccefsfully employed.

T H E other collection of his pofthumous pieces, publifhed in octavo, London MDCCXXII, contains " Reperto-
" rium;

" rium; or fome account of the tombs
" and monuments in the cathedral of
" Norwich;" where, as TENNISON obferves, there is not matter proportionate
to the fkill of the Antiquary.

THE other pieces are, " Anfwers to
" Sir WILLIAM DUGDALE's enquiries
" about the fens; A letter concerning
" Ireland; Another relating to urns
" newly difcovered; Some fhort ftric-
" tures on different fubjects:" and " A
" letter to a friend on the death of his
" intimate friend," publifhed fingly by
the author's fon in MDCXC.

THERE is inferted, in the BIOGRA-
PHIA BRITANNICA, " A letter con-
" taining inftructions for the ftudy of
" phyfick;" which, with the ESSAYS
here offered to the public, completes the
works of Dr. BROWNE.

To the life of this learned man, there
remains little to be added, but that in
MDCLXV he was chofen honorarv fellow
of the college of phyficians, as a man,
" Virtute et literis ornatiffimus, — emi-
" nently embellifhed with literature and
" virtue:" and, in MDCLXXI, received,

c 2

at

at Norwich, the honour of knighthood from CHARLES II ; a prince, who with many frailties and vices, had yet fkill to difcover excellence, and virtue to reward it, with fuch honorary diftinctions at leaft as coft him nothing, yet conferred by a king fo judicious and fo much beloved, had the power of giving merit new luftre and greater popularity.

THUS he lived in high reputation; till in his feventy-fixth year he was feized with a colick, which, after having tortured him about a week, put an end to his life at Norwich, on his birthday, October 19, MDCLXXXII. [a] Some of his laft words were expreffions of fubmiffion to the will of G O D, and fearlefnefs of death.

HE lies buried in the church of St. Peter, Mancroft, in Norwich, with this infcription on a mural monument, placed on the fouth pillar of the altar :

[a] BROWNE's Remains.   WHITEFOOT.

M. S.

Sir THOMAS BROWNE.

M. S.

Hic fitus eft THOMAS BROWNE, M. D.

Et Miles.

A° 1605. Londini natus

Generofa Familia apud Upton

In agro Ceftrienfi oriundus.

Schola primum Wintonienfi, poftea

In Coll. Pembr.

Apud Oxonienfes bonis literis

Haud leviter imbutus

In urbe hâc Nordovicenfi medicinam

Arte egregia, & fælici fucceffu profeffus,

Scriptis quibus tituli, R E L I G I O M E D I C I

Et P S E U D O D O X I A E P I D E M I C A aliifque

Per Orbem notiffimus.

Vir Prudentiffimus, Integerrimus, Doctiffimus;

Obiit Octobr. 19. 1682.

Pie pofuit mæftiffima Conjux

D^a. Doroth. Br.

Near the Foot of this Pillar

Lies Sir Thomas Browne, Kt. and Doctor in Phyfick,

Author of Religio Medici, and other Learned Books,

Who practic'd Phyfick in this City 46 Years,

And died Oct. 1682, in the 77 Year of his Age.

In Memory of whom

Dame *Dorothy Browne,* who had bin his Affectionate Wife

47 Years, caufed this Monument to be Erected.

C 3   B E-

BESIDES his lady, who died in
MDCLXXXV, he left a fon and three
daughters. Of the daughters nothing
very remarkable is known; but his fon,
EDWARD BROWNE, requires a particular mention.

HE was born about the year MDCXLII;
and after having paffed through the claffes of the fchool at Norwich, became
bachelor of phyfick at Cambridge; and
afterwards removing to Merton-College
in Oxford, was admitted there to the
fame degree, and afterwards made a
doctor. In MDCLXVIII he vifited part
of Germany; and in the year following
made a wider excurfion into Auftria,
Hungary, and Theffaly; where the
Turkifh Sultan then kept his court at
Lariffa. He afterwards paffed through
Italy. His fkill in natural hiftory made
him particularly attentive to mines and
metallurgy. Upon his return he publifhed an account of the countries thro'
which he had paffed; which I have
heard commended by a learned traveller, who has vifited many places after
him, as written with fcrupulous and
exact

exact veracity, such as is scarcely to be found in any other book of the same kind. But whatever it may contribute to the instruction of a naturalist, I cannot recommend it as likely to give much pleasure to common readers: for whether it be, that the world is very uniform, and therefore he who is resolved to adhere to truth, will have few novelties to relate; or that Dr. BROWNE was, by the train of his studies, led to enquire most after those things, by which the greatest part of mankind is little affected; a great part of his book seems to contain very unimportant accounts of his passage from one place where he saw little, to another where he saw no more.

UPON his return, he practised physick in London; was made physician first to CHARLES II, and afterwards in MDCLXXXII to St. Bartholomew's hospital. About the same time he joined his name to those of many other eminent men, in " A translation of Plu- " tarch's lives." He was first censor, then elect, and treasurer of the college

c 4   of

451

of phyficians; of which in MDCCV he
was chofen prefident, and held his office, till in MDCCVIII he died in a degree of eftimation fuitable to a man
fo varioufly accomplifhed, that King
CHARLES had honoured him with this
panegyrick, that " He was as learned
" as any of the college, and as well-
" bred as any of the court."

OF every great and eminent character, part breaks forth into publick view,
and part lies hid in domeftick privacy.
Thofe qualities which have been exerted in any known and lafting performances, may, at any diftance of time, be
traced and eftimated; but filent excellencies are foon forgotten; and thofe
minute peculiarities which difcriminate
every man from all others, if they are
not recorded by thofe whom perfonal
knowledge enabled to obferve them, are
irrecoverably loft. This mutilation of
character muft have happened, among
many others, to Sir THOMAS BROWNE,
had it not been delineated by his friend
Mr. WHITEFOOT, who " efteemed it
" an

" an efpecial favour of PROVIDENCE,
" to have had a particular acquaintance
" with him for two thirds of his life."
Part of his obfervations I fhall, therefore, copy.

" FOR a character of his perfon, his
" complexion and hair was anfwerable
" to his name; his ftature was mode-
" rate, and habit of body neither fat
" nor lean, but ἐυσάρκ☉.
" IN his habit of clothing, he had
" an averfion to all finery, and affected
" plainnefs, both in the fafhion and
" ornaments. He ever wore a cloke, or
" boots, when few others did. He
" kept himfelf always very warm, and
" thought it moft fafe fo to do, though
" he never loaded himfelf with fuch a
" multitude of garments, as Suetonius
" reports of AUGUSTUS, enough to
" clothe a good family.
" THE horizon of his underftanding
" was much larger than the hemifphere
" of the world: All that was vifible in
" the heavens he comprehended fo
" well, that few that are under them
" knew

" knew fo much: He could tell the
" number of the vifible ftars in his ho-
" rizon, and call them all by their
" names that had any ; and of the earth
" he had fuch a minute and exact geo-
" graphical knowledge, as if he had
" been by Divine Providence or-
" dained furveyor-general of the whole
" terreftrial orb, and its products, mine-
" rals, plants, and animals. He was fo
" curious a botanift, that befides the
" fpecifical diftinctions, he made nice
" and elaborate obfervations, equally
" ufeful as entertaining.

" His memory, though not fo emi-
" nent as that of Seneca or Scali-
" ger, was capacious and tenacious,
" infomuch as he remembred all that
" was remarkable in any book that he
" had read; and not only knew all per-
" fons again that he had ever feen at
" any diftance of time, but remem-
" bred the circumftances of their bodies,
" and their particular difcourfes and
" fpeeches.

" In the latin poets he remembred
" every thing that was acute and pun-
" gent;

" gent ; he had read moſt of the hiſto-
" rians, antient and modern, wherein
" his obſervations were ſingular, not
" taken notice of by common readers;
" he was excellent company when he
" was at leiſure, and expreſſed more
" light than heat in the temper of his
" brain.

" HE had no deſpotical power over
" his affections and paſſions, (that was
" a privilege of original perfection, for-
" feited by the neglect of the uſe of
" it;) but as large a political power
" over them, as any Stoick, or man of
" his time, whereof he gave ſo great
" experiment, that he hath very rarely
" been known to have been overcome
" with any of them. The ſtrongeſt that
" were found in him, both of the iraſ-
" cible and concupiſcible, were under
" the controul of his reaſon. Of ad-
" miration, which is one of them, be-
" ing the only product, either of igno-
" rance, or uncommon knowledge, he
" had more, and leſs, than other men,
" upon the ſame account of his know-
" ing more than others ; ſo that tho'
                                        " he

" he met with many rarities, he admi-
" red them not fo much as others do

" He was never feen to be tranf-
" ported with mirth, or dejected with
" fadnefs; always chearful, but rarely
" merry, at any fenfible rate; feldom
" heard to break a jeft; and when he
" did, he would be apt to blufh at the
" levity of it: his gravity was natural
" without affectation.

" His modefty was vifible in a na-
" tural habitual blufh, which was in
" creafed upon the leaft occafion, and
" oft difcovered without any obfervable
" caufe.

" They that knew no more of him
" than by the brifknefs of his writings,
" found themfelves deceived in their
" expectation, when they came in his
" company, noting the gravity and fo-
" briety of his afpect and converfation;
" fo free from loquacity, or much talka-
" tivenefs, that he was fomething diffi-
" cult to be engaged in any difcourfe;
" though when he was fo, it was al-
" ways fingular, and never trite or vul-
" gar. Parfimonious in nothing but his
" time,

" time, whereof he made as much
" improvement, with as little lofs as
" any man in it : when he had any to
" fpare from his drudging practice, he
" was fcarce patient of any diverfion
" from his ftudy ; fo impatient cf floth
" and idlenefs, that he would fay, he
" could not do nothing.

" SIR THOMAS underftood moft of
" the European languages ; viz. all that
" are in HUTTER's bible, which he
" made ufe of. The Latin and Greek
" he underftood critically ; the Oriental
" languages, which never were verna-
" cular in this part of the world, he
" thought the ufe of them would not
" anfwer the time and pains of learn-
" ing them ; yet had fo great a vene-
" ration for the matrix of them, viz.
" the Hebrew, confecrated to the Ora-
" cles of God, that he was not con-
" tent to be totally ignorant of it ; tho'
" very little of his fcience is to be
" found in any books of that primitive
" language. And tho' much is faid to
" be written in the derivative idioms of
" that tongue, efpecially the Arabick,
" yet

" yet he was fatisfied with the tranfla-
" tions, wherein he found nothing ad-
" mirable.

" In his religion he continued in
" the fame mind which he had declared
" in his firft book, written when he
" was but thirty years old, his RELI-
" GIO MEDICI, wherein he fully af-
" fented to that of the church of Eng-
" land, preferring it before any in the
" world, as did the learned GROTIUS.
" He attended the publick fervice very
" conftantly, when he was not with-
" held by his practice. Never miffed
" the facrament in his parifh, if he
" were in town. Read the beft Englifh
" fermons he could hear of, with libe-
" ral applaufe; and delighted not in
" controverfies. In his laft ficknefs,
" wherein he continued about a week's
" time, enduring great pain of the cho-
" lick, befides a continual fever, with
" as much patience as hath been feen
" in any man, without any pretence of
" Stoical apathy, animofity, or vanity of
" not being concerned thereat, or fuffer-
" ing

" ing no impeachment of happinefs.
" Nihil agis dolor.

" HIS patience was founded upon
" the chriftian philofophy, and a found
" faith of GOD's PROVIDENCE, and
" a meek and humble fubmiffion there-
" unto, which he expreffed in few
" words: I vifited him near his end,
" when he had not ftrength to hear or
" fpeak much; the laft words which I
" heard from him, were, befides fome
" expreffions of dearnefs, that he did
" freely fubmit to the will of GOD,
" being without fear: He had oft tri-
" umphed over the king of terrors in
" others, and given many repulfes in
" the defence of patients; but when his
" own turn came, he fubmitted with
" a meek, rational, and religious cou-
" rage.

" HE might have made good the
" old faying of Dat Galenus opes, had
" he lived in a place that could have
" afforded it. But his indulgence and
" liberality to his children, efpecially
" in their travels, two of his fons in
" divers countries, and two of his
" daugh-

" ters in France, ſpent him more than
" a little.   He was liberal in his houſe
" entertainménts, and in his charity; he
" leſt a comfortable, but no great eſtate,
" both to his lady and children, gained
" by his own induſtry.

" S u c h was his ſagacity and know-
" ledge of all hiſtory, antient and mo-
" dern, and his obſervations thereupon
" ſo ſingular, that it hath been ſaid by
" them that knew him beſt, that if
" his profeſſion, and place of abode,
" would have ſuited his ability, he
" would have made an extraordinary
" man for the privy-council, not much
" inferior to the famous P a d r e,
" P a u l o, the late oracle of the Ve-
" netian ſtate.

" T h o' he were no prophet, nor ſon
" of a prophet, yet in that faculty
" which comes neareſt it, he excelled,
" *i. e.* the ſtochaſtick, wherein he was
" ſeldom miſtaken, as to future events,
" as well publick as private; but not
" apt to diſcover any preſages or ſuper-
" ſtition."

" I t

Sir THOMAS BROWNE.

IT is obfervable, that he who in his earlier years had read all the books againſt religion, was in the latter part of his life averſe from controverſies. To play with important truths, to diſturb the repoſe of eſtabliſhed tenets, to ſubtilize objections, and elude proof, is too often the ſport of youthful vanity, of which maturer experience commonly repents. There is a time, when every wiſe man is weary of raiſing difficulties only to taſk himſelf with the ſolution, and deſires to enjoy truth without the labour or hazard of conteſt. There is, perhaps, no better method of encountering theſe troubleſome irruptions of ſcepticiſm, with which inquiſitive minds are frequently harraſſed, than that which BROWNE declares himſelf to have taken: " If there ariſe any doubts in my " way, I do forget them ; or at leaſt de- " fer them, till my better ſettled judg- " ment and more manly reaſon be able " to reſolve them : for I perceive, every " man's reaſon is his beſt OEDIPUS, " and will, upon a reaſonable truce, find " a way to looſe thoſe bonds, where-
d " with

" with the fubtilties of error have en-
" chained our more flexible and tender
" judgments."

THE foregoing character may be confirmed and enlarged, by many paffages
in the RELIGIO MEDICI; in which it
appears, from WHITEFOOT's teftimony,
that the author, though no very fparing
panegyrift of himfelf, has not exceeded
the truth, with refpect to his attainments
or vifible qualities.

THERE are, indeed, fome interior
and fecret virtues, which a man may
fometimes have without the knowledge of others; and may fometimes affume to himfelf, without fufficient reafons for his opinion. It is
charged upon BROWNE by Dr. WATTS,
as an inftance of arrogant temerity, that,
after a long detail of his attainments,
he declares himfelf to have efcaped
" the firft and father-fin of pride."
A perufal of the RELIGIO MEDICI will
not much contribute to produce a belief
of the author's exemption from this FA-
THER-SIN: pride is a vice, which pride
itfelf inclines every man to find in others,
and to overlook in himfelf.   As

As eafily may we be miftaken in eftimating our own courage, as our own humility; and, therefore, when BROWNE fhews himfelf perfuaded, that " he " could lofe an arm without a tear, or " with a few groans be quartered to " pieces," I am not fure that he felt in himfelf any uncommon powers of endurance; or, indeed, any thing more than a fudden effervefcence of imagination, which, uncertain and involuntary as it is, he miftook for fettled refolution.

" THAT there were not many ex- " tant, that in a noble way feared the " face of death lefs than himfelf, " he might likewife believe at a very eafy expence, while death was yet at a diftance; but the time will come to every human being, when it muft be known how well he can bear to die ; and it has appeared, that our author's fortitude did not defert him in the great hour of trial.

IT was obferved by fome of the remarkers on the RELIGIO MEDICI, that "the author was yet alive, and might grow
" worfe

" worfe as well as better :" it is, therefore, happy, that this fufpicion can be
obviated by a teftimony given to the
continuance of his virtue, at a time
when death had fet him free from danger of change, and his panegyrift from
temptation to flattery.

B u t it is not on the praifes of others,
but on his own writings, that he is to
depend for the efteem of pofterity; of
which he will not eafily be deprived,
while learning fhall have any reverence
among men : for there is no fcience, in
which he does not difcover fome fkill ;
and fcarce any kind of knowledge, pro-
fane or facred, abftrufe or elegant, which
he does not appear to have cultivated
with fuccefs.

H i s exuberance of knowledge, and
plenitude of ideas, fometimes obftruct
the tendency of his reafoning, and the
clearnefs of his decifions : on whatever
fubject he employed his mind, there
ftarted up immediately fo many images
before him, that he loft one by grafp-
ing another. His memory fupplied him
with fo many illuftrations, parallel or

de-

dependent notions, that he was always starting into collateral confiderations : but the fpirit and vigour of his perfuit always gives delight; and the reader follows him, without reluctance, thro' his mazes, in themfelves flowery and pleafing, and ending at the point origi- nally in view.

To have great excellencies, and great faults, " magnæ virtutes nec minora " vitia, is the poefy," fays our author, " of the beft natures." This poefy may be properly applied to the ftyle of BROWNE : It is vigorous, but rugged; it is learned, but pedantick ; it is deep, but obfcure; it ftrikes, but does not pleafe ; it commands, but does not al- lure : his tropes are harfh, and his combinations uncouth. He fell into an age, in which our language began to lcfe the ftability which it had obtained in the time of ELIZABETH; and was confidered by every writer as a fubject on which he might try his plaftick fkill, by moulding it according to his own fancy. MILTON, in confequence of this encroaching licence, began to intro-

duce

duce the Latin idiom: and BROWNE, though he gave lefs difturbance to our ftructures and phrafeology, yet poured in a multitude of exotick words; many, indeed, ufeful and fignificant, which, if rejected, muft be fupplied by circumlocution, fuch as COMMEN- SALITY for the ftate of many living at the fame table; but many fuperflu- ous, as a PARALOGICAL for an unrea- fonable doubt; and fome fo obfcure, that they conceal his meaning rather than explain it, as ARTHRITICAL ANA- LOGIES for parts that ferve fome ani- mals in the place of joints.

HIS ftyle is, indeed, a tiffue of many languages; a mixture of heterogeneous words, brought together from diftant regions, with terms originally appro- priated to one art, and drawn by vio- lence into the fervice of another. He muft, however, be confeffed to have augmented our philofophical diction; and in defence of his uncommon words and expreffions, we muft confider, that he had uncommon fentiments, and was not content to exprefs in many words

words

words that idea for which any language could fupply a fingle term.

But his innovations are fometimes pleafing, and his temerities happy: he has many " verba ardentia," forcible expreffions, which he would never have found, but by venturing to the utmoft verge of propriety; and flights which would never have been reached, but by one who had very little fear of the fhame of falling.

THERE remains yet an objection a-gainft the writings of BROWNE, more formidable than the animadverfions of criticifm. There are paffages, from which fome have taken occafion to rank him among Deifts, and others among Atheifts. It would be difficult to guefs how any fuch conclufion fhould be formed, had not experience fhewn that there are two forts of men willing to enlarge the catalogue of infidels.

IT has been long obferved, that an Atheift has no juft reafon for endea-vouring converfions; and yet none har-rafs thofe minds which they can influ-ence, with more importunity of folicita-

tion

tion to adopt their opinions. In proportion as they doubt the truth of their own doctrines, they are defirous to gain the atteftation of another underftanding ; and induftrioufly labour to win a profelyte, and eagerly catch at the flighteft pretence to dignify their fect with a celebrated name *.

THE others become friends to infidelity only by unfkilful hoftility : men of rigid orthodoxy, cautious converfation, and religious afperity. Among thefe, it is too frequently the practice, to make in their heat conceffions to Atheifm, or Deifm, which their moft confident advocates had never dared to claim or to hope. A fally of levity, an idle paradox, an indecent jeft, an unfeafonable objection, are fufficient, in the opinion of thefe men, to efface a name from the lifts of CHRISTIANITY, to exclude a foul from everlafting life.

---

* Therefore no hereticks defire to fpread
Their wild opinions like thefe epicures.
For fo their ftagg'ring thoughts are computed,
And other men's affent their doubt affures.
DAVIES.

Such

Such men are so watchful to censure, that they have seldom much care to look for favourable interpretations of ambiguities, to set the general tenor of life against single failures, or to know how soon any slip of inadvertency has been expiated by sorrow and retractation; but let fly their fulminations, without mercy or prudence, against slight offences or casual temerities, against crimes never committed, or immediately repented.

THE Infidel knows well, what he is doing. He is endeavouring to supply, by authority, the deficiency of his arguments; and to make his cause less invidious, by shewing numbers on his side: he will, therefore, not change his conduct, till he reforms his principles. But the zealot should recollect, that he is labouring, by this frequency of excommunication, against his own cause; and voluntarily adding strength to the enemies of truth. It must always be the condition of a great part of mankind, to reject and embrace tenets upon the authority of those whom they

think

think wifer than themfelves; and, therefore, the addition of every name to infidelity, in fome degree invalidates that
argument upon which the religion of
multitudes is neceffarily founded.

M E N may differ from each other in
many religious opinions, and yet all
may retain the effentials of C H R I S T I A-
N I T Y ; men may fometimes eagerly difpute, and yet not differ much from
one another: the rigorous perfecutors of
error, fhould, therefore, enlighten their
zeal with knowledge, and temper their
orthodoxy with C H A R I T Y ; that C H A-
R I T Y, without which orthodoxy is
vain; C H A R I T Y that " thinketh no
" evil,", but " hopeth all things," and
" endureth all things."

W H E T H E R B R O W N E has been numbered among the contemners of religion, by the fury of its friends, or the
artifice of its enemies, it is no difficult
tafk to replace him among the moft zealous P R O F E S S O R S of C H R I S T I A N I T Y.
He may, perhaps, in the ardour of his
imagination, have hazarded an expreffion, which a mind intent upon faults
may

may interpret into herefy, if confidered
apart from the reft of his difcourfe; but
a phrafe is not to be oppofed to volumes: there is fcarcely a writer to be
found, whofe profeffion was not divinity, that has fo frequently teftified his
belief of the SACRED WRITINGS, has
appealed to them with fuch unlimited
fubmiffion, or mentioned them with
fuch unvaried reverence.

I T is, indeed, fomewhat wonderful,
that HE fhould be placed without the
pale of CHRISTIANITY, who declares,
that " he affumes the honourable ftile
" of A CHRISTIAN," not becaufe it is
" the religion of his country," but becaufe " having in his riper years and
" confirmed judgment feen and exa-
" mined all, he finds himfelf obliged,
" by the principles of GRACE, and the
" law of his own reafon, to embrace
" no other name but this:" Who, to
fpecify his perfuafion yet more, tells us,
that " he is of the REFORMED RELI-
" GION; of the fame belief our SA-
" VIOUR taught, the APOSTLES diffe-
" minated, the Fathers authorized, and
                                    " the

" the Martyrs confirmed :" Who, tho'
" paradoxical in philofophy, loves in di-
" vinity to keep the beaten road ;" and
pleafes himfelf, that " he has no taint
" of herefy, fchifm, or error:" To
whom " where the Scripture is filent,
" the Church is a text; where that
" fpeaks, 'tis but a comment;" and who
ufes not " the dictates of his own rea-
" fon, but where there is a joint filence
" of both:" Who " bleffes himfelf,
" that he lived not in the days of mi-
" racles, when faith had been thruft
" upon him ; but enjoys that greater
" bleffing, pronounced to all that be-
" lieve and faw not." He cannot furely be charged with a defect of faith,
who " believes that our S a v i o u r was
" dead, and buried, and rofe again, and
" defires to fee him in his glory:" and
who affirms, that " this is not much to
" believe;" that " as we have reafon,
" we owe this faith unto hiftory;" and
that " they only had the advantage of a
" bold and noble faith, who lived be-
" fore his coming; and, upon obfcure
" prophecies and myftical types, could
" raife

" raife a belief." Nor can contempt of the pofitive and ritual parts of religion be imputed to him, who doubts, whether a good man would refufe a poifoned euchariſt ; and " who would violate his " own arm, rather than a church."

THE opinions of every man muſt be learned from himfelf : concerning his practice, it is fafeſt to truſt the evidence of others. Where thefe teſtimonies concur, no higher degree of hiſtorical certainty can be obtained ; and they apparently concur to prove, that BROWNE was A ZEALOUS ADHERENT TO THE FAITH OF CHRIST, that HE LIVED IN OBEDIENCE TO HIS LAWS, AND DIED IN CONFIDENCE OF HIS MERCY.

A. Pesne Pinx.t   G.L. Smith sc.

FREDERICK the III. King of PRUSSIA, &c.

THE

LITERARY MAGAZINE.

NUMB. VII.

From *October* 15, to *November* 15, 1756.

Memoirs of the King of Pruſſia.

HARLES FREDERICK the preſent king of *Pruſ-*
fia, whoſe actions and
deſigns now keep *Eu-*
rope in attention, is the
eldeſt ſon of *Frederick
William* by *Sophia Do-*
rothea, daughter of *George* the firſt, king
of *England*. He was born *January* 24,
1711-12. Of his early years nothing remarkable has been tranſmitted to us. As
he advanced towards manhood, he became
remarkable by his diſagreement with his
father.

The late king of *Pruſſia*, was of a diſpoſition violent and arbitrary, of narrow
views, and vehement paſſions, earneſtly engaged in little perſuits, or in ſchemes terminating in ſome ſpeedy conſequence, without any plan of laſting advantage to himſelf or his ſubjects, or any proſpect of diſtant events. He was therefore always
buſy though no effects of his activity ever
appeared, and always eager though he had
nothing to gain. His behaviour was to
the laſt degree rough and ſavage. The
leaſt provocation, whether deſigned or accidental, was returned by blows, which he
did not always forbear to the queen and
princeſſes.

From ſuch a king and ſuch a father it
was not any enormous violation of duty in
the immediate heir of a kingdom ſometimes to differ in opinion, and to maintain that difference with decent pertinacity.

Vol. I.

A prince of a quick ſagacity and compre-
henſive knowledge muſt find many practices in the conduct of affairs which he
could not approve, and ſome which he
could ſcarcely forbear to oppoſe.

The chief pride of the old king was to
be maſter of the talleſt regiment in Europe.
He therefore brought together from all
parts men above the common military
ſtandard. To exceed the height of ſix feet
was a certain recommendation to notice,
and to approach that of even a claim to
diſtinction. Men will readily go where
they are ſure to be careſſed, and he had
therefore ſuch a collection of giants as perhaps was never ſeen in the world before.

To review this towering regiment was
his daily pleaſure, and to perpetuate it was
ſo much his care, that when he met a tall
woman, he immediately commanded one
of his Titanian retinue to marry her, that
they might propagate procerity, and produce heirs to the fathers habilements.

In all this there was apparent folly, but
there was no crime. The tall regiment
made a fine ſhew at an expence not much
greater, when once it was collected, than
would have been beſtowed upon common
men. But the king's military paſtimes
were ſometimes more pernicious. He
maintained a numerous army of which he
made no other uſe than to review and to
talk of it, and when he, or perhaps his
emiſſaries ſaw a boy, whoſe form and
ſprightlineſs promiſed a future ſoldier, he

X x

or-

475

ordered a kind of a badge to be put about his neck by which he was marked out for the service, like the sons of christian captives in Turkey, and his parents were forbidden to destine him to any other mode of life.

This was sufficiently oppressive, but this was not the utmost of his tyranny. He had learned, though otherwise perhaps no very great politician, that to be rich was to be powerful, but that the riches of a king ought to be seen in the opulence of his subjects, he wanted either ability or benevolence to understand. He therefore raised exorbitant taxes from every kind of commodity and possession, and piled up the money in his treasury, from which it issued no more. How the land which had paid taxes once was to pay them a second time, how imposts could be levied without commerce, or commerce continued without money, it was not his custom to enquire. Eager to snatch at money and delighted to count it, he felt new joy at every receipt, and thought himself enriched by the impoverishment of his dominions.

By which of these freaks of royalty the prince was offended, or whether, as perhaps more frequently happens, the offences of which he complained were of a domestic and personal kind, it is not easy to discover. But his resentment, whatever was its cause, rose so high, that he resolved not only to leave his father's court, but his territories, and to seek a refuge among the neighbouring or kindred princes. It is generally believed that his intention was to come to England, and live under the protection of his uncle, till his father's death or change of conduct should give him liberty to return.

His design, whatever it was, he concerted with an officer of the army whose name was *Kat*, a man in whom he placed great confidence, and whom having chosen him for the companion of his flight, he necessarily trusted with the preparatory measures. A prince cannot leave his country with the speed of a meaner fugitive. Something was to be provided, and something to be adjusted. And, whether *Kat* found the agency of others necessary, and therefore was constrained to admit some partners of the secret; whether levity or vanity incited him to disburden himself of a trust that swelled in his bosom, or to shew to a friend or mistress his own importance; or whether it be in itself difficult for princes to transact any thing in secret, so it was that the king was in-

formed of the intended flight, and the prince and his favourite, a little before the time settled for their departure; were arrested, and confined in different places.

The life of princes is seldom in danger, the hazard of their irregularity falls only on those whom ambition or affection combines with them. The king after an imprisonment of some time, set his son at liberty, but poor *Kat* was ordered to be tried for a capital crime. The Court examined the cause and acquitted him; the king remanded him to a second trial and obliged his judges to condemn him. In consequence of the sentence thus tyrannically extorted, he was publicly beheaded, leaving behind him some papers of reflexions made in the prison, which were afterwards printed, and among others an admonition to the prince for whose sake he suffered, not to foster in himself the opinion of destiny, for that a providence is discoverable in every thing round us.

This cruel prosecution of a man who had committed no crime, but by compliance with influence not easily to be resisted, was not the only act by which the old king irritated his son. A lady with whom the prince was suspected of intimacy, perhaps more than virtue allowed, was seized, I know not upon what accusation, and, by the king's order, notwithstanding all the reasons of decency and tenderness that operate in other countries and other judicatures, was publicly whipped in the streets of Berlin.

At last, that the prince might feel the power of a king and a father in its utmost rigour, he was in 1733 married against his will to the princess Elizabetha Christina of Brunswick Lunenburg Bevern. He married her indeed at his father's command, but without professing for her either esteem or affection, and considering the claim of parental authority fully satisfied by the external ceremony, obstinately and perpetually during the life of his father, refrained from her bed. The poor princess lived about seven years in the court of Berlin, in a state which the world has not often seen, a wife without a husband, married so far as to engage her person to a man who did not desire her affection, and of whom it was doubtful whether he thought himself restrained from the power of repudiation by an act performed under evident compulsion.

Thus he lived secluded from public business, in contention with his father, in

476

lienation from his wife. This ſtate of uneaſineſs he found the only means of ſoftening. He diverted his mind from the ſcenes about him by ſtudies and liberal amuſements. The ſtudies of princes ſeldom produce great effects, for princes draw with meaner mortals the lot of underſtanding; and ſince of many ſtudents not more than one can be hoped to advance far towards perfection, it is ſcarcely to be expected that we ſhould find, that one a prince; that the deſire of ſcience ſhould overpower in any mind the love of pleaſure when it is always preſent or always within call; that laborious meditation ſhould be preferred in the days of youth to amuſements and feſtivity, or that perſeverance ſhould preſs forward in contempt of flattery, and that he in whom moderate acquiſitions would be extolled as prodigies, ſhould exact from himſelf that excellence of which the whole world conſpires to ſpare him the neceſſity.

In every great performance, perhaps in every great character, part is the gift of nature, part the contribution of accident, and part, very often not the greateſt part, the effect of voluntary election, and regular deſign. The king of Pruſſia was undoubtedly born with more than common abilities; but that he has cultivated them with more than common diligence was probably the effect of his peculiar condition, of that which he then conſidered as cruelty and misfortune.

In this long interval of unhappineſs and obſcurity he acquired ſkill in the mathematical ſciences, ſuch as is ſaid to put him on the level with thoſe who have made them the buſineſs of their lives. This is probably to ſay too much, the acquiſitions of kings are always magnified. His ſkill in poetry and in the French language have been loudly praiſed by Voltaire, a judge without exception, if his honeſty were equal to his knowledge. Muſick he not only underſtands but practiſes on the german flute in the higheſt perfection, ſo that according to the regal cenſure of Philip of Macedon, he may be aſhamed to play ſo well.

He may be ſaid to owe to the difficulties of his youth an advantage leſs frequently obtained by princes than literature and mathematics. The neceſſity of paſſing his time without pomp, and of partaking of the pleaſures and labours of a lower ſtation, made him acquainted with the various forms of life, and with the genuine paſſions, intereſts, deſires and diſtreſſes of

mankind. Kings without this help from temporary infelicity ſee the world in a miſt, which magnifies every thing near them, and bounds their view to a narrow compaſs, which few are able to extend by the mere force of curioſity. I have always thought that what Cromwel had more than our lawful kings, he owed to the private condition in which he firſt entered the world, and in which he long continued, in that ſtate he learned his art of ſecret tranſaction, and the knowledge by which he was able to oppoſe zeal to zeal, and make one enthuſiaſt deſtroy another.

The king of Pruſſia gained the ſame arts, and being born to fairer opportunities of uſing them, brought to the throne the knowledge of a private man without the guilt of uſurpation. Of this general acquaintance with the world there may be found ſome traces in his whole life. His converſation is like that of other men upon common topics, his letters have an air of familiar elegance, and his whole conduct is that of a man who has to do with men, and who is ignorant what motives will prevail over friends or enemies.

In 1740 the old king fell ſick, and ſpoke and acted in his illneſs with his uſual turbulence and roughneſs, reproaching his phyſicians in the groſſeſt terms with their unſkilfulneſs and impotence, and imputing to their ignorance or wickedneſs the pain which their preſcriptions failed to relieve. Theſe inſults they bore with the ſubmiſſion which is commonly paid to deſpotic monarchs, till at laſt the celebrated Hofman was conſulted, who fulling like the reſt to give eaſe to his majeſty was like the reſt treated with injurious language. Hofman, conſcious of his own merit, replied, that he could not bear reproaches which he did not deſerve; that he had tried all the remedies that art could ſupply, or nature could admit; that he was indeed a profeſſor by his majeſty's bounty, but that if his abilities or integrity were doubted, he was willing to leave not only the univerſity but the kingdom, and that he could not be driven into any place where the name of Hofman would want reſpect. The King however unaccuſtomed to ſuch returns, was ſtruck with conviction of his own indecency, told Hofman, that he had ſpoken well, and requeſted him to continue his attendance.

The king finding his diſtemper gaining upon his ſtrength, grew at laſt ſenſible that his end was approaching, and

or-

Ordering the prince to be called to his bed, laid feveral injunctions upon him, of which one was to perpetuate the tall regiment by continual recruits, and another to receive his efpoufed wife. The prince gave him a refpectful anfwer, but wifely avoided to diminifh his own right or power by an abfolute promife, and the king died uncertain of the fate of the tall regiment.

The young king began his reign with great expectations, which he has yet furpaffed. His father's faults produced many advantage to the firft years of his reign. He had an army of feventy thoufand men well difciplined, without any imputation of feverity to himfelf, and was mafter of a vaft treafure without the crime or reproach of raifing it. It was publicly faid in our houfe of commons, that he had eight millions fterling of our money, but, I believe, he that faid it had not confidered how difficultly eight millions wou'd be found in all the Pruffian dominions. Men judge of what they fee not by that which they fee. We are ufed to talk in England of millions with great familiarity, and imagine that there is the fame affluence of money in other countries, in countries whofe manufactures are few, and commerce little.

Every man's firft cares are neceffarily domeftic. The king being now no longer under influence or its appearance, determined now to act towards the unhappy lady who had poffeffed for feven years the empty title of the princefs of Pruffia. The papers of thofe times exibited the converfation of their firft interview; as if the king who plans campaigns in filence would not accommodate a difference with his wife, but with writers of news admitted as witneffes. It is certain that he received her as queen, but whether he treats her as a wife is yer in difpute.

In a few days his refolution was known with regard to the tall regiment, for fome recruits being offered him, he rejected them, and this body of giants by continued difregard mouldered away.

He treated his mother with great refpect, ordered that fhe fhould bear the title of queen mother, and that inftead of addreffing him as *his majefty*, fhe fhould only call him fon.

As he was paffing foon after between Berlin and Potfdam, a thoufand boys who had been marked out for military fervice, furrounded his coach, and cried out, *mer-*

ciful king deliver us from our flavery. He promifed them their liberty, and ordered the next day that the badge fhould be taken off.

He ftill continued that correfpondence with learned men, which he began when he was prince; and the eyes of all fcholars, a race of mortals formed for dependance, were upon him, as a man likely to renew the times of patronage, and to emulate the bounties of Lewis the fourteenth.

It foon appeared that he was refolved to govern with very little minifterial affiftance ; he took cognizance of every thing with his own eyes, declared that in all contrarieties of intereft between him and his fubjects, the public good fhould have the preference, and in one of the firft exertions of regal power banifhed the prime minifter and favourite of his father, as one that had *betrayed his mafter and abufed his truft.*

He then declared his refolution to grant a general toleration of religion, and among other liberalities of conceffion allowed the profeffion of *free majonry.* It is the great taint of his character that he has given reafon to doubt, whether this toleration is the effect of charity or indifference, whether he means to fupport good men of every religion, or confiders all religions as equally good.

There had fubfifted for fome time in Pruffia an order called the *order for favour,* which, according to its denomination, had been conferred with very little diftinction. The king inftituted the *order for merit,* with which he honoured thofe whom he confidered as deferving. There were fome who thought their merit not fufficiently recompenfed by this new title, but he was not very ready to grant pecuniary rewards. Thofe who were moft in his favour he fometimes prefented with fnuff-boxes, on which was infcribed, *amitie augmente te prix.*

He was, however, charitable if not liberal, for he ordered the magiftrates of the feveral diftricts to be very attentive to the relief of the poor, and if the funds eftablifhed for that ufe were not fufficient, permitted that the deficiency fhould be fupplied out of the revenues of the town.

One of his firft cares was the advancement of learning. Immediately upon his acceffion, he wrote to Rollin and Voltaire that he defired the continuance of their friendfhip, and fent for Mr. Maupertuis the

the principal of the French academicians who paffed a winter in Lapland to verify by the menfuration of a degree near the pole, the Newtonian doctrine of the form of the earth. He requefted of Maupertuis to come to Berlin to fettle an academy, in terms of great ardour and great condefcention.

At the fame time he fhewed the world that literary amufements were not likely, as has more than once happened to royal ftudents, to withdraw him from the care of the kingdom, or make him forget his intereft. He began by reviving a claim to Herftal and Hernal, two diftricts in the poffeffion of the bifhop of Liege. When he fent his commiffary to demand the homage of the inhabitants, they refufed him admiffion, declaring that they acknowledged no fovereign but the bifhop. The king then wrote a letter to the bifhop, in which he complained of the violation of his right, and the contempt of his authority, charged the prelate with countenancing the late act of difobedience and required an anfwer in two days.

In three days the anfwer was fent, in which the bifhop founds his claim to the two lordfhips, upon a grant of Charles the fifth, guarantied by France and Spain, alleges that his predeceffors had enjoyed this grant above a century, and that he never intended to infringe the rights of Pruffia; but as the houfe of Brandenburg had always made fome pretenfions to that territory, he was willing to do what other bifhops had offered, to purchafe that claim for an hundred thoufand crowns.

To every man that knows the ftate of the feudal countries, the intricacy of their pedigrees, the confufion of their alliances, and the different rules of inheritance that prevail in different places, it will appear evident, that of reviving antiquated claims there can be no end, and that the poffeffion of a century is a better title than can commonly be produced. So long a prefcription, fuppofes an acquiefcence in the other claimants, and that acquieficence fuppofes alfo fome reafon, perhaps now unknown, for which the claim was forborn. Whether this rule could be confidered as valid in the controverfy between thefe fovereigns may however be doubted, for the bifhop's anfwer feems to imply that the title of the houfe of Brandenburg had been alive by repeated claims, tho' the feizure of the territory had been hitherto forborn.

The king did not fuffer his claim to be fubjected to any altercations, but having publifhed a declaration in which he charged the bifhop with violence and injuftice, and remarked that the feudal laws allowed every man whofe poffeffion was withheld from him, to enter it with an armed force, he immediately difpatched two thoufand foldiers into the controverted countries, where they lived without coutroul, exercifing every kind of military tyranny, till the cries of the inhabitants forced the bifhop to relinquifh them to the quiet government of Pruffia.

This was but a petty acquifition, the time was now come when the king of Pruffia was to form and execute greater defigns. On the 9th of October 1740, half Europe was thrown into confufion by the death of Charles the fixth, Emperor of Germany, by whofe death all the hereditary dominions of the houfe of Auftria defcended, according to the pragmati cfanction, to his eldeft daughter, who was married to the duke of Lorrain, at the time of the emperor's death, duke of Tufcany.

By how many fecurities the pragmatic fanction was fortified, and how little it was regarded when thofe fecurities became neceffary: how many claimants ftarted up at once to the feveral dominions of the houfe of Auftria: how vehemently their pretenfions were enforced, and how many invafions were threatened or, attempted; the diftreffes of the emperor's daughter known for feveral years by the title only of the queen of Hungary, becaufe Hungary was the only country to which het claim had not been difputed: the firmnefs with which fhe ftruggled with her difficulties, and the good fortune by which fhe furmounted them: the narrow plan of this effay will not fuffer me to relate. Let them be told by fome other writer of more leifure and wider intelligence.

Upon the emperor's death, many of the German princes fell upon the Auftrian territories as upon a dead carcafe to be difmembered among them, without refiftance. Among thefe with whatever juftice, certainly with very little generofity, was the king of Pruffia, who having affembled his troops, as was imagined, to fupport the pragmatic fanction, on a fudden entered Silefia with thirty thoufand men, publifhing a declaration in which he difclaims any defign of injuring the rights of the houfe of Auftria, but urges his claim to

Si

479

Silefia, as arising *from antient conven-tions of family and confraternity between the houfe of* Brandenburgh, *and the prin-ces of* Silefia, *and other honourable titles.* He fays, the fear of being defeated by other pretenders to the Auftrian domi-nions, obliged him to enter Silefia with-out any previous expoftulation with the queen, and that he fhall *ftrennoufly efpoufe the interefts of the houfe of* Auftria.

Such a declaration was, I believe, in the opinion of all Europe, nothing lefs than he aggravation of hoftility by infult, and was received by the Auftrians with fuitable indignation. The king purfued his pur-pofe, marched forward, and in the fron-tiers of *Silefia* made a fpeech to his fol-lowers, in which he told them, that he con-fidered them rather " as friends than fub-
" jects, that the troops of Brandenburg
" had been always eminent for their
" bravery, that they would always fight
" in his prefence, and that he would re-
" compenfe thofe who fhould diftinguifh
" themfelves in his fervice, rather as a
" father than as a king."

The civilities of the great are never thrown away. The foldiers would na-turally follow fuch a leader with alacrity; efpecially becaufe they expected no op-pofition, but human expectations are fre-quently deceived.

Entering thus fuddenly into a country which he was fuppofed rather likely to protect than to invade, he acted for fome time with abfolute authority, but fup-pofing that this fubmiffion would not al-ways laft, he endeavoured to perfuade the queen to a ceffion of Silefia, imagining that fhe would eafily be perfuaded to yield what was already loft. He therefore ordered his minifters to declare at Vienna,
" that he was ready to guaranty all the
" German dominions of the houfe of
" Auftria." " That he would conclude
" a treaty with Auftria, Ruffia, and the
" maritime powers ;" " That he would
" endeavour that the duke of Lorrain
" fhould be elected emperor, and believed
" that he could accomplifh it," " That
" he would immediately advance to the
" queen two millions of florins," " That
" in recompenfe for all this he required
" Silefia to be yielded to him."

Thefe feem not to be the offers of a prince very much convinced of his own right. He afterwards moderated his claim, and ordered his minifter to hint at Vienna that half of Silefia would content him.

The queen anfwered, That though the king alleged as his reafon for entering Silefia, the danger of the Auftrian terri-tories from other pretenders, and endea-vours to perfuade her to give up part of her poffeffions for the prefervation of the reft, it was evident that he was the firft and only invader, and that till he entered in an hoftile manner, all her eftates were unmolefted.

To his promifes of affiftance fhe re-plied, that fhe fet an high value on th-king of Pruffia's friendfhip, but that fhe was already obliged to affift her againft invaders both by the golden bull, and the pragmatic fanction, of which he was a guarantee, and that if thefe ties were of no force fhe knew not what to hope from other engagements. Of his offers of alliances with Ruffia and the maritime powers, fhe obferved, that it could be never fit to alienate her dominions for the confolida-tion of an alliance formed only to keep them intire.

With regard to his intereft in the elec-tion of an emperor fhe expreffed her gra-titude in ftrong terms; but added that the election ought to be free, and that it muft be neceffarily embarraffed by contentions thus raifed in the heart of the empire. Of the pecuniary affiftance propofed fhe re-marks, that no prince ever made war to oblige another to take money, and that the contributions already levied in Silefia exceed the two millions offered as its pur-chafe.

She concluded, that as fhe values the king's friendfhip, fhe was willing to pur-chafe it by any compliance but the dimi-nution of her dominions, and exhorted him to perform his part in fupport of the pragmatic fanction.

The king finding negotiation thus in-effectual, pufhed forward his inrodes, and now began to fhow how fecretly he could take his meafures. When he called a council of war he propofed the queftion in a few words, all his generals wrote their opinions in his prefence upon feparate pa-pers, which he carried away, and examin-ing them in private formed his refolution without imparting it otherwife than by his orders.

He began not without policy to feize firft upon the eftates of the clergy, an or-der every where neceffary, and every where envied. He plundered the con-vents of their ftores of provifion, and told
them

them that he never had heard of any magazines erected by the apostles.

This insult was mean because it was unjust, but those who could not resist were obliged to bear it. He proceeded in his expedition, and a detachment of his troops took Jablunca, one of the strong places of Silesia, which was soon after abandoned for want of provisions, which the Austrian Hussars who were now in motion, were busy to interrupt.

One of the most remarkable events of the Silesia war, was the conquest of great Glogaw, which was taken by an assault in the dark, headed by prince Leopold of Anhalt Dessau. They arrived at the foot of the fortifications about twelve at night, and in two hours were masters of the place. In attempts of this kind many accidents happen which cannot be heard without surprize. Four Prussian grenadiers who had climbed the ramparts, missing their own company, met an Austrian captain with fifty-two men; they were at first frighted, and were about to retreat, but gathering courage, commanded the Austrians to lay down their arms, and in the terror of darkness and confusion were unexpectedly obey'd.

At the same time a conspiracy to kill or carry away the king of Prussia was said to be discovered. The Prussians published a memorial in which the Austrian court was accused of employing emissaries and assassins against the king; and it was alleged in direct terms, that one of them had confessed himself obliged by oath to destroy him, which oath had been given him in an aulic council in the presence of the duke of Lorrain.

To this the Austrians answered, that the character of the queen and duke was too well known not to destroy the force of such an accusation that the tale of the confession was an imposture; and that no such attempt was ever made.

Each party was now inflamed, and orders were given to the Austrian general to hazard a battle. The two armies met at Molwitz, and parted without a compleat victory on either side. The Austrians quitted the field in good order, and the king of Prussia rode away upon the first disorder of his troops without waiting for the last event. This attention to his personal safety has not yet been forgotten.

After this there was no action of much importance. But the king of Prussia irritated by opposition, transferred his interest in the election to the duke of Bava-

ria, and the queen of Hungary, now attacked by France, Spain, and Bavaria, was obliged to make peace with him at the expence of half Silesia, without procuring those advantages which were once offered her. [*To be continued in our next, with the head of the king of Prussia.*]

THE

LITERARY MAGAZINE.

NUMB. VIII.

From *November* 15, to *December* 15, 1756.

The Life of the King of Pruffia *continued from* p. 333.

O inlarge dominions has been the boaft of many princes, to difiufe happinefs and fecurity thro' wide regions has been granted to few. The king of Pruffia has afpired to both thefe honours, and endeavoured to join the praife of legiflator to that of conquerer.

To fettle property, to fupprefs falfe claims, and to regulate the adminiftration of civil and criminal juftice are attempts fo difficult and fo ufeful, that I fhall willingly fufpend or contract the hiftory of battles and fieges, to give a larger account of this pacific enterprize.

That the king of Pruffia has confidered the nature and the reafons of laws with more attention than is common to princes, appears from his differtation on the *Reafons for enacting and repealing Laws*. A piece which yet deferves notice, rather as a proof of good inclination than of great ability. For there is nothing to be found in it more than the moft obvious books may fupply, or the weakeft intellect difcover. Some of his obfervations are juft and ufeful, but upon fuch a fubject who can think without often thinking right? It is however not to be omitted, that he appears always propenfe towards the fide of mercy. ' If a poor man, (fays he) fteals in his want a watch, or a few pieces from one to

' whom the lofs is inconfiderable, is this a
' reafon for condemning him to death ?'

He regrets that the laws againft duels have been ineffectual, and is of opinion, that they can never attain their end, unlefs the princes of Europe fhall agree not to afford an Afylum to duellifts, and to punifh all who fhall infult their equals either by word, deed, or writing. He feems to fufpect this fcheme of being chimerical, ' Yet why, (fays he) fhould not perfonal ' quarrels be fubmitted to judges as well as ' queftions of pofleffion, and why fhould ' not a congrefs be appointed fc the ge- ' neral good of mankind, as well as for fo ' many purpofes of lefs importance.'

He declares himfelf, with great ardour againft the ufe of torture, and by fome mifinformation charges the Englifh that they ftill retain it.

It is perhaps impoffible to review the laws of any country without difcovering many defects and many fuperfluities. Laws often continue, when their reafons have ceafed. Laws made for the firft ftate of the fociety continue unabolifhed, when the general form of life is changed. Parts of the judicial procedure which were at firft only accidental become in time effential; and formalities are accumulated on each other till the art of litigation requires more ftudy than the difcovery of right.

The king of Pruffia examining the inftitutions of his own country thought them

such

E e e

ſuch as could only be amended by a general abrogation, and the eſtabliſhment of a new body of law, to which he gave the name of the CODE FREDERIC, which is comprized in one volume of no great bulk, and muſt therefore unavoidably contain general poſitions, to be accommodated to particular caſes by the wiſdom and integrity of the courts. To embarraſs juſtice by multiplicity of laws, or to hazard it by confidence in judges, ſeem to be the oppoſite rocks on which all civil inſtitutions have been wrecked, and between which legiſlative wiſdom has never yet found an open paſſage.

Of this new ſyſtem of laws, contracted as it is, a full account cannot be expected in theſe memoirs, but that curioſity may not be diſmiſſed without ſome gratification, it has been thought proper to epitomiſe the king's *plan for the reformation of his courts.*

'The differences which ariſe between members of the ſame ſociety may be terminated by a voluntary agreement between the parties, by arbitration, or by a judicial proceſs.

'The two firſt methods produce more frequently a temporary ſuſpenſion of diſputes than a final termination. Courts of juſtice are therefore neceſſary, with a ſettled method of procedure, of which the moſt ſimple is to cite the parties, to hear their pleas, and diſmiſs them with immediate deciſion.

'This however is in many caſes impracticable, and in others is ſo ſeldom practiſed that it is frequent rather to incur loſs than to ſeek for legal reparation, by entering a labyrinth of which there is no end.

'This tediouſneſs of ſuits keeps the parties in diſquiet and perturbation, rouſes and perpetuates animoſities, exhauſts the litigants by expence, retards the progreſs of their fortune, and diſcourages ſtrangers from ſettling.

'Theſe inconveniences, with which the beſt regulated polities of Europe are embarraſſed, muſt be removed not by the total prohibition of ſuits, which is impoſſible, but by contraction of proceſſes ; by opening an eaſy way for the appearance of truth, and removing all obſtructions by which it is concealed.

'The ordinance of 1667, by which Lewis XIV. eſtabliſhed an uniformity of Procedure through all his courts, has been conſidered as one of the greateſt benefits of his reign.

'The king of Pruſſia obſerving that each of his provinces had a different method of judicial procedure, propoſed to reduce them all to one form, which being tried with ſucceſs in Pomerania, a province remarkable for contention, he afterwards extended to all his dominions, ordering the judges to inform him of any difficulties which aroſe from it.

'Some ſettled method is neceſſary in judicial procedures. Small and ſimple cauſes might be decided upon the oral pleas of the two parties appearing before the judge : But many caſes are ſo entangled and perplexed as to require all the ſkill and abilities of thoſe who devote their lives to the ſtudy of the law.

'Advocates, or men who can underſtand and explain the queſtion to be diſcuſſed, are therefore neceſſary. But theſe men inſtead of endeavouring to promote juſtice and diſcover truth, have exerted their wits in the defence of bad cauſes, by forgeries of facts and fallacies of argument.

'To remedy this evil the king has ordered an inquiry into the qualifications of the advocates. All thoſe who practiſe without a regular admiſſion, or who can be convicted of diſingenuous practice are diſcarded. And the judges are commanded to examine which of the cauſes now depending have been protracted by the crimes and ignorance of the advocates, and to diſmiſs thoſe who ſhall appear culpable.

'When advocates are too numerous to live by honeſt practice they buſy themſelves in exciting diſputes, and diſturbing the community : the number of theſe to be employed in each court is therefore fixed.

'The reward of the advocates is fixed with due regard to the nature of the cauſe, and the labour required, but not a penny is received by them till the ſuit is ended, that it may be their intereſt, as well as that of the clients, to ſhorten the proceſs.

'No advocate is admitted in petty courts, ſmall towns, or villages; where the poverty of the people, and for the moſt part the low value of the matter conteſted, make diſpatch abſolutely neceſſary. In thoſe places the parties ſhall appear in perſon, and the judge make a ſummary deciſion.

'There muſt be likewiſe allowed a ſubordination of tribunals, and a power of appeal. No judge is ſo ſkilful and attentive as not ſometimes to err. Few are ſo honeſt as not ſometimes to be partial. Petty judges would become inſupportably tyrannical if they were not reſtrained by the fear of a ſuperior judicature, and their deciſions would be negligent or arbitrary if they were

were not in danger of ſeeing them examined and cancelled.

The right of appeal muſt be reſtrained, that cauſes may not be transferred without end from court to court; and a peremptory deciſion muſt at laſt be made.

'When an appeal is made to a higher court, the appellant is allowed only four weeks to frame his bill, the judge of the lower court being to tranſmit to the higher all the evidences and informations. If upon the firſt view of the cauſe thus opened it ſhall appear that the appeal was made without juſt cauſe, the firſt ſentence ſhall be confirmed without citation of the defendant. If any new evidence ſhall appear, or any doubts ariſe, both the parties ſhall be heard.

'In the diſcuſſion of cauſes altercation muſt be allowed; yet to altercation ſome limits muſt be put. There are therefore allowed a Bill, an Anſwer, a Reply, and a Rejoinder, to be delivered in writing.

'No cauſe is allowed to be heard in more than three different courts. To further the firſt deciſion, every advocate is enjoined under ſevere penalties not to begin a ſuit till he has collected all the neceſſary evidence. If the firſt court has decided in an unſatisfactory manner, an appeal may be made to the ſecond, and from the ſecond to the third. The proceſs on each appeal is limited to ſix months. The third court may indeed paſs an erroneous judgment, and then the injury is without redreſs. But this objection is without end and therefore without force. No method can be found of preſerving humanity from error, but of conteſt there muſt ſometime be an end; and he who thinks himſelf injured for want of an appeal to a fourth court, muſt conſider himſelf as ſuffering for the public.

'There is a ſpecial advocate appointed for the poor.

'The attornies who had formerly the care of collecting evidence and of adjuſting all the preliminaries of a ſuit, are now totally diſmiſſed; the whole affair is put into the hands of the advocates, and the office of an attorney is annulled for ever.

'If any man is hindered by ſome lawful impediment from attending his ſuit, time will be granted him upon the repreſentation of his caſe.'

Such is the order according to which civil juſtice is adminiſtered through the extenſive dominions of the king of Pruſſia; which if it exhibits nothing very ſubtle or profound, affords one proof more

that the right is eaſily diſcovered, and that men do not ſo often want ability to find, as willingneſs to practiſe it.

We now return to the war.

The time at which the queen of Hungary was willing to purchaſe peace by the reſignation of Sileſia, though it came at laſt, was not come yet. She had all the ſpirit, though not all the power of her anceſtors, and could not bear any thought of loſing any part of her patrimonial dominions to the enemies, which the opinion of her weakneſs raiſed every where againſt her.

In the beginning of the year 1742 the elector of Bavaria was inveſted with the imperial dignity, ſupported by the arms of France, maſter of the kingdom of Bohemia, and confederated with the Elector Palatine, and the elector of Saxony, who claimed Moravia; and with the king of Pruſſia, who was in poſſeſſion of Sileſia.

Such was the ſtate of the queen of Hungary, preſſed on every ſide, and on every ſide preparing for reſiſtance, ſhe yet refuſed all offers of accommodation, for every prince ſet peace at a price which ſhe was not yet ſo far humbled as to pay.

The king of Pruſſia was among the moſt zealous and forward in the confederacy againſt her. He promiſed to ſecure Bohemia to the emperor, and Moravia to the Elector of Saxony, and finding no enemy in the field able to reſiſt him, he returned to Berlin, and left Schwerin his general to proſecute the conqueſt.

The Pruſſians in the midſt of winter took Olmutz the capital of Moravia, and laid the whole country under contribution. The cold then hindred them from action, and they only blocked up the fortreſſes of Brinn and Spielberg.

In the ſpring the king of Pruſſia came again into the field, and undertook the ſiege of Brinn, but upon the approach of prince Charles of Lorrain retired from before it, and quitted Moravia, leaving only a garriſon in the capital.

The condition of the queen of Hungary was now changed. She was a few months before without money, without troops, incircled with enemies. The Bavarians had entered Auſtria, Vienna was threatened with a ſiege, and the queen left it to the fate of war, and retired into Hungary, where ſhe was received with zeal and affection, not unmingled however with that neglect which muſt always be born by greatneſs in diſtreſs. She bore the diſreſpect of her ſubjects with the ſame firmneſs as

the

the outrages of her enemies; and at laſt perſuaded the Engliſh not to deſpair of her preſervation by not deſpairing herſelf.

Voltaire in his late hiſtory has aſſerted that a large ſum was raiſed for her ſuccour by voluntary ſubſcriptions of the Engliſh ladies. It is the great failing of a ſtrong imagination to catch greedily at wonders. He was miſinformed, and was perhaps unwilling to learn by a ſecond enquiry, a truth leſs ſplendid and amuſing. A contribution was by news - writers upon their own authority, fruitleſly, and, I think, illegally propoſed. It ended in nothing. The parliament voted a ſupply, and five hundred thouſand pounds were remitted to her.

It has been always the weakneſs of the Auſtrian family to ſpend in the magnificence of empire thoſe revenues which ſhould be kept for its defence. The court is ſplendid, but the treaſury is empty, and at the beginning of every war advantages are gained againſt them, before their armies can be aſſembled and equipped.

The Engliſh money was to the Auſtrians as a ſhower to a field where all the vegetative powers are kept unactive by a long continuance of drowth. The armies which had hitherto been hid in mountains and foreſts ſtarted out of their retreats, and wherever the queen's ſtandard was erected, nations ſcarcely known by their names ſwarmed immediately about it. An army, eſpecially a defenſive army, multiplies itſelf. The contagion of enterprize ſpreads from one heart to another. Zeal for a native or deteſtation of a foreign ſovereign, hope of ſudden greatneſs or riches, friendſhip or emulation between particular men, or what are perhaps more general and powerful, deſire of novelty and impatience of inactivity fill a camp with adventurers, add rank to rank, and ſquadron to ſquadron.

The queen had ſtill enemies on every part, but ſhe now on every part had armies ready to oppoſe them. Auſtria was immediately recovered, the plains of Bohemia were filled with her troops, though the fortreſſes were garriſoned by the French. The Bavarians were recalled to the defence of their own country, now waſted by the incurſion of troops that were called barbarians, greedy enough of plunder, and daring perhaps beyond the rules of war, but otherwiſe not more cruel than thoſe whom they attacked. Prince *Loblowitz* with one army obſerved the motions of Broglio the French general in Bohemia,

and prince Charles with another put a ſtop to the advances of the king of Pruſſia.

It was now the turn of the Pruſſians to retire, they abandoned Olmutz, and left behind them part of their cannon and their magazines. And the king finding that Broglio could not long oppoſe prince Lobkowitz, haſtened into Bohemia to his aſſiſtance, and having received a reinforcement of twenty three thouſand men, and taken the caſtle of Glatz, which being built upon a rock ſcarcely acceſſible would have defied all his power had the garriſon been furniſhed with proviſions, he purpoſed to join his allies and proſecute his conqueſts.

Prince Charles ſeeing Moravia thus evacuated by the Pruſſians, determined to garriſon the towns which he had juſt recovered, and purſue the enemy, who by the aſſiſtance of the French would have been too powerful for Prince Lobkowitz.

Succeſs had now given confidence to the Auſtrians, and had proportionably abated the ſpirit of their enemies. The Saxons who had co-operated with the king of Pruſſia in the conqueſt of Moravia, of which they expected the perpetual poſſeſſion, ſeeing all hopes of ſudden acquiſition defeated, and the province left again to its former maſters, grew weary of following a prince, whom they conſidered as no longer acting the part of their confederate, and when they approached the confines of Bohemia took a different road, and left the Pruſſians to their own fortune.

The king continued his march, and Charles his purſuit. At Czaſlaw the two armies came in ſight of one another, and the Auſtrians reſolved on a deciſive day. On the 6th of May about ſeven in the morning, the Auſtrians began the attack, their impetuoſity was matched by the firmneſs of the Pruſſians. The animoſity of the two armies was much inflamed, the Auſtrians were fighting for their country, and the Pruſſians were in a place where defeat muſt inevitably end in death or captivity. The fury of the battle continued four hours, the Pruſſian horſe were at length broken, and the Auſtrians forced their way to the camp, where the wild troops who had fought with ſo much vigour and conſtancy, at the firſt of plunder forgot their obedience, nor had any man the leaſt thought but how to load himſelf with the richeſt ſpoils.

While the right wing of the Auſtrians was thus employed, the main body was left naked, the Pruſſians recovered from their con-

confuſion and regained the day. Charles was at laſt forced to retire, and carried with him the ſtandards of his enemies, the proofs of a victory which, though ſo nearly gained, he had not been able to keep.

The victory however was dearly bought, the Pruſſian army was much weakened, and the cavalry almoſt totally deſtroyed. Peace is eaſily made when it is neceſſary to both parties, and the king of Pruſſia had now reaſon to believe that the Auſtrians were not his only enemies. When he found Charles advancing he ſent to Broglio for aſſiſtance, and was anſwered that, ' he muſt have orders from Verſailles,' ſuch a deſertion of his moſt powerful ally diſconcerted him, but the battle was unavoidable.

When the Pruſſians were returned to their camp, the king hearing that an Auſtrian officer was brought in mortally wounded, had the condeſcenſion to viſit him. The Officer ſtruck with this act of humanity ſaid, after a ſhort converſation, ' I ' ſhould die, Sir, contentedly after this ' honour, if I might firſt ſhow my grati- ' tude to your majeſty by informing you ' with what allies you are now united, ' allies that have no intention but to de- ' ceive you.' The king appearing to ſuſ- pect this intelligence. ' Sir, (ſaid the ' Auſtrian) if you will permit me to ſend ' a meſſenger to Vienna, I believe the ' queen will not refuſe to tranſmit an ' intercepted letter now in her hands, which ' will put my report beyond all doubt.'

The meſſenger was ſent, and the letter tranſmitted, which contained the order ſent to Broglio, who was 1ſt, forbidden, To mix his troops on any occaſion with the Pruſſians. 2d, He was ordered to act al- ways at a diſtance from the king. 3d, To keep always a body of twenty thouſand men to obſerve the Pruſſian army. 4th, To obſerve very cloſely the motions of the king for important reaſons. 5th, To hazard nothing, but to pretend want of re-in- forcements, or the abſence of Belliſle.'

The king now with great reaſon con- ſidered himſelf as diſengaged from the confederacy, being deſerted by the Saxons, and betrayed by the French, he therefore accepted the mediation of king George, and in three weeks after the battle of Czar- ſlaw made peace with the queen of Hun- gary, who granted to him the whole pro- vince of Sileſia, a country of ſuch extent and opulence that he is ſaid to receive from it one third part of his revenues. By one of the articles of this treaty it is ſtipu-

lated, ' That neither ſhould aſſiſt the ene- ' mies of the other.'

The queen of Hungary thus diſentan- gled on one ſide, and ſet free from the moſt formidable of her enemies, ſoon per- ſuaded the Saxons to peace; took poſſeſſion of Bavaria; drove the emperor after all his imaginary conqueſts to the ſhelter of a neutral town, where he was treated as a fugitive; and beſieged the French in Prague, in the city which they had taken from her.

Having thus obtained Sileſia the king of Pruſſia returned to his own capital, where he reformed his laws, forbid the torture of criminals, concluded a defenſive alliance with England, and applied himſelf to the augmentation of his army.

This treaty of peace with the queen of Hungary was one of the firſt proofs given by the king of Pruſſia of the ſecrecy of his counſels. Belliſle the French general was with him in the camp as a friend and co- adjutor in appearance, but in truth a ſpy, and a writer of intelligence. Men who have great confidence in their own pene- tration, are often by that confidence de- ceived, they imagine that they can pierce thro' all the involutions of intrigue without the diligence neceſſary to weaker minds, and therefore ſit idle and ſecure; they believe that none can hope to deceive them, and therefore that none will try. Belliſle with all his reputation of ſagacity, though he was in the Pruſſian camp, gave every day freſh aſſurances of the king's adherence to the allies, while Broglio who commanded the army at a diſtance, diſcovered ſuffi- cient reaſons to ſuſpect his deſertion. Brog- lio was ſlighted and Belliſle believed, till on the 11th of June the treaty was ſigned, and the king declared his reſolution to keep a neutrality.

This is one of the great performances of polity which mankind ſeem agreed to celebrate and admire, yet to all this no- thing was neceſſary but the determination of a very few men to be ſilent.

From this time the queen of Hungary proceded with an uninterrupted torrent of ſucceſs, the French driven from ſtation to ſtation, and deprived of fortreſs after for- treſs, were at laſt encloſed with their two generals Belliſle and Broglio in the walls of Prague, which they had ſtored with all proviſions neceſſary to a town beſieged, and where they defended themſelves three months before any proſpect appeared of relief.

The Auſtrians having been engaged chiefly

chiefly in the field, and in ſudden and tumultuary excurſion rather than a regular war, had no great degree of ſkill in attacking or defending towns. They likewiſe would naturally conſider all the miſchiefs done to the city, as falling ultimately on themſelves, and therefore were willing to gain it by time rather than by force.

It was apparent that how long ſoever Prague might be defended, it muſt be yielded at laſt, and therefore all arts were tried to obtain an honourable capitulation. The meſſengers from the city were ſent back ſometimes unheard, but always with this anſwer, that no terms would be allowed, but that they ſhould yield themſelves priſoners of war.

The condition of the garriſon was in the eyes of all Europe deſperate, but the French, to whom the praiſe of ſpirit and activity cannot be denied, reſolved to make an effort for the honour of their arms. Maillebois was at that time encamped with his army in Weſtphalia. Orders were ſent him to relieve Prague. The enterpriſe was conſidered as romantic. Maillebois was a march of forty days diſtant from Bohemia, the paſſes were narrow, and the ways foul; and it was likely that Prague would be taken before he could reach it. The march was, however, begun, the army being joined by that of count Saxe conſiſted of fifty thouſand men, who, notwithſtanding all the difficulties which two Auſtrian armies could put in their way, at laſt entered Bohemia. The ſiege of Prague though not raiſed, was remitted, and a communication was now opened to it with the country. But the Auſtrians, by perpetual intervention, hindered the garriſon from joining their friends. The officers of Maillebois incited him to a battle, becauſe the army was hourly leſſening by the want of proviſions, but inſtead of preſſing on to Prague, he retired into Bavaria, and completed the ruin of the emperor's territories.

The court of France diſappointed and offended, conferred the chief command upon Broglio, who eſcaped from the beſiegers with very little difficulty, and kept the Auſtrians employed till Belliſle by a ſudden ſally quitted Prague, and without any great loſs joined the main army. Broglio then retired over the Rhine into the French dominions, waſting in his retreat the country which he had undertaken to protect, and burning towns and deſtroying magazines of corn with ſuch wantonneſs as gave reaſon to believe that he expected

commendation from his court for any miſchiefs done by whatever means.

The Auſtrians purſued their advantages, recovered all their ſtrong places, in ſome of which French garriſons had been left, and made themſelves maſters of Bavaria, by taking not only Munich the capital, but Ingolſtadt the ſtrongeſt fortification in the elector's dominions, where they found a great number of cannon and quantity of ammunition intended in the dreams of projected greatneſs for the ſiege of Vienna, all the archives of the ſtate, the plate and ornaments of the electoral palace, and what had been conſidered as moſt worthy of preſervation. Nothing but the warlike ſtores was taken away. An oath of allegiance to the queen was required of the Bavarians, but without any explanation whether temporary or perpetual.

The emperor lived at Francfort in the ſecurity that was allowed to neutral places, but without much reſpect from the German princes, except that upon ſome objections made by the queen to the validity of his election, the king of Pruſſia declared himſelf determined to ſupport him in the Imperial dignity with all his power.

This might be conſidered as a token of no great affection to the queen of Hungary, but it ſeems not to have raiſed much alarm. The German princes were afraid of new broils. To conteſt the election of an emperor once inveſted and acknowledged, would be to overthrow the whole Germanic conſtitution. Perhaps no election by plurality of ſuffrages was ever made among human beings, to which it might not be objected that voices were procured by illicit influence.

Some ſuſpicions, however, were raiſed by the king's declaration, which he endeavoured to obviate by ordering his miniſters to declare at London and at Vienna, that he was reſolved not to violate the treaty of Breſlaw. This declaration was ſufficiently ambiguous, and could not ſatisfy thoſe whom it might ſilence. But this was not a time for nice diſquiſitions, to diſtruſt the king of Pruſſia might have provoked him, and it was moſt convenient to conſider him as a friend, till he appeared openly as an enemy.

About the middle of the year 1744, he raiſed new alarms by collecting his troops and putting them in motion. The earl of Hindford about this time demanded the troops ſtipulated for the pro-
tection

tection of Hanover, not perhaps becauſe they were thought neceſſary, but that the king's deſigns might be gueſſed from his anſwer, which was, that troops were not granted for the defence of any country till that country was in danger, and that he could not believe the elector of Hanover to be in much dread of an invaſion, ſince he had withdrawn the native troops and put them into the pay of England.

He had, undoubtedly, now formed deſigns which made it neceſſary that his troops ſhould be kept together, and the time ſoon came when the ſcene was to be opened. Prince Charles of Lorrain having chaſed the French out of Bavaria, lay for ſome months encamped on the Rhine, endeavouring to gain a paſſage into Alſace. His attempts had long been evaded by the ſkill and vigilance of the French general, till at laſt, June 21, 1744, he executed his deſign, and lodged his army in the French dominions, to the ſurpriſe and joy of a great part of Europe. It was now expected that the territories of France would in their turn feel the miſeries of war, and the nation which ſo long kept the world in alarm, be taught at laſt the value of peace.

The king of Pruſſia now ſaw the Auſtrian troops at a great diſtance from him, engaged in a foreign country againſt the moſt powerful of all their enemies. Now, therefore, was the time to diſcover that he had lately made a treaty at Francfort with the emperor, by which he had engaged, 'that as the court of Vienna and 'its allies appeared backward to re-eſta- 'bliſh the tranquillity of the empire 'and more cogent methods appeared ne- 'ceſſary, he, being animated with a deſire 'of co-operating towards the pacification of 'Germany, ſhould make an expedition for 'the conqueſt of Bohemia, and to put it 'into the poſſeſſion of the emperor, his 'heirs and ſucceſſors for ever, in gratitude 'for which, the emperor ſhould reſign to 'him and his ſucceſſors, a certain num- 'ber of lordſhips, which are now part of 'the kingdom of Bohemia. His Impe- 'rial majeſty likewiſe guaranties to the 'king of Pruſſia the perpetual poſſeſſion 'of upper Sileſia, and the king guaran- 'ties to the emperor the perpetual poſſeſſion 'of upper Auſtria, as ſoon as he ſhall 'have occupied it by conqueſt.'

It is eaſy to diſcover that the king began the war upon other motives than zeal for peace, and that whatever reſpect he was willing to ſhew to the emperor,

he did not purpoſe to aſſiſt him without reward. In proſecution of this treaty he put his troops in motion, and according to his promiſe, while the Auſtrians were invading France, he invaded Bohemia.

Princes have this remaining of humanity, that they think themſelves obliged not to make war without a reaſon. Their reaſons are indeed not always very ſatisfactory. Lewis XIV. ſeemed to think his own glory a ſufficient motive for the invaſion of Holland. The Czar attacked Charles of Sweden, becauſe he had not been treated with ſufficient reſpect when he made a journey in diſguiſe. The king of Pruſſia having an opportunity of attacking his neighbour, was not long without his reaſons. On July 30, he publiſhed his declaration, in which he declares;

That he can no longer ſtand an idle ſpectator of the troubles in Germany, but finds himſelf obliged to make uſe of force to reſtore the power of the laws, and the authority of the emperor.

That the queen of Hungary has treated the emperor's hereditary dominions with inexpreſſible cruelty.

That Germany has been overrun with foreign troops, which have marched thro' neutral countries without the cuſtomary requiſitions.

That the emperor's troops have been attacked under neutral fortreſſes, and obliged to abandon the empire, of which their maſter is the head.

That the Imperial dignity has been treated with indecency by the Hungarian troops.

The queen declaring the election of the emperor void, and the diet of Francfort illegal, had not only violated the imperial dignity, but injured all the princes who have the right of election.

That he has no particular quarrel with the queen of Hungary, and that he deſires nothing for himſelf, and only enters as an auxiliary into a war for the liberties of Germany.

That the emperor had offered to quit his pretenſion to the dominions of Auſtria, on condition that his hereditary countries be reſtored to him.

That this propoſal had been made to the king of England at Hanau, and rejected in ſuch a manner as ſhewed that the king of England had no intention to reſtore peace, but rather to make his advantage of the troubles.

That

That the mediation of the Dutch had been deſired, but that they declined to interpoſe, knowing the inflexibility of the Engliſh and Auſtrian courts.

That the ſame terms were again offer'd at Vienna, and again rejected, that therefore the queen muſt impute it to her own council that her enemies find new allies.

That he is not fighting for any intereſt of his own, that he demands nothing for himſelf, but is determined to exert all his power in defence of the Emperor in vindication of the right of election, and in ſupport of the liberties of Germany which the Queen of Hungary would enſlave.

When this declaration was ſent to the Pruſſian miniſter in England, it was accompanied with a remonſtrance to the King, in which many of the foregoing poſitions were repeated, the Emperor's candour and diſintereſtedneſs were magnified; the dangerous deſigns of the Auſtrians were diſplayed; it was imputed to them as the moſt flagrant violation of the Germanick conſtitution, that they had driven the emperor's troops out of the empire; the public ſpirit and generoſity of his Pruſſian majeſty were again hardily declared; and it was ſaid that this quarrel having no connection with Engliſh intereſts, the Engliſh ought not to interpoſe.

Auſtria and all her allies were put into amazement by this declaration, which at once diſmounted them from the ſummit of ſucceſs, and obliged them to fight through the war a ſecond time. What ſuccours, or what promiſes Pruſſia received from France was never publicly known, but it is not to be doubted, that a prince ſo watchful of opportunity ſold aſſiſtance when it was ſo much wanted at the higheſt rate; nor can it be ſuppoſed that he expoſed himſelf to ſo much hazard only for the freedom of Germany, and a few petty diſtricts in Bohemia.

The French, who from ravaging the empire at diſcretion, and waſting whatever they found, either among enemies or friends, were now driven into their own dominions, and in their own dominions were inſulted and purſued, were on a ſudden by this new auxiliary reſtored to their former ſuperiority, at leaſt were diſburthened of their invaders, and delivered from their terrors. And all the enemies of the houſe of Bourbon ſaw with indignation and amazement the recovery of that power which they had with ſo much coſt and bloodſhed brought low, and which their animoſity and elation had diſpoſed them to imagine yet lower than it was.

The Queen of Hungary ſtill retained her firmneſs. The Pruſſian declaration was not long without an anſwer, which was tranſmitted to the European Princes with ſome obſervations on the Pruſſian miniſter's remonſtrance to the court of Vienna, which he was ordered by his maſter to read to the Auſtrian council, but not to deliver. The ſame caution was practiſed before when the Pruſſians after the Emperor's death invaded Sileſia. This artifice of political debate may, perhaps, be numbered by the admirers of greatneſs among the refinements of conduct, but as it is a method of proceeding not very difficult to be contrived or practiſed, as it can be of very rare uſe to honeſty or wiſdom, and as it has been long known to that claſs of men whoſe ſafety depends upon ſecreſy, though hitherto applied chiefly in petty cheats and ſlight tranſactions, I do not ſee that it can much advance the reputation of regal underſtanding, or indeed that it can add more to the ſafety than it takes away from the honour of him that ſhall adopt it.

The Queen in her anſwer, after charging the King of Pruſſia with breach of the treaty of Breſlaw, and obſerving how much her enemies will exult to ſee the peace now the third time broken by him, declares,

That ſhe had no intention to injure the rights of the electors, and that ſhe calls in queſtion not the event but the manner of the election.

That ſhe had ſpared the Emperor's troops with great tenderneſs, and that they were driven out of the empire only becauſe they were in the ſervice of France.

That ſhe is ſo far from diſturbing the peace of the empire, that the only commotions now raiſed in it, are the effect of the armaments of the King of Pruſſia.

Nothing is more tedious than public records when they relate to affairs which by diſtance of time or place loſe their power to intereſt the reader. Every thing grows little, as it grows remote, and of things thus diminiſhed it is ſufficient to ſurvey the aggregate without a minute examination of the parts.

(To be continued.)

THE
LITERARY MAGAZINE.
NUMB. IX.

From *December* 15, to *January* 15, 1757.

Life of the King of Pruſſia *continued from* p. 390, *and concluded.*

IT is eaſy to perceive that if the king of Pruſſia's reaſons be iufficient; ambition or animoſity can never want a plea for violence and invaſion. What he charges upon the queen of Hungary, the waſte of countries, the expulſion of the Bavarians, and the employment of foreign troops, is the unavoidable conſequence of a war inflamed on either ſide to the utmoſt violence. All theſe grievances ſubſiſted when he made the peace, and therefore they could very little juſtify its breach.

It is true that every prince of the empire is obliged to ſupport the imperial dignity, and aſſiſt the emperor when his rights are violated. And every ſubſequent contract muſt be underſtood in a ſenſe conſiſtent with former obligations, nor had the king power to make a peace on terms contrary to that conſtitution by which he held a place among the Germanic electors. But he could have eaſily diſcovered that not the emperor but the duke of Bavaria was the queen's enemy, not the adminiſtrator of the imperial power, but the claimant of the Auſtrian dominions. Nor did his allegiance to the emperor, ſuppoſing the emperor injured, oblige him to more than a ſuccour of ten thouſand men. But 10,000 men could not conquer Bohemia, and without the conqueſt of Bohe-

mia he could receive no reward for the zeal and fidelity, which he ſo loudly profeſſed.

The ſucceſs of this enterpriſe he had taken all poſſible precaution to ſecure. He was to invade a country guarded only by the faith of treaties, and therefore left unarmed, and unprovided of all defence. He had engaged the *French* to attack Prince *Charles* before he ſhould re-paſs the *Rhine*, by which the *Auſtrian* would at leaſt have been hindred from a ſpeedy march into *Bohemia*, they were likewiſe to yield him ſuch other aſſiſtance as he might want.

Relying therefore upon the promiſes of the *French*, he reſolved to attempt the ruin of the houſe of *Auſtria*, and in *Auguſt* 1744, broke into *Bohemia* at the head of an hundred and four thouſand men. When he entered the country he publiſhed a proclamation promiſing, That his army ſhould obſerve the ſtricteſt diſcipline, and that thoſe who made no reſiſtance ſhould be ſuffered to remain at quiet in their habitations. He required that all arms, in the cuſtody of whomſoever they might be placed, ſhould be given up, and put into the hands of public officers. He ſtill declared himſelf to act only as an auxiliary to the emperor, and with no other deſign than to eſtabliſh peace and tranquillity throughout *Germany* his dear country.

In this proclamation there is one paragraph of which I do not remember any precedent. He threatens that if any peaſant ſhall be found with arms he ſhall be hanged

VOL. I.

without

without further enquiry, and that if any lord fhall connive at his vaffals keeping arms in their cuftody, his village fhall be reduced to afhes.

It is hard to find upon what pretence the king of *Pruffia* could treat the *Bohemians* as criminals, for preparing to defend their native country, or maintain their allegiance to their lawful fovereign againft an invader, whether he appears principal or auxiliary, whether he profeffes to intend tranquillity or confufion.

His progrefs was fuch as gave great hopes to the enemies of *Auftria*; like *CÆSAR* he conquered as he advanced, and met with no oppofition till he reached the walls of *Prague*. The indignation and refentment of the queen of *Hungary* may be eafily conceived; the alliance of *Frankfort* was now laid open to all *Europe*, and the partition of the *Auftrian* dominions was again publicly projected. They were to be fhared among the emperor, the king of *Pruffia*, the elector palatine, and the landgrave of *Heffe*. All the powers of *Europe* who had dreamed of controling *France*, were awakened to their former terrors, all that had been done was now to be done again, and every court from the ftraits of *Gibraltar*, to the *Frozen Sea*, was filled with exultation or terror, with fchemes of conqueft or precautions for defence.

The king delighted with his progrefs, and expecting like other mortals, elated with fuccefs, that his profperity could not be interrupted, continued his march, and began in the latter end of *September* the fiege of *Prague*. He had gained feveral of the outer pofts, when he was informed that the convoy which attended his artillery was attacked by an unexpected party of the *Auftrians*. The king immediately went to their affiftance with the third part of his army, and found his troops put to flight, and the *Auftrians* hafting away with his cannons; fuch a lofs would have difabled him at once. He fell upon the *Auftrians* whofe number would not enable them to withftand him, recovered his artillery, and having alfo defeated *Bathicni* raifed his batteries, and there being no artillery to be played againft him, he deftroyed a great part of the city. He then ordered four attacks to be made at once, and reduced the befieged to fuch extremities that in fourteen days, the governor was obliged to yield the place.

At the attack commanded by *Schverin*,

a grenadier is reported to have mounted the baftion alone, and to have defended himfelf for fome time with his fword, till his followers mounted after him; for this act of bravery the king made him a lieutenant, and gave him a patent of nobility.

Nothing now remained but that the *Auftrians* fhould lay afide all thought of invading *France*, and apply their whole power to their own defence. Prince *Charles* at the firft news of the *Pruffian* invafion prepared to re-pafs the *Rhine*. This the *French*, according to their contract with the king of *Pruffia*, fhould have attempted to hinder, but they knew by experience that the *Auftrians* would not be beaten without refiftance, and that refiftance always incommodes an affailant. As the king of *Pruffia* rejoiced in the diftance of the *Auftrians* whom he confidered as entangled in the *French* territories; the *French* rejoiced in the neceffity of their return, and pleafed themfelves with the profpect of eafy conquefts while powers whom they confidered with equal malevolence fhould be employed in maffacring each other.

Prince *Charles* took the opportunity of bright moonfhine to repafs the *Rhine*, and *Noailles*, who had early intelligence of his motions, gave him very little difturbance, but contented himfelf with attacking the rear-guard, and when they retired to the main body ceafed his purfuit.

The king upon the reduction of *Prague* ftruck a medal, which had on one fide a plan of the town, with this infcription;

Prague taken by the king of Pruffia,
September 16, 1744;
For the third time in three years.

On the other fide were two verfes in which he prayed, *That his conquefts might produce peace.* He then marched forward with the rapidity which conftitutes his military character, took poffeffion of almoft all *Bohemia*, and began to talk of entering *Auftria* and befieging *Vienna*.

The queen was not yet wholly without refource. The elector of *Saxony*, whether invited or not, was not comprifed in the union of *Frankfort*, and as every fovereign is growing lefs as his next neighbour is growing greater, he could not heartily wifh fuccefs to a confederacy which was to aggrandize the other powers of *Germany*. The *Pruffians* gave him likewife a particular and immediate provocation to oppofe them, for when they departed to the conqueft of *Bohemia*, with all the elation
of

of imaginary fuccefs, they paffed through his dominions with unlicenfed and contemptuous difdain of his authority. As the approach of Prince *Charles* gave a new profpect of events, he was eafily perfuaded to enter into an alliance with the queen, whom he furnifhed with a very large body of troops.

The king of *Pruffia* having left a garrifon in *Prague,* which he commanded to put the burghers to death, if they left their houfes in the night, went forward to take the other towns and fortreffes, expecting perhaps that prince *Charles* would be interrupted in his march; but the *French* though they appeared to follow him either could not, or would not overtake him.

In a fhort time by marches preffed on with the utmoft eagernefs, *Charles* reached *Bohemia,* leaving the *Bavarians* to regain the poffeffion of the wafted plains of their country, which their enemies who ftill kept the ftrong places might again feize at will. At the approach of the *Auftrian* army the courage of the king of *Pruffia* feemed to have failed him. He retired from poft to poft, and evacuated town after town, and fortrefs after fortrefs, without refiftance, or appearance of refiftance, as if he was refigning them to the rightful owners.

It might have been expected that he fhould have made fome effort to fecure *Prague,* but after a faint attempt to difpute the paffage of the *Elbe,* he ordered his garrifon of eleven thoufand men to quit the place. They left behind them their magazines, and heavy artillery, among which were feven pieces of remarkable excellence, called the *Seven Electors.* But they took with them their field cannon and a great number of carriages laden with ftores and plunder, which they were forced to leave in their way to the *Saxons* and *Auftrians,* that harraffed their march. They at laft entered *Silefia* with the lofs of about a third part.

The king of *Pruffia* fuffered much in his retreat, for befides the military ftores, which he left every where behind him, even to the cloaths of his troops, there was a want of provifions in his army and confequently frequent defertions and many difeafes, and a foldier fick and killed was equally loft to a flying army.

At laft he re-entered his own territories, and having ftationed his troops in places of fecurity, returned for a time to *Berlin,* where he forbad all to fpeak either ill or well of the campaign.

To what end fuch a prohibition could conduce, it is difficult to difcover, there is no country in which men can be forbidden to know what they know, and what is univerfally known may as well be fpoken: It is true that in popular governments feditious difcourfes may inflame the vulgar, but in fuch governments they cannot be reftrained, and in abfolute monarchies they are of little effect.

When the *Pruffians* invaded *Bohemia,* and this whole nation was fired with refentment, the king of *England* gave orders in his palace that none fhould mention his nephew with difrepect; by this command he maintained the decency neceffary between princes, without enforcing and probably without expecting obedience but in his own prefence.

The king of *Pruffia's* edict regarded only himfelf, and therefore it is difficult to tell what was his motive, unlefs he intended to fpare himfelf the mortification of abfurd and illiberal flattery, which to a mind ftung with difgrace, muft have been in the higheft degree painful and difgufting.

Moderation in profperity, is a virtue very difficult to all mortals; forbearance of revenge, when revenge is within reach, is fcarcely ever to be found among princes. Now was the time when the queen of *Hungary* might perhaps have made peace on her own terms, but keennefs of refentment, and arrogance of fuccefs with-held her from the due ufe of the prefent opportunity. It is faid that the king of *Pruffia* in his retreat fent letters to prince *Charles,* which were fuppofed to contain ample conceffions, but were fent back unopened. The king of *England* offered likewife to mediate between them, but his propofitions were rejected at *Vienna,* where a refolution was taken not only to revenge the interruption of their fuccefs on the *Rhine* by the recovery of *Silefia,* but to reward the *Saxons* for their feafonable help by giving them part of the *Pruffian* dominions.

In the beginning of the year 1745 died the emperor *Charles* of *Bavaria,* the treaty of *Frankfort* was confequently at an end, and the king of *Pruffia* being no longer able to maintain the character of auxiliary to the emperor, and having avowed no other reafon for the war might have honourably withdrawn his forces, and on his own principles have complied with terms of peace: But no terms were offered him; the queen purfued him with the utmoft ardour of hoftility, and

M m m 2

the

the *French* left him to his own conduct, and his own destiny.

His *Bohemian* conquests were already loft, and he was now chased back into *Silesia*, where at the beginning of the year the war continued in an equilibration by alternate losses and advantages. In *April* the elector of *Bavaria* seeing his dominions overrun by the *Austrians*, and receiving very little succour from the *French*, made a peace with the queen of *Hungary* upon easy conditions, and the *Austrians* had more troops to employ against *Prussia*.

But the revolutions of war will not suffer human presumption to remain long unchecked. The peace with *Bavaria* was scarcely concluded when the battle of *Fontenoy* was loft, and all the allies of *Austria* called upon her to exert her utmost power for the preservation of the low countries, and a few days after the loss at *Fontenoy*, the first battle between the *Prussians* and the combined army of *Austrians* and *Saxons* was fought at *Niedburg* in *Silesia*.

The particulars of this battle were variously reported by the different parties, and published in the journals of that time; to transcribe them would be tedious and useless, because accounts of battles are not easily understood, and because there are no means of determining to which of the relations credit should be given. It is sufficient that they all end in claiming or allowing a complete victory to the king of *Prussia*, who gained all the *Austrian* artillery, killed four thousand, took seven thousand prisoners, with the loss, according to the *Prussian* narrative, of only sixteen hundred men.

He now advanced again into *Bohemia*, where, however, he made no great progress. The queen of *Hungary* though defeated was not subdued. She poured in her troops from all parts to the reinforcement of prince *Charles*, and determined to continue the struggle with all her power. The king saw that *Bohemia* was an unpleasing and inconvenient theatre of war, in which he should be ruined by a miscarriage, and should get little by a victory. *Saxony* was left defenceless, and if it was conquered might be plundered.

He therefore published a declaration against the elector of *Saxony*, and without waiting for reply, invaded his dominions. This invasion produced another battle at *Standentz*, which ended, as the former, to the advantage of the *Prussians*. The *Austrians* had some advantage in the beginning, and their irregular troops, who

are always daring and always ravenous broke into the *Prussian* camp, and carried away the military cheft. But this was easily repaired by the spoils of *Saxony*.

The queen of *Hungary* was still inflexible, and hoped that fortune would at last change. She recruited once more her army, and prepared to invade the territories of *Brandenburg*, but the king of *Prussia's* activity prevented all her designs. One part of his forces seized *Leipsic* and the other once more defeated the *Saxons*; the king of *Poland* fled from his dominions, prince *Charles* retired into *Bohemia*. The king of *Prussia* entered *Dresden* as a conqueror, exacted very severe contributions from the whole country, and the *Austrians* and *Saxons* were at last compelled to receive from him such a peace as he would grant. He imposed no severe conditions except the payment of the contributions, made no new claim of dominions, and, with the elector *Palatine*, acknowledged the duke of *Tuscany* for emperor.

The lives of princes, like the histories of nations, have their periods. We shall here suspend our narrative of the king of *Prussia*, who was now at the height of human greatness, giving laws to his enemies, and courted by all the powers of *Europe*. What will be the event of the present war it is yet too early to predict; his enemies are powerful, but we have seen those enemies once conquered, and there is no great reason to imagine that the confederacy against him will last long.

493

THE

ENGLISH WORKS

O F

ROGER ASCHAM,

PRECEPTOR to QUEEN ELIZABETH:

CONTAINING,

I. A REPORT of the AFFAIRS of GERMANY, and the Emperor CHARLES'S COURT.

II. TOXOPHILUS, or the SCHOOL of SHOOTING.

III. The SCHOOLMASTER, or perfect Way of bringing up Youth, illuftrated by the late learned Mr. UPTON.

IV. LETTERS to Queen ELIZABETH and others, now firft publifhed from the Manufcripts.

With NOTES and OBSERVATIONS, and the AUTHOR'S LIFE.

By JAMES BENNET,

Mafter of the Boarding-School at HODDESDON in HERTFORDSHIRE.

LONDON:

Printed for R. and J. DODSLEY, in Pall-Mall, and J. NEWBERY, in St. Paul's Church-Yard.
M, DCC, LXI.

THE

L I F E

O F

R O G E R   A S C H A M.

IT often happens to writers, that they are known only by their
works; the incidents of a literary life are feldom obferved, and
therefore feldom recounted ; but *Afcham* has efcaped the common
fate by the friendfhip of *Edward Graunt,* the learned mafter of *Weftminfter* fchool, who devoted an oration to his memory, and has marked the
various viciffitudes of his fortune. *Graunt* either avoided the labour of
minute inquiry, or thought domeftick occurrences unworthy of his notice ; or preferring the character of an orator to that of an hiftorian,
felected only fuch particulars as he could beft exprefs, or moft happily
embellifh. His narrative is therefore fcanty, and I know not by what
materials it can now be amplified.

Roger Afcham was born in the year **1515**, at *Kirby Wifke,* (or *Kirby
Wicke)* a village near *Northallerton* in *Yorkfhire,* of a family above the
vulgar. His father *John Afcham* was houfe-fteward in the family of
Scroop, and in that age, when the different orders of men were at a
greater diftance from each other, and the manners of gentlemen were
regularly formed by menial fervices in great houfes, lived with a very
confpicuous reputation. *Margaret Afcham,* his wife, is faid to have

b

been

497

been allied to many confiderable families, but her maiden name is not recorded. She had three fons, of whom *Roger* was the youngeft, and fome daughters; but who can hope, that of any progeny more than one fhall deferve to be mentioned? They lived married fixty-feven years, and at laft died together almoft on the fame hour of the fame day.

Roger having paffed his firft years under the care of his parents, was adopted into the family of *Antony Wingfield*, who maintained him, and committed his education, with that of his own fons, to the care of one *Bond*, a domeftick tutor. He very early difcovered an unufual fondnefs for literature by an eager perufal of *Englifh* books, and having paffed happily through the fcholaftick rudiments, was put, in 1530, by his patron *Wingfield*, to St. *John*'s college in *Cambridge*.

Afcham entered *Cambridge* at a time when the laft great revolution of the intellectual world was filling every academical mind with ardour or anxiety. The deftruction of the *Conftantinopolitan* empire had driven the *Greeks* with their language into the interiour parts of *Europe*, the art of printing had made the books eafily attainable, and *Greek* now began to be taught in *England*. The doctrines of *Luther* had already filled all the nations of the *Romifh* communion with controverfy and diffention. New ftudies of literature, and new tenets of religion, found employment for all who were defirous of truth, or ambitious of fame. Learning was at that time profecuted with that eagernefs and perfeverance which in this age of indifference and diffipation it is not eafy to conceive. To teach or to learn was at once the bufinefs and the pleafure of the academical life; and an emulation of ftudy was raifed by *Cheke* and *Smith*, to which even the prefent age perhaps owes many advantages, without remembering or knowing its benefactors.

Afcham foon refolved to unite himfelf to thofe who were enlarging the bounds of knowledge, and immediately upon his admiffion into the college, applied himfelf to the ftudy of *Greek*. Thofe who were zealous for the new learning, were often no great friends to the old religion; and *Afcham*, as he became a *Grecian*, became a proteftant. The re-formation was not yet begun, difaffection to popery was confidered as a crime juftly punifhed by exclufion from favour and preferment, and

498

and was not yet openly profeſſed, though ſuperſtition was gradually loſ-ing its hold upon the publick. The ſtudy of *Greek* was reputable enough, and *Aſcham* perſued it with diligence and ſucceſs equally con-ſpicuous. He thought a language might be moſt eaſily learned by teach-ing it; and when he had obtained ſome proficiency in *Greek*, read lec-tures, while he was yet a boy, to other boys who were deſirous of in-ſtruction. His induſtry was much encouraged by *Pember*, a man of great eminence at that time, though I know not that he has left any monuments behind him, but what the gratitude of his friends and ſcho-lars has beſtowed. He was one of the great encouragers of *Greek* learn-ing, and particularly applauded *Aſcham's* lectures, aſſuring him in a let-ter, of which *Graunt* has preſerved an extract, that he would gain more knowledge by explaining one of *Æſop's* fables to a boy, than by hearing one of *Homer's* poems explained by another.

Aſcham took his bachelor's degree in 1534, *February* 18, in the eigh-teenth year of his age; a time of life at which it is more common now to enter the univerſities than to take degrees, but which, according to the modes of education then in uſe, had nothing of remarkable prema-turity. On the 23d of *March* following, he was choſen fellow of the col-lege; which election he conſidered as a ſecond birth. Dr. *Metcalf*, the maſter of the college, *a man*, as *Aſcham* tells us, *meanly learned himſelf, but no mean encourager of learning in others*, clandeſtinely promoted his election, though he openly ſeemed firſt to oppoſe it, and afterwards to cenſure it, becauſe *Aſcham* was known to favour the new opinions; and the maſter himſelf was accuſed of giving an unjuſt preference to the northern men, one of the factions into which this nation was divided, before we could find any more important reaſon of diſſention, than that ſome were born on the northern and ſome on the ſouthern ſide of *Trent*. Any cauſe is ſufficient for a quarrel, and the zealots of the north and ſouth lived long in ſuch animoſity, that it was thought neceſſary at *Ox-ford* to keep them quiet by chuſing one proctor every year from each.

He ſeems to have been hitherto ſupported by the bounty of *Wingfield*, which his attainment of a fellowſhip now freed him from the neceſſity of receiving. Dependance, though in thoſe days it was more common, and therefore leſs irkſome than in the preſent ſtate of things, can never

b 2   have

have been free from difcontent; and therefore he that was releafed from it muft always have rejoiced. The danger is, left the joy of efcaping from the patron may not leave fufficient memory of the benefactor. Of this forgetfulnefs *Afcham* cannot be accufed; for he is recorded to have preferved the moft grateful and affectionate reverence for *Wingfield*, and to have never grown weary of recounting his benefits.

His reputation ftill increafed, and many reforted to his chamber to hear the *Greek* writers explained. He was likewife eminent for other ac-complifhments. By the advice of *Pember*, he had learned to play on mufical inftruments, and he was one of the few who excelled in the me-chanical art of writing, which then began to be cultivated among us, and in which we now furpafs all other nations. He not only wrote his pages with neatnefs, but embellifhed them with elegant draughts and il-luminations; an art at that time fo highly valued, that it contributed much both to his fame and his fortune.

He became mafter of arts in *March* 1537, in his twenty-firft year; and then, if not before, commenced tutor, and publickly undertook the education of young men. A tutor of one and twenty, however accom-plifhed with learning, however exalted by genius, would now gain little reverence or obedience; but in thofe days of difcipline and regularity, the authority of the ftatutes eafily fupplied that of the teacher; all power that was lawful was reverenced. Befides, young tutors had ftill younger pupils.

Afcham is faid to have courted his fcholars to ftudy by every incite-ment, to have treated them with great kindnefs, and to have taken care at once to inftill learning and piety, to inlighten their minds and to form their manners. Many of his fcholars rofe to great eminence, and among them *William Grindal* was fo much diftinguifhed, that by *Cheke*'s recommendation he was called to court as a proper mafter of languages for the lady *Elizabeth*.

There was yet no eftablifhed lecturer of *Greek*; the univerfity there-fore appointed *Afcham* to read in the open fchools, and paid him out of the publick purfe an honorary ftipend, fuch as was then reckoned fufficiently liberal:

liberal : a lecture was afterwards founded by King *Henry*, and he then quitted the fchools, but continued to explain *Greek* authours in his own college.

He was at firft an opponent of the new pronunciation introduced, or rather of the ancient reftored about this time by *Cheke* and *Smith*, and made fome cautious ftruggles for the common practice, which the credit and dignity of his antagonifts did not permit to defend very publickly, or with much vehemence : nor were they long his antagonifts ; for either his affection for their merit, or his conviction of the cogency of their arguments, foon changed his opinion and his practice, and he adhered ever after to their method of utterance.

Of this controverfy it is not neceffary to give a circumftantial account ; fomething of it may be found in *Strype*'s Life of *Smith*, and fomething in *Baker*'s Reflexions upon learning : it is fufficient to remark here, that *Cheke*'s pronunciation was that which now prevails in the fchools of *England*. Difquifitions not only verbal, but merely literal, are too minute for popular narration.

He was not lefs eminent as a writer of *Latin*, than as a teacher of *Greek*. All the publick letters of the univerfity were of his compofition ; and as little qualifications muft often bring great abilities into notice, he was recommended to this honourable employment not lefs by the neatnefs of his hand, than the elegance of his ftyle.

However great was his learning, he was not always immured in his chamber ; but being valetudinary, and weak of body, thought it neceffary to fpend many hours in fuch exercifes as might beft relieve him after the fatigue of ftudy. His favourite amufement was archery, in which he fpent, or, in the opinion of others, loft fo much time, that thofe whom either his faults or virtues made his enemies, and perhaps fome whofe kindnefs wifhed him always worthily employed, did not fcruple to cenfure his practice, as unfuitable to a man profeffing learning, and perhaps of bad example in a place of education.

To free himfelf from this cenfure was one of the reafons for which he publifhed, in 1544, his *Toxophilus*, or the Schole or Partitions of

I

Shooting,

Shooting, in which he joins the praise with the precepts of archery. He defigned not only to teach the art of fhooting, but to give an example of diction more natural and more truly *Englifh* than was ufed by the common writers of that age, whom he cenfures for mingling exotick terms with their native language, and of whom he complains, that they were made authours not by fkill or education, but by arrogance and temerity.

He has not failed in either of his purpofes. He has fufficiently vindicated archery as an innocent, falutary, ufeful, and liberal diverfion; and if his precepts are of no great ufe, he has only fhown by one example among many, how little the hand can derive from the mind, how little intelligence can conduce to dexterity. In every art practice is much; in arts manual practice is almoft the whole. Precept can at moft but warn againft errour, it can never beftow excellence.

The bow has been fo long difufed, that moft *Englifh* readers have forgotten its importance, though it was the weapon by which we gained the battle of *Agincourt*, a weapon which when handled by *Englifh* yeomen, no foreign troops were able to refift. We were not only abler of body than the *French*, and therefore fuperiour in the ufe of arms, which are forcible only in proportion to the ftrength with which they are handled, but the national practice of fhooting for pleafure or for prizes, by which every man was inured to archery from his infancy, gave us infuperable advantage, the bow requiring more practice to fkilful ufe than any other inftrument of offence.

Fire-arms were then in their infancy; and though battering pieces had been fome time in ufe, I know not whether any foldiers were armed with hand-guns when the *Toxophilus* was firft publifhed: they were foon after ufed by the *Spanifh* troops, whom other nations made hafte to imitate: but how little they could yet effect, will be underftood from the account given by the ingenious authour of the exercife for the *Norfolk* militia.

" The firft mufkets were very heavy, and could not be fired without " a reft; they had match-locks, and barrels of a wide bore, that car-
" ried

" ried a large ball and charge of powder, and did execution at a greater
" diftance.

" The mufketeers on a march carried only their refts and ammuni-
" tion, and had boys to bear their mufkets after them, for which they
" were allowed great additional pay.

" They were very flow in loading, not only by reafon of the un-
" wieldinefs of the pieces, and becaufe they carried the powder and
" balls feparate, but from the time it took to prepare and adjuft the
" match ; fo that their fire was not near fo brifk as ours is now. Af-
" terwards a lighter kind of match-lock mufket came into ufe, and they
" carried their ammunition in bandeliers, which were broad belts that
" came over the fhoulder, to which were hung feveral little cafes of
" wood covered with leather, each containing a charge of powder ; the
" balls they carried loofe in a pouch ; and they had alfo a priming horn
" hanging by their fide.

" The old *Englifh* writers call thofe large mufkets calivers : the har-
" quebuze was a lighter piece, that could be fired without a reft. The
" match-lock was fired by a match fixed by a kind of tongs in the fer-
" pentine or cock, which by pulling the trigger, was brought down
" with great quicknefs upon the priming in the pan ; over which there
" was a fliding cover, which was drawn back by the hand juft at the
" time of firing. There was a great deal of nicety and care required
" to fit the match properly to the cock, fo as to come down exactly true
" on the priming, to blow the afhes from the coal, and to guard the
" pan from the fparks that fell from it. A great deal of time was alfo
" loft in taking it out of the cock, and returning it between the fingers
" of the left hand every time that the piece was fired ; and wet weather
" often rendered the matches ufelefs."

While this was the ftate of fire-arms, and this ftate continued among
us to the civil war with very little improvement, it is no wonder that
the long bow was preferred by Sir *John Smith,* who wrote of the choice
of weapons in the reign of Queen *Elizabeth,* when the ufe of the bow
ftill continued, though the mufket was gradually prevailing. Sir *John
Hayward,*

2

Hayward, a writer yet later, has in his hiftory of the *Norman* kings endeavoured to evince the fuperiority of the archer to the mufketeer: however, in the long peace of King *James*, the bow was wholly forgotten. Guns have from that time been the weapons of the *Englifh*, as of other nations, and as they are now improved, are certainly more efficacious.

Afcham had yet another reafon, if not for writing his book, at leaft for prefenting it to King *Henry*. *England* was not then what it may be now juftly termed, the capital of literature, and therefore thofe who afpired to fuperiour degrees of excellence thought it neceffary to travel into other countries. The purfe of *Afcham* was not equal to the expence of peregrination ; and therefore he hoped to have it augmented by a penfion. Nor was he wholly difappointed; for the King rewarded him with an yearly payment of ten pounds.

A penfion of ten pounds granted by a king of *England* to a man of letters, appears to modern readers fo contemptible a benefaction, that it is not unworthy of enquiry what might be its value at that time, and how much *Afcham* might be enriched by it. Nothing is more uncertain than the eftimation of wealth by denominated money ; the precious metals never retain long the fame proportion to real commodities, and the fame names in different ages do not imply the fame quantity of metal; fo that it is equally difficult to know how much money was contained in any nominal fum, and to find what any fuppofed quantity of gold or filver would purchafe ; both which are neceffary to the commenfuration of money, or the adjuftment of proportion between the fame fums at different periods of time.

A numeral pound in King *Henry's* time contained, as now, twenty fhillings; and therefore it muft be inquired what twenty fhillings could perform. Bread-corn is the moft certain ftandard of the neceffaries of life. Wheat was generally fold at that time for one fhilling the bufhel : if therefore we take five fhillings the bufhel for the current price, ten pounds were equivalent to fifty. But here is danger of a fallacy. It may be doubted, whether wheat was the general bread-corn of that age ; and if rye, barley, or oats, were the common food, and wheat, as I

fufpect,

fufpect, only a delicacy, the value of wheat will not regulate the price of other things. This doubt is however in favour of *Afcham*; for if we raife the worth of wheat, we raife that of his penfion.

But the value of money has another variation, which we are ftill lefs able to afcertain : the rules of cuftom or the different needs of artificial life, make that revenue little at one time which is great at another. Men are rich and poor, not only in proportion to what they have, but to what they want. In fome ages, not only neceffaries are cheaper, but fewer things are neceffary. In the age of *Afcham*, moft of the elegancies and expences of our prefent fafhions were unknown : commerce had not yet diftributed fuperfluity through the lower claffes of the people, and the character of a ftudent implied frugality, and required no fplendour to fupport it. His penfion, therefore, reckoning together the wants which he could fupply, and the wants from which he was exempt, may be eftimated, in my opinion, at more than one hundred pounds a-year; which, added to the income of his fellowfhip, put him far enough above diftrefs.

This was an year of good fortune to *Afcham*. He was chofen orator to the univerfity on the removal of Sir *John Cheke* to court, where he was made tutor to Prince *Edward*. A man once diftinguifhed foon gains admirers. *Afcham* was now received to notice by many of the nobility, and by great ladies, among whom it was then the fafhion to ftudy the ancient languages. *Lee* archbifhop of *York* allowed him an yearly penfion; how much, we are not told. He was, probably about this time, employed in teaching many illuftrious perfons to write a fine hand, and among others *Henry* and *Charles*, dukes of *Suffolk*, the princefs *Elizabeth*, and prince *Edward*.

Henry VIII. died two years after, and a reformation of religion being now openly profecuted by King *Edward* and his council, *Afcham*, who was known to favour it, had a new grant of his penfion, and continued at *Cambridge*, where he lived in great familiarity with *Bucer*, who had been called from *Germany* to the profefforfhip of divinity. But his retirement was foon at an end; for in 1548 his pupil *Grindal*, the mafter

c   of

of the princefs *Elizabeth*, died, and the princefs, who had already fome acquaintance with *Afcham*, called him from his college to direct her ftudies. He obeyed the fummons, as we may eafily believe, with readinefs, and for two years inftructed her with great diligence ; but then being difgufted either by her or her domefticks, or perhaps eager for another change of life, he left her without her confent, and return- ed to the univerfity. Of this precipitation he long repented ; and as thofe who are not accuftomed to difrefpect, cannot eafily forgive it, he probably felt the effects of his imprudence to his death.

After having vifited *Cambridge*, he took a journey into *Yorkfhire* to fee his native place and his old acquaintance, and there received a letter from the court, informing him, that he was appointed fecretary to Sir *Richard Morifine*, who was to be difpatched as ambaffador into *Germany*. In his return to *London* he paid that memorable vifit to lady *Jane Gray*, in which he found her reading the *Phædo* in *Greek*, as he has related in his *Schoolmafter*.

In the year 1550 he attended *Morifine* to *Germany*, and wandered over a great part of the country, making obfervations upon all that appeared worthy of his curiofity, and contracting acquaintance with men of learning. To his correfpondent *Sturmius* he paid a vifit, but *Sturmius* was not at home, and thofe two illuftrious friends never faw each other. During the courfe of this embaffy, *Afcham* undertook to improve *Mori-fine* in *Greek*, and for four days in the week explained fome pages of *Herodotus* every morning, and more than two hundred verfes of *Sophocles* or *Euripides* every afternoon. He read with him likewife fome of the orations of *Demofthenes*. On the other days he compiled the letters of bufinefs, and in the night filled up his diary, digefted his remarks, and wrote private letters to his friends in *England*, and particularly to thofe of his college, whom he continually exhorted to perfeverance in ftudy. Amidft all the pleafures of novelty, which his travels fupplied, and in the dignity of his publick ftation, he preferred the tranquillity of private ftudy, and the quiet of academical retirement. The reafonablenefs of this choice has been always difputed ; and in the contrariety of human interefts and difpofitions, the controverfy will not eafily be decided.

4

He

He made a fhort excurfion into *Italy*, and mentions in his *School-mafter* with great feverity the vices of *Venice*. He was defirous of vifit-ing *Trent* while the council were fitting; but the fcantinefs of his purfe defeated his curiofity.

In this journey he wrote his *Report and Difcourfe of the Affaires in Germany*, in which he defcribes the difpofitions and interefts of the *German* princes like a man inquifitive and judicious, and recounts many parti-cularities which are loft in the mafs of general hiftory, in a ftyle which to the ears of that age was undoubtedly mellifluous, and which is now a very valuable fpecimen of genuine *Englifh*.

By the death of King *Edward* in 1553, the reformation was ftopped, *Morifine* was recalled, and *Afcham*'s penfion and hopes were at an end. He therefore retired to his fellowfhip in a ftate of difappointment and defpair, which his biographer has endeavoured to exprefs in the deepeft ftrain of plaintive declamation. *He was deprived of all his fupport*, fays *Graunt*, *ftripped of his penfion, and cut off from the affiftance of his friends, who had now loft their influence; fo that he had* NEC PRÆMIA NEC PRÆ-DIA, *neither penfion nor eftate to fupport him at* Cambridge. There is no credit due to a rhetorician's account either of good or evil. The truth is, that *Afcham* ftill had in his fellowfhip all that in the early part of his life had given him plenty, and might have lived like the other inhabitants of the college, with the advantage of more knowledge and higher repu-tation. But notwithftanding his love of academical retirement, he had now too long enjoyed the pleafures and feftivities of publick life, to return with a good will to academical poverty.

He had however better fortune than he expected, and, if he lamented his condition like his hiftorian, better than he deferved. He had during his abfence in *Germany* been appointed *Latin* fecretary to King *Edward*; and by the intereft of *Gardiner* bifhop of *Winchefter*, he was inftated in the fame office under *Philip* and *Mary*, with a falary of twenty pounds a year.

Soon after his admiffion to his new employment, he gave an extraor-dinary fpecimen of his abilities and diligence, by compofing and tran-

c 2

fcribing

fcribing with his ufual elegance, in three days, forty-feven letters to princes and perfonages, of whom cardinals were the loweft.

How *Afcham*, who was known to be a proteftant, could preferve the favour of *Gardiner*, and hold a place of honour and profit in Queen *Mary*'s court, it muft be very natural to inquire. *Cheke*, as is well known, was compelled to a recantation; and why *Afcham* was fpared, cannot now be difcovered. *Graunt*, at a time when the tranfactions of Queen *Mary*'s reign muft have been well enough remembered, declares, that *Afcham* always made open profeffion of the reformed religion, and that *Englesfield* and others often endeavoured to incite *Gardiner* againft him, but found their accufations rejected with contempt: yet he allows, that fufpicions and charges of temporization and compliance had fomewhat fullied his reputation. The authour of the *Biographia Britannica* conjectures, that he owed his fafety to his innocence and ufefulnefs; that it would have been unpopular to attack a man fo little liable to cenfure, and that the lofs of his pen could not have been eafily fupplied. But the truth is, that morality was never fuffered in the days of perfecution to protect herefy; nor are we fure that *Afcham* was more clear from common failings than thofe who fuffered more; and whatever might be his abilities, they were not fo neceffary but *Gardiner* could have eafily filled his place with another fecretary. Nothing is more vain, than at a diftant time to examine the motives of difcrimination and partiality; for the inquirer having confidered intereft and policy, is obliged at laft to omit more frequent and more active motives of human conduct, caprice, accident, and private affections.

At that time, if fome were punifhed, many were forborn; and of many why fhould not *Afcham* happen to be one? He feems to have been calm and prudent, and content with that peace which he was fuffered to enjoy; a mode of behaviour that feldom fails to produce fecurity. He had been abroad in the laft years of King *Edward*, and had at leaft given no recent offence. He was certainly, according to his own opinion, not much in danger; for in the next year he refigned his fellowfhip, which by *Gardiner*'s favour he had continued to hold, though not refident; and married *Margaret Howe*, a young gentlewoman of a good family.

He

508

ROGER ASCHAM.

He was diftinguifhed in this reign by the notice of Cardinal *Poole*, a man of great candour, learning, and gentlenefs of manners, and particularly eminent for his fkill in *Latin*, who thought highly of *Afcham*'s ftyle; of which it is no inconfiderable proof, that when *Poole* was defirous of communicating a fpeech made by himfelf as legate, in parliament, to the Pope, he employed *Afcham* to tranflate it.

He is faid to have been not only protected by the officers of ftate, but favoured and countenanced by the Queen herfelf; fo that he had no reafon of complaint in that reign of turbulence and perfecution: nor was his fortune much mended, when in 1558 his pupil *Elizabeth* mounted the throne. He was continued in his former employment, with the fame ftipend: but though he was daily admitted to the prefence of the Queen, affifted her private ftudies, and partook of her diverfions; fometimes read to her in the learned languages, and fometimes played with her at draughts and chefs; he added nothing to his twenty pounds a-year but the prebend of *Weftwang* in the church of *York*, which was given him the year following. His fortune was therefore not proportionate to the rank which his offices and reputation gave him, or to the favour in which he feemed to ftand with his miftrefs. Of this parfimonious allotment it is again a hopelefs fearch to inquire the reafon. The Queen was not naturally bountiful, and perhaps did not think it neceffary to diftinguifh by any prodigality of kindnefs a man who had formerly deferted her, and whom fhe might ftill fufpect of ferving rather for intereft than affection. *Graunt* exerts his rhetorical powers in praife of *Afcham*'s difintereftednefs and contempt of money; and declares, that though he was often reproached by his friends with neglect of his own intereft, he never would afk any thing, and inflexibly refufed all prefents which his office or imagined intereft induced any to offer him. *Camden*, however, imputes the narrownefs of his condition to his love of dice and cock-fights: and *Graunt* forgetting himfelf, allows that *Afcham* was fometimes thrown into agonies by difappointed expectations. It may be eafily difcovered from his *Schoolmafter*, that he felt his wants, though he might neglect to fupply them; and we are left to fufpect, that he fhewed his contempt of money only by lofing it at play. If this was his practice, we may excufe *Elizabeth*, who knew the domeftick character of her fervants, if fhe did not give much to him who was lavifh of a little.

However

However he might fail in his œconomy, it were indecent to treat with wanton levity the memory of a man who shared his frailties with all, but whose learning or virtues few can attain, and by whose excellencies many may be improved, while himself only suffered by his faults.

In the reign of *Elizabeth* nothing remarkable is known to have befallen him, except that, in 1563, he was invited by Sir *Edward Sackville* to write the *Schoolmaster*, a treatise on education, upon an occasion which he relates in the beginning of the book. This work, though begun with alacrity, in hopes of a considerable reward, was interrupted by the death of the patron, and afterwards sorrowfully and slowly finished, in the gloom of disappointment, under the pressure of distress. But of the authour's disinclination or dejection there can be found no tokens in the work, which is conceived with great vigour, and finished with great accuracy; and perhaps contains the best advice that was ever given for the study of languages.

This treatise he compleated, but did not publish; for that poverty which in our days drives authours so hastily in such numbers to the press, in the time of *Ascham*, I believe, debarred them from it. The printers gave little for a copy, and, if we may believe the tale of *Raleigh*'s history, were not forward to print what was offered them for nothing. *Ascham*'s book therefore lay unseen in his study, and was at last dedicated to Lord *Cecil* by his widow.

Ascham never had a robust or vigorous body, and his excuse for so many hours of diversion was his inability to endure a long continuance of sedentary thought. In the latter part of his life he found it necessary to forbear any intense application of the mind from dinner to bed-time, and rose to read and write early in the morning. He was for some years hectically feverish; and though he found some alleviation of his distemper, never obtained a perfect recovery of his health. The immediate cause of his last sickness was too close application to the composition of a poem, which he purposed to present to the Queen on the day of her accession. To finish this he forbore to sleep at his accustomed hours, till in *December* 1568 he fell sick of a kind of lingering disease, which *Graunt* has not named, nor accurately described. The most af-

flictive

flictive fymptom was want of fleep, which he endeavoured to obtain by the motion of a cradle. Growing every day weaker, he found it vain to contend with his diftemper, and prepared to die with the refignation and piety of a true Chriftian. He was attended on his deathbed by *Gravet* vicar of St. *Sepulchre*, and Dr. *Nowel*, the learned dean of St. *Paul*'s, who gave ample teftimony to the decency and devotion of his concluding life. He frequently teftified his defire of that diffolution which he foon obtained. His funeral-fermon was preached by Dr. *Nowel*.

Roger Afcham died in the fifty-third year of his age, at a time when, according to the general courfe of life, much might yet have been expected from him, and when he might have hoped for much from others: but his abilities and his wants were at an end together; and who can determine, whether he was cut off from advantages, or refcued from calamities? He appears to have been not much qualified for the improvement of his fortune. His difpofition was kind and focial; he delighted in the pleafures of converfation, and was probably not much inclined to bufinefs. This may be fufpected from the paucity of his writings. He has left little behind him, and of that little nothing was publifhed by himfelf but the *Toxophilus*, and the account of *Germany*. The *Schoolmafter* was printed by his widow, and the Epiftles were collected by *Graunt*, who dedicated them to Queen *Elizabeth*, that he might have an opportunity of recommending his fon *Giles Afcham* to her patronage. The dedication was not loft: the young man was made by the Queen's mandate fellow of a college in *Cambridge*, where he obtained confiderable reputation. What was the effect of his widow's dedication to *Cecil*, is not known: it may be hoped that *Afcham*'s works obtained for his family, after his deceafe, that fupport which he did not in his life very plenteoufly procure them.

Whether he was poor by his own fault or the fault of others, cannot now be decided; but it is certain that many have been rich with lefs merit. His philological learning would have gained him honour in any country, and among us it may juftly call for that reverence which all nations owe to thofe who firft roufe them from ignorance, and kindle among them the light of literature. Of his manners nothing can be

faid

511

said but from his own teſtimony and that of his contemporaries. Thoſe who mention him allow him many virtues. His courteſy, benevolence, and liberality, are celebrated; and of his piety we have not only the teſtimony of his friends, but the evidence of his writings.

That his *Engliſh* works have been ſo long neglected, is a proof of the uncertainty of literary fame. He was ſcarcely known as an authour in his own language till Mr. *Upton* publiſhed his *Schoolmaſter* with learned notes, which are inſerted in this edition. His other pieces were read only by thoſe few who delight in obſolete books; but as they are now collected into one volume, with the addition of ſome letters never printed before, the publick has an opportunity of recompenſing the injury, and allotting *Aſcham* the reputation due to his knowledge and his eloquence.

SOME ACCOUNT OF THE LIFE AND WRITINGS OF MR. WILLIAM COLLINS.

MR. William Collins was born at Chichester in Suffex, in the year 1721 : in which city his father was a reputable tradefman. He was admitted a fcholar of Winchefter college, Feb. 23, 1733. where he fpent feven years under the care of the learned Dr. Burton. In the year 1740, in confideration of his merit, he was placed firft in the lift of thofe fcholars who are elected from Winchefter college to New college in Oxford : but no vacancy happening at the latter, he was entered, the fame year, a commoner of Queen's college, Ox. and July 29, 1741. was elected a demy, or fcholar, of Magdalen college in the fame univerfity. At fchool he began to ftudy poetry and criticifm, particularly the latter. The following epigram, made by him while at Winchefter-fchool, difcovers a genius, and turn of expreffion, very rarely to be met with in juvenile compofitions.

TO

513

TO MISS AURELIA C—R,

ON HER WEEPING AT HER SISTER'S WEDDING.

CEafe, fair Aurelia, ceafe to mourn;
   Lament not Hannah's happy ftate;
You may be happy in your turn,
   And feize the treafure you regret.

With Love united Hymen ftands,
   And foftly whifpers to your charms;
" Meet but your lover in my bands,
   " You'll find your fifter in his arms."

His Latin exercifes were never fo much admired
as his Englifh.——At Oxford he wrote the epiftle
to Sir Thomas Hanmer, ·and Oriental eclogues,
which were firft publifhed in 1742, under the title
of Perfian eclogues. About the year 1743, he
left Oxford, having taken the degree of bachelor
of arts, weary of the confinement and uniformity
of an academical life; fondly imagining that a
man of parts was fure of making his fortune in
London; and ftruck with the name of author and
poet, without confulting his friends, he immediately removed to town, and rafhly refolved to
live

live by his pen, without undertaking the drudgery of any profeffion. Here he foon diffipated his fmall fortune, to compenfate for which, he pro-jected the hiftory of the revival of learning in Italy, under the pontificates of Julius II. and Leo X. His fubfcription for this work not anfwering his expectations, he engaged with a bookfeller, to tranflate Ariftotle's Poetics, and to illuftrate it with a large and regular comment. This fcheme alfo being laid afide, he turn'd his thoughts to dra-matic poetry, and being intimately acquainted with the manager, refolved to write a tragedy, which however he never executed. In the year 1746 he publifhed his odes; and fhortly after went abroad to our army in Flanders, to attend his uncle, colonel Martin, who, dying foon after his arrival, left him a confiderable fortune; which however he did not live long to enjoy, for he fell into a nervous diforder, which continued, with but fhort intervals, till his death, which happened in 1756. and with which diforder his head and intellects were at times affected.

For a man of fuch an elevated genius, Mr. Collins has wrote but little: his time was chiefly taken up in laying extenfive projects, and vaft de-figns, which he never even begun to put in execution.

We

515

We have been favoured with the following account of Mr. Collins by a gentleman, defervedly eminent in the republic of letters, who knew him intimately well.

Mr. Collins was a man of extenfive literature, and of vigorous faculties. He was acquainted not only with the learned tongues, but with the Italian, French, and Spanifh languages. He had employed his mind chiefly upon works of fiction, and fubjects of fancy; and, by indulging fome peculiar habits of thought, was eminently delighted with thofe flights of imagination which pafs the bounds of nature, and to which the mind is reconciled only by a paffive acquiefcence in popular traditions. He loved fairies, genii, giants, and monfters; he delighted to rove through the meanders of inchantment, to gaze on the magnificence of golden palaces, to repofe by the waterfals of Elyfian gardens. This was however the character rather of his inclination than his genius, the grandeur of wildnefs, and the novelty of extravagance, were always defired by him, but were not always attained. But diligence is never wholly loft: if his efforts fometimes caufed harfhnefs and obfcurity, they likewife produced in happier moments fublimity and fplendour. This idea, which he had formed of excellence, led him to oriental fictions, and allegorical imagery; and, perhaps,
while

516

while he was intent upon defcription, he did not fufficiently cultivate fentiment: his poems are the productions of a mind not deficient in fire, nor unfurnifhed with knowledge either of books or life, but fomewhat obftructed in its progrefs, by deviation in queft of miftaken beauties.

His morals were pure, and his opinions pious. In a long continuance of poverty, and long habits of diffipation, it cannot be expected that any character fhould be exactly uniform. There is a degree of want by which the freedom of agency is almoft deftroyed, and long affociation with fortuitous companions will at laft relax the ftrictnefs of truth, and abate the fervour of fincerity. That this man, wife and virtuous as he was, paffed always unentangled through the fnares of life, it would be prejudice and temerity to affirm. But it may be faid, that at leaft he preferved the fource of action unpolluted, that his principles were never fhaken, that his diftinctions of right and wrong were never confounded, and that his faults had nothing of malignity or defign, but proceeded from fome unexpected preffure, or cafual temptation.

The latter part of his life cannot be remembred but with pity and fadnefs. He languifhed fome years under that depreffion of mind which enchains the faculties without deftroying them,

and

and leaves reason the knowledge of right, without the power of purfuing it. Thefe clouds, which he found gathering on his intellects, he endeavoured to difperfe by travel, and paffed into France, but found himfelf conftrained to yield to his malady, and returned: he was for fome time confined in a houfe of lunatics, and afterwards retired to the care of his fifter in Colchefter, where death at laft came to his relief.

After his return from France, the writer of this character paid him a vifit at Iflington, where he was waiting for his fifter, whom he had directed to meet him: there was then nothing of diforder difcernable in his mind by any but himfelf, but he had then withdrawn from ftudy, and travelled with no other book than an Englifh teftament, fuch as children carry to the fchool; when his friend took it into his hand, out of curiofity to fee what companion a man of letters had chofen, " I have but one book," fays Collins, " but that " is the beft."

On the 3d ult. died, at Cofflect, the feat of Thomas Veale, Efq. in his way to London, the Reverend Mr. *Zachariah Mudge*, Prebendary of Exeter, and Vicar of St. Andrew's in Plymouth; a man equally eminent for his virtues and abilities, and at once beloved as a Companion, and reverenced as a Paftor. He had that general curiofity to which no kind of knowledge is indifferent or fuperfluous; and that general benevolence by which no order of men is hated or defpifed.

His principles, both of thought and action, were great and comprehenfive. By a folicitous examination of objections, and a judicious comparifon of oppofite arguments, he attained what enquiry never gives but to induftry and perfpicuity, a firm and unfhaken fettlement of conviction. But his firmnefs was without afperity; for knowing with how much difficulty truth was fometimes found, he did not wonder that many miffed it.

The general courfe of his life was determined by his profeffion. He ftudied the facred volumes, in the original languages, with what diligence and fuccefs his *Notes* upon the *Pfalms* give fufficient evidence. He once endeavoured to add the knowledge of Arabic to that of Hebrew; but finding his thoughts too much diverted from other ftudies, after fome time, defifted from his purpofe.

His difcharge of parochial duties was exemplary. How his *Sermons* were compofed may be learned from the excellent volume which he has given to the Public; but how they were delivered, can be known only to thofe that heard them; for as he appeared in the pulpit words will not eafily defcribe him. His delivery, though unconftrained, was not negligent, and though forcible was not turbulent; difdaining anxious nicety of emphafis, and laboured artifice of action, it captivated the hearer by its natural dignity; it roufed the fluggifh, and fixed the volatile; and detained the mind upon the fubject without directing it to the fpeaker.

The grandeur and folemnity of the Preacher did not intrude upon his general behaviour; at the table of his friends he was a companion communicative and attentive, of unaffected manners, of manly chearfulnefs, willing to pleafe, and eafy to be pleafed. His acquaintance was univerfally folicited, and his prefence obftructed no enjoyment, which religion did not forbid. Though ftudious he was popular, though argumentative he was modeft, though inflexible he was candid, and though metaphyfical yet orthodox.

of him in the " Anecdotes of Mr.
" Bowyer," and from the casual com-
munications I have happened to glean
from those who knew him.

STYAN THIRLBY, son of the Rev.
Mr. Thirlby, vicar of St. Malgaret's,
Leicester, was born about 1692. He
received his education at Leicester,
where he shewed great promises of future excellence. Among other early
productions of his ingenuity was a
Greek copy of verses "On the Queen
of Sheba's visit to Solomon." This was
an exercise, written by him at the school
of the Rev. Mr. Kilby, of Leicester,
who preserved it, and by whom his
proficiency was praised as very quick.
He went through my school, said Mr.
Kilby, *in three years, and his self-conceit was censured, as very offensive.—
He thought he knew more than all the
school. Perhaps,* said a gentlewoman to
whom this was told, *he thought rightly.*—
From his mental abilities no small degree of future eminence was presaged;
but the fond hopes of his friends were
unfortunately defeated by a temper
which was naturally indolent and quarrelsome, and by an unhappy addiction
to drinking.—From Leicester he was
removed to Jesus College, Cambridge,
where he published " An Answer to
" Mr. Whiston's Seventeen Suspicions
" concerning Athanasius, in his Histo-
" rical Preface, 1712:" "written," as
he says in the Preface, "by one very
" young, and, he may add, at such
" broken hours as many necessary avo-
" cations and a very unsettled state of
" health would suffer him to bestow
" upon them." It appears, by another
tract in this controversy, that he was
then "about 20 years old." He obtained a fellowship of his college by the
express desire of Dr. Ashton, who said
" he had had the honour of studying
" with him when young;" though he
afterwards spoke very contemptuously
of him * as the editor of " Justin
" Martyr," which appeared in 1723,
in folio; and the dedication to which has
always been considered as a masterly
production, in style particularly. After
Thirlby's

MR. URBAN,   *April* 8.
FROM a desire of contributing to
perpetuate the memory of a very
ingenious and learned English critic, I
am induced to send you such particulars
of the life of Dr. Thirlby as I have
been able to collect from what is said

* The proof of this assertion rests on an hitherto unpublished letter of Dr. Ashton, which
is here subjoined :—" You are much mistaken in thinking Thirlby wants some money from
" you (though in truth he wants); you are only taken in to adorn his triumph by a
" letter of applause, though I think you may spare that too; for he is set forth in his
" coach, with great ostentation, to visit his patron. I have not had the patience to read all
" his dedication, but have seen enough to observe, that it is stuffed with self-conceit, and
" an insolent contempt of others, Bentley especially, whom he again points out in p. 18,
" and treats in that page with the highest contempt, as he had done before in his preface.
" He

520

Thirlby's publication of Justin, Dr. Ashton, perhaps to shew him that he had not done all which might have been done, published, in one of the foreign Journals, "Some Emendations "of faulty Passages;" which when Thirlby saw, he said, slightly, that *any man who would, might have made them, and a hundred more.*—Thus far Thirlby went on in the divinity line; but his versatility led him to try the round of what are called the learned professions. His next pursuit was physic; and for a while he was called *Doctor.* While he was a nominal physician, he lived some time with the Duke of Chandos, as librarian; and is reported to have affected a perverse and insolent independence, so as capriciously to refuse his company when it was desired. It may be supposed that they were soon weary of each other.—He then studied the civil law, in which he lectured while the late Sir Edward Walpole was his pupil: but he was a careless tutor, scarcely ever reading lectures. The late learned Dr. Jortin, who was one of his pupils, was very early in life recommended by him to translate some of Eustathius's Notes for the use of "Pope's Homer;" and complained "that Pope, having accepted and approved his performance, never testified any curiosity or desire to see "him." The civil law line not pleasing him, though he became LL.D. he applied to common law, and had chambers taken for him in the Temple, by his friend Andrew Reid, with a view of being entered of that society, and being called to the bar; but of this scheme he likewise grew weary. He came, however, to London, to the house of his friend Sir Edward Walpole, who procured for him the office of a king's waiter in the port of London, in May 1741, a sinecure place, worth about 100l. per annum. Whilst in Sir Edward's house, he kept a miscellaneous book of memorables, containing whatever was said or done amiss by Sir Edward or any part of his family.—The remainder of his days were passed in private lodgings, where he lived very retired, seeing only a few friends, and

indulging, occasionally, in excessive drinking, being sometimes in a state of intoxication for five or six weeks together; and, as is usual with such men, appearing to be so even when sober; and in his cups he was jealous and quarrelsome.—"That man," says Mr. Clarke to Mr. Bowyer, speaking of Thirlby, "was lost to the republick of "letters very surprisingly; he went off, "and returned no more."—One of his pupils having been invited by him to supper, happened, as he was going away, to stumble at a pile of Justin, which lay on the floor in quires: Thirlby told him that he kicked down the books in contempt of the editor; upon which the pupil said, *It is now time to go away.*—Another acquaintance, who found him one day in the streets haranguing the crowd, and took him home by gentle violence, was ever afterwards highly esteemed by Thirlby for not relating the story.—He had originally contributed some notes to Theobald's Shakespeare, and afterwards talked of an edition of his own. Dr. Jortin undertook to read over that poet, with a view to mark the passages where he had either imitated Greek and Latin writers, or at least had fallen into the same thoughts and expressions. But Thirlby went no further than to write some abusive remarks on the margin of Warburton's Shakespeare, with a very few attempts at emendation, and those perhaps all in the first volume. In the other volumes he has only, with great diligence, counted the lines in every page. When this was told to Dr. Jortin, *I have known him,* said he, *amuse himself with still slighter employment; he would write down all the proper names that he could call into his memory.* His mind seems to have been tumultuous and desultory, and he was glad to catch any employment that might produce attention without anxiety; such employment, as Dr. Battie has observed, is necessary for madmen. The copy, such as it was, became the property of Sir Edward Walpole, to whom Thirlby bequeathed all his books and papers, and by whom it was lent to Dr Johnson, when he was preparing a

"He treats Meric Casaubon and Isaac Vossius in a manner not much different. He sticks "not to fling scorn upon Justin himself, as a trifling writer, beneath his dignity to consi-"der, and so absurd a reasoner as only *poffms hlore* can mend. I have read about sixty "pages of his performance, and am really ashamed to find so much self-sufficiency, and "insufficiency. I am almost provoked to turn critic myself, and let me tempt you to a "little laughter, by promising to shew you some conceits upon Justin, which are under no "name in Thirlby's edition." *Dr. Charles Ashton to Dean Moss,* 1723, MS.

valuable

valuable edition of "Shakspeare" for
the preſs. Dr. Thirlby died Dec. 19,
1753.—One of his colloquial topicks
was, *That Nature apparently intended a
kindof parity among her ſex*. "Some-
"times," ſaid he, "ſhe deviates a lit-
"tle from her general purpoſe, and
"ſends into the world a man of powers
"ſuperior to the reſt, of quicker intui-
"tion, and wider comprehenſion; this
"man has all other men for his ene-
"mies, and would not be ſuffered to
"live his natural time, but that his ex-
"cellence are balanced by his fail-
"ings. He that, by intellectual exal-
"tation, thus towers above his con-
"temporaries, is drunken, or lazy, or
"capricious; or, by ſome defect or
"other, is hindered from exerting his
"ſovereignty of mind; he is thus kept
"upon the level, and thus preſerved
"from the deſtruction which would
"be the natural conſequence of uni-
"verſal hatred."

1. SIR,   Oct. 10, 1782.
     While I am at Brighthelmſton, if
you have any need of conſulting me,
Mr. Strahan will do us the favour to
tranſmit our papers under his frank. I
have looked often into your "Anecdotes;" and you will hardly thank a lover
of literary hiſtory for telling you, that he
has been informed and gratified†. I
wiſh you would add your own diſcoveries and intelligence to thoſe of Dr.
Rawlinſon, and undertake the Supple-
ment to Wood. Think on it.
          I am, Sir, your humble ſervant,
                    SAM. JOHNSON,

† In a ſubſequent letter, dated Oct. 23, Dr. Johnſon adds, "I wiſh, Sir, you could
"could obtain ſome fuller information of Jortin, Markland, and Thirlby. They were
"three contemporaries of great eminence." It was in conſequence of this requeſt that I
drew up the account of Thirlby, which is printed in the Magazine for April 1784, p. 266;
which having been ſhewn to Dr. Johnſon in the ſtate of a proof ſheet, he added to it nearly
half of what is there printed. The Doctor's MS. is now before me, and begins with
"What I can tell of Thirlby, I had from thoſe who knew him; I never ſaw him in my
"life." The communication concludes with "This is what I can remember." I will
take this opportunity of adding, that, on my ſhewing Dr. Johnſon the "Remarks on his Life
"of Milton," which were publiſhed in 8vo. 1780, he wrote on the margin of p. 14, "In
"the account of London, I was deceived; partly by thinking the man too famous to be
"forgotten. Of the operation from the ["Literary] Magazine" "a POETICAL SCALE"],
"I was not the author. I fancy it was put in after. Had gained that work; for I not only
"did not write it, but do not remember it." J. N.

APPENDIX

TO

EARLY BIOGRAPHICAL WRITINGS

OF DR JOHNSON

The following passages are presented
in a clear form for the
reader's benefit

Continuation of the Life of Dr
  BOERHAAVE, from p.73

Having now qualified himself for
the Practice of Physick, he began
to visit Patients but without that
Encouragement c^h_w others, not equally
deserving, have sometimes met with.
His Business was, at first, not
great, and his Circumstances by no
means easy; but still superiour to
any Discouragement, he continued his
Search after Knowledge, and
determined that Prosperity, if ever
he was to enjoy it, should be the
Consequence, not of mean Art, or
disingenuous Solicitations, but of
real Merit, and solid Learning.
    His steady Adherence to his
Resolutions appears yet more
plainly from this Circumstance: He
was, while he yet remained in this
unpleasing Situation, invited by
one of the first Favourites of
K. William III. to settle at the
Hague, upon very advantageous
Conditions; but declined the Offer.
For having no Ambition but after
Knowledge, he was desirous of
living at liberty, without any
Restraint upon his Looks, his
Thoughts, or his Tongue, and at the
utmost Distance from all
Contentions, and State-Parties.
His Time was wholly taken up in
visiting the Sick, Studying, making
Chymical Experiments, searching
into every part of Medicine with
the utmost Diligence, teaching the
Mathematicks, and reading the
Scriptures, and those Authors who
profess to teach a certain Method of
loving God.*
    This was his Method of living
to the Year 1701, when he was recommended by Mr Van Berg to the
University, as a proper Person to
succeed Drelincurtius in the
Professorship of Physick, and
elected without any Solicitation on
his part, and almost without his
Consent, on the 18th of May.
    On this Occasion, having observed,
with Grief, that Hippocrates, whom he
regarded not only as the Father but
as the Prince of Physicians, was not
sufficiently read or esteemed by
young Students, he pronounced an
Oration, de commendando Studio
Hippocratico; by which he restored
that great Author to his just and
antient Reputation.

    *Circa hoc tempus, lautis
conditionibus, lautioribus promissis,
invitatus, plus vice simplici, a Viro
primariae dignationis, qui gratia
flagrantissima florebat Regis Gulielmi
III, ut Hagam Comitum sedem caperet
Fortunarum, declinavit constans.
Contentus videlicet vita libera,
remota a turbis, studiisque porro
percolendis unice impensa, ubi non
cogeretur alia dicere & simulare,
alia sentire & dissimulare: affectuum
studiis rapi, regi. Sic tum vita erat,
aegros visere, mox domi in Musaco se
condere, officinam Vulcaniam exercere;
omnes Medicinae partes acerrime
persequi; Mathematica etiam aliis
tradere; Sacra legere, & Auctores qui
profitentur docere rationem certam
amandi Deum.

    Boerhaave had now for nine Years
read physical Lectures, but without
the Title or Dignity of a Professor,
when by the Death of Professor Hotten,
the Professorship of Physick and
Botany fell to him of course.
    On this Occasion he asserted the
Simplicity and Facility of the Science
of Physick, in opposition to those
that think Obscurity contributes to
the Dignity of Learning, and that to
be admired it is necessary not to be
understood.
    His Profession of Botany made it
part of his Duty to superintend the
physical Garden, which improved so
much by the immense Number of new
Plants which he procured, that it
was enlarged to twice its original
Extent.

    *Aetas, labor, corporisque opima
pinguetudo, effecerant, ante annum,
ut inertibus refertum, grave, hebes,
plenitudine turgens corpus, anhelum
ad motus minimos, cum sensu
suffocationis, pulsu mirifice anomalo,
ineptum evaderet ad ullum motum.
Urgebat praecipue subsistens prorsus
& intercepta respiratio ad prima
somni initia: Unde somnus prorsus
prohibebatur, cum formidabili
strangulationis molestia. Hinc
Hydrops pedum, crurum, femorum,
scroti, praeputii, & abdominis.
Quae tamen omnia sublata. Sed dolor
manet in abdomine, cum anxietate
summa, anhelitu suffocante, &
debilitate incredibili: Somno pauco,
eoque vago, per somnia turbatissimo:
Animus vero rebus agendis impar.
Cum his luctor fessus nec emergo:
Patienter expectans Dei jussa,
quibus resigno data, quae sola amo,
& honoro unice.

    He published in 1707 Institutiones
Medicae, to which he added in 1708
Aphorismi de cognoscendis & curandis
morbis.
    1710, Index Stirpium in Horto
Academico.
    1719, De Materia Medica, &

Remediorum formulis Liber; and in
1727 a second Edition.
   1720, Alter Index Stirpium, &c.
adorned with Plates, and containing
twice the number of Plants as the
former.
   1722, Epistola ad Cl.Ruischium, qua
sententiam Malpighianam de glandulis
defendit.
   1724, Atrocis nec prius descripti
Morbi Historia Illustrissimi Baronis
Wassenariae.
   1725, Opera Anatomica &
Chirurgica Andreae Vesalii, with the
Life of Vesalius.
   1728, Altera atrocis rarissimique
Morbi Marchionis de Sancto Albano
Historia.
   Auctores de lue Aphrodisiaca, cum
tractatu praefixo.
   1731, Aretaei Cappadocis nova
Editio.
   1732, Elementa Chemiae.
   1734, Observata de Argento vivo,
ad Reg. Soc. & Acad. Scient.

Life of Dr Boerhaave: Page 35:
Footnote

   *Doctrinam sacris Literis
Hebraice & Graece traditam, solam
animae salutarem & agnovit & sensit.
Omni opportunitate profitebatur
disciplinam, quam Jesus Christus ore
& vita expressit, unice tranquillitatem dare menti. Semperque dixit
Amicis, pacem animi haud reperiundam
nisi in magno Mosis praecepto de
sincero Amore Dei & hominis bene
observato. Neque extra Sacra
monumenta uspiam inveniri, quod
mentem serenet. Deum pius adoravit,
qui est. Intelligere de Deo unice
volebat id, quod Deus de se
intelligit. Eo contentus ultra
nihil requisivit, ne Idololatria
erraret. In voluntate Dei sic
requiescebat, ut illius nullam omnino
rationem indagandam putaret. Hanc
unice supremam omnium legem esse
contendebat, deliberata constantia
perfectissime colendam. De aliis &
seipso sentiebat: Ut quoties criminis
reos ad poenas letales damnatos
audiret, semper cogitaret, saepe
diceret; "Quis'dixerit an non me fint
meliores? Utique, si ipse melior, id
non mihi auctori tribuendum esse
palam ajo, confiteor; sed ita
largienti Deo."

The Life of Admiral Drake: Page 45:
Text

   Continuation of the LIFE of
   Sir FRANCIS DRAKE, from p.396

When they had lain about an Hour in
this Place, they began to hear the
Bells of the Mules on each Hand, upon
which Orders were given, that the
Droves which came from Venta Cruz,
should pass unmolested, because they
carried nothing of great Value, and
those only be intercepted which were
travelling thither, and that none of
the Men should rise up till the
Signal should be given.

The Life of Sir Francis Drake: Page 51:
Text

   But this friendly Intercourse was
in appearance soon broken, for on the
next Day observing the Moors making
Signals from the Land, they sent out
their Boat, as before, to fetch them
to the Ship, and one John Fry leaped
ashore, intending to become an Hostage
as on the former Day, when immediately
he was seized by the Moors, and the
Crew observing great Numbers to start
up from behind the Rock with Weapons
in their Hands, found it Madness to
attempt his Rescue, and therefore
provided for their own Security by
returning to the Ship.
   Fry was immediately carried to the
King, who being then in continual Expectation of an Invasion from Portugal,
suspected that these Ships were sent
only to observe the Coast, and discover
a proper Harbour for the main Fleet;
but being informed who they were, and
whither they were bound, not only
dismissed his Captive, but made large
Offers of Friendship and Assistance,
which Drake, however, did not stay to
receive, but being disgusted at this
Breach of the Laws of Commerce, and
afraid of farther Violence, after
having spent some Days in searching
for his Man, in which he met with no
Resistance, left the Coast on Dec.31,
some time before Fry's Return, who
being obliged by this Accident to
somewhat a longer Residence among the
Moors, was afterwards sent home in a
Merchant's Ship.
   On Jan.16, they arrived at Cape
Blanc, having in their Passage taken
several Spanish Vessels. Here while
Drake was employing his Men in
catching Fish, of which this Coast
affords great Plenty, and various
Kinds, the Inhabitants came down to
the Sea-side with their Aliforges, or
Leather-Bottles, to traffick for
Water, which they were willing to
purchase with Ambergrise, and other
Gums. But Drake compassionating the
Misery of their Condition, gave them
Water whenever they asked for it, and
left them their Commodities to
traffick with, when they should be
again reduced to the same Distress,
without finding the same Generosity
to relieve them.
   Here having discharged some
Spanish Ships wh they had taken, towards the Isles of Cape Verd, and on
Jan.28, came to anchor before Mayo,
hoping to furnish themselves with
fresh Water; but having landed they
found the Town by the Water's Side
entirely deserted, and marching
farther up the Country, saw the
Vallies extremely fruitful, and
abounding with ripe Figs, Cocoes and
Plantains, but could by no means
prevail upon the Inhabitants to
converse or traffick with them: However they were suffered by them to
range the Country without Molestation,
but found no Water, except at such a
Distance from the Sea that the Labour
of conveying it to their Ships was
greater than it was at that time
necessary for them to undergo. Salt,
had they wanted it, might have been
obtained with less Trouble, being
left by the Sea upon the Sand, and

harden'd by the Sun, during the Ebb, in such Quantities, that the chief Traffick of their Island is carried on with it.

Jan.31. they passed by St Jago, an Island at that time divided between the Natives and the Portuguese, who first entering these Islands under the Show of Traffick, by degrees established themselves, claimed a Superiority over the original Inhabitants, and harrassed them with such Cruelty, that they obliged them either to fly to the Woods and Mountains, and perish with Hunger, or to take Arms against their Oppressors, and under the insuperable Disadvantages with which they contended, to die almost without a Battle in defence of their natural Rights, and antient Possessions.

Such Treatment had the Natives of St Jago received, which had driven them into the rocky Parts of the Island, from whence they made Incursions into the Plantations of the Portuguese, sometimes with Loss, but generally with that Success which Desperation naturally procures; so that the Portuguese were in continual Alarms, and lived with the natural Consequences of Guilt, Terror and Anxiety. They were wealthy, but not happy, and possessed the Island, but not enjoyed it.

They then sailed on within sight of Fogo, an Island so called from a Mountain, about the middle of it, continually burning, and like the rest inhabited by the Portuguese, two Leagues to the South of which lyes Brava, which has received its Name from its Fertility, abounding, tho' uninhabited, with all Kinds of Fruits, and watered with great Numbers of Springs and Brooks, which would easily invite the Possessors of the adjacent Islands to settle in it, but that it affords neither Harbour nor Anchorage.

The Life of Sir Francis Drake:
Page 55/56: Text

Drake, however, unwilling, as it seemed, to proceed to extreme Severities, offered him his Choice, either of being executed on the Island, or set ashore on the Main Land, or being sent to England to be tried before the Council; of which, after a Day's Consideration, he chose the first, alledging the Improbability of persuading any to leave the Expedition for the Sake of transporting a Criminal to England, and the Danger of his future State among Savages and Infidels. His Choice, I believe, few will approve: To be set ashore on the Main Land, was indeed only to be executed in a different Manner, for what Mercy could be expected from e Natives so incensed, but e most cruel and lingering Death? But why he should not rather have requested to be sent to England it is not so easy to conceive. In so long a Voyage he might have found a thousand Opportunities of escaping, perhaps with the Connivance of his Keepers, whose Resentment must probably in Time have given way to Compassion,

or at least by their Negligence, as it is easy to believe, they would, in Times of Ease and Refreshment, have remitted their Vigilance, at least he would have gained longer Life, and to make Death desirable seems not one of the Effects of Guilt. However, he was, as 'tis related, obstinately deaf to all Persuasions, and adhering to his first Choice, after having received the Communion, and dined chearfully with the General, was executed in the Afternoon, with many Proofs of Remorse, but none of Fear.

How far it is probable that Drake, after having been acquainted with this Man's Designs, sho[n]ld admit him into his Fleet, and afterwards caress, respect, and trust him; or that Doughtie, who is represented as a Man of eminent Abilities, should engage in so long and hazardous a Voyage with no other View than that of defeating it, is left to the Determination of the Reader. What Designs he could have formed with any Hope of Success, or to what Actions worthy of Death he could have proceeded without Accomplices, for none are mentioned, is equally difficult to imagine. Nor, on the other Hand, tho' the Obscurity of the Account, and the remote Place chosen for the Discovery of this wicked Project, seem to give some Reason for Suspicion, does there appear any Temptation, from either Hope, Fear, or Interest, that might induce Drake, or any Commander in his State, to put to death an innocent Man upon false Pretences.

(To be continued)

The Life of Sir Francis Drake:
Page 57/58: Text

From this Bay they were driven Southward to 55 Degrees, where, among some Islands, they stayed two Days to the great Refreshment of the Crew; but being again forced into the main Sea, they were tossed about with perpetual Expectations of perishing...

The Life of Sir Francis Drake, Page 63:
Text

The Men are generally naked, but the Women make a kind of Petticoat of Bulrushes, which they comb like Hemp, and throw the Skin of a Deer over their Shoulders. They are very modest, tractable and obedient to their Husbands.

Such is the Condition of this People, and not very different is, perhaps, the State of the greatest Part of Mankind. Whether more enlightened Nations ought to look upon them with Pity, as less happy than themselves, some Sceptics have made, very unnecessarily, a Difficulty of determining. More, they say, is lost by the Perplexities than gained by the Instruction of Science; we enlarge our Vices with our Knowledge, and multiply our Wants with our Attainments, and the Happiness of Life is better secured by the Ignorance of Vice than by the Knowledge of Virtue.

The Fallacy by which such reasoners have imposed upon themselves, seems to arise from the Comparison which they make, not between two Men equally inclined to apply the Means of Happiness in their Power, to the End for which Providence conferred them, but furnished in unequal Proportions with the Means of Happiness, which is the true State of savage and polished Nations, but between two Men, of which he to whom Providence has been most bountiful, destroys the Blessings by Negligence, or obstinate Misuse; while the other, steady, diligent, and virtuous, employs his Abilities and Conveniencies to their proper End. The Question is not whether a good Indian, or bad Englishman be most happy, but which State is most desirable, supposing Virtue and Reason the same in both.

Nor is this the only Mistake which is generally admitted in this Controversy; for these Reasoners frequently confound Innocence with the mere Incapacity of Guilt. He that never saw, or heard, or thought of strong Liquors, cannot be proposed as a Pattern of Sobriety.

This Land was named by Drake, Albion, from its white Cliffs, in which it bore some Resemblance to his Native Country, and the whole History of the Resignation of it to the English, was engraven on a piece of Brass, then nailed on a Post, and fixed up before their Departure, which being now discovered by the People to be near at hand, they could not forbear perpetual Lamentations. When the English on the 23d of July weigh'd Anchor, they saw them climbing to the Tops of Hills, that they might keep them in sight, and observed Fires lighted up in many parts of the Country, on which, as they supposed Sacrifices were offered.

Near this Harbour they touched at some Islands, where they found great Numbers of Seals, and despairing now to find any Passage through the Northern Parts, he after a general Consultation determined to steer away to the Moluccas, and setting Sail July 25th, he sail'd for sixty eight Days without Sight of Land; and on September 30th, arrived within View of some Islands, situate about eight Degrees Northward from the Line, from whence the inhabitants resorted to them in Canoes, hollowed out of the solid Trunk of a Tree, and raised at both ends so high above the Water, that they seemed almost a Simicircle; they were burnished in such a Manner that they shone like Ebony, and were kept steady by a piece of Timber, fixed on each side of them; with strong Canes, that were fastened at one End to the Boat, and at the other to the End of the Timber.

The first Company that came brought Fruits, Potatoes, and other things of no great Value, with an appearance of Trafick, and exchanged their Lading for other Commodities, with great shew of Honesty and Friendship, but having as they imagined, laid all Suspicion asleep, they soon sent another Fleet of Canoes, of which the Crews behaved with all the Insolence of Tyrants, and all the Rapacity of Thieves, for whatever was suffered to come into their Hands, they seemed to consider as their own, and would neither pay for it nor restore it, and at length finding the English resolved to admit them no longer, they discharged a Shower of Stones from their Boats, which Insult, Drake prudently and generously returned by ordering a Piece of Ordnance to be fired without hurting them, at which they were so terrify'd, that they leaped into the Water, and hid themselves under the Canoes.

Having for some Time but little Wind, they did not arrive at the Moluccas till the 3d of November, and then designing to touch at Tidore, they were visited, as they sailed by a little Island, belonging to the King of Ternate, by the Viceroy of the Place, who informed them, that it would be more Advantageous for them to have recourse to his Master for Supplies and Assistance than to the King of Ternate, who was in some Degree dependent on the Portugeze, and that he would himself carry the News of their Arrival, and prepare their Reception.

Drake was by the Arguments of the Viceroy prevailed upon to alter his Resolution, and on November 5, cast Anchor before Ternate, and scarce was he arrived, before the Viceroy with others of the chief Nobles, came out in three large Boats, rowed by forty Men on each side, to conduct the Ship into a safe Harbour, and soon after the King himself having received a Velvet Cloak by a Messenger from Drake, as a Token of Peace, came with such a Retinue and Dignity of Appearance as was not expected in those remote Parts of the World. He was received with Discharges of Cannons and every kind of Musick, with which he was so much delighted, that desiring the Musicians to come down into the Boat, he was towed along in it at the Stern of the Ship.

The King was of a graceful Stature, and regal Carriage, of a mild Aspect, and low Voice, his Attendants were dressed in white Cotton or Calicoe of whom some whose Age gave them a venerable Appearance, seemed his Counsellors, and the rest Officers or Nobles; his Guards were not ignorant of Fire Arms, but had not many among them, being equipped for the most Part with Bows and Darts.

The King having spent some Time in admiring the Multitude of New Objects that presented themselves, retired as soon as the Ship was brought to Anchor, and promised to return on the Day following, and in the mean Time, the Inhabitants having leave to traffick, brought down Provisions in great Abundance.

At the Time when the King was expected his Brother came aboard, to request of Drake that he would come to the Castle, proposing to stay himself as a Hostage for his return; Drake refused to go but sent some Gentlemen, detaining the King's Brother in the mean Time.

These Gentlemen were received by another of the King's Brothers, who conducted them to the Council-house near the Castle, in which they were directed to walk, there they found threescore Old Men, Privy Counsellors to the King, and on each side of the Door without, stood four old Men of foreign Countries, who served as Interpreters in Commerce.

In a short Time the King came from the Castle, dress'd in Cloth of Gold, with his Hair woven into gold Rings, a Chain of Gold upon his Neck, and on his Hands Rings very artificially set with Diamonds and Jewels of great Value; over his Head was born a rich Canopy, and by his Chair of State, on which he sat down when he had entered the House, stood a Page with a Fann set with Sapphires, to moderate the Excess of the Heat. Here he received the Compliments of the English, and then honourably dismissed them.

The Castle which they had some Opportunity of observing, seem'd of no great Force; it was built by the Portugeze, who attempting to reduce this Kingdom into absolute Subjection, murdered the King and intended to persue their Scheme by the Destruction of all his Sons; but the general Abhorence, which Cruelty and Perfidy naturally excites, armed all the Nation against them: and procured their total Expulsion from all the Dominions of Ternate, which from that Time increasing in Power, continued to make new Conquests, and to deprive them of other Acquisitions.

While they lay before Ternate, a Gentleman came on board attended by his Interpreter. He was dressed somewhat in the European Manner, and soon distinguished himself from the Natives of Ternate, or any Country that they had seen, by his Civility and Apprehension. Such a Visitant may easily be imagined to excite their Curiosity, which he gratified by informing them that he was a Native of China, of the Family of the King then reigning, and that being accused of a capital Crime, of which tho' he was innocent, he had not Evidence to clear himself, he had pétitioned the King that he might not be exposed to a Tryal, but that his Cause might be referred to divine Providence, and that he might be allowed to leave his Country, with a Prohibition against returning, unless Heaven, in Attestation of his Innocence, should enable him to bring back to the King some Intelligence, that might be to the Honour and Advantage of the Empire of China. In Search of such Information he had now spent three Years, and had left Tidore for the Sake of conversing with the English General, from whom he hoped to receive such Accounts as would enable him to return with Honour and Safety.

Drake willingly recounted all his Adventures and Observations, to which the Chinese Exile listened with the utmost Attention and Delight, and having fixed them in his Mind, thanked God for the Knowledge he had gained. He then proposed to the English General to conduct him to China, recounting, by Way of Invitation, the Wealth, Extent, and Felicity of that Empire; but Drake could not be induced to prolong his Voyage.

He therefore set sail on the 9th of Nov. in quest of some convenient Harbour, in a desart Island to refit his Ship, not being willing, as it seems, to trust the Generosity of the King of Ternate. Five Days afterwards he found a very commodious Harbour in an Island overgrown with Wood, where he repaired his Vessel and refreshed his Men without Danger or Interruption.

Leaving this Place the 12th of December, they sailed towards the Celebes; but having a Wind not very favourable, they were detained among a Multitude of Islands, mingled with dangerous Shallows, till Jan.9, 1580. When they thought themselves clear, and were sailing forwards with a strong Gale, they were at the Beginning of the Night surprized in their Course by a sudden Shock, of which the Cause was easily discovered, for they were thrown upon a Shoal, and by the Speed of their Course, fixed too fast for any Hope of escaping. Here even the Intrepidity of Drake was shaken, and his Dexterity baffled, but his Piety, however, remained still the same, and what he could not now promise himself from his own Ability, he hoped from the Assistance of Providence. The Pump was plied, and the Ship found free from new Leaks.

The next Attempt was to discover towards the Sea some Place where they might fix their Boat, and from thence drag the Ship into deep Water; but upon Examination it appeared that the Rock on which they had struck, rose perpendicularly from the Water, and that there was no Anchorage, nor any Bottom to be found a Boat's Length from the Ship. But this Discovery, with its Consequences, was by Drake wisely concealed from the common Sailors, lest they should abandon themselves to Despair, for which there was, indeed, Cause, there being no Prospect left but that they must there sink with the Ship, which must undoubtedly be soon dashed to Pieces; or perish in attempting to reach the Shore in their Boat; or be cut in Pieces by Barbarians if they should arrive at Land.

In the Midst of this Perplexity and Distress Drake directed that the Sacrament should be administered, and his Men, fortified with all the Consolation which Religion affords, then persuaded them to lighten the Vessel by throwing into the Sea Part of their Lading, which was chearfully complied with, but without Effect. At length, when their Hopes had forsaken them, and no new Struggles could be made, they were on a suden relieved by a Remission of the Wind, which having hitherto blown strongly against the Side of the Ship which lay towards the Sea, held it upright against the Rock; but when the Blast slackened (being then low Water) the Ship lying higher with that Part which rested on the Rock than with the other, and being born up no longer by the Wind, reeled into the deep Water, to the Surprize and Joy of Drake and his Companions.

This was the greatest, and most inextricable Distress which they had ever suffered, and made such an Impression upon their Minds, that for some Time afterwards they durst not adventure to spread their Sails, but went slowly forward with the utmost Circumspection.

They thus continued their Course without any observable Occurrence, till on the 11th of March they came to Anchor before the Island Java, and sending to the King a present of Cloath and Silks, received from him, in Return, a large Quantity of Provisions, and the Day following Drake went himself on Shore, and entertained the King with his Musick, and obtained Leave to store his Ship with Provisions.

The Island is governed by a great Number of petty Kings, or Raias, subordinate to one Chief; of these Princes three came on board together a few Days after their Arrival, and having upon their Return recounted the Wonders which they had seen, and the Civility with which they had been treated, incited others to satisfy their Curiosity in the same Manner, and Raia Donan, the Chief King, came himself to view the Ship with the warlike Armaments and Instruments of Navigation.

This Intercourse of Civilities some what retarded the Business for which they came; but at length they not only victualled their Ship, but cleansed the Bottom, which, in the long Course, was overgrown with a Kind of Shell-fish that impeded her Passage.

Leaving Java on March the twenty-sixth they sailed homewards by the Cape of Good Hope which they saw on June the fifth, on the fifteenth of August passed the Tropic, and on the 26th of September arrived at Plimouth, where they found that by passing through so many different Climates, they had lost a Day in their Account of Time, it being Sunday by their Journals, but Monday by the general Computation.

In this hazardous Voyage they had spent two Years ten Months and some odd Days, but were recompensed for their Toils by great Riches, and the uni[v]ersal Applause of their Countrymen, Drake afterwards brought his Ship up to Deptford, where Queen Elizabeth visited him on board his Ship, and conferred the Honour of Knighthood upon him;

The Life of Sir Francis Drake: Page 66: Text

The Transactions against ỹ Armada, 1588 are in themselves, far more memorable, but less necessary to be recited in this Succinct Narrative; only let it be remembered, that the Post of Vice-Admiral of England, to which Sir Francis Drake was then raised, is a sufficient Proof, that no Obscurity of Birth, or Meanness of Fortune, is unsurmountable to Bravery and Diligence.

In 1595 Sir Francis Drake, and Sir John Hawkins, were sent with a Fleet to the West Indies, which Expedition was only memorable for the Destruction of Nombre de Dios, and the Death of the two Commanders, of whom Sir Francis Drake died Jan.9, 1597, and was thrown into the Sea in a Leaden Coffin, with all the Pomp of naval Obsequies. It is reported by some, that the ill Success of this Voyage hastened his Death. Upon what this Conjecture is grounded does not appear, and we may be allowed to hope, for the Honour of so great a Man, that it is without Foundation, and that he whom no Series of Success could ever betray to Vanity, or Negligence, could have supported a Change of Fortune without Impatience or Dejection.

The Life of Dr Morin: Page 88: Text

This Regimen, extraordinary as it was, had many Advantages; for it preserved his Health, an Advantage which very few sufficiently regard; it gave him an Authority to preach Diet and Abstinence to his Patients; and it made him rich without the Assistance of Fortune; rich, not for himself, but for the Poor, who were the only Persons benefited by that artificial Affluence, which, of all others, is most difficult to acquire. It is easy to imagine that while he practised in the midst of Paris the severe Temperance of a Hermit, Paris differed no otherwise with regard to him, from a Hermitage, than as it supplied him with Books, and the Conversation of learned Men.

In 1662 he was admitted Doctor of Physic. About that time Dr Fagon, Dr Longuet, and Dr Galois, all eminent for their Skill in Botany, were employed in drawing up a Catalogue of the Plants in the Royal Garden, which was publish'd in 1665, under the Name of Dr Vallot, then first Physician; during the Prosecution of this Work, Dr Morin was often consulted, and from those Conversations it was that Dr Fagon conceived a particular Esteem of him, which he always continued to retain.

After having practised Physic some years, he was admitted Expectant at the Hotel Dieu, where he was regularly to have been made Pensionary Physician upon the first Vacancy; but mere unassisted Merit advances slowly, if, what is not very common, it advances at all. Morin had no Acquaintance with the Arts necessary to carry on Schemes of Preferment; the Moderation of his Desires preserved him from the Necessity of studying them, and the Privacy of his Life debar'd him from any Opportunity.

At last, however, Justice was done him in spite of Artifice and Partiality; but his Advancement added nothing to his Condition, except the Power of more extensive Charity; for all the Money which he received as a Salary, he put into the Chest of the Hospital, always, as he imagined, without being observed. Not content with serving the Poor for nothing, he paid them for being serv'd.

His Reputation rose so high in Paris, that Madamoiselle de Guise was desirous to make him her Physician, but it was not without difficulty that he was prevailed upon by his Friend, Dr Dodart, to accept the Place. He was by this new Advancement laid under the Necessity of keeping a Chariot, an Equipage very unsuitable to his Temper; but while he complied with those exterior Appearances which the Publick had a Right to demand from him, he remitted nothing of his former Austerity in the more private and essential Parts of his Life, which he had always the Power of regulating according to his own Disposition.

In two Years and a half the Princess fell sick, and was despaired of by Morin, who was a great Master of Prognosticks; at the time when she thought herself in no Danger, he pronounced her Death inevitable; a Declaration to the highest Degree disagreeable, but which was made more easy to him than to any other by his Piety, and artless Simplicity. Nor did his Sincerity produce any ill Consequences to himself; for the Princess affected by his Zeal, taking a Ring from her Finger, gave it him as the

last Pledge of her Affection, and rewarded him still more to his
Satisfaction, by preparing for Death
with a true Christian Piety. She left
him by Will an yearly Pension of two
thousand Livres, which was always
regularly paid him.

No sooner was the Princess dead,
but he freed himself from the Incumbrance of his Chariot, and retired to
St Victor without a Servant, having,
however, augmented his daily Allowance
with a little Rice boiled in Water.

Dodart, who had undertaken the
Charge of being ambitious on his
Account, procured him, at the Restoration of theAccademy in 1699, to be
nominated Associate Botanist; not
knowing, what he would doubtless have
been pleased with the Knowledge of, that
he introduced into that Assembly the Man
that was to succeed him in his Place of
Pensionary.

Dr Morin was not one who had upon
his Hands the Labour of adapting himself
to the Duties of his Condition, but
always found himself naturally adapted
to them. He had, therefore, no Difficul
ty in being constant at the Assemblies
of the Academy, notwithstanding the
Distance of Places, while he had
Strength enough to support the Journey.
But his Regimen was not equally
effectual to produce Vigour as to
prevent Distempers; and being 64 Years
old at his Admission, he could not
continue his Assiduity more than a Year
after the Death of Dodart, whom he
succeeded in 1707.

When Mr Tournefort went to pursue
his Botanical Enquiries in the Levant,
he desired Dr Morin to supply his Place
of Demonstrator of the Plants in the
Royal Garden, and rewarded him for the
Trouble, by inscribing to him a new Plant
which he brought from the East, by the
Name of Morina Orientalis, as he named
others the Dodarte, the Fagonne, the
Bignonne, the Phelipee. These are
Compliments proper to be made by the
Botanists, not only to those of their
own Rank, but to the greatest Persons;

The Life of Dr Morin: Page 89: Footnote

*The Practice of Dr Morin is for-
bidden, I believe, by every Writer that
has left Rules for the Preservation of
Health, and is directly opposite to that
of Cornaro, who, by his Regimen repaired
a broken Constitution, and protracted
his Life without any painful Infirmities
or any Decay of his intellectual
Abilities, to more than a hundred Years;
it is generally agreed, that as Men
advance in Years, they ought to take
lighter Sustenance, and in less
Quantities; and Reason seems easily to
discover that as the concoctive Powers
grow weaker, they ought to labour less.

The Life of Peter Burman: Page 92: Text

In this Visit to Paris he
contracted an Acquaintance, among

other learned Men, with the celebrated
Father Montfaucon, with whom he
conversed, at his first Interview,
under no other Character that than that
of a Traveller; but their Discourse
turning upon ancient Learning, the
Stranger soon gave such Proofs of his
Attainments, that Montfaucon declar'd
him a Traveller of uncommon Knowledge,
and confessed his Curiosity to know
his Name; which he no sooner heard,
than he sprung from his Seat, and
embracing him with the utmost Ardour,
expressed his Satisfaction at having
seen the Man whose Productions, of
various Kinds, he had so often praised;
and, as a real Proof of his Regard,
offered, not only to procure him an
immediate Admission to all the
Libraries of Paris, but to those in
remoter Provinces, which are not
generally open to Strangers, and undertook to ease the Expences of his
Journey by procuring him Entertainment
in all the Monastries of his Order.

This Favour Burman was hindered
from accepting, by the Necessity of
returning to Utretcht at the usual
Time of beginning a new Course of
Lectures, to which there was always so
great a Concourse of Students, as much
encreased the Dignity and Fame of the
University in which he taught.

He had already extended, to distant
Parts, his Reputation for Knowledge of
ancient History by a Treatise de
Vectigalibus Populi Romani, on the
Revenues of the Romans, and for his
Skill in Greek Learning, and in
ancient Coins, by a Tract called
Jupiter Fulgurator; and after his
Return from Paris, he published
Phædrus, first with the Notes of
various Comentators, and afterwards
with his own. He printed many Poems,
made many Orations upon different
Subjects, and procured an Impression
of the Epistles of Gudius and
Sarravius.

While he was thus employ'd, the
Professorships of History, Eloquence,
and the Greek Language, became vacant
at Leiden, by the Death of Perizonius,
which Burman's Reputation incited the
Curators of the University to offer
him upon very generous Terms, and
which, after some Struggles with his
Fondness for his native Place, his
Friends, and his Collegues, he was
prevailed on to accept, finding the
Solicitations from Leiden warm and
urgent, and his Friends at Utretcht,
though unwilling to be deprived of
him, yet not zealous enough for the
Honour and Advantage of their University, to endeavour to detain him
by great Liberality.

At his Entrance upon this new
Professorship, which was conferred
upon him in 1715, he pronounced an
Oration upon the Duty and Office of a
Professor of polite Literature. De
Publici Humanioris Disciplina
Professoris proprio officio et munere.
And shewed by the Usefulness and
Perspicuity of his Lectures, that he
was not confined to speculative
Notions on that Subject, having a
very happy Method of accommodating
his Instructions to the different
Abilities and Attainments of his
Pupils.

Nor did he suffer the publick
Duties of this Station to hinder him

from promoting Learning by Labours of a different Kind; for, besides many Poems and Orations which he recited on different Occasions, he wrote several Prefaces to the Works of others, and publish'd many useful Editions of the best Latin Writers, with large Collections of Notes from various Commentators.

He was twice Rector, or Chief Governor of the University, and discharged that important Office with equal Equity and Ability, and gained by his Conduct in every Station so much Esteem, that when the Professorship of History of the United Provinces became vacant, it was conferred on him, as an Addition to his Honours and Revenues, which he might justly claim; and afterwards, as a Proof of the Continuance of their Regard, and a Testimony that his Reputation was still encreasing they made him Chief Librarian, an Office which was the more acceptable to him, as it united his Business with his Pleasure, and gave him an Opportunity at the same Time of superintending the Library, and carrying on his Studies.

Such was the Course of his Life, till, in his old Age, leaving off his Practice of Walking and other Exercises, he began to be afflicted with the Scurvy, which discovered itself by very tormenting Symptoms of various Kinds; sometimes disturbing his Head with Vertigos, sometimes causing Faintness in his Limbs, and sometimes attacking his Legs with Anguish so excruciating, that all his Vigour was destroyed, and the Power of Walking entirely taken away, till at length his Left Foot became motionless. The Violence of his Pain produced irregular Fevers, deprived him of Rest, and entirely debilitated his whole Frame.

This tormenting Disease he bore, tho' not without some Degree of Impatience, yet without any unbecoming or irrational Despondency, and applied himself in the Intermission of his Pains to seek for Comfort in the Duties of Religion.

While he lay in this State of Misery he received an Account of the Promotion of two of his Grandsons, and a Catalogue of the King of France's Library, presented to him by the Command of the King himself, and expressed some Satisfaction on all these Occasions; but soon diverted his Thoughts to the more important Consideration of his external State, into which he passed on the 31st of March 1741, in the 73d Year of his Age.

He was a Man of moderate Stature, of great Strength and Activity, which he preserved by temperate Diet, without medical Exactness, and by allotting Proportions of his Time to Relaxation and Amusement, not suffering his Studies to exhaust his Strength, but relieving them by frequent Intermissions; a Practice consistent with the most exemplary Diligence, and which, he that omits will find at last, that Time may be lost, like Money, by unseasonable Avarice.

In his Hours of Relaxation he was gay, and sometimes gave Way so far to his Temper, naturally satirical, that he drew upon himself the Illwill of those who had been unfortunately the Subjects of his Mirth; but Enemies so provoked he thought it beneath him to regard or to pacify; for he was fiery but not malicious, disdained Dissimulation, and in his gay or serious Hours preserved a settled Detestation of Falshood. So that he was an open and undisguised Friend or Enemy, entirely unacquainted with the Artifices of Flatterers, but so judicious in the Choice of Friends, and so constant in his Affection to them, that those with whom he had contracted Familiarity in his Youth, had for the greatest Part his Confidence in his old Age.

His Abilities, which would probably have enabled him to have excelled in any Kind of Learning, were chiefly employ'd, as his Station required, on polite Literature, in which he arrived at very uncommon Knowledge, which, however, appears rather from judicious Compilations than original Productions. His Stile is lively and masculine, but not without Harshness and Constraint, nor, perhaps, always polished to that Purity which some Writers have attained. He was at least Instrumental to the Instruction of Mankind, by the Publication of many valuable Performances, which lay neglected by the greatest Part of the learned World, and if Reputation be estimated by Usefulness, he may claim a higher Degree in the Ranks of Learning than some others of happier Elocution, or more vigorous Imagination.

Life of the Earl of Roscommon: Page 386: Footnote

§
The present age is very little inclined to favour any accounts of this kind, nor will the name of Aubrey much recommend it to credit; it ought not, however, to be omitted, because better evidence of a fact cannot easily be found, than is here offered, and it must be by preserving such relations that we may at least judge how much they are to be regarded. If we stay to examine this account, we shall find difficulties on both sides; here is a relation of a fact given by a man who had no interest to deceive, and who could not be deceived himself; and here is, on the other hand, a miracle which produces no effect; the order of nature is interrupted to discover not a future, but only a distant event, the knowledge of which is of no use to him to whom it is revealed. Between these difficulties, what way shall be found? Is reason or testimony to be rejected? I believe what Osborne says of an appearance of sanctity, may be applied to such impulses or anticipations as this: Do not wholly slight them, because they may be true; but do not easily trust them, because they may be false.

* "He was at Dublin as much as ever distempered with the same fatal affection for play, which engaged him in one adventure that well

deserves to be related. As he returned to his lodgings from a gaming table, he was attacked in the dark by three ruffians, who were employed to assassinate him: The Earl defended himself with so much resolution, that he dispatch'd one of the aggressors; whilst a gentleman, accidentally passing that way, interpos'd, and disarmed another; the third secured himself by flight. This generous assistant was a disbanded officer of a good family, and fair reputation; who, by what we call the partiality of fortune, to avoid censuring the iniquities of the times, wanted even a plain suit of cloaths to make a decent appearance at the castle. But his lordship, on this occasion, presenting him to the Duke of Ormond, with great importunity prevailed with his grace, that he might resign his post of captain of the guards to his friend; which for about three years the gentleman enjoyed, and, upon his death, the Duke returned the commission to his generous benefactor." Fenton.

Life of the Earl of Roscommon: Page 387: Footnote

‖Mr Fenton has, in his notes upon Waller, given Roscommon a character too general to be critically just. 'In his writings, says he, we view 'the image of a mind, which was 'naturally serious and solid; richly 'furnished, and adorned with all the 'ornaments of art, and science; and 'those ornaments unaffectedly dis-'posed in the most regular and elegant 'order. His imagination might have, 'probably, been more fruitful and 'sprightly, if his judgment had been 'less severe: But that severity '(deliver'd in a masculine, clear, 'succinct stile) contributed to make 'him so eminent in the didactical 'manner, that no man with justice can 'affirm he was ever equalled by any of 'our nation, without confessing at 'the same time that he is inferior to 'none. In some other kinds of 'writing his genius seems to have 'wanted fire to attain the point of 'perfection; but who can attain it?' From this account of the riches of his mind, who would not imagine that they had been display'd in large volumes, and numerous performances? Who would not, after the perusal of this character, be surprised to find, that all the proofs of this genius, and knowledge, and judgment, are not sufficient to form a single book, or to appear otherwise than in conjunction with the works of some other writer of the same petty size?

Life of the Earl of Roscommon: Page
Text

386)
387)
388)

Having finish'd his affairs he returned to London, was made master

of the horse to the dutchess of York, and married the lady Frances, eldest daughter of the E. of Burlington, and widow of Colonel Courtnay. Here he formed a design of ⊤instituting a society for the refinement of the English language, but upon the commotions which were produced by King James's endeavours to introduce alterations in religion, he resolved to retire to Rome, alledging that it was best to sit next to the chimney when the chamber smoked. This journey was hindred by the gout, of which he was so impatient, that he admitted a repellent application from a French empiric, by which his distemper was driven up into his bowels,‡ and an end put to his life in 1684. His character as a writer is eminent: ‖ his works are, ‡ An Essay on translated Verse, a translation of the Art of Poetry, and some little poems, and translations.

Life of the Earl of Roscommon: Page 388: Footnotes

that he is, perhaps, the only correct writer in verse before Addison; and that if there are not so many or so great beauties in his composition, as in those of some contemporaries, there are at least fewer faults. Nor is this his highest praise; for Mr Pope has celebrated him as the only moral writer of King Charles's reign.

Unhappy Dryden! - in all Charles's days Roscommon only boasts unspotted lays.

‡ 'It was my Lord Roscommon's Essay 'on translated Verse, says Dryden, 'which made me uneasy, till I tried 'whether or no I was capable of follow-'ing his rules, and of reducing the 'speculation into practice. For many 'a fair precept in poetry is like a 'seeming demonstration in mathematics; 'very specious in the diagram, but 'failing in the mechanical operation. 'I think, I have generally observed 'his instructions; I am sure my reason 'is sufficiently convinc'd both of 'their truth and usefulness; which, 'in other words, is to confess no 'less a vanity than to pretend that I 'have, at least in some places, made 'examples to his rules.' This declaration of Dryden, will, I am afraid, be found little more than one of those cursory civilities, which one author pays to another; for when the sum of Lord Roscommon's precepts is collected, it will not be easy to discover, how they can qualify their reader for a better performance of translation, than might have been attained by his own reflexions. They are, however, here laid down, and disentangled from the ornaments with which they are embellished, and the digressions with which they are diversify'd.

    'Tis true, composing is the
        nobler part,
    But good translation is no easy art,
    For tho' materials have long since
        been found,

Yet both your fancy, and your hands
      are bound;
And by improving what was writ before,
Invention labours less, but
         judgment, more. -
      Each poet with a different talent
         writes,
One praises, one instructs, another
      bites.
Horace did ne'er aspire to Epick bays,
Nor lofty Maro stoop to Lyrick lays.
Examine how your humour is inclin'd,
And which the ruling passion of your
      mind;
Then, seek a poet who your way does
      bend,
And chuse an author, as you chuse a
      friend.
United by this sympathetick bond,
You grow familiar, intimate, and fond;
Your thoughts, your words, your
         stiles, your souls agree,
No longer his interpreter, but he. -

Take then a subject, proper to expound:
But moral, great, and worth a poet's
      voice,
For men of sense despise a trivial
      choice:
And such applause it must expect to
      meet,
As wou'd some painter, busy in a
      street,
To copy bulls and bears, and ev'ry sign
That calls the staring sots to nasty
      wine. -
      Take pains the genuine meaning to
         explore;
There sweat, there strain, tug the
      laborious oars
Search ev'ry comment that your care
      can find,
Some here, some there, may hit the
      poet's mind;
Yet be not blindly guided by the
      throng;
The multitude is always in the wrong.
When things appear unnatural or hard,
Consult your author, with himself
      compar'd.
Who knows what blessings Phoebus may
      bestow,
And future ages to your labour owe?
Such secrets are not easily found out,
But once discover'd, leave no room
      for doubt.
Truth stamps conviction in your
      ravish'd breast,
And peace and joy attend the glorious
      guest.
Yet if the shadow of a scruple stay,
Sure the most beaten is the safest
      way. -
      They who too faithfully on names
         insist,
Rather create than dissipate the mist;
And grow unjust by being over nice,
(For superstitious virtue turns to
      vice).
Let Crassus' ghost, and Labienus' tell
How twice in Parthian plains their
      legions fell;
Since Rome hath been so jealous of
      her fame,
That few know Pacerus or Monaeses'
      name. -
      And 'tis much safer to leave out
         than add,
Abstruse and mystick tho'ts you must ⎞
      express; ⎟
With painful care, but seeming   ⎬
      easiness;   ⎟
For truth shines brightest thro' the ⎠
      plainest dress.

Your author always will the best
      advise,
Fall when he falls, and when he
      rises, rise.

   He that can abstract his mind from
the elegance of the poetry, and confine
it to the sense of the precepts, will
find no other direction, than that the
author should be suitable to the trans-
lator's genius; that he should be such
as may deserve a translation; that he
who intends to translate him, should
endeavour to understand him; that
perspicuity should be studied, and
unusual or uncouth names sparingly
inserted, and that the stile of the
original should be copied in its
elevation and depression. These are
the rules which are celebrated as so
definite and so important, and for
the delivery of which to mankind, so
much honour has been paid.
Roscommon has, indeed, deserved his
honours, had they been given with
discernment, and bestowed not on the
rules themselves, but the art with
which they are introduced, and the
decorations with which they are
adorned.

Original Letters written by the late
Dr Johnson:
Page 522: Text:

Dr Thirlby died Dec.19, 1753. - One
of his colloquial topicks was, That
Nature apparently intended a kind of
parity among her sons.

Page 522: Footnote:

† In a subsequent letter, dated
Oct.28, Dr. Johnson adds, "I wish,
"Sir, you could obtain some fuller
"information of Jortin, Markland, and
"Thirlby. They were three contem-
"poraries of great eminence." It was
in consequence of this request that I
drew up the account of Thirlby, which
is printed in the Magazine for April
1784, p.260; which having been shewn
to Dr. Johnson in the state of a proof
sheet, he added to it nearly half of
what is there printed. The Doctor's
MS. is now before me, and begins with
"What I can tell of Thirlby, I had
"from those who knew him; I never saw
"him in my life." The communication
concludes with "This is what I can
"remember." I will take this
opportunity of adding, that, on my
shewing Dr. Johnson the "Remarks on his
"Life of Milton," which was published
in 8vo. 1780, he wrote on the margin
of p.14, "In the business of Lauder, I
"was deceived; partly by thinking the
"man too frantick to be fraudulent.
"Of this quotation from the ["Literary]
"Magazine"["a POETICAL SCALE"], I was
"not the author. I fancy it was put
"in after I had quitted that work; for
"I not only did not write it, but do
"not remember it." J.N.